MOON

USA NATIONAL PARKS

THE COMPLETE GUIDE TO ALL

59 PARKS

BECKY LOMAX

CONTENTS

1: JOSHUA TREE
2: ACADIA
3: DENALI
4: BRYCE CANYON
5: MOUNT RAINIER

DISCOVER THE USA NATIONAL PARKS

These 59 national parks are masterpieces spread across the United States. The artistry of nature paints their rain forests with mossy green, their lakes a vivid blue, and their canyons in shifting oranges and reds.

Their beauty is in their wildness. Cactus deserts bloom against the odds, and rugged mountains trap snow to feed rivers tumbling to oceans, where seascapes change with each tide. Wolves, grizzly bears, orcas, and eagles still rule the animal kingdom, much as they did when only Native Americans occupied these lands.

Their sights can only be described in superlatives: North America's highest peak, tallest waterfall, deepest lake, lowest elevation, and biggest trees.

Our parks provide moments of connection: hearing birds chatter, smelling fragrant trees, feeling the spray of waterfalls, touching rocks smoothed over by the centuries, and staring up into dark skies. These are the moments that let nature wash through us; that offer renewal of the human spirit.

Your trip to any of these national parks can be the start of a longer, life-enriching journey. Let it begin here.

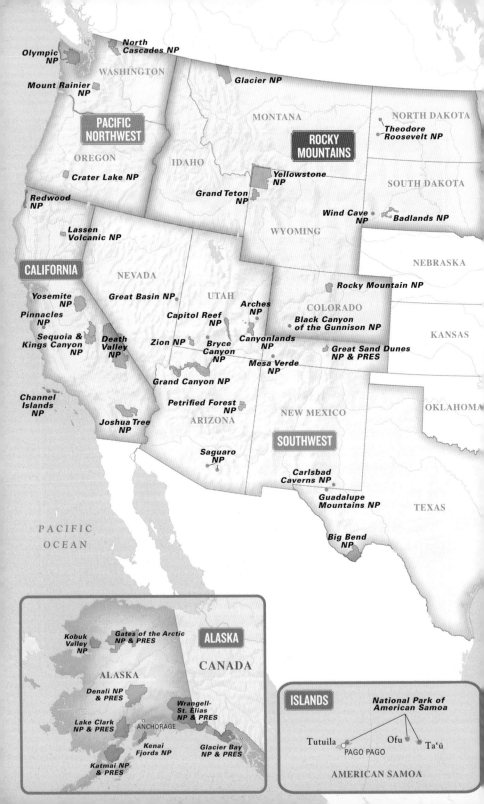

Top ⑩ *Experiences*

① SEE ICE CALVE IN GLACIER BAY

When moving ice becomes unstable, giant slabs of it crack off tidewater glaciers to crash into the frigid blue water of the park's fjords (page 89).

② WATCH OLD FAITHFUL BLOW IN YELLOWSTONE

Catch the most famous geyser in the country erupting like clockwork roughly every 90 minutes (page 441).

3

3 WANDER THROUGH WILDFLOWERS IN DEATH VALLEY

Death Valley blooms in ephemeral shows of yellow, purple, and white (page 146).

4 GO UNDERGROUND AT MAMMOTH CAVE

Explore this labyrinth—part of the longest cave system in the world—under electric lights, with handheld lanterns, or crawling through tight squeezes (page 611).

5 RAFT THROUGH THE GRAND CANYON

Sink into the rhythm of the river to cruise 277 miles of flatwater floats and crashing white water below immense canyon walls (page 276).

6 ADMIRE DELICATE ARCH

Walk to the base of this 60-foot-tall freestanding arch, a natural work of art painted by erosion and weathering (page 347).

7 GAZE UP AT REDWOODS IN SEQUOIA AND KINGS CANYON

Stand in awe at the base of the General Sherman Tree, a giant sequoia and the largest tree by volume in the world (page 135).

8

8 HIKE THE NARROWS IN ZION

Plod upstream in the rocky water of the North Fork of the Virgin River through a deep, narrow slot canyon of vertical cliffs (page 305).

9 TOUR ANCIENT CLIFF DWELLINGS IN MESA VERDE

Ancestral Pueblo people built houses, spiritual kivas, and storage rooms under overhanging cliffs. See these wondrous villages on ranger-led tours (page 370).

10 GATHER FOR FIREFLIES IN GREAT SMOKY

For two short weeks in late spring, synchronous fireflies gather here, flashing their bioluminescent lights in unison (page 588).

Where TO GO

ALASKA

Alaska contains some of the most rugged and wildest parks. In **Denali,** bus tours carry visitors deep into the park to see wolves, bears, moose, and the tallest peak in North America. Flightseeing gets visitors even closer to Denali mountain. See tidewater glaciers in **Glacier Bay** and **Kenai Fjords,** or fly above the Arctic Circle to **Gates of the Arctic and Kobuk Valley.** Watch brown bears fishing in **Katmai,** go fishing in **Lake Clark,** and hike to glaciers in **Wrangell-St. Elias.**

CALIFORNIA

The California parks span unique extremes: the marine environment of the **Channel Islands,** the desert badlands of **Death Valley,** and the bubbling mud pots of **Lassen Volcanic.** Two deserts collide in **Joshua Tree,** rocky spires shoot skyward in **Pinnacles,** and giant redwoods and sequoias pack into **Redwood** and **Sequoia-Kings Canyon.** The crowning park, **Yosemite,** shows off waterfalls in Yosemite Valley, far-reaching views from Glacier Point, and a cabled climb up the steep Half Dome.

PACIFIC NORTHWEST

Every one of the Pacific Northwest parks centers on mountains—from the volcano holding **Crater Lake** to high **Mount Rainier** spilling with glaciers to the icy peaks dominating the **North Cascades.** In **Olympic National Park,** you can drive into the alpine at Hurricane Ridge or go west to plunge into the lush Hoh Rain Forest and stroll rugged Ruby Beach.

SOUTHWEST

The parks of the Southwest show off nature's sculpture in the cliffs, fantastical hoodoos, and arches of **Bryce,** **Arches, Canyonlands,** and **Capitol Reef.** Belowground, the artistry continues with stalactites in **Carlsbad Caverns.** Even vegetation contains a rare beauty, with stately cacti in **Saguaro** and ancient bristlecones in **Great Basin.** Colors run rampant in the Painted Desert in the **Petrified Forest,** cliff dwellings of **Mesa Verde,** the giant sand dunes of **Great Sand Dunes,** the Chisos Mountains of **Big Bend,** and the desert peaks of **Guadalupe Mountains.** Two parks stand out as Southwest royalty. **Zion** features the Narrows, Zion Canyon, and the Zion-Mount Carmel Highway. **Grand Canyon** has overlooks of the gaping chasm along Hermit Road and at Desert View Watchtower, while the inner canyon lures hikers and boaters.

ROCKY MOUNTAINS

In the Rocky Mountains, the large, famous parks often overshadow the smaller ones. But these modest parks enchant in their own right—the narrow slot of **Black Canyon of the Gunnison,** colorful erosion of **Badlands,** boxwork of **Wind Cave,** and beloved badlands of **Theodore Roosevelt.** The large parks have earned fame for their iconic attractions. **Rocky Mountain** has its elk, Longs Peak, and Trail Ridge Road, the highest paved road in the country. **Glacier** has the scenic Many Glacier area, and the cliff-hugging Going-to-the-Sun Road. **Grand Teton** has wildlife and Teton Park Road. And **Yellowstone** has wildlife-watching, the Grand Canyon of the Yellowstone, and the priceless Old Faithful Geyser.

GREAT LAKES AND NORTHEAST

In the northeast is **Acadia** with its Park Loop Road, Jordan Pond House, and historic Carriage Roads.

GRAND CANYON

Like no other region, the Great Lakes contain parks that focus on water. In **Cuyahoga Valley,** Ohio, the canals preserve one of the nation's early water highways. In **Voyageurs,** Minnesota, the lake acreage rivals the amount of land. In **Isle Royale,** Michigan, the forested island wilderness is tucked away, isolated along Lake Superior.

THE SOUTH

From the Appalachian mountain parks such as **Shenandoah,** Virginia, to the coastal marine parks of **Biscayne** and **Dry Tortugas** in Florida, the national parks of the South include the subterranean world of **Mammoth Cave,** Kentucky; the swamps of **Congaree,** South Carolina; and the hot mineral springs of **Hot Springs,** Arkansas. Two jewels stand out: **Great Smoky Mountains** with Cades Cove, Cataloochee Valley, and Newfound Gap Road; and **Everglades** for wildlife-watching, canoeing or kayaking, and the Ten Thousand Islands.

ISLANDS

The Pacific Ocean and Caribbean Sea hold islands with lovely beaches. The **Virgin Islands** flank white-sand beaches with coral reefs and turquoise water. Located south of the equator, **American Samoa** likewise harbors impressive coral reefs. But in Hawaii, the national parks climb to great heights far above the beaches at **Haleakalā** and **Hawai'i Volcanoes.**

NATIONAL PARK PASSPORT STAMPS ▼▼▼

The National Park passport program, which launched in 1986, provides a way for visitors to collect free cancellation stamps for each park. Similar to passport stamps, each national park has a stamp that serves as a record of visiting that park. A few stamps feature a park icon; most name the park and date. Some also include the name of the visitors center. More than 400 properties in the national park system, including historical parks, monuments, and historical trails, participate in the program.

To collect stamps from all national parks, purchase a **national park passport book** (www.eparks.com) or use the passport stamp space provided on the chapter opener for each national park in this book.

Most parks will stamp your passport at the visitors center. In more remote parks, locations may vary. A location list is available online so you can determine in advance where you need to go.

Happy collecting!

NATIONAL PARKS PASS

Most national parks charge an entrance fee that is usually valid for seven days. To get the most bang for your buck, consider buying the **Interagency Annual Pass** ($80), which is good for all national parks and federal fee areas. Interagency passes are free for fourth graders in the United States, disabled persons, and military personnel. Seniors have two interagency pass options: Annual ($20), which is valid for one year, and Lifetime ($80).

FEE-FREE DAYS

Some national parks recognize several fee-free days annually, many of which fall on national or federal holidays. During fee-free days, the entrance fee for the national park is waived. Though dates may vary, most fee-free days include: Martin Luther King Day (Jan.), the first day of National Park Week (Apr.), National Public Lands Day (Sept.), and Veterans Day (Nov. 11). Consult individual park websites for current fee-free dates.

RESERVATIONS

To stay overnight inside the parks, make reservations for peak seasons (usually summer) **one year in advance.** This is especially true for lodges in Great Smoky Mountains, Grand Canyon, Rocky Mountain, Yosemite, Yellowstone, Grand Teton, Glacier, Zion, Olympic, and Acadia, as accommodations in these parks book up fast.

Most **campgrounds** accept reservations up to **six months in advance;** they fill quickly at popular locations such as Yosemite. Make any dinner, tour, or other activity reservations when booking your room or campsite.

LOTTERIES

Some activities require **lotteries** or advance reservations. Lotteries operate differently throughout the parks; most occur in winter or spring for the upcoming season. Lottery events include the **synchronous fireflies** in **Great Smoky Mountains;** hiking **Half Dome** and backpacking to the **High Sierra Camps** in **Yosemite;** driving a private vehicle on **the park road in Denali; snowmobiling** in **Yellowstone;** and private **rafting trips** in the **Grand Canyon.** For commercial river trips in the Grand Canyon, book **1-2 years in advance.**

SEASONS

High Season

Summer is often the best time to visit the national parks. As the winter snows disappear and temperatures begin to warm, the tourist crowds thicken and visitor services are in full swing. Park roads start to open, though snow may bury high-elevation roads into **July** and often returns to dust mountain peaks at the end of **September.**

The parks of the Southwest, however, are best in **spring** and **fall;** time your visit then to avoid the triple-digit temperatures of summer.

Low Season

Winter is often the low season, when park lodges, campgrounds, and restaurants **close for the season,** leaving minimal services for visitors. Some national parks in the South still enjoy year-round access thanks to their more moderate climates.

AVOID THE CROWDS

Our national parks are popular and rightly so. As visitation increases, however, so do the crowds. Following are some helpful tips to avoid the mayhem.

VISIT IN SHOULDER SEASON

Summer is often peak season, when crowds are at their strongest. Time your visit for **spring** or **fall** instead, or consider visiting the park in winter when snowy solitude offers a quiet respite. If you must tour in summer, opt for some of the least-visited national parks for a less harried experience.

ARRIVE EARLY MORNING OR LATE AFTERNOON

Rush hour at park entrance stations is 10am-4pm. To claim a coveted parking spot at prime sights and trailheads, arrive **before 9am** (in ultra-busy parks or on weekends, arrive before 8am).

Tour the most popular sights and the best-loved trails in the early morning or late afternoon, which avoids the crowds common during the busiest part of the day. Aim first for park areas that may require more time or energy to reach.

BEST FOR SOLITUDE

These parks offer some breathing room away from the crowds, with plenty of time to bask in the beauty of the landscape.

BLACK CANYON OF THE GUNNISON: The park's South Rim has popular overlooks, but the long drive to the North Rim means you might have the place to yourself.

CHANNEL ISLANDS: Most visitors arrive by boat and only stay for the day. Plan to camp overnight and you'll have an island nearly to yourself, especially on Anacapa (which has only seven campsites).

GATES OF THE ARCTIC: Access to this remote arctic park is only by air. Once you're dropped off, you can float or paddle a Wild and Scenic River or backpack through the trail-less wilderness.

GREAT BASIN: Few visit Great Basin, which means you can explore its caves or climb the trail to Wheeler Peak.

GUADALUPE MOUNTAINS: Stand alone on the highest summit in Texas as you overlook the Chihuahuan Desert.

HALEAKALĀ: Visitors flock to the summit of this volcano to watch the sun rise. After that, parking spots open up and crowds dissipate. Come for sunset instead, when there are fewer people.

ISLE ROYALE: This park is set in the midst of Lake Superior, where only canoes and sea kayaks can reach its private bays. Paddle alone around the island's 337 miles of shoreline.

NORTH CASCADES: Pick up a backcountry permit and stay overnight in a shoreline camp on Ross Lake. Backpack into the mountains to put down some solitary miles.

THEODORE ROOSEVELT: Most visitors head for the park's South Unit, but you can find secluded nooks in the badlands of the North Unit or at Roosevelt's favorite, the Elkhorn Ranch.

WRANGELL-ST. ELIAS: The largest national park in the United States is home to millions of acres of solitude, especially along its less traveled Nabesna Road.

Explore THE NATIONAL PARKS

Best HIKING

ACADIA

A bit of scrambling and aid from iron rungs, steps, and handrails on exposed segments gets you straight up to the apex of the **Beehive Loop Trail** for views of ocean and mountains.

DENALI

The view only gets bigger the higher you go on the steep **Eielson Alpine Trail,** which takes in vast mountainous wilderness and views of Denali when clouds dissipate.

GLACIER

This route tiptoes along the top-of-the-world **Highline Trail**—full of wildflowers and mountain goats—to historic Granite Park Chalet, where views sprawl 360 degrees.

GRAND CANYON

From the rim to Phantom Ranch, the **Bright Angel Trail** descends through eons of geology into canyon depths to cross the Colorado River.

GRAND TETON

Below the jagged summits of Teewinot and Mount Owen lie the epic views from Inspiration Point. A boat shuttle cuts the distance to this rocky bluff overlooking blue Jenny Lake.

GREAT SMOKY MOUNTAINS

Wooden steps, stone staircases, and elevated boardwalks make short work of the climb to **Andrews Bald,** a mountaintop meadow where views encompass the southern Smokies.

OLYMPIC

Wildflowers pave the path to the summit of **Hurricane Hill,** perched perfectly for northerly views of the Strait of Juan de Fuca into Canada and southerly views into the icy Mount Olympus.

ROCKY MOUNTAINS

The **Lumpy Ridge** loop passes Gem Lake, cradled under granite walls, followed by views of Estes Park, Longs Peak, and the Continental Divide.

▼ BRIGHT ANGEL TRAIL, GRAND CANYON

ANGELS LANDING, ZION

YOSEMITE

Expect to be showered by waterfalls on the **Mist Trail**'s scenery-laden ascent to thundering Vernal and Nevada Falls.

YELLOWSTONE

Fairy Falls is a two-for-one hike that rewards hikers with an overlook of the fiery arms radiating from Grand Prismatic Spring, followed by a ribbon waterfall in summer.

ZION

Zigzag your way up a series of short switchbacks to **Angels Landing,** where fixed chains assist you on the skinny path to the summit amid 1,000-foot drop-offs.

NEVADA FALL, YOSEMITE

FIND YOUR PARK

Which park is for you? If you want . . .

ACCESSIBILITY: Take the wheelchair-accessible boardwalk loop in Congaree.

BACKPACKING: Hike the Teton Crest Trail in Grand Teton and circle the Wonderland Trail in Mount Rainier.

BIKING: Pedal the historic canal towpath in Cuyahoga Valley.

BOATING: Paddle or boat around Kabetogama Lake in Voyageurs.

BOULDERING: Scale the rock piles at Hidden Valley in Joshua Tree.

CAVES: Tour the Natural Entrance to the Big Room in Carlsbad Caverns.

CROSS-COUNTRY SKIING: Glide the groomed tracks of Teton Park Road in Grand Teton.

DIVING: Explore sunken wrecks off Dry Tortugas.

FALL FOLIAGE: Take an autumn cruise along Skyline Drive in Shenandoah.

HORSEBACK RIDING: Saddle up at Glacier Creek Stables in Rocky Mountain.

HOT SPRINGS: Soak your worries away at Buckstaff Baths in Hot Springs.

RAIN FORESTS: Sink into the lush greenery at the Hoh Rain Forest in Olympic.

REDWOODS: Walk amid old-growth giants at Stout Memorial Grove in the Redwood State and National Parks.

ROCK CLIMBING: Dance up El Capitan's big walls in Yosemite.

SNORKELING: Swim through the coral reefs of the Virgin Islands.

SNOWMOBILING: Rumble along snowy paths to Old Faithful in Yellowstone.

VOLCANOES: Watch molten lava spew forth from Kilauea in Hawai'i Volcanoes.

WATERFALLS: Tour the valley waterfalls in Yosemite.

Best FOR WILDLIFE

BIRDING IN BIG BEND

A year-round **birding** mecca, Big Bend amps up with song in spring, when tropical birds arrive to breed. Catch the Colima warbler that nests in the Chisos Mountains, the only place in the United States it does so.

MARINELIFE IN THE CHANNEL ISLANDS

On these California islands, **sea lions** and **northern fur seals** rear pups in summer while **blue** and **humpback whales** surface offshore.

CARIBOU IN DENALI

From the bus tour on Denali Park Road, see a lone **wolf** cruising across tundra or a pack out hunting. Watch along river bottoms for **caribou.**

CROCODILES IN THE EVERGLADES

In a rare coexistence in the Everglades, you can bicycle or take a tram to see **crocodiles** and **alligators** in Shark Valley, plus scads of **egrets, ibis,** and **storks.**

WHALES IN GLACIER BAY

On a summer boat tour in Glacier Bay, catch a **humpback whale** flipping its tail above the water, an **orca** pointing its nose at the sky, or **bald eagles** scooping up fish in their talons.

GRIZZLIES IN GRAND TETON

Along the Moose-Wilson Road, see **grizzly bears** claw through berry bushes and moose feeding in ponds. Around Antelope Flats, spot **pronghorn** among the sagebrush.

▼ CARIBOU, DENALI

ELK HERD, ROCKY MOUNTAIN

MOOSE IN ISLE ROYALE

A haven for **moose** with willows galore, Isle Royale has enjoyed a surge of the giant, awkward-looking ungulates due to waning wolf populations.

BEARS IN KATMAI

From special viewing platforms, you can watch **brown bears** capture fish in the tumbling waters at Brooks Camp.

ELK IN ROCKY MOUNTAIN

In spring, newborn **elk** follow cows; and in fall, the park resounds with bugling as large-antlered bulls round up harems during the rut.

BISON IN YELLOWSTONE

A drive through Lamar or Hayden Valley will yield sightings of hundreds of **bison.** Go in May to see baby calves, known as "red dogs." Look also for **bears, wolves,** and **bighorn sheep.**

DARK SKIES

City lights drown out the stars for more than three-fourths of the U.S. population. Designated International Dark Sky Parks offer places where you can still see the Milky Way. Moonless nights are best. Some parks offer telescopes for viewing the starry skies. In August, watch for the annual Perseid meteor shower.

International Dark Sky Parks

Big Bend delights with deep views of countless constellations on a camping or backpacking trip.

Black Canyon of the Gunnison has a June astronomy festival.

Canyonlands offers night-sky programs with telescope viewing.

Capitol Reef holds the Heritage Starfest in October.

Death Valley has night-sky events in winter and spring. Take a moonlit hike at Mesquite Sand Dunes or Badwater Basin.

Glacier programs include Logan Pass Stargazing Nights and after-dark sky viewing at Apgar and St. Mary Visitor Centers.

Grand Canyon celebrates the skies with a June Star Party.

Joshua Tree draws campers for its Night Sky Festival in November.

Parks with dark skies events and stargazing

Night sky festivals and events: Acadia (Sept.), Bryce (June), Lassen (Aug.), Rocky Mountain (every two years), and Pinnacles (spring night hikes)

Great for stargazing: Arches, Badlands, Olympic, Great Basin, and Voyageurs

Best PARKS FOR KIDS

The National Park Service's **Junior Ranger Program** is one of the best activities for kids. The program includes a booklet, which children complete as they learn about each park and engage in fun activities (parents can participate). Kids then turn in their completed booklets at a visitors center to be sworn in as Junior Rangers and receive a national park badge or patch.

In addition to the Junior Ranger Program, specialty **naturalist programs** are great for kids. Look for **Wildlife Olympics** programs, where kids can test their physical skills and see how they stack up against animals. Check out **explorer backpacks** from the park visitors centers. Each pack comes equipped with goodies like lenses, field guides, and activities. The park visitors centers are filled with kids rooms, hands-on exhibits, and touchable learning programs.

YELLOWSTONE

Stop at the Madison Junior Ranger Station, where naturalists present short, family-friendly talks.

ARCHES

Take the whole family on a guided walk through Fiery Furnace. Kids will love scrambling up the rock.

GREAT SMOKY MOUNTAINS NATIONAL PARK

Join rangers to catch salamanders in Hen Wallow Falls.

ACADIA

The park's tidepools are great fun for kids.

GLACIER

Gaze through a special telescope that lets you look right into the sun.

GREAT SAND DUNES

Kids can sandboard down the majestic dunes of this giant sandbox.

PETRIFIED FOREST

It's the best place for tactile fun, as kids can touch the numerous fossilized plants and animals.

BISCAYNE

The marinelife in this watery park enchant children. To explore, all they need is a mask and snorkel.

▼ SANDBOARD DOWN GREAT SAND DUNES.

BEST PARKITECTURE

National park lodges reflect the architecture of their surrounding landscape. Many are National Historic Landmarks not to be missed.

Majestic Yosemite Hotel, Yosemite: Formerly the Ahwahnee Hotel, this wood and granite palace features stained glass windows, two glorious stone fireplaces, Native American designs, and a three-story beamed ceiling in the dining room with floor-to-ceiling views of Yosemite Valley.

Grand Canyon Lodge, Grand Canyon: Perched on the North Rim, the lodge's dining room and sunroom offer dramatic overlooks of the immense canyon.

Many Glacier Hotel, Glacier: Restored to its former glory, Many Glacier boasts mountain views, a large fireplace, and a double spiral staircase.

Jackson Lake Lodge, Grand Teton: Inside the modern lodge, the Mural Dining Room's floor-to-ceiling windows frame views of the Tetons that compete with the painted murals by Carl Roters.

Old Faithful Inn, Yellowstone: The five-story lobby is ringed with knob-by-wood balconies centered on a stone fireplace equal in height.

Paradise Inn, Mount Rainier: The Paradise Inn features a steep-pitched roof and an immense lobby flanked by stone fireplaces.

Bryce Canyon Lodge, Bryce Canyon: The stone-and-wood edifice sports an expansive porch that invites a long look at the surrounding woods.

Crater Lake Lodge, Crater Lake: The lodge's first story is built of stone, then topped by wood and a shingled roof. The Great Hall and the back porch both overlook deep-blue Crater Lake.

Lake Crescent Lodge, Olympic: A glass-paned sunroom and dining room nearly pull Lake Crescent inside this lodge.

▼ CRATER LAKE LODGE

Best SCENIC DRIVES

TRAIL RIDGE ROAD

The country's highest paved road climbs to a dizzying 12,183 feet, ascending into alpine tundra among the granite peaks that define **Rocky Mountains National Park.**

SKYLINE DRIVE

Skyline Drive winds through **Shenandoah**'s lush forests and across long ridgelines, surrounded by the golds, oranges, and reds of fall foliage.

GOING-TO-THE-SUN ROAD

Amid sawtooth peaks and deep valleys, this National Civil Engineering Landmark cuts through **Glacier**'s thousand-foot cliffs to climb to its high point at Logan Pass.

▼ BADLANDS LOOP ROAD

BADLANDS LOOP DRIVE

In a landscape chiseled by water and wind, this scenic drive through the **Badlands** crawls between spires and sharp canyons banded in varied colors.

RIM DRIVE

This undulating loop circles the rim of **Crater Lake** to take in the intense blues of the deepest lake in the United States.

PAINTED DESERT RIM DRIVE

The fields of petrified wood are backdropped by the pastel-hued badlands of the Painted Desert in **Petrified Forest National Park**.

PARK LOOP ROAD

From rocky coast to forested lakes, this loop around **Acadia**'s Mount Desert Island stacks up scenery, especially at sunrise or sunset on the spur up Cadillac Mountain.

TIOGA ROAD, YOSEMITE

BADWATER BASIN

Take in Zabriskie Point, Badwater Basin, and Artists Palette on **Death Valley**'s scenic road, which drops to 282 feet below sea level—the lowest elevation in North America.

NEWFOUND GAP ROAD

Bisecting the **Great Smoky Mountains,** this 33-mile ridgetop route provides epic views of the Smokies, roadside stops for scenic hikes, and spring wildflowers or autumnal colors.

TIOGA ROAD

Lined with subalpine lakes and granite peaks, **Yosemite**'s high-elevation road crests the Sierra to tour Tuolumne Meadows and Tioga Pass, with one of the best views of Half Dome.

SHARE THE LOVE:
THE BEST PICS IN THE PARKS

Look no further than these prime spots for the best photos to share on social media—they're guaranteed to make your friends jealous. Share your pics with other national park fans on Instagram at #nationalparkservice, #the59parks, #wildernessculture, #nps.explorer, and #travelwithmoon.

Glacier Point, Yosemite: This photo op makes it look as though you're on the top of an alpine peak . . . when you're really just three feet from the scenic walkway.

Roosevelt Arch, Yellowstone: This historic landmark has pedestrian doors, which make for fun angles when shooting the native rock arch. Paved sidewalks offer safe access.

Cadillac Mountain, Acadia: From the summit, capture the orange flames of sunrise or sunset with the golden glow glinting off water below amid pink granite slabs.

Watchman Overlook, Crater Lake: This overlook is the perfect spot for a top-of-the-world selfie backdropped by Wizard Island, the acute blue lake, and the caldera rim.

Mather Point, Grand Canyon: For the best color of Vishnu Temple and the immensity of the Grand Canyon, strike an early-morning pose at this promontory jutting above the abyss.

Zabriskie Point, Death Valley: Look like a total badass with a selfie taken in front of the craggy badlands. Go at sunrise to paint your pic with a depth of color.

GLACIER POINT

Mormon Row, Grand Teton: These historic weathered barns stand in the foreground of the sawtooth Teton Mountains, offering timeless pics. The best lighting is in the morning.

Wonder Lake, Denali: In late evening, catch the reflection of North America's tallest peak in this subalpine lake—you'll be one of the few that do.

The National Parks
AT A GLANCE

NAME	STATE	WHY GO	HIGH SEASON	FEE	VISITATION RANK	PAGE
Acadia ★	Maine	seacoast	May-Oct.	$30	7	534
Arches	Utah	arches	Mar.-Oct.	$30	16	344
Badlands	South Dakota	prairie badlands	Apr.-June	$25-30	23	504
Big Bend	Texas	the Rio Grande	Nov.-Apr.	$30	41	393
Biscayne	Florida	tropical waters	May-Sept.	none	39	644
Black Canyon of the Gunnison	Colorado	deep gorge	May-Sept.	$25-30	43	428
Bryce Canyon	Utah	hoodoos	Sept.-Oct.	$35	12	320
Canyonlands	Utah	canyon country	Mar.-May, Sept.-Nov.	$30	26	354
Capitol Reef	Utah	cliffs, geology	May-Sept.	$15-20	21	332
Carlsbad Caverns	New Mexico	caves	May-Sept.	$12-15	36	381
Channel Islands	California	islands	June-Aug.	none	42	192
Congaree	South Carolina	old-growth forest	Mar.-Aug.	none	50	625
Crater Lake	Oregon	deepest lake	summer	$25-30	27	207
Cuyahoga Valley	Ohio	history	Mar.-May	none	13	550
Death Valley	California	sand dunes, desert scapes	Sept.-May	$30	19	143
Denali ★	Alaska	Denali, the mountain	May-Sept	$10-15	30	39
Dry Tortugas	Florida	coral and sand islands	Dec.-Mar.	$15	53	650
Everglades ★	Florida	subtropical wilderness	Dec.-Mar.	$25-30	24	630
Gates of the Arctic	Alaska	wilderness	June-Aug.	none	59	94

★ indicates one of the most-visited parks in the country.

NAME	STATE	WHY GO	HIGH SEASON	FEE	VISITATION RANK	PAGE
Glacier ★	Montana	glaciers	June-Sept.	$35	10	482
Glacier Bay	Alaska	glaciers	May-Sept	none	35	85
Grand Canyon ★	Arizona	mile-deep canyon	May-Sept.	$35	2	259
Grand Teton ★	Wyoming	Teton mountains	June-Sept.	$35	9	460
Great Basin	Nevada	caves	May-Sept.	none	49	294
Great Sand Dunes	Colorado	sand dunes	May-Sept.	$20-25	38	375
Great Smoky Mountains ★	Tennessee/ North Carolina	Smoky Mountains	June-Aug., Oct.	none	1	581
Guadalupe Mountains	Texas	fossil reefs	Mar.-Sept.	$5-10	48	387
Haleakalā	Hawaii	volcanic summit	May-Sept.	$25-30	22	661
Hawai'i Volcanoes	Hawaii	volcanic activity	May-Sept.	$25-30	14	671
Hot Springs	Arkansas	hot springs	Sept.-May	none	15	616
Isle Royale	Michigan	freshwater island	Apr.-Oct.	$7	56	559
Joshua Tree	California	Joshua trees	Oct.-Apr.	$30	11	154
Katmai	Alaska	brown bears	July-Aug.	none	54	70
Kenai Fjords	Alaska	fjords, glaciers	June-Aug.	none	45	56
Kings Canyon	California	scenic byways	summer	$35	29	131
Kobuk Valley	Alaska	caribou, sand dunes	June-Aug.	none	58	94
Lake Clark	Alaska	wilderness	June-Sept.	none	57	65
Lassen Volcanic	California	volcanic land	Aug.-Sept.	$30	37	168
Mammoth Cave	Kentucky	cave	May-Oct.	none	34	610
Mesa Verde	Colorado	cliff dwellings	May-Sept.	$25-30	33	366
Mount Rainier	Washington	glacial peak	June-Sept.	$30	18	234
National Park of American Samoa	American Samoa	tropical forests, coral reef	June-Sept.	none	51	690
North Cascades	Washington	glacial scenery	June-Sept.	none	55	245
Olympic ★	Washington	rain forest	summer	$30	8	217

NAME	STATE	WHY GO	HIGH SEASON	FEE	VISITATION RANK	PAGE
Petrified Forest	Arizona	petrified trees	Feb.-May	$20-25	31	281
Pinnacles	California	volcanic peaks, talus caves	Mar.-Apr.	$30	47	185
Redwood	California	coast redwoods	summer	varies	40	176
Rocky Mountain ★	Colorado	high peaks, wildlife	May-Sept.	$35	4	409
Saguaro	Arizona	saguaros	Nov.-Mar.	$20-25	25	287
Sequoia	California	giant sequoias	summer	$35	20	131
Shenandoah	Virginia	Blue Ridge mountains	Sept.-Oct.	$30	17	600
Theodore Roosevelt	North Dakota	wildlife, badlands	May-Sept.	$30	28	521
Virgin Islands	U.S. Virgin Islands	coral reefs	Dec.-Mar.	none	44	681
Voyageurs	Minnesota	watery wilderness	May-Sept.	none	46	566
Wind Cave	South Dakota	caves	May-Sept.	none	32	514
Wrangell-St. Elias	Alaska	largest national park	June-Sept.	none	52	77
Yellowstone ★	Wyoming	geysers, volcanic scapes	June-Aug., Dec.-Mar.	$35	6	435
Yosemite ★	California	waterfalls, granite	summer	$35	5	109
Zion ★	Utah	canyons	May-Sept.	$35	3	301

▼ KENNICOTT GLACIER, WRANGELL-ST. ELIAS

ALASKA

Steep-walled fjords, charismatic bears, soaring eagles, and glaciers that creep down mountainsides into the sea: Alaska's national parks enchant with stunning scenery and wildlife. The eight parks may be a challenge to reach, with some only accessible by boat or air, but the rewards more than make up for the effort to see them. Within their vast wildernesses, you can find solitude amid stark beauty.

Crowning the state, Denali bests all other mountains as the tallest summit in North America. Blanketed year-round in ice, the immense peak reflects in Wonder Lake. Even when clouds bury the mountain, visitors can spot wolves, grizzly bears, caribou, and moose roaming through the taiga forest and tundra of Denali National Park.

◄ ALASKA RANGE

ALASKA

Beaufort Sea

Kobuk Valley NP

Gates of the Arctic NP & PRES

CANADA

ALASKA

FAIRBANKS

Denali NP & PRES

Wrangell-St. Elias NP & PRES

ANCHORAGE

Lake Clark NP & PRES

Kenai Fjords NP

Glacier Bay NP & PRES

JUNEAU

Katmai NP & PRES

Aleutian Islands

Gulf of Alaska

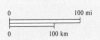

0		100 mi
0		100 km

The National Parks of
ALASKA

DENALI

This sweeping wilderness is great for wildlife viewing and spotting the tallest peak in North America (page 39).

KENAI FJORDS

The immense Harding Icefield spills with some 40 glaciers (page 56).

LAKE CLARK

The park is famous for three things: brown bear viewing, fly-fishing, and the cabin of naturalist Richard Proenneke (page 65).

GLACIER BAY

Experience untouched wilderness amid 3.3 million acres of rugged mountains, glaciers, fjords, and temperate rain forest (page 85).

KATMAI

Home to 2,200 brown bears, Katmai is the state's most iconic destination for bear viewing (page 70).

WRANGELL-ST. ELIAS

It's a magnet for mountaineers, birders, wildlife-watchers, backcountry hikers, and ghost town fans (page 77).

GATES OF THE ARCTIC

This vast, untouched wilderness spans about 8.4 million acres with no established roads, trails, or campgrounds (page 94).

KOBUK VALLEY

Charter a small plane to Kobuk Valley National Park and its staggering sand dunes (page 94).

1: CARIBOU, DENALI
2: CYLINDRICAL PINNACLES OF ICE, GLACIER BAY
3: GREAT KOBUK SAND DUNES, KOBUK VALLEY

Best OF THE PARKS

Flightseeing: Take a flightseeing trip around 20,310-foot Denali (page 43).

Bear viewing: View bears at Brooks Camp in Katmai, in Denali, and at Lake Clark (page 74).

Exit Glacier and Harding Icefield: Hike to the toe of Exit Glacier or up a mountainside overlooking the Harding Icefield (page 60).

McCarthy and Kennecott: Visit a quirky and isolated town that is joined by a neighboring "ghost mine town" (page 81).

Valley of Ten Thousand Smokes: Tour the desolate, ash-covered landscape created by the largest volcanic eruption of the 20th century (page 74).

PLANNING YOUR TRIP

Because Alaska is so big and the logistics of transport are challenging, plan at least **three weeks** to tour the national parks. Make lodging and campground **reservations** for in-park lodges a year in advance.

High season is **mid-June** through **early September.** You'll have the best weather, the richest landscape, the most touring and wildlife-viewing opportunities, and the most services available—along with the highest prices.

While you can drive to Denali, Kenai Fjords, and Wrangell-St. Elias, touring them may require shuttles, buses, and boat transportation. To visit Katmai, Lake Clark, Kobuk Valley, and Gates of the Arctic, you'll need to fly. To see Glacier Bay, take a ferry or plane to Gustavus and then head into the park via boat.

Anchorage offers the most accessible airport to the Alaskan parks.

▲ BEARS NEAR SILVER SALMON CREEK, LAKE CLARK

Road Trip

KENAI FJORDS, WRANGELL-ST. ELIAS, AND DENALI

Be ready to pound down wild miles in this epic road trip that links the three road-accessible national parks in Alaska. Fly into **Ted Stevens Anchorage International Airport** in Anchorage and **rent a car** capable of driving **gravel roads.**

Kenai Fjords

135 miles / 2.5 hours

From Anchorage, drive south for 2.5 hours to the east side of the Kenai Peninsula. In **Seward**, take Exit Glacier Road (aka Herman Leirer Rd.) to enter the park to see **Exit Glacier** and **Exit Glacier Nature Center.** From your two-night lodging accommodations in Seward, hop a full-day **boat tour** to see a tidewater glacier in **Aialik Bay.** Depart the following morning, unless you want to tack on the climb to the **Harding Icefield.**

NEAR HOLGATE GLACIER

Wrangell-St. Elias

377 miles / 7 hours

From Kenai Fjords, the route to Wrangell-St. Elias retraces the drive to Anchorage before following the Glenn Highway (AK 1) east to the Richardson Highway (AK 4) and the **Copper Center Visitor Center**. Overnight at a motel on the Richardson Highway. The

next morning, take the Edgerton Highway east to enter Wrangell-St. Elias on the unpaved **McCarthy Road**. At the bumpy road's terminus, walk into **McCarthy** to explore the funky town. Catch the shuttle and spend two nights at **Kennicott Glacier Lodge**. The next day, explore the **ghost mine** and hike to **Kennicott Glacier**.

Denali

335 miles / 9 hours or 2 days

From Wrangell-St. Elias, regain the Richardson Highway (AK 4) north to the **Denali Highway,** a mostly gravel 134-mile trek through the Alaska Range. At Cantwell, turn north on Parks Highway to the park entrance at **Denali Visitor Center**. Plan to overnight at one of the entrance hotels, then catch your transport the next morning to relax at **North Face Lodge** for several nights. En route, look for **wildlife** and explore **Eielson Visitor Center**. At the lodge, paddle **Wonder Lake**, hike, and gaze at the mountain **Denali**. To return to Anchorage, drive south on Parks Highway for 238 miles (4.25 hours).

1: DIXIE PASS, NEAR THE MCCARTHY ROAD, WRANGELL-ST. ELIAS
2: LYNX, DENALI
3: DENALI NATIONAL PARK NEAR EIELSON

DENALI NATIONAL PARK AND PRESERVE

Alaska

PASSPORT STAMPS ▼▼▼

WEBSITE:
www.nps.gov/dena

PHONE NUMBER:
907/683-9532

VISITATION RANK:
30

WHY GO:
See Denali, the highest peak in North America.

DENALI
NATIONAL PARK
AND PRESERVE

Lake Minchumina

Minchumina

North Fork Kuskokwim River

SNOHOMISH HILLS

Birch Creek

Slippery Cr.

McKinley River

Chilchukabena Lake

Kantishna River

River

Moose Creek

DENALI
NATIONAL PARK

Old Cache Lake

Spectacle Lake

DENALI
NATIONAL
PRESERVE

Big Lake

Highpower Creek

Castle Rocks
1,900ft

Herron River

Wilderness Boundary

Birch Creek

Wickersham Dome ▲

Kantishna
RANGER STATION ●
Wonder Lake
WONDER LAKE ⌂
MCKINLEY BAR TRAIL

DENALI WILDERNESS
within
DENALI NATIONAL PARK

Muddy River

Swift Fork

Slow Fork Hills

Tonzona River

Swift Fork

Foraker River

Straightaway Creek

Herron Glacier

A L A S K A

Mount Koven ▲

North Peak
19,470ft ▲

Kahiltna Dome ▲

Mount Crosson ▲

DENALI
South Peak
20,310ft ▲

Mount Hunter ▲

Mount Foraker
17,400ft ▲

Mount Stevens ▲

Heart Mountain
6,500ft ▲

Chedotlothna Glacier

Mount Russell
11,670ft ▲

Yentna Glacier

Lacuna Glacier

Kahiltna Glacier

Avalanche Spire
10,105ft ▲

Mount Goldie
6,315ft ▲

Surprise Creek

Dall Glacier

Mount Dall
8,756ft ▲

DENALI
NATIONAL PRESERVE

KICHATNA MOUNTAINS
Cathedral Spires

West Fork Yentna River

East Fork Yentna River

Chelatna Lake

Kahiltna Glacier

DUTCH HILLS

PETERS

Mount Kliskon
3,943ft ▲

Kahiltna River

Fairview Mountain
3,266ft ▲

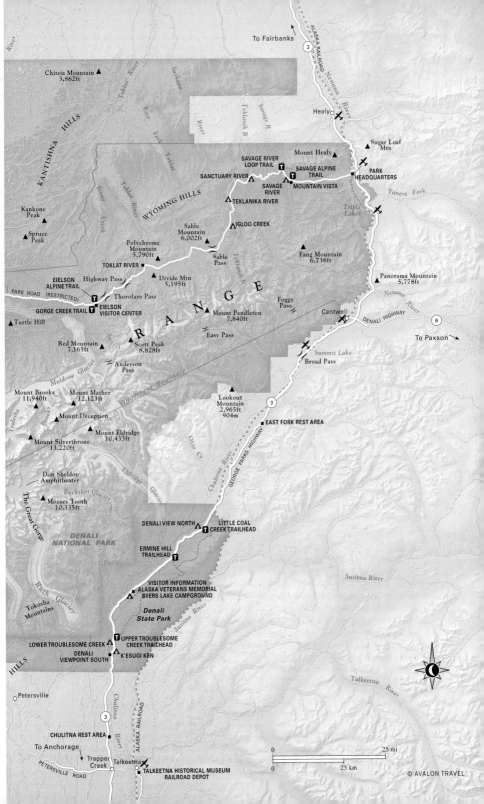

A visit to six-million-acre **DENALI NATIONAL PARK AND PRESERVE** is the trip of a lifetime, offering the easiest possible access to a vast swath of trackless wilderness. Pristine scenery is set against the backdrop of the Alaska Range and 20,310-foot Denali, the highest mountain in North America. Renowned for stellar opportunities to see bears, moose, caribou, Dall sheep, and wolves in the wild, the intact, protected ecosystem sits on the forefront of wilderness research and education. There's only one road, running just 92 miles into a park that measures almost 9,500 miles square. With a few exceptions, you can only drive the first 15 miles of the road in a private vehicle—but you can travel the entire distance in one of the park's many buses.

PLANNING YOUR TIME

The rugged, 92-mile **Denali Park Road** is the sole entrance into the park. You can only drive the first 15 miles of the road; with its restricted access, planning ahead is imperative. The only other way to travel the park road is via shuttle or tour bus, which require advance reservations.

Peak season (mid-May-mid-Sept.) is when services throughout the road system are fully operational. Once mid-September rolls around, many visitor-oriented activities and services—chief among them the "town" just outside the entrance to Denali National Park—shut down almost completely.

Advance reservations are required for the shuttle, tour, and camper buses and for the campgrounds (only two are accessible via the paved section of the park road) and park lodges. For specific travel dates in peak season, make bus, shuttle, and lodging reservations in December or January. If you have time and flexibility, you can book later, but if you wait to make shuttle reservations until your arrival at the park, you'll be put on a two-day waiting list.

ENTRANCE AND FEES

There is only one entrance to Denali, located at Mile 237 between Healy and Cantwell on George Parks Highway (AK 3). The entrance fee is $10-15 per person and is good for seven days. The fee is collected when reserving bus tickets and campsites; if you're not riding the bus or camping, pay the fee in person at the Denali Visitor Center.

VISITORS CENTERS

Denali has three main visitors centers and a couple of secondary visitor stations. Most are open from mid-May to mid-September; visitors centers deeper inside the park may open later. The **Murie Science and Learning Center** is the only visitors center open year-round. During the summer, public restrooms are available in all the park's visitors centers, with public-use pit toilets (basically, permanent outhouses) in the campgrounds.

The **Backcountry Information Center** (9am-6pm daily mid-May-mid-Sept.) and **Wilderness Access Center** (5am-7pm daily for bus departures and coffee, 7am-7pm for tickets) are both at Mile 1 of the Park Road. If you're here for a backcountry permit, head to the Backcountry Information Center; for bus tickets, to board a bus, or to arrange a stay in a campground, go to the Wilderness Access Center. If you need tickets or to check into a campground after hours, you can do so at the **Riley Creek Mercantile** (Mile 0.5 Park Rd.) until 11pm.

Denali Visitor Center

The **Denali Visitor Center** (Mile 1.5 Park Rd., 8am-6pm daily mid-May-mid-Sept.) is the main welcome center, with many ranger-led activities, an Alaska

Top ❸

❶ FLY OVER DENALI

Any trip into Denali National Park will be a phenomenal sightseeing adventure. But to really see the park—and Denali, the mountain—at their best, take a **flightseeing** trip. Even the most jaded Alaskan will subside into awe when "the High One" is front and center in the windshield. Many flightseeing operations also include a landing on a nearby glacier, so you can get out and walk on ground that only the world's most intrepid explorers have ever reached by other means. This is truly a once-in-a-lifetime splurge.

FLIGHTSEEING IN DENALI

❷ TOUR THE PARK BY BUS

With the exception of the road lottery and the early shoulder season, you can only drive to Mile 15 of the Park Road. If you want to go farther than that, you must take a bus. Most of the road is very narrow, with graded gravel and no shoulder, so it's a relief to let someone else do the driving while you keep an eye out for wildlife and scenery. Buses run into Denali National Park from mid-May to mid-September. The buses that go all the way to **Kantishna,** at the end of the road, usually don't start until June. Take along a daypack with additional clothing layers for changeable weather.

❸ WATCH WILDLIFE

Even if Denali, the mountain, is hiding behind the clouds, the park itself offers unparalleled views of dramatic scenery—from the towering, snow-clad Alaska Range to high tundra and swift-flowing glacier-fed streams—and great opportunities to see wildlife. Many visitors treat the bus ride into the park as a photo safari and come back with memories to last a lifetime. You can take the same approach on any trip into Denali, even if it's "just" a short day hike.

There are a few places you can direct your eyes—or binoculars—to help find the specific animals that interest you. Keep a sharp eye out for **moose** on the first 15 miles of the roadway, especially near streams; spot **caribou** near the last two miles; watch for **Dall sheep** on rocky areas above tree line; and look for **grizzly bears** everywhere, but especially above tree line. There are black bears in Denali National Park, too, but they tend to stay below tree line and aren't often seen. **Wolf** sightings are unpredictable, but this remains one of the best places in the state to view them.

DALL SHEEP

ONE DAY IN DENALI

If you only have one day in Denali, hop aboard the **shuttle bus** along Denali Park Road. The early-morning bus takes four hours to travel to **Eielson Visitor Center,** stopping en route for wildlife-watching. Upon reaching the visitors center, tour the exhibits and then join a ranger on the **Eielson Stroll** or opt for a more strenuous adventure on the **Eielson Alpine Trail.** If Denali is visible, you'll burn through plenty of photos before your evening return. For the trip, pack a few warm layers of clothing, lunch, snacks, water—and a camera.

Geographic bookstore and gift shop, a luggage check, the only restaurant in the park, and beautiful exhibits showcasing Denali's landscapes, wildlife, and natural history. The Alaska Railroad train depot is just a short walk away.

Murie Science and Learning Center

From mid-May to mid-September, the **Murie Science and Learning Center** (Mile 1.4 Park Rd., 9am-4:30pm daily year-round) acts as the primary welcome center. The science center also runs small-group interactive learning opportunities. Many of those programs are intended for local students, but if you plan ahead, you might be able to send young visitors on a once-in-a-lifetime field expedition through the **Alaska Geographic Field Institute** (www.akgeo.org).

Eielson Visitor Center

With million-dollar views of Denali (when it is visible), the **Eielson Visitor Center** (Mile 66 Park Rd., 9am-7pm daily June-mid-Sept.) offers services deep within the park, including daily ranger-led walks, interpretive exhibits, and a small art gallery. Many visitors make this their destination on the Park Road and hike one of the three nearby trails. Eielson Visitor Center has water, but no food.

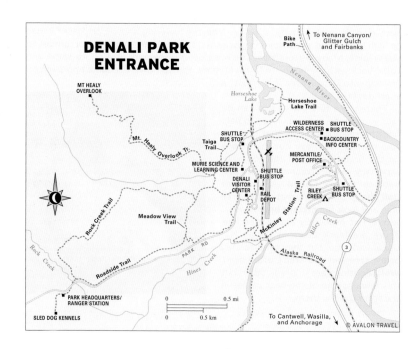

SLED DOG DEMONSTRATIONS

SIGHTS

DENALI, THE MOUNTAIN

At a whopping 20,310 feet in elevation, **Denali** is the tallest peak in North America. On clear days, it is visible from Anchorage, Fairbanks, and Talkeetna, although you can't see it from the park entrance because terrain is in the way! Once you're past Mile 9 of the Park Road, however, you have a chance of seeing the mountain—if it's "out." If you take a bus all the way to Mile 66 of the Park Road and the Eielson Visitor Center, where there won't be any folds of land between you and *the* mountain, you might even get stunning views of Denali (again, if it's "out").

The skies around Denali are often clear during the winter, but the mountain generates its own clouds during the summer, so on average, it may only be fully visible one day out of three. Don't give up, though—it's worth taking a chance to see it, and you have a better than 50-50 chance of getting at least a partial view of the mountain peeking out of the clouds. (Alaska's climate is changing, but you have a slightly better chance of seeing the mountain in the early summer rather than later in the year.)

Here's one thing that you shouldn't do: Don't march up to the Denali National Park rangers and announce that you'd like to hike the mountain itself. Plainly put, most people can't; any trip up Denali is a high-level mountaineering expedition that requires technical skill, equipment, and quite a bit of fitness. If you don't have the requisite skills, you can enlist the aid of a professional guiding service like the locally run **Alaska Mountaineering School** (13765 E. 3rd St., Talkeetna, 907/733-1016, www.climbalaska.org)—but you need to be willing to work hard, put in a lot of preparation beforehand, and learn a new skill set that might just save your life or those of your buddies.

WONDER LAKE

Wonder Lake is one of the most photogenic places for reflection pictures of Denali and the Alaska Range. The road that circles part of the 2.5-mile-long lake allows you the closest view of the mountain. Even if clouds preclude seeing the reflection, the lake provides good wildlife watching for moose and waterfowl. Even grizzlies swim across the lake. Swarms of mosquitoes cling to boggy ground in the area, so bring bug spray or head nets. To get to Wonder Lake requires an **11-hour round-trip shuttle ride.** The best views, made famous by photographs from the likes of Ansel Adams, are from the north end.

SLED DOG DEMONSTRATIONS

Denali is the only national park with a working kennel of sled dogs. You can tour the park kennels and visit the working huskies in free, 30-minute tours given several times daily

(June-Aug., limited schedule May and Sept.). The only catch is getting there. There's no parking at the kennels, so you have to either walk 1.5 miles (mostly uphill) or take the **Sled Dog Demonstration Shuttle** from the Denali Visitor Center bus stop, departing at least 40 minutes before each demonstration begins.

The kennels are also open year-round to visits (generally 8am-5pm) even if a tour isn't scheduled. During the winter, the kennels may be almost vacant when the dog teams are out working. Do not bring your pets—this would not be a fun bonding experience for them or for the sled dogs.

SCENIC DRIVE
DENALI PARK ROAD

When snowplowing is complete (late Mar. or early Apr.), the 92-mile **Denali Park Road** opens. In summer, rich patchworks of green forests and tundra flank broad braided rivers in gravel bars, while late August brings on yellows and reds. The road closes when winter returns (Sept.-Oct.).

Touring the first 15 miles of paved road to Savage River Rest Area will take about an hour without stops. This is as far as cars can go, with the exception of those with reservations at Teklanika Campground. Even though the mountain Denali is 70-plus miles away, you can still nab views through breaks in the taiga forest. When weather permits, you can spot it at **Mile 9** where the taiga breaks into tundra, again about 1.5 miles farther, and around **Savage River.** For wildlife, keep your eyes peeled for caribou and Dall sheep near the last two miles.

For those with **camping reservations at Teklanika Campground,** pass through the checkpoint at Savage River and continue another 14 miles beyond the pavement on the bumpy gravel road. Stop in early summer to look at wildflowers at **Primrose Ridge** (Mile 16) and scan for sheep. The road parallels the Teklanika River for several miles before the campground.

For those lucky ones who won the **road lottery,** permits allow driving as far as conditions allow. The narrow and shoulderless gravel road includes washboards and potholes. After crossing Sable Pass, brilliant green and orange colors flank hillsides from **Polychrome Overlook** (Mile 46). The braided **Toklat River** (Mile 52) spreads wide across the valley floor, often home to herds of caribou, before the road climbs over Highway Pass to **Stony Dome** (Mile 56) for

▼ TOKLAT RIVER

WINNING THE ROAD LOTTERY

The 92-mile road running into Denali National Park is only open to private vehicles until Mile 15—unless you're lucky enough to win the yearly road lottery. Anybody (including visitors from out of state or out of country) can apply for the lottery. The lucky winners can drive their own cars as far into the park as conditions permit.

The **lottery entry period** runs from May 1 to May 31 every year (www.recreation.gov) and the winning tickets are drawn in mid-June; if you win, you'll be notified by email and your credit card will be charged a $25 fee for the road permit. The driving period runs for four days, usually in September, and you're automatically assigned a day that your permit is valid. It's up to you to cover travel costs and logistics, and to provide the car.

Many rental car companies won't allow you to take their vehicles on gravel highways (including the Park Road), but **Alaska Auto Rental** (907/457-7368, www.alaskaautorental.com), which is based out of Fairbanks with a second office in nearby Healy, will. They also rent to drivers under 25 years of age.

a closer view of Denali. After popping over Thorofare Pass, the views of Denali only get bigger at **Eielson Visitor Center** (Mile 66) and **Wonder Lake** (Mile 87).

HIKING

Most of the maintained trails in Denali National Park are short, and the trails nearest the visitors centers are often crowded (by Alaska standards, anyway). But what these trails lack in length and sometimes privacy, they make up for in their beauty and scenic variety. If you want some company on the trail, rangers often lead hikes on the maintained paths and "Discovery Hikes" that go off-trail.

Hikers can access a few maintained trails off the paved section of **Denali Park Road.** (Vehicles are permitted on this section, so you can hit the trailhead whenever you want.) A free shuttle also runs to Savage River. A family-friendly trail, the mostly level **Savage River Loop** (1.7 mi. rt., 1 hr.) starts from the Savage River Day Use Area. Through

HIKING IN DENALI

Best Hike

EIELSON ALPINE TRAIL

1.6 MILES ROUND-TRIP
DURATION: 1.5 hours
ELEVATION CHANGE: 1,010 feet
DIFFICULTY: strenuous
TRAILHEAD: Eielson Visitor Center; access via park shuttle to Mile 66

The views just get bigger and bigger on this trail that climbs Thorofare Ridge north from Eielson Visitor Center. Three long switchbacks climb steeply to gain elevation. But soon, the trail departs the tundra to enter talus slopes and a seemingly barren alpine world, where tiny alpine wildflowers such as pink moss campion thrive tucked in the rocks. When Denali is visible, hikers often forget to look elsewhere, but the ridge overlooks the giant McKinley River that widens along the valley floor. The high alpine tundra harbors Dall sheep and grizzly bears along with marmots. While you can zip up and down, exploring the wide-open summit with 360-degree views is worth the additional time.

the glacier-carved river valley, the tundra trail goes downstream, crosses the river on a bridge, and returns. Or you can take the more strenuous four-mile **Savage Alpine Trail,** which goes up and over tundra slopes to the Savage River Campground.

The **Horseshoe Lake Trail** (3.2 mi. rt.) loops around a pretty lake of the same name. The trailhead is less than a mile into the park (near the railroad tracks) and goes to an overlook before dropping steeply to circle the lake. An additional 0.5-mile loop at the north end leads to the Nenana River.

Beyond the pavement on the Park Road, shuttle buses access other trailheads and let hikers hop on and off anywhere. At Mile 85, near Wonder Lake Campground, the level **McKinley River Bar Trail** (4.8 mi. rt.) goes through boggy meadows and spruce trees to terminate at the broad gravel expanse of the river bar.

RECREATION

BACKPACKING

Venturing off established trails and into the backcountry is one of the most glorious ways to see Denali. Due to the remote location and challenging terrain, which often involves crossings of swift, glacier-fed creeks, treat even a simple day trip as a serious backcountry expedition.

SAVAGE CANYON

BACKPACKING IN DENALI

To backpack in Denali—sleeping in a tent somewhere off in the tundra, with the midnight sun or a spangle of stars and aurora borealis glimmering overhead—you'll need a permit. First-come, first-served **backcountry permits** (free) are issued in person only at the **Backcountry Information Center** (Mile 1 Park Rd., 9am-6pm daily mid-May-mid-Sept.) 24 hours before your departure date. You will also receive a loaner bear-resistant food container, which is required while in the backcountry; return it within 48 hours of departing the backcountry.

The permit process takes about an hour and must be completed, in person, by all members of your party. To help you speed through the process, watch the wilderness safety video in the **Wilderness Access Center** (Mile 1 Park Rd.), which opens at 7am—two hours before the Backcountry Information Center opens. Then grab a copy of the worksheet from the back door of the Backcountry Information Center and fill it out in advance. Once the Backcountry Information Center opens, talk to a ranger, be assigned your unit number, buy maps, and purchase any bus tickets needed.

FLIGHTSEEING

Only a few carriers are authorized to make glacier landings in Denali National Park. They are:

Fly Denali (907/683-2359, www.flydenali.com) is the only provider that can depart straight from the park entrance (they base their aircraft in Anchorage, Talkeetna, and Healy).

Talkeetna Air Taxi (departing from Talkeetna; 800/533-2219, www.talkeetnaair.com)

Sheldon Air Service (departing from Talkeetna; 907/733-2321, www.sheldonairservice.com)

K2 Aviation (departing from Talkeetna; 800/764-2291, www.flyk2.com)

Kantishna Air Taxi (departing from Kantishna; 907/644-8222, www.katair.com, June-Sept., 303/449-1146 Oct.-May) provides air taxi services between Kantishna and the park entrance.

Temsco Air (877/789-9501, http://temscoair.com) also offers glacier landing tours to a glacier near the park and helicopter-supported hiking within the park. Small planes are an amazing adventure, but helicopters are even better: They can go closer, lower, and slower to terrain than a plane, and they can easily land in places that a plane pilot would never consider.

TOKLAT RIVER

BIKING

You can only drive the entirety of the Park Road if you're lucky enough to win the road lottery. But you can travel the entire Park Road—all 92 miles of it—on two wheels any time you like. You can rent a bike from most lodges near or inside the park, or use nearby **Denali Outdoor Center** (Mile 238.9 Parks Hwy., 888/303-1925 or 907/683-1925, www.denalioutdoorcenter.com). Make sure you bring proof that you paid your entrance fee at the Denali Visitor Center, or you may not get past Savage River at Mile 15.

If you want to overnight anywhere along the road, you'll need to book at one of the pricey all-inclusive lodges along the way, stay in one of the park's six bike rack-equipped campgrounds, or rough it like a backpacker (permit required). If you go the backpacking route you'll be required to carry a bear-resistant food container and conceal your bike off the road; if you lose your bike in the bushes, park officials won't help you hunt for it.

To extend your reach on a day trip, take a bus into the park to bike as far as you like on the road, then hop on a bus coming back. You can only take your bike on shuttle buses—not the narrated tour buses. Not all shuttles can take bikes, and those that do are limited to just two bikes at a time, so it's best to make **reservations** (www.reservedenali.com) or at least verify scheduling with a call to the shuttle operator (800/622-7275 or 907/272-7275).

RAFTING

Denali's swift, restless creeks make for dangerous crossings on foot—but that also translates to lots of fun for rafters. At Denali, rafting is on the Nenana River, which borders the park. **Denali Raft Adventures** (888/683-2234 or 907/683-2234, www.denaliraft.com) offers trips all the way from calm Class I water to boiling Class IV rapids. You choose between oar rafts (in which only the guide paddles) and paddle rafts (where every client pitches in, following commands from the guide).

Denali Outdoor Center (888/303-1925 or 907/683-1925, www.denalioutdoorcenter.com) is also excellent, with raft runs down Class III-IV rapids on oar or paddle rafts, plus lake and white-water kayaking trips.

WHERE TO STAY

INSIDE THE PARK

There are various bed-and-breakfasts and lodges near the entrance to Denali National Park but only a few lodges within the park. Most offer all-inclusive rates, with no TVs, no phones, and limited satellite Wi-Fi (if any). People come here to unplug or to splurge on a base-camp experience that lets them hike, bike, or paddle deep into the park without having to take a long bus ride or secure a backcountry camping permit. To overnight at private lodges requires taking a bus or flying to Kantishna, the airstrip at the road's terminus.

The **Denali Backcountry Lodge** (Mile 92 Park Rd., 800/808-8068, www.alaskacollection.com, from $529) is unique because it has no minimum stay. The rate includes lodging, three meals, twice-daily shuttle runs to nearby Wonder Lake, and extra activities like gold panning, mountain biking, morning yoga classes, and lake fishing. Ask for a room near the creek. If you want to avoid crowds of day-trippers, eat lunch early.

The **North Face Lodge** (907/683-2290, www.campdenali.com, from $1,800/3 nights) is the closest facility to the very popular backcountry camping destination of Wonder Lake, just 1.5 miles away on bicycle or by foot. The 15 hotel-style rooms all have electricity, private bathrooms, and running water, and an outdoor patio provides beautiful views of the Alaska Range. The all-inclusive rate covers meals, lodging, transportation from the railroad depot,

day and night programs that are heavy on hiking, and the use of outdoor gear, including canoes, bikes, and fishing equipment. There's a fixed schedule for arrivals, with only three-, four-, or seven-night stays allowed.

The same company runs **Camp Denali** (907/683-2290, www.campdenali.com, from $1,800/3 nights), where you pay the same rate to stay in rustic cabins lit by propane lamps and wood-stoves, with outhouses instead of flush toilets. A modern, shared bathroom and shower facility is available, but you'll have to take a five-minute walk to get there. Bonus: The camp sits right at tree line and has some amazing views, including Denali when it's "out."

There's just one real restaurant in Denali National Park: **Morino Grill** (Mile 1.5 Park Rd., mid-May-mid-Sept. daily 7:30am-5pm, limited hours during the shoulder season) is about 30 yards from the Denali Visitor Center. It offers boxed takeaway lunches and coffee all day long, plus made-to-order lunch and dinner.

You can purchase a limited selection of snacks at the **Wilderness Access Center** (Mile 1 Park Rd.), which also has a small coffee stand. The **Riley Creek Mercantile** (Mile 0.5 Park Rd., 907/682-9246) sells sandwiches, snacks, and limited groceries, along with camp fuel.

GRIZZLY BEARS

NAME	LOCATION	PRICE	SEASON	AMENITIES
Denali Backcountry Lodge	Kantishna	$529 and up	June-Sept.	lodge rooms, dining, shuttle
North Face Lodge	end of Denali Park Rd.	$1,800 and up	June-Sept.	hotel rooms, dining, transportation
Camp Denali	end of Denali Park Rd.	$1,800 and up	June-Sept.	cabins, pit toilets, shared bath
Riley Creek	Mile 0.25	$15-30	year-round	tent and RV sites
Savage River	Mile 14	$30-46	May-Sept.	tent, RV, and group sites
Sanctuary River	Mile 22	$15	May-Sept.	tent sites; camper bus
Teklanika River	Mile 29	$25	May-Sept.	tent and RV sites
Igloo Creek	Mile 35	$15	May-Sept.	tent sites; camper bus
Wonder Lake	Mile 85	$16	June-Sept.	tent sites; camper bus

Camping

There are six established campgrounds within Denali National Park. **Reservations** (800/622-7275 or 907/272-7275, www.reservedenali.com) are recommended for Riley Creek and Teklanika Campgrounds, located right inside the park entrance on either end of the paved section of the park road. **Riley Creek** has 147 campsites and an RV dump station (summer only), as well as cell and Internet reception. Camping is free in winter, when services are limited. One of the most coveted campgrounds in the park, **Teklanika River** has 53 campsites for tents or RVs. Book a three-night minimum stay so that you can drive to the campground. Then use the shuttle to hike or sightsee farther up the park road.

Savage River is reached by car or via the Savage River Shuttle. The campground has 33 tent and RV sites that can book up.

Three campgrounds can only be accessed via the **camper shuttle bus**. **Wonder Lake**, with 28 tent-only campsites, is the most popular regardless of its healthy mosquito population. Reservations (800/622-7275, www.reservedenali.com, $6 fee) are accepted. **Sanctuary River** (first come, first served) has six tent-only campsites while **Igloo Creek** (first come, first served) has seven tent-only campsites.

Basic camping items are available at **Riley Creek Mercantile** (Mile 0.5 Park Rd., 907/682-9246). To rent or buy backpacking equipment, contact **Denali Mountain Works** (Mile 239 Parks Hwy., 907/683-1542, http://denalimountainworks.com), 1.5 miles north of the park entrance along the Parks Highway. You can also rent gear from REI, which has locations in Fairbanks and Anchorage.

OUTSIDE THE PARK

Outside the park, on George Parks Highway (AK 3), a small community of seasonal visitor services and lodges clusters around the **entrance to Denali National Park.** Twelve miles north, **Healy** is the closest year-round town to the park entrance.

GETTING THERE

AIR

Alaska Airlines (800/252-7522, www.alaskaair.com) offers daily flights from Anchorage and Fairbanks. In Anchorage, **Ted Stevens Anchorage International Airport** (ANC, 5000 W. International Airport Rd., www.dot.alaska.gov) receives year-round service from Alaska Airlines, Delta, United, and Iceland Air, with seasonal service from JetBlue and Condor.

TOUR DENALI BY BUS.

RAIL

Unless you're planning to drive the Park Road or stay outside the park, taking the **Alaska Railroad** (800/544-0552, www.alaskarailroad.com) to Denali is one of the best rides in the state. The trip takes about 4 hours from Fairbanks or 7.5 hours from Anchorage.

CAR

Talkeetna, Anchorage, and Fairbanks are connected by the Parks Highway, which merges into the Glenn Highway as it nears Anchorage. If you're coming to Denali by car, the trip is 238 miles from Anchorage, theoretically a little more than four hours, but leave yourself at least five to make it up the Parks Highway, which is often congested by Alaska standards. The drive from Fairbanks is 125 miles or just over two hours if you don't run into construction or slow RVs.

Year-round gas stations are available in Cantwell (30 miles south of the park entrance) and Healy (11 miles north of the entrance). During the summer, you can also get gas at a seasonal station one mile north of the park entrance.

BUS

You can get to Denali on the **Park Connection** (800/266-8625, www.alaskacoach.com), one of the most established bus services in the state, with service all the way from Seward to Denali.

GETTING AROUND
DRIVING

You can only drive to Mile 15 of the Park Road. Fortunately, you don't really need a car to get around once you've made it to the park. Most housing comes with a free shuttle that will pick you up from the train depot, airport, or bus stop, and if you're taking a tour, most tour operators will happily pick you up from your hotel or from one of the free shuttle bus stops near the park entrance.

TOURS AND SHUTTLE BUSES

Tickets (800/622-7275 or 907/272-7275, www.reservedenali.com) for both tour buses and shuttle buses are sold through the park concessionaire and can be ordered as early as December 1 of the preceding year. This is also when the ticket prices, which fluctuate every year, are set. Get tickets online or at the **Wilderness Access Center** (Mile 1 Park Rd., 5am-7pm for bus departures and coffee, 7am-7pm for tickets). About two-thirds of shuttle reservations are sold in advance.

Narrated tour buses ($77-194) are guided by the drivers, who are also trained naturalists. They do stop for photo opportunities, but don't stop to let people hop on and off the bus. Trips range 5-12 hours, depending on how far

SAVAGE RIVER AREA

each bus goes into the park. Bus schedules fluctuate throughout the summer, but the staff at the Wilderness Access Center can fill you in. Lunch, snacks, and water are included.

Shuttle buses ($51 round-trip to Kantishna) aren't narrated, but they do stop for wildlife viewing and to let people hop on and hop off along the road. Schedules and where the buses start and stop vary quite a bit, so always double-check to make sure you don't miss the last bus back! Bring along food, snacks, and water.

Finally, the **camper bus** ($34 round-trip) is available only to people who are staying at an established campground or in the backcountry.

COURTESY BUSES

There are three courtesy buses near the park entrance—not to be confused with the tours that run deeper into the park. The entrance shuttles all operate daily during the summer season (roughly mid-May-mid-Sept.), and they're all free and wheelchair-accessible.

The **Savage River Shuttle** (marked "Woo Hoo!", 2 hrs. rt.) travels between the Denali Visitor Center, the Wilderness Access Center, and the Savage River area (Mile 14 Park Rd.). This is also the shuttle to the Savage River Campground. The round-trip takes about two hours.

The **Riley Creek Loop Shuttle** (marked "Nom Nom Nom!", 30 min. rt.) travels a loop between all the visitors centers near the park entrance, the Riley Creek Campground, and the Horseshoe Lake/Mount Healy trailhead.

The **Sled Dog Demonstration Shuttle** leaves from the Denali Visitor Center bus stop, departing at least 40 minutes before each demonstration begins.

THE DENALI HIGHWAY

If you just can't get enough of Alaska's glorious alpine scenery, there is no drive better than the **135-mile Denali Highway,** which runs east-west between the small community of Cantwell, on the Parks Highway, and the minuscule community of Paxson on the Richardson Highway. The road is mostly gravel and very rough in places, but tour buses navigate it—so if you're careful and go slow, it is almost always drivable in passenger vehicles. Because most of the road is above tree line, you'll be treated to nonstop views of glaciers, lakes, and the skirts of dense green trees that are slowly creeping higher on the peaks as the state warms. Wildlife sightings include moose, bear, and waterfowl.

THE NORTHERN LIGHTS

Fairbanks, Alaska, is one of the very best places for viewing the northern lights, or the aurora borealis. The lights, which are caused by electrically charged particles from the sun colliding with earth's atmosphere, can be seen directly overhead in Fairbanks, as opposed to down low on the horizon as you'd see them from the southern part of Alaska. One study showed that if you spend three nights actively looking for the northern lights in Fairbanks from September to April, when it's dark enough to actually see them, you have an 80 percent chance of success.

Visitors are sometimes disappointed to find that summer—Alaska's most hospitable season by far—is the worst possible time for seeing the aurora borealis. The sky just isn't dark enough. If the aurora is your thing, plan a trip to Fairbanks, Nome, or any community at similar latitude **September-April,** when skies are dark and the northern lights are more active.

There's no guarantee you'll see them while you're here—but if you take three or four days and use the following tips, you'll have better odds:

Plan to visit Nome, Fairbanks, or a community farther north (like Barrow); all three are at a high-enough latitude to see the lights overhead. You might still see the lights in more southerly parts of Alaska, but they're more likely to shine low on the horizon and may even be blocked by mountains.

Get as far away as you can from the city lights and any other light pollution. The darker the sky, the clearer your view of the lights will be. Chena Hot Springs is good place for viewing the northern lights: It's 60 miles out of town and offers heated viewing areas where you can watch for the lights all night long.

Ask for a wake-up call. Most hotels under the "aurora oval" (the latitude at which the aurora shines overhead) will happily let you know if the aurora comes out. You can also check the University of Alaska Fairbanks Geophysical Institute's aurora forecast at www.gi.alaska.edu/auroraforecast.

Be patient. The northern lights don't shine every night, but if you spend three nights under the aurora oval—when it's dark enough to see them, and you're actively looking for them—you have at least an 80 percent chance of seeing them.

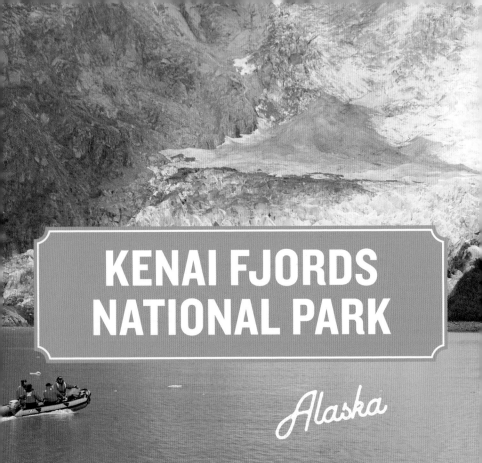

KENAI FJORDS NATIONAL PARK

Alaska

WEBSITE:
www.nps.gov/kefj

PHONE NUMBER:
907/422-0500

VISITATION RANK:
45

WHY GO:
Explore Alaskan fjords and the glaciers that shaped them.

PASSPORT STAMPS ▼▼▼

▲ ANCHOR GLACIER

KENAI FJORDS NATIONAL PARK is home to more than 670,000 acres of rugged glacier fjords. The park gets its name from the true fjords that line the coast—deep, steep-walled, narrow inlets gouged by ancient glaciers, perhaps the predecessors of the glaciers that now flow out of the park's immense Harding Icefield. Take a boat tour to see the caves up close and admire their striking rock formations. You'll have the added bonus of watching sea otters, humpback whales, and even gray whales during their March-mid-May migration.

The Harding Icefield covers more than half of the park—its 700 square miles spread over the Kenai Mountains with a thick blanket of ice. From the icefield, 38 glaciers spill east and west. These shrinking and thinning glaciers reveal the effects of climate change, despite the maritime weather that dumps 60 feet of snow annually on the icefield.

The collision of the marine fjord and icefield environment makes this national park unique. Its marine zone bounces with wildlife that includes puffins, bald eagles, black oystercatchers, Dall's porpoises, Steller's sea lions, and black bears. In the mountains above, creatures such as marmots, wolverines, moose, snowshoe hares, and mountain goats adapt to the cold.

Taking to the water—or to the air—is the easiest way to take in the high drama of this park.

PLANNING YOUR TIME

Kenai Fjords National Park is located just outside the town of Seward on the Kenai Peninsula in south-central Alaska. There are three easy ways to explore the park: **by air** on a flightseeing trip; **on foot,** via some of the state's most spectacular hiking trails; or **by tour boat** into the fjords. Most of the park is roadless wilderness, so you'll need to combine various modes of exploration.

June-August is the peak season for visiting. Services are reduced in May and September. Be prepared for cool, rainy weather in summer, though temperatures can climb to the low 70s. October-April offers cross-country skiing on the Exit Glacier Road, but rough seas preclude boat tours of the fjords.

ENTRANCE AND FEES

From Seward Highway (AK 9), the main vehicle entrance is via **Exit Glacier Road** (signed as Herman Leirer Rd.), three miles north of Seward. This is the only road that enters Kenai Fjords National Park. It takes about 20 minutes to drive to its end at the Exit Glacier Nature Center, where trails head to Exit Glacier, the closest glacier to reach on foot, and the Harding Icefield. There is no entrance fee.

VISITORS CENTERS

The **Kenai Fjords National Park Visitor Center** (1212 4th Ave., Seward, 907/422-0535, 9am-7pm daily Memorial Day-Labor Day, 9am-5pm daily mid-May-mid-Sept.) is in Seward, outside the park. It contains interpretive displays and an auditorium where the national park's many films are shown.

The modest **Exit Glacier Nature Center** (Herman Leirer Rd., 9am-7pm daily in summer) has a small selection of natural history displays. Ranger naturalists give daily talks and guide walks

KENAI FJORDS
NATIONAL PARK

TUSTUMENA
LAKE

Indian Glacier
5,720ft ▲

KENAI
NATIONAL
WILDLIFE
REFUGE

Tustumena Glacier

Truuli Glacier

5,269ft ▲

Chernof Glacier

5,288ft ▲

Sheep

River

Creek

5,873ft ▲

Chernof Gl

Fox

Bradley

River

Bradley

K   E   N   A   I

McCarty Glacier

6,340ft ▲

KACHEMAK BAY
STATE PARK

Glacier
Lake

Kachemak Bay

Bradley Lake

Kachemak
Creek   Kachemak Gl

Dinglestadt

Glacier

McCarty Fjord

Dixon Glacier

Nuka Glacier

Nuka

Native
Corporation

Portlock Glacier

Delight
Lake

KENAI NATIONAL
WILDLIFE REFUGE

Iceworm Peak
5,800ft ▲

Storm
Mountain
3,793ft ▲

River

North Arm

Black
Bay

Grewingk Glacier

Halibut

Creek

McCarty
Lagoon

KACHEMAK BAY
STATE PARK

Wosnesenski Gl

Yalik Glacier

4,540ft ▲

Beauty Bay

Native
Corporation

West Arm

Native
Corporation

Roaring Cove

Steep
Point

Petrof Glacier

Yalik Bay

Nuka Bay

McArthur

PYE
ISLANDS

Pass

Top ❸

HIKER AT EXIT GLACIER

① GAZE AT EXIT GLACIER

Exit Glacier is the only drive-to glacier in the park. Visit the **Exit Glacier Nature Center** to learn about glaciers, how they shape the landscape, and their glacial retreat. Then follow the wheelchair-accessible trail (1 mi. rt.) to the **Glacier View Overlook.** As Exit Glacier has melted, it has retreated back up its valley; it's now a longer walk to see it. (Trail signs mark its size at various years of its retreat.) In early summer, some of the ice will still be covered with winter snow. To see the exposed blue ice, plan a late-summer trip.

Exit Glacier is accessed via Exit Glacier Road (early May–mid-Nov.). In summer, avoid the clogged parking area and take the hourly **Exit Glacier Shuttle** from Seward. Rangers also lead daily walks in the area.

② FLY OVER HARDING ICEFIELD

There's a whole lot more park out there—670,000 acres of it—that you can take in from the air. **Flightseeing** allows for aerial viewing of fjords, marine and mountain environments, and the Harding Icefield; you can see crevasses, icefalls, and arms of glaciers extending miles from the icefield. Local air charters are based from the airport in Seward. (Planes do not land inside the park.)

③ TOUR THE FJORDS BY BOAT

Boat tours are one way to see some of the more than 400 miles of magical coastline in Kenai Fjords. Tides, waves, winds, storms, and glaciers pummel the coast into a rugged work of art containing caves, arches, and standing rocks called stacks. As tectonic plates pull the Kenai Fjords landmass down into the sea, the coastline forests sink into the seawater. You can see plenty in a half-day tour of **Resurrection Bay**—including seabird rookeries of cormorants, harlequin ducks, and kittiwakes—but the best tours visit a tidewater glacier in **Aialik Bay.**

HOLGATE GLACIER

ONE DAY IN THE KENAI FJORDS

Exit Glacier is an easy day trip by car. Follow Exit Glacier Road to the trailhead and hike 1-2 miles along the **Exit Glacier Trail** to peer at the ice. Fit hikers with more time can extend their trek to gaze at the **Harding Icefield.** From Seward, you can take a half-day **boat tour** of Resurrection Bay or visit a tidewater glacier in Aialik Bay.

to Exit Glacier. Parking can be limited 10:30am-3:30pm; plan to arrive in the morning or afternoon, when the light will make the glaciers appear bluer.

RECREATION

HIKING

If the weather is nice, tackle the **Harding Icefield Trail** (10 mi. rt., 5-6 hrs.), which starts from the Exit Glacier trailhead. The steep hike gains 3,300 feet in elevation on its way to overlooks of the Harding Icefield, a massive sheet of ice and snow that spawns some 40 glaciers. This hike of a lifetime is as challenging as it sounds. Black bear encounters are fairly common, and weather can change quickly.

If you want to hike on a glacier, book a trip with the meticulously trained guides from **Exit Glacier Guides**

(907/224-5569, www.exitglacierguides. com). They offer ice climbing on Exit Glacier plus multiday or heli-assisted ice climbing adventures, guided hikes, and camping trips.

KAYAKING

With the proper guidance, almost anybody can manage a stable sea kayak in the waters of Resurrection Bay. One of the best outfitters for both tours and equipment rental is **Sunny Cove Sea Kayaking Co.** (1304 4th Ave., Seward, 907/224-4426, www.sunnycove.com). **Liquid Adventures** (411 Port Ave., Seward, 907/224-9225, www.liquid-adventures.com) offers both paddling and stand-up paddleboard adventures and rentals.

▼ HARBOR SEALS

Best Hike

EXIT GLACIER TRAIL

1-2 MILES ROUND-TRIP
DURATION: 1 hour
ELEVATION CHANGE: negligible
DIFFICULTY: easy
TRAILHEAD: Exit Glacier Nature Center

The **Exit Glacier Trail** (1-2 mi rt., 1 hr.) offers a series of gentle loops on a broad, mostly level trail. A wheelchair-accessible portion of the trail leads 0.5 mile to **Glacier View Overlook,** where you can peer across the gravel outwash plain at the ice. For those willing to tackle a slightly more strenuous portion of trail, the **Toe of the Glacier** route departs the first loop to extend to two different points that drop onto the outwash plain; here, you can pick your way across the braided and rocky terrain to the toe of the glacier. From the spur trails that drop to the outwash plain, the **Edge of the Glacier Trail** (2.4 mi. rt., 4 hrs.) climbs steeply up bedrock to the side of the glacier, where you get the closest views of crevasses and blue ice.

DOGSLEDDING

Many of the flightseeing services that will take you into Kenai Fjords National Park offer some sort of a glacier dogsled adventure, including **Ididaride Sled Dog Tours** (12820 Old Exit Glacier Rd., 907/224-8607, www.ididaride. com, mid-May-mid-Sept.). You can tour the kennels, cuddle puppies, and take a two-mile cart or sled ride.

WHERE TO STAY

INSIDE THE PARK

Set amid the 1,700-acre Pedersen Lagoon Sanctuary on Aialik Bay, **Kenai Fjords Glacier Lodge** (800/334-8730, www.kenaifjordsglacierlodge.com, late May-early Sept., from $820 per person for 2 days and 1 night) is a modern ecolodge with 16 private cabins featuring full baths, electricity, and heat. The cabins are connected via boardwalks to the main lodge, which houses a dining room and lobby overlooking Pedersen Glacier. Transportation is by boat from Seward to the lodge. Stays include all meals, activities, and lodging.

Those willing to rough it in the wilderness can reap huge rewards of solitude, wildlife-watching, and scenery. Two rustic public-use cabins are located in Aialik Bay. Situated at the head of the bay in a spruce forest, the **Aialik Bay Cabin** sleeps four people in two wooden beds. Across the bay, Aialik

Glacier plunges to the water. Below the cabin, you can explore the rocky beach at low tide. In Holgate Arm off Aialik Bay, the **Holgate Cabin** sleeps six people in six wooden bunks. From the deck, you can stare right at Holgate Glacier and listen to the sounds of calving ice.

The cabins are equipped with a table, chairs, and a propane heater; there is no electricity and no running water (bring your own). Both cabins are surrounded by blueberries and salmonberries, which attract bears. Reaching the

BLACK BEAR

cabins means taking a boat (2 hours) or seaplane (30-35 minutes) to get there. Competition is keen—book **reservations** in early January (877/444-6777, www.recreation.gov, Memorial Day-Labor Day, $75 per night, 3-night max).

The **Exit Glacier Campground** (first come, first served, free) is a walk-in, tent-only campground located 0.25 mile before the Exit Glacier Nature Center. There are 12 sites and a central storage area for food and cooking items. Drinking water and pit toilets are available.

OUTSIDE THE PARK

Seward (www.seward.com) is the gateway to spectacular Kenai Fjords National Park. Located just outside the park, it has motels, campgrounds, restaurants, boat tours, flightseeing, and visitor services. It is also the site of the Kenai Fjords National Park Visitor Center.

GETTING THERE

AIR

The closest international airport is **Ted Stevens Anchorage International Airport** (ANC, 5000 W. International Airport Rd., www.dot.alaska.gov), which receives year-round service from Alaska Airlines, Delta, United, and Iceland Air, with seasonal service from Jet-Blue and Condor. Car rentals are available at the airport.

BOAT

Many cruise lines use Seward as their port of call for Anchorage. If you're a ferry buff, you're out of luck; this is one of the few port cities that the Alaska Marine Highway System does not serve.

RAIL

You can travel between Seward and Anchorage on the **Alaska Railroad** (800/544-0552, www.alaskarailroad.com). A one-way ticket for "adventure class" (coach class) starts at $105 for adults.

CAR

The scenic drive from Anchorage to Seward is 126 miles (2.5 hours). From Anchorage, head southeast on AK 1 to curve around Turnagain Arm, which separates the Kenai Peninsula from the mainland. In 87 miles, AK 1 exits right to Homer; continue straight as the road becomes AK 9 to its terminus 39 miles later in Seward. The route is known as the Seward Highway, a National Scenic Byway, and stays open year-round.

BEAR GLACIER

BEAR GLACIER

BUS

Several bus services ply the roads up and down the Kenai Peninsula. The best deal is from **Seward Bus Lines** (888/420-7788 or 907/563-0800, www.sewardbuslines.net, May-mid-Sept., from $40 one-way to Anchorage or Whittier), with two departures from Seward daily.

GETTING AROUND

The only road in the park is Exit Glacier Road (signed as Herman Leirer Rd.), three miles north of Seward. The road terminates in 8.4 miles at Exit Glacier.

FLIGHT TOURS

Local air charters include **Seward Helicopter Tours** (2210 Airport Rd., 888/476-5589 or 907/362-4354, www.sewardhelicopters.com), **Marathon Helicopters** (2210-B Airport Rd., 907/224-3616, www.marathonhelicopters.com), and **AA Seward Air Tours** (2300 Airport Rd., 907/362-6205 or 907/362-0046, www.sewardair.com), which uses small planes. All tour operators are based from the airport in Seward. Planes do not land inside the park.

BOAT TOURS

Two popular day-cruise operators are **Major Marine Tours** (1302 4th Ave., Seward, 800/274-7300 or 907/274-7300, www.majormarine.com) and **Kenai Fjords Tours** (800/808-8068, www.alaskacollection.com). Late March-late September, they run a similar series of half-day sightseeing cruises and full-day adventures. However, Kenai Fjords Tours is the only company that steps foot onto Fox Island. All boat tours depart from the harbor in Seward.

SHUTTLES

From Seward, the **Exit Glacier Shuttle** (call for reservations 907/224-5569 or 907/224-9225, www.exitglaciershuttle.com, $15 round-trip) offers hourly trips to and from the Exit Glacier Nature Center. **Alaska Shuttle Service** (907/947-3349, www.alaskashuttleservice.com) offers taxi, shuttle, and tour service up and down the Kenai Peninsula, usually with a four-person minimum.

TAXIS

Land, air, and water taxis service the community of Seward. Air taxis licensed through the park service can get you to remote locations in Kenai Fjords, dropping you off one day and picking you up at a scheduled time and place. Water taxis vary according to season due to rough seas in winter. **Seward Ocean Excursions** (907/599-0499, www.sewardoceanexcursions.com) is the only water taxi that offers year-round service. **Alaska Coastal Safari/Seward Water Taxi** (907/362-4101, www.sewardwatertaxi.com) is a one-man operation with a three-person minimum for each trip.

LAKE CLARK NATIONAL PARK AND PRESERVE

Alaska

PASSPORT STAMPS ▼▼▼

WEBSITE:
www.nps.gov/lacl

PHONE NUMBER:
907/781-2218

VISITATION RANK:
57

WHY GO:
Experience big wilderness.

▲ SALMON CREEK

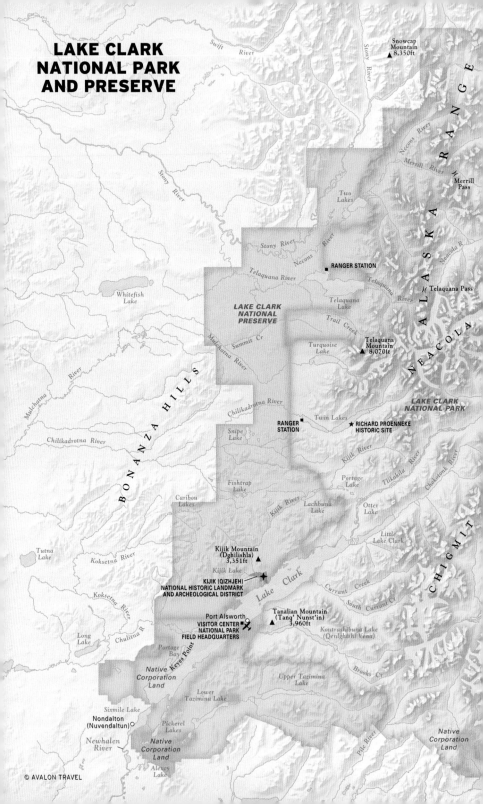

LAKE CLARK NATIONAL PARK AND PRESERVE

Swift River

Snowcap Mountain ▲ 8,350ft

Stony River

ALASKA RANGE

Stony River

Necons River

Merrill River

Merrill Pass

Neacola R.

Two Lakes

Stony River

Necons River

■ RANGER STATION

Telaquana River

Telaquana River

Telaquana Pass

Telaquana Lake

NEACOLA

Whitefish Lake

LAKE CLARK NATIONAL PRESERVE

Trail Creek

Telaquana River

River

Summit Cr.

Malchatna River

Turquoise Lake

Telaquana Mountain ▲ 8,070ft

LAKE CLARK NATIONAL PARK

River

Malchatna River

Chilikadrotna River

Twin Lakes

★ RICHARD PROENNEKE HISTORIC SITE

Chilikadrotna River

■ RANGER STATION

Snipe Lake

Kijik River

Tlikakila River

Chokotonk River

B O N A N Z A   H I L L S

Fishtrap Lake

Portage Lake

Otter Lake

Caribou Lakes

Kijik River

Lachbuna Lake

Little Lake Clark

Tutna Lake

Koksetna River

Kijik Mountain (Dghilishla) ▲ 3,351ft

Kijik River

Kijik Lake ★

Lake Clark

C H I G M I T

Koksetna River

KIJIK (QIZHJEH) NATIONAL HISTORIC LANDMARK AND ARCHEOLOGICAL DISTRICT

Currant Creek

South Currant Cr.

Long Lake

Chulitna R.

Port Alsworth VISITOR CENTER NATIONAL PARK FIELD HEADQUARTERS ✕

Tanalian Mountain (Tang' Nunst'in) ▲ 3,960ft

Kontrashibuna Lake (Qenlghishi Vena)

Portage Bay

Keyes Point

Native Corporation Land

Lower Tazimina Lake

Upper Tazimina Lake

Brooks Cr.

Sixmile Lake

Pickerel Lakes

Nondalton (Nuvendaltun) ○

Native Corporation Land

Pile River

Native Corporation Land

Newhalen River

Alexcy Lake

© AVALON TRAVEL

Rugged mountains, smoking volcanoes, and pristine waterways make up the wilderness of **LAKE CLARK NATIONAL PARK AND PRESERVE**. The park sits a short distance north of Katmai National Park, on the far side of Lake Iliamna, and is famous for three things: brown bear viewing, fly-fishing, and the cabin of naturalist Richard Proenneke. The park's wilderness offers backcountry adventures for the hardy.

PLANNING YOUR TIME

Lake Clark has no roads, campgrounds, or services. Getting here requires a flight from Anchorage or Homer to **Port Alsworth,** the park entrance. The peak season is **June-mid-September.** There is no entrance fee.

The small **Lake Clark Visitor Center** (907/781-2117, hours vary, daily late May-mid-Sept.) in Port Alsworth has voluntary backcountry registration forms (no permits required), bear canister rentals (free), Alaska Geographic books and maps, and films.

BEAR VIEWING

For top brown bear-viewing opportunities, charter a floatplane to fly to **Chinitna Bay, Crescent Lake,** or **Silver Salmon Creek.** Bear viewing is best June-early September.

DICK PROENNEKE'S CABIN

Naturalist **Richard Proenneke** built this cabin (daily June-Sept.) using only hand tools and lived in it for 30 years with no modern conveniences. He documented the building process in videos that have been collected in a DVD, *Alone in the Wilderness,* and his journals have been published in book form as *One Man's Wilderness*. Park rangers give cabin tours upon request. Getting here requires a 30-minute floatplane from Port Alsworth to Upper Twin Lake.

▼ KONTRASHIBUNA LAKE FROM THE SLOPES OF HOLEY MOUNTAIN

THE TANALIAN RIVER

RECREATION

Hiking trails leave Port Alsworth for **Tanalian Falls** and **Kontrashibuna Lake** (5 mi. rt.). At a trail junction midway, a strenuous climb shoots to the summit of **Tanalian Mountain** (4.8 mi. rt.), with big-view rewards of Lake Clark and the surrounding mountains.

Lake Clark offers plenty of shoreline for **kayakers** to paddle, and there are three National Wild and Scenic Rivers for skilled **white-water rafting** (Class III): the Tlikakila, Mulchatna, and Chilikadrotna. The rafting season runs June-September; trips span 70-230 miles.

Crescent Lake and Silver Salmon Creek are the top fishing spots, where you may cast for salmon in the company of bears. For guided fishing trips, contact **Redoubt Mountain Lodge** on Crescent Lake or **Silver Salmon Creek Lodge** at Silver Salmon Creek. Fishing season runs May-October.

In Port Alsworth, **Tulchina Adventures** (907/782-4720, www.tulchinaadventures.com) rents camping gear, paddling equipment, and motorized skiffs. It also maintains a campground and cabin rentals. For guided hiking, backpacking, kayaking, or rafting trips from Anchorage, contact **Alaska Alpine Adventures** (877/525-2577 or 907/351-4193, www.alaskaalpineadventures.com).

WHERE TO STAY

Lodges in Lake Clark are all privately owned and cater as much to fishing and kayaking as to bear viewing. **Silver Salmon Creek Lodge** (888/872-5666, www.silversalmoncreek.com, from $875) offers transport from Homer and Anchorage. **Redoubt Mountain Lodge** (907/776-7516, www.redoubtbaylodge.com, from $1,370) offers transport from Anchorage. Rates include use of gear.

Backcountry camping is permitted throughout the park. Primitive campsites at **Hope Creek** (free) are first come, first served. Other backcountry sites include **Upper** and **Lower Twin Lakes.**

For accommodations and services, stay outside the park in tiny **Port Alsworth** on the shore of Lake Clark.

GETTING THERE AND AROUND

Alaska Airlines (800/252-7522, www.alaskaair.com) services **Ted Stevens Anchorage International Airport** (ANC, 5000 W. International Airport Rd., www.dot.alaska.gov). From Anchorage, take an air taxi to Lake Clark National Park and Preserve.

Air taxis require reservations. From Anchorage, contact **Lake Clark Air** (907/781-2208, www.lakeclarkair.com) and **Lake and Peninsula Air** (907/345-2228, www.lakeandpenair.com). From Homer, contact **Adventure Airways** (907/299-7999, www.adventureairways.com), **Beluga Air** (907/235-8256, www.belugaair.com), or **Northwind Aviation** (907/235-7482, www.northwindak.com). **Lake Clark Air** (888/440-2281) and **Lake and Peninsula Air** (907/781-2228) maintain offices in Port Alsworth.

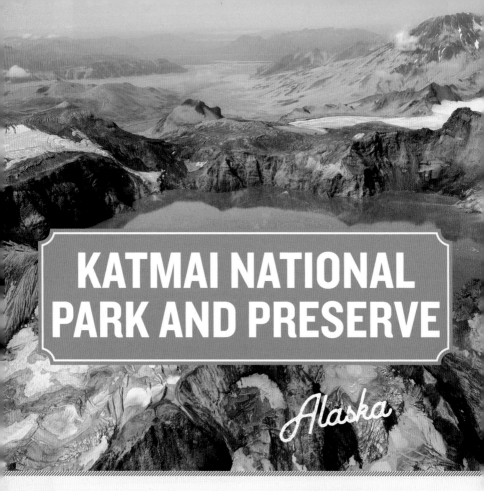

KATMAI NATIONAL PARK AND PRESERVE

Alaska

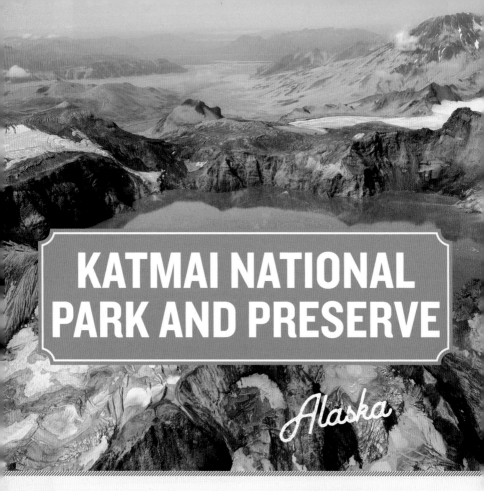

WEBSITE:
www.nps.gov/katm

PHONE NUMBER:
907/246-3305

VISITATION RANK:
54

WHY GO:
Watch brown bears
fish for salmon.

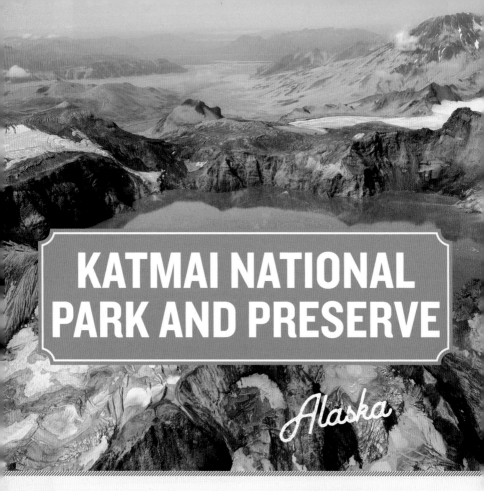

PASSPORT STAMPS ▼▼▼

▲ KATMAI CALDERA

Stretching southwest from the bottom of mainland Alaska, the Alaska Peninsula fractures into the volcanic Aleutian Islands. The biggest attraction here is bear viewing at **KATMAI NATIONAL PARK AND PRESERVE**. While Katmai may be the best-known bear-viewing location in the world, this four million-acre park includes phenomenal sea kayaking, world-class fishing, and one of the most stunning sights you'll ever see, the Valley of Ten Thousand Smokes. Alaska Native people lived here for thousands of years, their ancient homes marked by hundreds of depressions along the river.

PLANNING YOUR TIME

Inaccessible by road, Katmai National Park requires **air travel** to reach its remote wonders. Flights from **Anchorage** go to **King Salmon,** the service community located outside the park. From King Salmon, floatplanes head to Brooks Camp to watch bears catch fish in the river.

July and August are the nicest months to visit; limited travel and visitor services start in June and continue into September. Bear viewing is best July and September, while fishing is better in the shoulder seasons.

ENTRANCE AND FEES

The town of King Salmon serves as the jumping-off point into Katmai. Floatplanes depart here for **Brooks Camp,** the point of entry for most visitors.

MOUNT GRIGGS

There are no roads into the park and there is no entrance fee.

VISITORS CENTERS

The **King Salmon Visitor Center** (4 Bear Rd., King Salmon, 907/246-4250, www.fws.gov/refuge/Becharof, 8am-5pm daily in summer) serves as the park headquarters with information, a bookstore, and educational displays on the Alaska Peninsula's Native cultures and traditions, wildlife, and fishing.

The **Brooks Camp Visitor Center** (June-mid-Sept.) serves as the campground check-in and provides backcountry information for those heading beyond Brooks Camp. Books and maps are available at the center's Alaska Geographic store. Rangers lead daytime and evening programs, as well as an orientation on bear safety.

In the Valley of Ten Thousand Smokes, 23 miles southeast of Brooks Camp, the small outpost of **Robert F. Griggs Visitor Center** (summer only) overlooks the ash and pumice valley, fallout from the 1912 eruption of Novarupta. Rangers lead daily hikes to the valley floor with a steep climb on the return.

RECREATION

A bewildering number of guide services are authorized to operate within Katmai. If you want to narrow it quickly and ensure a good experience, stick with **Brooks Camp** or **Brooks Lodge** (907/243-5448, www.katmailand.com) for right-at-the-camp lodging and

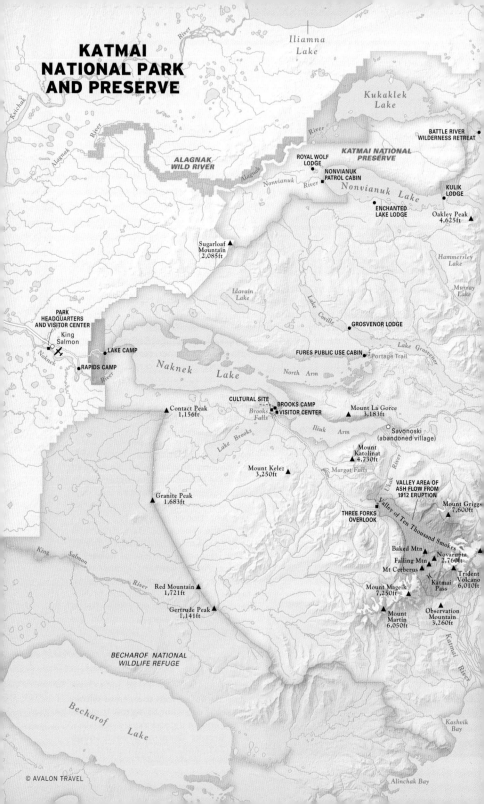

KATMAI NATIONAL PARK AND PRESERVE

Iliamna Lake

Kukaklek Lake

Alagnak

Kvichak

ALAGNAK WILD RIVER

BATTLE RIVER WILDERNESS RETREAT

KATMAI NATIONAL PRESERVE

ROYAL WOLF LODGE

NONVIANUK PATROL CABIN

Nonvianuk   *River*

Nonvianuk Lake

KULIK LODGE

ENCHANTED LAKE LODGE

Oakley Peak 4,625ft

Hammersley Lake

Sugarloaf Mountain 2,085ft

Idavain Lake

Murray Lake

Lake Coville

PARK HEADQUARTERS AND VISITOR CENTER

King Salmon

LAKE CAMP

GROSVENOR LODGE

Lake Grosvenor

FURES PUBLIC USE CABIN

Portage Trail

RAPIDS CAMP

Naknek   *Lake*

Naknek River

North Arm

CULTURAL SITE

BROOKS CAMP VISITOR CENTER

Brooks Falls

Lake Brooks

Contact Peak 1,156ft

Mount La Gorce 3,183ft

Iliuk Arm

Savonoski (abandoned village)

Mount Kelez 3,250ft

Mount Katolinat 4,730ft

Margot Falls

Ukak River

VALLEY AREA OF ASH FLOW FROM 1912 ERUPTION

Mount Griggs 7,600ft

Granite Peak 1,683ft

THREE FORKS OVERLOOK

Valley of Ten Thousand Smokes

Baked Mtn

Falling Mtn

Novarupta 2,760ft

Mt Cerberus

Trident Volcano 6,010ft

Katmai Pass

Mount Mageik 7,250ft

King   *Salmon*

River

Red Mountain 1,721ft

Gertrude Peak 1,141ft

Mount Martin 6,050ft

Observation Mountain 3,260ft

Katmai River

BECHAROF NATIONAL WILDLIFE REFUGE

Becharof Lake

Kashvik Bay

Alinchak Bay

© AVALON TRAVEL

COOK INLET

Kamishak Bay

Mcneil Falls   Mcneil Cove

Battle
Lake

Mcneil
Lake

Pirate
Lake

McNEIL RIVER
STATE GAME SANCTUARY

KAMISHAK SPECIAL USE AREA
(STATE OF ALASKA)

Kulik
Lake

Spotted Gl

Sukoi Bay

Cape
Douglas

Mount Douglas
7,063ft

Fourpeaked Gl

Fourpeaked
Mountain
6,903ft

KATMAI
NATIONAL
PARK

Wolverine Falls

Kaguyak
Crater

SWIKSHAK
PATROL CABIN

Swikshak
Bay

HALLO BAY
WILDERNESS CAMPS

Devils Desk
6,411ft

Kukak Volcano
6,700ft

Mount Denison
7,606ft

Mount Steller
7,300ft

Hallo Glacier

Ninagiak
Island

Hallo
Bay

KATMAI
WILDERNESS LODGE

Snowy Mountain
7,090ft

Kukak
Bay

Mount Katmai
6,715ft

Kaflia
Bay

Hidden
Harbor

Kuliak Bay

AMALIK BAY
PATROL CABIN

Kinak Bay

Missak Bay

Katmai Village
(abandoned)

Takli
Island

Dakavak
Bay

SHELIKOF STRAIT

AFOGNAK
ISLAND

Kupreanof Strait

Katmai
Bay

KODIAK
ISLAND

0   10 mi

0   10 km

Top ③

BROOKS RIVER, KATMAI

① WATCH BROWN BEARS

If you're going bear viewing, the most popular destination in Katmai is **Brooks Camp.** This National Historic Landmark includes the park visitors center, an established campground, an auditorium where rangers lead nightly chats in addition to their daytime guided hikes, and, if you want to spend the night within four walls, **Brooks Lodge.** From here you can hike to Brooks Falls and the three bear-viewing platforms lining the Brooks River, where brown bears feed on sockeye salmon. When the Falls Platform maxes out with people during prime seasons in July and September, you may need to wait for space, and rangers limit viewing time to one hour per person.

At Brooks Camp you can canoe or kayak Naknek Lake or hop the daily bus to Valley of Ten Thousand Smokes. This is also one of the park's hottest spots for fishing. Daily, ranger-led cultural walks go to archeological sites of house depressions and a reconstructed Alaska Native home.

② TOUR THE VALLEY OF TEN THOUSAND SMOKES

EXTINCT FUMAROLE NEAR KNIFE CREEK GORGE, VALLEY OF TEN THOUSAND SMOKES

The desolate, ash-covered **Valley of Ten Thousand Smokes** was created by the largest volcanic eruption of the 20th century. In 1912, the Novarupta volcano erupted for 60 hours, transforming the fertile Ukak River valley into the smoking landscape you see today.

To visit the valley, book the daylong Natural History Tour with park concessionaire **Katmailand** (907/243-5448, www.katmailand.com, daily early June-mid-Aug., advance reservations required, $51-96 per person). From Brooks Camp, a narrated tour bus travels 23 miles to the Overlook Cabin, where you'll stop for lunch, wildlife viewing, and a guided trek 1,000 feet down to the valley floor (3.4 mi. rt., strenuous).

For a guided backpacking trip through the valley, hire **Alaska Alpine Adventures** (877/525-2577 or 907/351-4193, www.alaskaalpineadventures.com), based in Anchorage.

③ FISH FOR SALMON

Katmai is renowned as a haven for anglers. During the June-September fishing season, the park's **Brooks Lodge** and **Grosvenor Lodge** offer 3-7-day guided fishing packages that include meals, lodging, and air travel from Anchorage. Cast your line for five species of salmon, plus rainbow trout, char, and arctic grayling.

THE VALLEY OF TEN THOUSAND SMOKES

fishing opportunities. From Anchorage, use **Alaska Alpine Adventures** (877/525-2577 or 907/351-4193, www.alaskaalpineadventures.com) for other activities such as hiking, backpacking, and paddling.

HIKING

Katmai has less than five miles of maintained trails. From Brooks Camp Visitor Center, a wheelchair-accessible trail leads to **Brooks Falls** (2.4 mi. rt.), where three viewing platforms provide a way to watch brown bears fishing for sockeye salmon. The more ambitious trail to **Dumpling Mountain** (3 mi. rt.) climbs 800 feet in elevation to views of Lake Brooks, Naknek Lake, the Brooks River, and Brooks Camp below.

KAYAKING AND CANOEING

Experienced sea kayakers go for the inland **Savonoski Loop.** Starting and finishing at Brooks Camp, the 80-mile route links two large lakes and two rivers. The route requires excellent skills to paddle the swift-moving wave trains, avoid obstacles in the Savonoski River, and portage kayaks 1.5 miles. Most paddlers do the loop in 4-7 days. Fure's Cabin provides an overnight option in the Bay of Islands, located in the North Arm of Naknek Lake.

WHERE TO STAY
INSIDE THE PARK

Most visitors will want to stay in Brooks Camp, where **Brooks Lodge** (877/737-1262, www.katmailand.com, June-mid-Sept., from $916) has 16 modern guest rooms with baths. Breakfast, lunch, and dinner are served buffet-style in the lodge dining room, which overlooks Naknek Lake. Bear-viewing platforms are nearby. The lodge offers daily tours to the Valley of Ten Thousand Smokes.

Grosvenor Lodge (877/737-1262, www.katmailand.com, June-mid-Sept., package rates apply), a fishing lodge on Grosvenor Lake, accommodates 4-6 guests in three cabins (with heat and electricity), a separate bathhouse, and a kitchen and dining area. The main lodge holds a lounge and bar.

Brooks Camp Campground (877/444-6777, www.recreation.gov, $12 June-Sept., $6 May and Sept.-Oct.) accommodates 60 tent campers and fills quickly. Reservations open in early January for the summer; July reservations book fast for the peak bear-viewing periods. Facilities include cooking shelters, fire rings, food storage boxes, water, and vault toilets. The campground has no designated sites—the open, grassy area is protected from bears by an electric fence.

MCNEIL RIVER STATE GAME SANCTUARY

Tucked outside the northern edge of Katmai National Park, **McNeil River State Game Sanctuary** was established in 1967 to protect the highest concentration of wild brown bears in the world. As you can imagine, that leads to some amazing bear-viewing opportunities. Guides and researchers have counted more than 70 brown bears near the McNeil River at one time. Bear viewing is best in July and mid-August, when chum salmon congregate at McNeil River Falls. A smaller number of bears swarm an early sockeye run up nearby Mikfik Creek.

A permit program limits visits to McNeil River Falls. Only 10 guided viewing permits are issued per day from early June to late August. **Permits** (907/267-2189, www.adfg.alaska.gov, $25 for lottery, $350 for permit) are assigned by lottery, which starts on March 2 of the prior year and ends on March 1 of the viewing year. Each permit is valid for four days. It's a four-mile round-trip hike to reach the falls.

If you don't win the permit lottery, apply for a camp-standby permit ($175), which is also valid for four days. The camp-standby permit allows you to stay in the sanctuary campground (tents only) and view bears from the campground and beach area. If somebody no-shows for a guided viewing trip, you can then take their spot.

This roadless sanctuary has no roads or modern amenities. Access is by chartered flight from Anchorage or Homer.

Backcountry camping in the Valley of Ten Thousand Smokes can be arranged with a one-way drop-off from Katmailand; some sites fringe the valley. Alternatively, hike 12 miles (one-way) from Valley Road to the primitive **Baked Mountain Huts** (first come, first served, free). No permits are required and there are no services.

Located in the Bay of Islands of Naknek Lake, rustic **Fure's Cabin** (877/444-6777, www.recreation.gov, June-Sept., $45) is a one-room, wood-heated cabin with no electricity. It sleeps six. Make reservations starting in early January.

OUTSIDE THE PARK

Services are located in the town of **King Salmon,** which has one hotel: the **Antlers Inn** (471 Alaska Peninsula Hwy., 888/735-8525 or 907/246-8525, www.antlersinnak.com, from $195).

GETTING THERE AND AROUND

King Salmon sits 290 miles southwest of Anchorage on the Alaska Peninsula, just off the west flank of Katmai National Park. You can only get here by plane. In summer, **Alaska Airlines** (800/252-7522, www.alaskaair.com) offers one flight daily from Anchorage to King Salmon. **PenAir** (800/448-4226 or 907/771-2640, www.penair.com) offers five or six flights from Anchorage in summer.

Upon arrival in King Salmon, take an air taxi with **Katmai Air** (800/544-0551, www.katmaiair.com, reserve in advance) into the park at Brooks Camp. Katmai Air also provides floatplane charters to other locations in the park.

Katmai has no public transportation. To get around, you'll need a boat or kayak, or to book a floatplane or tour bus to the Valley of Ten Thousand Smokes.

THE VALLEY OF TEN THOUSAND SMOKES

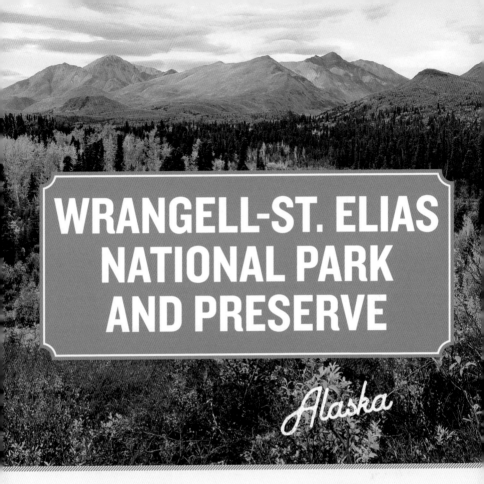

WRANGELL-ST. ELIAS NATIONAL PARK AND PRESERVE

Alaska

PASSPORT STAMPS ▼▼▼

WEBSITE:
www.nps.gov/wrst

PHONE NUMBER:
907/822-5234

VISITATION RANK:
52

WHY GO:
Visit the largest national park in the United States.

▲ CREEK TRAIL

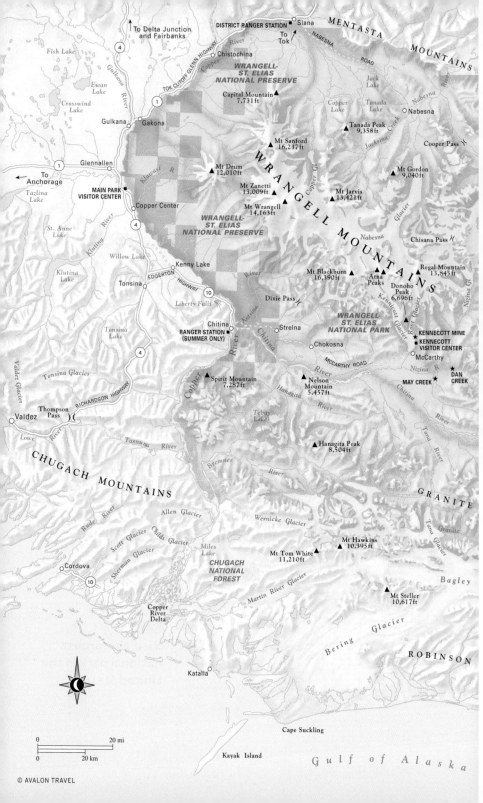

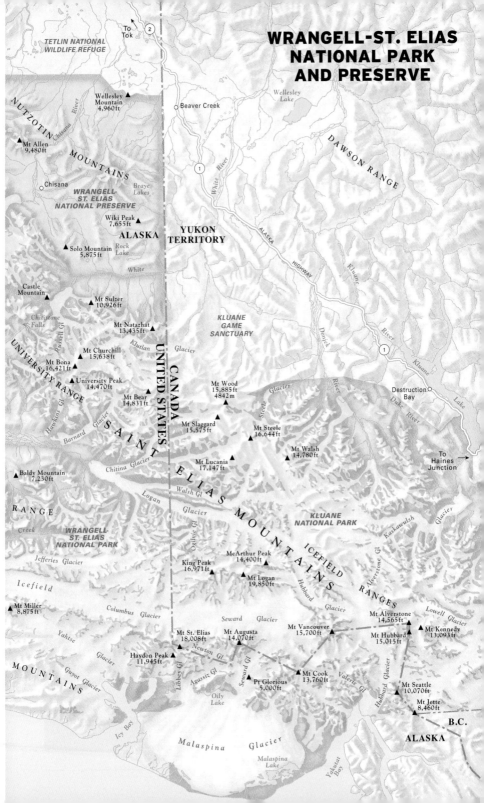

WRANGELL-ST. ELIAS NATIONAL PARK AND PRESERVE

To Tok

2

TETLIN NATIONAL WILDLIFE REFUGE

Beaver Creek

Wellesley Lake

DAWSON RANGE

NUTZOTIN MOUNTAINS

Wellesley Mountain 4,960ft

Mt Allen 9,480ft

Chisana

WRANGELL-ST. ELIAS NATIONAL PRESERVE

Braye Lakes

YUKON TERRITORY

White River

ALASKA HIGHWAY

Wiki Peak 7,655ft

ALASKA

Solo Mountain 5,875ft

Rock Lake

White

Castle Mountain

Chitistone Falls

Mt Sulzer 10,926ft

KLUANE GAME SANCTUARY

Mt Natazhat 13,435ft

1

Destruction Bay

Klutlan Glacier

UNIVERSITY RANGE

Mt Churchill 15,638ft

Mt Bona 16,421ft

University Peak 14,470ft

Mt Bear 14,831ft

Mt Wood 15,885ft 4842m

Steele Glacier

Donjek River

Kluane River

CANADA UNITED STATES

Mt Slaggard 15,575ft

Mt Steele 16,644ft

Mt Walsh 14,780ft

To Haines Junction

SAINT

Baldy Mountain 7,230ft

Chitina Glacier

Mt Lucania 17,147ft

Logan Glacier

Walsh Gl

ELIAS

RANGE

Creek

WRANGELL-ST. ELIAS NATIONAL PARK

Ogilvie Gl

KLUANE NATIONAL PARK

Kaskawulsh Glacier

Jefferies Glacier

MOUNTAINS

ICEFIELD RANGES

King Peak 16,971ft

McArthur Peak 14,400ft

Alverstone Gl

Icefield

Columbus Glacier

Mt Logan 19,850ft

Hubbard Glacier

Lowell Glacier

Mt Miller 8,875ft

Yahtse Glacier

Mt St. Elias 18,008ft

Mt Augusta 14,070ft

Mt Vancouver 15,700ft

Mt Alverstone 14,565ft

Mt Kennedy 13,093ft

Haydon Peak 11,945ft

Newton Gl

Mt Hubbard 15,015ft

Guyot Glacier

MOUNTAINS

Libbey Gl

Agassiz Gl

Seward Gl

Pt Glorious 5,000ft

Mt Cook 13,760ft

Valerie Gl

Hubbard Glacier

Mt Seattle 10,070ft

Icy Bay

Oily Lake

Mt Jette 8,460ft

B.C.

Malaspina Glacier

Malaspina Lake

Yakutat Bay

ALASKA

The largest national park in the United States, **WRANGELL-ST. ELIAS NATIONAL PARK AND PRESERVE** covers 13.2 million acres of pristine wilderness. With huge peaks and rivers of ice, it is a magnet for mountaineers aiming for the crowning glory of 18,008-foot Mount St. Elias. Serious backpackers come for solitude at turquoise lakes while wildlife watchers hone binoculars on bears, bison, mountain goats, and wolves. But access is difficult, with only two roads.

PLANNING YOUR TRIP

Wrangell-St. Elias National Park and Preserve sits snug against the Canadian border, 200 miles east of Anchorage. Paved roads skirt the park's western boundary, providing access to the gateway communities of Glennallen, Copper Center, Kenny Lake, and Chitina. Inside the park, most visitors beeline for the historic mining towns of **McCarthy** and **Kennicott,** accessible only by a long and difficult dirt road.

The best time to visit is **June-mid-September,** when balmy summers peak with highs in the 70s by July.

ENTRANCE AND FEES

The main entrance to the park is south of Glennallen along the paved **Richardson Highway** (AK 4), which runs through the town of Copper Center. There is no entrance station and no entrance fee.

VISITORS CENTERS

The **Copper Center Visitor Center** (Copper Center, mile 106.8 Richardson Hwy. at Glenn Hwy., 907/822-7250, 9am-6pm daily mid-May-mid-Sept., reduced spring/fall hours, closed winter) is 10 miles south of Glennallen. As the main park visitors center, it has exhibits, backcountry information, a bookstore, theater, and ranger talks. Next door, the Ahtna Cultural Center (year-round, hours vary) is a native heritage museum with a hand-built fish wheel. Outside, short paths visit scenic overlooks and rangers lead guided walks.

McCarthy Road has several spots for obtaining visitor information. Outside the park, stop at **Chitina Ranger Station** (mile 33, Edgerton Hwy., Chitina, 907/823-2205, 10am-4:30pm daily May-Sept.) for an update on road conditions. At the upper end of McCarthy Road, the unstaffed **McCarthy Road Info Station** (mile 59) has an orientation kiosk. Five miles north of McCarthy

KENNICOTT GLACIER AND STAIRWAY ICEFALL

KENNECOTT

in a historic schoolhouse, **Kennecott Visitor Center** (907/554-1105, 9:30am-6:30pm daily in summer) has ranger programs, exhibits, films, a bookstore, and backcountry information.

At the entrance to rugged Nabesna Road, stop at **Slana Ranger Station** (mile 0.5, 907/822-7401, 8am-5pm daily in summer) to find out road conditions. The station also has exhibits, a film, ranger programs, and backcountry information.

SIGHTS
MCCARTHY

A remote Alaskan homestead miles from pavement, **McCarthy** once supplied the mining district with necessities and services. Today, you'll find lodging, dining, a museum, and railroad memorabilia lining its 0.1-mile main street. McCarthy is a launch point for backcountry exploration, flightseeing, and guided trips, with hiking trails to glaciers and mines. Visitors are restricted to one access point—a wide footbridge over the Kennicott River with a 0.5-mile walk into town.

KENNECOTT

A five-mile road connects McCarthy with the ghost town of **Kennecott,** whose historic, bright red mine buildings are an eye-catching sight backdropped by the snowy Wrangell Mountains. In summer, **St. Elias Alpine Guides** (888/933-5427 or 907/554-4445, www.steliasguides.com) guides tours into the **Kennecott Mill** buildings. Most of the equipment is in surprisingly good condition and still works. With no private vehicle access, you must hike or bike to get here—or hop aboard the McCarthy-Kennicott shuttle van.

SCENIC DRIVES

Two rugged dirt roads reach into the Wrangell-St. Elias interior. While the roads are open year-round, they are full of potholes and washboards—if you drive too fast or have bald tires, expect a few flat tires. Fuel up in advance and bring a full-size inflated spare, jack, patch kit or Fix-a-Flat, and air compressor.

MCCARTHY ROAD

McCarthy Road (2-3 hrs. one-way) stretches 60 miles from Chitina to McCarthy, taking in raging rivers and turquoise lakes along the way. Stop to marvel at the **Kuskulana Bridge** (mile 17), a 775-foot expanse made even more impressive because it was built in 1910—and because you have to drive across it! Stop again at the huge **Gilahina Trestle** (mile 29) to admire its construction. Just before reaching the parking area, look for the Kennicott Glacier. The road terminates at the **Kennicott River Footbridge**.

The road is legendary for being narrow, rough, and full of sharp rocks and railroad spikes just waiting to puncture tires. Fill up on gas at Kenny Lake (AK 4) before making the trip.

NABESNA ROAD

Fuel up in Slana (Tok Cutoff Hwy., AK 1) for the 42-mile drive along **Nabesna Road** (3 hrs. rt.). Between miles 15 and 18, the rugged Wrangell Mountains come into view and you may spot **Mount Wrangell**, the park's only active volcano. **Kendesnii Campground,** at mile 28, is where many drivers turn around because the remaining road is rougher. Stop at the Slana Ranger Station for road updates, as washouts are frequent.

RECREATION

HIKING

The best hikes visit immense glaciers that resemble rivers of ice spilling from the Wrangell Mountains. To see the **Kennecott Glacier** (1.5 mi. one-way), hike the trail from the McCarthy Museum to the toe of the glacier. Views include multiple peaks, Gates Glacier, and Stairway Icefall. To see **Root Glacier** (2 mi. one-way), follow the trail from the Kennecott Visitor Center and across streams to the toe of the glacier.

St. Elias Alpine Guides (888/933-5427 or 907/554-4445, steliasguides.com) offers guided hikes to Root Glacier, guided ice climbing, backpacking, air-assisted hiking trips, river rafting, and mountaineering expeditions.

FLIGHTSEEING

In McCarthy, air taxis offer expeditions into the park. Go flightseeing with **Copper Valley Air Day Tours** (866/570-4200 or 907/822-4200, www.coppervalleyairservice.com) or **Wrangell Mountain Air** (800/478-1160, www.wrangellmountainair.com).

RAFTING

The silt-colored Kennicott River churns and boils beneath the footbridge toward McCarthy. **McCarthy River Tours & Outfitters** (907/554-1077, www.raftthewrangells.com, mid-May-mid-Sept) specializes in these turbulent waters, with single-day and multiday trips in the Copper River Valley. They also offer calmer paddleboarding and kayaking trips in the lake at the toe of Kennicott Glacier.

WRANGELL MOUNTAINS

FLOATPLANE

WHERE TO STAY

INSIDE THE PARK

For those seeking solitude, the park maintains 14 fly-in or snowmobile-in **backcountry cabins** (first come, first served) in remote locations.

McCarthy

The **McCarthy Lodge** (101 Kennicott Ave., 907/554-4402, www.mccarthy-lodge.com) has two accommodation options: the old boardinghouse of **Ma Johnson's Hotel** (from $229) and the **Lancaster Backpacker Hotel** (from $129). Bathrooms are shared. The lodge bistro serves local yak meat and wild-caught Copper River sockeye salmon. The **Golden Saloon**, where the town goes to socialize, serves pub fare. The lodge store sells ready-made sandwiches, ice cream, liquor, hardware, and limited groceries.

Kennecott

The nicest accommodations are at the **Kennicott Glacier Lodge** (800/582-5128, www.kennicottlodge.com, late May-mid-Sept., from $195). Guest rooms are in two buildings: 24 rooms in the lodge have shared baths and 20 rooms in the south wing have private baths. The dining room serves family-style breakfast, lunch, and dinner fare that some term "wilderness gourmet." Common areas are lined with historical artifacts from the Kennecott copper mine.

For a cozier experience, reserve one of the five **Blackburn Cabins** (907/231-6227, www.blackburncabins.com, year-round, from $150), which have two full beds, propane heaters, kitchens, and running water. Bike rentals, guided hikes, snow machine rentals, and guided trips are also available.

Camping

McCarthy Road has pullouts for camping (free) and two private campgrounds located before the footbridge at McCarthy. Only the aptly named **Glacier View Campground** (mile 58.9, McCarthy, 907/441-5737, www.glacierviewcampground.com, June-mid-Sept., $15) accepts reservations. It has a small open-air café and a bare-bones camp store.

At mile 27.8 on Nabesna Road, the primitive **Kendesnii Campground** (year-round, free) has 10 first-come, first-served campsites, but no drinking water. It is the only park service campground in the park. You can also camp at pullouts along the road.

OUTSIDE THE PARK

The gateway communities of **Glennallen, Copper Center, Kenny Lake,** and **Chitina** have limited services. Small motels, cabins, and campgrounds dot **Richardson Highway** (AK 4), **Glenn Highway** (AK 1), and **Tok Cutoff Road** (AK 1).

WRANGELL MOUNTAINS

GETTING THERE

AIR

The closest international airport is **Ted Stevens Anchorage International Airport** (ANC, 5000 W. International Airport Rd., www.dot.alaska.gov). Car rentals are available at the airport.

CAR

From Anchorage, it is a 180-mile drive on Glenn Highway (AK 1) to Glennallen. Two miles east of Glennallen, turn south onto Richardson Highway (AK 4); from there it's 10 miles to the Copper Center Visitor Center.

To reach McCarthy and Kennicott, continue south on Richardson Highway (AK 4) from Copper Center for 31 miles. Turn left (east) onto Edgerton Highway (AK 10) and drive 33 miles to the pavement's end at Chitina and the park entrance. From Chitina, follow the rough and unpaved McCarthy Road 60 miles east to McCarthy.

If Slana and Nabesna Road are your destination, follow Glenn Highway (AK 1) north from Glennallen for 73 miles.

SHUTTLE

From Anchorage, **Wrangell-St. Elias Tours** (907/390-0369, www.alaskayukontravel.com) runs a van shuttle to Glennallen, Chitina, and McCarthy. **Interior Alaska Bus Line** (800/770-6652, www.interioralaskabusline.com) travels to Glennallen.

GETTING AROUND

AIR

Wrangell Mountain Air (800/478-1160 or 907/554-4411, www.wrangellmountainair.com) operates thrice-daily flights in summer from Chitina to McCarthy.

CAR

From the park entrance at Chitina, **McCarthy Road** (60 mi., 2-3 hrs. one-way) goes to McCarthy and Kennicott. From the Tok Cutoff Road (AK 1), the rougher Nabesna Road (42 mi., 1.5 hrs. one-way) leads north of the mountains.

SHUTTLES

The **Kennicott Shuttle** (907/822-5292, www.kennicottshuttle.com, summer only, reservations required) picks up guests outside the park in Glennallen, Copper Center, Kenny Lake, or Chitina with transportation to McCarthy and Kennicott. **Wrangell-St. Elias Tours** (907/390-0369, www.alaskayukontravel.com) runs a shuttle van twice daily between Chitina and McCarthy.

At the Kennicott River, shuttles stop at the footbridge for the walk into McCarthy. In town, hop on the **McCarthy-Kennicott Shuttle** (907/554-4411, www.mccarthykennicottshuttle.com) to go into Kennicott.

GLACIER BAY NATIONAL PARK AND PRESERVE

Alaska

PASSPORT STAMPS ▼▼▼

WEBSITE:
www.nps.gov/glba

PHONE NUMBER:
907/697-2230

VISITATION RANK:
35

WHY GO:
Watch glaciers calve.

▲ MARGERIE GLACIER

Newak Glacier

Brabazon Range

Alsek River

SAINT ELIAS MOUNTAINS

CANADA
UNITED STATES

Tatshenshini River

Konamoxt Gl

Tatshenshini River

Towagh Glacier

Tsiatka Glacier

ALSEK RANGE

Tikke Glacier

Melburn Glacier

Mount Hay
8,870ft

Hay Glacier

Alsek Glacier

Alsek Lake

Alsek River

DRY BAY
RANGER STATION

GLACIER BAY
NATIONAL
PRESERVE

Dry
Bay

Deception Hills

Grand Plateau Glacier

Grand Pacific Glacier

Mount Lodge
10,530ft

Ferris Glacier

Mount Barnard
8,214ft

Tarr Inlet

Margerie Glacier

Mount Root
12,860ft

Gulf of Alaska

Mount
Fairweather
15,300ft

FAIRWEATHER

Mount Quincy
Adams
13,650ft

Inlet

Jaw
Point

Johns Hopkins

Mount Salisbury
12,000ft

Johns Hopkins Glacier

Mount Abbe
8,750ft

Cape
Fairweather

Fairweather Glacier

Lituya Mountain
11,750ft

RANGE

Johns Hopkins Glacier

Mount Orville
10,495ft

Mount
Bertha
10,204ft

Lituya Glacier

North Crillon Glacier

Mount
Crillon
12,726ft

Lituya Bay

Crillon
Lake

Mount La Perouse
10,728ft

La Perouse Glacier

PACIFIC OCEAN

Palma
Bay

Icy Point

Astrolabe
Point

GLACIER BAY
NATIONAL PARK
AND PRESERVE

0   10 mi

0   10 km

Death Valley

270 miles / 5 hours

Cross Yosemite's **Tioga Pass** heading east on Highway 120 before turning south on U.S. 395. From the Wild West town of **Lone Pine,** turn east onto Highway 190 to enter the park. Cruise along Highway 190 to **Panamint Springs.** An hour east is the aptly named park hub of **Furnace Creek,** a perfect base for touring **Badwater Drive** and **Zabriskie Point.**

Sequoia and Kings Canyon

340 miles / 6 hours

Exit Death Valley and head south on U.S. 395 toward Mojave, where you'll turn west on Highway 58. From Bakersfield, it's a straight shot north for 100 miles to the **Ash Mountain Entrance** of **Sequoia National Park.** Enjoy the scenic drive north on Generals Highway, stopping at **Moro Rock,** the **General Sherman Tree,** and the **Giant Forest Museum** (pick up tickets for **Crystal Cave!**). Bed down at the **John Muir Lodge** in Kings Canyon, where you're primed for visits to **Grant Grove** and the winding drive down **Kings Canyon Scenic Byway.**

1: ZABRISKIE POINT, DEATH VALLEY
2: MORO ROCK, SEQUOIA
3: REDWOOD CREEK AT KINGS CANYON SCENIC BYWAY, HIGHWAY 180, KINGS CANYON

GLACIER BAY NATIONAL PARK AND PRESERVE encompasses an enormous 3.3 million acres of land and water. Its craggy, snow-capped mountains, towering spruce and cedar trees, calving glaciers, and rich waters are hardly unique in Alaska, but this park is remarkable for several reasons.

The first is the pristine nature of the waters and lands; the waters, in particular, are some of the richest on earth, and Glacier Bay is one of the largest protected biosphere preserves in the world. Second, the solitude—cruise ships do visit the bay, but they never dock, and access is controlled during peak months.

Third, it's been less than 300 years since an enormously thick glacier covered much of this land. The bay was uncovered by a stunningly fast series of advances and retreats. Active tidewater glaciers from the Little Ice Age still push into the bay, but are receding at an alarming rate. Most of the bay's famed glaciers are thinning, shrinking, and becoming terrestrial glaciers.

Finally, this place is a rich, integral part of the Tlingit Alaska Native tradition, and park officials work closely with the tribes. One of their most notable successes was the opening of the Xunaa Shuká Hít (Huna House) clan house—the first permanent clan house in Glacier Bay since Tlingit villages were destroyed by a rapid glacier advance more than 250 years ago.

PLANNING YOUR TIME

Glacier Bay is virtually roadless. The park encompasses a 65-mile-long saltwater bay with multiple fjords hunkering between ice-laden mountains draped with glaciers that plunge into the tidewater. To see the glaciers requires **travel by air or water,** plus the logistics of several trip legs to get there. From **Juneau,** getting to the park entrance requires a ferry or a flight to **Gustavus,** a service town just outside the park that is unreachable by road. From Gustavus, taxis travel the short distance to Bartlett Cove, inside the park. From Gustavus or Bartlett Cove, boat tours enter Glacier Bay.

May-September is high season, with services in Gustavus and Bartlett Cove open. Despite moderate summer temperatures, erratic maritime weather systems deliver pervasive rains, especially around Bartlett Cove, which sees up to 70 inches annually. Bring rain gear and warm, quick-dry layers, including hat and gloves. For less rain, go in May or June.

There are three main areas to tour in Glacier Bay. The **Main Channel** contains the Marble Islands, where you might spot cliff-dwelling seabirds, sea lions, or summering humpback whales. At Tlingit Point, the waterways divide into two main arms.

The smaller **Muir Inlet** (sometimes called East Arm) contains multiple glaciers that are mostly terrestrial; McBride Glacier still reaches the tidewater, but Muir Glacier has melted with speedy recession back onto land.

The larger arm is **Glacier Bay,** known also as West Arm, where motorized boats and cruises can go. This arm holds the 35-mile-long Grand Pacific Glacier and the smaller Margerie Glacier, which calve off icebergs into the bay. Johns Hopkins and Gilman Glaciers produce submarine calving, where ice breaks off underwater to explode to the surface.

Top ③

1 CRUISE GLACIER BAY

Visitors can travel up the Main Channel or tour Glacier Bay's West Arm to view the tidewater glaciers. The only scheduled day tour in the park is the **Glacier Bay Tour** out of **Glacier Bay Lodge** (179 Bartlett Cove, 888/229-8687, www.visitglacierbay.com, daily in summer). National Park Service rangers narrate the eight-hour tour on high-speed catamarans. The tour takes in wildlife and the tidewater Grand Pacific and Margerie Glaciers. Lunch is included.

Cruise ships depart from West Coast and Alaskan cities to tour Glacier Bay. Two ships per day are allowed up the West Arm to spend four hours in the glacier areas. Cruise ships do not

MCBRIDE GLACIER

dock; sightseeing is only from the boat. Tour operators in Gustavus also offer day trips and longer overnight expeditions into Glacier Bay.

2 GO WHALE-WATCHING

From late June through September, whale-watching for humpback whales is phenomenal in the waters of Glacier Bay. Two of the best whale-watching tours are the half-day, naturalist-narrated **"Taz" Cross-Sound Express** (888/698-2726 or 907/321-2303, www.taz.gustavus.com), which also offers water-taxi services for kayakers and backpackers (the deck is large enough to handle large groups of kayaks), and the half-day **Wild Alaska Charters** tour (855/997-2704 or 907/697-2704, www.glacierbay.biz), limited to six passengers at a time.

3 KAYAK THE OPEN WATERS

Sea kayaking is enormously popular. **Glacier Bay Sea Kayaks** (Bartlett Cove, 907/697-2257, www.glacierbayseakayaks.com) has a concession for full- and half-day trips in the park and also provides gear rentals and trip-planning assistance to paddlers experienced enough to go without a guide. The **Beardslee Islands** are a popular destination, with great beach camping and wildlife viewing. Another great destination is **Muir Inlet**, where motorized boats are restricted, making this a prime place for quiet and solitude. Kayakers can use the daily Glacier Bay Tour boat as a water taxi to cut days off paddling time; they can also bring their own boats on the ferry from Juneau.

The folks at **Alaska Mountain Guides** (based in Haines, 800/766-3396 or 907/313-4422, www.alaskamountainguides.com) are renowned for their guided expeditions of five days or more. **Spirit Walker Expeditions** (800/529-2537, www.seakayakalaska.com) is also very popular for longer trips.

ONE DAY IN GLACIER BAY

If you must pack your Glacier Bay visit into one day, charter an early-morning flight from Juneau to Gustavus. Spend that night at **Glacier Bay Lodge,** then take the **Glacier Bay Tour** into Glacier Bay—it's the only way to see the wildlife and tidewater glaciers. The eight-hour tour boat returns in time to catch a late-afternoon flight back to Juneau.

ENTRANCE AND FEES

The park has no entrance station, but the official entrance is Bartlett Cove. There is no entrance fee.

VISITORS CENTERS

In Bartlett Cove, **Glacier Bay National Park Visitor Center** (Glacier Bay Lodge, 2nd fl., 907/697-2661, 11am-8pm daily late May-early Sept.) contains an Alaska Geographic bookstore and exhibits, including an underwater listening station and a kids corner. The theater has nightly educational programs, and ranger-guided walks depart for beachcombing or rain forest tours.

To go boating or camping in Glacier Bay, stop at the **Visitor Information Station** (Bartlett Cove, 907/697-2627, hours vary daily May-Sept.), adjacent to the public dock in Bartlett Cove. Attend an orientation covering the rigors of wilderness boating and camping, then pick up permits, maps, tide tables, and nautical charts.

SIGHTS
BARTLETT COVE

Bartlett Cove is Glacier Bay National Park's headquarters. Nestled at the south end of the bay, the enclave houses **Glacier Bay Lodge,** which contains the visitors center, hotel rooms, and a restaurant. The cove also has the **Huna Tribal House,** docks with boat services, kayak rentals, the **Visitor Information Station,** and a walk-in campground. Low tide is the perfect time to explore the intertidal zone around the cove, which is teeming with seaweed, algae, crabs, mollusks, and birds.

AERIAL VIEW OF GLACIER BAY NATIONAL PARK

HIKER AND GLACIER

HUNA TRIBAL HOUSE

The **Huna Tribal House** (12:30pm-5:30pm Mon.-Sat.) pays tribute to the Tlingit culture, which has a rich history in the lower bay. The building sports carvings and paintings that portray the history of Tlingit clans. Interpretive presentations (20 min.) are offered several times daily; weekly programs include guided walks and demonstrations on making dugout canoes. The house is located on the shoreline trail of Bartlett Cove, adjacent to Glacier Bay Lodge.

WHALE EXHIBIT

Stop at the outdoor pavilion near the Visitor Information Center to see the **Whale Exhibit,** home to the largest humpback whale skeleton in the United States. Known as Snow, this humpback whale was a regular summer resident in the bay for 26 years. Her 3,729-pound skeleton is more than 45 feet long.

RECREATION

HIKING

Glacier Bay has only 10 miles of designated hiking trails, including an easy stroll on the **Tlingit Trail** (0.5 mi. rt.) to the Huna Tribal House. A 0.25-mile trail goes along the beach to the Bartlett Cove Campground.

The **Forest Trail** (0.7 mi. one-way) is a wheelchair-accessible boardwalk trail that leads to two viewing decks overlooking a pond. Past the pond, a dirt trail continues to the campground and the beach before looping back to the starting point. Park rangers lead daily hikes on this trail.

The **Bartlett Lake Trail** (9.4 mi. rt., 7-8 hr.) climbs over moraine to tour spruce forests on its way to Bartlett Lake.

BOATING

Glacier Bay has 700 miles of shoreline for boaters to explore. June-August, private boat owners must secure a free permit (available online) to enter the waters of **Glacier Bay** and **Bartlett Cove.** Permits are good for up to 7 days; apply within 60 days of your planned arrival date. Don't dillydally, though—permits often "sell out" quickly from mid-June to early August. Motorized boats are limited to 25 craft per day in Glacier Bay. The public dock at Bartlett Cove has boater services.

FISHING

The waters of Glacier Bay and Icy Straits are enormously productive—this is one of the best places in the world for fishing—and the isolated location means you won't have to battle

SEA LIONS

rustic guest rooms with private baths. The lodge restaurant serves breakfast, lunch, and dinner; entrees specialize in Alaskan seafood. Bicycle rentals, fishing gear rentals, fishing licenses, and a laundry are available.

Bartlett Cove Campground (free, permit required, May-Sept.) offers serene tent camping with fantastic views over the water. It's a 0.25-mile walk to the 33-site campground; facilities include bear-resistant food caches, outhouses, and a warming shelter. Register at the Visitor Information Station near the private docks, follow an orientation, and then pick up your free camping permit. Campers can shower at Glacier Bay Lodge.

crowds. Book an all-inclusive, multiday fishing trip with **Glacier Bay Sportfishing** (907/697-3038, www.glacier-baysportfishing.com, lodging at the Gustavus Inn) or opt for a half-day to five-day trip with **Taylor Charters** (801/647-3401, www.taylorcharters-fishing.com). Glacier Bay Lodge rents fishing gear and sells licenses.

WHERE TO STAY

INSIDE THE PARK

The only accommodations inside the park are at **Glacier Bay Lodge** (179 Bartlett Cove, 888/229-8687, www.visitglacierbay.com, mid-May-early Sept., from $260). The facility has 48 small,

OUTSIDE THE PARK

Accommodations and dining options can be found in the picturesque community of **Gustavus,** 10 miles from the park entrance.

GETTING THERE

AIR

Alaska Airlines (800/252-7522, www.alaskaair.com, June-Aug.) offers seasonal service via a 30-minute flight from Juneau to Gustavus. From the airport in Gustavus, it's about 10 miles to the entrance of Glacier Bay National Park.

▼ SUNRISE ON THE FAIRWEATHER RANGE

A CRUISE SHIP APPROACHES MARGERIE GLACIER

Small planes, including seaplanes, hop between towns in southeast Alaska. They provide transportation, plus flightseeing trips. **Alaska Seaplanes** (907/789-3331, www.flyalaska-seaplanes.com) is based in Gustavus and Juneau. **Admiralty Air Service** (907/796-2000, www.admiraltyair-service.com) and **Ward Air** (907/789-9150, http://wardair.com) are based in Juneau.

BOAT

Cruise ships enter the bay but don't dock. The **Alaska Marine Highway System Ferry** (800/642-0066, www.dot.state.ak.us/amhs) offers twice-weekly service between Juneau and Gustavus, a 4.5-hour trip.

GETTING AROUND

Glacier Bay Lodge and most lodges in Gustavus provide shuttles from the airport or ferry terminal to the hotel. Taxis link the communities of Gustavus and Bartlett Cove; call **TLC Taxi** (907/697-2239, www.glacierbaytravel.com/tlctaxi) for service. The only road is the 10-mile link between Gustavus and Bartlett Cove, but if you need to rent a car, contact **Bud's Rent-a-Car** (907/697-2403).

GLACIER BAY NATIONAL PRESERVE

Glacier Bay is a remote and special place—so much so that UNESCO recognized it as a World Heritage Site and a Biosphere Reserve. That designation is thanks in part to **Glacier Bay National Preserve,** a small portion of the park tucked in the northeast corner. Bounded by the Gulf of Alaska and the Alsek River, this unique area is rich in wildlife. Recreation includes fishing, hunting, river rafting, and 60 miles of designated ATV trails.

To reach the remote preserve requires chartering an air taxi from Yakutat to one of two airstrips on the preserve. Visitors can camp in the wilderness (free) or reserve a small cabin rented by the Yakutat Ranger Station (907/784-3295, $25). Three small lodges operate concessions.

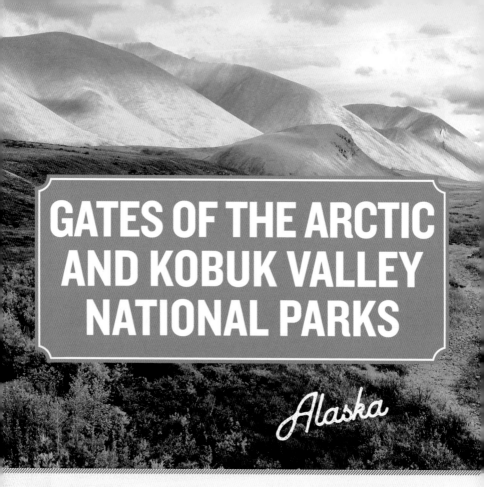

GATES OF THE ARCTIC AND KOBUK VALLEY NATIONAL PARKS

Alaska

GATES OF THE ARCTIC

WEBSITE:
www.nps.gov/gaar

PHONE NUMBER:
907/692-5494

VISITATION RANK:
59

WHY GO:
Visit a remote, raw wilderness.

KOBUK VALLEY

WEBSITE:
www.nps.gov/kova

PHONE NUMBER:
907/442-3890

VISITATION RANK:
58

WHY GO:
See migrating caribou and sand dunes.

PASSPORT STAMPS ▼▼▼

▲ KOBUK VALLEY

Two remote national parks claim places above Alaska's Arctic Circle. These roadless wildernesses see very few human footprints. The larger **GATES OF THE ARCTIC NATIONAL PARK AND PRESERVE** contains the wild Brooks Range, spilling with glaciers, huge rivers, tundra, and boreal forests.

The smaller **KOBUK VALLEY NATIONAL PARK** gains its fame from sand dunes made from ice age glaciers. Both have immense herds of caribou, plus tundra swans, musk ox, moose, wolves, and grizzly bears. The weather and the animals still rule here; we are simply transient visitors.

PLANNING YOUR TIME

These wilderness parks are devoid of trails, roads, campgrounds, lodging, visitor centers, and services. There are no entrance fees—or even entrances! All access is on foot or by bush plane. It's this very wildness that is the draw.

Winters are unforgivingly harsh and long. The best months to travel are **June-August.** Even during summer's short, mild weather, temperatures can drop well below freezing. Expect high winds, mosquitoes, and changeable weather.

Fairbanks is the jumping-off point for driving the Dalton Highway (AK 11), a rough dirt-road trek to the small service towns east of Gates of the Arctic. Fly-in guided trips depart from Anchorage, Fairbanks, Kotzebue, or Bettles. For visitors aiming to check off all U.S. national parks, the right outfitter can get you to Gates of the Arctic and Kobuk Valley on the same trip.

THE NOATAK RIVER

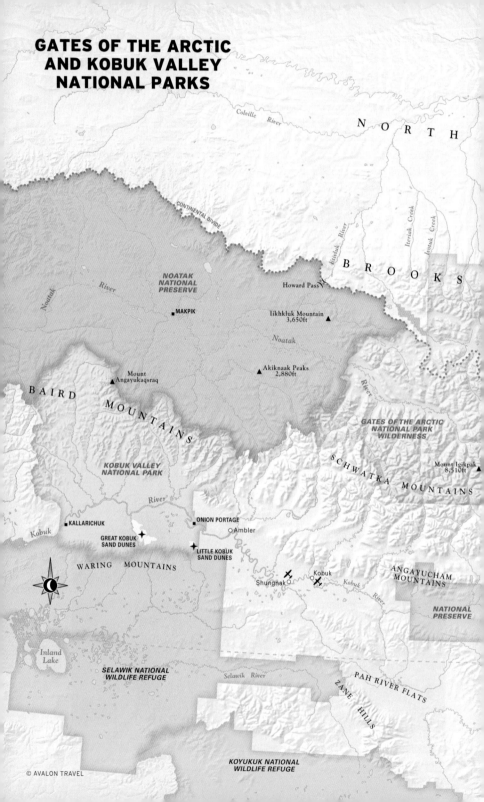

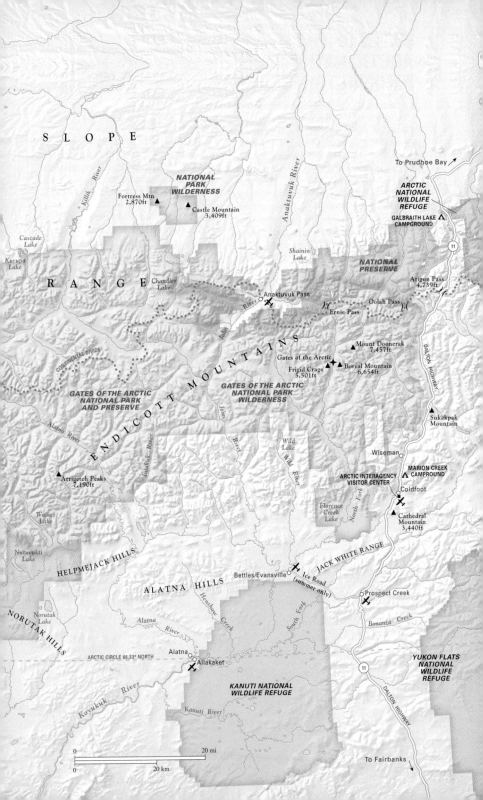

GATES OF THE ARCTIC NATIONAL PARK AND PRESERVE

Located in the Brooks Range at the foot of the needle-like Arrigetch Mountains, Gates of the Arctic National Park and Preserve is a vast, untouched wilderness that spans 8.4 million acres. Containing the northernmost mountain range in North America, it stretches west from the Dalton Highway through country where wildlife far outnumbers humans. Dense vegetation, marshes, frequent water crossings, glacial lakes, and soaring granite peaks make travel very challenging but beautifully remote.

PLANNING YOUR TIME

The closest "town" is the tiny hub of Bettles (population 12), accessible only by air or snow machine on the winter ice road.

Outside the park are three visitors centers. The **Arctic Interagency Visitor Center** (mile 175 Dalton Hwy., Coldfoot, 907/658-5209, hours vary daily, summer only) updates road conditions on the Dalton Highway, offers backcountry trip registration, and rents bear canisters. It also has films, exhibits, and a bookstore with maps.

Reachable only by air, the small **Bettles Ranger Station and Visitor Center** (in Bettles) has exhibits. The backcountry **Anaktuvuk Ranger Station** (summer hours vary) has an outdoor information kiosk.

RECREATION

Gates of the Arctic has flightseeing, remote camping, backpacking, pack rafting, river float trips, paddling, photography, fishing, and hunting; hire a guide for all activities. In addition to guides licensed for both parks, two companies provide guide services from Anchorage into Gates of the Arctic:

Alaska Alpine Adventures (877/525-2577 or 907/351-4193, www.alaskaalpineadventures.com) guides hiking, backpacking, and rafting trips.

Expeditions Alaska (770/952-4549, www.expeditionsalaska.com) owner Carl Donohue guides photography, backpacking, and pack rafting trips.

WHERE TO STAY

Outside the park, **Bettles Lodge** (Bettles, 907/692-5111, http://bettleslodge.com, year-round) has guest rooms,

▼ ARCTIC DIVIDE NEAR ANAKTUVUK PASS

GATES OF THE ARCTIC NATIONAL PARK AND PRESERVE

dining, flightseeing, guided backpacking and fishing, aurora viewing, and dogsledding.

On the Dalton Highway, small communities such as **Coldfoot** also have a few lodging and outfitter options. Campgrounds are at Galbraith Lake and Marion Creek.

GETTING THERE

From Fairbanks or Anchorage, **Ravn Alaska** (907/266-8394, www.flyravn. com) flies air taxis via Kotzebue to Bettles or Anaktuvuk Pass. **Wright's Air Service** (907/474-0502, www.wrightairservice.com) flies from Fairbanks to Bettles and Coldfoot.

GUIDE SERVICES

For most visitors, access is by bush plane. Professional guide services offer a safe (although pricey) way to experience the wonder of these arctic parks. Three companies are licensed to guide in Gates of the Arctic and Kobuk Valley:

Bettles Lodge (907/692-5111, http://bettleslodge.com) books flightseeing in both parks.

From Bettles airstrip, **Brooks Range Aviation** (800/692-5443 or 907/692-5444, http://brooksrange.com) offers flightseeing in both parks and guides backpacking, river floating, remote camping, hunting, and fishing trips.

From Fairbanks, **Arctic Wild** (907/479-8203, www.arcticwild.com) guides backpacking, pack rafting, hiking, and remote camping in both parks.

KOBUK VALLEY NATIONAL PARK

The 1.8-million-acre Kobuk Valley National Park gains its fame from its 25 square miles of massive sand dunes made by glaciers that ground their way through the land. Some dunes tower 100 feet high. More than a half-million caribou migrate through the dunes, many crossing the Kobuk River at Onion Portage where people still gather to harvest the animals much as they did 8,000 years ago.

PLANNING YOUR TIME

Kotzebue is the gateway for visiting Kobuk Valley. The multiagency **Northwest Arctic Heritage Center** (171 3rd Ave., 907/442-3890, 9am-6:30pm Mon.-Fri., 1pm-5pm Sat.) serves as the visitors center, nature center, and museum, plus headquarters for the park. Educational programs include classes in traditional native crafts. Spend an hour taking in the exhibits and get your national parks passport stamped for Kobuk Valley.

RECREATION

As the largest active dunes in the North American arctic, the Great Kobuk Sand Dunes and two lesser dunes cover about 20,500 acres. These wind-shaped relics show how the grinding power of ancient glaciers continue to change, even as grasses gain footholds in the sand. **Flightseeing** is the easiest way to see the dunes—on a flyover or landing to walk the sand.

To see the **Onion Portage caribou migration,** plan a trip around Labor Day to the Kobuk River. Charter a bush plane to get there, set up camp, and climb a hill to watch the show.

From Kotzebue, fly with **Arctic Backcountry Flying Service** (907/442-3200, www.arcticbackcountry.com) for flightseeing or guided fishing, backpacking, and float trips.

WHERE TO STAY

Outside the park, Kotzebue houses the modern, European-inspired **Nullaġvik Hotel** (306 Shore Ave., 907/442-3331, www.nullagvikhotel.com, from $259),

CAMPING ALONG THE SALMON RIVER

GREAT KOBUK SAND DUNES

whose name means "a place to sleep" in Inupiaq. Guest rooms have private baths and touches of Alaska Native art. One of the upper floors has an observation room overlooking Kotzebue Sound.

GETTING THERE

To reach Kobuk Valley, book a flight from Anchorage or Fairbanks to Kotzebue (there is no road access). From Kotzebue, charter a flight into the park. In summer, **Alaska Airlines** (800/252-7522, www.alaskaairlines.com) has daily flights from Anchorage. From Fairbanks or Anchorage, **Ravn Alaska** (907/266-8394, www.flyravn.com) flies to Kotzebue and then connects with Bettles. From Bettles, charter flights into Kobuk Valley are available from Ravn or **Bering Air** (800/478-3943 or 907/442-3943, www.beringair.com).

SIGHTS NEARBY

Noatak National Preserve (907/442-3890, www.nps.gov/noat) comprises the mountains around the Noatak River, a National Wild and Scenic River. Floating, fishing, and hunting are available.

Cape Krusenstern National Monument (907/442-3890, www.nps.gov/cakr) has wild coastal lagoons with archeological sites of human activity that date back 9,000 years.

ARCTIC NATIONAL WILDLIFE REFUGE

Established in 1960, the **Arctic National Wildlife Refuge** (ANWR, U.S. Fish and Wildlife Service, Fairbanks, 800/362-4546 or 907/456-0250) includes 19.64 million acres of land and water, more than 200,000 caribou, an unthinkable horde of mosquitoes, and one human settlement—the Iñupiat village of **Kaktovik** (population 250).

Bordered by Canada to the east, the Arctic Ocean to the north, and the Dalton Highway to the west, ANWR is so large that it spans varied ecological regions: boreal forest, alpine, coastal plain tundra, and coastal marine. It is home to grizzly bears, polar bears, musk oxen, and the highest concentration of nesting golden eagles in Alaska.

Only 1,500 people visit the refuge annually. ANWR remains a vast, largely trackless wilderness, an undisturbed spectrum of Arctic ecosystems that most human beings will never see in their lifetime.

CALIFORNIA

From redwood forests to snowcapped mountains, the California landscape is filled with overwhelming natural beauty and wide-open wilderness. The national parks here excel in superlatives: the tallest mountain in the continental United States, the lowest point in North America, and the highest waterfall in North America. They are a testament to powerful, earth-shaping forces that left their diverse handiwork across the region.

In Yosemite, waterfalls feather down faces of granite. Groves of giant sequoias tower above the trails in Sequoia and Kings Canyon. Along the Pacific coast, lush forests fill with coastal sequoias and islands harbor endemic marinelife. In between, you'll find dormant volcanoes, bone-dry deserts, and craggy alpine peaks begging exploration.

◄ GLACIER POINT, YOSEMITE

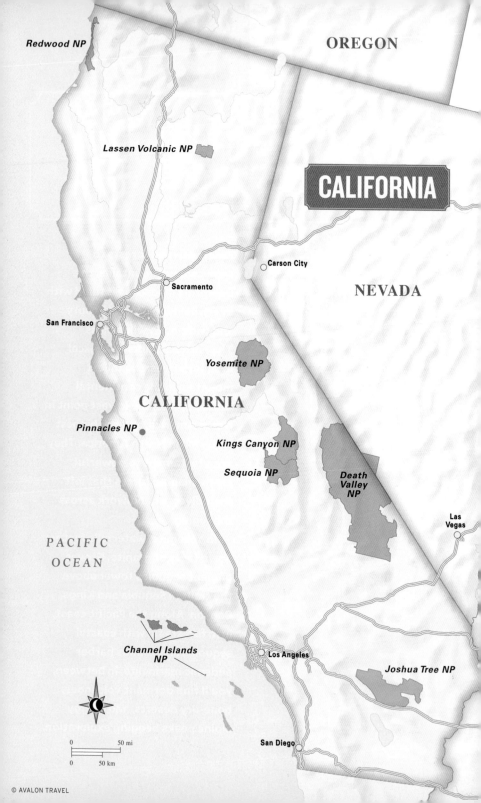

Redwood NP

OREGON

Lassen Volcanic NP

CALIFORNIA

Carson City

Sacramento

NEVADA

San Francisco

Yosemite NP

CALIFORNIA

Pinnacles NP

Kings Canyon NP

Sequoia NP

Death Valley NP

Las Vegas

PACIFIC OCEAN

Channel Islands NP

Los Angeles

Joshua Tree NP

San Diego

0   50 mi
0   50 km

© AVALON TRAVEL

The National Parks of
CALIFORNIA

YOSEMITE

Granite monoliths and plunging waterfalls are the hallmarks of this Sierra park that lures hikers, backpackers, and big-wall climbers (page 109).

SEQUOIA AND KINGS CANYON

These parks boast giant sequoia groves, numerous hiking trails, thriving wildlife, and smaller crowds than their more famous neighbor (page 131).

DEATH VALLEY

Sculpted sand dunes, crusted salt flats, and polished marble canyons pervade this park, which has both the Western Hemisphere's lowest and hottest spots (page 143).

JOSHUA TREE

The park's namesake trees and surreal appeal draw wildflower hounds, serious hikers, and hard-core rock climbers (page 154).

LASSEN

Geologic wonders include boiling mud pots, fumaroles, and a 10,462-foot volcano (page 168).

REDWOOD STATE AND NATIONAL PARKS

A series of state and national parks line the California coast, filled with groves of primordial giants (page 176).

PINNACLES

Climbers, hikers, and campers can't get enough of the huge rock formations, deep caves, and vertical topography in this tucked-away treasure (page 185).

CHANNEL ISLANDS

This series of islands has undeveloped beauty, stellar coastal views, and stunning sea caves for exploring by kayak (page 192).

1: BRIDGE OVER WOODS CREEK, KINGS CANYON
2: CINDER CONE, LASSEN
3: BALCONIES CAVE TRAIL, PINNACLES

Best OF THE PARKS

Yosemite Valley: Go to Yosemite's heart for El Capitan, Half Dome, and Bridalveil Fall (page 113).

Badwater Basin: Drive this scenic road for the best of Death Valley, including North America's lowest elevation (page 147).

Keys Ranch: Tour the well-preserved ruins of this former homestead, listed in the National Register of Historic Places (page 159).

General Sherman Tree: Admire the largest tree known on earth (page 135).

Lassen Peak: Climb to the summit of this active volcano (page 172).

GENERAL SHERMAN

PLANNING YOUR TRIP

California's best feature is its all-season appeal. Time your trip for **summer** and **early fall,** when Tioga Pass opens across the Sierra between Yosemite and Death Valley. Be aware that summer brings the most visitors, which will not only add to the crowds, but also to the traffic. To avoid the crowds, visit in **spring** when Yosemite's waterfalls are at their peak and fewer people populate the trails. In **winter,** Yosemite's roads are closed, including Highway 120 and the Tioga Pass. Snow can blanket the California mountains anytime between November and April.

The easiest places to fly into are **San Francisco** and **Los Angeles.** Book **hotels** and **rental cars** in advance for the best rates and availability, especially in the high season of summer. Reservations are essential for **campgrounds** in Yosemite.

1: GENERAL SHERMAN TREE, SEQUOIA
2: BRIDALVEIL FALL, YOSEMITE

Road Trip

YOSEMITE, DEATH VALLEY, AND SEQUOIA & KINGS CANYON

Start your trip in San Francisco, where you can fly into **San Francisco International Airport** and **rent a car.** This route is best traveled in **early summer** or **late fall** (June-Oct.), when Yosemite's Tioga Road (Hwy. 120) is open. If Tioga Road is closed, visit Sequoia and Kings Canyon before traveling south to enter Death Valley.

Yosemite

200 miles / 4 hours
Leave San Francisco at 8am to reach Yosemite by noon. The drive to the **Big Oak Flat Entrance** takes at least four hours; however, traffic, especially in summer and on weekends, can make it much longer.

Spend a day touring **Yosemite Valley,** seeing **Half Dome**, **El Capitan,** and **Yosemite Falls,** and then hike the **Mist Trail.** Spend a night under the stars at

UPPER YOSEMITE FALL

one of the park's campgrounds or indoors at the classic **Majestic Yosemite Hotel** (make reservations well in advance). In summer, take a scenic drive along Tioga Road and plan a hike at **Tuolumne Meadows.** Exit the park over Tioga Pass.

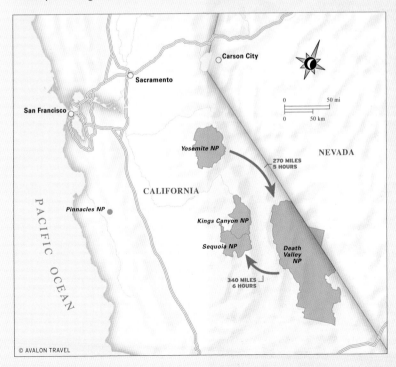

© AVALON TRAVEL

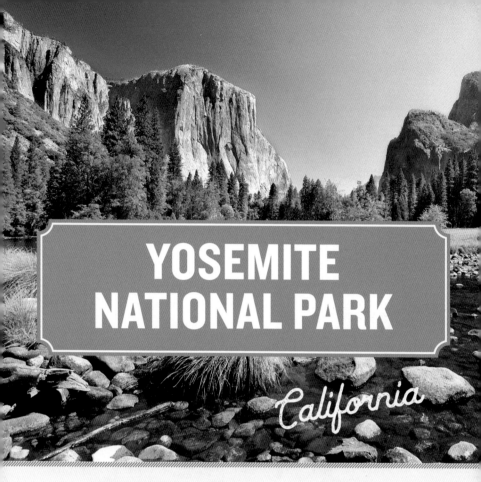

YOSEMITE NATIONAL PARK

California

PASSPORT STAMPS ▼▼▼

WEBSITE:
www.nps.gov/yose

PHONE NUMBER:
209/372-0200

VISITATION RANK:
5

WHY GO:
Admire waterfalls
and granite
cathedrals.

▲ MERCED RIVER AND EL CAPITAN

YOSEMITE
NATIONAL PARK

Of all the natural wonders that California has to offer, few are more iconic than this national park nestled within the Sierra Nevada. **YOSEMITE NATIONAL PARK** is a natural playground that has been immortalized in the photographs of Ansel Adams. The naturalist John Muir called it "the grandest of all the special temples of Nature I was ever permitted to enter." It was Muir who lobbied for national park designation in 1890 and who introduced its wonders to President Theodore Roosevelt in 1903. If this is your first visit, prepare to be overwhelmed.

PLANNING YOUR TIME

The first place most people go is Yosemite Valley (Hwy. 140, Arch Rock Entrance), the most visited region in the park, filled with sights, hikes, and services. Park in the Yosemite Village day-use lot and use the **park shuttle** (7am-10pm daily year-round, free) to get around. Plan at least 2-3 days just in **Yosemite Valley,** with an excursion to Glacier Point. With a week or more, explore Tuolumne Meadows (summer only) or Wawona.

Reservations for camping and lodging, as well as any permits, should be obtained up to **one year in advance.** It takes advance planning to score an overnight reservation in Yosemite Valley. **Half Dome Village** is your best bet for last-minute tent cabins, or you can try one of the first-come, first-served campgrounds.

Summer is high season, when traffic jams and parking problems plague the park. Use the free shuttles to reach popular sights and trailheads. Tuolumne Meadows and the Eastern Sierra are less congested, making them good summer options. **Spring** is best for waterfalls and wildflowers, and there are fewer crowds, as in **fall.** In **winter,** roads close and crowds are minimal. Chains may be required on any park road at any time.

ENTRANCES AND FEES

Yosemite is open daily year-round, though some roads close in winter. The entrance fee is $35 per vehicle ($30 motorcycle, $20 individual) and is valid for seven days. There are **five park entrances**:

Arch Rock (Hwy. 140): The main entrance accesses Yosemite Valley from the west (San Francisco, Sacramento). Once inside the park, Highway 140 becomes El Portal Road. Long lines form at the entrance station May-October; plan to arrive before 9am or after 5pm.

Big Oak Flat (Hwy. 120): This entrance accesses Yosemite Valley and Tuolumne Meadows (summer only) from the north (San Francisco, Sacramento). Inside the park, Highway 120 becomes Big Oak Flat Road.

South (Hwy. 41): This entrance provides access to Wawona from the south (Fresno, Los Angeles). Inside the park, Highway 41 becomes Wawona Road.

Tioga Pass (Hwy. 120): This High Sierra route is on the east side of Yosemite, 12 miles west of U.S. 395. Tioga Road accesses Tuolumne Meadows and the Eastern Sierra in summer. Tioga Pass is **closed in winter** (usually Oct.-May or early June).

Hetch Hetchy (off Hwy. 120): This is the only access to the Hetch Hetchy Reservoir and region. The entrance and Hetch Hetchy Road are open sunrise-sunset year-round.

VISITORS CENTERS

Valley Visitor Center

The **Valley Visitor Center** (Yosemite Village, 209/372-0299, shuttle stops 5 and 9, 9am-5pm daily year-round) has an interpretive museum in addition to information, books, maps, and

Top ❸

HALF DOME

❶ SCALE HALF DOME

One of Yosemite's most recognizable features rises high above the valley floor—**Half Dome.** This piece of a narrow granite ridge was polished to its smooth dome-like shape tens of millions of years ago by glaciers, giving it the appearance of half a dome. Hikers summit the dome with the assistance of a cable route first installed in 1919; it's terrifying to some and has been deadly for a few. Instead of climbing, view the iconic granite dome from the safety of the park road by taking the shuttle to **Mirror Lake,** where you can admire the giant from its base. Other good viewpoints include **Stoneman Meadow, Tunnel View** (Hwy. 41), and **Glacier Point.**

For those who are prepared, the most nontechnical climb requires a monumental day on **Half Dome** (14-16 mi. rt., 10-12 hrs., late May-early Oct. only, shuttle stop 16). The trail follows the Mist Trail to Nevada Fall and then is signed for Half Dome. Its 4,800-foot gain and descent is grueling. The final ultra-steep, 400-foot ascent is via metal hand cables that see a lineup of climbers. Once you stagger to the top, you'll find a restful expanse of stone on which to enjoy the scenery.

Do not attempt this trail lightly! It is not for young kids, anyone out of shape, or those unaccustomed to lengthy and strenuous high-altitude hikes. You must begin the trail *before sunrise* and turn around by 3:30pm. Do not climb the dome when the cables are down or when the trail is closed.

A **permit** (877/444-6777, www.recreation.gov, $10 reservation, $10 per person) is required. The park distributes 300 permits per day through an online lottery that starts in March.

❷ TOUR YOSEMITE VALLEY

The first place most people go is the floor of **Yosemite Valley.** It's the most visited spot in Yosemite, home to the towering granite walls of **El Capitan** and **Half Dome** and the plunging **Bridalveil Fall** and **Yosemite Falls.** It's also the starting point of many hikes, including the popular **Mist Trail.** From the valley floor, you can check out the visitors center, the theater, galleries, museum, hotels, and outdoor historical exhibits.

EL CAPITAN

❸ VIEW THE VALLEY FROM GLACIER POINT

In 1903, naturalist John Muir brought President Theodore Roosevelt to **Glacier Point**, igniting the president's passion for Yosemite. A drive or shuttle bus along Glacier Point Road (open June-Oct.) leads to a short, paved, wheelchair-accessible path with epic vistas across the entire valley and the High Sierra. Pose for a photo op in the footsteps of Muir and Roosevelt, then return to the valley floor via the Four-Mile Trail (4.8 mi. one-way).

ONE DAY IN YOSEMITE

With only one day, concentrate on the sights in Yosemite Valley, which is accessible year-round. Enter Yosemite National Park through the **Big Oak Flat** or **Arch Rock** entrances. Once in Yosemite Valley, hop aboard the **Valley Shuttle** for a scenic exploration of **Bridalveil Fall, El Capitan,** and **Half Dome.** The best way to experience Yosemite's beauty is on one of its many trails. Enjoy a leisurely stroll around **Mirror Lake,** scale a waterfall on the **Mist Trail,** or test your powers of endurance on the way to **Upper Yosemite Fall.**

schedules of ranger-led walks and talks. The complex includes the **Yosemite Museum** (9am-5pm daily, free), the **Ansel Adams Gallery** (9am-6pm daily summer, 10am-5pm daily winter), and the all-important public restrooms. A short walk from the visitors center leads to the re-created **Miwok Native American Village,** home to structures made by the Miwok tribe.

Behind the visitors center, the **Yosemite Theater** (Northside Dr., 7pm Sun.-Thurs. May-Sept., adults $8, children $4) presents programs and films, including the **John Muir Performances** starring Lee Stetson, Yosemite's resident actor.

Wawona Visitor Center at Hill's Studio

The **Wawona Visitor Center at Hill's Studio** (Wawona, 209/375-9531, 8:30am-5pm daily mid-May-mid-Oct.) is located in the former studio and gallery of Thomas Hill, a famous landscape painter from the 1800s. You can see his floor-to-ceiling paintings, gather information, get wilderness permits, and rent bear-proof canisters.

Tuolumne Meadows Visitor Center

The **Tuolumne Meadows Visitor Center** (Tioga Rd., 209/372-0263, 9am-6pm daily June-Sept.) is in a rustic building near the campground and the Tuolumne Meadows Store. Ranger talks are held in the parking lot through summer. Pick up permits and rent bear canisters at the **Tuolumne Meadows Wilderness Center** (8am-5pm daily June-Sept.), located along the road to Tuolumne Meadows Lodge (shuttle stop 3).

SIGHTS
YOSEMITE VALLEY
Bridalveil Fall

The trail to **Bridalveil Fall** (Southside Dr., 0.5 mi. rt.) is a pleasantly sedate uphill walk. Although the 620-foot waterfall runs year-round, its fine mist sprays most powerfully in the spring—expect to get wet! The trailhead has its own parking area, so it's one of the first sights people come to upon entering the park.

Yosemite Falls

Yosemite Falls (shuttle stop 6, Southside Dr.) is actually three separate waterfalls—Upper Fall, Lower Fall, and the middle cascades. This dramatic formation together creates one of the highest waterfalls in the world. The best time to visit is in **spring,** when snowmelt swells the river and creates a beautiful cascade that makes these falls famous. Walk to **Lower Yosemite**

YOSEMITE FALLS

EL CAPITAN

Fall (1.1 mi. rt., 30 min., easy) to enjoy the wondrous views of both Upper and Lower Yosemite Falls, complete with lots of cooling spray.

Mirror Lake

Mirror Lake (shuttle stop 17, end of Southside Dr., no vehicles) offers a stunningly clear reflection of the already spectacular views of Tenaya Canyon and the ubiquitous Half Dome. A short, level **hiking and biking path** (2 mi. rt., 1 hr., easy) circumnavigates the lake.

El Capitan

On the north side of the valley is 7,569-foot **El Capitan** (Northside Dr., west of El Capitan Bridge), a massive hunk of Cretaceous granite. This craggy rock face rises more than 3,000 feet above the valley floor and is accessible two ways: a long hike from **Upper Yosemite Fall** or rock-climbing the face. Most visitors, however, just gaze up adoringly from **El Capitan picnic area.**

WAWONA

The small town of **Wawona**, four miles from the South Entrance, is home to a lovely historical district with a hotel and restaurant, outdoor exhibits, and even a golf course.

Pioneer Yosemite History Center

The **Pioneer Yosemite History Center** (open daily year-round) is a rambling outdoor display area housing an array of historic vehicles and many of the original structures built in the park. Pass through the covered bridge to an uncrowded stretch of land where informative placards describe the history of Yosemite National Park through its structures. In summer, take a 10-minute tour by **horse-drawn carriage** (adults $5, kids $4), or check the *Yosemite Guide* for listings of living-history programs and live demonstrations.

Mariposa Grove of Giant Sequoias

The **Mariposa Grove** (Wawona Rd./Hwy. 41) offers a rare view of giant sequoia redwoods in the park. Several trails wind throughout the grove, allowing you to see some of the most impressive trees in a mile or less. Within the grove is the **Mariposa Grove Museum** (Upper Mariposa Grove), a replica of the cabin of Galen Clark, a former guardian of Yosemite National Park who is credited as the first nonnative to see Mariposa Grove.

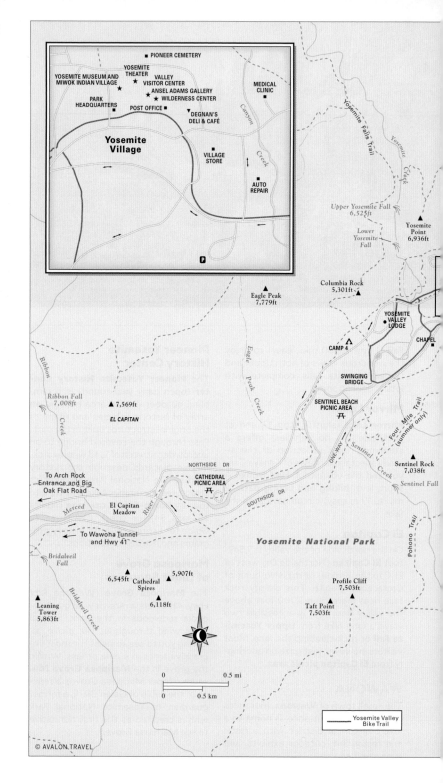

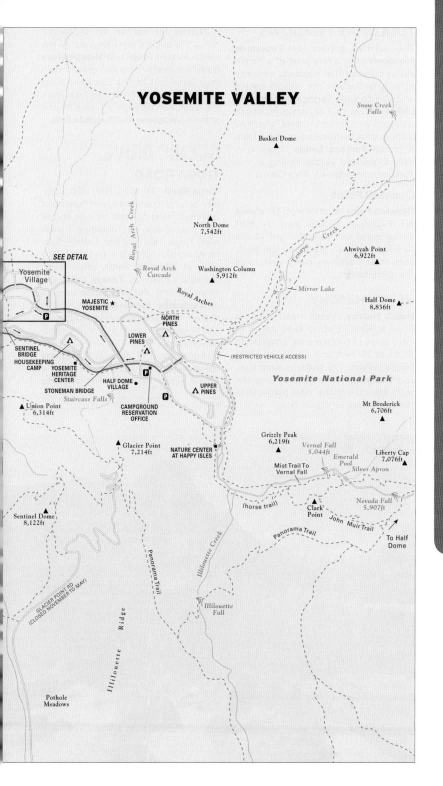

YOSEMITE VALLEY

Snow Creek Falls

Basket Dome ▲

North Dome
7,542ft ▲

Royal Arch Creek

Tenaya Creek

Ahwiyah Point
6,922ft ▲

SEE DETAIL

Yosemite
Village

Royal Arch
Cascade

Washington Column
5,912ft ▲

Mirror Lake

Half Dome ▲
8,836ft

**MAJESTIC
YOSEMITE** ★

Royal Arches

**NORTH
PINES** ⛺

(RESTRICTED VEHICLE ACCESS)

**LOWER
PINES** ⛺

Yosemite National Park

**SENTINEL
BRIDGE**

**HOUSEKEEPING
CAMP**

**YOSEMITE
HERITAGE
CENTER**

STONEMAN BRIDGE

**HALF DOME
VILLAGE**

**UPPER
PINES** ⛺

Mt Broderick
6,706ft ▲

Staircase Falls

▲ Union Point
6,314ft

**CAMPGROUND
RESERVATION
OFFICE**

Grizzly Peak
6,219ft ▲

▲ Glacier Point
7,214ft

**NATURE CENTER
AT HAPPY ISLES**

*Vernal Fall
5,044ft*

*Emerald
Pool*

Liberty Cap
7,076ft ▲

Mist Trail To
Vernal Fall

Silver Apron

*Nevada Fall
5,907ft*

Sentinel Dome
8,122ft ▲

(horse trail)

Clark
Point ▲

John Muir Trail

To Half
Dome

Panorama Trail

Illilouette Creek

Panorama Trail

GLACIER POINT RD
(CLOSED NOVEMBER TO MAY)

*Illilouette
Fall*

Illilouette Ridge

Pothole
Meadows

TUOLUMNE MEADOWS

The waving grasses of **Tuolumne Meadows** offer a rare peak at a fragile alpine meadow that supports a variety of wildlife. Park at the visitors center and walk to **Soda Springs and Parsons Lodge** (1.5 mi. rt., 1 hr., easy). From the trailhead at Lembert Dome, the trail leads past a carbonated spring to the historical **Parsons Lodge** (10am-4pm daily in season) before ending at the Tuolumne Meadows Visitor Center.

Olmsted Point

Olmsted Point (shuttle stop 12) shows off 9,926-foot Clouds Rest as Half Dome peeks out behind. Right at the parking lot, large glacial erratic boulders draw almost as many visitors as the point itself.

HETCH HETCHY

Hetch Hetchy (Hetch Hetchy Rd.) is home to Hetch Hetchy Reservoir, with 1,972 acres of surface area, a maximum depth of 312 feet, and a capacity of 117 billion gallons. The water is deep blue, and the gushing waterfalls along the sides are some of the most gorgeous in the whole park.

Named for Michael M. O'Shaughnessy, the original chief engineer of the Hetch Hetchy Project, **O'Shaughnessy Dam** is a massive curved gravity dam that turns part of the Tuolumne River into Hetch Hetchy Reservoir. Trails from the dam lead through a tunnel to the stunning **Wapama** and **Tuealula Falls.**

SCENIC DRIVE
TIOGA ROAD

Tioga Road (39 miles, Hwy. 120, summer only) is Yosemite's own "road less traveled," winding west to east across the High Sierra to Tuolumne Meadows, Tioga Pass, and the Eastern Sierra. Along the way, stop to take in the vista at **Olmsted Point,** stroll along the sandy beach at **Tenaya Lake,** and scramble atop **Pothole Dome** to gaze at **Tuolumne Meadows.** The road is dotted with campgrounds, trailheads, and scenic overlooks, plus a few natural wonders.

Anchoring the drive is **Tuolumne Meadows,** offering a rare peak at a fragile alpine meadow that supports

▼ HETCH HETCHY RESERVOIR

TUOLUMNE MEADOWS

a variety of wildlife. Across the road is the Tuolumne Meadows Visitor Center, a large campground, camp store and grill, and wilderness center.

From the west, Highway 120 becomes Big Oak Flat Road at the Big Oak Flat park entrance. In nine miles, at the left fork to Crane Flat junction, it becomes Tioga Road. The Tuolumne Meadows Visitor Center is 38 miles farther east. To get to Tioga Road from Yosemite Valley, take Northside Road to Big Oak Flat Road. At the Tioga Road junction, turn east.

HIKING
YOSEMITE VALLEY
Cook's Meadow

Soak in quintessential Yosemite Valley views from the easy **Cook's Meadow Loop** (1 mi. rt., 30 min., easy, shuttle stop 5 or 9). From the trailhead at the visitors center, you'll observe Ansel Adams's famous view of Half Dome from Sentinel Bridge and also the **Royal Arches** and Glacier Point. You can extend the hike into a bigger loop (2.25 mi. rt.) by circling both Cook's and Sentinel Meadows. Trail signs, and the plethora of other hikers, make it easy to find the turns.

Valley Loop Trail

The **Valley Loop Trail** (paved path beside Northside Dr. and Southside Dr.) traverses El Capitan Bridge, following the path of many old wagon roads and historical trails. From the Lower Yosemite Falls trailhead (shuttle stop 6), the **half loop** (6.5 mi. rt., 3 hrs., moderate) offers a half-day hike, while the **full loop** (13 mi. rt., 6 hrs., strenuous) spends a full day wandering the valley. Though paved, the route can be hard to follow; pick up a map at the visitors center.

Upper Yosemite Fall

One of the most strenuous, yet most rewarding, treks is **Upper Yosemite Fall** (7.2 mi. rt., 6-8 hrs., shuttle stop 7). From the trailhead at Camp 4, the climb steepens right away—2,700 vertical feet in just three miles. In one mile (and 1,000 feet), you'll reach **Columbia Rock** (2 mi. rt., 2-3 hours), with astonishing views of the valley below. The trail to the top of the falls follows stone steps with switchbacks and occasional railings, but much of the trail tends to be wet and slippery. Plan all day for this hike; bring plenty of water and snacks to replenish energy for the potentially tricky climb down.

GLACIER POINT

The road to Glacier Point is open late May-October, depending on snow. For one-way hikes from Glacier Point to the valley floor, make shuttle reservations with **Glacier Point Tour** (888/413-8869, www.travelyosemite.com).

Best Hike

MIST TRAIL

DISTANCE: 2.4-5.4 miles round-trip
DURATION: 3-6 hours
ELEVATION CHANGE: 1,050-2,000 feet
EFFORT: moderate
TRAILHEAD: Happy Isles

From the Happy Isles Nature Center (shuttle stop 16), the moderately strenuous **Mist Trail** climbs over steep, slick granite—including more than 600 stairs—to the top of **Vernal Fall** (2.4 mi. rt., 3 hrs.). Your reward is the stellar view of the valley below. Climb another two miles of switchbacks to the top of **Nevada Fall** (5.4 mi. rt., 6 hrs.) and return via the **John Muir Trail.** This popular trail is **closed in winter** due to ice and snow and can be dangerous in spring, when the river is at its peak. To get here, park in the day-use parking lot at Half Dome Village and board the free Yosemite Valley shuttle bus to Happy Isles.

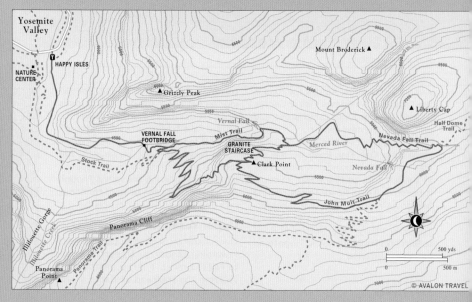

HIKING IN YOSEMITE'S HIGH SIERRA

Sentinel Dome and Taft Point

The trail to **Sentinel Dome** (2.2 mi. rt., 2-3 hrs., moderate) is a surprisingly easy walk considering the views you gain of the High Sierra. At the end of the trail, turn right and follow an old road through the forest. It's a steep but quick climb to the top of the dome. A left turn will bring you to **Taft Point and the Fissures** (2 mi. rt., 1 hr., moderate), unusual rock formations encountered en route to precarious vista points 2,000 feet above the valley.

The trailhead is six miles east of Bridalveil Creek Campground along Glacier Point Road.

VERNAL FALL, MIST TRAIL

Panorama Trail

The **Panorama Trail** (8.5 mi. one-way, 6 hrs., strenuous) runs from the Glacier Point trailhead to Yosemite Valley, with a 700-foot ascent and a 3,900-foot descent. Along the way, you'll see Illilouette Fall and Panorama Point, with views of Half Dome, Upper and Lower Yosemite Falls, and a sweeping vista of Yosemite Valley. The route finishes on the Mist Trail, picking up at Nevada and Vernal Fall.

Four-Mile Trail

A shuttle to Glacier Point means that you can descend to Yosemite Valley via the **Four-Mile Trail** (4.8 mi. one-way, 3-4 hrs., strenuous). The climb down affords views of Yosemite Falls and the valley that grow more spectacular with each switchback.

WAWONA

Wawona Meadow Loop

A flat walk along the **Wawona Meadow Loop** (3.5 mi. rt., 2 hrs., easy) sweeps around the lovely Wawona meadow and nine-hole golf course. The trailhead is at the Pioneer Yosemite History Center.

Chilnualna Falls

The trail to **Chilnualna Falls** (8.2 mi. rt., 5 hrs., strenuous) climbs 2,300 feet, following switchbacks up to the top of the falls. The top affords stunning views of Wawona below. The trailhead is at the Chilnualna Falls parking area.

TUOLUMNE MEADOWS AND TIOGA PASS

When Tioga Road opens (late May-June, depending on snow), the **Tuolumne Meadows Hiker Bus** (mid-June-mid-Sept., $2-3) offers car-free access to some trailheads.

Tuolumne Grove of Giant Sequoias

Aching to see some giant trees? The **Tuolumne Grove of Giant Sequoias** (2.5 mi. rt., 1.5 hrs., moderate) contains more than 20 mature giant sequoias. You have to climb 400 vertical feet back up from the grove to get to your car. The trailhead is at the junction of Tioga Road and Old Big Oak Flat Road.

▼ MARIPOSA GROVE, WAWONA

TENAYA LAKE

Tenaya Lake

The trail to **Tenaya Lake** (2.5 mi. rt., 1.5 hrs., easy, shuttle stop 9) offers sunny beaches and possibly the most picturesque views in all of Yosemite. The only difficult part is fording the outlet stream at the west end of the lake (the water gets chilly and can be deep).

May Lake and Mount Hoffman

May Lake (2 mi. rt., 1 hr., moderate, shuttle stop 11) sits peacefully at the base of the sloping granite of Mount Hoffman. The trail up to the lake gains a steady and steep 500 feet. For energetic hikers, a more difficult trail grunts 2,000 feet higher to the top of **Mount Hoffman** (6 mi. rt., 3-4 hrs., strenuous). Much of this walk is along granite slabs and rocky paths, but you'll have clear views of Cathedral Peak, Mount Clark, Half Dome, and Clouds Rest.

Elizabeth Lake

The trail to **Elizabeth Lake** (4.8 mi. rt., 4-5 hrs., strenuous, shuttle stop 5) begins at Tuolumne Campground (Loop B) and climbs almost 1,000 feet to the lake; most of the climb is during the first mile. Evergreens ring the lake and steep, granite Unicorn Peak rises high above.

North Dome

For an unusual look at a Yosemite classic, take the **North Dome Trail** (9 mi. rt., 4-5 hrs., strenuous) from the trailhead at Porcupine Creek through the woods and out to the dome. Getting to stare right at the face of Half Dome and Clouds Rest at what feels like eye level makes the effort worth it.

Cathedral Lakes

The trail to **Cathedral Lakes** (7 mi. rt., 4-6 hrs., strenuous, shuttle stop 7) climbs about 800 feet to picture-perfect lakes that show off the dramatic alpine peaks, surrounding lodgepole pines, and crystalline waters to their best advantage. The popular trailhead is on Tioga Road west of Tuolumne Meadows Visitor Center.

Gaylor Lakes

Gaylor Lakes Trail (2 mi. rt., 2 hrs., easy) starts at a thin-air 10,000 feet and climbs a steep 600 vertical feet up the pass to the Gaylor Lakes valley. Once in the valley, you can wander around five lovely lakes, stopping to admire the views out to the mountains surrounding Tuolumne Meadows or visiting the abandoned 1870s mine site above Upper Gaylor Lake. The trailhead is at the Tioga Pass Entrance.

CLIMBER ON MIDDLE CATHEDRAL ROCK

HETCH HETCHY

Wapama and Tueeulala Falls

Begin the hike to **Wapama Fall** (5 mi. rt., 2 hrs., moderate) by crossing O'Shaughnessy Dam, then following the Wapama Falls Trail through a tunnel and along the shore of the reservoir. Along the way, enjoy close-up views of spectacular **Tueeulala Fall.** For a longer hike, cross the wooden bridges under these falls to continue to beautiful **Rancheria Falls** (13.4 mi. rt., 7-8 hrs., strenuous).

Carlon Falls

The hike to **Carlon Falls** (4 mi. rt., 2 hrs., easy) begins in the Stanislaus National Forest, just past the Carlon Day Use Area. The trail soon enters the national park to follow the South Fork of the Tuolumne River. After a brief uphill climb, the payoff is lovely Carlon Falls.

RECREATION

BACKPACKING

Yosemite has bucket list backpacking routes, including the north end of the 211-mile **John Muir Trail** and 70 miles of the **Pacific Crest Trail.** A **wilderness permit** ($5 reservation, $5 per person) is required. Reserve a permit in advance online or pick up first-come,

first-served permits one day in advance at a permit issuing station. Bear canisters are required.

Yosemite's **High Sierra Camps** (888/413-8869, www.travelyosemite. com, July-early Sept.) offer tent cabins with amenities, breakfast and dinner in camp, and a sack lunch. Stay at **Merced Lake, Vogelsang, Glen Aulin, May Lake,** or **Sunrise Camp**—or visit all the camps in one 49-mile loop. Reservations are by lottery; applications are accepted in October for the following summer.

ROCK CLIMBING

El Capitan boasts a reputation as one of the world's seminal big-face climbs, a challenge that draws experienced rock climbers. For gear rental and guided rock climbing, use **Yosemite Mountaineering School** (209/372-8344, www.travelyosemite.com, 8:30am daily Mar.-Nov.). They also have beginner, intermediate, and advanced rock climbing classes for adults and children.

HORSEBACK RIDING

Big Trees Lodge Stable (Pioneer Yosemite History Center, Wawona Rd., 209/375-6502, www.travelyosemite.com, 7am-5pm daily June-Sept.) offers sedate two-hour horseback rides

THE MAJESTIC YOSEMITE HOTEL

around a historical wagon trail and more strenuous trips into the mountains. Reservations are recommended.

WINTER SPORTS

Yosemite Ski & Snowboard Area (Glacier Point Rd., 209/372-8430, www.travelyosemite.com, 9am-4pm daily mid-Dec.-early Apr.) offers rentals, lessons, and plenty of beginner downhill ski runs with enough intermediate runs to keep it interesting. The **Cross-Country Ski School** runs classes, rents gear, and guides cross-country ski tours, including an overnight trip to **Glacier Point Ski Hut.** A free **shuttle** runs between Yosemite Valley and the ski area twice daily in season.

Half Dome Village (Southside Dr., 209/372-8333, 3:30pm-9pm Mon.-Fri., noon-9:30pm Sat.-Sun. mid-Nov.-mid-Mar) has an outdoor ice-skating rink in winter with skate rentals.

WHERE TO STAY

INSIDE THE PARK

All Yosemite lodgings book quickly—up to one year in advance. Lodging **reservations** (888/413-8869, www.travelyosemite.com) for overnight accommodations are essential. Rates vary seasonally.

Yosemite Valley

Yosemite Valley is where everyone wants to be: It has the most services, lodging options, campgrounds, and restaurants.

Yosemite Valley Lodge (shuttle stop 8, year-round, from $235) has motel-style rooms and lodge rooms with king beds and balconies overlooking the valley. Enjoy the heated pool in the summer and free shuttles to the Glacier Point ski area in winter. The lodge has a post office, ATM, the **Mountain Room Restaurant** (5pm-8pm daily), **Mountain Room Lounge** (4:30pm-10pm Mon.-Fri., noon-10pm Sat.-Sun.), and **Food Court** (6:30am-8pm daily).

Built as a luxury hotel in the early 1900s, **The Majestic Yosemite Hotel** (shuttle stop 3, year-round, from $500) includes cottages and hotel rooms dripping with sumptuous appointments and Native American decor. A bonus is the stunningly elegant **Dining Room** (7am-10:30am, 11:30am-2:30pm, and 5:30pm-9pm Mon.-Sat., 7am-3pm and 5:30pm-9pm Sun.) with expansive ceilings, wrought-iron chandeliers, and a stellar valley view. Make reservations for all meals; dinner attire is resort style (long pants, collared shirts or blouses, dresses).

HALF DOME VILLAGE

Half Dome Village (shuttle stop 13, Mar.-Nov. and Dec.-Jan., Sat.-Sun. Jan.-Mar.) has a sprawling array of wood and tent cabins with or without heat, and with or without a private bath. The **Stoneman Motel** rooms have heat, private baths, and daily maid service. The three-sided tent cabins at **Housekeeping Camp** have cement walls, white canvas roofs, and a white canvas curtain separating the bedroom from a covered patio. Central bathrooms are available.

In Yosemite Village, **Degnan's Loft Pizza** (hours vary seasonally May-Sept.) serves pizza, soups, and appetizers. **Degnan's Deli** (7am-5pm daily year-round) offers an array of sandwiches, salads, and other takeout munchies. **Degnan's Café** (hours vary seasonally May-Sept.) sells coffee and baked goods. The **Village Grill Deck** (11am-6pm daily Apr.-Oct.) offers standard burgers and grilled food.

In Half Dome Village, the **Village Pavilion** (7am-10am and 5:30pm-8pm daily,) serves breakfast and dinner. There is also **Coffee Corner** (7am-11am daily Mar.-Nov.), the **Village Bar** (noon-10pm daily summer), **Pizza Deck** (noon-9pm daily Jan.-Nov.), and the **Meadow Grill** (11am-5pm daily summer).

Wawona

The charming **Big Trees Lodge** (Mar.-Nov. and mid-Dec.-early Jan., from

$150) opened in 1879. The black-and-white hotel complex includes a wraparound porch and on-site dining. Rooms (with bath and without) come complete with Victorian wallpaper, antique furniture, and a lack of in-room TVs and telephones.

The **dining room** (209/375-1425, 7:30am-10am, 11am-1:30pm, and 5pm-9pm) serves upscale California cuisine. Reservations are not accepted, so expect to wait for a table on high-season weekends. The common area offers seating, drinks, and live piano (Tues.-Sat.).

Tuolumne Meadows and Tioga Pass

White Wolf Lodge (Tioga Rd., mid-June-Sept., from $125) rents 24 heated canvas tent cabins and four wood cabins. The wood cabins include a private bath, limited electricity, and daily maid service, while the tent cabins share a central restroom and shower facility; all cabins include linens and towels. Amenities are few, but the scenery is breathtaking.

Tuolumne Meadows Lodge (Tioga Rd., early June-mid-Sept., from $125) offers charming wood-frame tent cabins in a gorgeous subalpine meadow setting with no electricity. Central facilities include restrooms, hot showers, and a **dining room** (209/372-8413, breakfast and dinner daily early June-mid-Sept.); dinner reservations are required.

Camping

Campground reservations (877/444-6777, www.recreation.gov, $12-26) are imperative. At 7am (Eastern time) on the 15th of each month, campsites become available for booking five months in advance. If you need a reservation for a specific day, get up early to call or check online diligently starting at 7am. If you're in the valley and don't have a campsite reservation, call the **campground status line** (209/372-0266) for a recording of what's available that day.

Yosemite Valley has three ultra-popular campgrounds with fierce competition for reservations: **Upper Pines** (238 sites), **Lower Pines** (60 sites), and **North Pines** (81 sites). Competition for the first-come, first-served sites at **Camp 4** (35 shared walk-in sites, tents only) is heavy spring-fall; a line forms long before the 8:30am registration at the kiosk opens.

Bridalveil Creek Campground (110 sites, first come, first served) is located midway up Glacier Point Road, a 45-minute drive from the valley. Its location along Bridalveil Creek makes it an appealing spot.

North of Wawona, the forested **Wawona Campground** (93 sites) offers scenic sites along the Tuolumne River. Reservations are accepted April-October (sites are first come, first served Oct.-Apr.).

Along Tioga Road, campgrounds for **Crane Flat** (166 sites), **Hodgdon Meadow** (105 sites, reservations accepted early Apr.-early Oct.), and **Tuolumne Meadows** (304 sites) book far in advance for summer. The remaining campgrounds are first come, first served: **Tamarack Flat** (52 sites), **White Wolf** (74 sites), **Yosemite Creek** (75 sites), and **Porcupine Flat** (52 sites).

OUTSIDE THE PARK

Gateway towns cluster the park entrances, offering accommodations, campgrounds, dining, and services. **Groveland** (Hwy. 120) is 26 miles from the Big Oak Flat Entrance. One mile outside the Hetch Hetchy Entrance, the **Evergreen Lodge** (33160 Evergreen Rd., Groveland, 209/379-2606, www.evergreenlodge.com) rents cabins.

El Portal (Hwy. 140) is less than four miles from the Arch Rock Entrance and 15 miles from Yosemite Valley, making it one of the closest places to overnight. **Mariposa** (Hwy. 140) lies about 30 miles from the Arch Rock Entrance and about 40 miles from Yosemite Valley.

Oakhurst (Hwy. 41) lies less than 15 miles from the South Entrance. **Fish Camp** (Hwy. 41) is 40 miles from Yosemite Valley via the South Entrance, a little over an hour's drive.

1: HALF DOME FROM SENTINEL BRIDGE
2: MARIPOSA GROVE, WAWONA
3: TAFT POINT

NAME	LOCATION	PRICE	SEASON	AMENITIES
Camp 4	Yosemite Valley	$6pp	year-round	tent sites
Upper Pines	Yosemite Valley	$26	year-round	tent and RV sites
North and Lower Pines	Yosemite Valley	$26	Mar.-Nov.	tent and RV sites
Half Dome Village	Yosemite Valley	$90-195	year-round	motel rooms, wooden cabins, tent cabins, dining
Housekeeping Camp	Yosemite Valley	$90	Apr.-Oct.	duplex camp units, showers
Yosemite Valley Lodge	Yosemite Valley	$235	year-round	hotel rooms, dining
Majestic Yosemite Hotel	Yosemite Valley	$500	year-round	hotel rooms, cottages, suites, dining
Bridalveil Creek	Wawona	$18	July-Sept.	tent and RV sites
Wawona	Wawona	$26	year-round	tent and RV sites
Big Trees Lodge	Wawona	$150	Apr.-Dec.	hotel rooms, dining
Tamarack Flat	Tuolumne Meadows	$12	June-Oct.	tent sites
Yosemite Creek	Tuolumne Meadows	$12	June-Sept.	tent sites
Porcupine Flat	Tuolumne Meadows	$12	July-Oct.	tent and RV sites
White Wolf	Tuolumne Meadows	$18	June-Sept.	tent and RV sites
Hodgdon Meadow	Tuolumne Meadows	$26	year-round	tent and RV sites
Crane Flat	Tuolumne Meadows	$26	July-Oct.	tent and RV sites
Tuolumne Meadows	Tuolumne Meadows	$26	June-Sept.	tent and RV sites
White Wolf Lodge	Tuolumne Meadows	$125	June-Sept.	wooden cabins, tent cabins, dining
Tuolumne Meadows Lodge	Tuolumne Meadows	$125	June-Sept.	tent cabins, dining

BIG OAK FLAT ENTRANCE

GETTING THERE

AIR

The closest international airports are **San Francisco International Airport** (SFO, U.S. 101, San Francisco, 650/821-8211 or 800/435-9736, www.flysfo. com), **Sacramento International Airport** (SMF, 6900 Airport Blvd., Sacramento, 916/929-5411, www.sacramento.aero), and **Reno-Tahoe International Airport** (RNO, 2001 E. Plumb Lane, Reno, NV, 775/328-6400, www.renoairport.com). Car rentals are available at all airports.

CAR

From the San Francisco Bay Area, it's a 4-5-hour drive to the park's west entrances of Arch Rock and Big Oak Flat for the quickest access to Yosemite Valley. Take I-580 east and continue east to I-205 and I-5 near Manteca. From Manteca, follow Highway 120 east through Groveland and the **Big Oak Flat Entrance** on the west side of the park. From Big Oak Flat, it's a 45-minute drive to Yosemite Valley.

Alternatively, from I-5 south take Highway 140 east through Merced to reach the **Arch Rock Entrance.** From

Arch Rock, it's a 30-minute drive to the valley. This is the **most popular and most crowded entrance** to Yosemite Valley. Plan to arrive before 9am or after 5pm to avoid long entrance lines.

From points south, enter the park through the **South Entrance** via Highway 41, a 1.5-hour drive north from Fresno. In four miles, Highway 41 becomes Wawona Road. From Wawona, it's another 1.5 hours to Yosemite Valley.

BUS

The **Yosemite Area Regional Transportation System** (YARTS, 877/989-2787, www.yarts.com) runs daily buses from Mariposa and Merced to Yosemite Valley. You can buy tickets on the bus, and no reservations are necessary. Buses run more frequently in summer.

GETTING AROUND

DRIVING

Driving in **Yosemite Valley** can be a crowded, congested experience. Parking lots and roadside pullouts fill early. Plan to arrive by 9am and leave your car in one of the three parking lots (Yosemite Village, Yosemite Falls, Half Dome Village), and then navigate the valley via the park's free shuttle.

EL CAPITAN

There are no **gas stations** in Yosemite Valley. The closest stations are in El Portal and at Crane Flat.

Glacier Point Road

Glacier Point is about an hour's drive from Yosemite Valley. From the Valley Visitor Center, drive 14 miles south to Chinquapin junction and turn left onto **Glacier Point Road** (closed Nov.-May). In winter (Dec.-Mar.), the first five miles of the road are plowed; chains may be required.

Tioga Road

Tioga Road (Hwy. 120) stretches from Crane Flat east to Tioga Pass, the east entrance to the park, where it becomes Tioga Pass Road. **The road is open only in summer.** To check weather conditions and road closures, call 209/372-0200. When the road is closed, there is no access to Tuolumne Meadows.

SHUTTLES

In summer—especially on weekends—traffic and parking in Yosemite Valley can be slow and stressful. Park your car at the Yosemite Village day-use lot and use the **Yosemite Valley shuttle** (7am-10pm daily year-round, free) to get around. Shuttles run every 10-20 minutes, stopping at Yosemite Valley Lodge, the Valley Visitor Center, Half Dome Village, all campgrounds, and the Happy Isles trailhead.

The **Glacier Point Tour** (888/413-8869, www.travelyosemite.com, 8:30am and 1:30pm daily May-Nov., $35-50) meets at Yosemite Valley Lodge to travel to Glacier Point Road when the road is open.

The summer-only **Tuolumne Meadows Hikers Bus** (209/372-1240, mid-June-Sept., $2-23) runs along Tioga Road between Olmsted Point and the Tuolumne Meadows Lodge. Service varies seasonally.

SIGHTS NEARBY

Mono Lake (Hwy. 120 and U.S. 395, www.monolake.org), east of Tioga Pass, is a saline and alkaline lake with strange-looking tufa towers. A one-mile interpretive trail ($3) winds through the South Tufa, one of the best places to view the spectacular towers.

Bodie State Historic Park (Hwy. 270, 13 miles east of U.S. 395, 760/647-6445, www.parks.ca.gov, 9am-6pm daily Apr.-Oct., 9am-4pm daily Nov.-Mar.) is the largest ghost town in California.

Devils Postpile National Monument (Minaret Vista Rd., Mammoth Lakes, 760/934-2289, www.nps.gov/depo, mid-June-mid-Oct.) is named for the strange natural rock formation found here—straight-sided hexagonal posts created by volcanic heat and pressure.

SEQUOIA AND KINGS CANYON

California

PASSPORT STAMPS ▼▼▼

WEBSITE:
www.nps.gov/seki

PHONE NUMBER:
559/565-3341

VISITATION RANK:
20 (Sequoia) and
29 (Kings Canyon)

WHY GO:
Explore giant sequoias,
underground caves,
and scenic byways.

▲ SEQUOIA AND KINGS CANYON
NATIONAL PARK

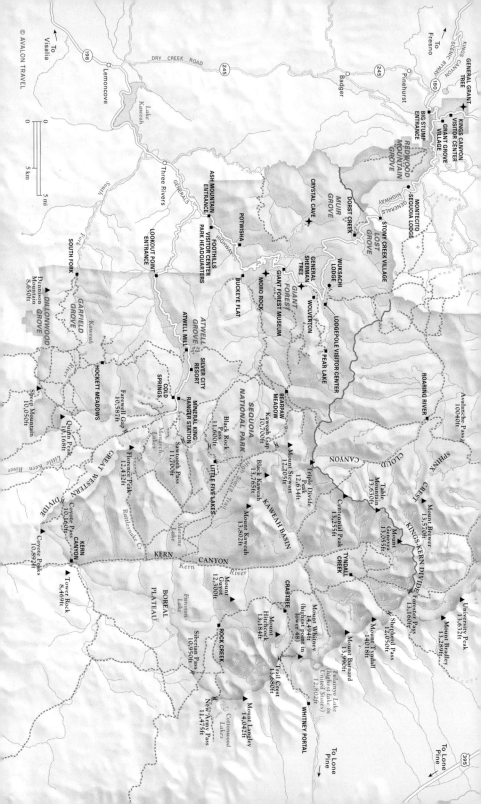

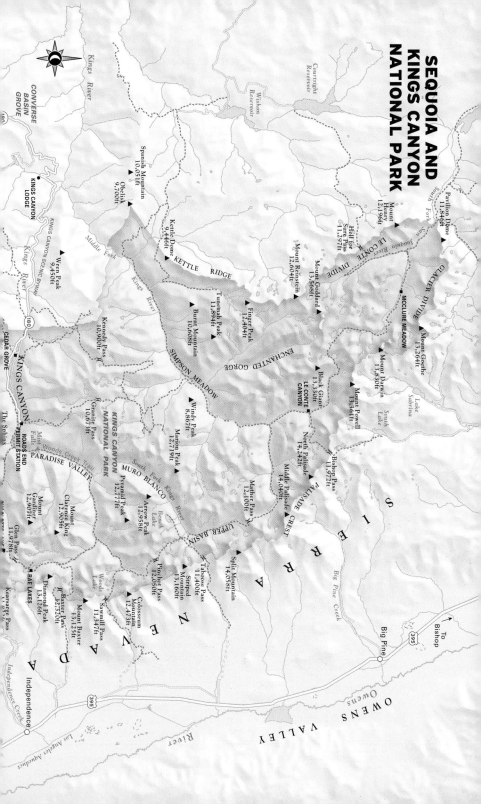

SEQUOIA AND KINGS CANYON NATIONAL PARKS house some of the tallest and oldest trees on earth. The parks span a vast vertical landscape, which climbs from 1,370 feet to the 14,494-foot summit of Mount Whitney, the highest peak in the contiguous United States. The parks combine for a huge acreage larger than Yosemite but see far smaller crowds. Much of their terrain is wild backcountry, accessible only by 800 miles of hiking trails, including the John Muir Trail and Pacific Crest Trail.

The parks share a boundary interspersed by the Sequoia National Forest and Giant Sequoia National Monument. To the north, Kings Canyon National Park encompasses a slice of the high Sierra Nevada with plunging canyons and alpine peaks. To the south, Sequoia National Park hosts acres of giant sequoia redwood groves as well as a stunning cave system.

PLANNING YOUR TIME

Located in central California, Sequoia and Kings Canyon are accessed by road only from the west side of the Sierra. *No roads enter the park from the Eastern Sierra and there is no way to drive across the Sierra from either park.*

Exploring the large parks takes time and requires long drives. Plan to stay 3-4 days to take some of the many epic hikes through the scenic redwood groves. In the main campgrounds, vacationers often set up a tent for one or two weeks and use the camp as a base for exploring the parks.

Due to vast elevation differences, weather varies with extremes. **Summer** is high season, when snow melts from cooler high-elevation trails and hot temperatures pervade the foothills. Winter dumps snow on the mountains, often closing park roads and making driving treacherous. Roads in Mineral King and Cedar Grove Kings Canyon close in winter.

ENTRANCES AND FEES

The entrance fee is $35 per vehicle ($30 motorcycle, $20 individual). There are two main entrances. From the west and north, the **Big Stump Entrance** (Hwy. 180) is the most direct route with the closest access to Kings Canyon

National Park, Grant Grove, and Generals Highway. From the south, the **Ash Mountain Entrance** (Hwy. 198) enters Sequoia National Park, where Highway 198 becomes Generals Highway.

VISITORS CENTERS

The **Kings Canyon Visitor Center** (83918 Hwy. 180 E., 559/565-4307, 9am-5pm daily summer, 9am-4pm daily winter) is in Grant Grove Village near the Big Stump entrance. This is the place to get maps and information on camping, hiking, wilderness permits, weather conditions, and road closures. Rangers offer interpretive programs, including snowshoe walks in winter.

Located near Cedar Grove Village in Kings Canyon, the **Cedar Grove Visitor Center** (559/565-3793, 9am-5pm daily summer) has books and maps and there are park rangers to answer questions.

At the **Lodgepole Visitor Center** (Generals Hwy., 559/565-4436, 7am-4:30pm daily summer) visitors can get books and maps, join a ranger talk or walk, pick up wilderness permits, and buy Crystal Cave tour tickets. It's about an hour's drive to Lodgepole from either park entrance.

The **Foothills Visitor Center** (559/565-4212, 8am-4:30pm daily year-round), one mile north of the Ash Mountain Entrance, serves as the park headquarters with a bookstore, exhibits, and ranger talks and walks. You can

Top 3

1 GAZE UP AT THE "GENERALS"

The **General Grant Tree** (north of Kings Canyon Visitor Center) is the second-largest tree by volume in the world and the nation's only living war memorial. The 1,700-year-old giant sequoia is 268 feet tall with a diameter of 40 feet and a volume of 46,608 cubic feet. The paved **General Grant Tree Trail** (0.6 mi. rt., 20 min., easy) leads to its namesake tree and the **Fallen Monarch,** an immense tree lying on its side and hollowed out in the middle. It also passes the 1872 **Gamlin Cabin,** the former living quarters of the grove's first ranger, and the **Centennial Stump,** which once hosted whole Sunday school classes on top of it.

GENERAL GRANT TREE, KINGS CANYON

The **General Sherman Tree** (Wolverton Rd., off Generals Hwy.) is, by sheer volume of wood, the largest known tree on earth. From the parking lot or shuttle stop at Wolverton Road, the one-mile trail with interpretive signs leads down to the viewing area. (This attraction can get crowded on summer weekends; visit on a weekday or early in the morning for a quieter experience.) A wheelchair-accessible trailhead with a shorter trail is on Generals Highway (south of Wolverton Rd.).

2 LEARN ABOUT GIANT SEQUOIAS AT THE GIANT FOREST MUSEUM

The **Giant Forest Museum** (Generals Hwy., 559/565-4480, 9am-4:30pm daily) is a lively place full of giant sequoias and touchable exhibits that provide context to these trees, such as the importance of fire in the life of a giant sequoia. Learn how the park used to look and why many of the buildings have been removed to make way for more trees. This is a great stop for families. Numerous hikes branch out into the surrounding Giant Forest Sequoia Grove.

3 GO UNDERGROUND AT CRYSTAL CAVE

Magical **Crystal Cave** (Cave Rd., near Giant Forest, May-Sept.) is one of the most beautiful of the 200 natural caves in the park. Its immense underground rooms fill with sparkling stalagmites and stalactites made of limestone that has metamorphosed over time into marble.

Access to the cave is by **guided tour only** (877/444-6777, www.recreation.gov, adults $16-18, kids $5-8). Tours range from 45 minutes to two hours, with longer adventures for serious spelunkers. Tickets are *not* sold at the cave entrance; purchase them in advance at the visitors centers or online. Tours fill quickly, so pick up tickets early in the morning.

The long, winding drive to the cave parking lot can take more than an hour and reaching the cave requires a steep and strenuous 0.5-mile walk; bring a warm layer of clothing for the 50-degree temperatures inside.

ONE DAY IN SEQUOIA & KINGS CANYON

Those short on time should head for the giant trees. Start with a walk around **General Grant Grove.** Then drive down Generals Highway to the **General Sherman Tree** and tour the **Giant Forest Museum.** If time permits, drive **Kings Canyon Scenic Byway** to Cedar Grove. Stop at canyon overlooks and hike the short **Zumwalt Meadow Trail.**

also buy Crystal Cave tickets or get a wilderness permit.

The **Mineral King Ranger Station** (559/565-3768, 8am-4pm daily summer) is located near the end of Mineral King Road. It has park information and wilderness permits.

SCENIC DRIVE

KINGS CANYON SCENIC BYWAY

North of Grant Grove Village, Highway 180 becomes the **Kings Canyon Scenic Byway** (35 miles) as it continues east through Cedar Grove. From its start at 6,600 feet, the road weaves down to 3,000 feet before climbing back up along the South Fork Kings River to 5,000 feet and terminating at Road's End. Ample roadside pullouts make it easy to stop and take in the tremendous views of the vast canyons that give the park its name.

The best stop is **Canyon View,** located one mile east of Cedar Grove Village. Look for the U-shaped canyon carved by glaciers, lodged between the soaring peaks flanking the Kings River. One mile farther east, walk a short path to the small, picturesque **Knapp's Cabin,** built in the 1920s by businessman George Knapp. The wheelchair-accessible **Roaring River Falls Trail** (0.5 mi. rt.) travels under a cool canopy of trees to rushing water squeezed through rock slots.

Cowering between North Dome and Grand Sentinel, **Roads End** is the end of the road in Kings Canyon. Beyond Roads End, the park is trails, canyons, forests, and lakes.

▼ KINGS CANYON

MIST FALLS

RECREATION
HIKING
Grant Grove

General Grant Grove is home to dozens of giant sequoias, the largest of which is the General Grant Tree. From the parking lot, take the **North Grove Loop Trail** (1.5 mi. rt., 1 hr., easy) along an old park road through the sequoia forest.

North of the Big Stump Entrance, the **Big Stump Trail** (2 mi. rt., 1 hr., easy) travels through a grove that was heavily logged in the late 19th century. Today, it is reclaiming its true nature as a sequoia grove. The route passes the **Mark Twain Stump,** the remains of a 26-foot-wide tree that was cut in 1891.

Redwood Mountain Sequoia Grove (in Redwood Canyon) is home to the largest grove of giant sequoias in the world. Walk down a short old roadbed to a trail junction and turn left to begin the **Hart Tree and Fallen Goliath Loop** (6.5 mi. rt., 3-4 hrs., moderate) across Redwood Creek and past the former logging site of Barton's Post Camp. About halfway around the loop, you'll come to a short spur trail that takes you to the **Hart Tree,** the largest in the grove and the 25th largest known in the world. **Fallen Goliath,** a little farther along, is another impressive sight. To reach the trailhead from Grant Grove, drive five miles south on Generals Highway to Quail Flat; turn right and drive 1.5 miles to Redwood Saddle. Turn left at the fork for the trailhead.

The trail to **Buena Vista Peak** (4 mi. rt., 2 hrs., moderate) makes a 450-foot ascent to the peak for views of the Western Divide, Mineral King, and Farewell Gap. The Buena Vista Trailhead is six miles south of Grant Grove.

The **Big Baldy Trail** (4.4 mi. rt., 2.5 hrs., moderate) climbs 640 feet to the granite summit of Big Baldy for views into Redwood Canyon. The trailhead is eight miles south of Grant Grove.

Cedar Grove

Kings Canyon Scenic Byway leads to trailheads for family-friendly hikes and big mountain adventures. One mile west of Roads End, the **Zumwalt Meadow Trail** (1.5 mi. rt., 1 hr., easy) leads through the lush meadow and continues through a grove of heavenly smelling incense cedar and pine trees along the Kings River.

From the Roads End Trailhead, the **Mist Falls Trail** (8 mi. rt., 4-5 hrs., moderate) begins with a sandy, dusty path to a granite junction. Turn north to climb steep switchbacks 1,500 vertical feet to the refreshing falls.

Best Hike

MORO ROCK

DISTANCE: 0.5 mile round-trip
DURATION: 30 minutes
ELEVATION CHANGE: 380 stairsteps
EFFORT: strenuous
TRAILHEAD: Moro Rock/ Crescent Meadow Rd.

The granite dome of **Moro Rock** stands starkly alone amid the landscape, providing an amazing vantage point for much of the park. Park in the lot at the base of the rock and climb the nearly 400 steps to the top (0.5 mi. rt., strenuous), holding onto the handrails for support. At the top, views extend into the canyons of the Great Western Divide and across the peaks of the Sierra Nevada. In summer, the road is closed to vehicles weekends and holidays, so take the free shuttle (9am-6pm).

Giant Forest and Lodgepole

Along the Generals Highway, short trails lead to big views and giant trees. From the Little Baldy Trailhead, the 700-foot ascent up 8,044-foot **Little Baldy** (3.4 mi. rt., 2-3 hrs., moderate) reaches the top of the granite dome to look down into the Giant Forest.

From the General Sherman Tree Trailhead, the wheelchair-accessible **Congress Trail** (2 mi. rt., 1 hr., easy) passes many of the park's most famous giant sequoias—Chief Sequoyah, General Lee, and President McKinley—as well as the House and Senate Groups.

At the Giant Forest Museum, the level **Big Trees Loop** (1.2 mi. rt., 1 hr., easy) circles Round Meadow. Interpretive panels make this a fun walk for kids and the paved boardwalk is wheelchair-accessible.

From Crescent Meadow parking lot, the **Crescent Meadow-Log Meadow Loop** (1.6 mi. rt., 1 hr., easy) lets hikers experience wildflowers as the trail passes Tharp's Log, the park's oldest cabin.

▼ TRAIL UP MORO ROCK

Foothills and Mineral King

At the southern entrance of Sequoia National Park, the Foothills area offers vigorous adventure with a big payoff. The **Marble Fork Trail** (7.4 miles, 4 hrs., strenuous) starts from Potwisha Campground on a forest road before winding upward through the woods 2,150 feet to sweeping views of the canyons and the water below. At a large slab that looks like white marble, you see the dramatic Marble Falls.

Hikes in the remote Mineral King area (Lookout Point Entrance, May-Nov.) are demanding and strenuous. The exception is the **Cold Springs Nature Trail** (1 mi. rt., 30 min.), an easy walk from the campground along the Kaweah River.

BACKPACKING

The premier backpacking trip in Kings Canyon is the **Rae Lakes Loop** (42 mi. rt., 5-7 days). From Roads End, the trail varies from flat and pleasant to mettle-testing rock scrambling, rugged switchbacks, and stream crossings. Along the way, you'll gain about 7,000 feet of elevation to reach 11,978-foot Glen Pass (snow covered until July) and the sparkling blue Rae Lakes; many hikers spend at least two nights here. The loop also takes in a portion of the John Muir and Pacific Crest Trails.

Wilderness permits ($15) are required, available from the visitors center or the **Roads End Permit Station** (7am-3:45pm daily late May-late Sept.). Permit quotas are enforced during high season and bear canisters are required.

HORSEBACK RIDING

In summer, saddle with **Grant Grove Stables** (559/335-9292 or 559/799-7247) or **Cedar Grove Pack Station** (Cedar Grove Village, 559/565-3464 or 559/337-2413). Cedar Grove also guides customized backcountry overnight trips.

WHERE TO STAY

INSIDE THE PARK

All park lodging and campgrounds fill on weekends and holidays and in June-early September. Make reservations in advance. For **campground reservations** (877/444-6777, www.recreation.gov, $18-22), book up to six months in advance.

Grant Grove

Grant Grove Cabins (866/807-3598, www.visitsequoia.com, year-round,

RAE LAKES

from $110) are rustic timber structures and tent cabins with private bathrooms or a shared central facility with public showers. The attractive yet simple **John Muir Lodge** (866/807-3598, www.visitsequoia.com, year-round, from $210) is a classic woodsy lodge with motel-style rooms. Nearby, **Grant Grove Restaurant** (Grant Grove Village, 7am-9pm daily) serves meals. Lodging reservations at Grant Grove fill 4-6 months in advance.

Montecito-Sequoia Lodge (63410 Generals Hwy., 559/565-3388 or 877/828-1440, www.sequoia-kingscanyon.com, year-round, from $120) is a rustic full-service resort with lodge rooms and cabins. In summer, Montecito operates primarily as a family camp, but rooms are available to non-campers. Rates are all-inclusive. The dining room hours vary daily year-round) serves breakfast, lunch, and dinner; dining reservations are accepted for hotel guests.

Three campgrounds cluster near Grant Village: **Sunset** (157 sites, May-Sept.), **Azalea** (110 sites, year-round), and **Crystal Springs** (36 sites, late May-early Sept.).

HIKING IN SEQUOIA NATIONAL PARK

Cedar Grove

Cedar Grove Lodge (Cedar Grove Village, 866/807-3598, www.visitsequoia.com, May-Oct., from $120) has 21 guest rooms with private baths and air-conditioning. Services include a **snack bar** (7:30am-8pm daily May-Oct.), gift shop, mini-mart, laundry, showers, and an ATM.

Several first-come, first-served campgrounds are near Cedar Grove Village: **Sheep Creek** (111 sites, late May-mid-Sept.), **Sentinel** (82 sites, May-mid-Nov.), and **Moraine** (121 sites, late June-early Sept.). **Canyon View** (late May-Sept., $40-60) has group sites by reservation.

Lodgepole

The **Wuksachi Lodge** (64740 Wuksachi Way, 866/807-3598, www.visitsequoia.com, year-round, from $215) offers upscale accommodations with facilities built in 1999. The on-site **Peaks Restaurant** (559/565-4070, 7am-10pm daily year-round) features sweeping forest views and serves three meals daily.

Lodgepole Village contains a large visitors center, market, the **Watchtower Deli** (11am-6pm daily May-Oct.), the **Harrison Grill** (9am-6pm daily Oct.-May), a gift shop, coin laundry, an ATM, shuttle services, and a post office. Many facilities close in winter.

Two campgrounds accept reservations: **Lodgepole Campground** (214 sites, May-Sept.), along the Kaweah River, and **Dorst Creek Campground** (late June-Labor Day, $22-60), along Generals Highway north of Wuksachi Village. Shuttles stop at both campgrounds.

Stony Creek Village has the **Stony Creek Lodge** (Generals Hwy., 877/828-1440, www.sequoia-kingscanyon.com, May-early Oct., from $160) with a **restaurant** (lunch and dinner), market/gift shop, an ATM, and a gas station (credit card, 24 hours daily). Nearby, two U.S. Forest Service campgrounds take reservations: **Stony Creek Campground** (50 sites, May-Oct.) and **Upper Stony Creek Campground** (23 sites, mid-May-mid-Sept.).

Foothills

Two campgrounds take reservations in summer: **Potwisha Campground** (42 sites, year-round) on the Kaweah River

HUME LAKE

and tent-only **Buckeye Flat** (28 sites, early Apr.-late Sept.), also in a lovely spot along the river. The primitive **South Fork Campground** (South Fork Dr., 10 sites, year-round, $12 May-Oct., free Oct.-May) is 13 miles off Highway 198 near Three Rivers. Sites are first come, first served; there are pit toilets, but no drinking water.

Mineral King

At Mineral King, the **Silver City Resort** (559/561-3223, www.silvercityresort.com, May-mid-Oct., from $275) has chalets and cabins. Two tent-only campgrounds (May-Oct., $12) are first come, first served: **Atwell Mill** (21 sites) and **Cold Springs** (40 sites). The Mineral King Ranger Station is next to Cold Springs.

Reaching the Mineral King area (Mineral King Rd., 25 miles east of Hwy. 198) requires driving a narrow, 22-mile road that takes at least 1.5 hours in good weather. Trailers and RVs are not recommended on the road.

OUTSIDE THE PARK

Visalia and **Three Rivers** have visitor services, lodging, and a summer shuttle into the park. The Hume Lake Ranger District of the Sequoia National Forest/Giant Sequoia National Monument (www.fs.fed.us) manages nearby campgrounds. Reservations are accepted for **Princess Campground** (Hwy. 180, June-Sept.) and **Hume Lake** (Generals Hwy., May-Sept.), 10 miles northeast of Grant Grove. **Tenmile** (Generals Hwy., May-Sept., $16), **Landslide** (Generals Hwy., summer only, $16), and **Convict Flat** (Hwy. 180, summer only, free) are first come, first served.

GETTING THERE

AIR

The closest international airport is **Fresno Yosemite International** (FAT, 559/621-4500, www.flyfresno.com), a 1-2-hour drive to either park entrance.

CAR

In the north, **Highway 198** enters Kings Canyon National Park; in the south, **Highway 180** enters Sequoia National Park. Both are linked by the slow, winding Generals Highway, which may close in winter. Park roads may require chains at any time. Check online or call the park for road conditions.

GETTING AROUND

DRIVING

Grant Grove is located in Kings Canyon National Park, four miles east of the Big Stump Entrance on Highway 180. **Cedar**

MOUNT WHITNEY

One of the most famous backpacking trips in Northern California is the trek to **Mount Whitney.** At 14,494 feet, Whitney is the highest peak in the continental United States, and this must-do trek draws intrepid hikers and climbers from around the world. Whitney also marks the southern end of the **John Muir Trail** and makes for a dramatic end or beginning for hikers doing the whole trail.

Mount Whitney is located at the far eastern edge of Sequoia National Park, just west of the town of Lone Pine. You can see the impressive peak from a few places in the backcountry of Sequoia and Kings Canyon, but you can't get there from within the parks. **There is no road that crosses the parks from west to east.** If you're coming from the west, you have to drive around the parks and enter from the eastern side.

Although Mount Whitney is a very challenging climb, with an elevation gain of more than 6,000 feet, it is not technical. You can climb the 10.7 miles of switchbacks all the way to the top of Mount Whitney and back in one day if you're in good shape and prepare properly for the journey. It's important to plan ahead, start early, and bring all the right safety gear for extreme weather.

Permits (760/873-2483, www.fs.fed.us/r5/inyo) are required for anyone entering the Mount Whitney Zone—even day hikers. Permit reservations are issued by lottery application (submitted Feb.-mid-Mar., 877/444-6777, www.recreation.gov).

The nearest campground is **Whitney Portal** (end of Whitney Portal Rd., 6 miles west of Lone Pine, 47 sites, late Apr.-late Oct., $21) in the Inyo National Forest seven miles from the trailhead. Make reservations (877/444-6777, www.recreation.gov). If you're planning to climb the summit, stay even closer at 25 walk-in sites located near the **Mount Whitney trailhead** (first come, first served, one-night limit) to wake up in the wee hours and start your ascent.

Grove is 30 miles northeast of Grant Grove on Kings Canyon Scenic Byway (Hwy. 180); only the first six miles of the road are open in winter (Oct.-Apr.).

Lodgepole is located on Generals Highway, 22 miles north of the Ash Mountain Entrance and 27 miles south of the Big Stump Entrance, about an hour's drive from either entrance. Wuksachi Village is two miles northwest of Lodgepole.

From Highway 198, the Ash Mountain Entrance accesses the **Foothills** area. To reach **Mineral King,** turn right onto Mineral King Road (two miles before the Ash Mountain Entrance) and drive 25 miles east (1.5 hrs.). The narrow and winding road does not permit RVs or trailers. Pass through the Lookout Point entrance (May-Oct., gate locked Nov.-Apr.) and pay the entrance fee at a self-serve kiosk.

No **gas** is sold in the national parks, but **Stony Creek Village** (Generals Hwy., 24 hrs. daily summer only) has gas pumps and accepts credit cards.

SHUTTLES

Sequoia National Park provides free summer **shuttle service** (9am-6pm daily late May-Sept.), stopping at Giant Forest Museum, Lodgepole Visitor Center, and Moro Rock, plus Dorst and Lodgepole Campgrounds. The **Visalia Shuttle** (reservations required, 877/287-4453, www.sequoiashuttle.com, late May-early Sept., $15 rt.) runs from Visalia and Three Rivers to Giant Trees Museum; the park entrance fee is included.

SIGHTS NEARBY

Giant Sequoia National Monument (www.fs.usda.gov) sits encased within the two parks and is home to 13 giant sequoia groves.

DEATH VALLEY NATIONAL PARK

California

PASSPORT STAMPS ▼▼▼

WEBSITE:
www.nps.gov/deva

PHONE NUMBER:
760/786-3200

VISITATION RANK:
19

WHY GO:
See sculpted sand dunes, hidden oases, and geologic discoveries.

▲ DEATH VALLEY SAND DUNES

DEATH VALLEY NATIONAL PARK

Located within the northern Mojave Desert, **DEATH VALLEY** boasts extreme temperatures and elevations. From the glaring salt flats of Badwater Basin 282 feet below sea level to snowcapped Telescope Peak at 11,049 feet, the park's complex geology spans eras of seas, volcanoes, tectonic forces, and fault lines.

Dotting the landscape are hidden springs, mining camps, ghost towns, petroglyphs, and the sacred spots of indigenous people who call the valley home. Decaying or preserved, battered by wind or watered by secret oases, these places stand as a testament to the frenzy of human hopes and the fury of imagination. Get out of the car to walk the twisting canyons, cool off near waterfalls, search for petroglyphs, and listen to the wilderness.

PLANNING YOUR TIME

Death Valley National Park is in southeastern California, with a small slice of the park in Nevada. Most of the park is accessible year-round. **Highway 190** bisects the park east to west, passing through the main park hub of Furnace Creek, an outpost of comfort and civilization.

Spring, fall, and **winter** are popular times to visit. Reservations for the few accommodations and campgrounds around Furnace Creek can be hard to come by; make lodging arrangements several months in advance. Summer is the off-season, with temperatures topping 120°F. Winter brings snow to the higher elevations and some roads may close, but the valley areas are pleasant and cool. In spring (Feb.-Apr.), the desert explodes with **wildflower blooms.**

Services are limited at Furnace Creek, Stovepipe Wells, and Panamint Springs. Before entering the park, stock up on food, gas, supplies, and especially water (two gallons of water per person per day).

ENTRANCES AND FEES

Highway 190 is the most efficient way to enter the park from east or west, and it accesses the most popular sights. The entrance fee is $30 per vehicle ($25 motorcycle, $15 individual) and is valid for seven days. Pay the entrance fee at self-pay kiosks or at ranger stations.

VISITORS CENTERS

The **Furnace Creek Visitor Center** (Furnace Creek, Hwy. 190, 9am-5pm daily Oct.-mid-June, 9am-6pm daily mid-June-Oct.) has exhibits, drinking water, information on park sights and activities, ranger programs, camping, and hiking. Buy park passes, permits, and park books from the on-site **Death Valley Natural History Association** (http://dvnha.org). Designated an International Dark Sky Park, the park hosts astronomy events and ranger-led stargazing programs in winter and spring.

Stovepipe Wells has a small ranger station with general park and backcountry information.

SIGHTS

DANTE'S VIEW

Dante's View (Dante's View Rd.) provides spectacular panoramic views of Death Valley. The Panamint Mountains rise dramatically from the stiflingly low Badwater Basin salt flats (282 feet below sea level) to 11,049-foot Telescope Peak, which is snowcapped much of the year.

20-MULE TEAM CANYON

The graded dirt **20-Mule Team Canyon Road** (Hwy. 190, east of Furnace Creek, 3 miles one-way) loops through a mudstone canyon past badlands and the site of historical mining prospects at

Top ❸

❶ FEEL THE BURN AT FURNACE CREEK

Furnace Creek (Hwy. 190) provides a good introduction for first-time visitors and includes access to many of the park's highlights: Zabriskie Point, Badwater Basin, and Artists Drive. **The Ranch at Death Valley** is home to a cabin and motel complex as well as restaurants, a general store, saloon, post office, golf course, horse stables, a **gas station,** restrooms, park headquarters, and a **visitors center.**

SUNRISE AT ZABRISKIE POINT

Built in 1883, the building that now houses the **Borax Museum** (760/786-2345, www.oasisatdeathvalley.com, 9am-9pm daily, donation) was once the assay office for the Monte Blanco Mine in what is now 20-Mule Team Canyon. It has exhibits on Native Americans, mining history, and the history of borax, the "white gold" of the valley. Outdoor exhibits include a 60-ton oil-burning locomotive that hauled borate.

One mile north of Furnace Creek, a short, paved path leads to the site of **Harmony Borax Works.** A 20-mule team wagon, the remains of a borax refinery, and interpretive signs tell the history of the site as a base for the 1883-1888 borax mining and processing operations. Faint, eroded remains of **borax haystacks** flank a 1.5-mile walk across the salt pan.

❷ SPY HIGH FROM ZABRISKIE POINT

Iconic **Zabriskie Point** (Hwy. 190, 7 miles south of Furnace Creek) overlooks otherworldly and eroded badlands from a high vantage point. A popular stop for photographers and other visitors, the colors kindle at sunrise and sunset, capturing the magnificent desolation of the valley.

❸ SINK LOW AT BADWATER BASIN

Badwater Basin (Badwater Rd., 17 miles south of Furnace Creek) is a Death Valley classic. The lowest point in North America at 282 feet below sea level, these vast salt flats encapsulate the mesmerizing yet unforgiving landscape of Death Valley. Walk out onto the salt flats to feel the sea of air and look for delicate salt-crystal formations. The blinding glare, emanating heat, and scale of humans next to the surrounding Black Mountains puts our existence into perspective.

BADWATER BASIN

ONE DAY IN DEATH VALLEY

Highway 190's paved route along **Badwater Road** makes for a perfect tour of the park. Stop at **Badwater Basin, Mesquite Sand Dunes,** and **Zabriskie Point** and make time for a short hike off **Artists Drive** or to **Darwin Falls.** Plan in advance for overnight accommodations in the Furnace Creek area.

20-Mule Team Canyon. When the road veers to the right, look to the left to see the site of the **Monte Blanco assay office,** a large wooden house built in 1883 to serve miners.

ARTISTS DRIVE

Named for its shifting palette of colors, the one-way loop **Artists Drive** (Badwater Rd.) rises along an alluvial fan fed by the Black Mountains. The colors, caused by the oxidizing of different metals on the volcanic rock, proffer a chaotic jumble of hues, including green, rose, yellow, purple, and red. Stop midway at **Artists Palette** for a scenic viewpoint. The scenic, paved nine-mile loop (one-way) starts on Badwater Road, five miles south of Furnace Creek.

DEVIL'S GOLF COURSE

Admire the controlled chaos of the **Devil's Golf Course** (Badwater Rd., 11 miles south of Furnace Creek) on the northern end of the eerie, stark salt flats of Badwater Basin. Devil's Golf Course is filled with spiky salt crystals—as groundwater seeps to the surface, it prompts the jagged pinnacles. Drive the graded dirt road to a small parking lot, where you can see the formations at closer range.

STOVEPIPE WELLS

Stovepipe Wells (Hwy. 190, www.escapetodeathvalley.com), a touring outpost built in 1926, still sits on the toll road that officially kicked off tourism in Death Valley. The road was originally built to join Stovepipe Wells with Lone Pine in the Sierra Nevada, and now serves as the park hub for this region, with a campground, hotel, restaurant, and gas station.

East of Stovepipe Wells, the wind-sculpted **Mesquite Flat Sand Dunes** rise above the desert floor to catch the light of the sky in smooth, unbroken crests and lines.

At **Devil's Cornfield,** mounded clumps of arrowweed plants stretch in neat rows along the sandy desert floor. The effect of the carefully plotted rows of salt-tolerant plants against the backdrop of the Funeral Mountains is surreal. In the spring, the haystacks blossom with blue tops.

As Highway 190 curves south, the Salt Creek area appears. A weathered, wheelchair-accessible boardwalk loop follows the miraculous **Salt Creek,** winding 0.5 mile toward pale, eroded mud hills through an expanse of pickleweed. This tiny riparian environment supports the endemic **Salt Creek pupfish.**

SCOTTY'S CASTLE

Scotty's Castle (Scotty's Castle Rd. at Hwy. 267, closed due to repairs) is an unlikely sight in this desert. The Spanish colonial-style mansion was built in 1922 by millionaires Albert and Bessie Johnson at the urging of Walter Edward Scott, better known as **Death Valley Scotty.** Scotty was an infamous Death Valley character who spun wild tales of gold deposits in the valley to lure investors. Ultimately his colorful personality proved to be the real investment.

The elaborate complex features a two-story house with stucco walls, a Spanish tile roof, and tiled walkways, plus an annex and a clock tower. The interior was fully furnished with the Johnsons' original possessions, including 1920s period furnishings, rich tapestries, mosaic tile work, arched doorways, and a spiral staircase.

Scotty's Castle is an hour's drive from Furnace Creek and Stovepipe Wells. The road may be closed due to damage and construction.

EUREKA DUNES

UBEHEBE CRATER

Perhaps 300 years ago, a powerful volcanic explosion created this colorful crater that measures 600 feet deep and 0.5 mile across. Park at the end of the paved access road to see **Ubehebe Crater** (Scotty's Castle Rd.). A hike (1.5 mi. rt.) allows you to peer down into the colorful depths of Ubehebe Crater, Little Hebe Crater, and other smaller craters.

THE RACETRACK

Despite its remoteness, many visitors make the long and difficult drive to **The Racetrack** (Racetrack Valley Rd.), an eerily dry lake bed scattered with the faint trails of rocks that skate across its surface. (Thin ice sheets cover the ground, acting as sails in a light wind, enough to propel the rocks across the surface and create the mysterious tracks.)

From the start of Racetrack Valley Road, it's a long but scenic haul along 26 miles of rutted, rocky washboard. You'll know you're getting close when you pass **Teakettle Junction** (19.4 miles). A high-clearance vehicle is usually adequate, but a 4WD vehicle may be necessary. Many people stay in Furnace Creek or Stovepipe Wells and turn the adventurous, 3-4-hour drive into a long day trip.

EUREKA DUNES

Isolated in the park's remote north, the beautiful and pristine **Eureka Dunes** (South Eureka Rd.) rise from the valley floor to cover an area three miles wide and one mile long. They are the tallest sand dunes in California, towering more than 680 feet from the enclosed valley floor. From their base, a climb into the dunes goes 0.5-2.5 miles and ascends 300-600 feet. Upon reaching the ridgeline, you are rewarded with sculpted dunes and sweeping views of the valley.

AGUEREBERRY POINT

Prospector Pete Aguereberry established Harrisburg camp in 1905, working what would become the **Eureka Mine.** Today, you can explore the original camp, visible from **Aguereberry Point Road.** Explore the remains of the Eureka Mine and Aguereberry's cabins just over the hill to the south behind the camp. The road continues toward epic views at **Aguereberry Point.**

WILDROSE CHARCOAL KILNS

The **Wildrose Charcoal Kilns** (Wildrose Canyon Rd.) are made of cut limestone, quarried locally and cemented with gravel, lime, and sand. They stand approximately 25 feet tall, their walls curving gracefully inward to form a

WILDROSE CHARCOAL KILNS

beehive shape. The Modock Consolidated Mining Company built them in 1877 to fuel the smelters of lead-silver mines in the Argus range to the west. Open, arched doorways lead to the interior of the now-defunct kilns; stomp around on the floors of each one to capture their hollow echoes.

SCENIC DRIVE
TITUS CANYON ROAD

From Highway 374 (Daylight Pass Rd.), six miles south of Beatty, the dirt and gravel **Titus Canyon Road** (27 mi.

one-way, 3 hrs.) sweeps through rugged rock formations, hangs over canyon views, skirts past **petroglyphs,** and even rolls through a **ghost town,** eventually passing through the grand finale: the canyon narrows. The narrows tower overhead, barely letting cars squeeze through before they open wide to reveal the barren Death Valley floor. A **high-clearance** vehicle is usually fine, but a 4WD vehicle may be needed in inclement weather.

▼ TITUS CANYON ROAD

Best Hike

DARWIN FALLS

DISTANCE: 2 miles round-trip
DURATION: 1.5 hours
ELEVATION CHANGE: 220 feet
EFFORT: easy
TRAILHEAD: Highway 190, west of Panamint Springs

The marvel of **Darwin Falls** is that they exist at all. The hike to the first falls is an easy and quick detour from Panamint Springs. A short one-mile walk along a canyon creek leads you to a sight to behold: actual water streaming over slanted bedrock. This is where most people stop. About 1.5 hours should get you to the falls and back in time for a nice lunch on the Panamint Springs patio.

RECREATION

HIKING

Off Badwater Road, **Golden Canyon** (2.5 mi. rt., 1.5 hrs., easy) has gentle grades that lead to sheer red walls with majestic creases. The mouth of the canyon begins along a gravel wash through short narrows with sedimentary and volcanic rocks on the passage walls. Then the canyon opens up to a gold corridor of badlands, both bright and desolate. At a fork about 1 mile in, go another 0.25 mile to the **Red Cathedral.** Hikers make a loop by continuing all the way to **Zabriskie Point** (6 mi. rt., 3 hrs., moderate) and returning via **Gower Gulch.**

Farther south on Badwater Road, **Natural Bridge** (0.7-1.4 mi. rt., 1 hr., easy) is one of the few natural bridges in the park. This hike is popular, so be prepared to share it. Natural Bridge spans a red-wall canyon that contrasts with the bright sky above. Look back toward Badwater Basin to see Telescope Peak in the distance.

Wildrose Canyon Road goes to two peak-bound trailheads. Near Wildrose Charcoal Kilns, a signed trail leads to **Wildrose Peak** (9 mi. rt., 5 hrs., moderate). The trail is intermittently steep up to the saddle, where you have sweeping views of Death Valley. Near Mahogany Flat, the hike up the highest peak in Death Valley—**Telescope Peak** (14 mi. rt., 8 hrs., strenuous)—is worth every switchback. The path climbs to 11,049 feet above Badwater Basin. Expect sweeping views of Death Valley to the east and Panamint Valley to the west.

BIKING

A paved bicycle path (2 mi. rt.) travels from Furnace Creek to Harmony Borax Works. More difficult rides include the hilly paved loop of **Artists Drive** (9 mi. one-way) and the exposed gravel loop of the **West Side Road** (up to 40 mi.) running along the valley floor. Mountain bikers can ride all 4WD roads. **Furnace Creek Ranch General Store** (760/786-3371, www.oasisatdeathvalley.com) rents mountain bikes; pickup and drop-off is at the gas station.

GOLF

At 214 feet below sea level, **Furnace Creek Golf Course** (Hwy. 190, 760/786-2345, www.oasisatdeathvalley.com) claims to be the lowest-elevation golf course in the world. Dotted with water, this 18-hole course is lined with palm and tamarisk trees.

WHERE TO STAY

INSIDE THE PARK

Lodging, dining, and camping are available in Furnace Creek (Hwy. 190, Death Valley, 800/236-7916, www.oasisatdeathvalley.com, year-round) at **The Inn at Death Valley** (from $500) and the **Ranch at Death Valley** (from $250); in **Stovepipe Wells Village** (51880 Hwy. 190, Death Valley, 760/786-2387, www.deathvalleyhotels.com, from $170), which includes the Toll Road Restaurant (7am-10am and 5:30pm-9pm daily) and Badwater Saloon (11:30am-close daily); and at **Panamint Springs Resort** (775/482-7680, 40440

SCENIC FOUR-WHEEL DRIVES

Hundreds of miles of unmaintained 4WD roads provide access to remote destinations in Death Valley. **Farabee's Jeep Rentals** in Furnace Creek rents 4WD vehicles and has up-to-date backcountry road information.

Cottonwood Canyon Road: West of Stovepipe Wells, this 19-mile primitive road travels deep into the Cottonwood Mountains. The road starts off spitting through semi-deep sand, eventually becoming more solid on washboard and gravel. It gets much rougher as it enters Cottonwood Canyon wash.

Echo Canyon to Inyo Mine: Between Furnace Creek and Zabriskie Point, this popular 19-mile round-trip road tours a scenic, winding canyon and ghost camp ruins. It requires a high-clearance vehicle for the first 3 miles to the canyon mouth and 4WD beyond to the mining camp.

Pleasant Canyon to Rogers Pass: From Panamint Valley Road, this rugged 4WD trek goes through Pleasant Canyon. You will drive directly in the creek en route to backcountry cabins and historic mining camps in the Western Panamint Mountains.

Racetrack Valley Road: High-clearance vehicles can make the long, white-knuckle drive 26 rocky miles into the Racetrack Valley from Ubehebe Crater, but 4WD may be necessary due to flooding and washouts. At **Teakettle Junction** at 19.4 miles, go west and south for 7 miles to **The Racetrack,** an eerily dry lake bed scattered with the faint trails of rocks that skate across its surface. Day trips take four hours; multiday trips can add on **Ubehebe Peak,** hidden mining camps like **Ubehebe Mine, Lost Burro Mine, Lippincott Mine,** and the **Goldbelt Mining District,** and even the occasional canyon.

Saline Valley Road: This rough yet graded dirt road travels 78 lonely miles from Death Valley-Big Pine Road near Big Pine to Highway 190, west of Panamint Springs. Although a high-clearance vehicle is suitable during good weather, 4WD is preferred to access the remote **Saline Valley** that contains sand dunes and Salt Lake. To drive the road takes the better part of a day without stops; for time to explore, allow at least three days, and camp at the centrally located, primitive **Warm Springs Camp.** The best times to visit are spring and fall. Summer sees blazing temperatures; in winter, rain and snow can render the Saline Valley Road impassable.

Warm Spring Canyon to Butte Valley: The lower canyon is easily accessible, following a good graded road the first 11 miles to Warm Springs Camp. The upper canyon is harder to reach and requires 4WD into Butte Valley.

Hwy. 190, Panamint Springs, www.panamintsprings.com, from $80).

There are nine national park campgrounds. **Furnace Creek** (154 sites, year-round, $22-36) is the only park campground that accepts **reservations** (877/444-6777, www.recreation.gov, Oct. 15-Apr. 15). From mid-April to mid-October, sites are first come, first served.

All other campgrounds are first come, first served and include: **Stovepipe Wells** (190 sites, mid-Sept.-mid-May, $14), **Mesquite Spring** (40 sites, year-round, $14), **Texas Springs** (92 sites, Nov.-May, $16), **Sunset** (270 sites, Nov.-May, $14), **Emigrant** (10 tent sites, year-round, free), **Wildrose** (23 sites, year-round, free), **Thorndike** (6 sites, Mar.-Nov., free) and **Mahogany Flat** (10 sites, Mar.-Nov., free).

All campgrounds can get very windy at night. If tent camping, stake all items properly. If relying on RV electrical hookups, don't be surprised by electricity surges and power outages.

OUTSIDE THE PARK

The gateway towns of **Lone Pine, Big Pine, Bishop, Ridgecrest**, and **Beatty, Nevada,** have limited accommodations and restaurants.

GETTING THERE AND AROUND

The park has no shuttles or public transportation—bring **your own vehicle**. For back-road excursions, rent 4WD rigs through **Farabee's** (Furnace Creek, 760/786-9872, http://farabeejeeps.com, mid-Sept.-mid-May); advance reservations are recommended.

Gas is sold inside the park, but prices are expensive. Fill up at one of the gateway towns instead.

AIR

The closest international airports are **Los Angeles International Airport** (LAX, 1 World Way, Los Angeles, 424/646-5252, www.lawa.org) and **McCarran International Airport** (LAS, 5757 Wayne Newton Blvd., Las Vegas, 702/261-5211, www.mccarran.com). The airports have car rentals.

CAR

From **Los Angeles,** take I-5 north toward Palmdale and Lancaster to Highway 14. Drive 120 miles north on Highway 14 to Indian Wells to join U.S. 395. Continue north on U.S. 395 for 42 miles to the town of Olancha. Turn right (east) onto Highway 190 and continue 45 miles to Panamint Springs. Stovepipe Wells lies 29 miles east of Panamint Springs; Furnace Creek is 53 miles east of Panamint Springs.

From **Las Vegas,** I-15 intersects with U.S. 95 north of the airport. Take U.S. 95 north for 88 miles to Lathrop Wells, Nevada. Turn left (south) onto Highway 373 and drive 24 miles southwest. Highway 373 becomes Highway 127 when it crosses into California. At the tiny outpost of Death Valley Junction, turn right (west) onto Highway 190 and continue west for 30 miles to the park hub at Furnace Creek.

SIGHTS NEARBY

Amargosa Opera House and Hotel (Hwy. 127, Death Valley Junction, 760/852-4441, www.amargosa-opera-house.com, 7am-10:30pm daily) is a historic (and haunted) hotel and restaurant that still hosts live performances.

Rhyolite is a ghost town that dates to 1904. Located seven miles outside the park boundary, the town's ruins include a beautiful mission-style train station, cemetery, mine ruins, and a house made of glass bottles.

Goldwell Open Air Museum (1 Golden St., 702/870-9946, www.goldwellmuseum.org, year-round, free) is a sculpture installation and art park located next to Rhyolite, sharing the land and the desert backdrop.

Ancient Bristlecone Pine Forest (760/873-2500, www.fs.usda.gov, 6am-10pm daily mid-May-Nov.), in the White Mountains east of Big Pine, has some of the oldest trees in the world, including the Methuselah Tree, dated 4,750 years old.

Trona Pinnacles (www.blm.gov) are remote tufa formations, a ghost lake set with alien spires. They are viewable from the Trona-Wildrose Highway at the south entrance to the park.

◄ THE RACETRACK FROM UBEHEBE PEAK

JOSHUA TREE
NATIONAL PARK

California

WEBSITE:
www.nps.gov/jotr

PHONE NUMBER:
760/367-5500

VISITATION RANK:
11

WHY GO:
Explore a desert landscape filled with jumbled boulders and Joshua trees.

PASSPORT STAMPS ▼▼▼

JOSHUA TREE's stunning, alien landscape both startles and charms. Powerful geologic forces have whipped the rocks here into twisted shapes and scrambled boulder piles. Among the eroded chaos, spiky Joshua trees reach out in unpredictable angles, forming jagged, moody backdrops to the dusty desert roads of the Mojave. Farther south, the landscape straddles the boundary between the Mojave and Colorado Deserts. The lower Colorado sits austere and arid, with wide alluvial fans guarding mountain canyons. Instead of Joshua trees, creosote bushes and spindly ocotillos dot the pristine desert wilderness.

Joshua Tree's surreal appeal draws casual day-trippers, spring wildflower hounds, serious hikers, and hard-core rock climbers in droves, all wanting to experience its beauty and strangeness. The park's location near major urban centers like Palm Springs and Los Angeles contributes to its popularity. Surrounding the park, the tiny towns of Joshua Tree and Twentynine Palms are filled with outsider art and alien-inspired feats of aeronautical engineering.

PLANNING YOUR TIME

Joshua Tree is in Southern California, east of Los Angeles and north of Palm Springs. Most visitors arrive via Highway 62 to enter the park on the west side near the town of Joshua Tree. From Joshua Tree, Park Boulevard connects with Twentynine Palms, the north entrance on Highway 62. Short spurs from Highway 62 take in the park's sights.

Visit during the cooler, if crowded, months of **October-April**; weekdays offer fewer crowds. The weather is gorgeous in spring and fall, but brutal in summer with average temperatures topping 100°F. In winter, the park is dusted by snow. For spring flowers, visit in late February-May.

Camping is the only overnight option inside the park. You'll need a **car,** a full tank of gas, and **water** (at least two gallons per person per day), as there are no services inside the park.

ENTRANCES AND FEES

The entrance fee is $30 per vehicle ($25 motorcycle and individual), which is good for seven days. All roads and entrance stations are open year-round, weather permitting. The park has three entrance stations:

West Entrance (Hwy. 62 and Park Blvd.) is in the town of Joshua Tree, south of the Joshua Tree Visitor Center. It sees the heaviest visitation; expect midday lines during peak season.

North Entrance (Hwy. 62 and Utah Trail) is in the town of Twentynine Palms near the Oasis Visitor Center.

South Entrance (Exit 168 off I-10) accesses the park's Colorado Desert and the less-visited Cottonwood Spring.

VISITORS CENTERS

The park's four visitors centers have information, exhibits, maps, natural history bookstores, water, and restrooms. Rangers lead patio talks and chats; you can also get schedules of ranger-led walks throughout the park.

Joshua Tree Visitor Center (6554 Park Blvd., Joshua Tree, 760/366-1855, 8am-5pm daily) is near the park's West Entrance. It has a bookstore with guides, maps, and gifts. There is also a restroom and a café (760/366-8200, 8am-5pm daily).

Black Rock Nature Center (9800 Black Rock Canyon Rd., Yucca Valley, 760/367-3001, 8am-4pm Sat.-Thurs., 8am-8pm Fri. Oct.-May) is a small

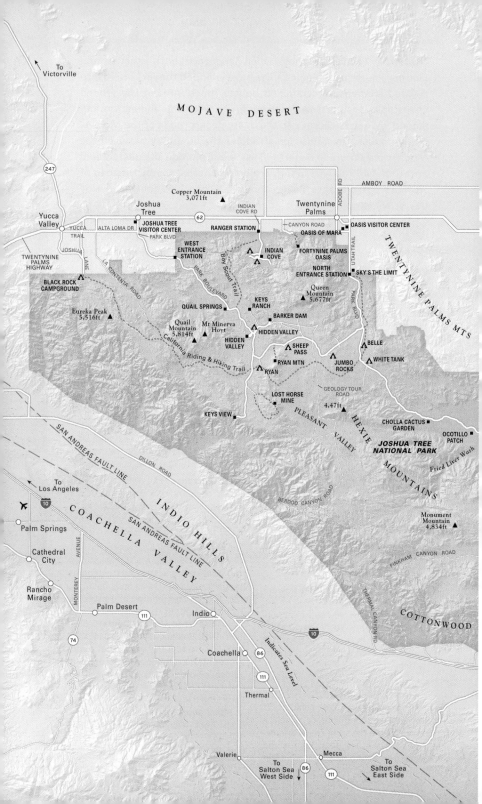

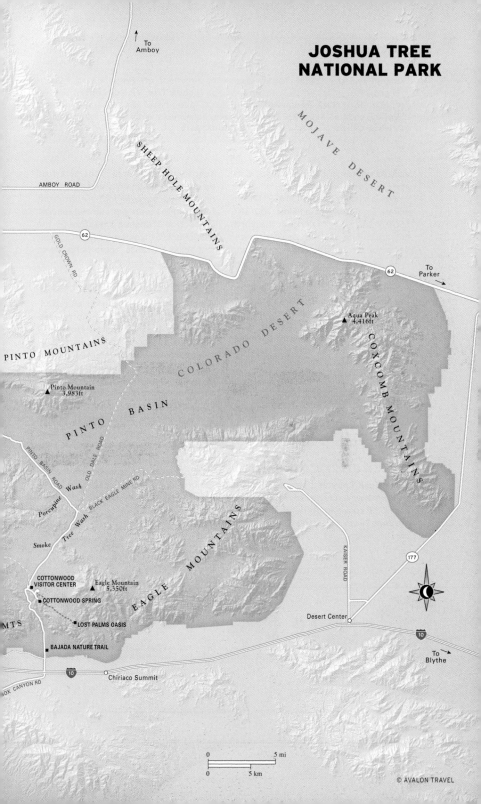

JOSHUA TREE NATIONAL PARK

To Amboy

MOJAVE DESERT

SHEEP HOLE MOUNTAINS

AMBOY ROAD

62

GOLD CROWN RD

62

To Parker

Aqua Peak
4,416ft

PINTO MOUNTAINS

COLORADO DESERT

COXCOMB MOUNTAINS

Pinto Mountain
3,983ft

PINTO BASIN

PINTO BASIN ROAD

OLD DALE ROAD

Porcupine Wash

BLACK EAGLE MINE RD

Smoke Tree Wash

EAGLE MOUNTAINS

KAISER ROAD

177

COTTONWOOD
VISITOR CENTER

Eagle Mountain
5,350ft

COTTONWOOD SPRING

MTS

LOST PALMS OASIS

Desert Center

BAJADA NATURE TRAIL

10

10

BOX CANYON RD

Chiriaco Summit

To Blythe

0   5 mi

0   5 km

© AVALON TRAVEL

ONE DAY IN JOSHUA TREE

If time is short, spend the day driving a scenic loop on the park road. From Highway 62, start with an introduction at **Joshua Tree Visitor Center.** Then cruise along **Park Boulevard,** stopping to hike one of the trails in **Hidden Valley,** such as **Skull Rock** or **Cap Rock.** Finish your auto tour at the **Oasis Visitor Center** with a walk to the **Oasis of Mara.**

visitors center in the Black Rock Canyon Campground area.

Oasis Visitor Center (74485 National Park Dr., Twentynine Palms, 760/367-5500, 8:30am-5pm daily) is at the North Entrance. The staffed visitors center has a bookstore with guides, maps, and gifts. Water, restrooms with flush toilets, and picnic tables are also available. An interpretive loop (0.5 mi. rt.) leads to the **Oasis of Mara,** a historic fan palm oasis with a large standing pool.

Cottonwood Visitor Center (Cottonwood Spring Rd., 8:30am-4pm daily) is at the south entrance of the park. There is a bookstore with guides, maps, and gifts. Water, restrooms with flush toilets, and picnic tables are also available. The visitors center is convenient to the Cottonwood Campground.

SIGHTS

BLACK ROCK CANYON

Black Rock Canyon (Joshua Lane) is in the northwest corner of Joshua Tree. It's home to a campground and several great hikes and offers easy access to the shops and restaurants of the Yucca Valley. The area is characterized by craggy rolling peaks and piñons, junipers, and oaks, giving it a different feel from the more popular Hidden Valley section of Joshua Tree. Though the Black Rock Canyon area is located near the West Entrance, there is no direct access into the center of the park.

COVINGTON FLATS

A series of lightly traveled and graded dirt roads in the park's northwestern corner tour **Covington Flats** (10.9 miles). This scenic drive leads to a sweeping overlook, several hiking trails, and some of the largest stands of Joshua trees, junipers, and piñon pines in the park. Access is off La Contenta Road.

EUREKA PEAK OVERLOOK

Follow signs to 5,521-foot **Eureka Peak Overlook** for sweeping panoramic views. From the summit, the Coachella Valley, Desert Hot Springs, and the San Jacinto Mountains lie southwest, while views to the north take in the Morongo Valley.

▼ COVINGTON FLATS

Top ❸

① CRUISE ALONG PARK BOULEVARD

From the West Entrance near the town of Joshua Tree, **Park Boulevard** delves deep into the Hidden Valley to emerge in the town of Twentynine Palms 25 miles later. This scenic drive takes in the most popular regions of the park, with access to Hidden Valley's **campgrounds, trailheads,** and **sights.**

BOARDED-UP WELL AT KEYS RANCH

② TOUR THE RUINS OF KEYS RANCH

From 1917 to 1969, homesteader, rancher, and miner Bill Keys carved out a desert domain that included a ranch house, schoolhouse, store, and workshop. Today, park rangers lead guided 90-minute tours of **Keys Ranch** (daily Oct.-May, adults $10, kids $5, under 6 free), the well-preserved ruins of the Desert Queen Ranch, a historic homestead near the Hidden Valley Campground. The tour is popular; purchase tickets on the day of the tour in person at Oasis Visitor Center (starting at 8:30am). Allow 40 minutes to drive the 22 miles from the visitors center to the ranch gate to meet your guide.

③ ROCK CLIMB IN HIDDEN VALLEY

From beginners to rock stars, climbers of all levels seek the park's vast array of traditional-style crack, slab, and steep-face climbing. More than 400 climbing formations and more than 8,000 recognized climbs make it a world-class destination. Some good places to watch climbers in action are the **Quail Springs** picnic area, **Hidden Valley Campground,** the **Wonderland of Rocks, Cap Rock, Jumbo Rocks, Indian Cove, Ryan Campground, Split Rock,** and **Live Oak.**

CAP ROCK

DESERT QUEEN MINE

HIDDEN VALLEY

Wonderland of Rocks

Dubbed the **Wonderland of Rocks,** this region is characterized by a wildly eroded maze of striking granite rock formations studded with secret basins, gorgeous views, and history. The Wonderland of Rocks covers the area southeast of Indian Cove Campground and northeast of Hidden Valley Campground. When you drive along Park Boulevard, its compelling rock formations are visible to the northeast. The closest driving points into the belly of the beast are the parking area for the **Barker Dam Nature Trail** (Park Blvd.) and **Indian Cove Campground** (Indian Cove Rd.).

Ryan Ranch

The homestead ruins of the **Ryan Ranch** (Park Blvd. near Ryan Campground) date to 1896. A 0.5-mile interpretive stroll leads to the remains of the ranch and its adobe bunkhouse, windmill, and outbuildings. A deeper search of the area reveals a pioneer cemetery and evidence of Native American grinding stones.

Keys View

Impressive vistas can be had from the lip of windswept **Keys View** (Keys View Rd.), a paved, wheelchair-accessible observation point in the Little San Bernardino Mountains. At the top, take in a panorama that stretches to the Salton Sea, Santa Rosa Mountains, San Andreas Fault, Palm Springs, San Jacinto Peak, and San Gorgonio Peak.

QUEEN VALLEY

The **Queen Valley** is a cross-section of Joshua Tree's greatest hits, with Joshua trees, mining ruins, Native American villages, scenic hikes, and views. A series of short dirt roads crisscrosses the Queen Valley, chugging through one of the largest pockets of Joshua trees in the park. Mining ruins range from large gold operations, like the Desert Queen Mine, to humbler affairs marked by the rusty remains of tent encampments. Established hiking trails follow a series of old mining roads to the **Desert Queen Mine, Lucky Boy Vista,** and the **Wall Street Mine.** To reach the Queen Valley area, follow the unpaved Queen Valley Road or Desert Queen Mine Road east to Pine City.

CHOLLA CACTUS GARDEN

Driving through the endless landscape of the Pinto Basin, the **Cholla Cactus Garden** (Pinto Basin Rd.) appears like an army of prickly planted teddy bears—their sheer numbers impress in this already surreal landscape. Stop to wander the 0.3-mile interpretive trail through a crop of strange flora.

COTTONWOOD SPRING

At the South Entrance, **Cottonwood Spring** (Cottonwood Spring Rd.) is a fan palm oasis. Its name comes from a surprising crop of native cottonwood trees that mix into the luxuriant vegetation surrounding the spring.

SCENIC DRIVE
GEOLOGY TOUR ROAD

The **Geology Tour Road** (18 miles) is a backcountry drive that descends south into the broad Pleasant Valley and an ancient dry lake. Enjoy views of the unique geologic phenomena, which includes dramatic erosion and uplifts. Pick up a free interpretive pamphlet from the Joshua Tree Visitor Center, which details the route with 16 numbered points of interest (also available from a small metal box at the start of the drive).

The first five miles of graded dirt road to Squaw Tank are passable by most cars (no RVs) in dry weather. Beyond Squaw Tank, the road is **4WD only** due to deep ruts, sand, and steep grades. Past Squaw Tank, the road completes a one-way loop clockwise along the Hexie Mountain foothills and through Pleasant Valley. You're committed to the two-hour drive once you start the loop.

RECREATION
HIKING

Joshua Tree offers fantastic hiking in an otherworldly landscape. Dehydration is the biggest danger while hiking in Joshua Tree. Always carry at least **two gallons of water per person per day** and hike during cooler times of the day, such as early morning or late afternoon. Never hike in summer or in midday heat.

Black Rock Canyon

This short trail rewards with panoramic views and desert knowledge. Hike the **Hi-View Nature Trail** (1.3 mi. rt., 1.5 hrs., moderate) clockwise to take in sweeping views of the Yucca Valley to the northeast, Black Rock Canyon to the south, and the San Bernardino Mountains, including the snowcapped 11,503-foot San Gorgonio Mountain to the west.

Hidden Valley

This is the **most popular area of the park,** as it accesses trails in Queen Valley, Hidden Valley, Quail Springs, and the Wonderland of Rocks. Expect filled parking lots and plenty of company on the trails.

The **Cap Rock Trail** (0.4 mi. rt., 20 min., easy) leads through whimsically eroded boulder formations, most notably a flat, cap-like rock balanced on top of a spectacular formation. This **wheelchair-accessible** trail is wide, flat, and made of hard-packed sandy dirt.

▼ BARKER DAM

Best Hike

BARKER DAM AND WALL STREET MILL

DISTANCE: 1.3-2.2 miles round-trip
DURATION: 1-1.5 hours
ELEVATION CHANGE: negligible
EFFORT: easy
TRAILHEAD: Barker Dam

Look for the signed trailhead off the Park Boulevard where the popular **Barker Dam Trail** (1.3 mi. rt., 1 hr., easy) loops through boulders to a small pond. The watering hole is a stop for migrating birds, bighorn sheep, and other wildlife.

From the trailhead in the Barker Dam parking area, the **Wall Street Mill Trail** (2.2 mi. rt., 1.5 hrs., easy) veers east, clearly marked with stone trail boundaries and occasional arrows. Along the way, you'll find abandoned cars and mining artifacts. A pink building marks the remains of the **Wonderland Ranch.** At the end of the trail are the **Desert Queen Well** ruins. A tall windmill, once used to pump water, still stands over piles of weathered timbers and an old tank.

Anthropomorphically named for its gaunt eye socket-like depressions, **Skull Rock** (1.7 mi. rt., 1.5 hrs., easy) marks a trail that winds through the scenic boulder- and plant-strewn landscape to hook over to Jumbo Rocks Campground. The trail follows the campground road until it crosses Park Boulevard to wind back through more boulders with views of the surrounding desert.

The **Hidden Valley Loop** (1 mi. rt., 45 min., easy) passes through granite boulders to emerge in scenic Hidden Valley, used for cattle grazing in the early-mid-1900s. The well-signed trail circles the small, enclosed valley, delving into the monzogranite boulder piles with tempting bouldering opportunities.

The trail to **Ryan Mountain** (3 mi. rt., 2.5 hrs., strenuous) climbs more than 1,000 feet in its ascent to the summit, where you are rewarded with panoramic views from the wind-scoured 5,457-foot vantage point.

A weathered stamp mill and the surrounding ruins (rock house foundations, equipment, and mining tunnels) are the highlight of the hike to **Lost Horse Mine** (4 mi. rt., 2-3 hrs., moderate). From the parking lot, the signed loop directs hikers counter-clockwise to climb the flank of stark Lost Horse Mountain through a mix of Joshua trees, yucca, and juniper. The path passes the **Optimist Mine** (only a stone chimney and scattered artifacts remain) and climbs precipitously, giving way to sweeping views toward the northeast. **Lost Horse Mine** comes into view below. Although the mill and tunnels are fenced off, remains of rock houses and artifacts make this an interesting place to explore.

SKULL ROCK

LOST HORSE MINE

Indian Cove

The **49 Palms Oasis** (3 mi. rt., 2-3 hrs., moderate) is surrounded by native fan palms secluded in a rocky canyon. From the trailhead, the path climbs over a ridge and then winds down through arid hills. The trail passes through a flinty landscape that gives no indication of its secret oasis until you are close enough to see it nestled against the jagged hills.

Cottonwood Spring

The well-signed **Mastodon Peak Loop** (3 mi. rt., 2 hrs., moderate) affords dramatic desert views stretching as far as the Salton Sea. The nature trail leaves the Cottonwood Spring parking area to head northwest, reaching a junction at 0.5 mile. Turn right to continue toward the base of the foothills. Just past the junction, concrete foundations mark the site of the old **Winona Mill.** From the base of the mountains, the trail climbs toward the peak and the remains of the **Mastodon Mine,** clinging to the hillside. Enjoy sweeping views west toward the Cottonwood Mountains. Continue the loop down the mountain to a fork; turn right and finish at scenic **Cottonwood Spring.**

The **Lost Palms Oasis Trail** (7.5 mi. rt., 5-6 hrs., strenuous) undulates through striking desert scenery before dropping down to a secluded canyon and the largest collection of fan palms in the park. The exposed trail starts from scenic **Cottonwood Spring** and ripples over an up-and-down landscape dominated by a series of ridges and washes. The trail edges into the foothills of the Eagle Mountains before emerging to overlook a steep canyon and the Lost Palms Oasis, a watering hole for bighorn sheep and other wildlife. The steep trail continues to the boulder and palm-strewn canyon floor, a great place to take a break before the return.

BIKING

The paved **Park Boulevard** (25 mi.) offers prime cycling through the park's most spectacular scenery between the West Entrance in Joshua Tree to the North Entrance near Twentynine Palms. **Pinto Basin Road** (30 mi.), the other paved park road, cuts through the Pinto Basin's open desert with scenery that's

CHOLLA CACTUS ALONG PINTO BASIN ROAD

ROCK CLIMBING IN JOSHUA TREE

less rewarding than Park Boulevard, but also more lightly traveled.

Bike rentals are located outside the park's West Entrance in the town of Joshua Tree at **Joshua Tree Bicycle Shop** (6416 Hallee Rd., Joshua Tree, 760/366-3377, www.joshuatreebicycleshop.com, 10am-6pm Mon.-Sat.).

ROCK CLIMBING OUTFITTERS

Joshua Tree lures rock climbers. Four trails (Barker Dam Loop, Boy Scout Trail, Willow Hole, and Wonderland Wash) knife short distances into the **Wonderland of Rocks,** where rock climbing trails are signed and established.

Climber's Coffee (Hidden Valley Campground, 8am-10am Sat.-Sun. mid-Oct.-Apr.) offers the opportunity to meet Joshua Tree's climbing ranger and glean information from other climbers. To get in on the action, take a group class or a private, guided climb through one of several outfitters:

Joshua Tree Rock Climbing School (760/366-4745, www.joshuatreerockclimbing.com) offers year-round rock climbing classes and private guided outings.

Cliffhanger Guides (760/401-5033, www.cliffhangerguides.com) specializes in custom guided rock climbing half-day and full-day adventures.

WILLOW HOLE TRAIL

Vertical Adventures (800/514-8785, www.vertical-adventures.com) has 1-5-day courses, private instruction, and guided climbing.

Climbing Life Guides (760/780-8868, www.joshuatreeclimbinglifeguides.com) lead rock climbing and teach technical climbing.

To gear up for your rock climbing adventure, check out one of the three outfitters located on the main drag in Joshua Tree:

Nomad Ventures (61795 Twentynine Palms Hwy., Joshua Tree, 760/366-4684, www.nomadventures.com)

Coyote Corner (6535 Park Blvd., Joshua Tree, 760/366-9683, www.jtcoyotecorner.com)

Joshua Tree Outfitters (61707 Twentynine Palms Hwy., Joshua Tree, 760/366-1848, http://joshuatreeoutfitters.com).

HORSEBACK RIDING

With more than 250 miles of equestrian trails and trail corridors, horseback riding is a great way to experience Joshua Tree National Park—if you bring your own horse. Two campgrounds offer equestrian camping with overnight areas for stock animals: **Ryan Campground** (760/367-5545, $15, no water), in centrally located Hidden Valley, and **Black Rock Canyon** (877/444-6777, www.recreation.gov, $20, water available) in Joshua Tree's northwest corner. Reservations are required.

If you're not bringing your own horse, **Joshua Tree Ranch** (760/366-5357, www.joshuatreevillage.com, $35 per hour pp) offers guided private and group trail rides from their ranch, located less than two miles from the park's West Entrance.

WHERE TO STAY
INSIDE THE PARK

There are no accommodations or food inside the park. The only option is camping. Black Rock, Jumbo Rocks, Indian Cove, and Cottonwood accept **reservations** (877/444-6777, www.recreation.gov, $15-20) six months in advance for October-May. The remaining campgrounds are first-come,

JUMBO ROCKS CAMPGROUND

first-served and are open year-round. Campgrounds start to fill by Thursday most weekends **October-May**. In summer, all campgrounds are first-come, first-served.

Black Rock Campground (reservations Oct.-May), in the northwest corner of Joshua Tree, is a good choice for first-time visitors, as drinking water is available and the location offers easy access to Yucca Valley for supplies.

Hidden Valley, on the south end of the Wonderland of Rocks, is popular with rock climbers—and everyone else. Sites are at a premium here.

Jumbo Rocks is the largest campground in the park and its sites fill quickly at this convenient location along Park Boulevard. **Nearby Belle** and **White Tank**, off Pinto Basin Road, are both first-come, first-served.

Indian Cove (reservations Oct.-May) has both group and RV sites on the north edge of the Wonderland of Rocks. Access is from Highway 62.

Cottonwood Campground (reservations Oct.-May) is near the south entrance to the park, off I-10.

Sheep Pass (reservation only) is a tent-only group campground off Park Boulevard, between **Ryan** and Jumbo Rocks.

OUTSIDE THE PARK

Outside the park, find lodging and dining in **Yucca Valley,** the town of **Joshua Tree,** and **Twentynine Palms.** Backcountry camping is permitted on BLM land, and the town of Joshua Tree has a private RV park.

GETTING THERE

AIR

The closest airport is **Palm Springs Airport** (PSP, 3400 E. Tahquitz Canyon Way, 760/318-3800, www.palmsprings-ca.gov). International travelers should fly into **Los Angeles International Airport** (LAX, 1 World Way, Los Angeles, 424/646-5252, www.lawa.org).

CAR

Yucca Valley is the best place to fuel up before entering the park. The small town has several major car rental agencies available.

The **West Entrance** (Hwy. 62) to Joshua Tree is located 40 miles (1 hr.) north of Palm Springs and 145 miles (3-4 hrs.) east of Los Angeles. From I-10 near Palm Springs, head north on Highway 62 for 30 miles to the town of Joshua Tree. Turn south on Park Boulevard and follow the road into the park.

The **North Entrance** (Hwy. 62) is farther east near Twentynine Palms. From Joshua Tree, drive 16 miles east along Highway 62 then turn south on Utah Trail.

The **South Entrance** (I-10) is located about 60 miles (1 hr.) east of Palm

NAME	LOCATION	PRICE	SEASON	SITES	AMENITIES
Black Rock	Black Rock Canyon	$20	year-round; reserve Oct.-May	99	tent/RV and horse sites, flush toilets, drinking water, dump station
Hidden Valley	Hidden Valley	$15	year-round	44	tent/RV sites, vault toilets
Ryan	Hidden Valley	$15	year-round	31	tent and horse sites, vault toilets
Sheep Pass	Hidden Valley	$25-50	year-round	6	group tent sites, vault toilets
Jumbo Rocks	Hidden Valley	$15	year-round; reserve Oct.-May	124	tent/RV sites, vault toilets
Belle	Hidden Valley	$15	Oct.-May	18	tent sites, vault toilets
White Tank	Hidden Valley	$15	year-round	15	tent/RV sites, vault toilets
Indian Cove	Indian Cove	$20	year-round; reserve Oct.-May	101	tent/RV sites and group sites, vault toilets
Cottonwood	Cottonwood Spring	$20	year-round; reserve Oct.-May	62	tent/RV and group sites, flush toilets, drinking water, dump station

Springs along I-10 and 160 miles (4 hrs.) east of Los Angeles. From I-10, turn north on Cottonwood Spring Road to enter the park.

GETTING AROUND

Most visitors drive into the park from the west entrance and follow the main Park Road to sights and trailheads in the Hidden Valley. In peak season, congestion at trailheads and parking areas may be a problem.

The **Road Runner Shuttle Service** (www.jtnproadrunner.org) departs from the Joshua Tree and Oasis Visitor Centers, stopping at popular areas in the Hidden Valley section of the park. Shuttles run every two hours (8am-4pm daily); a park pass is required.

SIGHTS NEARBY

The Integratron (2477 Belfield Blvd., Landers, 760/364-3126, www.integratron.com, $35) is a spherical wood dome imbued with an amazing sound resonance. Book a sound bath (1 hr.) and listen to crystal bowl harmonies followed by recorded music for relaxation and meditation.

Giant Rock (3 miles north of the Integratron) is the largest freestanding boulder in the world. It stands seven stories high and covers 5,800 square feet of ground.

The **Noah Purifoy Outdoor Desert Art Museum** (63030 Blair Ln., Joshua Tree, www.noahpurifoy.com, sunrise-sunset daily, free) exhibits twisted and stacked sculptures in metal, plywood, porcelain, paper, cotton, and glass mediums across 10 acres of an otherworldly artscape.

Pioneertown (Pioneertown Rd.) was a popular Wild West filming destination in the 1940s and 1950s. It continues as a family-friendly attraction. The adjacent **Pappy & Harriet's Pioneertown Palace** (53688 Pioneertown Rd., 760/365-5956, www.pappyandharriets.com) serves great barbecue with live bands nightly in the set's original cantina.

LASSEN VOLCANIC NATIONAL PARK

California

WEBSITE:
www.nps.gov/lavo

PHONE NUMBER:
530/595-4480

VISITATION RANK:
37

WHY GO:
Explore a volcanic
landscape.

▲ MANZANITA LAKE, LASSEN
VOLCANIC NATIONAL PARK

LASSEN VOLCANIC NATIONAL PARK is one of the oldest national parks—it's also one of the remotest and most primitive. The rugged weather and geographic isolation have preserved a largely unspoiled wilderness. Encased within the park is Mount Lassen, an active volcano with a history of eruptions, the last of which took place in 1914-1917. A partial loop drive through the park follows the stark slopes and jagged rocks of the most recent eruption to an enormous volcano crater. Ample hiking trails, lovely ponds, and plentiful campsites let visitors settle in to enjoy the panoramas of Mount Lassen.

PLANNING YOUR TIME

Located in Northern California, this high-elevation park is only accessible during the short **summer** months when snow melts and daytime temperatures rise to the 80s and 90s. Snow chokes the area October-June, closing the main road through the park. Most visitors arrive in **August** and **September.** Those short on time stick to the park's paved loop road.

ENTRANCES AND FEES

There are two park entrances, both located on Highway 89. The **northwest entrance** (summer only) is at the junction of Highways 89 and 44 near Manzanita Lake. The **southwest entrance** (open year-round) is accessed from Highway 36 and travels north through the park from the Kohm Yah-mah-nee Visitor Center.

The entrance fee is $30 per vehicle ($25 motorcycle, $15 individual) and is good for seven days. In winter, the park road is closed.

VISITORS CENTER

The **Kohm Yah-mah-nee Visitor Center** (21800 Lassen National Park Hwy., Mineral, 530/595-4480, 9am-5pm daily Apr.-Oct., 9am-5pm Wed.-Sun. Nov.-Mar.) has interactive exhibits, a cafe, and a souvenir shop, and a bookstore. Outside, strategically placed benches offer gorgeous views of the mountains and a short interpretive trail tours the paved walkways. Rangers lead programs, including snowshoe walks in winter.

SIGHTS

SULPHUR WORKS

The **Sulphur Works** boardwalk leads to loud boiling mud pots and a small steaming stream that sends up occasional bursts of boiling water. From the southwest entrance station, drive along the park road to the parking area north of the Kohm Yah-mah-nee Visitor Center.

SUMMIT LAKE

Lassen is dotted with tiny lakes. One of the most popular (and most easily accessible) is **Summit Lake**. The bright and shining small lake attracts campers to its two campgrounds and an easy walk navigates its waters and the plantlife. Follow one of the small trails

SULPHUR WORKS

LASSEN VOLCANIC NATIONAL PARK

LASSEN
NATIONAL FOREST

Badger

Table Mountain
6,919ft

To
Redding

Nobles Emigrant Trail

Dwarf Forest

Chaos Jumbles

Reflection
Lake

VOLCANO ADVENTURE
YOUTH CAMP

LOST CREEK GROUP CAMP

ENTRANCE
STATION

Manzanita
Lake

MANZANITA LAKE
CAMPGROUND

CHAOS CRAGS AND
CHAOS JUMBLES

Crags Lake

Lava

8,530ft

CHAOS CRAGS

Lava

Manzanita Creek

Lassen
Creek

Hat
Creek

Anklin Meadows

HOT ROCK

Raker Peak
7,483ft

Hat Creek

DEVASTATED AREA

Devastated Area

HAT
CREEK
TRAILHEAD

Dersch Meadows

Hat Mountain
7,695ft

LASSEN
NATIONAL FOREST

Crescent Crater
8,645ft

LASSEN VOLCANIC
WILDERNESS

Paradise Meadows

Shadow
Lake

SUMMIT LAKE TRAILHEAD

SUMMIT LAKE NORTH

Summit Lake

SUMMIT LAKE SOUTH

Summit

North Fork Bailey Creek

Blue Lake Canyon

Loomis Peak
8,658ft

Crescent
Cliff

LASSEN PEAK
10,457ft

Soda
Lake

Eagle Peak
9,222ft

LASSEN PEAK TRAILHEAD

ROAD'S
HIGH POINT
8,512ft

Cliff
Lake

Reading Peak

Pilot Pinnacle
8,886ft

Lake Helen

Emerald
Lake

Mount Diller
9,087ft

Ridge
Lakes

BUMPASS
TRAILHEAD

Bumpass
Mountain
8,753ft

Upper Meadow

KINGS CREEK
PICNIC AREA

KINGS
CREEK
TRAILHEAD

Kings Creek
Falls

Kings

Diamond Pk
7,968ft

Little Hot Springs Valley

SULPHUR WORKS

Hydrothermal
Areas

Sifford
Lakes

Brokeoff
Mountain

Forest
Lake

Mill Creek
Falls

Bumpass Creek

Crumbaugh
Lake

LASSEN VOLCANIC
WILDERNESS

Devils Kitchen

KOHM YAH-MAH-NEE
VISITOR CENTER

SOUTHWEST

Conard Meadows

Twin Meadows

Panther Creek

ENTRANCE STATION

Mount Conard
8,204ft

Drake
Lake

Mill Creek

Ridge
Lake

Huckleberry
Lake

Blue Lake

To
Mineral

LASSEN
NATIONAL FOREST

To Hwy 44

Prospect Peak
8,338ft

Butte Creek

Bathtub Lake

BUTTE LAKE

Butte Lake

Sunrise Peak
7,139ft

Flat

Pacific Crest Trail

Soap Lake

Emigrant Lake

Nobles Emigrant Trail

Cinder Cone
6,907ft

Fantastic Lava Beds

Lava

Lava

Widow Lake

Ash Butte
7,577ft

Big Bear Lake

Cluster Lakes

Silver Lake

Feather Lake

Little Bear Lake

Fairfield Peak
7,272ft

Snag Lake

Teal Lake

LASSEN VOLCANIC WILDERNESS

Lower Twin Lake

Rainbow Lake

Mount Hoffman
7,883ft

Red Cinder Cone
8,008ft

Upper Twin Lake

Swan Lake

Echo Lake

Hidden Lake

Cameron Meadow

Grassy Creek

LASSEN VOLCANIC NATIONAL PARK

Crater Butte
7,267ft

Grassy Swale

Horseshoe Lake

Jakey Lake

Inspiration Point

Crystal Cliffs
7,548ft

Pilot Mountain
7,175ft

Kings Creek

Crystal Lake

Glen Lake

Island Lake

Saddle Mountain
7,638ft

Indian Lake

Juniper Lake

East Lake

Corral Meadow

Flatiron Ridge

DRAKESBAD GUEST RANCH

WARNER VALLEY

WARNER VALLEY TRAILHEAD

JUNIPER LAKE

Bonte Peak
7,777ft

Boiling Springs Lake

Hot Springs Creek

Pacific Crest Trail

MOUNT HARKNESS FIRE LOOKOUT TOWER

Hydrothermal Areas

Terminal Geyser

Sifford Mountain
7,408ft

Little Willow Lake

Kelly Mountain

Warner Valley

Willow Lake

To Chester

To Chester

0   1 mi
0   1 km

© AVALON TRAVEL

Top ❸

BUMPASS HELL

❶ TOUR LASSEN VOLCANIC SCENIC BYWAY

From the southwest entrance, the **park road** (Hwy. 89, open June–early Oct.) twists and turns for 30 miles through a volcanic landscape. The stunning drive climbs to 8,512 feet below the summit of Lassen Peak. Scenic pullouts en route offer places for viewing and photographing the scenery. South of Lassen Peak, the road has multiple switchbacks; north of the peak, there are fewer curves.

❷ WALK THROUGH BUMPASS HELL

North of the Sulphur Works, **Bumpass Hell** is packed with hydrothermal activity. Walk the partial boardwalks along the **Bumpass Nature Trail** (3 mi. rt., 2 hrs., moderate) to peek at boiling mud pots, fumaroles, steaming springs, and bubbling pools. The strong smell of sulfur proves that this volcano is far from extinct.

❸ SCALE THE SUMMIT OF LASSEN PEAK

Majestic **Lassen Peak** stretches 10,457 feet into the sky. The craggy and broken mountain peak is all that's left after the 1915 eruption—hence the lack of vegetation. Climb 2.5 miles to the summit or simply settle for multiple views of its raw landscape from pullouts on the park road. The Lassen Peak Parking Area and Viewpoint offers the closest look.

LASSEN PEAK

Best Hike

LASSEN PEAK TRAIL

DISTANCE: 4.8 miles round-trip
DURATION: 3-5 hours
ELEVATION CHANGE: 1,957 feet
EFFORT: strenuous
TRAILHEAD: Lassen Peak

The **Lassen Peak Trail** is the park's must-do hike. From the Lassen Peak trailhead, this loose rock path climbs 1,957 feet to the highest point on Lassen Peak via a starkly beautiful, unusual trail. Long views extend across the park and beyond. Along the way, exhibits explain the fascinating scenery of volcanic remains, lakes, wildlife, and rock formations. Due to the high elevation, the trail tends to be cool even in summer heat; sea-level visitors may feel winded.

down to the edge of the water to eke out a spot on the miniscule beach.

DEVASTATED AREA

When Lassen Peak blew its top in 1915, the eruption destroyed a tremendous part of the mountain. Boiling mud and explosive gases tore off the side of the peak, killing all the vegetation in the area. A hail of lava rained down, creating new rocks—ranging in size from gravel to boulders—across the north side of the mountain. Today, the **Devastated Area** north of Summit Lake offers an interpretive, wheelchair-accessible walk (0.5 mi. rt.) through a small part of the disrupted mountainside to see some of the world's youngest rocks, plus renewing vegetation.

CHAOS CRAGS AND JUMBLES

In the northwest corner of the park, a massive rock avalanche about 300 years ago created the broken **Chaos Jumbles**. The avalanche was so big and came down so fast that it trapped a pocket of air underneath. The regrowth of the living landscape has allowed a greater variety of competing plants to get a foothold. Today, visitors can enjoy the broader-than-average variety of coniferous trees at the park road pullout.

LOOMIS MUSEUM

Near the northwest entrance is the **Loomis Museum** (530/595-6140, 9am-5pm Fri.-Sun. mid-May-mid-June, 9am-5pm daily mid-June-Oct., free). The interpretive museum shows the history of Mount Lassen, focusing heavily on the 1914-1915 eruptions photographed by B. F. Loomis. The photos offer a rare chance to see the devastation and following stages of regrowth on the volcanic slopes.

RECREATION
HIKING

From the trailhead (13 miles north of the southwest entrance), the **Kings Creek Falls Trail** (3 mi. rt., 2 hrs., moderate) treks downhill to waterfalls. Admire the small cascade and pool before beginning the 700-foot climb back up.

From the Summit Lake trailhead, a forested path runs the length of Summit Lake to **Echo Lake** (4.4 mi. rt., 2-3 hrs., moderate). With a gentle elevation gain of only 500 feet, the pleasant walk reaches Echo Lake in 2.2 miles with views of Lassen Peak.

From the trailhead (south of the southwest entrance station), **Brokeoff Mountain** (7.4 mi. rt., 5-7 hrs., strenuous) grunts up a 2,600-foot ascent from a mile-high starting point. This is one of the toughest hikes, but the reward is big panoramic views.

For a radical change of scenery, take the **Cinder Cone Trail** from Butte Lake (4-5 miles, moderate). The trail rises 800 vertical feet over two miles; to lengthen the hike, walk down the south side of the cone. Geology and photography buffs will like this hike, which shows off some of the more interesting and less-seen volcanic history of Mount Lassen.

ONE DAY IN LASSEN

Visitors short on time can enjoy most of the park's sights by cruising along the **Lassen Volcanic Scenic Byway.** Pick up the park's road guide from the visitor center and enjoy the 30-mile road trip!

BACKPACKING

Lassen offers backpacking through a volcanic landscape dotted with scenic lakes. Wilderness permits are required on the **Pacific Crest Trail** (available at the visitors center, bear canister required). For families and beginning backpackers, an 11-mile loop from the Summit Lake trailhead takes in seven lakes; short side trips add more lakes.

WHERE TO STAY

INSIDE THE PARK

Lassen has few in-park accommodations, most of them campgrounds (one with cabins). Four developed campgrounds are accessible via the paved park road; the remaining primitive campgrounds are via dirt roads. **Reservations** (877/444-6777, www.recreation.gov) are highly recommended six months in advance for **Manzanita Lake, Summit Lake,** and **Butte Lake.** All campsites have picnic tables and fire pits.

Near the northwest entrance, **Manzanita Lake** (May-Oct., $24) is the largest campground and has flush toilets, potable running water, an RV dump station, and showers. Trailers and campers up to 35 feet are allowed. Reservations go fast for the rustic cabins ($70-95) that line the north shore of the lake. The **Manzanita Lake Camper Store** (8am-6pm daily May-Sept., hours vary seasonally) sells hot food and snacks.

At 7,000 feet, **Summit Lake North and South** (late June-Sept., $20-22) are split on either side of Summit Lake, with scenery and prime hiking. The two developed campgrounds have flush toilets; bring water for drinking and washing.

Near the Kohm Yah-mah-nee Visitors Center, **Southwest Walk-In** (first come, first served, year-round, $10-16) has tent-only campsites that are reached via a short, paved walk from the parking area (RVs can park in the lot). In summer, there are flush toilets

▼ BROKEOFF MOUNTAIN

and drinking water; fees are reduced in winter when the water is shut off.

The **Lassen Cafe & Gift** (Kohm Yah-mah-nee Visitor Center, 530/595-3555, 9am-4pm daily Apr.-May, 9am-5pm June-Oct.) sells burgers, pizza, coffee, and ice cream.

In the park's remote northeast corner, accessed from Highway 44, a gravel road reaches the 6,100-foot **Butte Lake** (June-Oct., $15). The large campground has pit toilets, but no drinking water. Trailers and RVs are limited to 35 feet. The nearby Butte Lake has a boat launch and hiking trails.

Located on the park's east side, a rough dirt road leads to **Juniper Lake** (north of Chester, June-Oct., $12). Located next to 6,752-foot Juniper Lake, the campground has pit toilets and no drinking water. A boat launch sits about 1.5 miles north. Hiking trails encircle the lake.

North of Chester, a dirt road accesses small **Warner Valley** (June-Sept., $16), which has pit toilets and drinking water. Trailers are not allowed. Nearby hiking trails showcase volcanic features.

Located near the southwest entrance station, the **Drakesbad Guest Ranch** (Warner Valley Rd., Chester, 866/999-0914, www.drakesbad.com, June-mid-Oct., from $189) is an all-inclusive ranch with horseback riding, swimming, and fishing.

OUTSIDE THE PARK

The nearest lodgings are about 9 miles south in **Mineral** and in the tiny town of **Chester,** 25 miles east of the southwest entrance on Highways 89/36.

GETTING THERE AND AROUND

AIR

The closest international airport is **Sacramento International Airport** (SMF, 6900 Airport Blvd., Sacramento, 916/929-5411, www.sacairports.org), where car rentals are available.

CAR

Lassen Volcanic National Park is located 150-175 miles (3 hrs.) north of Sacramento. Take I-5 north to Red Bluff, then follow Highway 36 east for 43 miles past Mineral. Turn left onto Highway 89, which leads to the southwest park entrance.

Highway 89 becomes the main road through the park; the visitors center, campgrounds, trailheads, and lakes cluster along it. It is closed from late October to May, June, or July, depending on weather and snowfall.

The park has no public transportation; exploration requires a vehicle. Manzanita Lake Campground store has the only **gas** station. Otherwise, gas up en route in Red Bluff, Chester, or Susanville.

SIGHTS NEARBY

Mount Shasta (County Hwy. A10, Mount Shasta City), a dormant volcano that last erupted in 1786, towers 14,162 feet above the region and offers camping, hiking trails, and winter sports.

LASSEN VOLCANIC NATIONAL PARK

REDWOOD NATIONAL AND STATE PARKS

California

WEBSITE:
www.nps.gov/redw

PHONE NUMBER:
707/465-7335

VISITATION RANK:
40

WHY GO:
Feel small beneath
coast redwoods.

▲ REDWOOD NATIONAL PARK

Of all the natural wonders California has to offer, it's the redwoods that inspire pure awe. The towering coastal redwoods *(Sequoia sempervirens)* grow along the state's rugged north coast. The best places to explore extensive wild groves of these gargantuan treasures are in the **REDWOOD NATIONAL AND STATE PARKS**, which line the coast from Eureka to Crescent City. Along U.S. 101, the cluster of state and national parks lure travelers with numerous hiking trails, forested campgrounds, kitschy tourist traps, and some of the tallest and oldest trees on the continent.

PLANNING YOUR TIME

The Redwood National and State Parks meander 40 miles along the northern California coast between Crescent City in the north and the old logging town of Eureka in the south. In addition to **Redwood National Park**, this parkland includes three state parks—**Prairie Creek Redwoods, Del Norte Coast Redwoods,** and **Jedediah Smith Redwoods.** Combined, the region encompasses most of California's northern redwood forests.

Summer is the busiest season, with cool temperatures in the 40s-60s, fog, and damp weather. Fall, winter, and early spring (Oct.-Apr.) can deliver copious rain.

ENTRANCES AND FEES

U.S. 101 connects the multiple park entrances. Redwood National Park has no entrance fee; however, Prairie Creek Redwoods, Del Norte Coast Redwoods, and Jedediah Smith Redwoods State Parks collect entrance and day-use fees.

VISITORS CENTERS

Four visitors centers offer information, exhibits, maps, ranger-led talks and walks, and restrooms.

Thomas H. Kuchel Visitor Center (U.S. 101, Orick, 707/465-7765, 9am-5pm daily spring-fall, 9am-4pm daily winter) is the largest facility, with a ranger station, maps, advice, permits for backcountry camping, and books. In the summer, rangers lead talks and coast walks.

Prairie Creek Visitor Center (Newton B. Drury Scenic Pkwy., 707/488-2039, 9am-5pm daily summer, 9am-4pm Thurs.-Mon. fall-spring) includes a small interpretive museum that describes the history of the California redwood forests. A tiny bookshop adjoins the museum.

Hiouchi Visitor Center (Hwy. 199, Hiouchi, 707/458-3294, 9am-5pm daily summer, 9am-4pm daily winter) has backcountry permits, a park movie, and a picnic area.

Jedediah Smith Visitors Center (U.S. 101, Hiouchi, 707/458-3496, 9am-5pm daily summer) has information and materials about all of the nearby parks.

SIGHTS
REDWOOD NATIONAL PARK

This iconic park harbors old-growth groves of coastal sequoias. These sacred places spur the imagination with their lush, verdant beauty.

PRAIRIE CREEK REDWOODS STATE PARK

Prairie Creek Redwoods State Park (Newton B. Drury Scenic Pkwy., 707/488-2039, www.parks.ca.gov, sunrise-sunset daily, day use $8) has miles of wild beach, roaming wildlife, and a popular hike through a one-of-a-kind fern-draped canyon. Prairie Creek offers a sampler platter of the best natural elements of California's North Coast.

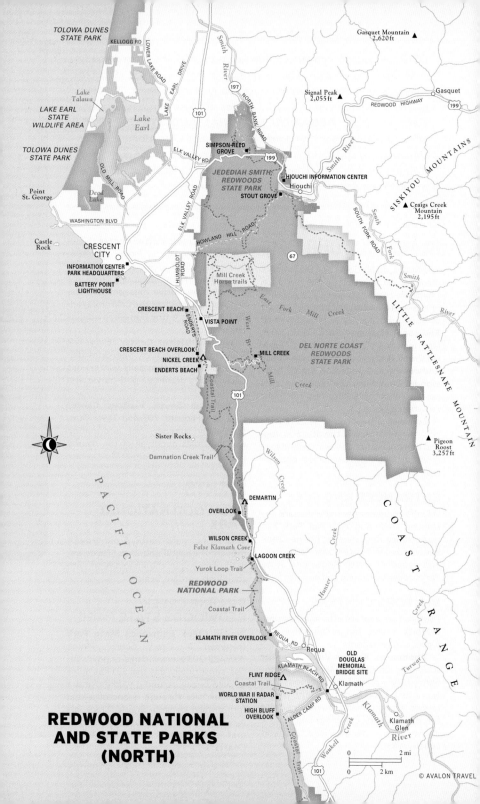

REDWOOD NATIONAL AND STATE PARKS (NORTH)

© AVALON TRAVEL

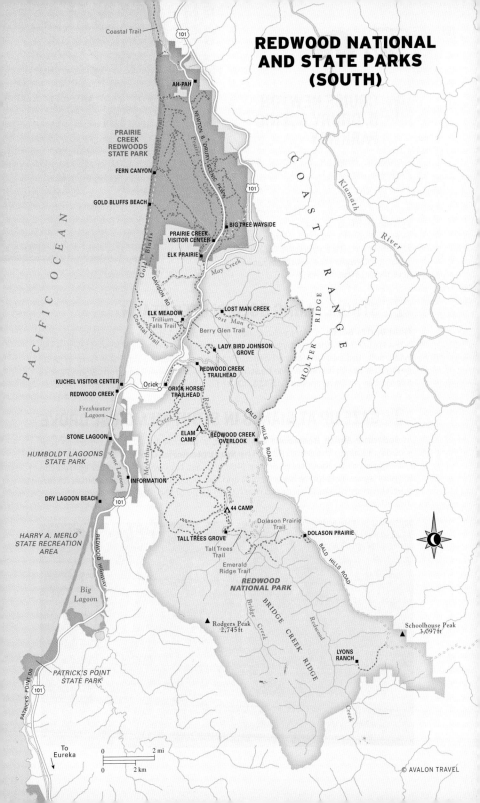

REDWOOD NATIONAL AND STATE PARKS (SOUTH)

Coastal Trail

101

AH-PAH

PRAIRIE CREEK REDWOODS STATE PARK

FERN CANYON

GOLD BLUFFS BEACH

BIG TREE WAYSIDE

PRAIRIE CREEK VISITOR CENTER

ELK PRAIRIE

Newton B. Drury Scenic Pkwy

Prairie Creek

101

May Creek

COAST RANGE

Klamath River

HOLTER RIDGE

DAVISON RD

Coastal Trail

ELK MEADOW
Trillium Falls Trail

LOST MAN CREEK

Lost Man Cr.

Berry Glen Trail

LADY BIRD JOHNSON GROVE

REDWOOD CREEK TRAILHEAD

KUCHEL VISITOR CENTER

REDWOOD CREEK

Orick

ORICK HORSE TRAILHEAD

Freshwater Lagoon

PACIFIC OCEAN

Gold Bluffs

McArthur Creek

Redwood Creek

BALD HILLS ROAD

STONE LAGOON

Stone Lagoon

ELAM CAMP

REDWOOD CREEK OVERLOOK

HUMBOLDT LAGOONS STATE PARK

INFORMATION

DRY LAGOON BEACH

101

44 CAMP

Dolason Prairie Trail

DOLASON PRAIRIE

HARRY A. MERLO STATE RECREATION AREA

TALL TREES GROVE

Tall Trees Trail

Emerald Ridge Trail

BALD HILLS ROAD

REDWOOD HIGHWAY

Big Lagoon

REDWOOD NATIONAL PARK

BRIDGE CREEK RIDGE

Rodgers Peak 2,745 ft

Bridge Creek

Redwood Creek

Schoolhouse Peak 3,097 ft

LYONS RANCH

PATRICK'S POINT DR

PATRICK'S POINT STATE PARK

101

To Eureka

0   2 mi

0   2 km

© AVALON TRAVEL

Top ❸

① CRUISE NEWTON B. DRURY SCENIC PARKWAY

Gorgeous **Newton B. Drury Scenic Parkway** parallels U.S. 101 through the redwoods. Along the parkway, old-growth redwoods line the road and offer an up-close view of the forest ecosystem, with a grove or a trailhead every hundred yards for further exploration. The north entrance is four miles south of Klamath; the south entrance is six miles north of Orick.

NEWTON B. DRURY SCENIC PARKWAY

② STROLL ALONG GOLD BLUFFS BEACH

Gold Bluffs Beach is truly wild. Lonely waves pound the shore, a spikey grove of Sitka spruce tops the nearby bluffs, and herds of Roosevelt elk frequently roam the wide, salt-and-pepper-colored beach. Prospectors found gold flakes here in 1850, giving the beach its name. The beach, part of Prairie Creek Redwoods State Park, is accessible via Davison Road off U.S. 101 at Elk Meadow.

③ GAZE UP AT GIANTS IN STOUT MEMORIAL GROVE

In **Jedediah Smith Redwoods State Park,** a pristine forest of old-growth redwoods sits along the Smith River. The **Stout Memorial Grove** is home to some of the biggest and oldest trees on the North Coast that were somehow spared the loggers' saws. This grove is very quiet and less populated than others, since its far-north latitude makes it harder to reach than some of the other big redwood groves in California.

STOUT MEMORIAL GROVE IN JEDEDIAH SMITH REDWOOD STATE PARK

ONE DAY IN THE REDWOODS

A drive along U.S. 101 on the Redwood Highway gets you up close to the looming trees. Make your first stop at the **Thomas H. Kuchel Visitor Center** to learn about the giant trees, then take a walk to the beach. Walk the **Lady Bird Johnson Trail** in Redwoods National Park then drive north to the otherworldly **Newton B. Drury Scenic Parkway** in Prairie Creek Redwoods State Park.

Stop at the **Big Tree Wayside,** home to the 304-foot-high **Big Tree.** Its life was almost cut short by a homesteader who wanted to cut it down to use the stump as a dance floor. Follow the short, five-minute loop trail near the Big Tree to see other neighboring giants.

Look for a herd of **Roosevelt elk** at Elk Prairie, a stretch of open grassland along the southern end of the parkway. This subspecies of elk stands up to five feet high and weighs up to 1,000 pounds. The best times to see the elk are early morning and around sunset. During the mating season (Aug.-Oct.), the bugling of the bulls fills the air.

DEL NORTE COAST REDWOODS STATE PARK

South of Crescent City, **Del Norte Coast Redwoods State Park** (Mill Creek Campground Rd. off U.S. 101, 707/465-7335, www.parks.ca.gov, day use $8) encompasses a variety of ecosystems, including eight miles of wild coastline, second-growth redwood forest, and virgin old-growth forests. Del Norte State Park has no visitors center, but you can get information from the **Crescent City Information Center** (1111 2nd St., Crescent City, 707/465-7306, 9am-5pm daily spring-fall, 9am-4pm daily winter).

JEDEDIAH SMITH REDWOODS STATE PARK

The **Jedediah Smith Redwoods State Park** (U.S. 199, 9 miles east of Crescent City, 707/465-7335, www.parks.ca.gov, day use $8) is the northernmost of the redwoods parks. It preserves a pristine forest of old-growth redwoods along the Smith River in the **Stout Memorial Grove.**

▼ ROOSEVELT ELK

PRAIRIE CREEK BRIDGE

RECREATION
HIKING
Redwood National Park

The most popular place to get close to the trees is the **Lady Bird Johnson Loop** (Bald Hills Rd., 1.4 mi. rt., 1 hr., easy). The level loop provides an intimate view of the redwood and fir forests that define this region, and spring visitors get treated to rhododendron blooms. Pick up an interpretive brochure at the trailhead.

The cool, dark **Trillium Falls Trail** (Davison Rd. at Elk Meadow, 2.5 mi. rt., 1.5 hrs., easy-moderate) has striking redwoods and a small, moss-flanked waterfall that is lovely any time of year, but best in spring when the water volume peaks. The trail gets its name from the white trillium that bloom in spring.

The **Lost Man Creek Trail** (east of Elk Meadow, 1 mile off U.S. 101, 1-22 mi. rt., easy-difficult) has it all. The first half-mile is perfect for wheelchairs and families with small children. But as the lush redwood-and-fern-lined trail rolls along, grades get steeper and more challenging. To reach the Lost Man Creek picnic grounds at 11 miles requires ascending more than 3,000 feet of elevation and crossing several streams. Bikes are permitted on this trail.

To sink into a full day of enchantment in this moist forest, hike the **Redwood Creek Trail** (Bald Hills Rd. spur off U.S. 101, 16 mi. rt., 7-9 hrs., strenuous), which follows Redwood Creek to the **Tall Trees Grove.** Two bridges over the river are installed in summer only (May-Sept.) along the route.

Prairie Creek Redwoods State Park

Near Gold Bluffs Beach, **Fern Canyon Loop** (0.7 mi. rt., 30 min., easy) runs through a narrow canyon carved by Home Creek. Ferns, mosses, and other water-loving plants grow thick up the sides of the canyon, creating a beautiful vertical carpet of greenery (scenes from *Jurassic Park 2* and *Return of the Jedi* were filmed here).

The **James Irvine Loop** and **Miners' Ridge** (12.4 mi. rt., 7 hrs., moderate) starts from the visitors center on the **James Irvine Trail** and reaches the beach. Return on the **Miner's Ridge Trail.** As you head out, bear right when you can, following the trail through enormous trees until it joins Fern Canyon Trail. Turn left when you get to the coast and walk along Gold Bluffs Beach for 1.2 miles to the campground, turning east to head back on the more demanding trail toward the visitors center.

Del Norte Coast Redwoods State Park

In summer, Mill Creek Campground is the trailhead for several trails (access is from U.S. 101 when the campground is closed). The **Trestle Loop Trail** (1 mi. rt., 30 min., easy) trots along a defunct railroad route from the logging era with trestles and other artifacts along the way. It's a good place to tour second-growth redwoods. A leisurely walk on the **Nature Loop Trail** (1 mi. rt., 30 min., easy) educates visitors with interpretive signage about the unique redwood trees and ecosystem.

Jedediah Smith Redwoods State Park

A shady hike beneath 1,000-year-old redwoods, the **Simpson Reed Loop** (1 mi. rt., 30 min., easy) descends to the banks of the Smith River, where fallen trees create pools for fish. Look for red-legged frogs on the damp forest floor.

From the Hiouchi Visitor Center and Jedediah Smith Campground, paths cross a summer footbridge over the turquoise Smith River to access several trailheads. To hike north along the river, take the **Hiouchi Trail** (2 mi. rt., 1 hr., moderate) through old-growth redwoods into a streamside environment of wild berries and Pacific madrone.

For a more aggressive trek along a salmon stream, follow the **Mill Creek Trail** (7.5 mi. rt., 4 hrs., strenuous) upstream through old-growth redwoods to unpaved Howland Hill Road. Fall brings on reds and golds of big-leaf maples along the clear stream.

The **Boy Scout Tree Trail** (Howland Hill Rd., 5.2 mi. rt., 3 hrs., moderate) is usually quiet with few hikers, and its gargantuan forest will make you feel truly tiny. A spur at the end of the trail leads to a double-trunked redwood tree. The trail ends at Fern Falls.

BACKPACKING

Hikers can don an overnight pack on the Redwood Creek Trail for a 2-3-day trip. Designated campsites are at **Elam Camp** (3 sites) and **44 Camp** (4 sites), plus a segment along the river with large gravel bars that has dispersed camping. The northern section of the **California Coastal Trail** (CCT, www.californiacoastaltrail.info) runs through Redwood National Park and has primitive backcountry sites. The trail is reasonably well marked with signs featuring the CCT logo.

Backcountry camping is allowed by permit (free), available in person from the visitors centers.

WHERE TO STAY

INSIDE THE PARKS

Redwood National Park has no designated campgrounds, but several state park campgrounds take **reservations** (800/444-7275, www.reservecalifornia.com, mid-May-Sept., $35) during the busy summer season. Book reservations six months in advance to guarantee a spot. Outside of summer,

▼ REDWOOD NATIONAL PARK

campgrounds are first come, first served. Sites include picnic tables, fire pits, flush toilets, showers, and food storage lockers, but no hookups.

Tucked under ancient redwoods, **Elk Prairie Campground** (Prairie Creek Redwoods, 127011 Newton B. Drury Scenic Pkwy., year-round) has 75 sites for tents and RVs. A campfire area is an easy walk north of the campground, with evening programs hosted by rangers and volunteers.

Gold Bluffs Beach Campground (Prairie Creek Redwoods, Davison Rd., year-round) has 26 beachfront sites for tents only with wide ocean views.

Mill Creek Campground (Del Norte Redwoods, U.S. 101, mid-May-Sept.) has 145 sites for tents and RVs spread beneath young redwoods.

Jedediah Smith Campground (Jedediah Smith Redwoods, U.S. 199, Hiouchi, year-round) has 86 sites for tents and RVs under old-growth redwoods on the banks of Smith River. Most sites are near the River Beach Trail. Reservations are advised, especially for summer.

OUTSIDE THE PARKS

Small towns dot the coast along U.S. 101. Look for accommodations and restaurants in **Crescent City, Trinidad, Garberville, Eureka,** and **Arcata.**

GETTING THERE AND AROUND

The Redwood National and State Parks line 40 miles of U.S. 101. There is no public transportation; a vehicle is required for exploration.

AIR

The closest airport is the small regional **Del Norte County Airport/Jack McNamara** (CEC, 250 Dale Rupert Rd., Crescent City, 707/464-7288, http://flycrescentcity.com). The closest international airports are **San Francisco International Airport** (SFO, U.S. 101, San Mateo, 800/435-9736, 650/821-8211, www.flysfo.com) and **Sacramento International Airport** (SMF, 6900 Airport Blvd., 916/929-5411, www.sacairports.org), both a six-hour drive from the parks.

CAR

From San Francisco, take U.S. 101 north to Leggett, where it meets with Highway 1. Follow U.S. 101 north to Orick, where you'll find the Thomas H. Kuchel Visitor Center.

From Sacramento, take I-5 north to Highway 299 west, which ends in Arcata. Turn north on U.S. 101 to Orick. The 330-mile drive will take about 5-6 hours.

Prairie Creek Redwoods is 9 miles north of Orick on U.S. 101. The Newton B. Drury Scenic Parkway parallels U.S. 101 as an alternate route.

Del Norte Coast Redwoods is on U.S. 101, 19 miles north of Prairie Creek Redwoods. The park entrance is on Hamilton Road, east of U.S. 101.

To reach Jedediah Smith Redwoods State Park, follow north along U.S. 101 to U.S. 199. Turn left onto U.S. 199 and continue east for 9 miles.

SIGHTS NEARBY

Humboldt Redwoods State Park (17119 Avenue of the Giants, Weott, 707/946-2409, www.parks.ca.gov or www.humboldtredwoods.org, 9am-5pm daily Apr.-Oct., 10am-4pm daily Nov.-Mar.) lines the **Avenue of the Giants** (Hwy. 254, between Weott and Myers Flat), paralleling U.S. 101 and the Eel River for 32 miles between Garberville and Scotia.

Patrick's Point State Park (4150 Patrick's Point Dr., Trinidad, 707/677-3570, www.parks.ca.gov, day use $8) is a rambling coastal park with campgrounds, trails, and beaches.

Richardson Grove State Park (1600 U.S. 101, 707/247-3318, www.parks.ca.gov, daily sunrise-sunset, day use $8) is the first of the old-growth redwoods heading north on U.S. 101. It has a visitors center and campground.

Trees of Mystery (15500 U.S. 101 N., 707/482-2251 or 800/638-3389, www.treesofmystery.net, June-Aug. daily 8am-7pm, Sept.-Oct. daily 8:30am-6:30pm, Nov.-May daily 9am-5pm), a roadside tourist stop, offers a SkyTrail gondola ride through the old-growth redwoods, a palatial gift shop, and a little-known gem: a Native American museum.

PINNACLES
NATIONAL PARK

California

PASSPORT STAMPS ▼▼▼

WEBSITE:
www.nps.gov/pinn

PHONE NUMBER:
831/389-4485

VISITATION RANK:
47

WHY GO:
Scramble up volcanic peaks and through talus caves.

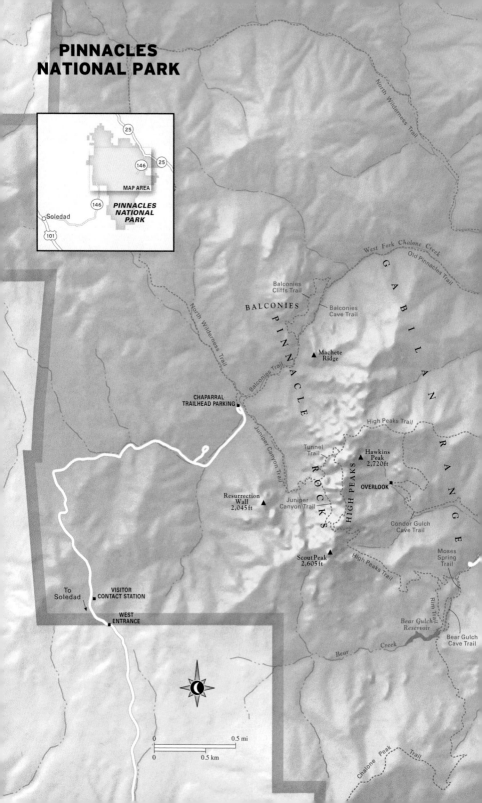

PINNACLES
NATIONAL PARK

MAP AREA

25

146 **25**

**PINNACLES
NATIONAL
PARK**

146

Soledad

101

North Wilderness Trail

West Fork Chalone Creek

Old Pinnacles Trail

Balconies
Cliffs Trail

BALCONIES

Balconies
Cave Trail

G A B I L A N

North Wilderness Trail

P I N N A C L E

Machete
Ridge

Balconies Trail

High Peaks Trail

CHAPARRAL
TRAILHEAD PARKING

Tunnel
Trail

Hawkins
Peak
2,720 ft

R A N G E

Juniper Canyon Trail

Resurrection
Wall
2,045 ft

Juniper Canyon Trail

R O C K S

HIGH PEAKS

OVERLOOK

Condor Gulch
Cave Trail

Moses
Spring
Trail

Scout Peak
2,605 ft

High Peaks Trail

To Soledad

VISITOR
CONTACT STATION

WEST
ENTRANCE

Rim Trail

Bear Gulch
Reservoir

Bear Gulch
Cave Trail

Bear   Creek

0   0.5 mi

0   0.5 km

Chalone Peak   Trail

Chock-full of natural castles of rock spires, towers, walls, canyons, and caves, **PINNACLES NATIONAL PARK** rises above the Gabilan Mountains on the east side of the Salinas Valley. A natural wonder created by volcanic activity, Pinnacles was a national monument until it was elevated to national park status in 2013. This stunning 26,000-acre park of intricate geology has more than 30 miles of hiking trails. It also holds some of the world's largest talus caves, created when boulders become lodged in its narrow canyons. Along its rock faces climbers ascend cracks and nubbins. With a unique blend of flora and fauna, Pinnacles is home to California condors, Townsend's big-eared bats, California red-legged frogs, 100 species of wildflowers, and 400 bee species.

PLANNING YOUR TIME

East of the Salinas Valley, in the parched hills of the Gabilan Mountains, Pinnacles National Park (5000 Hwy. 146, Paicines) attracts hikers, rock climbers, cave explorers, and birders. True to its name, the park is studded with huge rock formations jutting into the sky.

The weather is generally warm and dry throughout the year, but is blazing hot in summer. **Spring** (Mar.-Apr.) is high season, when visitors flood the park for rare access to the upper and lower Bear Gulch Caves. Regardless of when you visit, it is essential to bring plenty of water with you on the trails.

ENTRANCES AND FEES

Pinnacles National Park has two entrances, both accessed via Highway 146. No roads connect the two entrances. The **east entrance** accesses the park campground and popular Bear Gulch Day Use Area, with multiple trail options. On the **west side** is a ranger station parking area that closes at night. The west entrance is only accessible when the park gate (7:30am-8pm daily) is open. There are no services or campgrounds on the west side.

The entrance fee is $30 per vehicle ($25 per person on foot or bicycle).

VISITORS CENTERS

Located on the east side of the park, the **Pinnacles Visitor Center** (831/389-4485, 9:30am-5pm daily) is the main source of information for visitors and campers. The **Bear Gulch Nature Center** (10am-4pm Sat.-Sun. Jan-May), located in the Bear Gulch Day Use Area, has wildlife and nature exhibits.

The west entrance hosts the **West Pinnacles Visitor Contact Station** (831/389-4427, 9am-4:30pm Sat.-Sun.), where you can pay the entrance fee; however, there are no services.

RECREATION

HIKING

Pinnacles has more than 30 miles of hiking trails and is home to two **talus caves,** which are open seasonally to hikers. Both close during specific periods to protect the park's hibernating colonies of Townsend bats. Exploring the caves is fun; a self-guided hike through the caves requires some scrambling through narrow passageways, which may be wet in early spring. Flashlights or headlamps are required. Check at the visitors center first to confirm that the caves are open.

One of the best ways to experience the geology of Pinnacles is via the west side's **Juniper Canyon Loop** (4.3 mi. rt., 2-3 hrs., strenuous), which leads hikers through a steep, narrow traverse of the High Peaks. Begin on the Juniper Canyon Trail to climb 2,605-foot Scout Peak, where you may spot a condor soaring overhead. The loop then swings through High Peaks before returning to the trailhead.

Top ❸

❶ SCRAMBLE UP BEAR GULCH CAVE

BEAR GULCH CAVE

From the Bear Gulch Day Use Area, a series of well-signed, connected trails leads to **Bear Gulch Cave** (2.2 mi rt., 1.5 hrs., moderate). The high rocky walls of this talus cave slope inward as the 0.7-mile path meanders past lodged boulders and along Bear Creek. Exiting the upper portion of the cave, the trail climbs to scenic **Bear Gulch Reservoir,** a convenient spot to catch your breath and enjoy a quick lunch.

To start, head out on the **High Peaks Trail;** turn left onto the **Moses Spring Trail** to reach the entrance to the **Bear Gulch Cave Trail.** The return loop follows the **Rim Trail** back to the High Peaks Trail; turn right to return to the day-use area, or left to scale the High Peaks Trail (6.7 miles, strenuous).

Mid-May to mid-July, a gate closes the upper portion of Bear Gulch Cave to protect the hibernating colony of Townsend bats. Access to both upper and lower Bear Gulch Cave is open to hikers for only a few weeks in March and October.

❷ CRAWL THROUGH BALCONIES CAVE

The **Balconies Cave** (1.2-2.5 mi. rt., 30-90 min., moderate) can be reached via a 0.6-mile trail from the west side parking area or on a level 2.5-mile trail from the **Old Pinnacles Trailhead** parking area on the east side. The Balconies Cave offers a fun, 0.4-mile scramble through a series of stacked boulders, a shorter but more tactile and hands-on exploration of the park's talus caves. The Cave Trail exits into a loop with the **Balconies Cliffs Trail** (an option for claustrophobic hikers) for a 1.4-mile return to the west side.

It's possible to turn this trail into a loop by taking the **High Peaks Trail to Balconies Cave Loop** (8.4 mi. rt., 4-5 hrs., strenuous) into the heart of the park. Start with the High Peaks Trail on the east side, as the elevation gain is significantly easier.

❸ HIKE THE HIGH PEAKS TRAIL

DISTANCE: 6.7 miles round-trip

DURATION: 4-5 hours

ELEVATION CHANGE: 1,425 feet

EFFORT: strenuous

TRAILHEAD: Bear Gulch Day Use Area

The star trail in the park is the **High Peaks Trail,** a tough haul to the top of the park's volcanic pinnacles with views across multiple counties. The 0.7-mile portion of the trail climbs across the rock-strewn ridgeline via steps carved into the rock with handrails for support. It's almost like a beginner's version of Yosemite's famed Half Dome hike. Multiple trails connect with the High Peaks Trail, making it possible to finish a loop of the entire park via the **Balconies Cave Trail** (8.4 mi. rt., 4-5 hrs., strenuous) or the **Condor Gulch Trail** (5.3 mi. rt., 3 hrs., strenuous).

BALCONIES CAVE TRAIL

From the east side, hikers can reach the Bear Gulch Cave via the **Moses Spring Trail** (2.2 mi. rt., 1.5 hrs., moderate) to Bear Gulch Reservoir. From the reservoir, the **Chalone Peak Trail** (9 mi. rt., 4-5 hrs., strenuous) continues 3.3 miles to 3,304-foot North Chalone Peak.

The **Old Pinnacles Trail** (Old Pinnacles Trailhead, 5.3 mi. rt., 2-3 hrs., moderate) tours Balconies Cave via Machete Ridge and the Balconies Cliffs. For a more intense hike from this end of the park, the **Condor Gulch-High Peaks Loop** (Bear Gulch Day Use Area, 5.3 mi. rt., 3 hrs., strenuous, 1,300-foot elevation gain) trots through multiple rock formations.

ROCK CLIMBING

Most of the park's best rock climbing is on the east side, where routes range from beginner to advanced, but the rock here is volcanic breccia and prone to weakness. The **Tourist Trap** and the **Discovery Wall** are the closest climbs from the Bear Gulch Day Use Area. For more information, visit **Friends of Pinnacles** (www.pinnacles.org), an organization dedicated to climbing at Pinnacles.

WHERE TO STAY
INSIDE THE PARK

The **Pinnacles Campground** (877/444-6777, www.recreation.gov, year-round, tents $23, RVs $36) is located at the east entrance and has 99 tent sites, 36 RV sites, and 14 group sites. Most are shaded by oaks and all come with a picnic table, fire ring, and bathrooms, with showers nearby. There is a dump station to accommodate RVs and all sites have electrical hookups. The camp store sells food and necessities.

OUTSIDE THE PARK

Accommodations and dining options are located in **Salinas, Soledad,** and **King City.**

GETTING THERE

Pinnacles has two entrances, but no roads connect them—making the drive from one to the other a two-hour endeavor. To reach the **east entrance** from the north, take U.S. 101 to Highway 25 through the town of Hollister. After another 30 miles, turn right on Highway 146 to the park entrance. From San Francisco, the trip is 130 miles and takes nearly 2.5 hours. From Monterey, it is 75 miles and 1.5 hours.

PINNACLES NATIONAL PARK

For the **west entrance,** continue south on U.S. 101, past Salinas to Highway 146 in Soledad. Take Highway 146 east for a very slow 14 miles. There are no services at this entrance. The trip from Monterey, via Highway 68, is 60 miles, taking a little over an hour.

GETTING AROUND

There is limited parking on both the east and west side lots. On weekends, a free **shuttle** stops at the Pinnacles Visitor Center and the Bear Gulch area on the east side of the park. Plan to board the shuttle early (before 10am) to avoid the hour-plus wait on weekends.

CALIFORNIA CONDORS

With wings spanning 10 feet from tip to tip, California condors are some of the area's most impressive natural treasures. The largest flying bird in North America, their presence here is a story of hope and testament to the success of conservation efforts. In the early 1980s, the condor population had dropped to a low of 22 raptors, due to their susceptibility to lead poisoning and through deaths caused by electric power lines, habitat loss, and hunting. A captive breeding program was initiated for this highly endangered species and, after more than 30 years, there are now more than 400 California condors.

The jutting spires of Pinnacles are home to about 60 California condors, bred in captivity and then released into the wild. If you're lucky, you might even spy one flying overhead on one of the park's rugged hiking trails. (Look for a tracking tag on the bird's wing to determine that you are actually looking at a California condor and not a big turkey vulture, plentiful in the park.)

CHANNEL ISLANDS NATIONAL PARK

California

WEBSITE:
www.nps.gov/chis

PHONE NUMBER:
805/658-5730

VISITATION RANK:
42

WHY GO:
Paddle and hike an
island sanctuary.

PASSPORT STAMPS ▼▼▼

▲ INSPIRATION POINT,
ANACAPA ISLAND

The remote **CHANNEL ISLANDS** are only accessible by boat or plane, but the hardy souls who visit these jeweled islands are treated to uncrowded trails, isolated beaches, and an extensive marine sanctuary. Kelp forests offshore sway in the ocean's surge as pumpkin-colored garibaldi (the California state fish) swim past rocks dotted with multicolored sea urchins. Onshore, rare species, including the island fox and the island scrub-jay, roam freely. Day-trippers can explore, hike, kayak, snorkel, and even scuba dive.

PLANNING YOUR TIME

The five Channel Islands lie off the central California coast, accessible by boat or plane from Santa Barbara and Ventura. The most visited islands are **Anacapa,** a dramatic five-mile spine jutting out from the sea, and **Santa Cruz,** California's largest island at 24 miles long and 6 miles wide. The second-largest island, **Santa Rosa,** is difficult to access because of consistently strong winds. The smaller **San Miguel** is accessible spring-fall by permit only. **Santa Barbara** is the smallest and southernmost of the islands.

You can visit Anacapa, Santa Cruz, and to a lesser degree Santa Rosa on day trips (boats depart at 9am, return at 4pm); only trips to Santa Cruz and Anacapa are available year-round.

Summer (June-Aug.) is high-season for recreational activities such as snorkeling, diving, and kayaking. Wildlife migrations take place in **spring** and **fall.**

Sailing to the islands takes 1-4 hours, and tough winds can crop up on the open water. While weather varies daily, daytime temperatures hang in the mid-60s with nights dropping by only 10-15 degrees.

ENTRANCES AND FEES

There is no entrance fee to visit Channel Islands; however, you must buy a ticket on a boat or plane departing from Santa Barbara or Ventura.

VISITORS CENTERS

There is no main visitors center. Instead, visit the **Robert J. Lagomarsino Channel Islands National Park Visitor Center** (1901 Spinnaker Dr., Ventura, 805/658-5730, www.nps.gov/chis, 8:30am-5pm daily) in Ventura Harbor Village before heading to the islands. It

▼ MARINELIFE ABOUNDS IN THE CHANNEL ISLANDS.

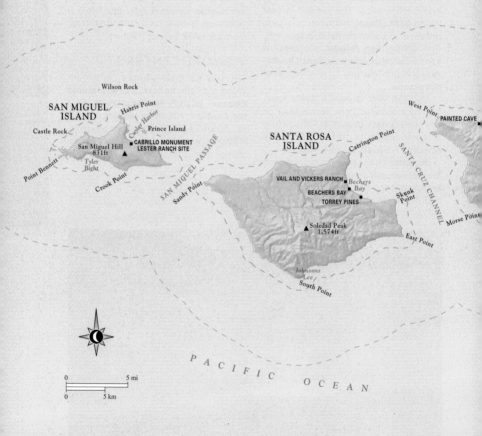

CHANNEL ISLANDS
NATIONAL PARK

POINT CONCEPTION

SANTA YNEZ MOUNTAINS

Santa Ynez Peak
4,298ft

154

101

1

101

SANTA BARBARA CHANNEL

Wilson Rock

SAN MIGUEL
ISLAND

Harris Point

Cuyler Harbor

Prince Island

Castle Rock

San Miguel Hill
831ft

CABRILLO MONUMENT
LESTER RANCH SITE

Tyler
Bight

Point Bennett

Crook Point

SAN MIGUEL PASSAGE

Sandy Point

SANTA ROSA
ISLAND

Carrington Point

West Point

PAINTED CAVE

SANTA CRUZ CHANNEL

VAIL AND VICKERS RANCH

Bechers
Bay

BEACHERS BAY

TORREY PINES

Skunk
Point

Morse Point

Soledad Peak
1,574ft

East Point

Johnsons
Lee

South Point

PACIFIC OCEAN

0   5 mi

0   5 km

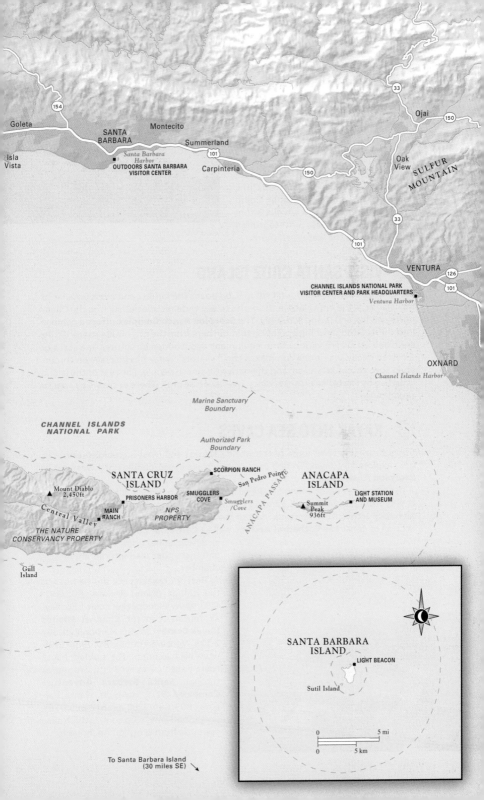

Top ③

① DAY TRIP TO ANACAPA ISLAND

Five miles long and 0.25 mile wide, **Anacapa** is actually three islets on the east end of the main island. **East Anacapa,** a desert-like island with steep cliffs, houses the stunning Inspiration Point, **Anacapa Lighthouse,** a small visitors center, and **Arch Rock,** a 40-foot-high rock window in the waters offshore.

ANACAPA LIGHTHOUSE

② VISIT SANTA CRUZ ISLAND

Santa Cruz Island (year-round, 90 min. by boat), the largest and most popular of the islands, is the only place in the world to see endemic species such as the Channel Island fox and island scrub-jay. The **Scorpion Ranch Complex** offers a glimpse into the isolated ranching operation that ran here from the mid-1800s to the 1980s; sprinkled about are various farm equipment and wooden structures in a state of arrested decay. Inside the complex, a small visitors center has displays on threatened species, conservation, and the native Chumash people. The rest of the island is owned by the Nature Conservancy (www.nature.org), where access is by special permit only.

③ KAYAK INTO SEA CAVES

Santa Cruz Island has some of the world's largest and most incredible sea caves, best explored by kayak. To find easy-to-reach sea caves, paddle northwest out of **Scorpion Anchorage.**

Anacapa has outstanding sea kayaking, but due to rugged cliffs, water access is only from East Anacapa's Landing Cove. Paddle out to **Arch Rock,** the 40-foot-high rock arch in the waters just east of the islet, or to **Cathedral Cove.** This scenic section of coast has **Cathedral Arch** as well as **Cathedral Cave,** reachable by kayak during higher tides. The cave has five entrances that lead into an impressive chamber.

Reserve kayak space on the boat to the islands (Island Packers, 805/642-1393, www.islandpackers.com). For kayak rentals, contact **Channel Islands Kayak Center** (3600 S. Harbor Blvd., Ste. 2-108, Ventura Harbor, 805/984-5995, www.cikayak.com). For guided kayak tours to sea caves on Santa Cruz, book through **Santa Barbara Adventure Company** (32 E. Haley St., Santa Barbara, 805/884-9283 or 877/885-9283, www.sbadventureco.com), which also operates from Scorpion Anchorage.

ANAPACA ISLAND

Best Hike

INSPIRATION POINT

1.5 MILES ROUND-TRIP
DURATION: 1 hour
EFFORT: easy
TRAILHEAD: Landing Cove,
East Anacapa

If you have seen a photo of the Channel Islands on a calendar or postcard, most likely that is the spectacular view from **Inspiration Point.** On the way, the trail includes stops at Pinniped Point and Cathedral Cove, where you can view sea lions stacked like sandbags on pocket beaches hundreds of feet down. From this high vantage point on the west end of the island, Middle Anacapa Island and West Anacapa Island rise out of the ocean like a giant sea serpent's spine. Below, the healthy blue-green ocean is spotted with rust-colored kelp forests. Overhead and below, gulls soar and do aerial acrobatics. In the distance, the large mass of Santa Cruz Island bulges out from behind the other Anacapa Islands. With a bench, Inspiration Point is a place to sit and soak in the view and the solitude of the Channel Islands. In a word, Inspiration Point is inspiring.

has a bookstore, displays of marinelife, exhibits, and a 25-minute introductory film on the islands. The **Outdoors Santa Barbara Visitor Center** (113 Harbor Way, Santa Barbara, 805/456-8752, http://outdoorsb.sbmm.org, 11am-5pm Sun.-Fri., 9am-3pm Sat.) also has information about the national park and the Channel Islands National Marine Sanctuary.

SANTA ROSA ISLAND

Fewer visitors reach the rugged and windy **Santa Rosa Island,** (Apr.-early Nov., 3 hrs. by boat), whose mountainous spine rises to 1,574-foot Soledad Peak with views of neighboring Santa Cruz Island and the mainland coastline. The island's white-sand beaches and coastal lagoons seem virtually untouched, as is the Torrey pine forest, home to some of the rarest pines in the world.

SAN MIGUEL

The westernmost island in the chain, **San Miguel Island** (April-early Nov., 4 hrs. by boat) has exceptional wildlife, especially at **Point Bennett,** where an estimated 30,000 seals and sea lions reside. Most visitors arrive at **Cuyler Harbor,** a large half-moon bay on the northeast side. Tidepools await at the east end of the scenic two-mile-long white-sand beach. Western gulls,

California brown pelicans, cormorants, and Cassin's auklets nest on Prince Island, which sits in the mouth of the harbor. On a bluff above the harbor, an inscribed stone cross is dedicated to Juan Rodríguez Cabrillo, the Portuguese explorer who anchored here in 1542.

SANTA BARBARA

At one square mile, **Santa Barbara** (Apr.-early Nov., 3 hrs. by boat) is the smallest of the islands and a rare stop. This southernmost island has warm water for swimming, diving, snorkeling, and kayaking, and is home to impressive seabird colonies, including one of the world's largest colonies of Xantus's murrelets.

RECREATION

HIKING

Anacapa is home to the flat **Inspiration Point Loop** (1.5 mi. rt., 1 hr., easy), which circles the island. The **Lighthouse Trail** (0.5 mi. rt., 20 min., easy) climbs to a viewpoint.

For coastal scenery, cliff-top views to the mainland, and whale-watching, Santa Cruz Island can't be beat. Walk along the **Cavern Point Loop** (2 mi. rt., 2 hrs., moderate). The **Smugglers Cove Trail** (7.5 mi. rt., 4 hrs., strenuous) follows an old ranch road across the eastern interior to a south-facing beach. Even if you don't find the elusive island scrub-jay on **Scorpion Canyon Loop** (4.5 mi. rt., 3 hrs., moderate), you'll tour a unique canyon followed by a series of stunning vistas.

The **Water Canyon Beach Trail** (3 mi. rt., 1.5 hrs., easy) leads to a white-sand beach. The **East Point Trail** (16 mi. rt., 8 hrs., strenuous) takes in the Torrey pine forest and beaches of Santa Rosa Island. The **Lobo Canyon Trail** (9 mi. rt., 5 hrs., strenuous) leads to a water-sculpted canyon resembling those in the Southwest.

On San Miguel, hike inland from Cuyler Harbor through a canyon with native vegetation to the **Lester Ranch Site** (2 mi. rt., 1 hr., moderate) to see the remains of a cistern, root cellar, and the living-room chimney in a rubble pile.

Hike the **Arch Point Trail** (1 mi. rt., 30 min., moderate) to view the 130-foot-high arch on Santa Barbara Island's northern tip. For wildlife, walk to **Elephant Seal Cove** (2.5 mi. rt., 1.5 hrs., moderate) or **Sea Lion Rookery** (2 mi. rt., 1 hr., moderate), where steep cliffs overlook sea mammal colonies. To view the whole island, take the **Signal Peak Trail** (3 mi. rt., 1.5 hrs., moderate) to the island apex at 634 feet.

SNORKELING AND SCUBA DIVING

Santa Cruz Island offers fine snorkeling and scuba diving in Scorpion Harbor. The kelp east and west of the Scorpion Anchorage Pier are rich in sealife, while the wreck of the **USS Peacock**, a World War II minesweeper 50 yards off Scorpion Rocks in 40-60 feet of water, captivates divers. Rent snorkel gear from **Santa Barbara Adventure Company** (805/884-9283 or 877/885-9283, www.sbadventureco.com) in Scorpion Harbor.

To dive the island's other spots, you'll need your own boat or to a charter dive boat. Schedule diving trips from Ventura Harbor with **Peace Dive Boat** (1691 Spinnaker Dr., G Dock, 805/650-3483, www.peaceboat.com) or **Truth Aquatics** (301 W. Cabrillo Blvd., 805/962-1127, http://truthaquatics.net).

WHERE TO STAY
INSIDE THE PARK

There are no accommodations, food, or services on the Channel Islands. **Camping** (877/444-6777, www.recreation

▼ SANTA CRUZ ISLAND

ANACAPA ISLAND

.gov, $15) is the only overnight option. All campsites have picnic tables and access to pit toilets.

On Santa Cruz Island, **Scorpion Ranch Campground** is a 0.5-1-mile walk from the pier at Scorpion Anchorage. The lower campground (22 sites) sits in a eucalyptus-shaded canyon, while the upper loop (3 sites, 6 group sites) is spread in a meadow—but it's twice as far to lug your camping gear. The campgrounds have drinking water and food storage boxes. From Prisoners Harbor, a strenuous 3.5-mile hike goes to the **Del Norte Backcountry Campsite,** a remote spot in an oak grove.

The other islands have primitive campgrounds with no drinking water; bring water with you. A 0.5-mile hike on East Anacapa includes 154 stairs to reach the **Anacapa Campground** (7 sites), which is quite sun- and wind-exposed. A steep one-mile hike uphill reaches **San Miguel Campground** (9 sites). From the visitors center, a steep 0.5-mile hike connects with **Santa Barbara Island Campground** (10 sites). On Santa Rosa, a level 1.5-mile hike accesses the **Water Canyon Campground** (15 sites), where backcountry beach camping (mid-Aug.-Dec.) is allowed on the undeveloped coastline.

OUTSIDE THE PARK

Accommodations and restaurants are plentiful in **Ventura** and **Santa Barbara.**

GETTING THERE

Most visitors reach Channel Islands National Park by hopping a boat run by **Island Packers Cruises** (1691 Spinnaker Dr., Ste. 105B, Ventura Harbor, 805/642-1393, www.islandpackers.com). Schedules change seasonally. The crossing time ranges 1-4 hours, based on distance and conditions. Some landings require climbing steel ladders to docks and then stairs to reach the island tops.

Anacapa: By boat (year-round, 90 min.), Anacapa requires debarking by climbing up a steel ladder and then ascending stairs to the island top.

Santa Cruz: The two primary points of entry onto Santa Cruz are at **Scorpion Anchorage** and **Prisoners Harbor.** After a 90-minute boat ride from Ventura, travelers offload either by climbing a steel ladder to a short shore pier or via skiff landings.

Santa Rosa: Boats debark at Santa Rosa, where visitors must climb a 20-foot steel-rung ladder to reach flat land. Year-round flights to the island take 25 minutes.

San Miguel: Boat trips can experience potentially rough seas and skiff landings require waterproof gear.

Santa Barbara: Boat travel requires a skiff transfer with a climb up a steel-rung ladder, then laboriously trudging up 0.25 mile of steps to crest the island top.

Channel Island Aviation (305 Durley Ave., Camarillo, 805/987-1301, www.flycia.com) has flights to Santa Rosa Island.

PACIFIC NORTHWEST

Oregon's only national park, Crater Lake's startlingly blue water is ringed by steep rock cliffs.

Washington's three national parks cling to mountains that are home to glaciers.

Olympic National Park is filled with rain forests, enormous old-growth trees, and rocky tidepools on the Pacific coast.

Looming above Seattle, 14,411-foot Mount Rainier lures climbers to scale its summit while backpackers hike the wildflower meadows and forests of the Wonderland Trail.

North Cascades National Park covers wild mountain country that includes hiking trails, more than 300 glaciers, and the fjord-like Lake Chelan.

◄ SOL DUC FALLS, OLYMPIC NATIONAL PARK

CANADA

North
Cascades NP

PACIFIC
OCEAN

Olympic
NP

Seattle

Olympia

WASHINGTON

Mount Rainier
NP

Portland

Salem

PACIFIC
NORTHWEST

OREGON

Crater Lake NP

0   50 mi
0   50 km

© AVALON TRAVEL

The National Parks of
THE PACIFIC NORTHWEST

CRATER LAKE, OR

The caldera from a catastrophic volcanic eruption 6,600 years ago now contains the nation's deepest and bluest lake (page 207).

OLYMPIC, WA

Wet, lush, and wild, the park is filled with rain forests housing world-record trees, a rugged coastline, and a mountain range that begs hiking (page 217).

MOUNT RAINIER, WA

The king of the Cascades, this glacier-crowned peak towers over the surrounding countryside (page 234).

NORTH CASCADES, WA

These jagged peaks comprise one of the wildest places in the Lower 48. Get a taste of the scenery on the beautiful North Cascades Highway (page 245).

1: JAMES ISLAND, RIALTO BEACH, OLYMPIC
2: LUPINE BELOW LITTLE TAHOMA, MOUNT RAINIER
3: CRATER LAKE, OREGON

Best OF THE PARKS

Crater Lake Rim Drive: Circle the rim of this lake-filled caldera (page 211).

Hoh Rain Forest: Walk under some of the tallest trees in the world in this rain forest (page 221).

Hurricane Ridge: Take in majestic alpine views that get even more impressive if you continue on one of several hiking trails (page 221).

Ruby Beach: Enjoy a winning combination of beauty and accessibility at this Pacific beach (page 221).

Wildflowers at Paradise: Relish icy Mount Rainier framed by fields of wildflowers in summer (page 238).

North Cascades Highway: Navigate the beautiful curves, reservoirs, forests, and peaks of this well-maintained highway (page 249).

PLANNING YOUR TRIP

Plan at least **10 days** to tour all four parks or **one week** for the Washington parks. Make lodging and campground **reservations** inside the parks one year in advance. **Winter** closes many of the roads in this region, with limited access to a handful of locations and services.

Summer is prime time for Washington and Oregon. From mid-June to September, the days are long and the temperatures seldom climb above the mid-80s. Snow melts from mountain passes and high-altitude hiking trails, usually by July. The sunny, mild days are great for kayaking.

Seattle provides the most central access to Olympic, Mt. Rainier, and North Cascades National Parks.

1: SUNSET AT HURRICANE RIDGE
2: NORTH CASCADES HIGHWAY

Road Trip

MOUNT RAINIER, OLYMPIC, AND NORTH CASCADES

Launching from **Seattle,** this road trip makes a grand loop that includes a ferry ride across Puget Sound, traveling from the mountains to the coast for a rich taste of Washington's best.

Mount Rainier

BENCH LAKE, MOUNT RAINIER

86 miles / 2 hours

From **Seattle,** get an early start for the two-hour drive to the **White River Entrance** in the northeast corner of Mount Rainier National Park. A winding road climbs to **Sunrise**, a hub of park activity and the highest point on the mountain accessible by car. Get your bearings at the visitors center, have lunch at the cafeteria, and then head out for a couple of hours of alpine hiking.

Drive to Paradise for dinner and overnighting at **Paradise Inn.** In the morning, tour the visitors center, explore the wildflower meadows, and hike to **Bench Lake** or **Plummer Peak**. The next day, exit the park via **Longmire.**

Olympic

157 miles / 3.5 hours

Say goodbye to Rainier as you head west toward Olympic National Park. Stop at **Lake Quinault,** at the southern end of the park, where you'll experience the lush, primordial forest. Drive up the coast on U.S. 101 to dine and overnight at **Kalaloch Lodge**.

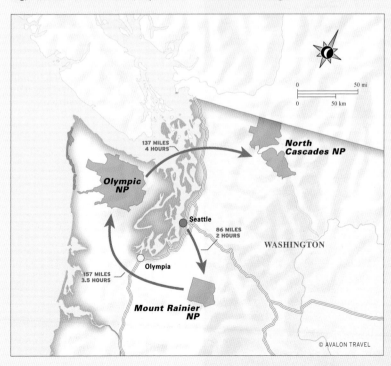

137 MILES
4 HOURS

North Cascades NP

Olympic NP

50 mi

50 km

Seattle

86 MILES
2 HOURS

WASHINGTON

Olympia

157 MILES
3.5 HOURS

Mount Rainier NP

© AVALON TRAVEL

In the morning, drive north to **Ruby Beach,** a classic example of Washington's misty, pebble-strewn coastline. Continue north on U.S. 101 to glacier-carved **Lake Crescent.** Spend the afternoon floating on its tranquil, turquoise-green waters before overnighting at **Lake Crescent Lodge** or in Port Angeles.

The next morning, drive to the only part of the Olympic Mountains that's accessible by car: **Hurricane Ridge.** Stop at **Hurricane Ridge Visitor Center** and walk to **Hurricane Hill** for immense views. Depart the Olympics in the early afternoon to drive to Port Townsend (1 hr.) to catch the 35-minute ferry (fee, reservations required) across Puget Sound to Coupeville on Whidbey Island.

North Cascades

137 miles / 4 hours

After debarking on Whidbey Island, drive north to cross Deception Pass Bridge to the mainland. Your next stop is **Marblemount,** two hours east on Highway 20, where you'll spend the night. In the morning, follow the **North Cascades Highway** as it slices 30 miles across the park. Stop at **North Cascades Visitor Center** before taking a boat tour of **Diablo Lake.** Back on the highway, head east to visit **Ross Lake Overlook.** Go as far as **Washington Pass** for views of Liberty Bell and Early Winter Spires before returning to your lodging for the night. The next day, it's a two-hour drive back to Seattle.

1: VIEWS INTO OLYMPIC NATIONAL PARK
2: KAYAKING ON CRESCENT LAKE
2: DIABLO LAKE TRAIL, NORTH CASCADES

CRATER LAKE NATIONAL PARK

Oregon

PASSPORT STAMPS ▼▼▼

WEBSITE:
www.nps.gov/crla

PHONE NUMBER:
541/594-3000

VISITATION RANK:
27

WHY GO:
Visit a sapphire-blue lake in the heart of a sunken volcano.

▲ CRATER LAKE

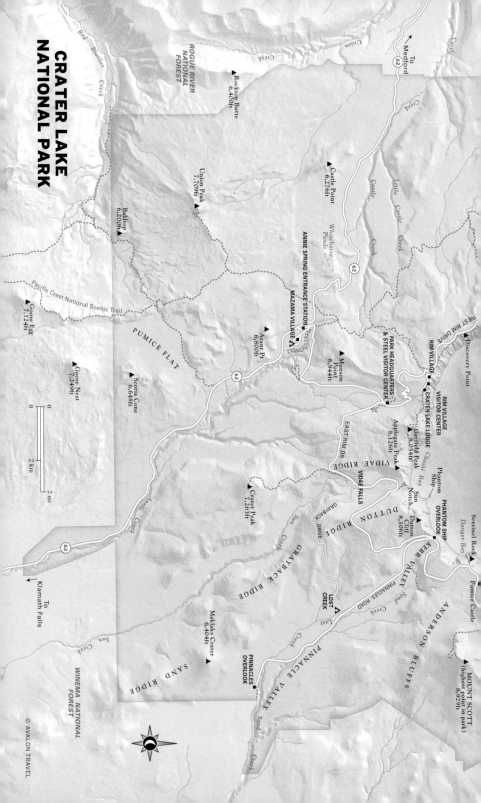

CRATER LAKE
NATIONAL PARK

ROGUE RIVER
NATIONAL
FOREST

Red Blanket Creek

▲ Rockton Butte
6,400ft

Union Creek

Castle Creek

Little Castle Creek

Castle Creek

To
Medford

62

To Medford

▲ Castle Point
6,276ft

Whitehorse
Ponds

▲ Union Peak
7,709ft

Baldtop
6,200ft

62

ANNIE SPRING ENTRANCE STATION

MAZAMA VILLAGE

Pacific Crest National Scenic Trail

▲ Goose Egg
7,124ft

PUMICE FLAT

▲ Goose Nest
7,249ft

▲ Scoria Cone
6,648ft

62

▲ Arant Pt
6,800ft

▲ Munson
Point
6,944ft

PARK HEADQUARTERS
& STEEL VISITOR CENTER

WEST RIM DRIVE

Discovery Point

RIM VILLAGE
RIM VILLAGE
VISITOR CENTER

CRATER LAKE LODGE

▲ Garfield Peak
8,054ft

▲ Applegate Peak
8,126ft

Chaski Bay

Sun
Notch

Phantom
Ship

PHANTOM SHIP
OVERLOOK

EAST RIM DR

VIDAE RIDGE

VIDAE
FALLS

▲ Dutton
Hill
8,106ft

Sentinel Rock
Danger Bay

DUTTON RIDGE

0

2 km

2 mi

Annie Creek

GRAYBACK RIDGE

GRAYBACK DRIVE

Sun Creek

▲ Crater Peak
7,263ft

Sand Creek

LOST
CREEK

PINNACLES ROAD

KERR VALLEY

Pumice Castle

ANDERSON BLUFFS

62

To
Klamath Falls

SAND RIDGE

▲ Maklaks Crater
6,404ft

PINNACLES
OVERLOOK

Lost Creek

PINNACLE VALLEY

Sand Creek

▲ MOUNT SCOTT
(highest point in park)
8,929ft

WINEMA
NATIONAL
FOREST

© AVALON TRAVEL

N

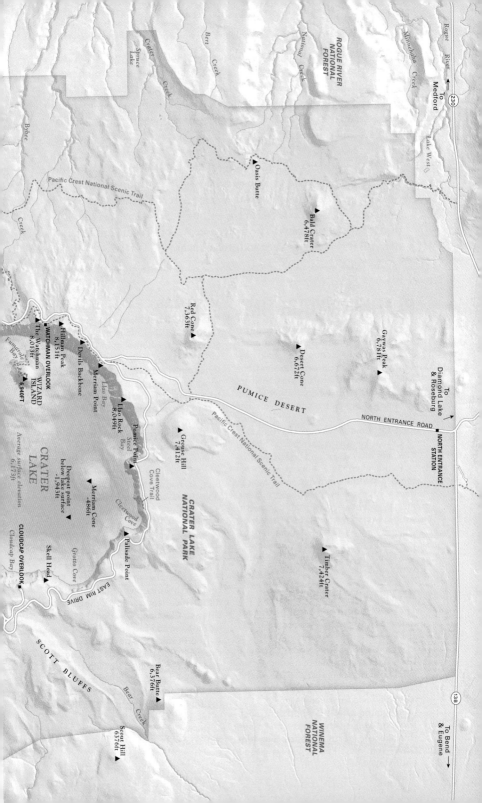

ROGUE RIVER
NATIONAL
FOREST

To
Medford

230

Rogue River

Minnehaha Creek

Lake West

National Creek

Bert Creek

Spruce Lake

Creek

Creek

Oasis Butte

Pacific Crest National Scenic Trail

Creek

Bald Crater
6,478ft

Red Cone
7,363ft

Gaywas Peak
6,781ft

To
Diamond Lake
& Roseburg

Desert Cone
6,672ft

PUMICE DESERT

NORTH ENTRANCE ROAD

NORTH ENTRANCE
STATION

Hillman Peak
8,151ft
WATCHMAN OVERLOOK
The Watchman
8,013ft
WIZARD
ISLAND
6,940FT

Pacific Crest National Scenic Trail

Devils Backbone

Merriam Point

Llao Bay

Llao Rock
8,049ft

Steel Bay

Pumice Point

Grouse Hill
7,412ft

Cleetwood
Cove Trail

Deepest point
below surface
1,943ft

Merriam Cone
486ft

Cleetwood
Cove

CRATER
LAKE

Average surface elevation
6,173ft

Grotto Cove

Skell Head

Palisade Point

EAST RIM DRIVE

CLOUDCAP OVERLOOK

Cloudcap Bay

CRATER LAKE
NATIONAL
PARK

Timber Crater
7,424ft

SCOTT BLUFFS

Bear Butte
6,370ft

Bear Creek

Scout Hill
6376ft

WINEMA
NATIONAL
FOREST

To Bend
& Eugene

138

High in the Cascades lies the crown jewel of Oregon: **CRATER LAKE**, the country's deepest lake at 1,943 feet. Its surface glimmers like a polished sapphire placed inside a volcano that blew and then collapsed thousands of years ago. Crater Lake's extraordinary hues are produced by the depth and clarity of the water and its ability to absorb all the colors of the spectrum (except the shortest wavelengths, blue and violet).

When visitors crest into the crater for the first time and spot the lake, its blueness and immense expanse hits with a sudden burst of stark beauty. "Wow" expressions are afterthoughts. One of the first national parks created in the country, Crater Lake preserves a pristine water habitat within a volcano. A loop road circles the caldera, offering scenic drives and stellar hikes.

PLANNING YOUR TIME

Crater Lake National Park is southern Oregon's top destination. **Summer** (May-Sept.) weekends are peak season, when the loop drive around the caldera clogs with traffic. Most visitors schedule their trip when the whole loop is open to drive—from early summer (late May-late June) until winter snows (mid-Oct.-mid-Nov.) bury the road.

Crater Lake is located high in the Cascade Mountains and erratic weather is prevalent. July, August, and September see the warmest and sunniest days with highs in the 60s. Spring and fall yo-yo between rain and snow. In winter, wet snowstorms pelt the park—which averages 43 feet of annual snowfall—and clouds can block your view of the lake. Check the park webcams to verify visibility.

ENTRANCES AND FEES

The park's **South** and **West Entrances** (Hwy. 62) are open year-round; a pay station for both is at Annie Creek near Mazama Village. The **North Entrance** (Hwy. 138) is open mid-June-mid-October. The entrance fee is $25-30 per vehicle ($20-25 motorcycle, $12-15 individual) and is valid for seven days.

In winter, only the South Entrance is open to reach the south rim to see the lake; the North Entrance, East Rim Drive, and West Rim Drive are closed until May-June.

VISITORS CENTERS

The tiny **Rim Village Visitor Center** (9:30am-6:30pm daily late May-late Sept., shorter hours spring and fall) is in Rim Village near Crater Lake Lodge. It has a few exhibits and a bookstore. A rock stairway behind the building leads to **Sinnott Memorial Overlook,** with one of the best views of the lake. Daily ranger talks are held.

The **Steel Visitor Center** (9am-5pm daily late Apr.-early Nov., 10am-4pm daily early Nov.-late Apr.) is located below Rim Village near park headquarters. It has a film, exhibits, information, maps, backcountry permits, and a bookstore.

SCENIC DRIVE

The **Rim Drive** (summer only) is a scenic tour of the sunken caldera. From the North Junction, go left onto **East Rim Drive.** Head a mile off the East Rim Drive to **Cloudcap Overlook;** Oregon's highest paved road will take you there. At the **Pumice Castle Overlook,** spot the bright orange "castle" on the cliff wall. It's especially vibrant in the early evening, when the sun lights it up. At the **Phantom Ship Overlook,** try to spy the tiny island in this big lake; it's really 170 feet tall. East Rim Drive finishes at the park headquarters and Steel Visitor Center.

Top 3

1 CIRCLE THE CRATER ON THE RIM DRIVE

The 33-mile scenic **Rim Drive** (summer only), divided into a longer East Rim and a shorter West Rim, offers a scenic cruise around the glistening lake. If you're seeing Crater Lake for the first time, drive into the park from the north for the most dramatic perspective. After crossing through a pumice desert, the road climbs to higher elevations until it overlooks the blue lake.

THE PHANTOM SHIP

From the North Junction, follow **East Rim Drive,** stopping at pullovers along the way to the park headquarters and Steel Visitor Center. A highlight is the **Phantom Ship Overlook**.

From park headquarters, you continue your tour on **West Rim Drive,** which takes in the historic **Crater Lake Lodge** and **Watchman Overlook,** for picture-perfect views of Wizard Island.

2 TAKE A BOAT TOUR TO WIZARD ISLAND

Due to the caldera's steep, avalanche-prone slopes, only one trail leads down to the lake itself, and it is the only way to reach the tour boat. **Volcano Boat Cruises** (888/774-2728, www.craterlakelodges.com, daily July-mid-Sept.) launches a narrated cruise to Wizard Island, with three hours of exploration on the tiny dot of land. A boat shuttle offers access for self-explorers as well. All boats depart from Cleetwood Cove, accessible only by a steep trail.

3 CLIMB WATCHMAN PEAK

DISTANCE: 1.6 miles round-trip

DURATION: 1.5 hours

ELEVATION CHANGE: 420 feet

EFFORT: strenuous

TRAILHEAD: Watchman Overlook

From a trailhead 3.8 miles northwest of Rim Village, park rangers often lead sunset hikes up **Watchman Peak**. The trail climbs 420 feet to a fire lookout overlooking Wizard Island.

VIEW OF CRATER LAKE FORM THE TOP OF WATCHMAN PEAK

ONE DAY IN CRATER LAKE

Thanks to the scenic **Rim Drive**, visitors who only have one day can circle the entire loop. Stop at overlooks to enjoy the lake for various vantages and squeeze in at least one short hike to **Sun Notch** or **Watchman Peak.**

From the junction at park headquarters, climb the switchbacks on **West Rim Drive** to a junction. Go right onto the spur to visit the **Sinnott Memorial Overlook** and historic **Crater Lake Lodge.** Return to the junction to continue onto West Rim Drive. In about a mile, stop at **Discovery Point** (a great sunrise location), where a gold prospector stumbled upon the lake while riding his mule. Farther along West Rim Drive, **Watchman Overlook** offers good views of Wizard Island and an outstanding sunset location.

Those entering from the north should drive the East Rim followed by the West Rim; those entering from park headquarters should drive the West Rim followed by the East Rim. The entire loop is open in summer only, with the road plowed and accessible mid-June to early November. Drive clockwise around the lake, which makes pulling off at more than 30 viewpoints easier. Plan at least three hours for the drive.

RECREATION

HIKING

West Rim Drive

Just east of Crater Lake Lodge, the **Garfield Peak Trail** (3.6 mi. rt., 2-3 hrs., strenuous) climbs an imposing ridge with wildflower displays of phlox, Indian paintbrush, and lupine, as well as frequent sightings of eagles and hawks. The route tops out at Garfield Peak, which provides a 360-degree view of the crater and the lake 1,888 feet below.

East Rim Drive

A half mile east of park headquarters, the **Castle Crest Wildflower Loop** (0.5 mi. rt., 20 min., easy) is one of the best places to view the mid-July-mid-August flora. A short loop with lots of visual punch goes to **Sun Notch** (0.8 mi. rt., 45 min., easy), 4.4 miles east of park headquarters. This loop climbs 150 feet through a meadow to overlook the Phantom Ship and Crater Lake.

From the Pinnacles Road, a well-graded dirt path goes through old-growth forest to **Plaikni Falls** (2 mi. rt., 1 hr., easy), a cascade that rolls down a glacier-carved cliff. To view the falls at the end requires a short, steep grunt uphill.

Only the **Cleetwood Cove Trail** (2.2 mi. rt., 1.5 hrs., strenuous) cuts through Crater Lake's plunging rim to reach the lakeshore. Near the boat dock, you can swim in the crystal-clear lake water. But be ready for frigid cold and a return climb that gains 700 feet in elevation. A hike to **Wizard Island Summit** (2.3 mi. rt., 2 hrs., strenuous) requires a boat ride (fee) and a 770-foot climb. Once at the top, you can peer into the crater while circumnavigating the rim on a flat trail. Drop-offs are steep, but the views go all directions.

GARFIELD PEAK TRAIL

CYCLISTS RIDE THE RIM DRIVE.

From a trailhead 14 miles east of park headquarters, a trail ascends to the top of 8,926-foot **Mount Scott** (4.4 mi. rt., 3 hrs., strenuous), the highest peak in the park. Lake views and perspectives on a dozen Cascade peaks are the rewards at the end of the trek that gains 1,250 feet.

BICYCLING

The 33-mile paved **Rim Drive** around Crater Lake is a cyclist's dream ride. But it's no lazy pedal. Flying downhills swoop immediately into steep, long uphill climbs as the rolling road tours around the lake. Elevation gain for the entire loop nearly reaches 4,000 feet. Much of the road is narrow with minimal shoulders, so it is only for cyclists experienced with riding with cars at their elbows.

Most cyclists opt for a clockwise loop from park headquarters to get the monster climbs done early in the ride. Due to colossal amounts of snow in winter, the road is only open to bikers in summer and fall. September usually has two car-free days on the East Rim for prime cycling, and often cyclists are permitted to ride portions of the road in June after the plows have removed snow but before they are open to cars. Bring your own bicycle; the closest rentals are in Ashland, 75 miles away.

WINTER SPORTS

When snow buries the park in winter, services and activities are cut to a minimum. However, many cross-country skiers, snowshoers, and winter campers enjoy this solitude. Park rangers lead **snowshoe hikes** (1pm Sat.-Sun., 1pm daily Christmas week, weather permitting). Ski and snowshoe rentals are available at Rim Village.

Winter trekkers must be prepared to blaze their own cross-country trails and contend with frequent snowstorms. Inquire about trail, avalanche, and weather conditions at the visitors center before embarking. Circling the lake takes two or three days, even in good weather. Only highly skilled winter hikers or skiers should attempt this 33-mile route, which requires a beacon, probe, and shovel for traversing avalanche paths.

WHERE TO STAY
INSIDE THE PARK

Lodging is concentrated on the southern edge of the lake at **Rim Village;** opening and closing dates vary. Most services are open mid-May to mid-October. Make lodging and camping **reservations** (888/774-2728, www.crater-lakelodges.com) one year in advance.

VIEW FROM CRATER LAKE LODGE

The **Crater Lake Lodge** (late May-mid-Oct., from $205) is hewn of local wood and stone with massive picture windows of the lake and decor echoing its 1915 origins. Many of the 71 rooms have expansive views of the lake, while less expensive rooms face Upper Klamath Lake and Mount Shasta. The lobby's large stone fireplace serves as a gathering spot on chilly evenings. The **dining room** (7am-10:30am, 11:30am-2:30pm, and 5pm-10pm daily, hours vary seasonally, dinner reservations advised) serves Pacific Northwest cuisine. A bar menu offers drinks and appetizers in the lobby or on the porch overlooking the lake.

At Mazama Village (7 miles south of the rim), the **Cabins at Mazama Village** (late May-late Sept., $155) have rooms with 1-2 queen beds and a bath; there are no TVs, phones, or air-conditioning. The **Annie Creek Restaurant** (7am-10:30am, 11am-4pm, and 5pm-9pm daily mid-June-Labor Day, shorter hours spring and fall) serves American-style comfort food.

Mazama Campground (Mazama Village, June-late Sept., $23-32) accepts reservations for some of its more than 200 sites; all other sites are first come, first served. Facilities include drinking water, flush toilets, and showers (fee). **Lost Creek Campground** (Pinnacles Rd., July-Oct., first come, first served, $10) has 16 tent-only sites with drinking water and vault toilets.

The **Rim Village Cafe** (9am-8pm daily summer, shorter hours fall-spring) is open year-round and sells grab-and-go sandwiches, salads, and rice bowls.

OUTSIDE THE PARK

Accommodations, restaurants, and services are available in **Ashland.** Several national forests surrounding Crater Lake have campgrounds.

GETTING THERE

AIR

The closest international airport is **Rogue Valley International-Medford Airport** (MFR, 1000 Terminal Loop Pkwy., Medford, 541/772-8068 or 800/882-7488, www.jacksoncountyor.org), served by United, Horizon, and Allegiant. Car rentals are available at the airport.

TRAIN

Amtrak (800/872-7245) has a station 70 miles east at Klamath Falls (1600 Oak Ave., 541/884-2822). The **Crater Lake Trolley** (541/882-1896, www.craterlaketrolley.net) runs a shuttle from the Amtrak station to Rim Village (late June-early Oct.).

CAR

The only year-round access to Crater Lake is from the south via **Highway 62.**

CRATER LAKE WITH WIZARD ISLAND

To reach Crater Lake from Grants Pass, head for Gold Hill and take Highway 234 until it meets Highway 62. As you head up Highway 62, the road makes a horseshoe bend through the Cascades, starting at Medford and ending 20 miles north of Klamath Falls.

The northern route via **Highway 138** (Roseburg to U.S. 97, south of Beaver Marsh) is usually closed by snow mid-October-July, as is the park's north entrance.

GETTING AROUND

There is no public transportation within the park. Most visitors tour the 33-mile Rim Drive in private vehicles.

BOAT TOURS

Volcano Boat Cruises (888/774-2728, www.craterlakelodges.com, daily July-mid-Sept.) offers narrated tours on the lake. Tickets are sold up to 24 hours in advance via touch-screen kiosks in Crater Lake Lodge or Annie Creek Gift Shop in Mazama Village. Kiosk sales shut down two hours before departure; after that, you can pick up any remaining tickets at the Cleetwood Trailhead until 45 minutes before departure. A limited number of tickets are available by **reservation requests** online. Choose between two boat tours:

Two-hour narrated excursions (6 departures daily, 9:30am-3:45pm, adults $42, kids $28) cruise counterclockwise around the perimeter of the lake and do not stop at Wizard Island.

Five-hour narrated cruises (departs 9:45am and 12:45pm daily, adults $58, kids $37) make a three-hour stop for hiking at Wizard Island.

If you just want to get to Wizard Island for three hours of self-guided

TAKE A BOAT RIDE ON CRATER LAKE.

THE GEOLOGY OF CRATER LAKE

Geologically speaking, the name *Crater Lake* is a misnomer. Technically, Crater Lake lies in a caldera, which is produced when the center of a volcano caves in on itself. In this case, the cataclysm occurred 6,600 years ago with the destruction of formerly 12,000-foot-high Mount Mazama. Klamath Native American legend, which tells of a fierce battle between the chiefs of the underworld and the world aboveground causing explosions and ashfall, roughly parallels the scientific explanation for Crater Lake's formation.

The aftereffects of this great eruption left huge, deep drifts of ash and pumice deposited over a wide area up to 80 miles from the volcano. The pumice deserts to the north of the lake and the deep ashen canyons to the south are the most dramatic examples. So thick and widespread is the pumice that water percolates through too rapidly for plants to survive, creating reddish pockets of bleakness in the otherwise green forest. In the southern canyons, hot gases bubbling up through the ash created the eerie gray hoodoos that hardened into rocklike towers. While water washed away the loosely packed ash, creating the steep canyons visible today, these hoodoos have withstood centuries of erosion.

Following the volcanic activity, the caldera filled with water over thousands of years. The lake is self-contained, fed only by snow and rain, with no outlets other than evaporation and seepage.

Wizard Island, a large cinder cone that rises 760 feet above the surface of the lake, offers evidence of volcanic activity since the caldera's formation. The true crater at the top of the island is the source of the lake's name. The **Phantom Ship,** a smaller island formed from lava, is a much older feature.

Although Crater Lake often records the coldest temperatures in the Cascades, the lake itself has only frozen over once since records have been kept. The surface of the lake can warm up past the 60°F mark during the summer. The deeper water stays around 38°F, although scientists have discovered 66°F hot spots 1,400 feet below the lake's surface.

Rainbow trout, kokanee (a landlocked salmon), and crayfish were introduced to the lake many years ago by humans; crayfish are now threatening the lake's native newts. Some types of mosses and green algae grow more than 400 feet below the lake's surface, a world record for these freshwater species.

exploration, take the **boat shuttle** (departs 8:30am and 11:30am daily, adults $33, kids $21).

Allow 90 minutes to drive the 12 miles from Rim Village to the Cleetwood trailhead. Prepare to hike the **Cleetwood Trail** (1.1 mi. one way, 30-45 min., strenuous) 700 feet down to **Cleetwood Cove dock,** where boat tours depart. Dress warmly, as the lake is cool.

TROLLEY TOURS

The **Crater Lake Trolley** (541/882-1896, www.craterlaketrolley.net, 10am-3pm daily mid-June-mid-Oct., tours vary June and Sept.-Oct., $24-27 adults, $17 kids) takes a two-hour tour along Rim Drive with stops at scenic viewpoints. The natural gas-powered trolleys are ADA-compliant and feature commentary by a guide. Purchase tickets in advance from a trolley parked by the Community House at Rim Village, near the Crater Lake Lodge.

SIGHTS NEARBY

Oregon Caves National Monument (Hwy. 46, 541/592-2100, www.nps.gov/orca, 9am-6pm daily summer, hours vary spring and fall) has stalactites and stalagmites deep inside a mountain, plus the unexpected pleasure of a classic mountain lodge.

Diamond Lake (Diamond Lake Ranger District, 541/498-2531, www.fs.usda.gov) has three campgrounds, boat launches, and an 11-mile paved bike trail that loops the ultra-scenic lake surrounded by volcanic peaks.

OLYMPIC
NATIONAL PARK

Washington

PASSPORT STAMPS ▼▼▼

WEBSITE:
www.nps.gov/olym

PHONE NUMBER:
360/565-3130

VISITATION RANK:
8

WHY GO:
Wander amid old-growth temperate rain forests.

▲ HURRICANE HILL,
OLYMPIC NATIONAL PARK

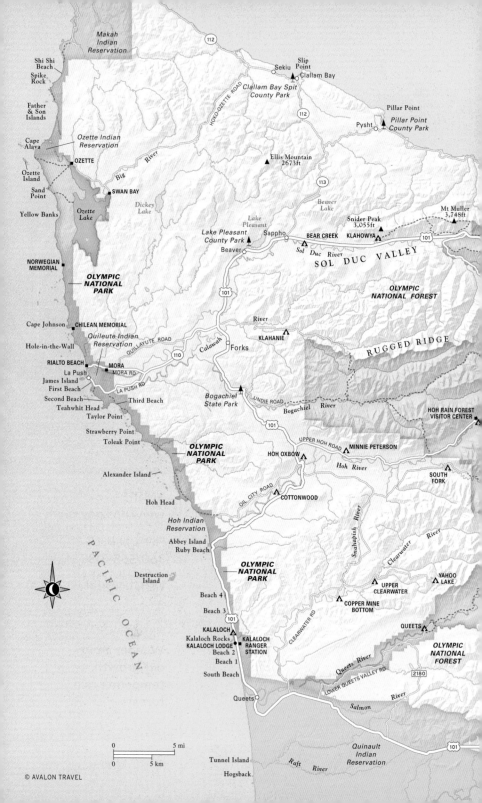

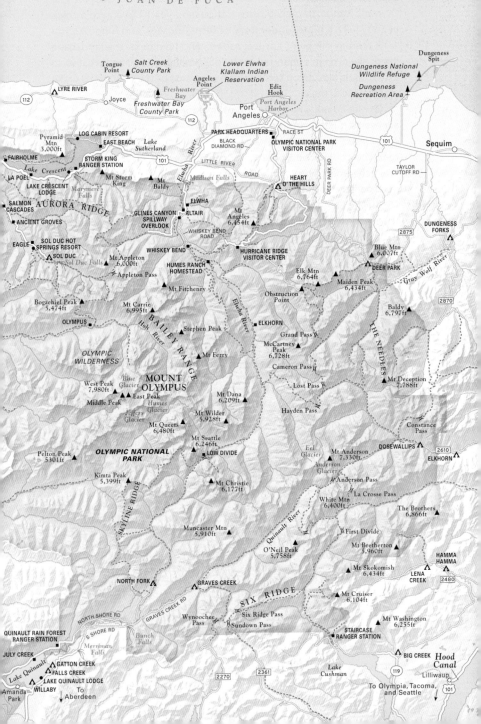

OLYMPIC NATIONAL PARK

STRAIT OF JUAN DE FUCA

Ferry to Victoria,
British Columbia,
Canada

Tongue
Point

Salt Creek
County Park

Freshwater
Bay

Lower Elwha
Klallam Indian
Reservation

Dungeness National
Wildlife Refuge

Dungeness
Spit

Dungeness
Recreation Area

Angeles
Point

Ediz
Hook

Port Angeles Harbor

LYRE RIVER

Joyce

Freshwater Bay
County Park

Port
Angeles

112

Pyramid
Mtn
3,000ft

LOG CABIN RESORT

EAST BEACH

Lake
Sutherland

PARK HEADQUARTERS

BLACK
DIAMOND RD

RACE ST

OLYMPIC NATIONAL PARK
VISITOR CENTER

101

Sequim

FAIRHOLME

STORM KING
RANGER STATION

Lake Crescent

101

Elwha River

LITTLE RIVER

DEER PARK RD

TAYLOR
CUTOFF RD

LA POEL

LAKE CRESCENT
LODGE

Mt Storm
King

Mt
Baldy

Madison Falls

ROAD

Heart
O' THE HILLS

2875

DUNGENESS
FORKS

SALMON
CASCADES

Marymere
Falls

AURORA RIDGE

ELWHA

ALTAIR

Mt
Angeles
6,454ft

Blue Mtn
6,007ft

ANCIENT GROVES

GLINES CANYON
SPILLWAY
OVERLOOK

WHISKEY BEND
ROAD

DEER PARK

Gray Wolf River

EAGLE

SOL DUC HOT
SPRINGS RESORT

WHISKEY BEND

HURRICANE RIDGE
VISITOR CENTER

Elk Mtn
6,764ft

Maiden Peak
6,434ft

2870

SOL DUC

Sol Duc Falls

Mt Appleton
6,000ft

Appleton Pass

HUMES RANCH
HOMESTEAD

Obstruction
Point

Baldy
6,797ft

Bogachiel Peak
5,474ft

Mt Fitzhenry

Mt Carrie
6,995ft

Hoh River

ELKHORN

Grand Pass

THE NEEDLES

OLYMPUS

Stephen Peak

BAILEY RANGE

McCartney
Peak
6,728ft

Mt Deception
7,788ft

OLYMPIC
WILDERNESS

Mt Ferry

Cameron Pass

Lost Pass

West Peak
7,980ft

Blue
Glacier

MOUNT
OLYMPUS

Mt Dana
6,209ft

Hayden Pass

Middle Peak

East Peak

Humes
Glacier

Jeffers
Glacier

Mt Queets
6,480ft

Mt Wilder
5,928ft

Constance
Pass

Pelton Peak
5,301ft

OLYMPIC NATIONAL
PARK

Mt Seattle
6,246ft

LOW DIVIDE

Eel
Glacier

Mt Anderson
7,330ft

DOSEWALLIPS

2610

ELKHORN

Anderson
Glacier

Kimta Peak
5,399ft

SKYLINE RIDGE

Mt Christie
6,177ft

Anderson Pass

La Crosse Pass

White Mtn
6,400ft

The Brothers
6,866ft

Muncaster Mtn
5,910ft

Quinault River

First Divide

Mt Bretherton
5,960ft

HAMMA
HAMMA

O'Neil Peak
5,758ft

Mt Skokomish
6,434ft

LENA
CREEK

2480

NORTH FORK

GRAVES CREEK

SIX RIDGE

Mt Cruiser
6,104ft

NORTH SHORE RD

GRAVES CREEK RD

Wynoochee
Pass

Six Ridge Pass

STAIRCASE
RANGER STATION

Mt Washington
6,255ft

QUINAULT RAIN FOREST
RANGER STATION

S SHORE RD

Bunch
Falls

Sundown Pass

BIG CREEK

Hood
Canal

JULY CREEK

Merriman
Falls

119

Lilliwaup

GATTON CREEK

FALLS CREEK

LAKE QUINAULT LODGE

Lake Quinault

WILLABY

Amanda
Park

To
Aberdeen

2270

2361

Lake
Cushman

To Olympia, Tacoma,
and Seattle

101

OLYMPIC NATIONAL PARK's massive rain forest stretches across the Hoh, Queets, and Quinault river valleys to the west of the Olympic Range. Immense trees a thousand years old create a thick canopy with a moist understory of ferns, mosses, and fungi. As you walk among the giant spruce, cedars, and hemlocks, the landscape looks like it hasn't changed in the past millennium. The forest is so lush it feels like, if you took a nap by the side of the trail, you'd wake up covered in moss.

On the coast, a narrow strip of national park land provides easy access to mist-shrouded beaches where winter storm-watching is considered a recreational activity. From sea level to nearly 8,000 feet, the park spans a breadth of ecosystems—from craggy coastal starfish pools to humid rain forests, from mountain lakes and glaciated peaks to colorful wildflower meadows.

On the eastern side of the park, ancient trees cloak steep ridges that lead to rugged peaks. From Hurricane Ridge, you can gaze into the core of the park where serrated peaks drip with small glaciers that culminate in the highest point in the park—the crown of Mount Olympus.

PLANNING YOUR TIME

This 1,400-square-mile park lies in the center of the Olympic Peninsula and includes a 70-mile stretch of the Pacific coastline. With multiple entrance points placed far apart, the easiest access is via U.S. 101, which loops nearly around the park. Most of the park's interior is inaccessible by car, but is the province of hikers, backpackers, and climbers.

With a lot of driving, **four days** will get you to the main sights. Plan one week to 10 days to best soak up the area's riches. Lodging in the park is limited so most visitors make use of the surrounding gateway towns: **Port Angeles, Port Townsend, Sequim,** and **Forks.** Book summer **reservations** in these areas one year in advance.

The park is open year-round. **Summer** is the most popular time to visit, when it's dry and temperatures range 75-85 degrees. Avoid the big summer crowds by visiting in off-season or hiking in more remote locations.

Fall-spring, some roads, campgrounds, and facilities close and the threat of rain is ever-present—bring rain gear. Come winter, low-elevation temperatures stay above freezing while upper elevations like Hurricane Ridge amass snow.

ENTRANCES AND FEES

The entrance fee is $30 per vehicle ($25 motorcycle, $15 individual) and is good for seven days. There is no fee to enter parts of the park crossed by U.S. 101, such as at Lake Crescent and along the coastline south from Ruby Beach.

There are six entrance stations staffed daily May-September: **Heart O' the Hills/Hurricane Ridge** (Hurricane Ridge Rd.); **Elwha** (Olympic Hot Springs Rd.); **Hoh** (Upper Hoh Rd.); **Ozette** (Hoko-Ozette Rd.); **Sol Duc** (Sol Duc Rd.); and **Staircase** (Staircase Rd.).

Entrance stations are unstaffed in the off-season (Sept.-May); use the self-serve pay stations instead.

VISITORS CENTERS

Olympic National Park has four visitors centers with exhibits, information and schedules, maps, and bookstores. Kids can choose from two Junior Ranger

Top 3

1 STEP INTO THE HOH RAIN FOREST

The **Hoh Rain Forest** is the best place to explore the park's lush rain forest environment. A drive up the Hoh River proffers views of the dark canopy and shaded understory, but walking through the rain forest yields a vastly different experience—damp woods, earthy scents, fields of moss, and every shade of green imaginable.

HOH RAIN FOREST

2 GO HIGH ON HURRICANE RIDGE

Hurricane Ridge is the only car-accessible route to high vistas inside the Olympic Mountains. From Port Angeles, **Hurricane Ridge Road** (daily May-mid-Oct., Fri.-Sun. Nov.-Mar., chains required in winter) snakes up the mountainside for 17 picturesque miles at an easy 7 percent grade. The road climbs amid big scenery to alpine trails, fields bursting with wildflowers, and shrieking marmots. As the road nears the summit, you'll reach the **Hurricane Ridge Visitor Center,** which has an observation desk for peak-gazing. Look north for views of the blue Strait of Juan de Fuca glimmering 5,000 feet below. To the south lie ice-draped citadels and Mount Olympus, the park's highest peak.

3 EXPLORE TIDEPOOLS AT RUBY BEACH

Sea stacks and driftwood decorate **Ruby Beach,** which transitions from rocky ground to red sand as waves crash on the beach. From the parking area overlook, the paved **Ruby Beach Trail** (0.5 mi. rt., 20 min.) leads through woods and tall undergrowth down to the tidal zone. Come at low tide, when you have clear passage up and down the beach to explore tidepools full of mussels, starfish, and urchins and observe sea otters in the water. Look for the famous hole in a sea stack next to Cedar Creek.

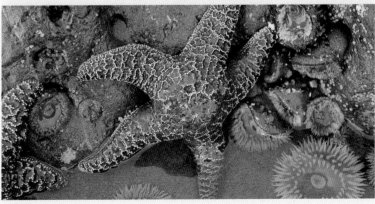

STARFISH, RUBY BEACH

ONE DAY IN OLYMPIC

Spend the night in **Port Angeles** so you can get an early start for your one day in the park. Start with a drive up to **Hurricane Ridge,** followed by a stop for lunch at **Crescent Lake Lodge.** Then cruise through the **Hoh Rain Forest** and finish with a stroll along **Ruby Beach.**

booklets (free) or pick up a **Discovery Backpack** ($5 donation) for in-the-field explorations.

Olympic National Park Visitor Center

The **Olympic National Park Visitor Center** (3002 Mount Angeles Rd., Port Angeles 360/565-3130, 7:30am-6pm daily summer, hours vary fall-spring) has park-wide information and hands-on exhibits for kids and shows a park film. Inside, the **Wilderness Information Center** (360/565-3100, daily Apr.-Oct.) is where to go for weather updates, trail reports, overnight permits ($8 per person per night), and bear canisters.

Hurricane Ridge

The **Hurricane Ridge Visitor Center** (9am-6pm daily late June-Sept., hours and days vary Oct.-May) has an observation deck, self-guided nature trails, and ranger-led walks in summer. It is located 17 miles south of Port Angeles on the summit of Hurricane Ridge.

Hoh Rain Forest

The **Hoh Rain Forest Visitor Center** (360/374-6925, 9am-5pm daily mid-May-Sept., hours and days vary May-Oct.) has a bookstore, an information desk, and ranger-led interpretive walks and presentations. It is located at the end of the Upper Hoh Road, 31 miles southeast of Forks.

Kalaloch

The small **Kalaloch Ranger Station** (156954 U.S. 101, Forks, 360/962-2283, hours vary daily late June-Sept., Tues.-Sat. mid-May-late June) is the best resource for the Olympic coast.

HURRICANE RIDGE

KAYAKING ON CRESCENT LAKE

SIGHTS

ELWHA VALLEY

Visitors come to the **Elwha Valley** to see the Elwha River's transformation. Between Port Angeles and Lake Crescent, follow the Elwha River Road south into the park. Just before reaching the entrance station, a paved, wheelchair-accessible 200-foot path leads to **Madison Falls.**

From the **Glines Canyon Spillway Overlook** (Whiskey Bend Rd. off Elwha River Rd.), look down on the remnants of the Elwha Dam to witness the old reservoir as it returns to forest. Early in the 20th century, two dams harnessed the river's power for paper milling in Port Angeles. Since the removal of the dams in 2011-2014, the water is being coaxed back to its old channels and salmon now swim upstream.

LAKE CRESCENT

Lake Crescent is the place to go for tranquil beauty. Follow U.S. 101 south as it cuts into the park along the 12-mile-long glacier-carved lake. Set in a trough of steep old-growth forest, Lake Crescent is more than 600 feet deep. The translucent turquoise-green water is startlingly clear; at some points, visibility on the lake's surface extends to 60 feet, making it a popular spot for paddlers and anglers. Enjoy the lake from its three **picnic areas,** a campground, the **Crescent Lake Lodge, Log Cabin Resort,** or two **boat launches.**

NatureBridge (415/992-4700, www.naturebridge.org) is an environmental education center with a facility near the lodge. It has weekend family programs (spring-summer) and two-week science camps for teens (summer).

SOL DUC VALLEY

West of Lake Crescent on U.S. 101, paved **Sol Duc Hot Springs Road** (pronounced "Saul Duck") leads into the park along the Sol Duc River. With old-growth forest looming on either side, the road is a beautiful 12-mile drive. Hiking here feels like something out of a fairy tale, with beams of sunlight breaking through high tree branches to dapple the forest floor.

In five miles, stop at a viewing platform overlooking **Salmon Cascades** where you can watch steelhead trout in spring and Coho salmon in fall as they fly through the air, struggling to climb a small waterfall on their way upstream.

Near the end of the road, **Sol Duc Hot Springs Resort** (12076 Sol Duc Rd., 888/896-3818, www.olympicnationalparks.com, Apr.-mid-Oct., day passes $15 adults, $10 kids) feels like a suburban rec center plopped down in the middle of the woods. You can soak in three cement pools with temperatures ranging 99-104 degrees Fahrenheit (bathers often go au natural). One large, non-thermal swimming pool offers shared space for sunbathers, swimmers, and kids.

LAKE OZETTE

At eight miles long and three miles wide, **Lake Ozette** is the third-largest natural lake in Washington. The area from its eastern shore to the coastline is part of the national park and includes a picnic area, boat launch, and campground on the north shore.

KALALOCH

The name **Kalaloch** (CLAY-lock) derives from a Quinault term meaning "sheltered landing." This coastal portion of Olympic National Park stretches between the Hoh Indian Reservation and the Quinault Reservation, providing easy access to beaches that maintain a wild feel.

Seven points along U.S. 101 can get you down to the water. Stop first at the north-end viewpoint to overlook **Ruby Beach.** From here, six numbered points access the beach from south to north. **Beach Four** is good for tidepooling, and in summer park rangers conduct guided tours of the tidepools. Next up is **Kalaloch Beach,** 7.5 miles south of Ruby. Between Kalaloch Campground and Kalaloch Lodge, Kalaloch Creek enters the ocean where the **Kalaloch Rocks** sit offshore. **South Beach** is the southernmost beach in the park.

QUEETS RAIN FOREST

South of Kalaloch, the paved and gravel Upper Queets Valley Road leads 27 miles into the **Queets Rain Forest.** This off-the-beaten-path region of the park is the province of campers, hikers, and anglers casting into the Queets River. At the road's terminus is the huge **Queets Sitka Spruce**—the largest spruce in the world by volume. The 248-foot-tall wonder is almost 15 feet in diameter at its base.

QUINAULT RAIN FOREST

The **Quinault Rain Forest** is just as rainy and impressive as the Hoh. Its forest includes some huge trees, like the **Quinault Lake Spruce,** the world's largest Sitka spruce by girth. Look for it on the easy **Big Sitka Spruce Tree Trail** (0.6 mi. rt., 30 min.), located on the South Shore Road at the lake's east end. However, the most impressive tree is on the North Shore—one of the world's largest red cedars lies on the **Big Cedar Trail** (0.4 mi. rt., 20 min., easy).

WILLABY CREEK FLOWS INTO LAKE QUINAULT

Best Hike

HURRICANE HILL TRAIL

DISTANCE: 3.2 miles round-trip
DURATION: 2 hours
ELEVATION CHANGE: 700 feet
EFFORT: moderate
TRAILHEAD: Hurricane Hill Road parking lot, 1.5 miles west of Hurricane Ridge Visitor Center

The **Hurricane Hill Trail** takes you through summer fields of wildflowers, where you may have to struggle with the impulse to throw your arms wide and belt out the opening bars of "The Sound of Music." The paved, wide trail with a couple of interpretive signs climbs out of the forest into high alpine meadows on a path that steepens the farther you go. En route, you may encounter mountain goats. At the 5,757-foot ridge, immense views spread around you. To the south, the Olympic Mountains spread in layers. You can see the glaciers flanking Mount Olympus, the highest peak in the park. To the north, look straight down on Port Angeles and the Strait of Juan de Fuca, which separates the United States from Canada. On clear days, you can even see Mount Baker and Glacier Peak. Go early in the day, as parking fills for this hike.

At the center of the rain forest sits the 240-foot-deep **Lake Quinault,** a glacier-fed natural reservoir of the Quinault River. Placid and beautiful, the lake harbors **Lake Quinault Lodge** (on the South Shore), which is listed in the National Register of Historic Places. You can boat, fish, and swim in summer or just hang out watching the rain the rest of the year.

Hikers and campers follow the **Quinault Rain Forest Loop Drive** (31 miles) to access trailheads and campsites. The road travels around the lake and up one side of the Quinault River and back down the other. The upper portions of North Shore and South Shore Roads are dirt.

HIKING

HURRICANE RIDGE AND THE NORTH SIDE

Opposite the visitors center, easy paths let you absorb the beauty. Two wheelchair-accessible paved trails go to **Big Meadow** (0.5 mi. rt., 20 min.) for mountain views and **Cirque Rim** (1 mi. rt.,

45 min., wheelchair assistance may be needed) overlooking the Strait of Juan de Fuca. The partly paved **High Ridge Loop** (0.7 mi. rt., 30 min.) climbs to Sunrise Point for views in all directions.

Klahhane Ridge

From the Hurricane Ridge visitors center, an out-and-back traverse to **Klahhane Ridge** (7.6 mi. rt., 4 hrs., strenuous) packs in big views in both directions, scads of wildflower meadows, and resident mountain goats and marmots. After passing the Switchback Trail, the last mile steepens to climb 800 feet to the ridge.

Grand Valley

An upside-down trail descends into **Grand Valley** (8.2-13 mi. rt., 4-8 hrs., strenuous), demanding an 1,800-foot climb back up on the return. The route starts with a stunning high traverse south on Lillian Ridge before dropping into the valley cradling three lovely lakes—**Moose Lake** (8.2 mi. rt.), **Grand Lake** (8.7 mi. rt.), and **Gladys Lake** (9.2 mi. rt.), the last above the tree line. The route passes talus and wildflower meadows and culminates at **Grand Pass** (13 mi. rt.) for big views. The trailhead is at the end of the Obstruction Point Road.

Royal Basin

The Upper Dungeness Trail enters the park to reach **Royal Lake** (16 mi. rt., 8 hrs., strenuous), tucked below the craggy Needles and Mount Deception. The trail follows Royal Creek into the rugged Royal Basin, a glaciated bowl of forest, meadows, talus slopes, and waterfalls. Beyond the lake, small tarns, lingering snowfields, Shelter Rock, and wildflowers speckle the alpine wonderlands of the upper basin. The **Upper Dungeness Trailhead** is located outside the park, south of Sequim. You'll need a Northwest Forest Pass and an early start to park at the crowded trailhead parking lot.

ELWHA VALLEY
Humes Ranch Loop

The **Humes Ranch Loop** (6.5 mi. rt., 3 hrs., moderate) takes a shady, wooded walk past two long-abandoned early-20th-century homesteads—**Michael's Cabin** and **Humes Ranch.** A short spur goes to **Goblin Gates,** a picturesque spot where the Elwha River rushes between two rocky outcroppings. The trailhead is at the end of the gravel Whiskey Bend Road, off Olympic Hot Springs Road.

Boulder Lake Trail

The **Boulder Lake Trail** is used to access **Olympic Hot Springs** (5 mi. rt., 2.5 hrs., easy), but follow it farther to reach **Boulder Lake** (10 mi. rt.). The path starts with a gentle climb along a former roadbed through old-growth forest. After crossing Boulder Creek, the hot springs appear. (On weekends, you may have to wait for space in a pool.) Continue on to reach the beautiful green-tinted Boulder Lake with Boulder Peak looming above. The trailhead is at the end of Olympic Hot Springs Road.

LAKE CRESCENT
Marymere Falls

From Storm King Ranger Station, a gentle walk in the woods culminates at the 90-foot **Marymere Falls** (1.8 mi. rt., 1 hr., easy). After 0.5 mile on the Marymere Falls Trail is the turnoff for **Mount Storm King** (4.2 mi. rt., 3 hrs., strenuous), a steep 1,700-foot ascent on a switchback trail. Partway up, a viewpoint looks down on Lake Crescent.

Spruce Railroad Trail

On East Shore Road, the **Spruce Railroad Trail** (2-8 mi. rt., 1-4 hrs., easy) takes a lakeside route along the north shore of Lake Crescent. The repurposed railroad track trail was once used for hauling Sitka spruce—you even go through a tunnel.

WATERFALL VIEWS INTO OLYMPIC NATIONAL PARK

HOH RAIN FOREST

Devil's Punchbowl (1 mile from the trailhead) is a calm cove surrounded by tall bluffs and crossed by a picturesque bridge with a postcard-worthy view of Mount Storm King. The cove is a popular swimming hole; bring your suit for a dip. This trail is now a segment of the **Olympic Discovery Trail**, a shared trail for walkers and cyclists with a paved 6.5-mile extension that is wheelchair-accessible.

SOL DUC VALLEY

Lover's Lane Trail

At Sol Duc Hot Springs Resort, the **Lover's Lane Trail** (5.8 mi. rt., 3 hrs., easy) offers an easy, scenic loop through lush terrain along the banks of the Sol Duc River. As you cross the river to head back downstream, Sol Duc Falls roars while making a two-level, 50-foot drop. The best viewing is from the bridge, where you're close enough to get spritzed with a gentle mist.

Sol Duc Falls Trail

To reach Sol Duc Falls with a shorter walk, drive to the terminus of Sol Duc Road to hike the **Sol Duc Falls Trail** (1.6 mi. rt., 1 hr., easy). The crowning hike loops **Seven Lakes Basin and High Divide** (18.2 mi. rt., 9 hrs., strenuous) with a 3,050-foot climb past subalpine lakes and wildflower meadows to a goat-trail traverse across Bogachiel Peak with spectacular views of Mount Olympus and Blue Glacier.

HOH RAIN FOREST

From the visitors center, follow the **Mini-Trail** (0.25 mile), an accessible loop with interpretive signage. The evocatively named **Hall of Mosses Trail** (0.8 mi. rt., 30 min.) loops past 200-foot firs, big-leaf maples festooned with moss, and licorice ferns that carpet the forest floor. The **Spruce Nature Trail** (1.2 mi. rt., 45 min.) leads through the forest to the banks of the Hoh River.

LAKE OZETTE AND THE COAST

Shi Shi Beach

For isolated coastal beauty, head through the Makah Reservation to **Shi Shi Beach** (4-9 mi. rt., 2-5 hrs., easy, $10 pass required). A partial boardwalk path cuts through damp woods to a steep, rope-assisted descent to the beach. The sandy 2.5-mile crescent flecked with driftwood is best at low tide for tidepools of starfish and sea urchins. **Point of Arches,** a group of massive, intricate sea stacks, sits at the south end.

To reach Shi Shi Beach (pronounced "shy shy"), take Cape Flattery Road west of Neah Bay for 2.5 miles and turn south onto Hobuck Beach Road. After crossing the Sooes River the road becomes Sooes Beach Road to reach the trailhead.

BACKPACKING IS A POPULAR ACTIVITY IN THE PARK.

Cape Alava

The draw at Lake Ozette is the coastline and its impressive wildlife. **Cape Alava** (6.6 mi. rt., 3.5 hrs., easy) plods on a cedar boardwalk through forest and wet prairie to the westernmost point of the Lower 48, passing the site of a **Makah village.** The beach is strewn with rocks, driftwood, and a ship anchor that washed ashore. About a mile south of Cape Alava are the **Wedding Rocks,** with Indian petroglyphs depicting whales, fertility figures, and a European ship.

The **Sand Point Trail** (6 mi. rt., 3 hrs., easy) travels mostly over boardwalk to reach the beach at a southern point. The **Ozette Triangle** (9 mi. rt., 5 hrs., easy) connects the Cape Alava Trail to the Sand Point Trail, adding three miles of walking along the beach.

A **ranger station** (360/963-2725, daily June-Sept.) at the end of Hoko-Ozette Road marks the trailhead for the two routes.

EAST SIDE

Upper Lena Lake

The trail to Lena Lake crowds with weekend hikers, but those who hike to **Upper Lena Lake** (14 mi. rt., 7-8 hrs., strenuous) will find plenty of breathing room along with subalpine wildflowers,

huckleberries, and views of the Brothers, a pair of rugged peaks. The demanding route climbs 3,900 feet. From U.S. 101 north of Hoodsport, take the Hamma Hamma River Road (#25) to the trailhead.

Staircase Rapids Loop

The **North Fork of the Skokomish River Trail** passes Pacific rhododendrons, vibrant mossy old growth, and waterfalls offering multiple destinations. At one mile in, turn south to cross the river for the **Staircase Rapids Loop** (2 mi. rt., 1 hr., easy) to admire a big fallen cedar tree. The trailhead is at the Staircase Ranger Station, at the end of the twisting dirt road.

RECREATION

BACKPACKING

The park's backcountry is a backpacker's paradise. Long, forested valley trails top out on stunning subalpine passes with a riot of colorful wildflowers in summer. The best two- or three-day trips head to **Royal Basin** (16 mi. rt.), **Grand Valley** (8.2-13 mi. rt.), **Seven Lakes Basin-High Divide Loop** (18.2 mi. rt.), and the **Ozette Triangle** (9 mi. rt.).

On the west side, the most popular backpacking trips last 3-5 days. The **Hoh River Trail** (35 mi. rt.) combines a gentle rain forest walk with a climb past a 100-foot canyon on the way to Glacier Meadows, where wildflowers intersperse among glacial moraine as Mount Olympus looms above. For long beach treks, watch the tides for **Rialto Beach to Cape Alava** (44 mi. rt.) or **Third Beach to Hoh River** (32 mi. rt.).

Permits are required and can be picked up 24 hours in advance from the **Wilderness Information Center** (3002 Mount Angeles Rd., 360/565-3100, daily Apr.-Oct., $8). **Reservation requests** start March 15 for May-September trips.

CLIMBING

The end of the Hoh River Trail is the most popular launching point for experienced mountaineers to scale 7,980-foot **Mount Olympus** (late June-early Sept.), the tallest peak in the park. It's a technically demanding scramble over glaciers and a rock spire at the summit, requiring ice axes, harnesses, ropes, and crampons. Permits are not required for climbing, but are required for backcountry camping.

Several companies guide climbs: **Mountain Madness** (800/328-5925, www.mountainmadness.com), **International Mountain Guides** (360/569-2609, www.mountainguides.com).

KAYAKING AND RAFTING

Several lakes make for exceptional paddling. Lake Crescent, Lake Ozette, and Lake Quinault have boat launches for motorboats and other watercraft. **Lake Crescent Lodge** and **Log Cabin Resort** rent kayaks, rowboats, canoes, and paddleboards for Lake Crescent. For Lake Quinault, **Lake Quinault Lodge** rents kayaks, paddleboards, canoes, and rowboats.

Guided float trips hit the rivers. **Adventures through Kayaking** (2358 U.S. 101, 360/417-3015, www.atkayaking.com) leads kayak or paddleboard tours on Lake Crescent and provide lessons and rentals. **Rainforest Paddlers** (360/374-5254, www.rainforestpaddlers.com) leads trips on the Hoh, Sol Duc, and Elwha Rivers. They also guide kayak trips on the Hoh and in an estuary near La Push.

FISHING

Lake Crescent contains Beardslee rainbows, Crescenti cutthroats, and abundant kokanee runs May-October. The **Sol Duc River** has steelhead, salmon, and trout.

▼ ROCK CAIRNS, RIALTO BEACH

SNOWSHOEING ON HURRICANE RIDGE

WINTER SPORTS

With 400 inches of snow annually, **Hurricane Ridge** becomes a winter playground December-March. You can downhill ski, cross-country ski, snowboard, tube, and snowshoe. Hurricane Ridge Road is open to uphill traffic Friday-Sunday (9am-4pm), weather permitting (carry tire chains).

For downhill skiing and snowboarding, **Hurricane Ridge Ski and Snowboard Area** (848/667-7669, www.hurricaneridge.com, 10am-4pm Sat.-Sun. Dec.-Mar., pass required) operates two rope tows and a Poma lift and rents tubes for sliding. A gift shop rents downhill skis, cross-country skis, and snowshoes.

Ranger-led **snowshoe walks** (2pm Sat.-Sun. Dec.-Mar., adults $7, children $3) last 1.5 hours and include snowshoes. Sign up 30 minutes before the start time at the Hurricane Ridge Visitor Center.

WHERE TO STAY

INSIDE THE PARK

For summer stays, make **reservations** (888/896-3818, www.olympicnationalparks.com) one year in advance at four lodges.

Lake Crescent

The historic **Lake Crescent Lodge** (416 Lake Crescent Rd., 360/928-3211, May-early Jan., from $190) has cabins with fireplaces, motel rooms, and lodge rooms with shared baths. The lodge **restaurant** (7am-2:30pm and 5pm-9pm daily) overlooks the lake and has a bar and gift shop.

At the north end of Lake Crescent, the **Log Cabin Resort** (3183 E. Beach Rd., 360/928-3325, late May-Sept., from $110) has cabins, a few large chalets, and an RV campground. The modest on-site **restaurant** (8am-11am, noon-4pm, and 5pm-9pm daily) serves breakfast, lunch, and dinner.

Sol Duc

Sol Duc Hot Springs Resort (12076 Sol Duc Rd., 360/327-3583, Mar.-Oct., from $180) consists of RV campsites and 32 no-frills cabins next to the hot springs complex; some rooms have kitchens. The resort's **Springs Restaurant** (7am-10:30am, 11am-4pm, and 5pm-9pm daily) and **Poolside Deli** (11:30am-4:30pm daily) serve cafeteria-style breakfast, lunch, and dinner.

Lake Quinault

Built in 1926, **Lake Quinault Lodge** (345 South Shore Rd., 360/288-2900, year-round, from $245) is a classic national park hotel with rooms in the original lodge, a newer building with larger rooms, or a small annex. The lodge's **Roosevelt Dining Room** (7:30am-3pm and 5pm-9pm daily) serves breakfast, lunch, and dinner.

Kalaloch

Kalaloch Lodge (157151 U.S. 101, 360/962-2271, www.thekalalochlodge.com, year-round, from $200) sits on a bluff overlooking the ocean. Accommodations include Bluff Cabins, smaller Kalaloch Cabins, and guest rooms in the main lodge. The lodge's **Creekside**

NAME	LOCATION	PRICE	SEASON	AMENITIES
Heart O' the Hills	Hurricane Ridge	$20	year-round	tent and RV sites
Fairholme	Lake Crescent	$20	May-Oct.	tent and RV sites
Lake Crescent Lodge	Lake Crescent	$190	May-Jan.	cabins, motel and lodge rooms, dining
Log Cabin Resort	Lake Crescent	$110	May-Sept.	cabins, chalets, RV sites, dining
Sol Duc	Sol Duc	$21-24	Mar.-Oct.	tent and RV sites
Sol Duc Hot Springs Resort	Sol Duc	$180	Mar.-Oct.	cabins, RV sites, dining
Ozette	Lake Ozette	$20	year-round	tent and RV sites
Hoh	Hoh Rain Forest	$20	year-round	tent and RV sites
Lake Quinault Lodge	Lake Quinault	$245	year-round	lodge rooms, dining
Kalaloch Campground	Kalaloch	$22		tent and RV sites
Kalaloch Lodge	Kalaloch	$200	year-round	cabins, lodge rooms, dining
Mora	Rialto Beach	$20	year-round	tent and RV sites
Staircase	Staircase	$20	May-Oct.	tent and RV sites

Restaurant (8am-8pm daily) serves breakfast, lunch, and dinner, with reservations essential in summer.

Campgrounds

Only two campgrounds accept **reservations** (877/444-6777, www.recreation.gov) in summer. **Sol Duc Campground** (82 sites) near Sol Duc Hot Springs and popular **Kalaloch Campground** (170 sites) on the ocean. All remaining campgrounds are first come, first served: **Heart O' the Hills Campground** (105 sites) near Hurricane Ridge; **Fairholme Campground**

KALALOCH

MOUNTAIN VIEWS OF OLYMPIC NATIONAL PARK

(88 sites) near a noisy highway; **Hoh Campground** (78 sites) near the Hoh visitors center; **Ozette Campground** (15 sites); **Mora Campground** (94 sites) two miles from Rialto Beach; and **Staircase** (49 sites) on the Skokomish River.

Primitive campgrounds (no drinking water, $15) include: **Deer Park** (Deer Park Rd., June-mid-Oct., 14 tent-only sites), **South Beach** (May-Sept., 55 sites), **Graves Creek** (year-round, 30 tent-only sites), **North Fork** (North Shore Rd., year-round, 9 tent-only sites), and **Queets** (Upper Queets River Rd., year-round, 20 sites).

OUTSIDE THE PARK

Port Angeles, Port Townsend, and **Sequim** serve as gateway towns for the north side of Olympic National Park. Tiny **Forks** and **Kalaloch** are bases for exploring the park's coastal side. **Hoodsport** is a small eastside base with minimal services.

GETTING THERE

AIR

The closest international airport is **Seattle-Tacoma International Airport** (SEA, 800/544-1965 or 206/787-5388, www.portseattle.org/seatac). Car rentals are at the airport.

BUS

Olympic Bus Lines (800/457-4492, http://olympicbuslines.com) operates the Dungeness Line between Sea-Tac airport and Port Angeles, with three stops in Seattle. The four-hour ride travels twice eastbound and twice westbound per day.

CAR

From Seattle, drive south on I-5 through Tacoma, then turn north on Highway 16 to Bremerton. From Bremerton, take Highway 3 north to Highway 104 where it meets up with U.S. 101 north to Port Townsend and Port Angeles. Port Angeles is on U.S. 101, 19 miles north of the Hurricane Ridge Visitor Center in Olympic National Park. Plan 2.5-3 hours for the drive of 125 miles.

FERRY

From Seattle, **Washington State ferries** (206/464-6400, www.wsdot.wa.gov) depart for Bainbridge Island and Bremerton. Both connect by highways to U.S. 101.

GETTING AROUND

Driving along U.S. 101 will give you plenty of views of trees with snippets of the beach, but you'll see little of the mountains and rain forest in the heart of the park. Lots of driving is required between park regions and you'll need to take paved spur roads to visit them. Check the road and weather hotline (360/565-3131) for travel conditions.

From Port Angeles, **Hurricane Ridge** is 19 miles (45 min.) south of downtown, where Race Street becomes Mount Angeles Road and then Hurricane Ridge Road. About 11 miles (20 min.) southwest of Port Angeles, U.S. 101 reaches the **Elwha** entrance to the park via Olympic Hot Springs Road. West of Port Angeles, U.S. 101 reaches the southern side of **Lake Crescent** in 21 miles (30 min.) and the **Sol Duc** entrance in 30 miles (1 hr.) via Sol Duc Road.

To reach **Lake Ozette,** turn off Route 112 just west of Sekiu onto Hoko-Ozette Road and drive 21 miles south to the road's end.

To get to the **Hoh Rain Forest,** take U.S. 101 to Upper Hoh Road and drive 18 miles to the visitors center. It's about 90 miles (2 hrs.) from Port Angeles.

Along U.S. 101 on the coast, **Kalaloch** is 90 miles (2.5 hrs.) south of Port Angeles. **Ruby Beach** is on the northernmost point of the Kalaloch coast, eight miles north of Kalaloch Lodge and 27 miles south of Forks.

U.S. 101 skirts the western edge of **Lake Quinault** 35 miles (45 min.) south of Kalaloch. The Quinault Rain Forest is accessed off the North Shore or South Shore Roads. It's a 120-mile drive (3.3 hrs.) from Port Angeles.

SIGHTS NEARBY

Museum at the Makah Cultural and Research Center (Makah Indian Reservation, 1880 Bayview Ave., Neah Bay, 360/645-2711, http://makahmuseum.com, 10am-5pm daily) features artifacts from the Lake Ozette archeological site.

Cape Flattery (Neah Bay, http://makah.com, Makah Recreation Pass required) is the northwesternmost point in the Lower 48, accessible via a wild hike to four observation decks overlooking the Pacific.

SUNLIGHT STREAMS THROUGH SOL DUC

MOUNT RAINIER NATIONAL PARK

Washington

WEBSITE:
www.nps.gov/mora

PHONE NUMBER:
360/569-2211

VISITATION RANK:
18

WHY GO:
Visit the most glaciated peak in the contiguous United States.

PASSPORT STAMPS ▾▾▾

▲ MOUNT RAINIER NATIONAL PARK

MOUNT RAINIER NATIONAL PARK is the most impressive geographical landmark in the Pacific Northwest. With an elevation of 14,411 feet, the ice-coned volcano is the tallest peak in the Cascade Mountains, which stretch from Canada to California. Tumbling from its cone are the most glaciers of any peak in the Lower 48. Throughout much of Washington, it dominates the horizon, making it an integral part of the state's identity.

At Paradise and Sunrise—the two highest car-accessible points—the towering summit feels within your grasp, just one flower-filled meadow away. But it looms 8,000-9,000 feet overhead. Splayed around its flank, idyllic hiking trails and twisting mountain roads tour abundant old-growth forests, waterfalls, alpine lakes, and fields of brilliant wildflowers.

PLANNING YOUR TIME

About 100 miles south of Seattle, Mount Rainier beckons. Visitors come to explore the park's five developed areas. In the center of the park, **Paradise** tucks south of Rainier's peak while **Sunrise** lies northeast. Both offer elevated locations with big views, visitors centers, and trailheads. South of Paradise is **Longmire,** with a hotel, restaurant, and museum. In the southeast corner, near the Stevens Canyon entrance, **Ohanapecosh** has a visitors center and campground. In the rainy northwest corner, **Carbon/Mowich** gets very little traffic; it's where hikers, bikers, and campers go to escape the crowds.

The majority of visitors come during the mild **summer** season (late June-Sept.) when temperatures hang in the 60s and 70s. July-August sees long midday lines at the Nisqually and White River entrance stations, and parking lots fill at Sunrise, Paradise, and popular trailheads. Plan to go early in the day or on a weekday for more solitude. Fall and spring are rainy and cool; in winter, most of the park lies buried under snow.

ENTRANCES AND FEES

There are three entrance stations: the **Nisqually Entrance** (open year-round) at the southwest corner, the **Stevens Canyon Entrance** (late May-mid-Sept.) at the southeast corner, and the **White River Entrance** (late June-mid-Oct.) to the northeast. For the remote **Carbon/Mowich** area, pay fees in a drop box or at the ranger station.

The entrance fee is $30 per vehicle ($25 motorcycle, $15 individual) and is good for seven days.

VISITORS CENTERS

At Paradise, the **Henry M. Jackson Visitor Center** (360/569-6571, 10am-5pm daily May-mid-June and Sept., 10am-7pm daily mid-June-Aug., 10am-5pm Sat.-Sun. Oct.-Apr.) is a modern take on traditional alpine design. Inside, watch an introductory park film, see exhibits, and have a bite at the snack bar. The center is the starting point for ranger-led daily nature walks in summer and weekend snowshoe treks in winter.

At Sunrise, the historic log cabin **Sunrise Visitor Center** (360/663-2425, 10am-6pm daily July-early Sept.) houses natural history displays and has telescopes to check out Mount Rainier's glaciers. Rangers answer questions and lead daily nature walks; the information desk has times and destinations. Across the parking lot, **Sunrise Day Lodge** has a gift shop and a cafeteria.

At the Stevens Canyon entrance is the tiny **Ohanapecosh Visitor Center** (360/569-6581, hours vary June-Sept.). In summer, rangers lead nature walks several times a week. You can pick up trail maps and consult with rangers about explorations.

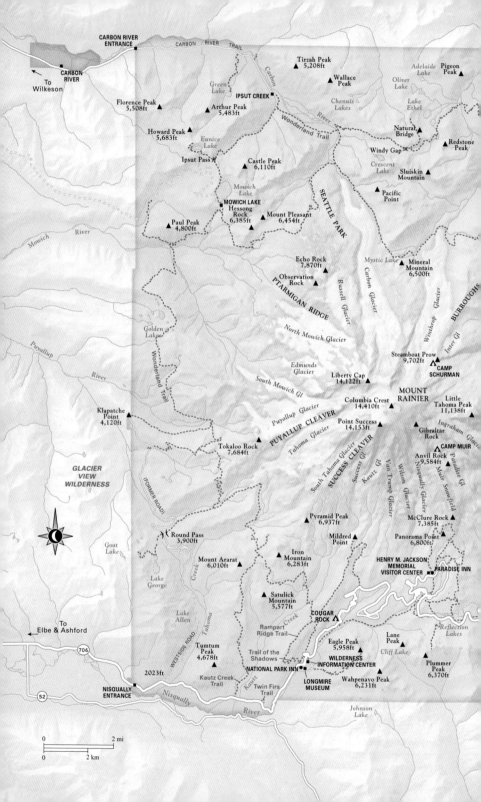

MOUNT RAINIER NATIONAL PARK

MT. BAKER-SNOQUALMIE
NATIONAL FOREST

Scarface
6,108ft ▲   Lake
            Eleanor

Slide Mountain
6,339ft ▲

CRYSTAL MOUNTAIN
SKI AREA
AND RESORT

Brown Peak
6,322ft ▲

Skyscraper
Mountain
7,078ft ▲

Forest
Lake

Marcus Peak
6,962ft ▲

Rover
Lake

SOURDOUGH MOUNTAINS

SUNRISE RIDGE

MATHER MEMORIAL PARKWAY

Pacific Crest National Scenic Trail

Frozen
Lake

SUNRISE
DAY LODGE   Dege Peak
             7,008ft ▲

SUNRISE
VISITOR CENTER

EMMONS VISTA

Shadow
Lake

WHITE RIVER

WHITE RIVER
ENTRANCE

Crystal
Lake

Placer
Lake

MOUNTAIN

White River

410

MATHER MEMORIAL PARKWAY   410

American River

Emmons Glacier

Baker
Point ▲

GOAT ISLAND MOUNTAIN

GOVERNORS RIDGE

510

Deadwood
Lakes

WENATCHEE
NATIONAL
FOREST

Tamanos
Mountain
6,790ft ▲

Ghost
Lake

Chinook Pass
5,432ft

MOUNT RAINIER
NATIONAL PARK

Fryingpan Glacier

Sarvant Glaciers

Panhandle
Gap
6,800ft ▲

Owyhigh
Lakes

Cayuse Pass
4,694ft

Tipsoo
Lake

Dewey
Lake

Whitman Glacier

Barrier Peak
6,514ft ▲

Swamp
Lake

Cowlitz Gl.

Cowlitz Rocks
7,450ft ▲

Double Peak
6,199ft ▲

COWLITZ   DIVIDE

Wonderland Trail

Ohanapecosh River

Chinook Creek

123

Seymour Peak
6,337ft ▲

American
Lake

Cougar
Lake

Pacific Crest National Scenic Trail

Fan Lake

Shriner Peak
5,834ft ▲

Bald Rock
5,411ft ▲

Crag
Lake

Marsh
Lakes

BOX
CANYON

Grove of the
Patriarchs Trail

Three
Lakes

Bench Lake

Snow
Lake

STEVENS CANYON
ENTRANCE

Carlton Creek

Stevens Peak
6,510ft ▲

Unicorn Peak
6,917ft ▲

Blue Lake

Muddy Fork Cowlitz River

OHANAPECOSH
VISITOR CENTER

Jug Lake

GIFFORD PINCHOT
NATIONAL FOREST

Ohanapecosh River

123

To
Packwood

© AVALON TRAVEL

Top ❸

TRAILS IN PARADISE

❶ SOAK IN THE PARADISE VIEWS

At 5,400 feet, with glacier-clad Rainier standing before you, **Paradise** is a gorgeous, understandably crowded spot. Late July and August is the prime time for viewing the peak framed by fields of wildflowers. This is the busiest place in the park and on weekends the large parking lot packs out.

❷ SPY MOUNT RAINIER FROM SUNRISE

The **Sunrise** area occupies a subalpine plateau with spectacular views of the northeast side of Mount Rainier—the towering summit feels just beyond your grasp. It's one of the most popular destinations within the park, but the window for visiting is narrow—the road up is usually open only from late June or early July through early September.

❸ HIKE THE SKYLINE TRAIL

For impressive views of Rainier from Glacier Vista and Panorama Point, the **Skyline Trail** (5.5 mi. rt., 4.5 hrs., strenuous) climbs 1,700 feet, waltzing above timberline; it draws scads of hikers. With some exposure and steep lingering snowfields on the upper part, this trail is not for acrophobes.

MOUNT RAINIER FROM THE SUNRISE AREA

ONE DAY IN MOUNT RAINIER

Drive the scenic park road to **Paradise** or **Sunrise** and concentrate your time there. Stop at scenic pullouts en route, tour the visitors centers, and tackle a hike to soak up the mountain's splendor.

At Longmire's **Wilderness Information Center** (360/569-6650, 7:30am-5pm daily mid-May-mid-Oct.) you can get passes for and information about backcountry hiking and camping, plus suggestions for hikes.

SIGHTS

LONGMIRE

Longmire is home to the **Longmire Museum** (360/569-6575, 9am-5pm daily May-Sept., off-season hours vary). The small facility, located in the original park headquarters, contains displays on the park's natural history, along with exhibits of basketry, a small totem pole, and photos from the park's early days. It's seven miles from the Nisqually entrance in the park's southwest corner.

PARADISE

The 13-mile drive from Longmire to Paradise ascends through evergreen forests where periodic openings provide down-valley and up-mountain vistas. Three miles before Paradise, stop at the pullout overlooking **Narada Falls,** where a steep trail leads to the plunge pool at its base.

Built in 1916, **Paradise Inn** (mid-May-early Oct.) is an imposing wooden lodge built in the style of many national park hotels, with the highlights found in the public spaces. The lobby is impressive, with high ceilings, stone fireplaces, and mountain views. A stay here is a step back in time—there are no TVs, phones, or WiFi. Just views for days.

OHANAPECOSH

The Ohanapecosh area consists of a visitors center and campground in the heavily wooded southeast corner of the park near the Stevens Canyon entrance. To get here from Paradise, cruise east on 19-mile **Stevens Canyon Road** (open June-October), which is packed with scenery.

Begin by passing **Reflection Lakes** and then wind through forests and past more small lakes, with views of Mount Rainier and the Cascades shooting between the trees.

A pullout along the way offers side views of the multi-tiered **Martha Falls,** which end with a 145-foot plunge. For a closer look, pull off the road where it intersects with the **Wonderland Trail,** 0.5 mile west of the falls pullout. Take the trail to the bridge at the falls' base.

The road cuts across the slopes of Stevens Canyon to follow Stevens Creek downhill. At **Box Canyon,** a short trail leads to a footbridge spanning the deep, narrow gorge created by the **Muddy Fork of the Cowlitz River.** By the time you get to the junction with Route 123, the road is deep within old-growth forests of Douglas fir and western hemlock at an elevation of 2,200 feet.

SUNRISE

At 6,400 feet, **Sunrise** (road open late June or early July-early Sept.) is the highest point in the park reachable by car—and getting here is part of the fun. From the White River entrance station off Route 410, the road climbs for 11 miles on switchbacks lacing through evergreen forests to emerge into meadows with all-encompassing vistas. The subalpine plateau has spectacular views of Rainier's two largest glaciers (Emmons and Winthrop), and large numbers of **elk** congregate during summer and fall.

CARBON/MOWICH

The remote **Carbon/Mowich** area tucks into the park's rain forest-like northwest corner that sees fewer visitors. Reach it by taking Route 165 south from Buckley to Carbonado and crossing the Carbon River Gorge Bridge to a junction. The left fork onto Carbon River Road goes to the park's border, where the washed-out road becomes a trail for six miles of walking or biking. The right fork ventures 17 potholed gravel miles on Mowich Lake Road to **Mowich Lake** (open June-Sept.), the largest and deepest body of water in the park. The lake has a picnic area, tent-only campground, and several trails.

RECREATION

HIKING

The prime hiking season runs July-September after most of the snow is gone. Wildflowers usually peak late July-August.

Longmire

Across the road from Longmire National Inn, the **Trail of the Shadows** (0.7 mi. rt., 30 min., easy) takes a stroll around the meadow where Longmire's resort once stood. Cutting off from this trail, a longer loop continues up **Rampart Ridge** (4.6 mi. rt., 2.5 hrs., moderate) to a majestic view over the Nisqually River far below, then joins the Wonderland Trail. Go clockwise for better views of Rainier.

With a 1,200-foot ascent comes the reward of **Comet Falls** (3.8 mi. rt., 2 hrs., strenuous), a 301-foot-tall ribbon. Part of the trail ascends a rocky face on log steps. Locate the trailhead halfway between Longmire and Paradise west of Christine Falls.

PINNACLE PEAK TRAIL

Paradise

Among the area's spiderweb of subalpine forest and meadow trails, the easiest is the **Nisqually Vista Trail** (1.2 mi. rt., 45 min., moderate), which leads through flamboyant florals to overlook the Nisqually River and Glacier.

Between Paradise and Stevens Canyon, the **Pinnacle Peak Trail** (2.5 mi. rt., 2 hrs., strenuous) starts at the Reflection Lakes parking lot to climb to the saddle between Pinnacle and Plummer Peaks for huge Rainier views. The trail, which often retains snow into July, gains 1,100 feet to the saddle, where adept scramblers can add on Plummer Peak. From a trailhead one mile east of Reflection Lakes, a less steep trail filled with bear grass and flowers in late summer chugs to **Bench and Snow Lakes** (2.5 mi. rt., 1.5 hrs., moderate).

Ohanapecosh

West of the Stevens Canyon entrance station, the **Grove of the Patriarchs Loop** (1.5 mi. rt., 1 hr., easy) crosses the crystalline Ohanapecosh River via a suspension bridge onto an island of virgin old-growth trees. Some of the oldest trees in the state, these thousand-year-old Douglas firs, western hemlocks, and western red cedars tower over ferns.

From Ohanapecosh Campground, the **Silver Falls Loop** (3 mi. rt., 2 hrs., easy) follows the river through old-growth forest to the 75-foot Silver Falls and a side spur leading to the former site of Ohanapecosh Hot Springs Resort.

A rigorous grind up a steep, shadeless ridge goes to 5,834-foot **Shriner Peak Lookout** (8 mi. rt., 5 hrs., strenuous). Big, 360-degree views from the peak make it worth the effort. Find the trailhead 3.5 miles north of the Stevens Canyon Entrance on the west side of the road.

Sunrise

From the Sunrise Visitor Center parking lot, trails gain views of Rainier's biggest glaciers. The **Sunrise Nature Trail** (1.5 mi. rt., 1 hr., easy) takes a self-guided loop. The **Shadow Lakes Loop** (3.7 mi. rt., 2 hrs., moderate) drops to a rim overlooking the White River valley and then follows the ridge to Shadow Lake,

SHADOW LAKE AT SUNRISE

VIEW OF MT. RAINIER FROM SUMMERLAND

returning via Frozen Lake and Sourdough Ridge. The trail to 7,181-foot **Mount Fremont Lookout** (5.6 mi. rt., 3 hrs., strenuous) trots up Sourdough Ridge to Frozen Lake before branching off to the north, where mountain goats sometimes hang around the summit. A gentler climb to **Dege Peak** (7 mi. rt., 3.5 hrs., moderate) goes east on Sourdough Ridge for views of Mount Baker to the north and Mount Adams to the south.

From the White River Campground, the **Glacier Basin Trail** (6.5 mi. rt., 6 hrs., strenuous) gains 1,700 feet to pop out of the forest in an idyllic basin of meadows cradling a glacial tarn. Views take in the Wedge and Mount Ruth on Rainier. Add a side spur (1 mi. rt.) to go up the moraine to see Emmons Glacier, the largest of Rainier's glaciers.

You must get here early to claim a parking spot for the best-of-the-best hike to **Summerland** (9 mi. rt., 5 hrs., strenuous). The trail follows Fryingpan Creek and then switchbacks up to reach prolific wildflower meadows below Little Tahoma and Rainier. The trailhead is three miles west of the White River entrance.

Carbon/Mowich

To escape crowds, drive the 17-mile, rough-graveled Mowich Lake Road (located near Carbonado on Hwy. 165 south of Buckley) to Mowich Lake. Climbing 1,700 feet to **Spray Park** (8 mi. rt., 4 hrs., moderate) takes in Spray Falls on a short spur trail and wildflower meadows with a backdrop of the ice-capped Rainier. The less demanding trail to **Tolmie Peak Lookout** (7.5 mi. rt., 4 hrs., moderate) gains 1,100 feet to pass Eunice Lake before zipping up switchbacks to a big view of Rainier.

BACKPACKING

A 93-mile loop circling Mount Rainier, the **Wonderland Trail** traverses passes, forests, streams, and alpine meadows—all with changing views of the icy mountain. The strenuous trail has copious ups and downs (22,000 feet of elevation gain), including several short stretches with 3,500-foot changes. Backpackers need 10-14 days for the entire loop. You can start at multiple trailheads and choose from 18 designated trailside camps and three front-country campgrounds for overnighting.

Wilderness permits are required. Due to heavy competition for permits, get **reservations** ($20) online starting March 15. For first-come, first-served permits on your day of departure, go early in person to the Longmire or White River Wilderness Information Centers, Jackson Visitor Center, or Carbon River Ranger Station. Most of the route is snow-free **late June to mid-October**.

CLIMBING

For climbers, Mount Rainier is a premier summit and training peak, where raging winds, whiteouts, avalanches, hidden crevasses, rockfall, and altitude increase the hazard. About 10,000 people attempt the summit every year; less than half succeed. DIY trips require fluency in rock climbing, navigation, glacier travel, and crevasse rescue. Ropes, harnesses, crampons, and ice axes are vital. Most climbs launch from Paradise to overnight at Camp Muir before clambering via Disappointment Cleaver and Ingraham Glacier to the highest point at the Columbia Crest. A second common route goes from White River Campground onto the Inter and Emmons Glaciers to overnight at Camp Schurman before ascending the Emmons and Winthrop Glaciers.

Climbing the peak usually requires two days. Fees include a **climbing cost recovery fee** ($32-47) and a reservation for a **wilderness permit for overnighting** ($20). Once in the park, you must also obtain a **climbing permit** (free) from the Paradise Climbing Information Center or White River Wilderness Information Center within 24 hours of departure.

For guided climbs, contact **Alpine Ascents International** (206/378-1927, www.alpineascents.com), **International Mountain Guides** (360/569-2609, www.mountainguides.com), or **Rainier Mountaineering Inc.** (888/892-5462, www.rmiguides.com).

WINTER SPORTS

In winter, most visitors head to **Paradise** (Dec.-Apr.) to play in a supervised **snow-play** area. Bring your own soft sliding toys, such as inner tubes and saucers. Snow-buried roads become routes for **cross-country skiers** and **snowshoers.** Many beginners ski the ungroomed road or trails to Nisqually Vista, Narada Falls, or Reflection Lakes.

Rent skis, avalanche beacons, snowshoes, and other winter gear from the **Longmire General Store** (360/569-2275, 10am-5pm daily in winter). You can also arrange ski lessons and tours.

From Jackson Visitor Center, rangers lead **snowshoe walks** (free) on winter weekends and holidays. Snowshoes are free to use during these walks.

WHERE TO STAY
INSIDE THE PARK

With limited lodging, **reservations** (855/755-2275, www.mtrainierguest-services.com) are mandatory; book one year ahead for summer stays.

In Longmire, the **National Park Inn** (360/569-2411, year-round, from $126) has 25 guest rooms; some share bathrooms. The **dining room** (7am-11am, 11:30am-4:30pm, and 5pm-7pm) serves three meals daily.

GROVE OF THE PATRIARCHS

Erected in 1916 at Paradise, **Paradise Inn** (360/569-2413, mid-May-early Oct., $123-185) is an imposing timber lodge with an impressive lobby, high ceilings, stone fireplaces, and mountain views. The guest rooms share bathroom facilities and tight quarters. The **dining room** (7am-9:30am, noon-2pm, and 5:30pm-8pm daily) serves lunch and dinner.

There are small eateries at **Paradise Camp Deli** (Jackson Visitor Center, 10am-6:45pm daily mid-June-Sept., 10am-4:45pm daily May-mid-June and Sat.-Sun. Oct.-Apr.) and **Sunrise Day Lodge Snack Bar** (10am-7pm daily late June-early Sept.). **Longmire General Store** (360/569-2411, 9am-8pm daily mid-June-Aug., 10am-5pm daily Sept.-mid-June) sells snacks.

Two campgrounds accept **reservations** (877/444-6777, www.recreation.gov) up to six months in advance. **Cougar Rock** (mid-May-mid-Sept., $20), between Longmire and Paradise, has 173 tent and RV sites. **Ohanapecosh** (mid-May-early Oct., $20), south of the Stevens Canyon entrance, has 188 tent and RV sites. Amenities include drinking water, flush toilets, and dump stations, but no hookups.

Two campgrounds are first come, first served. **White River** (late June-late Sept., $20), along the road to Sunrise, has 112 tent and RV sites. The primitive **Mowich Lake Campground** (early July-early Oct., free) has 10 walk-in tent platforms.

OUTSIDE THE PARK

The surrounding towns of **Ashford, Greenwater,** and **Enumclaw** have limited amenities. More options lie farther north in **Seattle** or **Tacoma**.

GETTING THERE

AIR

Seattle-Tacoma International Airport (SEA, 800/544-1965 or 206/787-5388, www.portseattle.org/seatac), served by about two dozen airlines, is closest to the park. **Portland International Airport** (PDX, 7000 NE Airport Way, Portland, OR, 877/739-4636, www.pdx.com) is farther from the park,

just across the Oregon border. Both airports have car rentals.

CAR

From Seattle (85 miles, 2 hrs.), drive south on I-5 to exit 127. Go east on Highway 512. Turn south on Highway 7 to Elbe and turn east on Highway 706 to Ashford and the **Nisqually Entrance** (open year-round), the busiest entrance. To reach the **White River Entrance** (summer only), the closest entrance to Seattle, drive to Enumclaw to Highway 410. **Stevens Canyon** (usually open May-Nov.) is farthest from the Seattle area.

From Portland (131 miles, 2.5 hrs.), drive north on I-5 to exit 68. Go east on U.S. 12 to Morton, then north on Highway 7 to Elbe. Go east on Highway 706 to Ashford and the **Nisqually Entrance.**

GETTING AROUND

The park has no public transportation and **no gasoline.** You'll need a car gassed up to get around.

In winter, most of the park roads close due to snow (Oct. or Nov.-May or June). The Nisqually Entrance and the road from Nisqually through Longmire to Paradise remains open year-round. In winter, vehicles are required to carry tire chains, and the road to Paradise closes nightly and can remain closed during the day.

SIGHTS NEARBY

Mount St. Helens National Volcanic Monument (Rte. 504, 360/274-2100, http://parks.state.wa.us, 9am-5pm daily mid-May-mid-Sept., hours and days shorten in spring, fall, and winter) has a visitors center with exhibits about the 1980 volcanic eruption and trails through the blast zone.

Crystal Mountain Resort (33914 Crystal Mountain Blvd., Enumclaw, 360/663-2265, www.crystalmountainresort.com, daily June-Sept., Nov.-Apr.) has winter skiing and snowboarding, plus summer sightseeing and hiking. The Mount Rainier Gondola whisks riders in both seasons to the summit for stunning views of Mount Rainier.

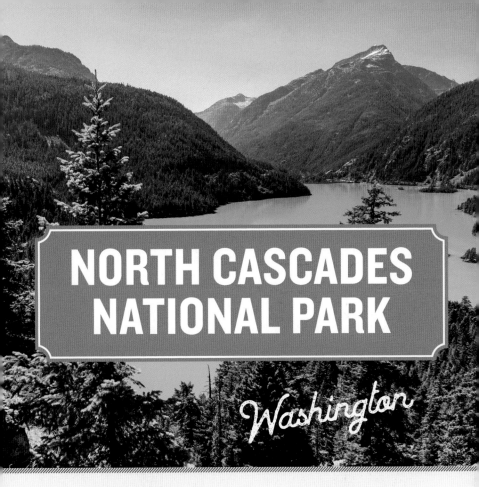

NORTH CASCADES
NATIONAL PARK

Washington

PASSPORT STAMPS ▼▼▼

WEBSITE:
www.nps.gov/noca

PHONE NUMBER:
360/854-7200

VISITATION RANK:
55

WHY GO:
Rugged glaciated scenery.

▲ DIABLO LAKE, NORTH CASCADES NATIONAL PARK

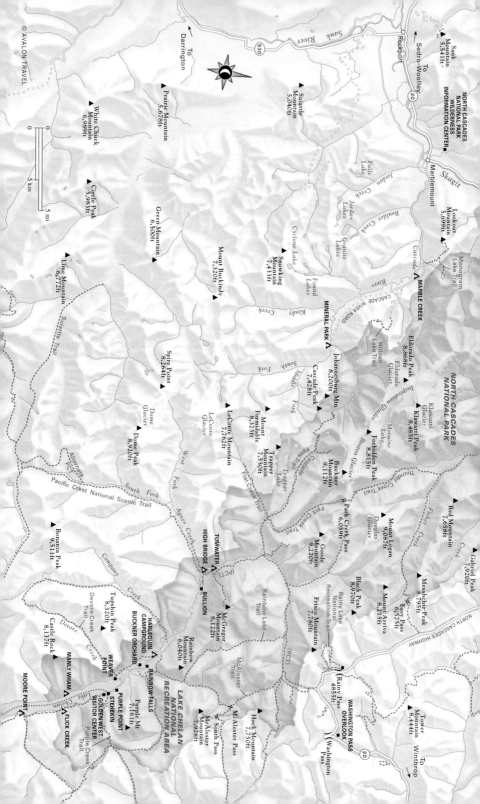

More than 300 glaciers still cling to the mountains within **NORTH CASCADES NATIONAL PARK**, by far the greatest concentration in the Lower 48. But climate forces are rapidly altering the landscape by melting glaciers and increasing fires. Because so much of the park requires access via foot or boat, driving the North Cascades Highway is the most popular visitor activity. The sprawling park also tacks on the recreation areas of Ross Lake and upper Lake Chelan. Most of the park is a vast wilderness; those who venture into its remote reaches discover turquoise lakes, crevassed glaciers, and ice-chewed peaks.

PLANNING YOUR TIME

North Cascades National Park lies north of Seattle and east of Bellingham. Most visitors spend their time at three destinations: the **North Cascades Highway,** which bisects the park; **Ross Lake**; and upper **Lake Chelan.**

Late June-September is the prime time to visit—the North Cascades Highway is open, and temperatures are in the 60s-90s. Fall colors arrive in October-early November. Late November-April, snow pounds the park, closing 44 miles of the North Cascades Highway.

ENTRANCES AND FEES

Most visitors access the park via Route 20 east from **Marblemount** or west from Winthrop. There is no official entrance station and there is no entrance fee.

VISITORS CENTERS

North Cascades Visitors Center (Rte. 20, milepost 120, 9am-5pm daily mid-May-Sept., 9am-5pm Sat.-Sun. mid-Apr.-mid-May and Oct.), near the town of Newhalem, contains exhibits, a bookstore, theater, and wheelchair-accessible trails.

SIGHTS

DIABLO LAKE

Turquoise **Diablo Lake** glistens behind Diablo Dam on the Skagit River. From the **North Cascades Environmental Learning Center** (1940 Diablo Dam Rd., 206/526-2599, www.ncascades.org) on the lake's north shore, **lake tours** (360/854-2589, www.seattle.gov, July-mid-Sept., adults $30-42, kids half price, reservations required) on a glass-ceilinged boat frequently sell out. The **Diablo Lake Lunch Tour** (Thurs.-Mon., 4 hrs., 10:15am check-in) and **Diablo Lake Afternoon Cruise** (Fri.-Sun., 2.5 hrs., 1pm check-in) take in waterfalls, peaks, and two dams. The **Diablo Lake Ferry** (daily 8:30am and 3pm, $20) gets hikers and day-trippers up-lake.

DIABLO LAKE

LAKE CHELAN

ROSS LAKE

The 540-foot-high **Ross Lake Dam** holds back 24-mile-long **Ross Lake.** You can see the lake from **Ross Lake Overlook** (milepost 135) on the North Cascades Highway. The only road to **Ross Lake National Recreation Area** is via Hope, British Columbia, on a 40-mile route to **Hozomeen Campground** and **boat launch.**

Near the lake's south end, **Ross Lake Resort** (206/386-4437, www.rosslakeresort.com, mid-June-Oct.) rents canoes, kayaks, motorboats, and fishing gear to day-trippers. It also has lodging and a water taxi service to trailheads and lakeshore campsites. To get to the resort takes about one hour in three stages: Diablo Lake Ferry, a resort land shuttle ($8), and a short boat ride up-lake.

LAKE CHELAN

Lake Chelan National Recreation Area adjoins the park's south end. Only hikers and boaters can reach the isolated hamlet of **Stehekin** (steh-HEE-kin), 50 miles up Lake Chelan. Most Stehekin day visitors arrive on the **Lady of the Lake** or **Lady Express** (509/682-4584, http://ladyofthelake.com, daily May-mid-Oct., 3-5 days weekly mid-Oct.-Apr., 8:30am-2:45pm or 6pm, adults $41-61, kids half price) to have lunch. You can overnight at the rustic lodge, or camp on the lake.

SCENIC DRIVE
NORTH CASCADES HIGHWAY

The **North Cascades Highway** (Route 20, May-late Nov.) slices 30 miles across the park. East of the park, the road climbs to its highest point and two dramatic passes; most visitors drive the 21 miles from the east entrance to Washington Pass Overlook before turning around. In winter (late Nov.-Apr.), snow and avalanches close the road from Ross Dam to the eastern side of Washington Pass (mileposts 134-178).

From Marblemount, the road heads east past the turnoff to **North Cascades Visitor Center** and the quiet company town of **Newhalem.** Next to **Skagit General Store** (milepost 120) is **Old Number Six,** a 1928 Baldwin steam locomotive that hauled passengers and supplies to the Skagit River dams in pre-highway days. A short walk on the **Trail of the Cedars** (1 mi. rt., 30 min., easy) tours 1,000-year-old trees.

East of Newhalem, the highway climbs along the three dams and reservoirs—Gorge, Diablo, and Ross—that form the centerpiece of **Ross Lake National Recreation Area.** Stop at the overlook for **Gorge Creek Falls** to see it plunging into the gorge. Pull over next to peer down on the turquoise waters

NORTH CASCADES NATIONAL PARK

of **Diablo Lake,** and then continue east to **Ross Lake Overlook.**

After the road exits the national park, it climbs through Okanogan National Forest along Granite Creek to crest 4,855-foot **Rainy Pass** and 5,477-foot **Washington Pass.** From the latter pass, a short, paved trail goes to viewpoints of 7,720-foot **Liberty Bell**—the symbol of the North Cascades Highway—and **Early Winter Spires.** From the passes, the highway spirals down into the Methow Valley to Winthrop, 30 miles eastward.

RECREATION

HIKING

The **Sourdough Lookout Trail** (10.4 mi. rt., 6 hrs., strenuous) gains 4,870 feet on a switchback-loaded climb to the summit, where sumptuous views take in lakes and peaks. From the North Cascades Environmental Learning Center, the **Diablo Lake Trail** (7.6 mi. rt., 4 hrs., moderate) leads to Ross Dam; you can chop the mileage in half by returning via the Diablo Lake ferry.

From the North Cascades Highway at Rainy Pass (Northwest Forest Passes required), one trailhead leads to three destinations. A flat, accessible trail goes to glacier-fed **Rainy Lake** (2 mi. rt., 1 hr., easy). The **Lake Ann Trail** (3.4 mi. rt., 2 hrs., moderate) reaches a cirque lake rimmed by larches that turn gold in fall. The **Maple Pass Loop** (7.5 mi. rt., 4 hrs., strenuous) gains 2,200 feet for a ridgeline traverse. From a trailhead between Rainy and Washington Passes, the **Blue Lake Trail** (4 mi. rt., 2 hrs., moderate) traipses through subalpine meadows to emerald waters surrounded by a trio of spectacular summits: Liberty Bell, Whistler Mountain, and Cutthroat Peak.

From Marblemount, follow the rugged Cascade River Road for 23 miles to the trailhead for **Cascade Pass** (7.4 mi. rt., 5 hrs., strenuous), one of the park's finest hikes. Upon reaching the pass, a 360-degree view spreads out with peaks, glaciers, and summer wildflower meadows. Before embarking, check road conditions at the Wilderness Information Center.

BACKPACKING

A two-day trip (13.4 mi. rt.) climbs to wildflower-strewn Cascade Pass and farther up **Sahale Arm to Sahale Glacier,** where camps tuck into rocks and the views claim glaciers and peaks for miles. For a 4-5-day loop (35 mi. rt.), tackle a portion of the Pacific Northwest Trail to cross **Hannegan Pass,** traverse **Copper Ridge,** drop to the **Chilliwack River,** and return over the pass;

camp at Boundary, Copper Lake, Indian Creek, and Copper Creek.

Backcountry permits are free in advance from the **North Cascades Wilderness Information Center** (7280 Ranger Station Rd., Marblemount, 360/854-7245, 7am-6pm daily July-Aug., 8am-5pm daily May-June and Sept.). Apply March 15-May 15 for an **advance reservation** ($20) in summer and fall.

WHERE TO STAY

INSIDE THE PARK

Spend the night at rustic resorts for a serious dose of peace and quiet. Make reservations a year in advance for these prized getaways that are only accessible by boat or on foot.

Ross Lake Resort (206/386-4437, http://rosslakeresort.com, mid-June-Oct., from $195) has cabins and bunkhouses that float on the water. Cabins have full kitchens with shared barbecue grills. The resort rents motorboats, kayaks, and canoes and has a water taxi service to trailheads and campsites along the lakeshore.

The **North Cascades Lodge at Stehekin** (855/685-4167, http://lodgeatstehekin.com, from $145) has lodge rooms (May-Oct.) and units with kitchens (year-round). Amenities include a convenience store, kayak rentals, and a **restaurant** that serves three meals daily (mid-May-mid-Oct.).

The only food is at **Skagit General Store** (milepost 120, Newhalem, 206/386-4489, 10am-5pm daily mid-May-Oct., 10am-5pm Mon.-Fri. Nov.-mid-May).

Several campgrounds line North Cascades Highway. Most have potable water and pit or flush toilets, but no showers or hookups. Make **reservations** (877/444-6777, www.recreation.gov) up to six months in advance for **Newhalem Creek** (milepost 120, mid-May-mid-Oct., 111 sites, $16) and **Colonial Creek** (milepost 130, mid-May-mid-Oct., 142 sites, $16).

Find first-come, first-served campgrounds at **Goodell Creek** (milepost 119, year-round, 19 sites, small RVs only, $16) and tiny, primitive **Gorge Lake** (milepost 126, year-round, 6 sites, free).

Accessible only from British Columbia, **Hozomeen Campground** (Silver/Skagit Rd., first come, first served, mid-May-Oct., 75 sites, free) sits at the north end of Ross Lake. The 40-mile rough, graveled Silver/Skagit Road goes south from Hope, British Columbia, to this remote campground in the United States.

The park has **boat-in backcountry campsites** on Diablo Lake (launch at Colonial Creek), Ross Lake (launch at Hozomeen Campground), and Lake Chelan near Stehekin (launch at Chelan or 25-Mile Creek State Park). Pick up backcountry camping permits (free) 24 hours before departure from the **North Cascades Wilderness Information Center** (7280 Ranger Station Rd., Marblemount, 360/854-7245, 7am-6pm daily July-Aug., 8am-5pm daily May-June and Sept.) or the nearest ranger station. Make **reservations** (Mar. 15-May 15, $20) for summer.

OUTSIDE THE PARK

Accommodations, food, and services are in **Bellingham, Burlington, Mount Vernon, Sedro-Wooley, Concrete,** and **Marblemount.** To the east, look for services in **Winthrop, Twisp,** and **Chelan.**

GETTING THERE AND AROUND

AIR

The closest international airport is **Seattle-Tacoma International Airport** (SEA, 800/544-1965 or 206/787-5388, www.portseattle.org/seatac). The airport has car rentals.

CAR

A car is essential for getting around and across the North Cascades. It's a 125-mile (3 hrs.) drive from Seattle to the North Cascades Visitor Center in Newhalem. From Seattle, drive 65 miles north on I-5 to Burlington. Exit onto Route 20 and continue 60 miles east to the park entrance.

SOUTHWEST

Across the Southwest, cliffs and canyons dominate the mysterious landscape. Here, the national parks range from red-rock spires to river-cut canyons, water pockets, and arches. You can even slide down sand dunes and explore underground caves. This land of variety is littered with unique sights: petrified trees in badlands, giant saguaros in desert, and ancient bristlecone pines in mountains.

Three prominent canyons top the parks. Zion tucks a narrow slot into soaring, colorful walls. In Bryce Canyon, a geologic fairyland of rock spires rises beneath high cliffs. At the Grand Canyon, layers of geologic history transport visitors back in time millions of years. Along the way, national monuments, captivating parks, and scenic stops all vie for your attention.

◄ MESA ARCH, CANYONLANDS

NEVADA

Salt Lake City

WYOMING

Cheyenne

Rocky Mountain NP

Great Basin NP

UTAH

Arches NP

Denver

COLORADO

Capitol Reef NP

Canyonlands NP

Black Canyon of the Gunnison NP

Bryce Canyon NP

Zion NP

Great Sand Dunes NP & PRES

Grand Canyon NP

Mesa Verde NP

Santa Fe

Petrified Forest NP

Albuquerque

ARIZONA

Phoenix

NEW MEXICO

Saguaro NP

Carlsbad Caverns NP

El Paso

Guadalupe Mountains NP

SOUTHWEST

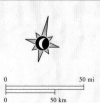

| 0 | 50 mi |
| 0 | 50 km |

TEXAS

Big Bend NP

© AVALON TRAVEL

The National Parks of
THE SOUTHWEST

GRAND CANYON, AZ

The massive, mile-deep canyon is a wonder. Hike its rim or descend into the inner canyon (page 259).

PETRIFIED FOREST, AZ

A scenic drive tours pastel badlands strewn with petrified wood (page 281).

SAGUARO, AZ

The Sonoran Desert houses unique forests with saguaros older than humans (page 287).

GREAT BASIN, NV

You can go high on 13,063-foot Wheeler Peak or dive underground into the Lehman Caves (page 294).

ZION, UT

Sheer cliffs and monoliths stretch high into the heavens (page 301).

BRYCE, UT

Unique red and pink hoodoos shoot up from a steep mountainside (page 320).

CAPITOL REEF, UT

Waterpocket Fold rises from the desert in an enormous wrinkle of rock (page 332).

ARCHES, UT

Delicate rock arches create windows in the scenery (page 344).

CANYONLANDS, UT

Expansive vistas, trails, and scenic back roads take in hundreds of miles of canyon country (page 354).

MESA VERDE, CO

The park's geometric stone-and-mortar cliff dwellings echo the area's long human history (page 366).

GREAT SAND DUNES, CO

This 150,000-acre park holds the continent's tallest sand dunes (page 375).

CARLSBAD CAVERNS, NM

Expansive underground caves contain delicate, lacy stalactites (page 381).

GUADALUPE MOUNTAINS, TX

The summit of the highest point in Texas overlooks multihued canyons and deserts (page 387).

BIG BEND, TX

This mountain, canyon, and desert park yields colorful cacti, tropical birds, and views into Mexico (page 393).

1: VIEWPOINT ALONG THE RIM, GRAND CANYON
2: DESERT VARNISH, ZION
3: DUNES BACKDROPPED BY CLEVELAND PEAK, GREAT SAND DUNES

Best OF THE PARKS

Hermit Road: Make your way west along the forested rim of the Grand Canyon to the stone cottage of Hermit's Rest (page 263).

Desert View Watchtower: See one of architect Mary Colter's finest accomplishments—a rock tower standing tall on the edge of the Grand Canyon (page 263).

The Narrows: Hike the bed of the Virgin River between high, fluted walls—only 20 feet apart in some places—where little sunlight penetrates and mysterious side canyons beckon (page 305).

Sunrise and Sunset Points: Walk a stretch of the Rim Trail between these two viewpoints for stunning views of Bryce Canyon (page 324).

Delicate Arch: Admire the most awe-inspiring of Arches National Park's namesake rock formations, which rises from a slickrock bluff (page 347).

Grand View Point: Perch yourself on top of 1,000-foot cliffs at this dramatic vista, with Canyonlands spread out beneath your feet (page 359).

Cliff Dwelling Tours: Tour North America's largest cliff dwelling, whose preserved walls offer a spectacular glimpse into the lives of the Ancestral Puebloans (page 370).

PLANNING YOUR TRIP

Plan at least **one week** to tour a selection of Southwest parks; to hit all of the parks, you'll need 2-3 weeks. Make lodging and campground **reservations** up to one year in advance for accommodations inside the parks. Summer temps bake this region into an arid crisp, but the shoulder seasons of **spring** and **fall** offer more pleasant temperatures, along with slightly fewer people. Winter **closes the road** between Zion and Bryce, the east entrance and North Rim of Grand Canyon, part of Mesa Verde, and higher elevations of Great Basin.

Sale Lake City and Las Vegas provide the best access to many Southwest national parks.

▲ DESERT VIEW WATCHTOWER

Road Trip

You can visit the major national parks of the Southwest by driving a loop of roughly 1,200 miles. Fly into **Las Vegas, Nevada,** and then rent a car and hit the road! Make reservations well in advance for all park lodges or campgrounds.

VIRGIN RIVER VALLEY, ZION NATIONAL PARK

Zion and Bryce

235 miles / 4.5 hours

From Las Vegas, drive 165 miles (3 hrs.) northeast to **Zion** where barren, towering rock walls surround a verdant oasis. Explore iconic attractions like **Court of the Patriarchs,** the **Emerald Pools,** and the **Narrows.** Spend the night in the **Zion Lodge.**

A 70-mile (1.5 hrs.) drive leads to **Bryce Canyon,** famed for its red and pink hoodoos—delicate fingers of stone rising from a steep mountainside. Explore the rim at spots like **Inspiration Point,** take a short hike below the rim on the **Queen's Garden Trail,** and watch the sun set over the canyon. Stay the night at the **Lodge at Bryce Canyon.**

Capitol Reef

120 miles / 2.5 hours

Leave Bryce by 8am for the drive to Capitol Reef, where the Fremont River carves a magnificent canyon through **Waterpocket Fold.** For hikers, it offers a leafy, well-watered sanctuary from the park's otherwise arid landscapes. Take the **21-mile scenic drive** (1.5 hrs.) to **Capitol Gorge** to see the petroglyphs, pioneer register, and natural water tanks.

© AVALON TRAVEL

Arches and Canyonlands

145 miles / 2.5 hours

From Capitol Reef, drive 145 miles (2.5 hrs.) to **Moab,** gateway to Arches and Canyonlands. Spend one day in **Arches** driving the park road to see windows through the solid rock. Stop to walk to four arches at **The Windows** and hike to **Delicate Arch.**

In vast **Canyonlands,** the Colorado River tunnels through an otherworldly landscape of sandstone. Drive 25 miles (40 min.) to the **Island in the Sky District** to explore viewpoints like **Shafer Canyon Overlook.** Stop at the visitors center and hike the short **Grand View Trail,** overlooking Monument Basin before returning to Moab.

Mesa Verde

146 miles / 3 hours

From Moab, drop southeast into Colorado to reach Mesa Verde. Stop at the visitors center to purchase tickets for a ranger-led tour of one of the cliff dwellings: **Cliff Palace, Balcony Palace,** or **Long House.** If time permits, drive to Wetherill Mesa to walk through several archeological sites or visit **Chapin Mesa Archeological Museum.** Overnight at **Far View Lodge.**

Grand Canyon

278 miles / 5 hours

From Mesa Verde, aim for the South Rim of Grand Canyon. Enter the park at the **east entrance** to stop at **Desert View Watchtower** and **Grandview Point** for your first views of the immense canyon before driving to Grand Canyon Village and touring the visitors center. Catch the sunset from **Yavapai Point** and spend the night at **El Tovar** or the **Bright Angel Lodge.** In the morning, take the shuttle to **Hermit's Rest** and walk the rim between two viewpoints on the return before driving from Grand Canyon back to Las Vegas (280 mi., 4.5 hrs.).

1: SHAFER CANYON OVERLOOK, ISLAND IN THE SKY DISTRICT, CANYONLANDS
2: LONG HOUSE ON WETHERILL MESA, MESA VERDE
3: DESERT VIEW WATCHTOWER, GRAND CANYON

GRAND CANYON NATIONAL PARK

Arizona

PASSPORT STAMPS ▼▼▼

WEBSITE:
www.nps.gov/grca

PHONE NUMBER:
928/638-7888

VISITATION RANK:
2

WHY GO:
Enjoy rim-side views,
inner canyon trails,
and rafting the
Colorado.

▲ MATHER POINT

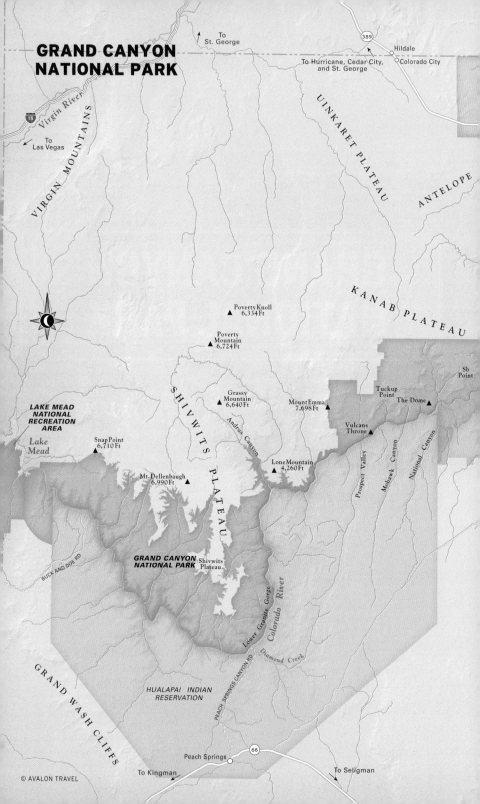

GRAND CANYON NATIONAL PARK

To St. George

389

Hildale
Colorado City

To Hurricane, Cedar City,
and St. George

15 Virgin River

To Las Vegas

VIRGIN MOUNTAINS

UINKARET PLATEAU

ANTELOPE

KANAB PLATEAU

Poverty Knoll
6,334 Ft

Poverty
Mountain
6,724 Ft

SHIVWITS PLATEAU

Grassy
Mountain
6,640 Ft

Andrus Canyon

Mount Emma
7,698 Ft

Tuckup
Point

Sb
Point

The Dome

Vulcans
Throne

LAKE MEAD
NATIONAL
RECREATION
AREA

Lake
Mead

Snap Point
6,710 Ft

Lone Mountain
4,260 Ft

Prospect Valley

Mohawk Canyon

National Canyon

Mt. Dellenbaugh
6,990 Ft

GRAND CANYON
NATIONAL PARK

Shivwits
Plateau

BUCK AND DOE RD

Lower Granite Gorge

Colorado River

Diamond Creek

GRAND WASH CLIFFS

HUALAPAI INDIAN
RESERVATION

PEACH SPRINGS CANYON RD

Peach Springs

66

To Kingman

To Seligman

© AVALON TRAVEL

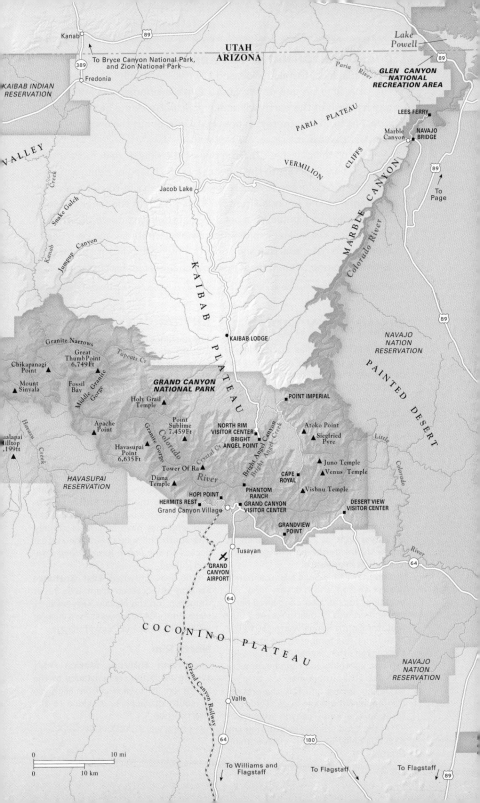

GRAND CANYON NATIONAL PARK must be seen to be believed. It is 1 mile deep, 18 miles wide, and 277 river miles long. Standing for the first time on one of the South Rim's overlooks, the immense, gaping gash in the earth will make your pulse skip a beat in utter awe. The brash vastness conjures questions about the universe and humans' place in it.

Gaze at the massive rift from one of the rims or gain more intimacy by descending into the inner canyon by hiking or riding a mule down to the Colorado River. Strong hikers climb rim-to-rim with an overnight at the famous Phantom Ranch deep in the inner gorge. Rafters can hire a guide for a once-in-a-lifetime trip down the great river, riding the roiling rapids and camping on its serene beaches. From rim to river, sunrises and sunsets glow with brilliant shades of pink and orange, a reminder of just how changeable this landscape is.

PLANNING YOUR TIME

The Grand Canyon lies across northern Arizona, practically straddling the border with Utah. Most visitors head to the South Rim, where 2-3 days is enough time to see the sights, watch a sunset, and day-hike. To visit the North Rim, add 1-2 days and plan for a five-hour drive from the South Rim. The South Rim is open year-round, while the North Rim is open mid-May through mid-October.

It's vital to plan and make reservations at least **six months in advance,** even if you're just on the South Rim. To ride a mule into the inner canyon, or to stay overnight at Phantom Ranch or one of the inside-the-park lodges, book **13 months in advance.**

Summer (May-Sept.) is the park's busiest season, and it is *very* busy. Expect lines for shuttles, congested parking, and crowds at overlooks. At 7,000 feet, the South Rim is warm (60s-70s) in summer, but temperatures in the inner canyon often exceed 110°F. Late-afternoon lightning and thundershowers may also strike in summer.

During **spring** and **fall**, the crowds thin and are more laid-back. Temperatures in the inner canyon range 80-97°F; the rims are pleasant during the day, but chilly at night with morning frost.

ENTRANCES AND FEES

The entrance fee is $35 per vehicle ($30 motorcycle, $20 individual) and is good for seven days to both the North and South Rims. There are two entrances on the South Rim and one on the North Rim. It is a five-hour drive (220 miles) between the South Rim and the North Rim.

South Rim

South Rim entrances are open daily year-round, 24 hours per day. From Williams, visitors drive 60 miles along Route 64 to the **South Entrance Station.** This is the busiest entrance in the park and may have long lines midday. The south entrance offers the closest access to the South Rim's Grand Canyon Village.

The less crowded **East Entrance Station** is accessed from U.S. 89 at Cameron (on the Navajo Reservation). Here, Route 64 heads west for a leisurely 25 miles to Grand Canyon Village.

North Rim

The **North Entrance Station** (May 15-Oct. 15) is the sole entrance to the North Rim. It is reached from Highway 67 south of Jacob Lake, close to the Utah border.

Top ❸

HERMIT'S REST

① TOUR HERMIT ROAD

On the South Rim, the Hermit Road viewpoints are some of the best in the park, especially for sunsets. The park's **free shuttle** (5am-sunset daily Mar.-Nov.) travels seven miles along Hermit Road from Grand Canyon Village to **Hermit's Rest**. The two-hour round-trip stops at eight viewpoints along the way; return buses stop only at Mohave, Pima, and Hopi Points. Catch the shuttle at the **Hermit's Rest Transfer Stop,** west of the Bright Angel Lodge. Hermit Road opens to cars December-February, when you can drive your vehicle to most of the viewpoints.

② DESCEND INTO THE INNER CANYON

Spending time inside the canyon offers unparalleled intimacy with diurnal changes of color, blooming cacti, crawly creatures, and rugged terrain cut by the roaring Colorado River. While you can **day hike** or **ride a mule** below the rim, other options invite grander exploration: Enter the lottery for an overnight stay at **Phantom Ranch;** backpack the canyon's rugged trails, overnighting at **designated backcountry campsites** like Cottonwood, Bright Angel, and Indian Gardens; or **float the Colorado River** on a guided raft trip. A **permit**

PHANTOM RANCH

($8 per person per night, $10 reservation fee) is required to enter the inner canyon. Apply online or contact the South Rim Backcountry Information Center (928/638-7875, 8am-5pm daily).

   Note: Descending to the river and back to the rim in one day is *not physically possible nor advised*.

③ GAZE OUT FROM DESERT VIEW WATCHTOWER

One of Mary Colter's greatest constructions is this Puebloan-inspired structure along Desert View Drive, a 25-mile drive east from the village. **Desert View Watchtower** (9am-5pm daily, hours vary seasonally) is an artful homage to smaller Anasazi-built towers found in the Four Corners region. You reach the tower's high, windy deck by climbing the twisting, steep steps curving around the open middle, past walls painted with visions of Hopi lore and religion by Hopi artist Fred Kabotie. (Pick up *The Watchtower Guide* in the gift shop on the bottom floor for interpretations of the figures and symbols.) From the top of the watchtower, the South Rim's highest viewpoint, the whole arid expanse opens up, and you feel something like a lucky survivor at the very edge of existence, even among the crowds.

ONE DAY IN GRAND CANYON

One day at Grand Canyon will only taunt you to return for longer. Plan to tour the South Rim by entering through the east entrance. Check out the **Desert View** sights, then drive to **Grand Canyon Village** and have lunch at **El Tovar.** After lunch, hop the **Hermit Road Shuttle,** getting off to hike a segment of the **South Rim Trail.** If you can, linger until sunset to catch the color from **Hopi Point.**

VISITORS CENTERS

South Rim

The South Rim has two main visitors centers. **Grand Canyon Visitor Center** (Grand Canyon Village, 9am-6pm daily) is the park's main welcome and information center. The visitors center's theater screens a 20-minute orientation film about the canyon.

The **Desert View Visitor Center** (9am-5pm daily) sits on Desert View Point about 25 miles east of Grand Canyon Village. This is the stop for those entering the park from the east entrance. Both visitors centers have bookstores, information, maps, and brochures. Ranger programs change seasonally. Kids can also participate in the educational Junior Ranger Program.

South Rim also has two other information stations:

The **Verkamp's Visitor Center** (Grand Canyon Village, 8am-5pm daily, hours vary seasonally) has an information desk and park exhibits in addition to crafts and park souvenirs.

Canyon View Information Plaza (9am-5pm daily), near Mather Point, has outdoor displays on the history of the canyon.

North Rim

The **North Rim Visitor Center** (8am-6pm daily May 15-Oct. 15) is located near Grand Canyon Lodge and Bright Angel Point. Stop here for park maps, brochures, and exhibits on North Rim science and history. A bookstore is on site and rangers offer a full program of talks and guided hikes.

SIGHTS

SOUTH RIM

The South Rim is the most developed portion of Grand Canyon National Park. It is home to **Grand Canyon Village Historical District,** a small assemblage of hotels, restaurants, gift shops, and lookouts that offer some of the best viewpoints of the canyon. You can also see some of Arizona's most evocative buildings, all of them National Historic Landmarks.

The South Rim Road has 19 named viewpoints, from the eastern Desert View to the western Hermit's Rest. The best and easiest way to see the canyon viewpoints is to park your car and take

▼ DESERT VIEW WATCHTOWER

MATHER POINT

the park's free shuttle or walk along the **Rim Trail.**

Mather Point

Mather Point is named for the first National Park Service director, Stephen T. Mather. Walking out onto the two railed-off rocks will make you feel like you're hovering on the edge of the canyon's abyss. The point can get busy, especially in the summer. Leave your car at the large parking area and walk along the **Rim Trail** west to Yavapai Point and the Geology Museum, the best place to learn about the canyon's geology.

Yavapai Point and Geology Museum

First opened in 1928, **Yavapai Point and Geology Museum** (8am-6pm daily winter, 8am-8pm daily summer, free) is a limestone-and-pine museum designed by architect Herbert Maier. The site for the stacked-stone structure was handpicked by canyon geologists as best for viewing the various strata. Inside are displays about canyon geology and a huge topographic relief map of the canyon.

Hopi House

Designed by architect Mary Colter, the 1905 **Hopi House** (928/638-2631, 8am-5pm daily, hours vary seasonally) used Hopi workers and local materials to build what is now a gift shop and Native American arts museum. The Harvey Company even hired the famous Hopi-Tewa potter Nampeyo to live here with her family while demonstrating her artistic talents and Hopi lifeways to tourists. This is one of the best places in the region for viewing and buying Hopi, Navajo, and Pueblo art (though most of the art is quite expensive), and even items made by Nampeyo's descendants are on view and for sale here.

El Tovar Hotel

El Tovar was the South Rim's first great hotel. Designed in 1905 by Charles Whittlesey for the Santa Fe Railroad, El Tovar has the look of a Swiss chalet and a log-house interior, watched over by the wall-hung heads of elk and buffalo; it is at once rustic, cozy, and elegant. This Harvey Company jewel has hosted dozens of rich and famous canyon visitors over the years, including George Bernard Shaw and presidents Teddy Roosevelt and William Howard Taft. Inside you'll find two gift shops, a cozy lounge, and El Tovar's restaurant, the best in the park.

Bright Angel Lodge

Off the lobby of the rustic **Bright Angel Lodge** is a small History Room (7am-10pm daily) with fascinating exhibits about Fred Harvey, architect

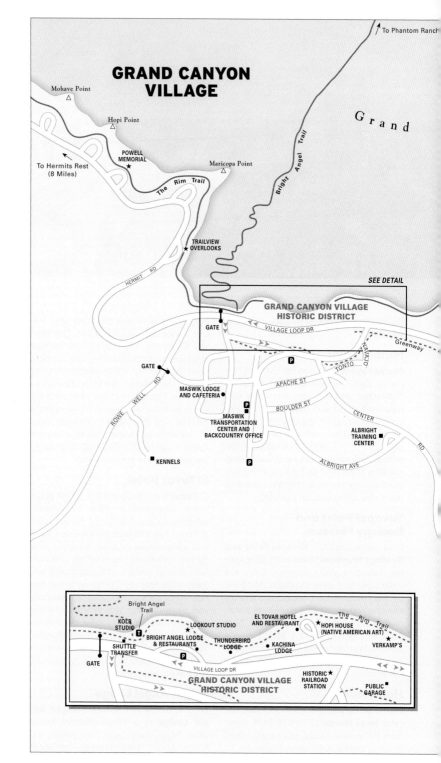

GRAND CANYON VILLAGE

To Phantom Ranch

Grand

Mohave Point

Hopi Point

POWELL MEMORIAL

To Hermits Rest (8 Miles)

Maricopa Point

The Rim Trail

Bright Angel Trail

HERMIT RD

TRAILVIEW OVERLOOKS

SEE DETAIL

GRAND CANYON VILLAGE HISTORIC DISTRICT

GATE

VILLAGE LOOP DR

Greenway

NAVAJO

GATE

WELL RD

ROWE

MASWIK LODGE AND CAFETERIA

APACHE ST

TONTO

BOULDER ST

CENTER

MASWIK TRANSPORTATION CENTER AND BACKCOUNTRY OFFICE

ALBRIGHT TRAINING CENTER

RD

KENNELS

ALBRIGHT AVE

Bright Angel Trail

KOLB STUDIO

LOOKOUT STUDIO

EL TOVAR HOTEL AND RESTAURANT

The Rim Trail

HOPI HOUSE (NATIVE AMERICAN ART)

SHUTTLE TRANSFER

BRIGHT ANGEL LODGE & RESTAURANTS

THUNDERBIRD LODGE

KACHINA LODGE

VERKAMP'S

GATE

VILLAGE LOOP DR

GRAND CANYON VILLAGE HISTORIC DISTRICT

HISTORIC RAILROAD STATION

PUBLIC GARAGE

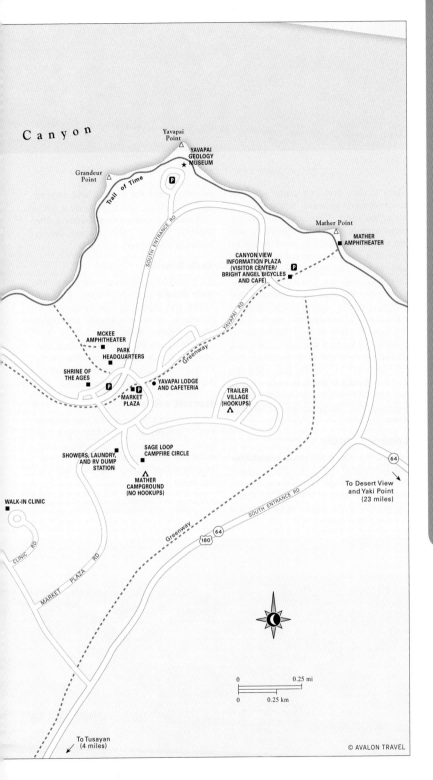

Canyon

Yavapai Point

YAVAPAI GEOLOGY MUSEUM

Grandeur Point

Trail of Time

P

SOUTH ENTRANCE RD

Mather Point

MATHER AMPHITHEATER

CANYON VIEW INFORMATION PLAZA (VISITOR CENTER/ BRIGHT ANGEL BICYCLES AND CAFE)

P

YAVAPAI RD

MCKEE AMPHITHEATER

PARK HEADQUARTERS

Greenway

SHRINE OF THE AGES

P

P

YAVAPAI LODGE AND CAFETERIA

MARKET PLAZA

TRAILER VILLAGE (HOOKUPS)

SAGE LOOP CAMPFIRE CIRCLE

SHOWERS, LAUNDRY, AND RV DUMP STATION

MATHER CAMPGROUND (NO HOOKUPS)

WALK-IN CLINIC

CLINIC RD

64

To Desert View and Yaki Point (23 miles)

Greenway

180 64

SOUTH ENTRANCE RD

MARKET PLAZA RD

0   0.25 mi

0   0.25 km

To Tusayan (4 miles)

© AVALON TRAVEL

HERMIT'S REST

Mary Colter, and the early years of southwestern tourism. You'll see Colter's "geologic fireplace," a 10-foot-high re-creation of the canyon's varied strata. The stones were collected from the inner canyon by a geologist and then loaded on the backs of mules for the journey out. The fireplace's strata appear exactly like those stacked throughout the canyon walls, equaling a couple of billion years of earth-building from bottom to rim. The lodge includes a collection of small cabins just to the west of the main building. The cabin closest to the rim was once the home of **Bucky O'Neill,** an early canyon resident and prospector who died while fighting with Teddy Roosevelt's Rough Riders in Cuba.

Lookout Studio

Mary Colter designed the **Lookout Studio** (9am-5pm daily), a little stacked-stone watchhouse that seems a mysterious extension of the rim. The stone patio jutting out over the canyon is a popular place for photos and canyon gazing. Built in 1914 to provide a comfortable but "indigenous" building, the lookout now contains a store selling books and souvenirs.

Kolb Studio

Built in 1904 right on the canyon's rim, **Kolb Studio** (8am-7pm daily) was the home and studio of the famous Kolb Brothers, pioneer canyon photographers, moviemakers, river rafters, and entrepreneurs. Inside are a gift shop, gallery, and display about the brothers, who in 1912 rode the length of the Colorado in a boat with a movie camera rolling.

Hermit's Rest

Hop on and off the park's free shuttle bus (5am-sunset daily Mar.-Nov.) to tour the seven scenic miles along Hermit Road, from Grand Canyon Village to Hermit's Rest. Along the way, epic vistas await.

▼ FOOTPATH TO POWELL POINT

CAPE ROYAL ON THE NORTH RIM

Trailview Overlook is the first stop, with views of Bright Angel Trail twisting down into the canyon and across the plateau to overlook the Colorado River.

Maricopa Point provides a vast, mostly unobstructed view of the canyon all the way to the river. To the west, look for the rusted remains of the Orphan Mine.

Powell Point holds a memorial to explorer and writer John Wesley Powell, who led the first and second river expeditions through the canyon in 1869 and 1871. The point is a good spot for sunset views.

Hopi Point offers sweeping views of the western canyon. It is the most popular viewing point for sunsets. North across the canyon is Isis Temple and the Temple of Osiris.

Mohave Point peers down into the Colorado River. Also visible are the 3,000-foot red and green cliffs named **The Abyss.** Below the viewpoint you can see the red-rock mesa called the Alligator.

Pima Point is the last viewpoint, with wide-open views to the west and the east.

The final stop on the Hermit Road is the enchanting rest house called **Hermit's Rest** (9am-5pm daily, hours vary seasonally). Inside the low-slung stone cabin, a huge, yawning fireplace dominates the warm, rustic front room, outfitted with a few chairs and a Navajo blanket or two splashing color against the gray stone. Outside, the views of the canyon and down the Hermit's Trail are spectacular.

Tusayan Museum and Ruin

The **Tusayan Museum** (9am-5pm daily, free) has a small exhibit on the canyon's early human settlers. Find the museum 3 miles west of Desert View and 22 miles east of Grand Canyon Village, located near an 800-year-old Ancestral Puebloan ruin with a self-guided trail and regularly scheduled ranger walks.

NORTH RIM

It's all about the scenery here at 8,000 feet on the North Rim. The often-misty canyon and thick, old-growth forest along its rim command attention. Stop at three developed viewpoints, each offering a slightly different look at the canyon.

Bright Angel Point looks over Bright Angel Canyon with a view of Roaring Springs, the source of Bright Angel Creek and fresh water for the North Rim and inner canyon. At 8,803 feet, **Point Imperial** is the highest point on the North Rim with the best all-around view of the canyon. **Cape Royal,** a 23-mile one-way drive across the Walhalla Plateau, **looks** toward the South Rim.

Grand Canyon Lodge

Perched on the edge of the north rim, **Grand Canyon Lodge** (www.grand-canyonforever.com) is a rustic log-and-stone structure built in 1927-1928. Its warm Sun Room frames the canyon through huge picture windows. At sunset, head out to the back patio to watch the sun sink over the canyon. Right near the door leading out to the patio is sculptor Peter Jepson's charming life-size bronze of **Brighty,** a famous canyon burro and star of the 1953 children's book *Brighty of the Grand Canyon* by Marguerite Henry.

SCENIC DRIVES
DESERT VIEW DRIVE

The South Rim's **Desert View Drive** (25 miles) heads east of Grand Canyon Village to exit via the park's east entrance. Along the way, canyon viewpoints offer scenic vistas with fewer crowds. Take a side road to reach **Grandview Point** overlook at 7,400 feet. The site where the original canyon lodge once stood takes in a sweeping bend in the Colorado River. To the east, look for the 7,844-foot monument called the Sinking Ship, and to the north look for Horseshoe Mesa.

Moran Point, east of Grandview, offers impressive views of the canyon and the river. (The point is named for the great painter Thomas Moran.) Directly below, you'll see Hance Rapid, one of the largest on the river. Next you'll come to **Lipan Point,** with its wide-open vistas and the best view of

the river from the South Rim. At **Desert View,** climb the namesake watchtower to catch a faraway glimpse of sacred Navajo Mountain near the Utah-Arizona border, the most distant point visible from within the park.

CAPE ROYAL SCENIC DRIVE

On the North Rim, Cape Royal Scenic Drive (23 miles) boasts dramatic views. From Grand Canyon Lodge to Cape Royal, the paved road wends through mixed conifer and aspen forests on the **Walhalla Plateau.** Short trails go to stunning viewpoints of the canyon. Plan at least half a day for the drive and bring water and snacks.

Leave the lodge just before dawn to watch the sun rise from **Point Imperial,** a three-mile side road at the beginning of Cape Royal Road. Continue along the drive to **Vista Encantadora** (Charming View) as it rises above Nanokoweap Creek. Just beyond is **Roosevelt Point,** where you can hike the easy 0.2-mile **Roosevelt Point Trail** to a view worthy of the man who saved the Grand Canyon.

The drive terminates at **Cape Royal** at 7,865 feet. To see an expansive and unbounded view of the canyon, walk the **Cape Royal Trail** (0.6 mi. rt., 20 min.). On a clear day, you can spot the South Rim's Desert Watchtower way across the gorge, and the river far below. Along the trail, you'll pass the rock arch called **Angel's Window.**

▼ LIPAN POINT

SOUTH KAIBAB TRAIL

HIKING

This is arid country. Avoid hiking mid-day (10am-4pm) and carry at least one gallon of water per person. All canyon trails descend—which means it will take twice as long to climb back up. Hiking to the canyon bottom and back in one day *is not possible nor advised.*

SOUTH RIM

South Kaibab Trail

Steep and shadeless but relatively short, the **South Kaibab Trail** has fewer crowds plus the possibility of spotting bighorn sheep, deer, and California condors. **Ooh Aah Point** (1.8 mi. rt., 1-2 hrs.) has great views of the canyon from steep switchbacks. **Cedar Ridge** (3 mi. rt., 2-4 hrs.) grabs views of O'Neill Butte

and Vishnu Temple. **Skeleton Point** (6 mi. rt., 4-6 hrs.), with views of the Colorado River, is as far as you can go in one day. The trailhead is located east of the village near Yaki Point; take the shuttle bus on the Kaibab Trail Route.

Hermit Trail

The moderate **Hermit Trail** (6.2 mi. rt., 3-4 hrs.) leads to some less visited areas of the canyon. The section to the secluded, green **Dripping Springs** is one of the best day hikes in the canyon for mid-level to expert hikers. Start on the Hermit Trail's steep, rocky, almost stair-like switchbacks; look for the **Dripping Springs Trailhead** after about 1.5 miles. Veer left and follow the trail along a ridgeline across Hermit Basin; the unobstructed views are awe-inspiring. In about one mile, reach

YAKI POINT

Best Hike

BRIGHT ANGEL TRAIL

DISTANCE: 1.5-9.5 miles round-trip
DURATION: 2-9 hours
ELEVATION GAIN: 3,060 feet
EFFORT: moderate to difficult
TRAILHEAD: Grand Canyon Village on the South Rim

The **Bright Angel Trail** is the most popular trail into the Grand Canyon. Many visitors walk a short stretch down Bright Angel just to get a feeling of what it's like below the rim. Hiking down, you quickly leave behind the crowded rim and enter a sharp, arid landscape, twisting down switchbacks on a path that is sometimes rocky underfoot. The trail is steep and it doesn't take long for the rim to look very far away and those rim-top people to look like scurrying ants.

The hike to **Mile-and-a-Half Resthouse** (3 mi. rt., 2-4 hrs.) offers a good introduction to the steep, twisting trail. A little farther on is **Three-Mile Resthouse** (6 mi. rt., 4-6 hrs.). Both rest houses have water (available seasonally). A rather punishing day hike, beautiful **Indian Garden** (9 mi. rt., 6-9 hrs.) is a cool, green oasis in the arid inner canyon. *Due to heat, this route is not recommended in the summer.*

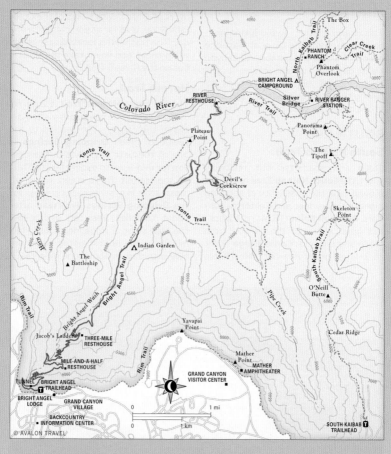

© AVALON TRAVEL

BRIGHT ANGEL TRAIL

the junction with the Boucher Trail and continue west for 0.5 mile up a side canyon to Dripping Springs, a shock of fernlike greenery off a rock overhang with spring water trickling into a small collecting pool. The hike back up is punishing, and there's no water on the trail.

Rim Trail

The **Rim Trail** (12.8 mi. one-way, 5-7 hrs.) is the best way to see the South Rim. The mostly paved trail runs from the **South Kaibab** trailhead and through Grand Canyon Village, ending at **Hermit's Rest.** It hits major sights and overlooks along the way.

With 16 **shuttle stops,** you can hop on and off the trail at your pleasure. Past the Bright Angel trailhead, the path becomes a dirt single-track between Powell Point and Monument Creek Vista. Walk to **Yavapai Point** (2 mi. one-way, 1 hr.) for stunning views of the canyon from the Yavapai Observation Station. The stretch from Grand Canyon Village to **Hopi Point** (2.2 mi. one-way, 1 hr.) is best at sunset.

NORTH RIM

It's cool on the high, forested North Rim, making hiking in summer less of a chore. There are a few easy rim trails, including the **Transept Trail** (4 mi. rt., 2 hrs.), which travels through forest from the Grand Canyon Lodge to the campground and provides a good introduction to the North Rim.

TRANSEPT CANYON FROM THE WIDFORSS TRAIL

TONTO TRAIL

Uncle Jim Trail

The easy **Uncle Jim Trail** (5 mi. rt., 2.5 hrs.) winds through old stands of spruce and fir, sprinkled with quaking aspen, to Uncle Jim Point, where you can let out your best roar into the canyon known as Roaring Springs.

Widforss Trail

The easy and mostly flat **Widforss Trail** (10 mi. rt., 5 hrs.) leads along the Transept Canyon through ponderosa pine, fir, and spruce, with a few stands of aspen mixed in, to Widforss Point, where you can stare across the great chasm and rest before heading back. For a shorter interpretive hike, follow the first half of the trail using the guide available at the visitors center.

North Kaibab Trail

The difficult **North Kaibab Trail** is the only North Rim route into the inner canyon and the Colorado River. A short jog down to **Coconino Overlook** (1.4 mi. rt., 1-2 hrs.) offers views of the San Francisco Peaks and the South Rim. Lower destinations include **Supai Tunnel** (4 mi. rt., 3-4 hrs.), which was blasted out of the rock in the 1930s by the Civilian Conservation Corps, and **Redwall Bridge** (5.2 mi. rt., 4-6 hrs.), which was built in 1966 after a flood.

Strong hikers can descend the North Kaibab to **Roaring Springs** (9.4 mi. rt., 6-8 hrs.). The springs fall headlong out of the cliff to spray mist and rainbows into the hot air. Start your hike early and bring plenty of water. The 3,000-foot climb back out of the canyon is difficult. In summer, there is water at the trailhead, Supai Tunnel, and Roaring Springs.

The North Kaibab Trailhead is a few miles north of Grand Canyon Lodge. Take the **hiker's shuttle** (5:30am and 6am daily, $7) from the lodge. Purchase tickets 24 hours in advance.

RECREATION
BACKPACKING

The inner canyon beckons backpackers with rugged trails and a number of **designated backcountry campsites** including Cottonwood, Bright Angel, and Indian Garden. Designated campsites also flank the Kaibab Trail and Tonto Plateau between Indian Garden and Hermit Trail.

▶ NORTH KAIBAB TRAIL

BACKPACKING RIM-TO-RIM

This classic journey begins on the South Rim at the **Bright Angel** or **South Kaibab Trailhead** to cross the Colorado River and connect with the North Rim via the **North Kaibab Trailhead**. Most backpackers plan 3-4 days for the trip and rely on **Trans-Canyon Shuttle** (928/638-2820, www.trans-canyonshuttle. com, twice daily each direction, May 15-Oct. 15, $90) for the five-hour return drive back to the starting rim. Advanced planning and physical preparation are imperative for this trip.

Lining the Bright Angel and North Kaibab Trails are three developed campgrounds with restrooms, drinking water, and campsites with picnic tables, pack poles, and food storage bins. From the South Rim, the Bright Angel Trail descends 9.5 miles (4,460 feet) to **Bright Angel Campground** near the Colorado River and Phantom Ranch. A much steeper plunge, South Kaibab Trail drops 8 miles over 4,860 feet to the same point.

From the North Rim, the **North Kaibab Trail** cruises 14.2 miles into the canyon with the greatest elevation change (5,850 feet). The most common rim-to-rim route connects the Bright Angel and North Kaibab Trails, with a two-night stay at Bright Angel Campground to explore and rest.

For hikers climbing out of Bright Angel Campground, a predawn start is a must. Due to the extreme elevation gains, many choose to break the uphill grunt into two days by camping at **Indian Garden** on the Bright Angel Trail or at **Cottonwood** on the North Kaibab Trail. (The South Kaibab Trail has no camping. Due to its steep, waterless pitch, it is recommended only for descents.)

A **permit** ($10, plus $8 pp per night) is required and it's not easy to get. The park receives 30,000 requests for backcountry permits annually, but issues only 13,000. To apply for a permit, visit the park website for an application, submission dates (usually six months in advance), and regulations. For more information, contact the South Rim Backcountry Information Center (928/638-7875, 8am-5pm daily).

BRIGHT ANGEL TRAIL

BIKING

When **Hermit Road** (7 miles one-way, Mar.-Nov.) closes to cars it remains open to cyclists who can ride from Grand Canyon Village to Hermit's Rest. To make a loop, opt for the paved **Hermit Road Greenway Trail** (2.8 miles one-way), a portion of the Rim Trail from Monument Creek Vista to Hermit's Rest.

Near the Grand Canyon Visitor Center, **Bright Angel Bicycles and Café** (928/679-0992, www.bikegrandcanyon. com, 6am-8pm daily Apr.-Nov., 7am-7pm daily Dec.-Mar.) rents bikes, safety equipment, and trailers. They also offer guided bike tours of the South Rim.

RIVER TRIPS

River rafters place the trip along the Colorado River through the Grand Canyon at the top of their bucket lists. Huge

▼ RAFTING THE COLORADO

MULE RIDES

white-water rapids alternate with placid turquoise pools. At night, star-filled evenings accompany campers as owls hoot deep in the gorge. Rafting season runs **April-October.** Guided river trips range from three days to three weeks on dories, motorized rafts, oared rafts, or paddle rafts. Some trips include a hike down one of the corridor trails to the river. Book six months to one year in advance.

The best place to start is the **Grand Canyon River Outfitters Association** (www.gcroa.org), a nonprofit group of about 16 licensed river outfitters monitored and approved by the National Park Service. Each has a good safety record and similar rates.

MULE RIDES

Grand Canyon mules have been dexterously picking along the skinny trails, loaded with packs and people, for generations. Weight and age restrictions apply. On the South Rim, **Xanterra** (888/297-2757, www.grandcanyonlodges.com) leads mule rides along the **East Rim** (3 hrs., $145) or down the Bright Angel Trail into the canyon to overnight at **Phantom Ranch** (1-2 nights, $588-840, meals included). Make reservations 13 months in advance.

On the North Rim, **Canyon Trail Rides** (435/679-8665, www.canyonrides.com, May 15-Oct. 15) go to Uncle Jim's Point. You can also take a mule down into the canyon along the North Kaibab Trail to the Supai Tunnel.

WHERE TO STAY

INSIDE THE PARK
South Rim

Xanterra (303/297-2757 or 888/297-2757, www.grandcanyonlodges.com) operates five lodges in Grand Canyon Village. Make reservations 13 months in advance for stays April-October and 6 months in advance in other seasons.

El Tovar (from $217) is a 1905 National Historic Landmark near the rim with 78 rooms and suites. The hotel's **restaurant** (928/638-2631, 6:30am-11am, 11:30am-2pm, and 5pm-10pm daily, reservations required) serves some of the best food in Arizona. A comfortable cocktail lounge resides off the lobby with a window on the canyon. A mezzanine sitting area overlooks the log-cabin lobby, and a gift shop sells Native American art and crafts.

Bright Angel Lodge (from $95) retains a rustic character that fits perfectly with the wild canyon just outside.

NAME	LOCATION	PRICE	SEASON	AMENITIES
Mather Campground	South Rim	$18	year-round	tent sites
Trailer Village	South Rim	$45	year-round	RV sites
Bright Angel Lodge	South Rim	$95-217	year-round	hiker rooms, hotel rooms, cabins, dining
Maswik Lodge	South Rim	$215	year-round	motel rooms, cabins, dining
Yavapai Lodge	South Rim	$150-185	year-round	motel rooms, dining
Kachina Lodge	South Rim	$225-243	year-round	motel rooms
Thunderbird Lodge	South Rim	$225-243	year-round	motel rooms
El Tovar	South Rim	$217-354	year-round	hotel rooms, dining
Desert View Campground	East Rim	$12	May-mid-Oct	tent sites
North Rim Campground	North Rim	$18-25	May 15-Oct. 31	tent sites
Grand Canyon Lodge	North Rim	$135-205	May 15-Oct. 15	cabins, motel rooms, dining
Indian Garden	Inner Canyon	permit required	year-round	hike-in tent sites
Bright Angel	Inner Canyon	permit required	year-round	hike-in tent sites
Cottonwood	Inner Canyon	permit required	year-round	hike-in tent sites
Phantom Ranch	Inner Canyon	$51-149	year-round	hike-in dorms, cabins, food

Most lodge rooms have only one bed and no TVs. Utilitarian "hiker" rooms have refrigerators and share showers. The lodge's cabins have private baths, TVs, and sitting rooms. There are three drinking and dining options: The **Arizona Room** (928/638-2631, 11:30am-3pm and 4:30pm-10pm daily Mar.-Dec.) serves southwestern dishes in a stylish yet casual atmosphere, the **Harvey House Cafe** (928/638-2631, 6:30am-10pm daily) plates standard rib-sticking food, and the **Bright Angel Fountain** (11am-5pm daily in season) has fast food, hot dogs, and ice cream.

Kachina Lodge and **Thunderbird Lodge** (both from $225) both offer basic rooms with TVs, safes, private baths, and refrigerators.

Maswik Lodge (303/297-2757, www.grandcanyonlodges.com, from $215) has motel-style rooms with TVs, private baths, and refrigerators. (The lodge's south section is under construction.) The hotel has the cafeteria-style **Maswik Food Court** (928/638-2631, 6am-10pm daily) and a sports bar.

Delaware North (877/404-4611, www.visitgrandcanyon.com) operates **Yavapai Lodge** (11 Yavapai Lodge Rd., from $150) near Market Plaza. The basic motel has air-conditioning, refrigerators, and TVs. The West Section has no air-conditioning but is pet-friendly. The lodge **restaurant** (6am-10pm daily) has a limited menu of hot and cold sandwiches. For RVers, the **Trailer Village** ($45) has hookups. The **Canyon Village Market** (8am-7pm daily, hours vary seasonally) sells groceries, camping supplies, and deli foods.

INDIAN GARDEN CAMPGROUND

North Rim

Built in the late 1930s, the **Grand Canyon Lodge** (928/638-2611 or 888/297-2757, www.grandcanyonforever.com, mid-May-mid-Oct., from $135) is the only hotel on the North Rim. It has several small, comfy lodge rooms and dozens of cabins with private bathrooms; some have gas fireplaces.

The rustic log-and-stone lodge has a large central lobby, a **Dining Room** (6:30am-10am, 11:30am-2:30pm, and 4:30pm-9:30pm daily mid-May-mid-Oct., dinner reservations required), deli, saloon, gift shop, general store, and gas station.

Inner Canyon

Designed in 1922 by Mary Colter for the Fred Harvey Company, **Phantom Ranch** (888/297-2757, www.grandcanyonlodges.com, dorms $51, cabin $149) has the only accommodations inside the canyon. Located near the mouth of Bright Angel Canyon, the complex is shaded by cottonwoods that were planted in the 1930s by the Civilian Conservation Corps. Phantom Ranch has several rustic, air-conditioned cabins and dormitories, one for men and one for women; both offer restrooms with showers.

The lodge's Phantom Ranch Canteen sells beer and lemonade (with air-conditioning!). The Canteen offers two meals daily: breakfast (eggs, pancakes, and bacon) and dinner, with a choice of steak, stew, or vegetarian. It also offers a boxed lunch with a bagel, fruit, and salty snacks. Meal reservations are required.

Reservations are on a lottery system (www.grandcanyonlodges.com/lodging/phantom-ranch/lottery). Lottery reservations begin 15 months in advance.

Camping

The South Rim has two campgrounds. **Mather Campground** (877/444-6777, www.recreation.gov, $18) has more than 300 campsites, plus coin-operated showers and laundry. The village is a 15-minute walk and a shuttle stop is nearby. The campground typically fills by noon in summer. Reservations are accepted March-mid-November for up to six months in advance. One loop stays open in winter with limited services.

Near the park's east entrance, **Desert View Campground** (first come, first served, May-mid-Oct., $12) has 50 sites for tents and small trailers.

The **North Rim Campground** (877/444-6777, www.recreation.gov, $18-25) has campsites near the rim, with showers and a coin-operated laundry. Reserve sites six months in advance.

OUTSIDE THE PARK

Plentiful accommodations, restaurants, and services are available in **Tusayan, Williams,** and **Flagstaff.**

GETTING THERE
AIR

Most visitors fly into **Phoenix Sky Harbor International Airport** (PHX, 3400 E. Sky Harbor Blvd., 602/273-3300, www.skyharbor.com), rent a car, and drive about 3.5 hours north to the South Rim. **Grand Canyon Airlines** (www.grandcanyonairlines.com) has flights from Boulder City, Nevada, near Las Vegas, to Grand Canyon Airport at Tusayan, but no car rentals.

BUS

Arizona Shuttles (928/350-8466, www.arizonashuttle.com) offers service from Flagstaff to the Grand Canyon (daily Mar.-Oct., $60 rt.). Connections also go between Phoenix's Sky Harbor Airport and Flagstaff ($48 one-way) several times a day.

From Tusayan, a free **shuttle** (8am-9:30pm daily Mar. 1-Sept. 30) runs from the National Geographic IMAX theater into the park to the Grand Canyon Visitor Center. Purchase your entrance ticket at the IMAX before getting on the shuttle.

TRAIN

From Williams, the **Grand Canyon Railway** (800/843-8724, www.thetrain.com, $65-220 rt.) takes about 2.5 hours to reach the South Rim Depot. Fiddlers often stroll through the restored historic cars; on some trips, there's even a mock train robbery complete with bandits on horseback.

CAR

Most visitors drive to the park's South Rim from **Flagstaff** or **Williams,** entering through the south or east gates. The **south entrance** is the busiest; traffic backs up during summer. The quickest way to the south entrance is via Route 64 from Williams (60 miles). From Flagstaff, take U.S. 180 through the forest past the San Francisco Peaks to merge with Route 64 at Valle (80 miles) to get to the entrance.

To reach the **east entrance,** take U.S. 89 north from Flagstaff to Cameron, then take Route 64 west to the entrance. Entering through the east entrance lands you at Desert View, Desert View Watchtower, and Tusayan Museum and Ruin.

GETTING AROUND
SOUTH RIM

Driving is unnecessary on the South Rim thanks to the park's shuttle service and the walkable Rim Trail. When visiting in the summer, park your vehicle early in the day and use the park's shuttle system to get around. The **Backcountry Information Center** has a large parking lot; the southern portion can accommodate RVs and trailers. If you're just visiting for the day, drive into the village and park your car in El Tovar parking lot or the large lot at **Market Plaza.**

The park operates an excellent free **shuttle service** with buses fueled by compressed natural gas. The shuttle runs from sunrise until about 9pm; however, there is no shuttle that travels east from Grand Canyon Village to the east entrance.

NORTH RIM

The drive from the South Rim to the North Rim is 215 miles (5 hrs.). Route 67 from Jacob Lake to the North Rim typically closes to vehicles from late November until May.

The **Trans Canyon Shuttle** (928/638-2820, www.trans-canyonshuttle.com, $90 one-way, reservations required) makes a twice-daily round-trip excursion between the North and South Rims.

To get from the Grand Canyon Lodge to the North Kaibab Trailhead, take the **Hikers Shuttle** ($4-7), which leaves the lodge twice daily in early morning. Buy tickets the day before at the lodge.

SIGHTS NEARBY

Pipe Spring National Monument (406 N. Pipe Spring Rd., Fredonia, 928/643-7105, www.nps.gov/pisp) guides tours on the ranch and homestead to show what life was like on the lonely 19th-century frontier.

Vermillion Cliffs National Monument (435/688-3200, www.blm.gov) features an undeveloped area of striking red cliffs, petroglyphs, dirt roads, and oddities such as little cliff dweller structures built of red rock. House Rock is built under a huge overhang.

Glen Canyon National Recreation Area (928/608-6200, www.nps.gov/glca) is famous for houseboating on Lake Powell, a man-made lake formed by the Glen Canyon Dam. At **Lee's Ferry,** you can dip your toes in the mighty Colorado River.

Hualapai Skywalk (888/868-9378 or 928/769-2636, www.grandcanyonwest.com), at Eagle Point on the Hualapai Reservation, extends 4,000 feet above the Grand Canyon floor on a glass-bottom viewing bridge.

PETRIFIED FOREST NATIONAL PARK

Arizona

PASSPORT STAMPS ▼▼▼

WEBSITE:
www.nps.gov/pefo

PHONE NUMBER:
928/524-6228

VISITATION RANK:
31

WHY GO:
See petrified trees loaded with colorful quartz crystal.

▲ SONSELA MEMBER OVERLOOKING BLUE MESA MEMBER

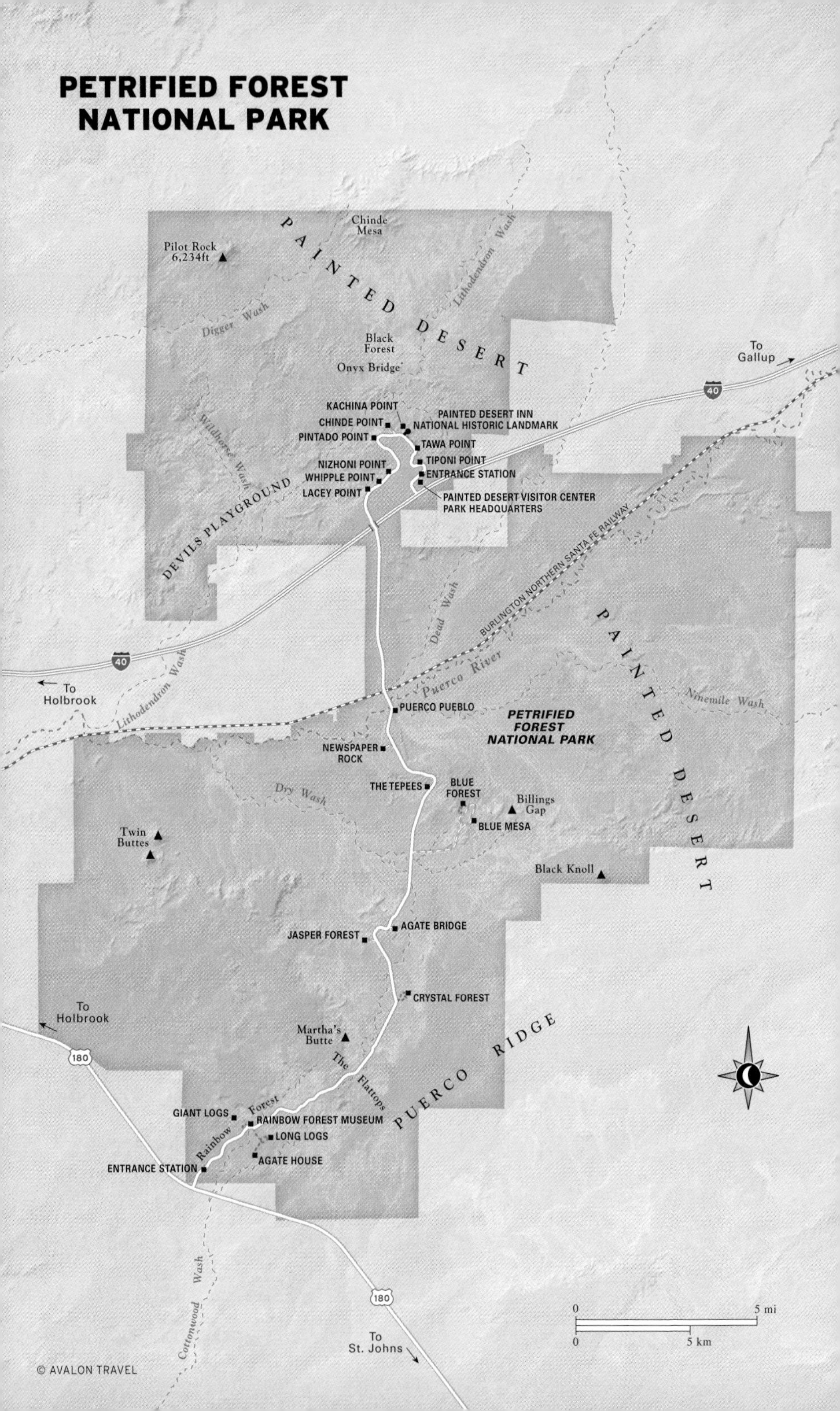

PETRIFIED FOREST
NATIONAL PARK

Chinde Mesa

Pilot Rock
6,234ft ▲

PAINTED DESERT

Digger Wash

Black Forest

Onyx Bridge

To Gallup

Lithodendron Wash

40

KACHINA POINT
CHINDE POINT ■   ■ PAINTED DESERT INN
PINTADO POINT ■   NATIONAL HISTORIC LANDMARK
                    ■ TAWA POINT
NIZHONI POINT ■   ■ TIPONI POINT
WHIPPLE POINT ■   ■ ENTRANCE STATION
LACEY POINT ■
                    ■ PAINTED DESERT VISITOR CENTER
                       PARK HEADQUARTERS

DEVILS PLAYGROUND

Wildhorse Wash

Dead Wash

BURLINGTON NORTHERN SANTA FE RAILWAY

40

← To
Holbrook

Litholendron Wash

Puerco River

PAINTED DESERT

Ninemile Wash

PUERCO PUEBLO ■

PETRIFIED
FOREST
NATIONAL PARK

NEWSPAPER ■
ROCK

Dry Wash

THE TEPEES ■   BLUE ■
                FOREST
                         ▲ Billings
                            Gap
                ■ BLUE MESA

Twin ▲
Buttes ▲

Black Knoll ▲

JASPER FOREST ■   ■ AGATE BRIDGE

← To
Holbrook

■ CRYSTAL FOREST

Martha's ■
Butte

The Flattops

PUERCO RIDGE

180

GIANT LOGS ■
  ■ RAINBOW FOREST MUSEUM
  ■ LONG LOGS
Rainbow Forest
  ■ AGATE HOUSE

ENTRANCE STATION ■

Cottonwood Wash

180

To
St. Johns

0		5 mi
0		5 km

© AVALON TRAVEL

What once was a swampy forest frequented by ancient oversized reptiles is now **PETRIFIED FOREST NATIONAL PARK**, a blasted scrubland strewn with quartz-wrapped logs some 225 million years old. Each petrified log possesses a smooth, multicolored splotch or swirl seemingly unique from the rest. You can walk among the logs on several easy, paved trails. For a bigger picture of the park, drive through the pastel-hued badlands of the Painted Desert on a scenic drive between the north and south entrances.

The park's proximity to Winslow and to Route 66 have made it a popular southwestern tourist attraction since the late 19th century. The lore and style of that golden age of tourism pervades the park with a pleasant nostalgia. It also adds an extra, unexpected contrast to the overwhelming age of the logs and geology around you.

PLANNING YOUR TIME

Petrified Forest National Park is in northeast Arizona, approximately 116 miles east of Flagstaff. **Spring** (Feb.-May) is the best time to be in Arizona's lowland deserts. The weather is gorgeous, often in the high 70s and 80s. It typically stays triple-digit hot from summer deep into October; yet this is the busy tourist season, where lowlanders seek escape from the heat. By November the weather cools off, and in December-February a kind of winter enters the desert.

The park is bisected by I-40. For a one-day visit, follow the paved, 26-mile road between the north and south entrances.

Note that Arizona does not observe daylight saving time. The park stays on Mountain Standard Time year-round.

ENTRANCES AND FEES

The entrance fee is $20-25 per vehicle ($15-20 motorcycle, $10-15 individual) and is valid for seven days. Two entrances access the park. The **north entrance** is just beyond Painted Desert Visitor Center off I-40 (exit 311). The **south entrance** is off Highway 180.

PETROGLYPHS

VISITORS CENTERS

The park has two visitors centers with maps of all the sightseeing stops. **Painted Desert Visitor Center** (7am-7pm daily summer, shorter hours fall-spring) is at the north entrance. The **Rainbow Forest Museum** (8am-7pm daily summer, shorter hours fall-spring) is at the south entrance and has some amazing fossils and displays about the dinosaurs that once ruled this land.

SCENIC DRIVE

To see this understated masterpiece of a national park, drive the **26-mile park road** (open 7am-7:30pm daily summer, shorter hours fall-spring), stopping at the pullouts along the colorful badlands. Add in several short hikes to sate your appetite for more sights. Start at the North Entrance and the **Painted Desert Visitor Center,** where the road enters the Painted Desert. You'll pass several viewpoints, including **Tawa Point,** where the views are long, subtle, colorful, and barren.

Two miles from the north entrance, stop at the **Painted Desert Inn National Historic Landmark** (Kachina Point, 9am-4pm daily) for one of the most dramatic petroglyphs in the state—a large, stylized mountain lion etched into a slab of rock. Enter the Painted Desert Inn to gaze at the evocative,

mysterious murals full of Hopi mythology and symbolism. The murals were painted by the great Hopi artist Fred Kabotie. Redesigned by Mary Colter, the great genius of southwestern style and elegance, the inn was a restaurant and store operated by the Fred Harvey Company just after World War II; before that, it was a rustic, out-of-the-way hotel and taproom built from petrified wood. Upon reimagining the Pueblo Revival-style structure for modern visitors, Colter commissioned Kabotie to decorate the inn's walls.

Past the inn is **Pintado Point,** offering one of the best views of this strange landscape. Before you cross over the usually dry Puerco River and the Santa Fe Railroad tracks, look for the rusted husk of a **1932 Studebaker** sitting alone off the side of the road. This artifact marks the line that old Route 66 once took through the park, roughly visible now in the alignment of the power lines stretching west behind the car.

Cross I-40 and continue south to the **Newspaper Rock** petroglyphs; some of the 650 petroglyphs are viewable through spotting scopes from a spur road to the overlook. Farther on, the **Puerco Pueblo ruin** preserves the cultural legacy of the people that once lived and thrived on this high desert plain. Continuing south through the

▼ PUERCO PUEBLO

BLUE MESA LOOP

Petrified Forest, look out for the hard-to-miss red-and-gray formations aptly named **The Tepees.** Farther south, the **Agate Bridge** pullout features a 110-foot-long bridge made of petrified logs. Nearby, there's an entire fallen petrified forest scattered around the otherwise barren stretch called **Jasper Forest.** The scenic road tour terminates at the **Rainbow Forest Museum.**

RECREATION
HIKING

Accessible from the park's scenic road are several short side hikes that offer a deeper connection with the landscape.

Between Tawa Point and Kachina Point, you can walk the unpaved **Painted Desert Rim Trail** (1 mi. rt., 30 min.) for lovely views of this wondrous, exotic, and colorful landscape. From the Puerco Pueblo parking area, the paved **Puerco Pueblo Loop** (0.3 mi. rt., 45 min.) leads to petroglyphs and a 100-room pueblo that is 600 years old.

From the Blue Mesa Sun Shelter, follow the **Blue Mesa Loop** (1 mi. rt., 45 min.) to its main attraction: strange blue bentonite clay cliffs, worn and sculpted into fantastic shapes. Prepare for a steep descent and a climb on the return hike.

▼ PAINTED DESERT RIM TRAIL

For petrified logs with shiny crystals, hike from the Crystal Forest parking area on the paved **Crystal Forest Loop** (0.75 mi. rt., 30 min.).

Several short hikes depart from the Rainbow Forest Museum. For a short walk on a paved trail, take the **Giant Logs Trail** (0.4 mi. rt., 30 min.) to visit the park's largest petrified trees. The partially paved **Long Logs Loop** (2.6 mi. rt., 1 hr.) heads south of the road to see some of the park's longest and most numerous petrified trees in a logjam. A spur trail goes to **Agate House**, a pueblo built from petrified wood about 700 years ago.

BICYCLING

Cyclists can ride the 26-mile park road, but must exercise caution—many drivers are staring at the views instead of the road. Mountain bikers can ride a section of Old Route 66 that lacks pavement and the first portion of the Long Logs Loop.

WHERE TO STAY

INSIDE THE PARK

There are no campgrounds or lodgings inside the park. Backcountry camping is permitted in the park's wilderness area (free permit required). The only place to get a meal is the south entrance's Fred Harvey Company restaurant, **Painted Desert Diner** (928/524-3756, 8am-4pm daily, which serves delicious fried chicken, Navajo tacos, burgers, and other road-food favorites in a cool Route 66 retro dining room. The south entrance visitors center sells snacks.

OUTSIDE THE PARK

Accommodations and restaurants are available in the nearby towns of **Holbrook** and **Winslow**; however, **Flagstaff** offers the best variety of each and the most services.

GETTING THERE AND AROUND

There is no public transportation to or within the park. Only one road traverses the park, running 26 miles between the north and south entrances.

BLUE MESA PETRIFIED WOOD

AIR

The closest international airport is **Phoenix Sky Harbor International Airport** (PHX, 3400 E. Sky Harbor Blvd., 602/273-3300, www.skyharbor.com). From Phoenix, you'll need to rent a car and drive almost four hours to the park entrance. **Flagstaff Pulliam Airport** (FLG, 6200 S. Pulliam Dr., 928/556-1234, www.flagstaff.az.gov) is serviced by American Eagle Airlines. The drive from Flagstaff takes two hours to reach either park entrance.

CAR

Approaching Petrified Forest National Park by car from the west, take I-40 toward Holbrook (exit 285 or 286) and continue through the small town's dilapidated downtown. From Holbrook, take U.S. 180 for 21 miles to the south entrance. From the east, take I-40 to exit 311 and the north entrance.

SIGHTS NEARBY

Meteor Crater (I-40 and Meteor Crater Rd., 928/289-4002, www.meteorcrater.com, 7am-7pm in summer, 8am-5pm fall-spring) is a large hole in the ground born from the collision of an asteroid with the high-desert grasslands about 50,000 years ago.

Homolovi Ruins State Park (I-40 to U.S. 87 North at Winslow, 928/289-4106, http://azstateparks.com) has more than 300 archaeological sites, as well as tours, hiking trails, and a campground.

SAGUARO
NATIONAL PARK

Arizona

PASSPORT STAMPS ▼▼▼

WEBSITE:
www.nps.gov/sagu

PHONE NUMBER:
520/733-5153

VISITATION RANK:
25

WHY GO:
See stately saguaros in the Sonoran Desert.

▲ SAGUARO NATIONAL PARK

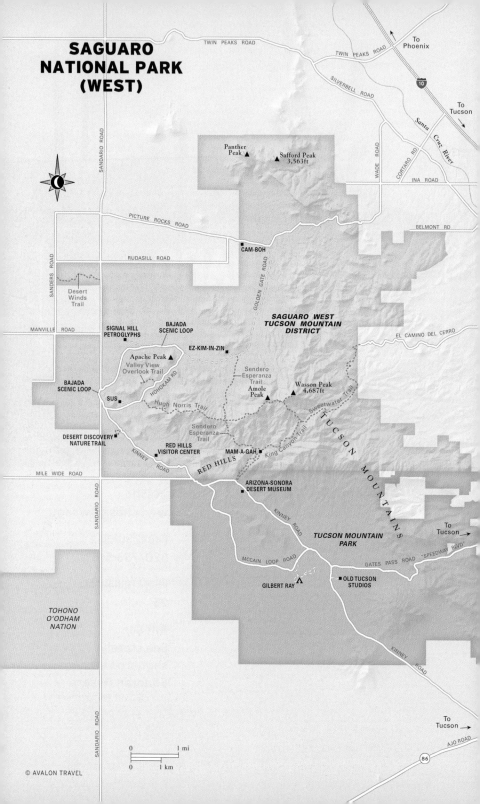

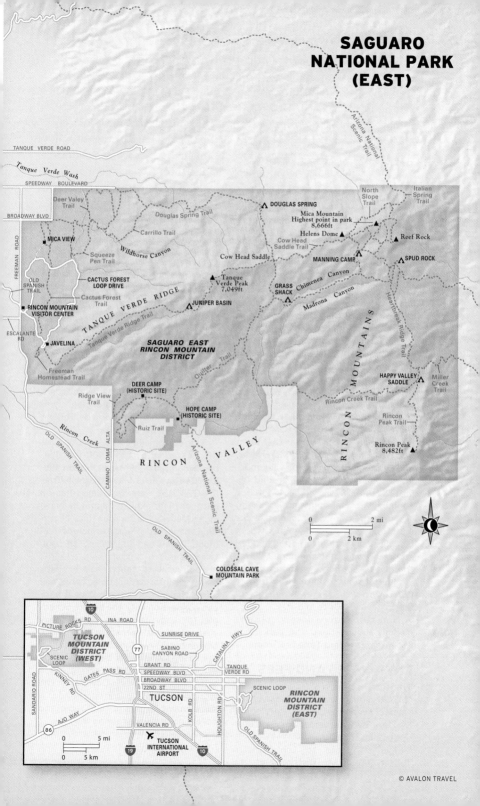

This is where the icon of arid America holds court. The country's largest cacti, the saguaro (pronounced sa-WAH-ro), grow slowly, achieving arms and full stature at around 125 years old. Some extend to 50 feet tall. **SAGUARO NATIONAL PARK** serves as a sanctuary for the regal cacti, with a western section at the base of the Tucson Mountains and a larger eastern section at the base of the Rincon Mountains. Together they protect a magnificent slice of Sonoran Desert landscape, including large saguaro forests surrounded by thick underbrush of ocotillo, prickly pear, cholla, mesquite, and palo verde. If you want to see an accessible and wondrous example of the Sonoran Desert at its best, there are few better places to go.

PLANNING YOUR TIME

Saguaro National Park is split by the city of Tucson in southern Arizona. Both the east (Rincon Mountains) and west (Tucson Mountains) sections are worth visiting. If you have time only for one, make it the eastern section, which is older and larger. Despite the park's proximity to Tucson, you'll need a car to visit either section.

Peak season is **November through March.** If you want to hit the wildflower blooms, plan for late February or March. The best times to visit are March-May and September-November, when moderate temperatures hover around 85-95°F. In summer, the desert is too hot, zooming into triple digits even in shade. Temperatures are a bit cooler in the mountains. In July and August, count on near-daily late-afternoon thunderstorms. Though hot and humid during the day, these monsoon months are a wonderful time to be alive in the Sonoran Desert. In winter, temperatures dip to the mid-50s to mid-70s.

Note that Arizona does not observe daylight saving time. The park is on Mountain Standard Time year-round.

ENTRANCES AND FEES

The entrance fee is $20-25 per vehicle ($15-20 motorcycle, $10-15 individual), valid for seven days at both sections of the park. Park entrances are open sunrise to sunset daily.

The entrances to the western Tucson Mountain District and the eastern Rincon Mountain District are a 35-60-minute drive apart across the city of Tucson. The 33-mile drive can take 30 minutes to one hour.

VISITORS CENTERS

Start your tour of the western Tucson Mountain District at the large **Red Hills Visitor Center** (2700 N. Kinney Rd., 520/733-5158, 9am-5pm daily), where you can learn about the ancient symbiotic friendship between the Tohono O'odham and the saguaro.

The eastern Rincon Mountain District is backed by the 8,600-foot Rincon Mountains. The small **Rincon Visitor Center** (3693 S. Old Spanish Trail, 520/733-5153, 9am-5pm daily) has an outdoor plant exhibit, helpful in learning to identify the Sonoran flora. Nighttime ranger-led programs include full-moon walks and stargazing through telescopes.

Each visitors center has exhibits, maps and information, bookstores, and a film that narrates the Native American connection with the desert. Schedules for ranger-led walks and talks vary year-round, but generally take place November-May. Junior Ranger Programs are available for kids and include earning a badge and checking out a self-guided Discovery Day Pack. The Not So Junior Ranger Program adds a fun element for parents and seniors to collect points while touring the park.

TUCSON MOUNTAIN DISTRICT

SCENIC DRIVES

TUCSON MOUNTAIN DISTRICT

A good way to see the western section of the park, especially in the heat of summer, is to drive the two-way **Bajada Loop** (6 mi.) through a thick saguaro forest. The route is graded dirt and can get dusty, but you can also walk or bike the loop. When driving the south side of the loop, stop at the **Valley View Overlook Trail,** where an easy 0.8-mile round-trip path rises to an expansive view of the Avra Valley, the saguaro-lined desert, and the skulking rock mountains. On the north side of the loop, take a 0.3-mile round-trip walk to the **Signal Hill Picnic Area** to see ancient petroglyphs.

RINCON MOUNTAIN DISTRICT

The easiest way to see the eastern section of the park is to drive very slowly along the **Cactus Forest Loop Drive** (8 mi. one-way). The route begins at the visitors center and winds up across the bajada. The desert here is gorgeous, especially after a rainstorm or early in the morning during the wildflower bloom months. On the loop's east side, stop at two overlooks to see the **Sonoran Desert** and the **Cactus Forest**. On the north side of the loop, walk the 0.25-mile paved **Desert Ecology Trail** to learn about life in the desert. On the east side, stop at the **Rincon Mountain Overlook** to take in the views.

HOHOKAM PETROGLYPHS ON SIGNAL HILL

RECREATION

HIKING

Both sections of Saguaro National Park offer superior desert hiking. In the Tucson Mountain District, a strenuous but beautiful hike goes up 4,687-foot **Wasson Peak** (7.5 mi. rt., 3-4 hrs.), the highest in the Tucson Mountains. It's a great way to spend a Sonoran Desert morning. You can get there by picking up the **King Canyon Trail** just across Kinney Road near the Arizona-Sonora Desert Museum. It's about 3.5 miles to the top of the peak, hiking on switchbacks through typical bajada desert. Then, you can make it a loop by heading down the **Hugh Norris Trail** to its junction with the **Sendero Esperanza Trail** and taking the **Gold Mine Trail** back to the car.

There are easier and less steep trails around the park. An easy one to take with kids is the **Signal Hill Petroglyphs Trail** (0.5 mi.), a modest climb to a collection of boulders with several petroglyphs on display. If you continue on the flat, easy trail, you'll go through some wonderful desert with a good chance to see wildlife.

In the park's eastern section, there are several 3-5-mile loop hikes that will take you through all of the best parts of the sprawling cactus forests. The **Cactus Forest Trail** (2 mi. rt., 1 hr.) is an easy, mostly flat trail among the green-armed giants.

BICYCLING

In the western Tucson Mountains, the gravel **Bajada Loop** (6 miles) offers an opportunity to pedal through a forest thick with saguaros. The only downside is contending with copious dust kicked up from cars. Many cyclists prefer the paved **Cactus Forest Loop Drive** (8 miles one-way) in the eastern Rincon Mountains. Mountain bikers can ride the **Cactus Forest Trail** (2.5 miles), a single-track, two-way path that bisects Cactus Forest Loop Drive.

CACTUS BLOOM

SAGUARO CACTI

WHERE TO STAY

There are no developed campgrounds within the park. Backcountry camping is permitted at six primitive campgrounds in the **Saguaro Wilderness Area;** a permit ($8) is required. The closest developed campground is the **Gilbert Ray Campground** (8451 W. McCain Loop, off Kinney Rd., 520/883-4200, $10-20) in Tucson Mountain Park near the Tucson Mountain District. The city of **Tucson** is filled with plentiful accommodations, restaurants, and services.

GETTING THERE AND AROUND

AIR

Tucson International Airport (TUS, 7250 S. Tucson Blvd., 520/573-8100, www.flytucson.com) hosts six airlines (including American, Delta, Southwest, and Alaska Airlines) flying to 18 destinations. It's a small but efficient airport, with daily nonstop flights throughout the United States.

CAR

To reach the park's **Tucson Mountain District** (west) from I-10, take Speedway Boulevard west to Kinney Road. Turn right and drive four miles. At the junction with Mile Wide Road, veer right to continue on Kinney Road. The Red Hills Visitor Center will appear in one mile.

To reach the **Rincon Mountain District** from I-10, exit the freeway east onto Houghton Road. Drive eight miles north to Escalante Road and turn right. Continue two miles to Old Spanish Trail and turn left to enter the park.

PUBLIC TRANSPORTATION

For bus service to Tucson, there's the **Greyhound** bus station (801 E. 12th St. near Broadway and Euclid, 520/792-3475, www.greyhound.com).

The **Amtrak** (400 N. Toole Ave., 800/872-7245, www.amtrak.com) station in downtown Tucson is served by the Sunset Limited and Texas Eagle lines.

The City of Tucson operates the **Sun Tran** (4220 S. Park Ave., 520/792-9222, www.suntran.com, 6am-7pm Mon.-Fri., 8am-5pm Sat.-Sun.) bus line with stops all over Tucson. But routes do not extend to the parks.

No public transportation is available from Tucson to the parks or inside the parks.

SIGHTS NEARBY

Arizona-Sonora Desert Museum (2021 N. Kinney Rd., 520/883-2702, www.desertmuseum.org, 7:30am-5pm daily Mar.-Sept., 7:30am-10pm Sat. June-Aug., 8:30am-5pm daily Oct.-Feb.) is home to thousands of saguaros standing tall above the hot, rocky landscape, surrounded by pipe-cleaner-like ocotillo and fuzzy cholla, creosote, and prickly pear.

GREAT BASIN
NATIONAL PARK

Nevada

WEBSITE:
www.nps.gov/grba

PHONE NUMBER:
775/234-7331

VISITATION RANK:
49

WHY GO:
Explore ancient
bristlecone pines and
limestone caves.

▲ WHEELER PEAK

GREAT BASIN NATIONAL PARK is the only national park in Nevada. Carved out of Humboldt National Forest, its mountainous slopes contain groves of 4,000-year-old bristlecone pines, the oldest living organisms on the planet. The trees' ability to survive in an arid, harsh climate and poor soil yields their longevity. Underground within the quartzite limestone are the corridors of the Lehman Caves, carved by water over millions of years. Thanks to its high elevation, the park also contains the only permanent glacier-like ice in the state.

You can drive on the highest road in Nevada to camp at almost 10,000 feet on Wheeler Peak. With minimal light pollution, the upper elevations of this International Dark Sky Park are spread with brilliant stars. Day hikes tour the peak, ice, and bristlecone pines. The air is fresh, the views are grand, and the vibe is reverent in this hallowed temple of wilderness.

PLANNING YOUR TIME

Great Basin National Park straddles the Nevada-Utah state line near the end of U.S. 50, "the Loneliest Road" in east-central Nevada. It's a remote park far from anywhere else. Many visitors treat the park as a day trip, viewing the caves and driving to the peak before continuing on their way elsewhere. Those who spend a few days here can acclimate for the hike to the 13,063-foot summit of Wheeler Peak.

BRISTLECONE PINE

The park crowds with visitors on **summer** (May-Sept.) weekends, when the weather is mild, with highs of 85°F and lows of 55°F (mosquito season runs June-July). Make reservations for cave tours or risk being turned away. Fall and spring can be cool but pleasant, while winter brings snow to the mountain peaks.

ENTRANCE AND FEES

The entrance to the park is along Highway 488 (Lehman Caves Rd.), which ends at the Lehman Caves Visitor Center. There is no entrance station and no entrance fee.

VISITORS CENTERS

The **Lehman Caves Visitor Center** (5500 W. Hwy. 488, 8am-5pm daily year-round) is where you can purchase cave tour tickets, peruse exhibits, watch an orientation film, and pick up park information. In summer, free evening **astronomy programs** (7pm Sat.) include a ranger presentation followed by telescope viewing of celestial objects clearly rendered thanks to the park's dark skies. When the full moon brightens the sky, rangers guide **moonlight hikes** instead (free, tickets at visitors center). The park's sky programs culminate in a three-day **Astronomy Festival** (late Sept.).

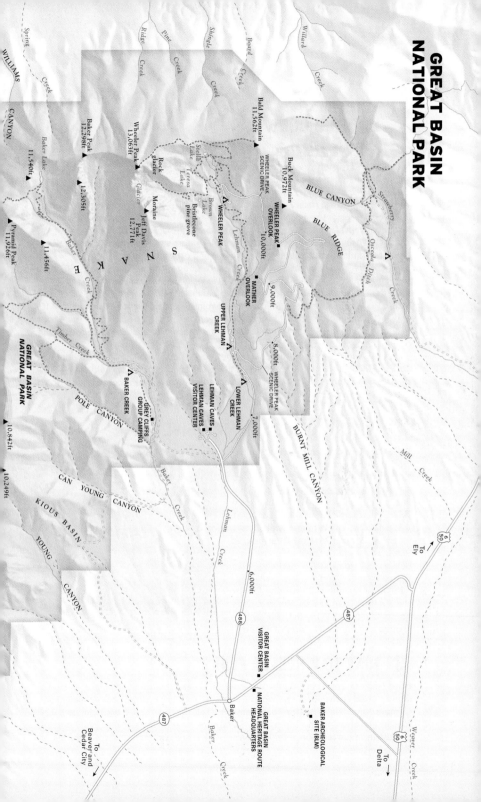

GREAT BASIN
NATIONAL PARK

WILLIAMS CANYON

Spring Creek

Baker Creek

Ridge Creek

Pine Creek

Shingle Creek

Board Creek

Willard Creek

Bald Mountain
11,562ft ▲

Baker Peak
12,298ft ▲

Wheeler Peak
13,063ft ▲

Rock glacier

Stella Lake

Teresa Lake

Glacier

Moraine

Brown Lake

Jeff Davis Peak
12,771ft ▲

Bristlecone pine grove

WHEELER PEAK

11,540ft ▲

12,305ft ▲

Baker Creek

11,455ft ▲

Pyramid Peak
11,926ft ▲

S N A K E

Buck Mountain
10,972ft ▲

WHEELER PEAK SCENIC DRIVE

WHEELER PEAK OVERLOOK
10,000ft ■

BLUE CANYON

BLUE RIDGE

Strawberry Creek

Osceola Ditch

■ MATHER OVERLOOK
9,000ft

Lehman Creek

8,000ft
WHEELER PEAK SCENIC DRIVE

UPPER LEHMAN CREEK

LOWER LEHMAN CREEK

7,000ft

GREAT BASIN NATIONAL PARK

Timber Creek

POLE CANYON

BAKER CREEK

GREY CLIFFS GROUP CAMPING ■

LEHMAN CAVES VISITOR CENTER ■

LEHMAN CAVES

Baker Creek

10,842ft ▲

CAN YOUNG CANYON

KIOUS BASIN

10,249ft ▲

YOUNG CANYON

BURNT MILL CANYON

Mill Creek

Lehman Creek

6,000ft

To Ely

56
6 50 US

488

487

GREAT BASIN VISITOR CENTER ■

GREAT BASIN NATIONAL HERITAGE ROUTE HEADQUARTERS ■

BAKER ARCHEOLOGICAL SITE (BLM) ■

Baker

487

To Beaver and Cedar City

Baker Creek

To Delta

Weaver Creek

6 50 US

Top ❸

LEHMAN CAVES

❶ TOUR UNDERGROUND CAVES

Five hundred million years ago, Nevada sat under a shallow sea, teeming with creatures like the ichthyosaur (now Nevada's official state fossil). Eons of pressure changes, incessant heating and cooling cycles, erosion, and calcification acted on that primordial seabed—pushing it into mountain ranges, changing sandstone into marble, and cutting deep gashes in the rock. The result, countless calcite dribbles later, is the **Lehman Caves,** with ornate stalagmites, stalactites, "soda straws," and other features.

There are two cave tours. The 60-minute **Lodge Room Tour** (adults $8, ages 5-15 and seniors $4, children under 5 free) is less than 0.5 mile long and is perfect for kids. The tour passes through three main cave rooms—the Gothic Palace, the Music Room, and the Lodge Room. The 90-minute **Grand Palace Tour** (adults $10, ages 5-15 and seniors $5) is limited to children older than age 5. The 0.6-mile tour includes the Lodge Room Tour with additional access to the Grand Palace, which holds the Parachute Shield.

Tours usually run 9am-4pm. In summer, tours depart daily every two hours; in spring and fall, tours reduce to twice daily. In winter, a tour is only held Friday-Sunday. **Reservations** (877/444-6777, www.recreation.gov) are recommended up to six months in advance.

❷ TAKE A SCENIC SUMMIT DRIVE

Wheeler Peak Scenic Drive (June-Oct., weather permitting) switchbacks 13 miles along Lehman Creek toward 13,063-feet Wheeler Peak. From tree line to summit, it takes your breath away. This extraordinary drive curves at 8,500 feet where Wheeler Peak comes into view. Stop at **Mather Overlook,** at 9,000 feet, where the views are even better. The road keeps climbing, with the peak ahead and the vast valley behind, until reaching the parking lot for the Summit Trail. The scenic drive ends one mile later at Wheeler Peak Campground at a breath-sucking 9,886 feet.

WHEELER PEAK SCENIC DRIVE

❸ HIKE TO WHEELER PEAK

Hardy hikers set their sights on Wheeler Peak, though its trails are usually snow-buried until mid-June. From the Summit Trail parking area near Wheeler Peak Campground, the **Wheeler Peak Summit Trail** (8.6 mi. rt., 5-6 hrs.) climbs 3,000 feet in elevation to the top of the 13,063-foot peak. Start early to avoid getting caught in midafternoon thunderstorms, which are common and treacherous on the mountain.

WHEELER PEAK ON THE SUMMIT TRAIL

Located outside the park, the **Great Basin Visitor Center** (57 N. Hwy. 487, Baker, 8am-5:30pm daily Apr.-Oct.) sells cave tour tickets, shows a film, and features exhibits on park flora, fauna, and cave formations.

HIKING

Located at the visitors center, the **Mountain View Nature Trail** (0.3 mi., 20 min.) is a gentle stroll that passes **Rhodes Cabin,** a historical exhibit. Pick up a trail guide at the visitors center to learn about juniper, piñon pine, mountain mahogany, mistletoe, limestone, and marble.

On **Wheeler Peak,** two trails offer greater exploration. The **Bristlecone and Glacier Trail** (4.6 mi. rt., 2-3 hr.) links an interpretive trail with Great Basin's only glacier. From the trailhead, the interpretive path travels 1.4 miles, circling a sanctuary of bristlecone pines; watch these ancient beings cling to life with a precarious yet tenacious grip. Past the temple of the pines, the Glacier Trail becomes steep and rocky over the next mile. Soon you enter a cirque, a valley carved by the extant glacier at the head, bookended by sheer cliffs, with the summit of Wheeler Peak in full view. Starting 0.25 mile from Wheeler Peak Campground, the **Alpine Lakes Trail** (2.7 mi., 2 hrs.) passes Teresa and Stella Lakes with easy grades and views of mighty peaks.

At the end of Baker Creek Road is the trailhead for the steep **Baker Lake and Johnson Lake Loop Trail** (13 mi., 7 hrs.). Reach scenic Baker Lake in five miles. Continuing to Johnson Lake requires a one-mile climb over the 10,800-foot Johnson Pass below Pyramid Peak. Several points on the trail provide 360-degree vistas, including inspiring looks at Baker Peak and Wheeler Peak. Just before Johnson Lake are the remains of the Johnson Lake Mine, now reduced to a few cabin ruins, discarded mining equipment, and a 1,000-foot aerial tramway.

TRAIL TO WHEELER PEAK

WHERE TO STAY

INSIDE THE PARK

The park has five developed **campgrounds** ($12) with vault toilets, picnic tables, drinking water, and tent pads. Most sites are first come, first served. There are no lodging accommodations.

At 7,500 feet, **Lower Lehman Creek** (11 sites) is favored by trailers and RVs for its easy year-round access. At 7,800 feet, **Upper Lehman Creek Campground** (22 sites, May-Oct.) has better scenery than Lower Lehman. Near the summit of Wheeler Peak Scenic Drive at 9,886 feet is **Wheeler Peak Campground** (37 sites, May-Oct.); due to the altitude, some people find difficulty sleeping and breathing here. **Baker Creek Campground** (38 sites, May-Oct.) is located at 7,530 feet off of gravel Baker Creek Road. **Grey Cliffs Campground** (16 sites, 877/444-6777, www.recreation.gov, May-early Sept.) sits at 7,530 feet on Baker Creek Road and accepts site **reservations.**

Along **Snake Creek Road** (year-round, free) are primitive campsites with fire grates and picnic tables (no water). The sites are difficult to reach, are muddy in spring, and are snow-covered in winter.

Inside the visitors center, the **Lehman Caves Cafe** (8am-5pm daily Apr.-Oct., shorter hours spring and fall, $10-20) serves breakfast and lunch. Try the "incredible ice cream sandwich," a double scoop crammed between a giant pair of oatmeal cookies, easily big enough for two.

OUTSIDE THE PARK

The tiny town of **Baker**, five miles from the park entrance, has a couple of accommodation and dining options. **Ely,** 70 miles northwest, is the largest nearby town with more services.

GETTING THERE AND AROUND

AIR

The nearest major international airports are **Salt Lake City International Airport** (SLC, 776 North Terminal Dr., 801/575-2400, www.slcairport.com), 230 miles northeast in Salt Lake City, Utah, and **McCarran International Airport** (LAS, 5757 Wayne Newton Blvd., 702/261-5211, www.mccarran.com), 300 miles south in Las Vegas, Nevada. **Reno-Tahoe International Airport** (RNO, 2001 E. Plumb Ln., 775/328-6400, www.renoairport.com) is almost 400 miles west on the other side of Nevada, about a 6-7-hour drive. Car rentals are available at all airports.

CAR

There is no public transportation into or within the park; a car is necessary. Access is via U.S. 50, also known as "the Loneliest Road." From the junction of U.S. 50, Highway 487 heads south for five miles to the town of Baker. At Baker, take Highway 488 (Lehman Caves Rd.) west for five miles into the park.

SIGHTS NEARBY

Cathedral Gorge State Park (111 Cathedral Gorge State Park Rd., Panaca, 775/728-4460, http://parks.nv.gov/parks) has interpretive exhibits, ranger programs, a campground, shaded picnic areas, drinking water, restrooms, and scenic hikes.

BRISTLECONE PINE TRAIL

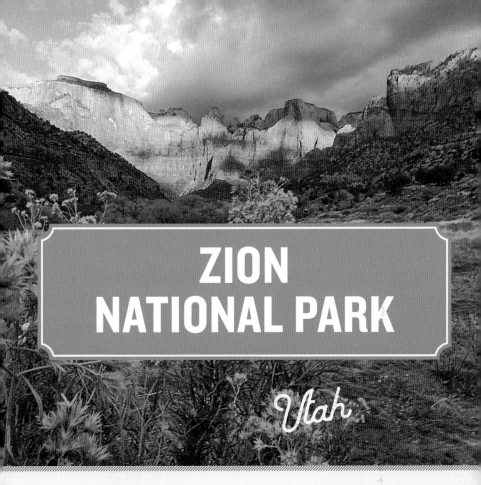

ZION
NATIONAL PARK

Utah

PASSPORT STAMPS ▼▼▼

WEBSITE:
www.nps.gov/zion

PHONE NUMBER:
435/772-3256

VISITATION RANK:
3

WHY GO:
Explore one of
the West's most
impressive canyons.

▲ ZION NATIONAL PARK

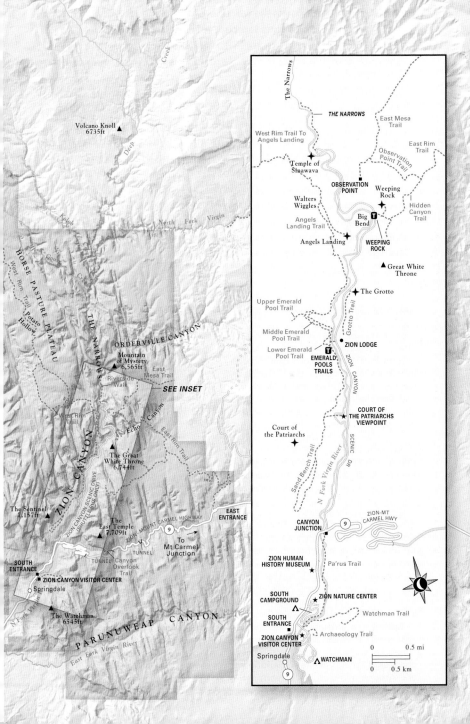

ZION NATIONAL PARK

From skinny slot canyons through which you can barely squeeze to the large, monolith-flanked canyons of the Virgin River, **ZION NATIONAL PARK** packs the wonders of the eroded Southwest into a compact area. Color runs rampant: pale beige, yellows, pinks, oranges, reds, and chocolate are in its sandstone scenery. Here, energetic streams and other forces of erosion created finely sculptured rock. Little trickles of water percolating through massive chunks of sandstone left markedly un-desert-like habitats, enabling an incredible variety of plants to find niches.

When you visit Zion, the first thing to catch your attention will be the sheer 2,000-foot cliffs and great monoliths of Zion Canyon. Yet the longer you stay, the more your attention focuses on the park's intricacies. In this portion of the Grand Staircase of Utah, a variety of geologic structures tickle the eyes, from freestanding arches to the patterned sandstone of Checkerboard Mesa and even a petrified forest. Due to nearly 5,000 feet of elevation variation, four major vegetation zones contain a huge biodiversity, from lush fern grottos to aspen trees. It's a landscape to soak up for days.

PLANNING YOUR TIME

Zion National Park is in southwest Utah, 86 miles southwest of Bryce Canyon National Park. Visitors usually drop in at the visitors center, travel the Zion Canyon Scenic Drive, and take short walks on the Weeping Rock or Riverside Walk Trail. A stay of two days or longer lets you take in more of the grand scenery and hike other inviting trails.

Crowds come spring, summer, and fall into Zion Canyon, and many people check off that one main canyon as "seeing the park." But as impressive as it is, Zion Canyon is only a small slice of this national park. Roads venturing into other sections—Kolob Canyons and Kolob Terrace Road to Lava Point—see far fewer people, have breathing room, and offer equally enchanting scenery.

Summer (May-Sept.) is the busiest season, with midday lines at the entrance to Zion Canyon, the shuttle stops, and Zion Canyon Visitor Center.

Spring and **autumn** are the choice seasons for the most pleasant temperatures. They are also good for the best chances of seeing wildlife and wildflowers. Around mid-October to early November, cottonwoods and other trees blaze with color. Summer temperatures in the canyons can be uncomfortably hot, with highs hovering above 100°F.

In **winter,** nighttime temperatures drop to near freezing, and weather tends to be unpredictable. Snow may block some of the high-country trails and the road to Lava Point, but the rest of the park is open and accessible year-round.

ENTRANCE AND FEES

Two entrances reach the Zion Canyon section of the park. From **Springdale,** enter the south end of Zion Canyon near the visitors center and the Zion Canyon shuttle buses. During summer, this entrance backs up with long lines. Avoid the lines by taking the free shuttle from Springdale.

From the east, come in on the **Zion-Mount Carmel Highway,** pass through a long tunnel, and then pop into Zion Canyon a few miles north of the visitors center. Large RVs and bicycles must heed special regulations for the long tunnel.

The entrance fee is $35 per vehicle ($30 motorcycle, $20 individual) and is valid for seven days.

Top ❸

① EXPLORE ZION CANYON

The highlight for most visitors is **Zion Canyon,** which is approximately 2,400 feet deep. Zion Canyon Scenic Drive winds along the canyon floor and the North Fork of the Virgin River past some of the most spectacular scenery in the park. During the spring, summer, and early fall, a **shuttle bus** ferries vis-

NIGHTFALL IN ZION CANYON

itors along this route; you can drive it in winter. Hiking trails branch off to lofty viewpoints and narrow side canyons. Adventurous souls can continue on foot past the road's end and into the eerie depths of the Virgin River Narrows in upper Zion Canyon.

② RIVER-HIKE THE NARROWS

Hike *inside* the Virgin River, between high, fluted walls where little sunlight penetrates and mysterious side canyons beckon. There's no trail, and you'll be wading much of the time in the river, which is usually knee- to chest-deep. A good half-day trip begins at the end of the Riverside Walk (shuttle stop: Temple of Sinawava) and

follows the Narrows 1.5 miles (about 2 hours) upstream to Orderville Canyon, then back the same way. Orderville Canyon makes a good destination in itself. No permit is needed if you're just going partway in and back in one day, but a permit *is* required to hike the entire Narrows (16 mi. one-way, 12 hrs. to 2 days). Early summer (mid-June-mid-July) and early autumn (mid-Sept.-mid-Oct.) are the best times to go.

Savvy Narrows hikers rent special canyoneering shoes. You may also want hiking poles for stability, neoprene socks for warmth, dry bags for your gear, and dry suits in cool weather. Read up on hiking the Narrows on the park's website or from the handout at Zion Canyon Visitor Center.

THE VIRGIN RIVER

3 DRIVE ZION-MOUNT CARMEL HIGHWAY

A land of sandstone slickrock, hoodoos, and narrow canyons dominates the east side of the park. You can see much of the dramatic scenery along the 10-mile **Zion-Mount Carmel Highway** (Hwy. 9) between the East Entrance Station and Zion Canyon. Built in the late 1920s, the highway features scenic views, overlooks, switchbacks, two tunnels, and unique geological features. It's worth driving both directions, but the westbound route yields a spectacular descent into Zion Canyon—first through a 530-foot tunnel, then a 1.1-mile tunnel, followed by a series of six switchbacks descending 800 feet to the canyon floor. During summer, a stream of traffic piles across the highway, which often makes sightseeing take 1-2 hours one-way.

Highlights on the eastern plateau include views of the White Cliffs and Checkerboard Mesa. Checkerboard Mesa's distinctive pattern is caused by a combination of vertical fractures and horizontal bedding planes, both accentuated by weathering. It may be the tallest sandstone cliff in the world.

The highway's spectacular tunnels were built for smaller automobiles, and the curves in the long tunnel force large vehicles into the oncoming lane. Most RVs, buses, trailers, and fifth wheels, and some truck-campers, will require traffic control with rangers stationed on both ends of the tunnel closing down travel in one direction for one-way driving. While the route is open 24/7, RVs can only access the tunnel when traffic control rangers are present (8am-8pm daily May-early Sept., shorter hours rest of the year).

VISITORS CENTERS

Zion Canyon

The sprawling **Zion Canyon Visitor Center** (8am-6pm daily mid-Apr.-late May and Sept.-early Oct., 8am-7pm daily late May-Aug., 8am-5pm daily early Oct.-mid-Apr.) is located between the Watchman and South Campgrounds. Staff members can answer questions about trails, provide updates on the weather, and arrange a shuttle to remote trailheads.

The **backcountry desk** opens at 7am daily (late Apr.-late Nov.) and a backcountry shuttle board allows hikers to coordinate transportation between trailheads. The bookstore is stocked with an excellent selection of books and topographic and geologic maps. During summer, the visitors center entrance can have long waiting lines; go early or late for fewer crowds.

Kolob Canyons

The **Kolob Canyons Visitor Center** (8am-5pm daily mid-Mar.-mid-Oct., 8am-4:30pm daily mid-Oct.-mid-Mar.) is a good place for information on exploring the Kolob region. Hikers can learn current trail conditions and obtain

KOLOB CANYONS

the permits required for overnight trips and Zion Narrows day trips. The visitors center and the start of Kolob Canyons Road are just off I-15 exit 40.

ZION-MT. CARMEL HIGHWAY

ONE DAY IN ZION

Park your car at **Zion Canyon Visitor Center.** Enjoy the exhibits, then jump on the **free park shuttle** for a stroll on the **Riverside Walk** or **Weeping Rock Trail.** Jump off the shuttle at Zion Lodge for lunch at the **Red Rock Grill.** Then take a longer hike: **Hidden Canyon** is lots of fun and won't utterly deplete experienced hikers. If you don't hike much, the trails to the **Emerald Pools** are easier. **Springdale** is just a short walk or shuttle bus ride from the park entrance, and it has several very good restaurants, shops, and galleries.

SIGHTS

ZION NATURE CENTER

Zion Nature Center (shuttle stop 2, 1pm-6pm daily late May-mid-Aug.) houses natural history programs for kids, including Junior Ranger activities for ages 6-12. It's at the northern end of South Campground, an easy walk along the Pa'rus Trail from the Zion Canyon Visitor Center or the Human History Museum.

ZION HUMAN HISTORY MUSEUM

The **Zion Human History Museum** (shuttle stop 2, 10am-6pm daily mid-Apr.-late May, 9am-7pm daily late May-early Sept., 9am-6pm early Sept.-early Oct., 10am-5pm early Oct.-mid.-Apr.) focuses on southern Utah's cultural history, with a film introducing the park plus exhibits on Native American and Mormon history. It's the first shuttle stop after the visitors center.

COURT OF THE PATRIARCHS

The **Three Patriarchs** (shuttle stop 4), a trio of peaks to the west, overlook Birch Creek. They are known as (from left to right) Abraham, Isaac, and Jacob. Mount Moroni, the reddish peak on the far right, partly blocks the view of Jacob. Although the official viewpoint is a beautiful place to relax and enjoy the view, you'll get an even better view if you cross the road and head about 0.5 mile up the Sand Bench Trail.

THE GROTTO

The Grotto (shuttle stop 6) is a popular place for a picnic. From here, a trail leads south to Zion Lodge; across the road, the Kayenta Trail links up with the Emerald Pools Trails farther south. A right turn on the trail connects north to the West Rim Trail, which leads to Angels Landing.

WEEPING ROCK

Weeping Rock (shuttle stop 7) is home to hanging gardens and many moisture-loving plants, including the striking Zion shooting star. The rock "weeps" because this is a junction between porous Navajo sandstone and denser Kayenta shale. Water trickles down through the sandstone, and, when it can't penetrate the shale, moves laterally to the face of the cliff. Several trails, including the short and easy Weeping Rock Trail, start here.

BIG BEND

Big Bend (shuttle stop 8) is where you'll see rock climbers on the towering walls. Pull out your binoculars to watch their moves on the face of the vertical walls.

TEMPLE OF SINAWAVA

The last shuttle stop is at the **Temple of Sinawava** (shuttle stop 9), where 2,000-foot-tall rock walls stretch skyward from the Virgin River. The **Riverside Walk,** a paved wheelchair-accessible path, heads one mile upstream to the Virgin Narrows, a place where the canyon becomes too narrow for even a sidewalk to squeeze alongside. From here, hikers wade up the **Narrows.**

SCENIC DRIVES

KOLOB CANYONS ROAD

Kolob Canyons Road (I-15 at exit 40) is in the extreme northwestern corner of the park. From the Kolob Canyons

TEMPLE OF SINAWAVA

Visitor Center, the paved scenic drive winds five miles past the dramatic Finger Canyons of the Kolob to the terminus at Kolob Canyons Viewpoint. The road has many pullouts where you can stop to admire the scenery as it climbs 1,300 feet in elevation. The first part of the drive follows the 200-mile-long Hurricane Fault that forms the west edge of the Markagunt Plateau. Look for the tilted rock layers deformed by friction as the plateau rose nearly one mile. At four miles up, the route crosses Lee Pass, named after John D. Lee of the infamous Mountain Meadows Massacre; he's believed to have lived nearby for a short time after the massacre. At the road's end, you can climb 0.5 mile to 6,369-foot **Timber Creek Overlook,** where views encompass the Pine Valley Mountains, Zion Canyons, and distant Mount Trumbull.

KOLOB TERRACE ROAD

From the town of Virgin on Highway 9, **Kolob Terrace Road** (early June-early Nov.) accesses a high plateau roughly parallel to and west of Zion Canyon. The steep road runs 23 miles north through ranchland and up a narrow tongue of land, with drop-offs on either side. After reaching a high plateau, the land widens. The Hurricane Cliffs rise from the gorge to the west, and the back side of Zion Canyon's big walls are to the east.

At Lava Point Road, turn right and follow the dirt road 1.8 miles east to reach 7,890-foot **Lava Point** and its tiny, primitive campground. A panorama takes in the Cedar Breaks area to the north, the Pink Cliffs to the northeast, Zion Canyon Narrows and tributaries to the east, the monoliths of Zion Canyon to the southeast, and Mount Trumbull on the Arizona Strip to the south. Lava Point is a good place to cool off in summer—temperatures are about 20°F cooler than in Zion Canyon. Aspen, ponderosa pine, Gambel oak, and white fir grow here. Expect the trip from Virgin to Lava Point to take about one hour.

North of Lava Point, Kolob Terrace Road ends in 3.5 miles at **Kolob Reservoir**, a popular boating and fishing destination.

HIKING
ZION CANYON
Watchman Trail

SHUTTLE STOP: Zion Canyon Visitor Center

From a trailhead north of Watchman Campground, the **Watchman Trail** (2.4 mi. rt., 2 hrs., easy) climbs 370 vertical feet to a bench below Watchman Peak, the prominent mountain southeast of the visitors center. Views encompass lower Zion Canyon and the town of Springdale. The well-graded trail follows a side canyon past some springs, then ascends to the overlook.

Pa'rus Trail

SHUTTLE STOPS: Zion Canyon Visitor Center and Canyon Junction

The paved **Pa'rus Trail** (2 mi. one-way, 1 hr., easy) runs from the South Campground to the Canyon Junction shuttle bus stop. For most of its distance, it skirts the Virgin River and makes for a nice early-morning or evening stroll. The wheelchair-accessible trail is also open to bicycles and pets.

Sand Bench Trail

SHUTTLE STOPS: Court of the Patriarchs and Zion Lodge

The **Sand Bench Trail** (1.7 mi. rt., 1-2 hrs., easy) has good views of the Three Patriarchs, the Streaked Wall, and other monuments of lower Zion Canyon. There is an elevation gain of 500 feet.

Emerald Pools Trails

SHUTTLE STOP: Zion Lodge

Spring-fed pools, small waterfalls, and views of Zion Canyon make this climb to the **Emerald Pools** (1-3 hrs., easy-moderate) worthwhile. Don't

▼ SUNSET OVER THE WATCHMAN

THE EAST RIM TRAIL

expect solitude, as these relatively easy trails are quite popular. From the footbridge at Zion Lodge, you have a choice of three trails. The easiest is the paved, wheelchair-accessible trail to the **Lower Pool** (1.2 mi. rt.), a recessed alcove with hanging gardens and misty falls. To reach it, turn right after the footbridge. From the Lower Pool, continue to the **Middle Pools** (1.8 mi. rt.), a pair of pools at the base of small waterfalls. Views take in the landmarks of Zion Canyon. You can loop back to the footbridge via a direct route from the Middle Pools. To reach the Middle Pools directly from the footbridge, turn left instead. A steep up-and-back, 0.4-mile spur trail leads from the Middle Pool to **Upper Emerald Pool** (2.6 mi. rt.). This magical spot has a white-sand beach and towering cliffs rising above.

Weeping Rock Trail

SHUTTLE STOP: Weeping Rock

A favorite with visitors, the paved but steep **Weeping Rock Trail** (0.5 mi. rt., 20 min., easy) winds upward past lush vegetation and wildflowers to a series of cliffside springs above an overhang. Thousands of water droplets glisten in the afternoon sun. The springs emerge where water seeping through more than 2,000 feet of Navajo sandstone meets a layer of impervious shale. Signs along the way identify trees and plants.

Observation Point Trail

SHUTTLE STOP: Weeping Rock

This highly scenic trail climbs 2,150 feet to 6,507-foot **Observation Point** (7.2 mi. rt., 4-6 hrs., strenuous) on the edge of Zion Canyon. The first of many switchbacks begins a short way up from the trailhead at the Weeping Rock parking area. The junction for the Hidden Canyon Trail appears after 0.8 mile. Several switchbacks later, the trail enters sinuous Echo Canyon. At the halfway point, the trail joins the **East Rim Trail.** Head left on the East Rim Trail to

ECHO CANYON

Best Hike

WEST RIM TRAIL TO ANGELS LANDING

DISTANCE: 5.4 miles round trip
DURATION: 4-5 hours
ELEVATION CHANGE: 1,488 feet
EFFORT: strenuous
TRAILHEAD: The Grotto

Not for acrophobes, the trail up to Angels Landing tiptoes along a narrow rib with cliff drop-offs on both sides. But for those up for the challenge, it's a hike full of entertainment with huge rewards. The finale puts you on a high-elevation point in the middle of Zion Canyon with 360-degree views, including the Great White Throne and the Organ. This is not a trail for solitude; in fact, some days, hundreds of people hike this trail. You may have to wait in places for people to pass or descend pitches where there's only room for one hiker.

After crossing the bridge over the North Fork of the Virgin River, the route heads north along two miles of pavement on the West Rim Trail. As the hot trail ascends the narrow Refrigerator Canyon between Angels Landing and Cathedral Mountain, the air cools a bit. After the ravine comes a beautiful piece of stonework trail that is fun to hike; Walter's Wiggles zigzags for 21 short switchbacks up to Scout Lookout. From the lookout saddle, you'll turn off the West Rim Trail toward Angels Landing to climb a half mile along the top of the rib. Along steeper pitches and narrow stairsteps, chains bolted into the rock serve as handholds. The rib plunges vertically off both sides, leading to the last skinny ramps to the summit.

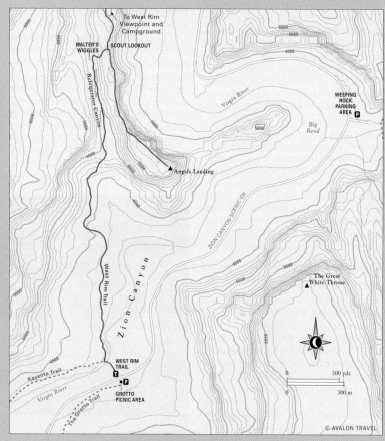

ANGELS LANDING

climb slickrock slopes above Echo Canyon with many fine views. Parts of the trail cut right into the cliffs, work done in the 1930s by the Civilian Conservation Corps. You'll reach the rim at last after steady climbing. Then it's an easy 0.6-mile jaunt through a forest of piñon pine, juniper, Gambel oak, manzanita, sage, and some ponderosa pine to Observation Point. Impressive views take in Zion Canyon below and mountains and mesas all around.

THE WEST RIM TRAIL

Hidden Canyon

SHUTTLE STOP: Weeping Rock

Inside narrow **Hidden Canyon** (5 mi. rt., 3-4 hrs., strenuous) await small sandstone caves, a little natural arch, and diverse plant life. The high walls, rarely more than 65 feet apart, block sunlight except for a short time at midday. From Weeping Rock parking area, climb about 1,000 feet, first going 0.8 mile to the signed junction, then turning right for 0.7 mile to the canyon entrance. Footing can be a bit difficult in places because of loose sand, but chains provide handholds on the more exposed sections. Steps chopped into the rock just inside Hidden Canyon help bypass some deep pools. After heavy rains and spring runoff, the creek forms a small waterfall at the canyon entrance. The canyon is about one mile long and mostly easy walking, although the trail fades away. Look for the arch on the right about halfway up the canyon.

Riverside Walk

SHUTTLE STOP: Temple of Sinawava

This is one of the most popular hikes in the park and is also one of the easiest. The paved and nearly level Riverside Trail (2 mi. rt., 1 hr., easy) begins at the end of Zion Canyon Scenic Drive and winds upstream along the river to the Virgin River Narrows. The first half of the trail is wheelchair-accessible.

ZION-MOUNT CARMEL HIGHWAY

The fun **Canyon Overlook Trail** (1 mi. rt., 1 hr., moderate) starts on the road east of Zion Canyon and features great views from the heights without the stiff climbs found on most other Zion trails. The trail winds in and out along the ledges of Pine Creek Canyon, which opens into a great valley. Panoramas at trail's end take in lower Zion Canyon in the distance. A sign at the viewpoint identifies Bridge Mountain, Streaked Wall, East Temple, and other features. The Great Arch of Zion—termed a blind arch because it's open on only one side—lies below; the arch is 580 feet high, 720 feet long, and 90 feet deep.

KOLOB CANYONS

You're likely to have the trails to yourself in this quiet section of the park. Access these hikes from the Kolob Canyons Road, which begins south of Cedar City off I-15.

Taylor Creek Trail (5.8 mi. rt., 3-4 hrs., moderate) heads upstream into the canyon of the Middle Fork of Taylor Creek. The destination is Double Arch Alcove and a dry fall that blocks the way (water flows over it during spring runoff and after rains). The trailhead is two miles from the Kolob Canyons Visitor Center.

A trail 3.1 miles from the visitors center follows the **South Fork of Taylor Creek** (2.4 mi. rt., 1.5 hrs., moderate) as it goes upstream beneath steep canyon walls.

The 287-foot span on **Kolob Arch** makes it one of the world's largest arches. Kolob's height is more than 300 feet and its vertical thickness is 75 feet. To see the arch, you have a choice of two trails. **La Verkin Creek Trail** (14 mi. rt., 7-8 hrs., strenuous) begins at Lee Pass and drops into Timber Creek. It then crosses over hills to La Verkin Creek (flows year-round) and turns up side canyons to the arch. The 950-foot ascent back to the trailhead can be hot and tiring. You can also hike to Kolob Arch on the **Hop Valley Trail** (7 mi. one-way, 3.5-4 hrs.), reached from Kolob Terrace Road.

▼ KOLOB ARCH

WATERFALLS NEAR KOLOB ARCH

KOLOB TERRACE

From the Lava Point Trailhead, the **West Rim Trail** (June-early Nov.) offers two hiking options. You can walk the trail as an out-and-back trek into Potato Hollow (13 mi. rt., 6-7 hrs., strenuous). From the high elevation, you'll overlook Wildcat Canyon. Or hike the trail one-way (13.3 mi., 6-8 hrs., strenuous) beyond Potato Hollow southeast to Zion Canyon. Many hikers do this as a point-to-point hike by setting up a shuttle (contact the visitors center backcountry desk). While the total route drops 3,600 feet in elevation, 3,000 feet of that plunges in a knee-pounding descent in the last six miles to the Grotto.

From the Lava Point Campground, take **Barney's Trail** (1 mi.) from site #2 to the trailhead or access the trailhead from Highway 9 in Virgin via Kolob Terrace Road and Lava Point Road.

RECREATION
BACKPACKING

For two-day backpacking trips, **Kolob Arch** (14 miles) makes a great destination, while the **West Rim Trail** offers a point-to-point 13-mile trip. Hands down, the best two-day trip is on the **Narrows** (16 miles) from the "top down," but competition for permits is cutthroat.

CANYONEERS SCALE ZION'S WALLS AND CLIFFS.

Overnight hikers must obtain **backcountry permits** ($15-25, https://zion-permits.nps.gov) in person one day in advance from the park's visitors centers or by reservation online three months in advance. For backcountry trailheads outside Zion Canyon, consult the visitors center's **backcountry desk** for shuttle options.

Shuttles are available from **Zion Rock and Mountain Guides** (435/772-3303, www.zionrockguides.com) and **Zion Adventure Company** (435/772-1001, www.zionadventures.com).

The Narrows

Permits (https://zionpermits.nps.gov) are required for overnight hikes in the Narrows—from the "top down" starting at Chamberlain's Ranch and hiking downstream to the Riverside Walk. Visit the backcountry desk at the visitors center the day before you plan to hike or the morning of your hike (7am-noon) to apply. Only one-night stays are allowed. No camping is permitted below Big Springs.

The following Springdale outfitters rent specially designed river-hiking boots, along with neoprene socks, walking sticks, and dry suits, for hiking the **Narrows.** They also lead tours and provide shuttle service to Chamberlain's Ranch.

Zion Adventure Company (36 Lion Blvd., Springdale, 435/772-1001, www.zionadventures.com)

THE NARROWS

Zion Outfitter (7 Zion Park Blvd., Springdale, 435/772-5090, www.zion-outfitter.com)

Zion Guru (795 Zion Park Blvd., Springdale, 435/632-0432, www.zionguru.com)

Zion Rock and Mountain Guides (1458 Zion Park Blvd., Springdale, 435/772-3303, www.zionrockguides.com)

BIKING

On the stretch of park road between the visitors center and Canyon Junction (where the Zion-Mount Carmel Highway meets Zion Canyon Scenic Drive) the paved **Pa'rus Trail** is open to cyclists for easy family pedaling. Bike parking is plentiful at the visitors center, Zion Lodge, and most trailheads. Outside the Zion Canyon area, **Kolob Terrace Road** is a good place for cyclists to pound down the miles to Kolob Reservoir (44 mi. rt.). Bike rentals and maps are available in Springdale at **Zion Outfitter** (95 Zion Park Blvd., 435/772-5090, http://zionoutfitter.com).

HORSEBACK RIDING

Trail rides on horses and mules leave from the corral near **Zion Lodge** (435/679-8665, www.canyonrides.com, mid-Mar.-Oct.) and head down the Virgin River. A one-hour trip goes to the Court of the Patriarchs, and a half-day ride follows the Sand Bench Trail.

WHERE TO STAY

INSIDE THE PARK

Zion Lodge

Within the park, lodging is limited to Zion Lodge and the three park campgrounds. Rustic **Zion Lodge** (shuttle stop 5, 888/297-2757, www.zionlodge.com, year-round, from $210) has accommodations in hotel rooms near the main lodge or in cute cabins (gas fireplaces but no TV). Reservations can be made up to 13 months in advance and they book fast for April-October.

The lodge's **Red Rock Grill** (435/772-7760, 6:30am-10:30am, 11:30am-3pm, and 5pm-10pm daily, dinner reservations required) offers a southwestern and Mexican-influenced menu for breakfast, lunch, and dinner. The **Castle**

Dome Café serves decent fast food, including salads and coffee.

Camping

Two campgrounds lie inside the south entrance to Zion Canyon. **Watchman Campground** (877/444-6777, www.recreation.gov, year-round, $20-30) has 164 sites, some with electrical hookups. **South Campground** (Mar.-Nov., $20) has 126 first-come, first-served sites. Both campgrounds have drinking water, but no showers, and they fill on major holidays and in summer. Plan to arrive by 8am to score a spot. Campers have access, via the park's free shuttles, to restaurants and showers in Springdale.

Up Kolob Terrace Road, primitive **Lava Point Campground** (May-Sept., free) has six first-come, first-served sites with pit toilets, but no drinking water. The campground is a 90-minute drive from Zion Canyon.

OUTSIDE THE PARK

Near the park's south entrance are several small towns with good services for travelers. **Springdale** has the widest range of services, including excellent lodgings and restaurants; **Rockville** has a few B&Bs; and **Hurricane** is a hub for less expensive chain motels. **St. George** offers many places to stay and eat.

GETTING THERE

AIR

Salt Lake City is convenient as a terminus for travelers who want to make a road-trip loop tour through all of Utah's parks. **Salt Lake City International Airport** (SLC, 776 N. Terminal Dr., 801/575-2400, www.slcairport.com) is located 300 miles north of the park.

Consider flying into **McCarran International Airport** (LAS, 5757 Wayne Newton Blvd., 702/261-5211, www.mccarran.com) in Las Vegas, Nevada, instead of Salt Lake. McCarran is well served by major domestic airlines, and by smaller or "no-frills" carriers. It is a 163-mile drive to the park. Car rentals are available at either airport.

DESERT BIGHORN SHEEP

CAR

To get to the south entrance of Zion National Park from Salt Lake City, take I-15 south for 300 miles; the driving time is about four hours. From Las Vegas, it's just 120 miles northeast on I-15 to St. George, with Zion just 43 miles farther on Highway 9.

A separate entrance for Kolob Canyons is reached via Kolob Canyons Road, which begins off I-15 (exit 40) at the Kolob Canyons Visitor Center.

A fourth entrance is accessed by the Kolob Terrace Road at the town of Virgin on Highway 9.

GETTING AROUND

DRIVING

Zion Canyon Scenic Drive is only open to private vehicles December-early February. The road may close when parking spots fill.

February-late November, Zion Canyon Scenic Drive is closed to private vehicles and access is via shuttle bus. In summer, visitors park at Zion Canyon Visitor Center, where the small lot usually fills by 10am. To avoid congestion, park in Springdale and take the free shuttle into the park.

The Kolob Canyons area in the park's northwest corner has its own entrance. Reach this area via **Kolob Canyons Road,** which begins just off I-15 at exit 40.

To visit a less traveled part of the park, take Highway 9 north to the tiny town of Virgin on the **Kolob Terrace Road.** The road goes to backcountry sites and Lava Point, but has no entrance station or visitors center.

SHUTTLE BUS

Within Zion Canyon, free **shuttle buses** (7am-7:45pm daily Mar.-late May, 6am-8:30pm daily late May-late Sept., 7am-6:45pm daily late Sept.-Oct., 7am-6pm daily early Nov.) provide frequent service through the park. There are actually two separate bus lines: One line travels between Springdale and the park entrance, while the other bus line starts at the visitors center and runs the length of Zion Canyon Road, stopping at scenic overlooks, trailheads, and Zion Lodge. You can transfer between the two shuttle systems at Zion Canyon Visitor Center. The buses run frequently and are wheelchair-accessible; pets are not allowed.

November-February, the buses are out of service and private vehicles are allowed into Zion Canyon.

ZION-MOUNT CARMEL TUNNEL

On Zion-Mount Carmel Highway, most RVs (including buses, trailers, fifth wheels, and some truck-campers) will require oncoming traffic to be stopped to allow one-way travel through the mile-long tunnel. Drivers must time their trips for when traffic control rangers are present (8am-8pm daily May-early Sept., shorter hours rest of the year).

RVs are measured at the entrance station where, if you are within the vehicle limits, a **permit** ($15) will be issued for travel through the tunnel while rangers manage one-way traffic for your passage. The fee is good for two trips through the tunnel within seven days. Height, width, and length restrictions will ban access for the largest RVs, forcing alternate routes into the park. Bicycles and pedestrians are not allowed in the tunnel.

TOURS

The **Zion Canyon Field Institute** (435/772-3264, www.zionpark.org) runs educational programs ranging from animal tracking to photography to archaeology.

BRYCE CANYON NATIONAL PARK

Utah

WEBSITE:
www.nps.gov/brca

PHONE NUMBER:
435/834-5322

VISITATION RANK:
12

WHY GO:
Spy sculpted hoodoos
and colorful hues.

PASSPORT STAMPS ▼▼▼

In **BRYCE CANYON NATIONAL PARK**, a geologic fairyland of rock spires rises beneath the high cliffs of the Paunsaugunt Plateau. This intricate maze, eroded from a soft limestone, glows with warm shades of reds, oranges, pinks, yellows, and creams. The rocks provide a continuous show of changing color throughout the day as the sun's rays and cloud shadows move across the landscape. Looking at these rock formations is like looking at puffy clouds in the sky; it's easy to find images in the shapes of the rocks. Some see the natural rock sculptures as Gothic castles; others as Egyptian temples, subterranean worlds inhabited by dragons, or vast armies of a lost empire.

Bryce Canyon isn't a canyon at all, but the largest of a series of massive amphitheaters cut into the Pink Cliffs. In Bryce Canyon National Park, you can gaze into the depths from viewpoints and trails on the plateau rim, but a whole different world awaits those hiking down the steep trails among the spires. A scenic drive traces the length of the park and passes many overlooks and trailheads. Off-road, the nearly 36,000 acres of Bryce Canyon National Park offer many opportunities to explore spectacular rock features, dense forests, and expansive meadows.

PLANNING YOUR TIME

Bryce Canyon is in southern Utah, between Zion National Park and Grand Staircase-Escalante National Monument. Allow a full day to tour the park, stopping at visitors centers, cruising the scenic drive, and taking a few short walks. Sunsets and sunrises reward overnight visitors, while moonlit nights reveal yet another spectacle.

September-October are choice hiking months—the weather is at its best and the crowds are at their smallest, although nighttime temperatures in late October can dip well below freezing. The park's elevation ranges 6,600-9,100 feet, so it's usually much cooler here than at Utah's other national parks. Expect pleasantly warm days in summer, frosty nights in spring and autumn, and snow at almost any time of year. The visitors center, scenic drive, and a campground stay open year-round, but the busy season is April-October, when reservations are a good idea.

▼ THE SNOW-COVERED AMPHITHEATER

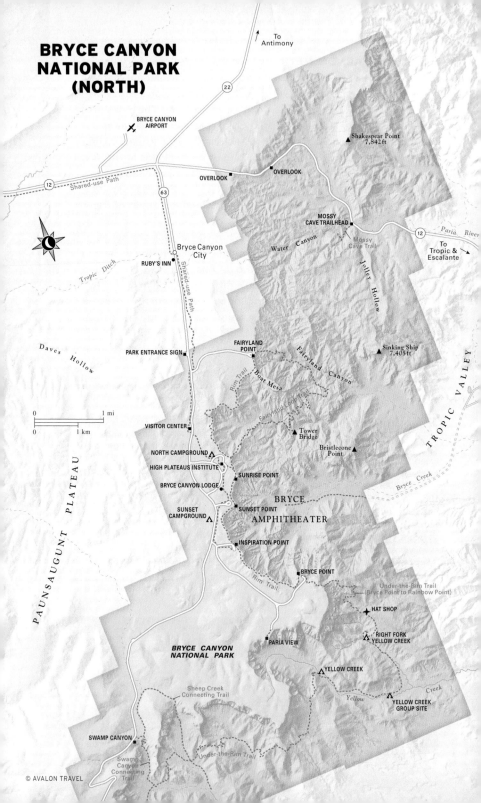

BRYCE CANYON NATIONAL PARK (NORTH)

To Antimony

22

BRYCE CANYON AIRPORT

Shakespear Point 7,842ft

12 Shared-use Path

OVERLOOK OVERLOOK

63

MOSSY CAVE TRAILHEAD

Water Canyon

Mossy Cave Trail

Bryce Canyon City

12 Paria River

RUBY'S INN

To Tropic & Escalante

Jolley Hollow

Tropic Ditch

Daves Hollow

Shared-use Path

FAIRYLAND POINT

PARK ENTRANCE SIGN

Sinking Ship 7,405ft

Fairyland Canyon

Rim Trail

Boat Mesa

Fairyland Loop Trail

TROPIC VALLEY

0   1 mi
0   1 km

VISITOR CENTER

Tower Bridge

Bristlecone Point

NORTH CAMPGROUND

HIGH PLATEAUS INSTITUTE

SUNRISE POINT

BRYCE CANYON LODGE

Bryce Creek

BRYCE AMPHITHEATER

SUNSET CAMPGROUND

SUNSET POINT

INSPIRATION POINT

Under-the-Rim Trail (Bryce Point to Rainbow Point)

PAUNSAUGUNT PLATEAU

Rim Trail

BRYCE POINT

HAT SHOP

RIGHT FORK YELLOW CREEK

PARIA VIEW

BRYCE CANYON NATIONAL PARK

YELLOW CREEK

Yellow   Creek

YELLOW CREEK GROUP SITE

Sheep Creek Connecting Trail

SWAMP CANYON

Swamp Canyon Connecting Trail

Under-the-Rim Trail

© AVALON TRAVEL

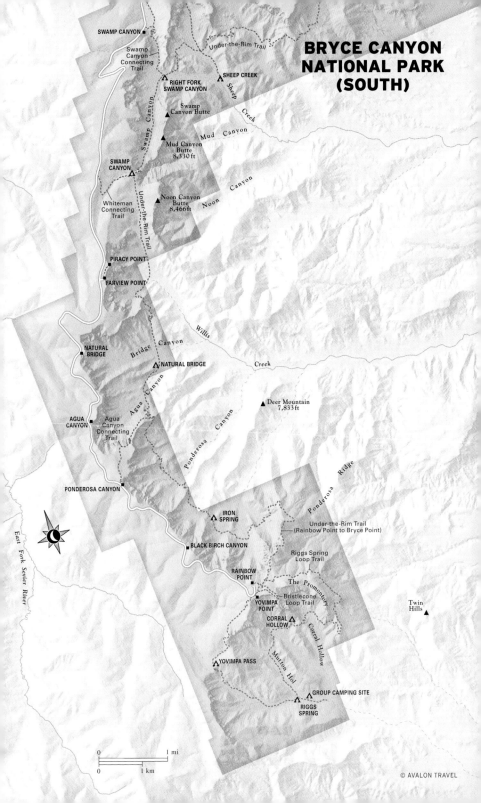

BRYCE CANYON NATIONAL PARK (SOUTH)

SWAMP CANYON

Swamp Canyon Connecting Trail

Under-the-Rim Trail

RIGHT FORK SWAMP CANYON

SHEEP CREEK

Sheep

Creek

Swamp Canyon Butte

Mud Canyon

Mud Canyon Butte 8,330 ft

Swamp Canyon

SWAMP CANYON

Whiteman Connecting Trail

Under-the-Rim Trail

Noon Canyon

Noon Canyon Butte 8,466 ft

PIRACY POINT

FARVIEW POINT

Willis

NATURAL BRIDGE

Bridge Canyon

NATURAL BRIDGE

Creek

Agua Canyon

Deer Mountain 7,833 ft

AGUA CANYON

Agua Canyon Connecting Trail

Ponderosa Canyon

PONDEROSA CANYON

Ponderosa Ridge

IRON SPRING

Under-the-Rim Trail (Rainbow Point to Bryce Point)

East Fork Sevier River

BLACK BIRCH CANYON

Riggs Spring Loop Trail

RAINBOW POINT

The Promontory

Bristlecone Loop Trail

YOVIMPA POINT

CORRAL HOLLOW

Corral Hollow

Twin Hills

YOVIMPA PASS

Mutton Hol

GROUP CAMPING SITE

RIGGS SPRING

0   1 mi

0   1 km

© AVALON TRAVEL

Top ❸

❶ TAKE IN PANORAMAS FROM SUNRISE AND SUNSET POINTS

Sunrise and Sunset Points lie about one mile south of the visitors center and are connected by a 0.5-mile paved section of the **Rim Trail.** Panoramas from each point take in large areas of Bryce Amphitheater and beyond. The lofty Aquarius and Table Cliff Plateaus rise along the skyline to the northeast; you can see the same colorful Claron Formation in cliffs that faulting has raised about 2,000 feet higher.

VIEW FROM SUNSET POINT

❷ VIEW HOODOOS FROM INSPIRATION POINT

To visit a fantastic maze of hoodoos in the Silent City, drive Bryce Point Road two miles. At the first spur road, turn left after the turnoff to reach **Inspiration Point**. Weathering along vertical joints has cut many rows of narrow gullies, some more than 200 feet deep. A short but steep 0.2-mile walk ascends Upper Inspiration Point

HOODOO ROCK FORMATIONS

❸ TOP OUT AT YOVIMPA AND RAINBOW POINTS

The land drops away in rugged canyons and fine views at the end of the scenic drive (17 miles south of the visitors center). At an elevation of 9,115 feet, this is the highest area of the park. Yovimpa and Rainbow Points are only a short walk apart yet offer different vistas. Hikes in this area include the **Bristlecone Loop Trail,** the **Riggs Spring Loop Trail,** and the **Under-the-Rim Trail.**

VIEW OF THE VALLEY FROM BRISTLECONE LOOP TRAIL, RAINBOW POINT

ONE DAY IN BRYCE CANYON

Get up early and catch the free park shuttle so you don't miss the scene at **Sunrise Point.** If you don't want to hike down (and climb back up), take a walk along the **Rim Trail.** Plan to picnic at **Rainbow Point,** at the end of the parkway, with views over much of southern Utah. After lunch, descend from the rim on the **Navajo Loop Trail.** At the bottom of the loop, turn onto the **Queen's Garden Trail** and follow that back up to the rim. The Rim Trail connects the two trailheads. For dinner, the **Lodge at Bryce Canyon** has the best food in the area.

ENTRANCE AND FEES

The entrance fee is $35 per vehicle ($30 motorcycle, $20 individual) and is good for seven days. The park entrance is on Highway 63; fee stations are inside the park adjacent to the visitors center.

VISITORS CENTERS

At the **visitors center** (8am-8pm daily May-Sept., 8am-6pm daily Apr. and Oct., 8am-4:30pm daily Nov.-Mar.), geologic exhibits illustrate how the land was formed and how it has changed. Historical displays interpret the Paiute people, early explorers, and the first settlers. Rangers present a variety of naturalist programs, including short hikes (mid-May-early Sept.). From the turnoff on Highway 12, follow signs past Ruby's Inn into the park; the visitors center is a short distance farther on the right.

▼ SUNRISE AT BRYCE POINT

SCENIC DRIVE

The 18-mile park road is a scenic drive with spurs shooting eastward to impressive overlooks that also serve as trailheads into the canyons (overlooks are listed north to south).

FAIRYLAND POINT

From **Fairyland Point,** whimsical forms line Fairyland Canyon a short distance below, beckoning you to descend into the "fairyland." To reach the turnoff, drive south 0.3 mile inside the park boundary, then turn east and go one mile.

BRYCE POINT

Four miles south of the visitors center, **Bryce Point** offers views of the south end of Bryce Amphitheater and expansive scenery to the north and east. To reach **Paria View,** backtrack 0.5 mile and turn left. From this overlook, cliffs drop precipitously into the headwaters

of Yellow Creek, a tributary of the Paria River. You can see a section of the Under-the-Rim Trail winding up a hillside near the mouth of the amphitheater below. Distant views take in the Paria River Canyon, White Cliffs (of Navajo sandstone), and Navajo Mountain.

FARVIEW POINT

The sweeping panorama of **Farview Point** takes in a lot of geology. You'll see levels of the Grand Staircase that include the Aquarius and Table Cliff Plateaus to the northeast, Kaiparowits Plateau to the east, and White Cliffs to the southeast. Look beyond the White Cliffs to see a section of the Kaibab Plateau that forms the north rim of the Grand Canyon in Arizona. The point is nine miles south of the visitors center.

NATURAL BRIDGE

This large **Natural Bridge** spans 54 feet and is 95 feet high. Despite its name, the arch was formed by weathering from rain and freezing water, not by stream erosion like a true natural bridge. Once the opening reached ground level, runoff began to enlarge the hole and to dig a gully through it. It is just off the road to the east, 1.7 miles past Farview Point.

AGUA AND PONDEROSA CANYONS

You can admire sheer cliffs and hoodoos from the **Agua Canyon** overlook. With a little imagination, you may be able to pick out the Hunter and the Rabbit below. The **Ponderosa Canyon** overlook (1.8 miles east) offers a panorama similar to that at Farview Point. Turn off 1.4 miles past Natural Bridge.

RECREATION

HIKING

The **Rim Trail** (11 mi. rt., 5-6 hrs., easy) follows the edge of Bryce Amphitheater for 5.5 miles between Fairyland and Bryce Points. Most people just walk sections of it on leisurely strolls or use the trail to connect with other routes. The 0.5-mile section near the lodge between Sunrise and Sunset Points is paved and nearly level; other parts are gently rolling.

The **Fairyland Loop Trail** (8 mi. rt., 4-5 hrs., strenuous) winds in and out of colorful rock spires in the northern part of Bryce Amphitheater and includes

▼ A RED SANDSTONE NATURAL BRIDGE

STUNNING CHINA WALL

views of Tower Bridge. The route gains and loses elevation several times, including the climb to exit to the rim (2,309 feet), making the trail feel much longer. You can start the loop from Fairyland Point or Sunrise Point, connecting the two via the Rim Trail.

From Sunset Point, you'll drop 520 vertical feet down the **Navajo Loop Trail** (1.5 mi. rt., 1.5 hrs., moderate) through a narrow canyon. At

the bottom, the loop leads into deep, dark **Wall Street**—an even narrower 0.5-mile-long canyon—and then returns to the rim.

Peekaboo Loop Trail (5.5 mi. rt., 4 hrs., strenuous) is full of surprises at every turn—and there are lots of turns. The trail tours the southern part of Bryce Amphitheater, which has some of the most striking rock features. You can also start from Bryce Point (6.5 mi. rt.),

HIKE THE NAVAJO LOOP TRAIL.

Best Hike

QUEEN'S GARDEN TRAIL

DISTANCE: 1.8 miles round-trip
DURATION: 1.5 hours
ELEVATION CHANGE: 320 feet
EFFORT: easy-moderate
TRAILHEAD: Sunrise Point

A favorite of many people, this trail drops from Sunrise Point through impressive features in the middle of Bryce Amphitheater to a hoodoo resembling a portly Queen Victoria. This is the easiest excursion below the rim. The Queen's Garden Trail also makes a good loop hike with the **Navajo Loop** and **Rim Trails;** most people who do the loop prefer to descend the steeper Navajo and climb out on Queen's Garden for a 3.5-mile hike. Trails also connect with the **Peekaboo Loop Trail** and go to the town of Tropic.

from Sunset Point (5.5 mi. rt. via Navajo Loop Trail), or from Sunrise Point (7 mi. rt. via Queen's Garden Trail). This is the only trail in the park where horses are permitted.

The **Hat Shop Trail** (4 mi. rt., 3 hrs., moderate), an area of delicate spires capped by erosion-resistant rock, makes a good day-hike destination on the Under-the-Rim Trail. Begin at Bryce Point, descending on the Under-the-Rim Trail for about two miles. The return climb gains 900 feet.

HOODOOS

The easy **Bristlecone Loop Trail** (1 mi. rt., 30 min., easy) begins from either Rainbow or Yovimpa Point and goes to ancient bristlecone pines—some 1,800 years old—along the rim. Viewpoints include the Four Corners.

One of the park's more challenging day hikes, the **Riggs Spring Loop** (8.5 mi. rt., 5 hrs., strenuous) begins at Rainbow Point and descends into canyons in the southern area of the park. Great views of the hoodoos, lots of aspen trees, a couple of pretty meadows, and views off to the east highlight this hike. A shortcut bypassing Riggs Spring saves 0.75 mile.

HORSEBACK RIDING

Canyon Trail Rides (Lodge at Bryce Canyon, 435/679-8665, www.canyonrides.com, Apr.-Oct.) offers guided two-hour and half-day rides near Sunrise Point. Both rides descend to the canyon floor; the longer ride follows the Peekaboo Loop Trail. **Ruby's Horseback Adventures** (435/834-5358 or 866/782-0002, www.horserides.net, Apr.-Oct.) offers horseback riding in and near Bryce Canyon with 1.5-hour, half-day, and full-day trips.

WHERE TO STAY

INSIDE THE PARK

Travelers may have a hard time finding accommodations and campsites April-October. Advance reservations at lodges, motels, and the park campground are a good idea; otherwise, plan to arrive by late morning.

The **Lodge at Bryce Canyon** (877/386-4383, http://brycecanyonforever.com, Apr.-Oct., rooms from $203, cabins $221) is the only lodge inside the park. Accommodations include lodge suites, motel-style guest rooms, and lodgepole pine cabins. Activities include horseback rides, park tours, evening entertainment, and ranger talks; a gift shop sells souvenirs. Make reservations 13 months in advance for this historic landmark.

The lodge's **dining room** (7am-10:30am, 11:30am-3pm, and 5:30pm-10pm daily Apr.-Oct., $13-34) is classy and atmospheric, with a large stone fireplace, white tablecloths, and good food. A short walk from the main lodge is **Valhalla Pizzeria and Coffee Shop** (6am-10pm daily mid-May-mid-Oct.).

The park has two campgrounds. The **North Campground** is just past the visitors center; the best sites are a few yards downhill from the Rim Trail. The **Sunset Campground** is about 2.5 miles farther on the right, across the road from Sunset Point. **Reservations** (877/444-6777, www.recreation.gov, May-Sept., $20 tents, $30 RVs) are accepted for some sites six months in advance. The remaining sites are first come, first served; arrive by noon to claim a spot.

Backcountry camping is available on the Under-the-Rim and Riggs Spring Loop Trails. A permit is required ($5-15) from the visitors center.

OUTSIDE THE PARK

Motels cluster near the park entrance road, but do not offer much for the money. The town of **Tropic** has a cache of motels lining Main Street (Hwy. 12) and several pleasant B&Bs. **Panguitch** is a stopover on the road between Zion and Bryce Canyon National Parks, with reasonably priced motels and good dining. The Dixie National Forest has three Forest Service campgrounds.

On Highway 63 north of the park boundary, **Best Western Ruby's Inn** (26 S. Main St., 435/834-5341 or 866/866-6616, www.rubysinn.com, from $95) offers year-round services including a hotel, dining, and a general store, as well as recreational outfitters, entertainment, and shopping. Many tour bus groups bed down here.

▼ HIKE AMID NATURAL SPIRES.

THE HOODOOS

The park's landscape originated about 60 million years ago as sediments in a large body of water, named Lake Flagstaff by geologists. Silt, calcium carbonate, and other minerals settled on the lake bottom. These sediments consolidated and became the Claron Formation, a soft, silty limestone with some shale and sandstone. Lake Flagstaff had long since disappeared when the land began to rise as part of the Colorado Plateau uplift about 16 million years ago. Uneven pressures beneath the plateau caused it to break along fault lines into a series of smaller plateaus at different levels, collectively known as the Grand Staircase. Bryce Canyon National Park occupies part of one of these plateaus—the Paunsaugunt.

The spectacular Pink Cliffs on the park's east edge contain the famous erosional features known as hoodoos, carved in the Claron Formation. Variations in hardness of the rock layers result in these strange features, which seem almost alive. Water flows through cracks, wearing away softer rock around hard, erosion-resistant caps. Finally, a cap becomes so undercut that the overhang allows water to drip down, leaving a "neck" of rock below the harder cap. Traces of iron and manganese provide the distinctive coloring.

The hoodoos continue to change—new ones form and old ones fade away. Despite appearances, wind plays little role in creating the landscape; it's the freezing and thawing, snowmelt, and rainwater that dissolve weak layers, pry open cracks, and carve out the forms. The plateau cliffs, meanwhile, recede at a rate of about one foot every 50-65 years; look for trees on the rim that now overhang the abyss. Listen, and you might hear the sounds of pebbles falling away and rolling down the steep slopes.

GETTING THERE

AIR

Salt Lake City is the travel hub for Utah. Delta Airlines and all other major airlines have regular flights into **Salt Lake City International Airport** (SLC, 776 N. Terminal Dr., 801/575-2400, www.slcairport.com). It is a four-hour drive (270 miles) via I-15 south to the park. **McCarran International Airport** (LAS, 5757 Wayne Newton Blvd., 702/261-5743, www.mccarran.com) in Las Vegas is another option, with a four-hour drive via I-15 north to the park. Car rentals are available at both airports.

CAR

Bryce Canyon National Park is just south of the incredibly scenic Highway 12, between Bryce Junction and Tropic. To reach the park from Bryce Junction (7 miles south of Panguitch at the intersection of U.S. 89 and Hwy. 12), head

▲ HOODOOS OF BRYCE CANYON

BRYCE'S HOODOOS

14 miles east on Highway 12 to the park turnoff. From Escalante, it's about 50 miles west on Highway 12 to the turnoff for Bryce. From Highway 12, turn south onto Route 63 for the final three miles into the park (winter snows occasionally close this section). Both approaches have spectacular scenery.

GETTING AROUND

You can drive your own vehicle into Bryce Canyon National Park. However, if you do drive into the park, trailers cannot go past Sunset Campground. For day visitors, trailer parking is available at the visitors center. For free **parking** to catch shuttles, park at the visitors center or near Ruby's Inn, outside the park entrance.

SHUTTLE BUS

During the summer, the National Park Service runs the **Bryce Canyon Shuttle** (every 15-20 minutes 8am-8pm daily mid-May-mid-Oct., shorter hours off-season, free) from the shuttle parking and boarding area at the intersection of Highways 12 and 63 to the visitors center, with stops at Ruby's Inn and Ruby's Campground. From the visitors center, the shuttle travels to the park's developed areas, including all the main amphitheater viewpoints, Sunset Campground, and the Bryce Canyon Lodge.

TOURS

Free **shuttle bus tours** (435/834-5290, 9am and 1:30pm daily early May-mid-Oct., reservations required at Ruby's Inn, Ruby's Campground, or the shuttle parking area) of the park go all the way to Rainbow Point. **Ruby's Inn** (26 S. Main St., 866/866-6616, www.rubysinn. com) is filled with recreational outfitters, along with vendors who organize hayrides, barn dances, and chuckwagon dinners.

Bryce Canyon Airlines (Ruby's Inn, 435/834-8060) offers scenic flightseeing tours by both plane and helicopter. A 35-minute airplane tour ($175 pp, 2-person minimum) provides a good look at the surroundings.

SIGHTS NEARBY

Coral Pink Sand Dunes State Park (435/648-2800, reservations 800/322-3770, www.stateparks.utah.gov, day use $8, camping $20), west of Kanab, is home to sand dunes that reach heights of several hundred feet and cover about 2,000 acres.

Kodachrome Basin State Park (801/322-3770 or 800/322-3770, www.stateparks.utah.gov, $19 tents, $28 RVs with hookups) offers beautiful campsites. From Bryce, take Highway 12 east to Cannonville, then go 9 miles south to the park.

CAPITOL REEF NATIONAL PARK

Utah

WEBSITE:
www.nps.gov/care

PHONE NUMBER:
435/425-3791

VISITATION RANK:
21

WHY GO:
See spectacular cliffs
and colorful geology.

▲ CAPITOL REEF NATIONAL PARK

Although **CAPITOL REEF NATIONAL PARK** receives less attention than Utah's other national parks, it is a special place in its own right, with excellent hiking and splendid scenery. Sculpted rock layers in a rainbow of colors put on a fine show. The Waterpocket Fold—so named for the many small pools of water trapped by the tilted strata—extends 100 miles between Thousand Lake Mountain in the north and Lake Powell in the south. The most spectacular cliffs and rock formations of the Waterpocket Fold form Capitol Reef, named for the white Navajo sandstone between Pleasant Creek and the Fremont River.

Roads and hiking trails in the park provide access to the colorful rock layers. You'll also see remnants of human history—petroglyphs and storage bins of the prehistoric Fremont people, a schoolhouse and other structures built by Mormon pioneers, and several small uranium mines from the 20th century.

PLANNING YOUR TIME

Capitol Reef National Park flanks Highway 24, a major east-west road south of I-70 in south-central Utah. Travelers short on time will enjoy a quick stop at the visitors center and a drive on Highway 24 through an impressive cross section of Capitol Reef cut by the Fremont River.

You can see more of the park on the Scenic Drive, a narrow, paved road that heads south from the visitors center. The drive passes beneath spectacular cliffs of the reef and enters Grand Wash and Capitol Gorge Canyons; allow at least 1.5 hours for the 21-mile round-trip and any side trips.

In **summer** (May-Sept.), expect hot days (highs in the upper 80s and low 90s) and cool nights. Late-afternoon thunderstorms are common in July-August; impending storms are warnings for flash flooding. Winter brings cool days (highs in the 40s) and night temperatures in the low 20s and teens. Snow accents the colored rocks while rarely hindering traffic on the main highway. Snow may halt winter travel on the back roads and trails, but it soon melts when the sun comes out.

ENTRANCES AND FEES

The entrance fee is $20 per vehicle ($15 motorcycle, $10 individual). The entrance fee is only collected for vehicles on the Scenic Drive; a self-pay kiosk is just past the campground. Though Highway 24 bisects Capitol Reef National Park, driving the road is free.

VISITORS CENTER

At the **Capitol Reef Visitors Center** (Hwy. 24, 8am-6pm daily mid-May-Sept., 8am-4:30pm daily Oct.-May), a 15-minute film introduces Capitol Reef's history, wildlife, and geology. Hikers can pick up trail maps and checklists of plants, birds, mammals, and wildlife. Rangers offer talks, campfire programs, and the Junior Ranger Program (Easter through Oct.). Capitol Reef is an International Dark Sky Park and you can see the Milky Way on moonless nights and at ranger-led astronomy programs. The visitors center is at the turnoff for Fruita Campground and the Scenic Drive.

SIGHTS

From the west, **Highway 24** drops from the broad mountain valley near Torrey onto Sulphur Creek, with dramatic rock formations soaring to the horizon. A

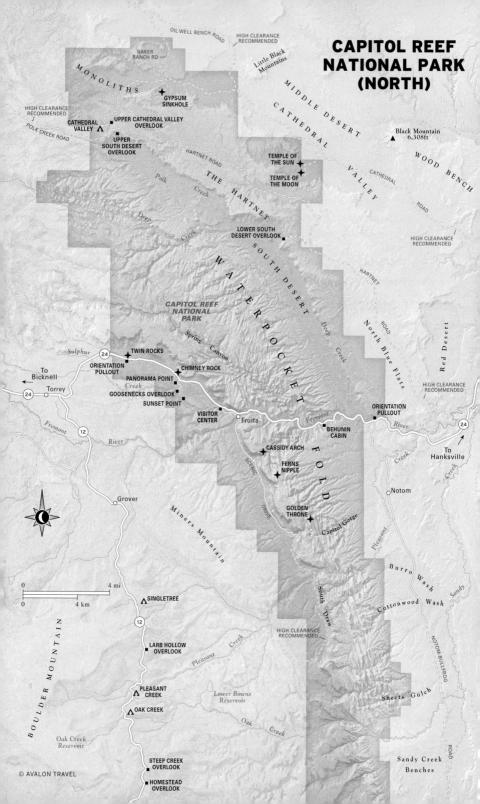

CAPITOL REEF NATIONAL PARK (NORTH)

OIL WELL BENCH ROAD

HIGH CLEARANCE RECOMMENDED

Little Black Mountains

MIDDLE DESERT

CATHEDRAL

MONOLITHS

BAKER RANCH RD

★ GYPSUM SINKHOLE

HIGH CLEARANCE RECOMMENDED

POLK CREEK ROAD

CATHEDRAL VALLEY ⛺

■ UPPER CATHEDRAL VALLEY OVERLOOK

UPPER SOUTH DESERT OVERLOOK

HARTNET ROAD

THE HARTNET

Polk Creek

Deep Creek

WOOD BENCH

Black Mountain ▲ 6,308ft

TEMPLE OF THE SUN ✦

TEMPLE OF THE MOON ✦

CATHEDRAL VALLEY

MIDDLE DESERT

LOWER SOUTH DESERT OVERLOOK ■

HIGH CLEARANCE RECOMMENDED

SOUTH DESERT

HARTNET

ROAD

WATERPOCKET

CAPITOL REEF NATIONAL PARK

Spring Canyon

Deep Creek

North Blue Flats

Red Desert

Sulphur

24

TWIN ROCKS ★

ORIENTATION PULLOUT

CHIMNEY ROCK ★

To Bicknell

Creek

PANORAMA POINT ■

Torrey

24

GOOSENECKS OVERLOOK ■

SUNSET POINT ■

VISITOR CENTER ○

Fruita

FOLD

Fremont River

HIGH CLEARANCE RECOMMENDED

ORIENTATION PULLOUT ■

River

24

Fremont

12

River

BEHUNIN CABIN ▪

To Hanksville

SCENIC

★ CASSIDY ARCH

FERNS NIPPLE ★

Creek

Grover

Miners Mountain

DRIVE

GOLDEN THRONE ★

Capitol Gorge

Notom ○

Pleasant

Burro Wash

Cottonwood Wash

Sandy

0   4 mi

0   4 km

△ SINGLETREE

12

South Draw

NOTOM-BULLFROG ROAD

LARB HOLLOW OVERLOOK ■

Pleasant

Creek

HIGH CLEARANCE RECOMMENDED

Sheets Gulch

BOULDER MOUNTAIN

△ PLEASANT CREEK

△ OAK CREEK

Lower Bowns Reservoir

Oak Creek

Oak

Creek

Oak Creek Reservoir

STEEP CREEK OVERLOOK ■

Sandy Creek Benches

HOMESTEAD OVERLOOK ■

© AVALON TRAVEL

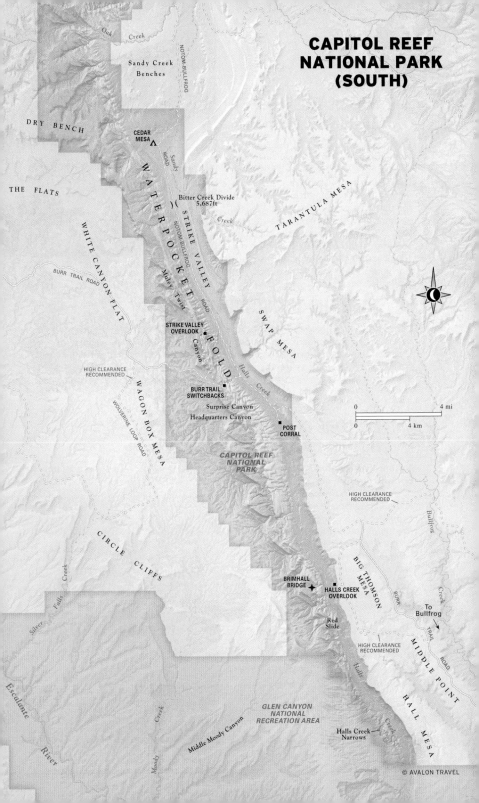

CAPITOL REEF
NATIONAL PARK
(SOUTH)

Oak   Creek

Sandy Creek
Benches

NOTOM-BULLFROG

DRY   BENCH

CEDAR
MESA

Sandy ROAD

THE   FLATS

Bitter Creek Divide
5,687ft

Creek

TARANTULA MESA

WHITE CANYON FLAT

BURR TRAIL ROAD

W A T E R P O C K E T

NOTOM-BULLFROG ROAD

STRIKE VALLEY

Muley Twist

SWAP MESA

STRIKE VALLEY
OVERLOOK

F O L D

Canyon

Halls   Creek

HIGH CLEARANCE
RECOMMENDED

WAGON BOX MESA

WOLVERINE LOOP ROAD

BURR TRAIL
SWITCHBACKS

Surprise Canyon
Headquarters Canyon

0   4 mi
0   4 km

POST
CORRAL

CAPITOL REEF
NATIONAL
PARK

HIGH CLEARANCE
RECOMMENDED

C I R C L E   C L I F F S

Bullfrog

BIG THOMSON MESA

BURR

BRIMHALL
BRIDGE
HALLS CREEK
OVERLOOK

Creek

Silver Falls Creek

Red
Slide

To
Bullfrog

HIGH CLEARANCE
RECOMMENDED

TRAIL   ROAD

Escalante

GLEN CANYON
NATIONAL
RECREATION AREA

Halls

M I D D L E   P O I N T

Creek

River

Middle Moody Canyon

Moody

Halls Creek
Narrows

Creek

H A L L   M E S A

© AVALON TRAVEL

Top ③

① WATCH THE SUN SET AT SUNSET POINT

Enjoy panoramic views of the Fremont River gorge, the Capitol Reef cliffs, and the distant Henry Mountains at **Sunset Point.** Plan your evening around viewing the sunset; it's worth hanging out for the whole show. From the Goosenecks Overlook parking area, it's an easy 0.3-mile hike across the slickrock to Sunset Point. There's a sign at the trailhead. Bring a flashlight and use caution when hiking back in the dark.

SUNSET FROM SUNSET POINT

② TOUR THE SCENIC DRIVE

Turn south from **Highway 24** at the visitors center to experience some of the reef's best scenery and to learn more about its geology. You can do a quick tour with stops on the out-and-back **Scenic Drive** (16-21 mi. rt., 1.5 hrs.), but several hiking trails may tempt you to extend your stay. Before embarking on the drive, pick up a brochure at the visitors center for descriptions of geology along the road. While the Scenic Drive is paved, side roads have gravel surfaces.

③ EXPLORE GEOLOGY ALONG NOTOM-BULLFROG ROAD

Notom-Bullfrog Road crosses some of the younger geologic layers of the **Waterpocket Fold.** The northernmost 10 miles of the road have been paved, and about 25 miles are paved on the southern end near Bullfrog, a settlement on the shores of Lake Powell. The rest of the road is dirt and gravel, and it can get pretty washboarded and bumpy. The turnoff from Highway 24 is 9.2 miles east of the visitors center. Stops along the drive (north to south) include: **Notom Ranch** (Mile 4.1), a private ranch; **Burrow Wash** (Mile 8.1); and **Cottonwood Wash** (Mile 9.3). The pavement ends at **Five Mile Wash** (Mile 10.4). The dirt road reenters the park at Mile 20 with options to explore **Cedar Mesa Campground** (Mile 22.3), **Burr Trail Road** (Mile 34.1), and **Surprise Canyon** (Mile 36). Notom-Bullfrog Road exits the park for good at Mile 37.5 to end at Bullfrog Marina in Glen Canyon National Recreation Area (Mile 70).

GEOLOGIC FORMATIONS ON THE NOTOM-BULLFROG ROAD, THE WATERPOCKET FOLD

huge amphitheater of stone rings the basin, with formations such as **Twin Rocks, Chimney Rock,** and the **Castle** glowing in deep red and yellow tones. Ahead, the canyon narrows as the Fremont River slips between the cliffs to carve its chasm through Waterpocket Fold.

PANORAMA POINT

Take in the sweeping view from **Panorama Point** (2.5 miles west of the visitors center). To reach the point, follow signs south to Panorama Point. Enjoy views of Capitol Reef, the distant Henry Mountains to the east, and looming Boulder Mountain to the west.

GOOSENECKS OVERLOOK

The Goosenecks of Sulphur Creek are located on a gravel road one mile south of Panorama Point. A 0.1-mile walk leads to the **Goosenecks Overlook** on the rim with dizzying views of the creek below. An easy trail leads 0.3 mile to **Sunset Point** for views of the Capitol Reef cliffs and the distant Henry Mountains.

FRUITA

The Fruita area contains a breadth of history stretching along the narrow Fremont River canyon. On the north side of Highway 24 is the **Fruita Schoolhouse,** a one-room log structure that housed grades one through eight in 1896. The school closed in 1941 due to a lack of students. Although the schoolhouse is locked, you can peer inside the windows and take photos.

Just east, on a northside pullout, are panels of the **Fremont petroglyphs**; several mountain sheep and human figures with headdresses decorate the cliff. View more petroglyphs by walking left and right along the cliff face. Farther east, another northside pullout shows where Elijah Cutlar Behunin used blocks of sandstone to build the **Behunin Cabin** around 1882. For several years, Behunin, his wife, and 11 of their 13 children shared this sturdy but small cabin (the kids slept outside). A window allows a look inside the dirt-floored structure, but no furnishings remain.

In the **Fruita Historic District,** south of the visitors center on the Scenic Drive, you'll pass orchards and several of Fruita's buildings. A **blacksmith shop** displays tools, harnesses, farm machinery, and Fruita's first tractor. **Ripple Rock Nature Center** has activities and exhibits for kids, many centering on pioneer life. Typical of rural Utah farmhouses of the early 1900s, the **Gifford Farmhouse** houses cultural demonstrations; handmade baked goods, gifts, and a picnic area are also available.

AUTUMN IN THE FRUITA HISTORIC DISTRICT

THE WATERPOCKET FOLD

About 65 million years ago, well before the Colorado Plateau uplifted, sedimentary rock layers in south-central Utah buckled, forming a steep-sided monocline, a rock fold with one very steep side in an area of otherwise nearly horizontal layers. A monocline is a "step-up" in the rock layers along an underlying fault. The rock layers on the west side of the Waterpocket Fold have been lifted more than 7,000 feet higher than the layers to the east. The 100-mile-long fold was then subjected to millions of years of erosion, which slowly removed the upper layers to reveal the warped sedimentary layers at its base. Continued erosion of the sandstone has left many basins, or "water pockets," along the fold. These seasonal water sources, often called "water tanks," are used by desert animals, and they were a water source for prehistoric people. Erosion of the tilted rock layers continues today, forming colorful cliffs, massive domes, soaring spires, stark monoliths, twisting canyons, and graceful arches. Getting a sense of the Waterpocket Fold requires some off-pavement driving. The best viewpoint is along **Burr Trail Road,** which climbs up the fold between Boulder and Notom-Bullfrog Road.

NATURAL WATER TANKS ABOVE CAPITOL GORGE

CATHEDRAL VALLEY

Only the most adventurous travelers enter the remote canyons and desert country of the park's northern district of Cathedral Valley. Four-wheel drive roads lead through stately sandstone monoliths, volcanic remnants, badlands country, many low mesas, and vast sand flats. The district's two main roads—**Hartnett Road** and **Cathedral Road** (aka Caineville Wash Rd.)—combine with a short stretch of Highway 24 to form a loop, with a campground at their junction. The **Upper Cathedral Valley Trail,** just below the campground, is a one-mile walk offering excellent views of the Cathedrals.

GRAND WASH

The Scenic Drive leaves the Fremont River valley and climbs up a desert slope, with the rock walls of the Waterpocket Fold rising to the east. Turn off the pavement toward the east to explore **Grand Wash,** a dry channel etched through the sandstone. A dirt road follows the twisting gulch for one mile, with sheer rock walls rising along the sandy streambed. At the road's end, an easy hiking trail follows the wash 2.5 miles to its mouth along Highway 24.

Back on the paved road, continue south past **Slickrock Divide**, to where the rock lining the reef deepens into a ruby red and erosion forms odd columns and spires that resemble statuary. The **Egyptian Temple** is one of the most striking and colorful features with its white-topped red rock.

CAPITOL GORGE

From the end of the pavement, this eastward gravel road tours the narrow, twisting **Capitol Gorge**, the route of the main state highway through south-central Utah for 80 years. From the terminus, an easy one-mile saunter down the gorge will take day hikers past petroglyphs and a "register" rock where pioneers carved their names.

PLEASANT CREEK ROAD

Near the beginning of the Capitol Gorge Road, the dirt **Pleasant Creek Road** (high-clearance vehicles recommended) heads south below the face of the reef. After three miles, the road ends at Pleasant Creek. The creek's perennial waters begin high on Boulder Mountain to the west and cut a scenic canyon completely through Capitol Reef.

◄ GRAND WASH IN THE WATERPOCKET FOLD

HICKMAN BRIDGE

HIKING

HIGHWAY 24

Many day hikes begin within a short drive of the visitors center. **Chimney Rock** (3.6 mi. rt., 2.5 hrs., moderate) is a fluted spire of dark red rock capped by a block of hard sandstone. The loop trail ascends from the parking lot on the north side of the highway 590 feet in elevation to a ridge overlooking Chimney Rock. The trailhead is three miles west of the visitors center.

The **Hickman Bridge Trail** (1.8 mi. rt., 1.5 hrs., moderate) includes a 133-foot natural bridge that spans a small streambed. The trail follows the Fremont River's green banks a short distance before gaining 380 feet in the climb to the bridge. The last section of trail follows a dry wash shaded by cottonwood, juniper, and piñon pine trees. You'll pass under the bridge (eroded from the Kayenta Formation) at trail's end. The trailhead is two miles east of the visitors center.

For a longer option, take the Hickman Bridge Trail for 0.25 mile, then turn right at the signed fork. A splendid overlook above Fruita beckons hikers to climb 1,100 feet on the **Rim Overlook Trail** (4.6 mi. rt., 3.5 hrs., strenuous). Panoramic views take in the Fremont River valley below, the great cliffs of Capitol Reef above, the Henry Mountains to the southeast, and Boulder Mountain to the southwest.

Continue another 2.2 miles to reach **Navajo Knobs** (9.4 mi. rt., 4-5 hrs., strenuous), a 1,620-foot ascent from the trailhead. Rock cairns lead the way over slickrock along the rim of the

CHIMNEY ROCK

Best Hike

GRAND WASH TRAIL

DISTANCE: 4.5 miles round-trip
DURATION: 2-3 hours
ELEVATION CHANGE: 200 feet
EFFORT: easy
TRAILHEAD: 4.7 miles east of the visitors center on Highway 24

One of only five canyons cutting complete-ly through the reef, Grand Wash offers easy hik-ing, great scenery, and an abundance of wildflow-ers. There's no trail—just follow the dry riverbed. (Flash floods can occur during storms.) Only a short distance from Highway 24, canyon walls rise 800 feet above the floor and narrow to as little as 20 feet in width; this stretch of trail is known as the Narrows. After the Narrows, the wash widens, and wildflowers grow every-where. The Cassidy Arch trailhead is two miles from Highway 24.

Waterpocket Fold. A magnificent pan-orama at trail's end takes in much of southeastern Utah.

THE SCENIC DRIVE

From the Fruita blacksmith shop, the **Fremont Gorge Overlook** trail (4.6 mi. rt., 2.5 hrs., strenuous) crosses a love-ly native prairie on Johnson Mesa and steeply climbs 1,090 feet to the over-look above the Fremont River.

Across the road from the Fruita Campground, **Cohab Canyon Trail** (3.4 mi. rt., 2 hrs., moderate) follows steep switchbacks during the first 0.25 mile, with gentler grades on the 400 feet to the top. Turn right at the top on the **Frying Pan Trail** to Cassidy Arch (3.5 mi. rt., 2 hrs., moderate).

From the Fruita Campground am-phitheater, the **Fremont River Trail** (2 mi. rt., 1.5 hrs., moderate) passes or-chards along the Fremont River. The trail climbs sloping rock strata to a viewpoint on Miners Mountain where sweeping views take in Fruita, Boulder Mountain, and the reef.

GRAND WASH

Off Grand Wash Road, the **Cassidy Arch Trail** (3.4 mi. rt., 2-3 hrs., strenuous) climbs 670 feet for views of Grand Wash, the great domes of Navajo sandstone, and the arch itself. The trail ascends the north wall of Grand Wash, then winds across slickrock to a vantage point close to the arch.

The **Old Wagon Trail** (3.8 mi. rt.) crosses a wash, then ascends steadily through piñon and juniper woodland on Miners Mountain. After 1.5 miles, the trail leaves the wagon road and goes north 0.5 mile to a high knoll for the best views of the Capitol Reef area. Look for the trailhead on the west side of the Scenic Drive 0.7 mile south of Slickrock Divide, between Grand Wash and Capitol Gorge.

Fremont petroglyphs appear on the **Capitol Gorge Trail** (2 mi. rt., 1.5 hr., easy); turn left after 0.1 mile. The narrows of Capitol Gorge close in at 0.3 mile. In 0.5 mile, look for a pioneer register on the left; it consists of the names and dates of early travelers and ranchers scratched in the canyon wall. At 0.75 mile, look left for natural water tanks typical of those in the Waterpocket Fold. The trailhead is at the terminus of Capital Gorge Road, at the end of the Scenic Drive.

From the same parking area, the **Golden Throne Trail** (4 mi. rt., 4 hrs., strenuous) turns left to climb 1,100 feet in a steady grade to a viewpoint of the Golden Throne, a massive monolith of yellow-hued Navajo sandstone capped by a thin layer of red Carmel Formation.

WHERE TO STAY
INSIDE THE PARK

There are no accommodations or restaurants inside the park. Camping is the only overnight option.

Surrounded by orchards and lush grass, **Fruita Campground** (year-round, $20) has 71 sites for tents and RVs, with drinking water (May-Oct.) and heated restrooms, but no showers or hookups. The first-come, first-served sites often fill by early afternoon in the busy May-October season.

Two year-round, primitive campgrounds have first-come, first-served sites, but no water. The **Cedar Mesa Campground** (5 sites, year-round, free) is in the park's southern district, just off the dirt Notom-Bullfrog Road. From the visitors center, drive east 9.2 miles

▼ CASSIDY ARCH

A BOARDWALK-LINED TRAIL THROUGH THE GORGE

on Highway 24, then turn right and continue 22 miles on Notom-Bullfrog Road. **Cathedral Valley Campground** (6 sites, year-round, free) serves the park's northern district near the Hartnett Junction, about 30 miles north of Highway 24.

Backcountry camping is allowed in the park; obtain a free backcountry permit at the visitors center.

OUTSIDE THE PARK

At the junction of Highways 12 and 24, 11 miles west of the visitors center, the town of **Torrey** has several excellent lodgings and a good restaurant. Several Forest Service campgrounds are south of Torrey on Boulder Mountain along Highway 12.

GETTING THERE AND AROUND

AIR

The closest international airport is **Salt Lake City International Airport** (SLC, 776 N. Terminal Dr., 801/575-2400, www.slcairport.com), 220 miles north via I-15 to Highways 89 and 24. Rental cars are available.

CAR

There is no public transportation into or within the park; you'll need a car. Travelers coming from Zion and Bryce should head north on Highway 12 from the town of Boulder. Twisty Highway 12 will take you over Boulder Mountain to Highway 24 at the town of Torrey; Capitol Reef is just 11 miles east.

SIGHTS NEARBY

Grand Staircase-Escalante National Monument (435/644-1300, https://blm.gov) contains a vast, scenic collection of slickrock canyon lands and desert, prehistoric village sites, Old West ranchland, arid plateaus, and miles of back roads linking stone arches, mesas, and abstract rock formations.

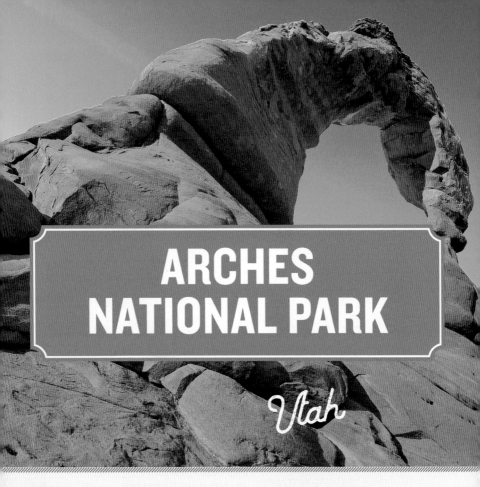

ARCHES NATIONAL PARK

Utah

WEBSITE:
www.nps.gov/arch

PHONE NUMBER:
435/719-2299

VISITATION RANK:
16

WHY GO:
Hike amid natural
sandstone arches.

PASSPORT STAMPS ▼▼▼

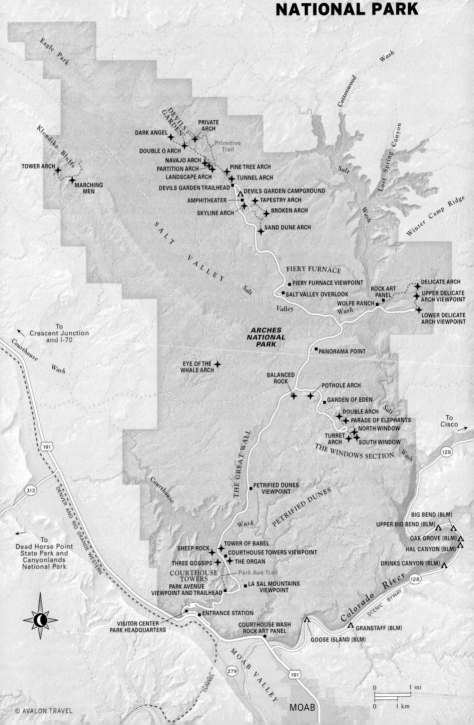

ARCHES NATIONAL PARK

Eagle Park

Wash

Cottonwood

Klondike Bluffs

DEVIL'S GARDEN

Dark Angel

PRIVATE ARCH

Primitive Trail

DOUBLE O ARCH

NAVAJO ARCH

PARTITION ARCH

LANDSCAPE ARCH

PINE TREE ARCH

TUNNEL ARCH

TOWER ARCH

MARCHING MEN

DEVILS GARDEN TRAILHEAD

DEVILS GARDEN CAMPGROUND

AMPHITHEATER

TAPESTRY ARCH

SKYLINE ARCH

BROKEN ARCH

SAND DUNE ARCH

SALT VALLEY

Salt

Salt

Wash

Last Spring Canyon

Winter Camp Ridge

FIERY FURNACE

FIERY FURNACE VIEWPOINT

SALT VALLEY OVERLOOK

Valley

WOLFE RANCH

Wash

ROCK ART PANEL

DELICATE ARCH

UPPER DELICATE ARCH VIEWPOINT

LOWER DELICATE ARCH VIEWPOINT

To Crescent Junction and I-70

Courthouse

Wash

ARCHES NATIONAL PARK

EYE OF THE WHALE ARCH

PANORAMA POINT

BALANCED ROCK

POTHOLE ARCH

GARDEN OF EDEN

DOUBLE ARCH

PARADE OF ELEPHANTS

NORTH WINDOW

TURRET ARCH

SOUTH WINDOW

THE WINDOWS SECTION

Salt

Wash

To Cisco

191

313

DENVER AND RIO GRANDE WESTERN

To Dead Horse Point State Park and Canyonlands National Park

THE GREAT WALL

Courthouse

Wash

PETRIFIED DUNES VIEWPOINT

PETRIFIED DUNES

128

BIG BEND (BLM)

UPPER BIG BEND (BLM)

OAK GROVE (BLM)

HAL CANYON (BLM)

DRINKS CANYON (BLM)

SHEEP ROCK

TOWER OF BABEL

COURTHOUSE TOWERS VIEWPOINT

THREE GOSSIPS

THE ORGAN

COURTHOUSE TOWERS

Park Ave Trail

PARK AVENUE VIEWPOINT AND TRAILHEAD

LA SAL MOUNTAINS VIEWPOINT

Colorado River

SCENIC BYWAY

128

ENTRANCE STATION

VISITOR CENTER PARK HEADQUARTERS

COURTHOUSE WASH ROCK ART PANEL

GRANSTAFF (BLM)

GOOSE ISLAND (BLM)

279

MOAB VALLEY

191

TUNNEL

MOAB

0   1 mi

0   1 km

© AVALON TRAVEL

A concentration of rock arches of marvelous variety has formed within the maze of sandstone fins at **ARCHES NATIONAL PARK**, one of the most popular parks in the United States. Balanced rocks and tall spires add to the splendor. Paved roads and short hiking trails provide easy access to some of the more than 1,500 arches in the park. If you're short on time, a drive to the Windows Section (23.5 miles round-trip) affords a look at some of the largest and most spectacular arches. To visit all the stops and hike a few short trails would take all day.

Most of the early settlers and cowboys that passed through the Arches area paid little attention to the scenery. In 1923, however, a prospector by the name of Alexander Ringhoffer interested officials of the Rio Grande Railroad in the scenic attractions at what he called Devils Garden (now known as Klondike Bluffs). The railroad men liked the area and contacted Stephen Mather, who was the first director of the National Park Service. Mather started the political process that led to designating two small areas as a national monument in 1929, but Ringhoffer's Devils Garden wasn't included until later. The monument grew in size over the years and became Arches National Park in 1971. The park now comprises 76,519 acres—small enough to be appreciated in one day, yet large enough to warrant extensive exploration.

PLANNING YOUR TIME

Located in southeastern Utah, about four hours from Salt Lake City, Arches is easy to reach via U.S. 191. Due to its proximity to Island in the Sky in Canyonlands National Park, most visitors go to both on the same trip. Its position just outside Moab gives it loads of options for lodging, camping, and dining; make reservations, as the town packs out in spring and fall. With no food services inside the park, you'll enjoy your time much more by packing a lunch and bringing one.

March through October is high season. **Fall** and **spring** are the most popular times to visit, as daytime temperatures are moderate. Real desert heat sets in during late May-early June. Temperatures then soar into the 90s and 100s at midday, although the dry air makes the heat more bearable. Early morning is the choice time for summer travel. Autumn begins after late-summer rains end and lasts into November or even December; days are bright and sunny with ideal temperatures, but nights become cold.

ENTRANCES AND FEES

The sole entrance to Arches is five miles north of downtown Moab on U.S. 191. Expect long entrance lines mid-day March-October. The entrance fee is $30 per vehicle ($25 motorcycle, $15 individual) and is good for seven days.

VISITORS CENTERS

Past the park entrance, the expansive **visitors center** (7:30am-6pm daily Mar.-Sept., 8am-5:30pm daily Oct., 8am-4:30pm daily Nov., 9am-4pm daily Dec.-Feb.) provides a good introduction to the area. Exhibits identify rock layers, describe geologic and human history, and illustrate some of the wildlife and plants in the park. Staff members can answer questions, issue backcountry permits, and sign you up for a ranger-led tour in the Fiery Furnace area.

Top ❸

① GAZE OUT FROM DELICATE ARCH

The park's iconic feature, **Delicate Arch** (Wolfe Ranch Rd.) stands in a magnificent setting atop gracefully curving slickrock. A moderately strenuous 3-mile round-trip hike leads to the arch, but another perspective can be gained by driving 1.2 miles beyond Wolfe Ranch and looking for the small arch high above. A short wheelchair-accessible trail and a slightly longer, steeper trail (0.5 mi. rt.) provide views onto the arch.

DELICATE ARCH

② EXPLORE MORE ARCHES AT THE WINDOWS

The Windows area holds four arches. From the Windows parking area, a series of short and easy trails lead to the massive arches. Take the Windows trailhead to walk below **North Window**, **South Window**, and **Turret Arch**. **Double Arch**, a short walk from the second trailhead, has two arches framing a large opening overhead. On the way back to the main park road, stop at **Garden of Eden Viewpoint** for a panorama of the Salt Valley.

SOUTH WINDOW

③ HIKE INTO THE DEVILS GARDEN

The **Devils Garden** trailhead, picnic area, and campground are located near the end of the main park road. Devils Garden offers fine scenery and **more arches** than any other section of the park. A hiking trail leads past large sandstone fins to Landscape Arch and six other named arches. This is one of the most popular areas in the park and is worth planning your time around.

BALANCED ROCK

SIGHTS

MOAB FAULT

A pullout for **Moab Fault** offers an amazing view of Moab Canyon and its huge fault. The rock layers on this side of the canyon have slipped down more than 2,600 feet in relation to the other side.

PARK AVENUE

Great sandstone slabs form a skyline on each side of **Park Avenue**, a dry wash version of the famed New York City street. A trail goes one mile down the wash to the North Park Avenue trailhead. Midway, the large rock monoliths of **Courthouse Towers** rise on the west, followed by the sandstone towers forming the **Three Gossips**. You can also see these from the road at Courthouse Towers Viewpoint.

BALANCED ROCK

The gravity-defying **Balanced Rock** is a boulder more than 55 feet high that rests precariously atop a 73-foot pedestal. For a closer peek at it, take the 0.3-mile trail that encircles it.

FIERY FURNACE

A viewpoint off the park road offers a look into the **Fiery Furnace,** closely packed pink, orange, and red sandstone fins that form a maze of deep slots with many arches and at least one natural bridge. (The Fiery Furnace gets its name from sandstone fins that can turn flaming red at sunrise or sunset.) Sign up at the visitors center for a **ranger-led hike**

▼ COURTHOUSE TOWERS

SKYLINE ARCH

within fins. A slightly longer trail (1.6 miles round-trip) crosses a field to **Broken Arch**. (Up close, you'll see that the arch isn't really broken.)

SKYLINE ARCH

In 1940, a giant boulder fell from the opening of **Skyline Arch,** doubling the size of the arch in just seconds. The 0.4-mile **Skyline Arch Trail** leads nearer to the base of the arch.

SCENIC DRIVE

Arches has one **main park road** (36 miles) that cruises past fantastical monoliths and the artistry of weathered red rocks. From the visitors center, the road begins a long but well-graded climb up the cliffs to the northeast. After cresting onto the mesa top, you'll gaze out onto a landscape loaded with geological sights thrusting up from the sagebrush desert. Short, paved spurs turn off to sightseeing features and trailheads. The road terminates at Devils Garden trailhead and campground.

Between March and October, expect traffic congestion and full parking lots. Go early or later in the day for less traffic or you may need to bypass some sights.

(3 hrs., strenuous, Mar.-Oct., $10) into the Fiery Furnace.

BROKEN AND SAND DUNE ARCHES

Two short trails lead to these smaller arches. From the park road, a 0.4-mile walk on red sand leads to the small, ground-level **Sand Dune Arch** tucked

SAND DUNE ARCH

ONE DAY IN ARCHES

With the park's scenic drive and short hikes, even those who have only one day can explore its easily accessed arches. Drive the main park road to the Windows area, where you can walk to **North Window** and **South Window**. Stop to walk a little of **Park Avenue** before driving to the trailhead for the park and Utah icon—the freestanding **Delicate Arch**.

RECREATION

HIKING

Devils Garden Loop

A full tour of **Devils Garden** (7.2 mi. rt., 4 hrs., moderate) leads to eight arches and a vacation's worth of scenic wonders. From the trailhead, you'll see two arches off a side trail to the right: **Tunnel Arch,** with its relatively symmetrical opening, and **Pine Tree Arch,** named for a piñon pine that once grew inside. Continue on the main trail to **Landscape Arch,** which has an incredible 306-foot span that is one of the longest unsupported rock spans in the world. For a shorter and easier hike, turn around at Landscape Arch (2 mi. rt., 1 hr.).

Beyond Landscape Arch, the trail narrows to reach the remains of **Wall Arch,** which collapsed in 2008. A short side trail branches off to the left beyond the stubs of Wall Arch to **Partition Arch** and **Navajo Arch.** The main trail continues northwest and ends at **Double O Arch**. Double O has a large, oval-shaped opening and a smaller hole underneath. **Dark Angel** is a distinctive rock pinnacle 0.25 mile northwest; cairns mark the way. Beyond Double O, a primitive trail loops back to Landscape Arch via Fin Canyon and adds one mile.

Fiery Furnace Trail

A labyrinth of red sandstone, the **Fiery Furnace** is open only to those joining a **ranger-led hike** (3 hrs., twice daily Mar.-Oct., adults $10, kids $5) or to experienced hikers with **permits** (adults $6, kids $3). The hike is moderately strenuous and involves steep ledges, squeezing through narrow cracks, a couple of jumps, and hoisting yourself up off the ground. There is no turning back once the hike starts, so make sure you're physically prepared and properly equipped. **Reservations** (877/444-6777, www.recreation.gov) for the ranger-led hike are accepted up to six months in advance and often fill.

DOUBLE O ARCH

THE FIERY FURNACE

Best Hike

DELICATE ARCH TRAIL

DISTANCE: 3 miles round-trip
DURATION: 2 hours
ELEVATION CHANGE: 500 feet
EFFORT: strenuous
TRAILHEAD: Wolfe Ranch

Hiking to the base of **Delicate Arch** is a highlight. A bit of pioneer history survives nearby at **Wolfe Ranch,** a weather-beaten cabin built in 1906 by John Wesley Wolfe. Shortly after the trailhead at Wolfe Ranch, a spur trail leads to some Ute petroglyphs depicting horses, their riders, and a few bighorn sheep. The first stretch of the main trail is broad, flat, and not especially scenic, except for a good display of spring wildflowers. Soon, the trail climbs steeply up onto the slickrock and the views open up, spanning the park and the La Sal Mountains in the distance. The arch sits in a magnificent setting atop gracefully curving slickrock.

BIKING

The rolling terrain of the main park road appeals to road cyclists. Relatively fit mountain bikers can go for the 24-mile ride to **Tower Arch** and back via a dirt road. From the Devils Garden parking area, take Salt Valley Road for about 7.5 miles. Turn left onto a jeep road that leads to the "back door" to Tower Arch.

ROCK CLIMBING

Rock climbers find plenty of drool-worthy cracks and nubbins in the park. Most go for the sheer stone faces of **Park Avenue** or **Owl Rock,** the small, owl-shaped tower located on the Windows Road. Stop by the visitors center for a free **permit** (https://archespermits.nps.gov) or visit **Pagan Mountaineering** (59 S. Main St., Moab, 435/259-1117, www.paganclimber.com), a climbing and outdoor-gear store in Moab, for more information.

▼ SUNSET AT DELICATE ARCH

MOAB

The largest town in southeastern Utah, **Moab** makes an excellent base for exploring Arches and Canyonlands National Parks and the surrounding canyon country. The slickrock canyons seem made for exploration by bike, and people come from all over the world to pedal the backcountry. River trips on the Colorado River are nearly as popular, and a host of other outdoor recreational diversions—from horseback riding to 4WD jeep exploring to skydiving—combine to make Moab one of the most popular destinations in Utah.

The **Moab Information Center** (25 E. Center St., 435/259-8825, www.discovermoab.com, 8am-7pm Mon.-Sat., 9am-6pm Sun. Apr.-Sept.) is an excellent source for information about the area's recreational options. **Canyonlands Field Institute** (435/259-7750 or 800/860-5262, http://cfimoab.org) leads weekend day hikes (mid-Apr.-mid-Oct., $40-45, including transportation and fees) at various locations near Moab; join one of these to really learn the area's natural history.

Mountain Biking

Most people come to Moab to mountain bike **mid-March-late May,** and then again **mid-September-October.** The interconnected **MOAB Brand Trails,** comprising loops and spur trails, form a trail system with several options that are especially good for beginners or riders who are new to slickrock. Several bicycle rental shops offer daylong mountain bike excursions in addition to rentals: **Rim Tours** (1233 S. U.S. 191, 435/259-5223, www.rimtours.com); **Magpie Cycling** (800/546-4245, www.magpieadventures.com); **Western Spirit Cycling** (478 Mill Creek Dr., 435/259-8732, www.westernspirit.com); and **Escape Adventures** (Moab Cyclery, 391 S. Main St., 800/596-2953, www.escapeadventures.com).

Rafting

Outfitters offer both laid-back and exhilarating day trips, as well as longer multiday trips. Rafting season runs **April-September.** Most do-it-yourself river-runners obtain their permits by applying in January-February for a March drawing; the Moab Information Center's BLM ranger can advise on this process. The following outfitters offer a variety of rafting options:

Adrift Adventures (378 N. Main St., 800/874-4483, www.adrift.net)

Canyonlands Field Institute (800/860-5262, http://cfimoab.org)

Canyon Voyages (211 N. Main St., 866/375-7364, www.canyonvoyages.com)

Moab Adventure Center (225 S. Main St., 866/904-1163, www.moabadventurecenter.com)

Navtec Expeditions (321 N. Main St., 800/833-1278, www.navtec.com)

Red River Adventures (1140 S. Main St., 877/259-4046, www.redriveradventures.com)

Sheri Griffith Expeditions (800/332-2439, www.griffithexp.com)

Tag-A-Long Expeditions (452 N. Main St., 800/874-4483, www.tagalong.com)

Camping

There are 26 **BLM campgrounds** ($10-15) in the Moab area. Although these spots can't be reserved, sites are abundant enough that campers can usually get a site. The campgrounds are concentrated on the banks of the Colorado River—along Highway 128 toward Castle Valley, along Highway 279 toward the potash factory, and along Kane Creek Road—and at the Sand Flats Recreation Area near the Slickrock Bike Trail. Only a few of these campgrounds can handle large RVs; none have hookups, and few have piped water. For a full list of BLM campgrounds and facilities, visit www.discovermoab.com.

DEVILS GARDEN CAMPGROUND

WHERE TO STAY
INSIDE THE PARK

Come prepared with a picnic lunch; there are no accommodations or food inside the park.

Devils Garden Campground (877/444-6777, www.recreation.gov, year-round, $25) is an excellent place to camp, with some sites tucked under rock formations and others offering great views—but it's extremely popular. Plan accordingly and reserve a site well in advance for stays March-October; campers without reservations are out of luck. A camp host is on-site, and firewood is available ($5). In winter, sites 1-24 are available on a first-come, first-served basis.

OUTSIDE THE PARK

Moab is the gateway for accommodations, food, services, and camping. Bureau of Land Management (BLM) campsites are on Route 313, just west of U.S. 191, on the way to Canyonlands National Park's Island in the Sky District, and along the Colorado River on Route 128, which runs northeast from U.S. 191 at the north end of Moab.

GETTING THERE AND AROUND
AIR

Salt Lake City International Airport (SLC, 776 N. Terminal Dr., 801/575-2400, www.slcairport.com) is 234 miles north of Moab. The four-hour drive follows I-15, U.S. 6, I-70, and U.S. 191. Rental cars are available. **Boutique Air** (855/268-8478, www.boutiqueair.com) provides daily scheduled air service between **Canyonlands Field** (CNY, U.S. 191, 16 miles north of Moab, 435/259-4849, www.moabairport.com) and Salt Lake City and Denver.

CAR

Arches National Park is 26 miles south of I-70 and 5 miles north of Moab, both off U.S. 191. If you're driving from Moab, allow 15 minutes to reach the park, as there is often slow-moving RV traffic along the route.

TOUR

Canyonlands Field Institute (800/860-5262 or 435/259-7750, http://cfimoab.org) guides one-day and multiday educational adventures and programs in Arches.

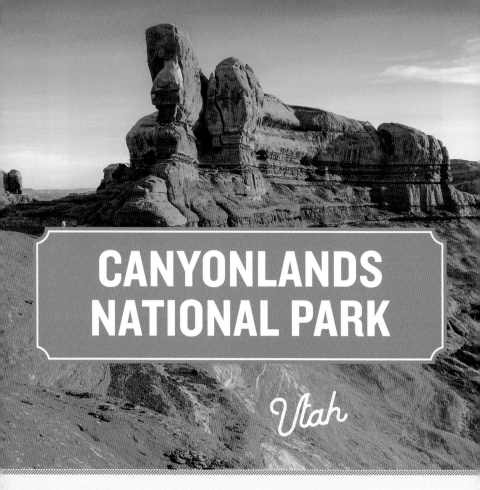

CANYONLANDS
NATIONAL PARK

Utah

WEBSITE:
www.nps.gov/cany

PHONE NUMBER:
435/719-2313

VISITATION RANK:
26

WHY GO:
Explore Utah's
canyon country.

▲ CANYONLANDS NATIONAL PARK

Utah's canyon country puts on a supreme performance in this vast park, which spreads across 527 square miles. The deeply entrenched Colorado and Green Rivers collide at its heart, then rage south as the mighty Colorado roars through tumultuous Cataract Canyon. The rivers split the park into distinct districts full of serrated cliffs, spires, boulders, and colorful rock that lights up at sunrise and sunset. Desert mesas plunge thousands of feet into canyon webs, some of which have seen little to no human exploration. In places, petroglyphs pay tribute to ancient people.

You won't find elaborate park facilities—most of **CANYONLANDS NATIONAL PARK** remains a primitive backcountry park prized by hikers, backpackers, mountain bikers, 4WD explorers, and river rafters. In fact, paved roads only go to limited places in two districts. To sink into the wondrous solitude and detail of the canyons, plan a multiday backcountry trip, self-supported or guided from companies in Moab. This is one wilderness with breathing space, beauty, and a dark night sky spread with a zillion stars.

PLANNING YOUR TIME

Canyonlands is divided into four districts and a separate noncontiguous unit. The Colorado and Green Rivers form the **Rivers** district and divide Canyonlands National Park into three other regions. **Island in the Sky** lies between the Colorado and Green Rivers, **The Maze** is to the southwest, and **The Needles** is to the southeast. The small **Horseshoe Canyon Unit**, farther west, preserves astounding petroglyphs and ancient rock paintings. If you're short on time, Island in the Sky is the best choice.

No roads directly connect the districts. Visitors must leave the park to drive from one district to another. Due to Canyonlands' proximity to Arches National Park, most visitors combine visits to the two national parks.

Spring (Mar.-May) and **fall** (Sept.-Nov.) are the best times to visit; arm yourself with insect repellent late spring-midsummer. In summer, temperatures can climb to more than 100°F. Winter days tend to be bright and sunny, with nighttime temperatures in the teens or below zero and snow and ice may close roads and trails.

ENTRANCES AND FEES

Each district has its own entrance. The entrance fee is $30 per vehicle ($25 motorcycle, $15 individual) and is good for seven days. A variety of **permits** (https://canypermits.nps.gov) are required for backcountry exploration.

Day-use permits (free) are required for 4WD vehicles, motorcycles, and bicycles on the White Rim Road and Elephant Hill. Day-use permits are available online one day in advance.

Overnight backcountry permits ($30 for 5-7 people) are required for any overnight excursions into Canyonlands' backcountry on foot, bike, or a 4WD vehicle. Apply online up to four months in advance. Reservations are recommended, especially for backpacking trips into the White Rim or the Needles.

River permits ($30 per trip, $20 per person) are required for day trips and overnights by rafters, kayakers, and canoers. Permits are first come, first served. Apply online or at a visitors center up to four months in advance.

VISITORS CENTERS

While the **Moab Information Center** (25 E. Center St., Moab, 435/259-8825, www.discovermoab.com, 8am-7pm

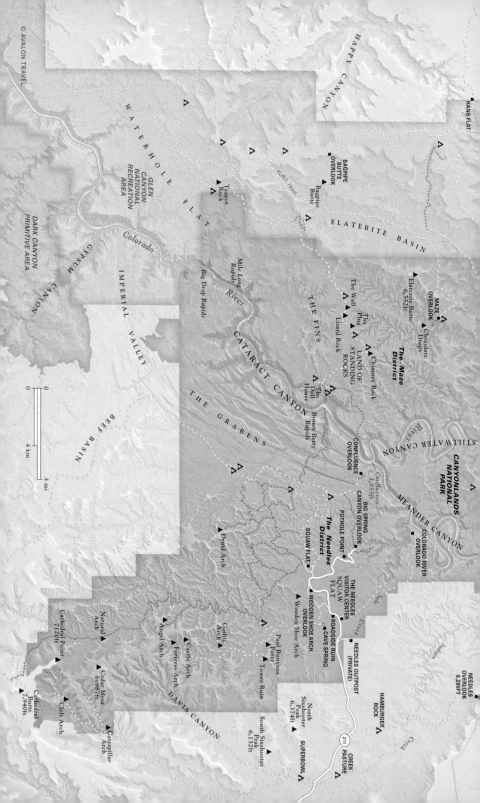

CANYONLANDS NATIONAL PARK

GREAT GALLERY
PICTOGRAPHS

Horseshoe
Canyon Unit

HORSESHOE CANYON

Barrier Creek

Natural Arch

ORANGE CLIFFS

THE SPUR

Cleopatras
Chair

GLEN
CANYON
NATIONAL
RECREATION
AREA

Buttes
of the Cross

Anderson
Bottom

PANORAMA
POINT OVERLOOK

Ekker
Butte

Green

WHITE RIM RD

River

Fort
Bottom

Potato
Bottom

Hardscrabble
Bottom

Upheaval
Bottom

Green
River

MINERAL CANYON

MINERAL ROAD

Upheaval
Canyon
Trail

The
Breaks

HORSETHIEF POINT

WHITE

Steer Mesa

Candlestick
Tower

UPHEAVAL DOME

HOLEMAN SPRING
CANYON OVERLOOK

Upheaval
Dome

WHALE
ROCK

TAYLOR CANYON

Moses and
Zeus

TAYLOR TRAIL

RIM

Green

Junction
Butte

WILLOW FLAT

GREEN RIVER
OVERLOOK

ORANGE CLIFFS
OVERLOOK

Island In
The Sky
District

Aztec
Butte

MESA ARCH

CANDLESTICK
TOWER OVERLOOK

BUCK CANYON
OVERLOOK

GRAND VIEW
POINT OVERLOOK

MONUMENT
BASIN

WHITE RIM RD

Washer
Woman

Airport
Tower

ISLAND IN THE SKY
VISITOR CENTER

SHAFER CANYON
OVERLOOK

SHAFER TRAIL ROAD

313

WHITE RIM

Colorado

MEANDER CANYON

Little Bridge
Canyon

Musselman
Arch

GOOSENECK
OVERLOOK

DEAD HORSE
POINT OVERLOOK

VISITOR CENTER

DEAD HORSE
POINT
STATE PARK

LONG CANYON

LOCKHART CANYON

Pyramid
Butte

POTASH ROAD

Potash

River

279

ANTICLINE
OVERLOOK

ONE DAY IN CANYONLANDS

Begin your day at the **Island in the Sky Visitor Center,** which overlooks an 800-foot-deep natural amphitheater. After a six-mile drive south, you'll find the trail for the easy walk to **Mesa Arch,** which rewards you with one of the most dramatic vistas in Utah: an arch on the edge of an 800-foot cliff. For lunch, hit the picnic area at **Grand View Point,** another six miles south, for astonishing views over red-rock canyons. After lunch, take a longer hike from a trailhead near the visitors center on the **Neck Springs Trail.**

Mon.-Sat., 9am-6pm Sun. mid-Mar.-Nov.) is outside the national park, it's the best place to get oriented due to its central location between Island in the Sky, Needles, and Arches National Park. The center has brochures, maps, and books as well as someone to answer questions.

Island in the Sky

The **Island in the Sky Visitor Center** (8am-6pm daily late Apr.-mid-Sept., limited hours spring and fall, closed late Dec.-early Mar.) is located just before the neck crosses to Island in the Sky. It has maps, a bookstore, exhibits, a short park film, and permits. Rangers offer programs spring-fall with intermittent stargazing events.

The Needles

Stop at the **Needles Visitor Center** (west end of Hwy. 211, 8am-6pm daily spring and fall, 8:30am-4pm daily July-Aug.) for information on hiking, back roads, permits, maps, brochures, books, and a film. When the office is closed, you'll find information posted outside.

The Maze

The Maze is served by the tiny **Hans Flat Ranger Station** (8am-4:30pm daily year-round).

ISLAND IN THE SKY

Island in the Sky is a triangle of mesas and canyons between the Green and Colorado Rivers. Paved roads lead to impressive overlooks along the upper mesa rim, while trails access geologic features. Below the rim, the White Rim 4WD Road makes a loop above the rivers on a route favored by mountain bikers. To reach Island in the Sky from Moab, drive 32 miles north on Highway 191 and southwest on Route 313 to the visitors center.

SCENIC DRIVES

Shafer Canyon

From the visitors center, the road heads south (6 mi. one-way). First, turn into **Shafer Canyon Overlook** to look down

▼ SHAFER CANYON ROAD

Top **3**

① WATCH SUNRISE BENEATH MESA ARCH

MESA ARCH AT SUNRISE

The Island in the Sky district's **Mesa Arch** (0.5 mi. rt., 30 min., easy) follows an easy loop to a Navajo sandstone arch perched on the rim of a sheer 800-foot cliff. For the best photo-op, arrive by sunrise and watch the glowing orb peek between the narrow arch's gap.

② GAZE OUT FROM GRAND VIEW POINT

Island in the Sky's Grand View Point Road tours 12 miles of overlooks like Candlestick Tower, Buck Canyon, and Orange Cliffs. The road's terminus holds the best view at **Grand View Point,** a 6,080-foot perch. Monument Basin lies below, and countless canyons, the Colorado River, the Needles, and mountain ranges beckon in the distance.

VIEW FROM THE GRAND VIEW POINT

③ GLIMPSE PICTOGRAPHS IN HORSESHOE CANYON

An outstanding day trip, **Horseshoe Canyon** contains exceptional prehistoric rock art. Ghostly life-size pictographs in the **Great Gallery** and rock art left by the subsequent Fremont and Ancestral Puebloans provide an intriguing look into the past. The **Horseshoe Canyon Trail** (6.4 mi. rt., 4-5 hrs., moderately strenuous) drops on a path to a long, sandy wash slog to the gallery.

THE GREAT GALLERY AT HORSESHOE CANYON

GREEN RIVER

on the twisting Shafer Trail Road that goes to the White Rim 4WD Road 1,200 feet below. Continuing south, the mesa squeezes into a narrow land bridge just wide enough for the road.

Upheaval Dome

From the main park road, turn north on **Upheaval Dome Road** (10 mi. rt.). The best viewpoint is located on the dirt spur road that goes 1.5 miles to **Green River Overlook**. Views plunge thousands of feet to the river oxbows below. Back on the main road, you can drive to the terminus to see **Upheaval Dome**, which requires hiking.

White Rim Road

White Rim Road lies below the sheer cliffs of Island in the Sky. Travel along the winding road presents a constantly changing panorama of rock, canyons, river, and sky. You'll see all three levels of Island in the Sky: high plateaus, the White Rim, and the rivers.

Only 4WD vehicles with high clearance can make this **100-mile trip** (2-3 days), camping by permit along the way. Driving is slow and winding; a few steep, single-lane, rocky, or sandy sections pose white-knuckled driving. The road has no services or developed water sources, so have plenty of fuel and water with some to spare. From the visitors center on Route 313, the east entrance is Shafer Trail Road one mile north, and the west entrance is Mineral Bottom Road, aka Horsethief Trail, 9 miles north.

HIKING

Shafer Canyon

The **Neck Spring Loop** (5.8 mi. rt., 3-4 hrs., strenuous) begins near the Shafer Canyon Overlook on the main park road, but heads down the opposite side of the road into Taylor Canyon to Neck Springs and Cabin Springs. Then, it climbs 760 feet in elevation back to the road 0.5 mile south of the start.

Grand View Point

On the Grand View Point Road one mile before the end, the **White Rim Overlook Trail** (1.8 mi. rt., 1 hr., easy) trots east along a peninsula to an overlook of Monument Basin and beyond. From the road's end, the **Grand View Point Trail** (2 mi. rt., 1 hr., easy) continues for more vistas from the southernmost tip of Island in the Sky.

Upheaval Dome

One mile northwest of the junction with Upheaval Dome Road, **Aztec Butte** (2 mi. rt., 1 hr., easy) is one of the few areas at Island in the Sky with Native American ruins. The route climbs 200 vertical feet to the top of the butte for a good panorama of the mesa top. About 4.4 miles northwest of the junction, the **Whale Rock Trail** (1 mi. rt., 30 min., easy) climbs 100 feet up a sandstone hump near the outer rim of Upheaval Dome.

At the road's terminus, trails go for views of Upheaval Dome, a geological curiosity of a fantastically deformed

Best Hike

MESA ARCH TRAIL

DISTANCE: 0.25 mile one-way
DURATION: 30 minutes
ELEVATION CHANGE: 80 feet
EFFORT: easy
TRAILHEAD: Grand View Point Road

This easy trail leads to a spectacular arch on the rim of the mesa. On the way, the road crosses the grasslands and scattered juniper trees of Gray's Pasture. A trail brochure available at the start describes the ecology of the mesa. The sandstone arch frames views of rock formations below and the La Sal Mountains in the distance. Photographers come here to catch the sun (or moon) rising through the arch.

pile of rocks. The crater is about 3 miles across and 1,200 feet deep. The **Crater View Trail** (1.8 mi. rt., 1.5 hrs., easy) leads to two overlooks on the rim of Upheaval Dome. Energetic hikers can reach Upheaval Dome via the **Syncline Loop Trail** (8.3 mi. rt., 5-7 hrs., strenuous), which circles completely around the dome, dropping and climbing 1,200 feet. Halfway around, the trail intersects with the **Upheaval Dome Canyon Trail** (add 3 mi. rt., 2 hrs.) to go into the crater itself.

MOUNTAIN BIKING

Mountain bikers rank the **White Rim Road** as one of the region's best routes. Endurance riders do the 100-mile-loop in one epic day, but most prefer to tour the route in 3-4 days (self-supported or with vehicle support to haul water and gear). Be prepared to handle emergencies and flat tires on your own. **Permits** are required for both single-day and overnight trips. Bike shops, rentals, and guides are based in Moab.

THE NEEDLES

The Needles district showcases some of the finest rock sculptures in Canyonlands National Park. Spires, arches, and monoliths appear in almost any direction you look. Prehistoric ruins and rock art exist in a greater variety and quantity than anywhere else in the

BIKING THE WHITE RIM TRAIL, ISLAND IN THE SKY DISTRICT

park. A paved road, several 4WD roads, and many hiking trails offer a variety of ways to explore the Needles. From Moab, reach the Needles by traveling south on U.S. 191 for 40 miles and then turning right on Route 211, going 34 miles to the visitors center.

SCENIC DRIVES

From the visitors center, the paved park road into the Needles (6.5 mi. one way) doesn't have the giant views like Island in the Sky, but rather short walks to sights.

Stops go to **Roadside Ruin** (0.3 mi. rt.) to see the well-preserved granary left by Ancestral Puebloan people, **Cave Spring Trail** (0.6 mi. rt.) for a clockwise interpretive loop that provides an introduction to the park's geology, and **Pothole Point Trail** (0.6 mi. rt.) to visit dissolved sandstone holes. The road terminates at **Big Spring Canyon Overlook**.

High-clearance 4WD rigs can explore beautiful canyon scenery, arches, and Native American rock-art sites.

Salt Creek Canyon Road

Salt Creek Canyon Road (26 mi. rt.) begins near Cave Spring Trail, crosses sage flats, and then heads deep into this spectacular canyon; included is a side trip to 150-foot-high Angel Arch. Salt Canyon is frequently closed due to quicksand after flash floods in summer and shelf ice in winter. **Horse Canyon Road** (13 mi. rt., permit required) turns left shortly before the mouth of Salt Canyon for a side trip to Tower Ruin.

Colorado Overlook Road

Starting at the visitors center, the **Colorado Overlook Road** (14 mi. rt.) follows Salt Creek west to Lower Jump Overlook. It then bounces across slickrock to a view of the Colorado River. The road is very rough the last 1.5 miles.

HIKING

The Needles has outstanding day hiking and backpacking (overnight trips require permits for preassigned

▼ POTHOLE POINT

campsites). Interconnected trails loop through Lost, Squaw, Big Springs, and Elephant Canyons with routes including sandy washes, slickrock passes and ramps, cairned routes, exposed ledges, rock-hewn foot holes, and ladders. The best routes make loops, which you can do in either direction. Always ask the rangers about current sources of water, and treat it before drinking.

Squaw Flat Trailhead

From the Squaw Flat Trailhead, the **Squaw Canyon-Lost Canyon Loop** (8.7 mi. rt., 4-5 hrs., moderate) climbs over a slickrock pass. Most of the trail goes through wash bottoms, where water supports abundant vegetation; you may need to wade. You can also loop the other direction to connect **Squaw Canyon and Big Spring Canyon** (6.8 mi. rt., 3-4 hrs., moderate) via a steep slickrock climb over red and white sandstone.

Elephant Hill Trailhead

Chesler Park is a lovely desert meadow that contrasts with the surrounding red and white spires that gave the Needles its name. **Chesler Park Trail** (6 mi. rt., 3-4 hrs., moderate) winds through sand and slickrock before ascending a small pass through spires to overlook Chesler Park and return on the same route.

Starting with the Chesler Park Trail, the **Chesler Park Loop** (11 mi. rt., 6-7 hrs., strenuous) circles the park and includes the unusual **Joint Trail,** which squeezes through a 0.5-mile-long narrow crack.

To reach **Druid Arch** (11 mi. rt., 6-7 hrs., strenuous), climb into Elephant Canyon and follow the chasm—flanked with large white-domed red rocks—to the head, where the final pitch ascends to view the freestanding arch.

Big Spring Canyon Overlook Trailhead

The **Confluence Overlook Trail** (11 mi. rt., 6 hrs., moderate) goes west on a shadeless trail to a fine viewpoint overlooking the Green and Colorado Rivers 1,000 feet below. The trail crosses Big Spring and Elephant Canyons and follows a jeep road for a short distance.

THE MAZE

Few visitors make it to the wild country of the Maze. Only the rivers, a handful of 4WD roads, and hiking trails provide access. Due to the difficulty of travel, most visitors come for a minimum of three days. Regardless of mode of travel, explorers need a **backcountry permit** for overnight trips. All travelers need to be able to handle emergencies and flat tires and be self-sufficient. Experienced hikers can explore the "maze" of canyons on unmarked routes. The Maze has **no developed water sources.** Vehicle travelers need to bring their own water; hikers can filter water from springs in some canyons.

Getting here from Moab involvs 135 miles of driving via I-70, Route 24, and a 46-mile 2WD dirt road to **Hans Flat Ranger Station** (435/259-2652, 8am-4:30pm daily). No services are available, so gas up before reaching the Maze.

SCENIC DRIVES

Only 4WD, high-clearance rigs should tackle the rough roads of the Maze, which require slow travel. Check conditions first with a ranger before starting out. Avoid travel during or after rains, as rock and clay surfaces can be slippery.

All routes will cross the narrow **Flint Trail 4WD Road** (2.8 mi. one way), located 14 miles south of the Hans Flat ranger station. Stop at the signed overlook at the top to scout for vehicles headed up, as the road has few places to pass. All campsites are primitive.

From Hans Flat Ranger Station, a rough, rocky trek with switchbacks, drop-offs, and steep pitches leads to the **Maze Overlook** (60 mi. rt., 6 hrs.) for views down into the intricate canyons. From the ranger station, those going to the **Land of Standing Rocks** (74 mi rt., 10 hrs., 3 campsites) to see striking features of the Wall, Standing Rock, and Chimney Rock jutting up from the desert mesa should carry extra gas, a spare tire, and vehicle repair gear. Be prepared for extremely rough road after Teapot Rock Camp. The road continues on to the tall, rounded spires of **The Doll House** (add on 10 mi. rt., 2 hrs., 3 campsites) and views of the Colorado River.

The Maze is only for self-sufficient, experienced hikers who can read maps, hike strenuous trails, and have 4WD high-clearance vehicles. Actual trails are minimal; cairned routes and some worn trails connect the mesa with the canyon bottoms, where unmarked routes follow sandy washes. A few places require using hands and feet to climb or descend boulders; bring a 25-foot rope to haul packs up or down these. Due to the remoteness, most hikers opt for multiday backpacking trips, camping is in designated zones rather than at specific campsites.

From the Maze Overlook, the **Maze Overlook Trail** (2 mi. rt., 2 hrs.) drops over a Class IV boulder into the South Fork of Horse Canyon. Once in the canyon, walk around to the Harvest Scene, a group of prehistoric pictographs (add 3 mi. rt.). Two miles east of the bottom of the Flint Trail Road, the steep **Golden Stairs** (4 mi. rt., 3-4 hrs., 1 car campsite at top) drops to the Land of Standing Rocks Road for good views of Ernies Country and the Fins. From the Doll House, the **Spanish Bottom Trail** (2.4 mi. rt., 2-3 hrs.) drops 1,260 vertical feet to Spanish Bottom beside the Colorado River. A thin trail leads downstream into Cataract Canyon and the first of a long series of rapids. To see the confluence instead from the Doll House, hike the **Colorado-Green River Overlook Trail** (10 mi. rt., 5-7 hrs.) north to a viewpoint.

THE RIVERS

The Rivers district includes long stretches of the **Green** and **Colorado Rivers.** River floating provides one of the best ways to experience the inner depths of the park. Above the confluence, the rivers have flat water for paddlers in canoes, sea kayaks, and rafts. Below the confluence, the volume of water squeezes through 14-mile Cataract Canyon with Class III-IV white water. Boaters need permits.

For ease, commercial trips take care of everything. The following outfitters in Moab are authorized by the National Park Service. Most offer single-day and multiday trips.

COLORADO RIVER

Adrift Adventures (378 N. Main St., 435/259-8594 or 800/874-4483, www.adrift.net)

Sheri Griffith Expeditions (2231 S. Hwy. 191, 503/259-8229 or 800/332-2439, www.griffithexp.com)

Tag-A-Long Expeditions (452 N. Main St., 435/259-8594 or 800/874-4483, www.tagalong.com)

Western River Expeditions (225 S. Main St., 801/942-6669 or 866/904-1160, www.westernriver.com)

WHERE TO STAY
INSIDE THE PARK
Island in the Sky

Located on Murphy Point Road, the **Willow Flat Campground** (year-round, $15, no water or hookups) has only 12 sites available on a first-come, first-served basis; sites fill up early in all seasons except winter.

The Needles

Located three miles south of the visitors center, **Squaw Flat Campground** (year-round, $20) has 26 sites, many snuggled under the slickrock. Rangers present evening programs at the campfire circle spring-autumn. Some campsites are reservable during spring and fall (877/444-6777, www.recreation.gov); otherwise, they are first come, first serve.

The Maze

The Maze has **nine camping locations** with a 15-person, three-vehicle limit. A backcountry permit is required. Expect to share your site with others, especially in the popular spring months.

OUTSIDE THE PARK

With scads of lodging, restaurants, and services, **Moab** is a Utah tourist town. Book reservations for spring and fall six months in advance.

Near the Island in the Sky District, the year-round campground at **Dead Horse Point State Park** (800/322-3770, www.reserveamerica.com, book four months in advance) fills daily February-November. Primitive Bureau of Land Management (BLM) campsites flank Route 313.

Just outside the Needles district, **Needles Outpost** (435/459-0777, www.needlesoutpost.com, mid-Mar.-late Oct.) has campsites without hookups. Nearby BLM land also offers a number of places to camp, including two first-come, first-served campgrounds in the Canyon Rims Special Recreation Management Area.

GETTING THERE AND AROUND

The closest airport is **Salt Lake City International Airport** (SLC, 776 N. Terminal Dr., 801/575-2400, www.slcairport.com), 234 miles north of Moab. The four-hour drive follows I-15, U.S. 6, I-70, and U.S. 191. Rental cars are available; however, 4WD vehicles with high clearance are preferred. **Boutique Air** (855/268-8478, www.boutiqueair.com) provides daily scheduled air service between **Canyonlands Field** (CNY, U.S. 191, 16 miles north of Moab, 435/259-4849, www.moabairport.com) and Salt Lake City and Denver.

CAR

Island in the Sky

From Moab, drive 10 miles north on U.S. 191 and turn left (west) onto Route 313. If you are coming in from I-70, drive 20 miles south on U.S. 191 from exit 182 to reach the junction. Continue on this paved road for 22 miles west, and then south, to reach the park entrance. From Moab, allow 45 minutes to reach the park.

The Needles

To reach the Needles district, drive 40 miles south from Moab (or 14 miles north from Monticello) on U.S. 191, and then turn west onto Highway 211 for 38 miles.

The Maze and Horseshoe Canyon

South of I-70, Route 24 and Route 95 access dirt roads to the western canyons. The easiest way in is the dirt, washboarded 2WD road from Route 24 to Hans Flat Ranger Station (46 mi.). Beyond there, a 2WD dirt road goes north to Horseshoe Canyon (32 mi.), and extremely rugged 4WD, high-clearance roads go to Maze destinations (30-47 mi.).

TOURS

Canyonlands Field Institute (800/860-5262 or 435/259-7750, http://cfimoab.org) guides one-day and multiday educational adventures and programs.

SIGHTS NEARBY

Dead Horse Point State Park (435/259-2614, www.stateparks.utah.gov, $10 day use) has a campground and hiking trails to spectacular canyon and Colorado River overlooks near Island in the Sky.

BLM Newspaper Rock Historical Monument (Hwy. 211, near the Needles) hosts a profusion of petroglyphs, while three miles west **Indian Creek** has world-class rock climbing, with close to 1,000 routes and splitter cracks, most 5.10 and above.

Canyon Rims Recreation Area (www.blm.gov), between Moab and the Needles, houses the Needles and Anticline Overlooks, which offer magnificent panoramas.

Natural Bridges National Monument (www.nps.gov/nabr, $10), south of the Needles, preserves some of the finest examples of natural stone architecture.

Goblin Valley State Park (435/275-4584, https://stateparks.utah.gov, daily 6am-10pm, $13 day use) has fields of alien-looking hoodoos, hiking, and a campground west of the Maze.

MESA VERDE
NATIONAL PARK

Colorado

WEBSITE:
www.nps.gov/meve

PHONE NUMBER:
970/529-4465

VISITATION RANK:
33

WHY GO:
Ancient Puebloan
cliff dwellings.

PASSPORT STAMPS ▼▼▼

▲ MESA VERDE NATIONAL PARK

At **MESA VERDE NATIONAL PARK,** nearly 5,000 archaeological sites spread across a large, beautiful mesa whose higher elevations receive more precipitation than the surrounding valleys. Thanks to this increased moisture, cooler temperatures, and better soils, pinyon and juniper trees thrive. This forested mesa gains its name from the Spanish phrase translated as "green table."

This mesa holds 600 intricate, multistory cliff dwellings tucked into enormous sandstone alcoves. The dwellings offer keen insight into the lives of the ancient people who once farmed the mesa tops and lived in the tiny mud-brick rooms. Petroglyphs offer further hints to their culture and way of life, which lasted about 700 years. The Puebloans mysteriously disappeared by AD 1300. Today, 26 tribes maintain special connections with this remarkable history.

PLANNING YOUR TIME

Mesa Verde National Park is situated in southwestern Colorado, near the Four Corners of Colorado, Utah, Arizona, and New Mexico. It's easy to link a visit to Mesa Verde with several nearby national monuments. The region boasts impressive ruins and acre upon acre of gorgeous slickrock scenery, where crimson and white sandstone monoliths tower above vegetation and secluded archaeological sites.

The park's main draw is its remarkable cliff dwellings. **Balcony House, Cliff Palace,** and **Long House** can only be visited on ranger-guided tours. (Sadly, Spruce Tree House, the park's best-preserved dwelling, is closed due to danger from rockfalls.) In summer, it's not always possible to visit both Balcony House and Cliff Palace on the same day due to high demand for tours. Consider staying longer, or visit **Long House** (road open May-mid-Oct.), the park's second-largest dwelling, instead.

Tour season varies **spring-fall** (May-Sept.); tours are not offered in winter. Tickets are only available in person up to two days in advance. Pick up tour tickets upon arrival at the park's visitors center, as the tour schedule will dictate your sightseeing.

This area can be hot in summer with temperatures in the 90s; summer afternoon thunderstorms can dole out lightning. Spring and fall, when 60-75°F is the norm, are ideal times to visit. In spring, the cottonwoods along the sparse creeks begin to leaf out. In autumn, leaves turn gold and the distant mountaintops are dusted with fresh snow. Winter nights are chilly, but the daytime temperatures are usually pleasantly cool. Expect snowstorms November-April.

ENTRANCE AND FEES

The park entrance is accessed via one clearly signed road that branches south from U.S. 160. Upon turning onto the park entrance road, the visitors center appears on the left; this is where you'll pay the entrance fee January-March. The actual park entrance station is 0.5 mile farther down the park road; pay the entrance fee here late March-December.

In summer, the entrance fee is $25-30 per vehicle ($20-25 motorcycle, $12-15 individual). All entrance fees are valid for seven days.

VISITORS CENTER

The **Mesa Verde Visitor and Research Center** (7:30am-7pm daily late May-early Sept., shorter hours in winter) is housed in a scenic LEED building. Pick up tour tickets and view exhibits on the Ancestral Puebloan people, original art, and sculptures. Facilities include a bookstore, restrooms, and Wi-Fi.

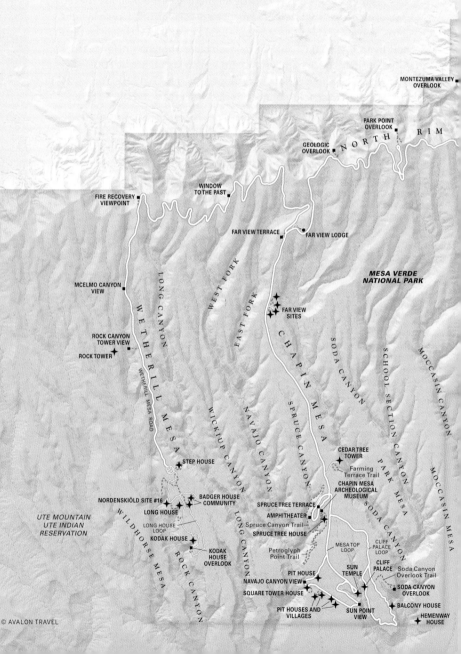

MESA VERDE
NATIONAL PARK

To Dove Creek

To Shiprock

Cortez

MONTEZUMA VALLEY
OVERLOOK

PARK POINT
OVERLOOK

GEOLOGIC
OVERLOOK

NORTH RIM

FIRE RECOVERY
VIEWPOINT

WINDOW
TO THE PAST

FAR VIEW TERRACE

FAR VIEW LODGE

WEST FORK

MESA VERDE
NATIONAL PARK

MCELMO CANYON
VIEW

LONG CANYON

EAST FORK

FAR VIEW
SITES

ROCK CANYON
TOWER VIEW

ROCK TOWER

WETHERILL MESA

CHAPIN MESA

SODA CANYON

SCHOOL SECTION CANYON

MOCCASIN CANYON

WETHERILL MESA ROAD

WICKIUP CANYON

NAVAJO CANYON

SPRUCE CANYON

PARK MESA

MOCCASIN MESA

CEDAR TREE
TOWER

Farming
Terrace Trail

CHAPIN MESA
ARCHEOLOGICAL
MUSEUM

SODA CANYON

STEP HOUSE

NORDENSKIÖLD SITE #16

BADGER HOUSE
COMMUNITY

SPRUCE TREE TERRACE

UTE MOUNTAIN
UTE INDIAN
RESERVATION

WILDHORSE MESA

LONG HOUSE

LONG HOUSE
LOOP

KODAK HOUSE

KODAK
HOUSE
OVERLOOK

LONG CANYON

AMPHITHEATER

Spruce Canyon Trail

SPRUCE TREE HOUSE

ROCK CANYON

Petroglyph
Point Trail

MESA TOP
LOOP

CLIFF
PALACE
LOOP

CLIFF
PALACE

Soda Canyon
Overlook Trail

PIT HOUSE

SUN
TEMPLE

SODA CANYON
OVERLOOK

NAVAJO CANYON VIEW

SQUARE TOWER HOUSE

BALCONY HOUSE

PIT HOUSES AND
VILLAGES

SUN POINT
VIEW

HEMENWAY
HOUSE

© AVALON TRAVEL

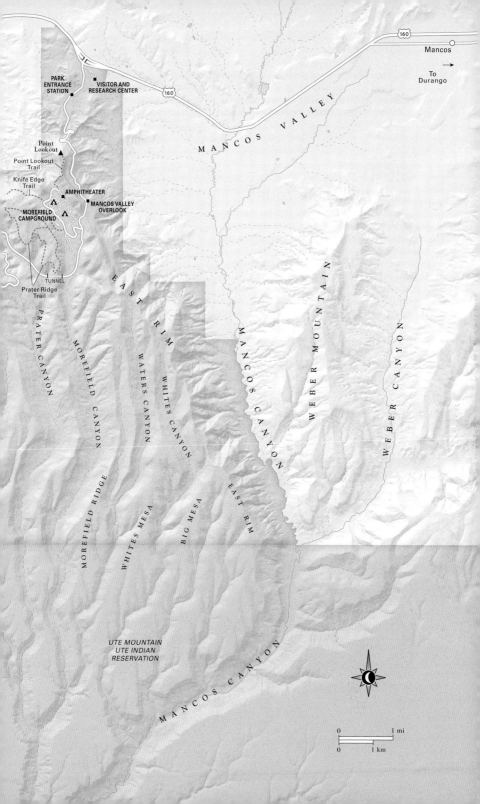

160

Mancos

To
Durango

PARK
ENTRANCE
STATION

VISITOR AND
RESEARCH CENTER

160

M A N C O S   V A L L E Y

Point
Lookout

Point Lookout
Trail

Knife Edge
Trail

AMPHITHEATER

MOREFIELD
CAMPGROUND

MANCOS VALLEY
OVERLOOK

TUNNEL

Prater Ridge
Trail

P R A T E R   C A N Y O N

E A S T   R I M

M O R E F I E L D   C A N Y O N

W A T E R S   C A N Y O N

W H I T E S   C A N Y O N

M A N C O S   C A N Y O N

W E B E R   M O U N T A I N

W E B E R   C A N Y O N

M O R E F I E L D   R I D G E

W H I T E S   M E S A

B I G   M E S A

E A S T   R I M

UTE MOUNTAIN
UTE INDIAN
RESERVATION

M A N C O S   C A N Y O N

0   1 mi

0   1 km

ONE DAY IN MESA VERDE

If you only have half a day, drive the park road south to the Chapin Mesa area, where you can see some of the mesa-top sites at **Far View** and take a tour of either **Cliff Palace** or **Balcony House.** If you can spend a full day, add in an afternoon at **Chapin Mesa Archeological Museum** and walk the **Petroglyph Point Trail.**

SIGHTS

CLIFF DWELLING TOURS

After living on the mesa top for nearly 600 years, the Ancestral Puebloans began building pueblos beneath the area's impressive overhanging cliffs. The structures range greatly in size, from one-room storage areas to entire villages. One of the first things that you'll notice is how cramped the rooms feel to modern visitors; the average Ancestral Puebloan male stood five feet, four inches tall and the average female was about five feet tall.

Tickets ($5) for daily tours can be purchased in person up to two days in advance. Ticket locations include the Colorado Welcome Center (928 E. Main St., Cortez, 970/565-4048, www.colorado.com, 9am-5pm daily) and the Mesa Verde Visitor and Research Center. Limited tickets are available at Chapin Mesa Archeological Museum (20 miles south of the park entrance, 8am-6:30pm daily early Apr.-mid-Oct.).

Other cliff dwellings tours can be booked up to six months in advance (877/444-6777, www.recreation.gov, $5-25) and include a **Twilight Tour of Cliff Palace** and **Sunrise Tour of Balcony House.** Tours also go through **Oak Tree House, Yucca House,** and **Mug House.**

Cliff Palace

The largest of the dwellings is **Cliff Palace** (daily late May-mid-Sept.), with more than 150 rooms and 20 circular kivas (distinctive circular pits used for

▼ CLIFF PALACE

BALCONY HOUSE

performing cultural rituals). Considering that three-quarters of the park's 600 cliff dwellings contain just 1-5 rooms, Cliff Palace is exceptionally big, a true neighborhood where an estimated 100 people once lived.

Balcony House

With just 40 rooms, nearby **Balcony House** (daily late Apr.-Oct.) is an intermediate-sized complex. To access their mesa-top gardens, the villagers used hand- and footholds carved into the sandstone, as well as tall wooden ladders. You'll climb a 32-foot modern version of this during the tour. This adventurous outing involves down-climbing a 100-foot staircase into the canyon and clambering through a 12-foot-long, 18-inch-wide tunnel.

Long House

The park's second-largest cliff dwelling is **Long House** (daily mid-May-late Oct. weather permitting). Excavated between 1959 and 1961, the Long House includes about 150 rooms and 21 kivas whose beams date to 1145 AD. Archaeologists believe that 150-175 people once lived beneath the shadow of its 300-foot-long alcove. Of special note is a well-preserved, triangular tower rising four stories from floor to ceiling at the western end of the alcove. Visiting the site requires walking 2.3 miles

round-trip from Wetherill Mesa Kiosk to the Long House trailhead. You'll climb two 15-foot ladders as part of the tour.

FAR VIEW

A self-guided stroll to **Far View House** (1.5 mi. rt., 1-2 hrs.) visits several Pueblo villages, including eye-catching spiral petroglyphs at the **Pipe Shrine House.** Located four miles north of the Chapin Mesa Archeological Museum, the unnamed trail is open 8am-sunset year-round.

FAR VIEW COMMUNITY RUINS

WETHERILL MESA

Two self-guided walks depart from the Wetherill Mesa Kiosk at the terminus of Wetherill Mesa Road (daily May-Oct. weather permitting). From the kiosk, walk one mile (round-trip) to reach the **Step House** (9am-4pm), where you can walk around a cliff dwelling and see a pit house and petroglyphs. Accessible from the same kiosk is the **Badger House Trail** (2.5 mi. rt., 1.5-2 hrs.), which visits four mesa-top archeological sites.

CHAPIN MESA ARCHEOLOGICAL MUSEUM

The **Chapin Mesa Archeological Museum** (8am-6:30pm daily May-mid Oct., reduced hours in winter, free) shows a 25-minute orientation film and has a series of educational exhibits that include prehistoric artifacts, dioramas, and other cultural and historical items. It's located on Chapin Mesa, 21 miles south of the park entrance.

SCENIC DRIVES

NORTH RIM

The curvy **North Rim Road** (11 mi. one way) tiptoes along canyon rims between Morefield Campground and Far View Lodge. It goes through a tunnel and passes three overlooks: Montezuma Valley, Park Point, and Geologic Overlook, each offering a different take on the rugged mesa-and-canyon scenery. Of the three, Park Point at 8,572 feet is the highest point in the park, with a 360-degree view where you can see the four states of the Four Corners. This road accesses Chapin Mesa and Mesa Top Loop Roads plus Wetherill Mesa Road.

MESA TOP LOOP ROAD

Mesa Top Loop Road (daily 8am-sunset, 6 mi.) tours several overlooks such as Navajo Canyon and Sun Point, which offer plunging views down adjacent canyons. Self-guided stops include several pit houses and the ceremonial Sun Temple, which may have been an observatory for the sky. Mesa Top Loop Road is 21 miles south of the park entrance, beyond the Chapin Mesa Archeological Museum.

WETHERILL MESA

Wetherill Mesa Road (8am-7pm daily May-Oct. weather permitting) tours a long, protruding peninsula of land bordered by impressive canyons whose sandstone cliffs host many natural alcoves. Ancestral Puebloans took

▼ MESA VERDE NATIONAL PARK IN SUMMER

PETROGLYPH POINT TRAIL

advantage of many of these landmarks to build storage buildings and homes in their protective shadows. Stop at overlooks to take in McElmo Canyon and Rock Canyon Tower. At the road's terminus at Wetherill Mesa Kiosk, you can hike to Step House or Badger House. The road is located on the west side of the park, 27 miles from the visitors center.

RECREATION

HIKING

The crowded **Petroglyph Point Trail** (2.4 mi. rt., 1.5 hr.) accesses close-up views of ancient rock art, including hunting scenes, spirals, and dainty handprints. The less-peopled **Spruce Canyon Trail** (2.4 mi. rt., 1.5 hrs.) descends into the canyon to cross a seasonal trickle stream on small bridges before climbing about 500 feet back up.

The trailhead is gated. Register at the Chapin Mesa Archeological Museum to hike either trail and check gate hours.

BICYCLING

Cyclists enjoy the thrill of the park's curvy roads and their steep climbs and descents, but they come with challenges: narrow roadways, no shoulders, broken pavement, and congested traffic. Riding early or late in the day is a more pleasant experience. All roads in the park permit bicycles, with the exception of Wetherill Mesa Road.

Rangers lead a **bike-and-hike adventure tour** (Wed. and Sun., late May-early Sept., 9 mi. rt., 4.5 hrs.) to several archeological sites, including Long House. The tour bicycles two-thirds of the distance and hikes the remaining one-third. Reservations are required (877/444-6777, www.recreation. gov, $15). Bring your own bicycle or rent a bike in Cortez or Durango before you enter the park.

WHERE TO STAY

INSIDE THE PARK

Located 15 miles south of the park entrance, **Far View Lodge** (970/529-4421 or 800/449-2288, www.visitmesaverde.com, mid-Apr.-mid-Oct., from $130) is the only lodging option in the park. It has 150 southwestern-styled rooms that lack TVs but have sweeping views and free Wi-Fi. Rates include a full breakfast; dinner is available at the **Mesa Verde Metate Room Restaurant** (5pm-9:30pm daily in season); reservations are strongly recommended.

The 267-site **Morefield Campground** (late Apr.-mid-Oct., $31) is located four miles south of the park entrance. Some sites can be reserved in advance. Amenities include flush toilets, showers, a camp store, laundry, and a dump station.

The casual, self-service **Far View Terrace Café** (0.25 mile south of Far View Lodge, 7am-8pm daily mid Apr.-early Oct.) has reasonably priced food, including Navajo tacos and fresh coffee. Farther up the road, near the Chapin Mesa Archeological Museum, the **Spruce Tree Terrace Café** (9am-6:30pm daily year-round) is a convenient place to grab a bite of barbecue. Near the Morefield Campground, the **Knife Edge Café** (7am-10am, 11am-2pm, and 4:30pm-7pm daily) is known for its pancake-and-sausage breakfasts.

OUTSIDE THE PARK

Located 10 miles from the park entrance, the small town of **Cortez** offers basic services in between the area's many monuments.

GETTING THERE

AIR

The closest international airport is **Denver International Airport** (DEN, 8500 Peña Blvd., Denver, 303/342-2000, www.flydenver.com). **Durango-La Plata County Airport** (DRO, 1000 Airport Rd., Durango, 970/382-6050, www.flydurango.com) offers daily service by United Airlines and American Airlines, including nonstop service to Denver. Car rentals are available.

Animas Transportation (2023 Main Ave., Durango, 970/259-1315, www.animastransportation.com) will shuttle a carload to the park on a per-mile basis, which works out to about $150 one-way.

CAR

The east-west U.S. 160 connects Mesa Verde National Park with Durango, 35 miles east of the park entrance, and Cortez, 10 miles west.

GETTING AROUND

There is no public transportation within the park. You'll need a car to get around and the roads are steep, extremely curvy, and narrow with no shoulders. **Gas** is available at the campground. Inside the park (about 15 miles south of U.S. 160), the road splits: one branch turns west toward Wetherill Mesa, while the main road continues south to Chapin Mesa, the location of Balcony House and Cliff Palace.

Guided bus tours (Aramark, 800/449-2288, www.visitmesaverde. com, daily mid-Apr.-mid-Oct, $39-47) are an option for touring the park. The 700 Years Tour takes in the Cliff House and other sites. The Far View Tour climbs Park Point and goes to the Sun Temple and Spruce Tree Overlook. Purchase tickets in advance online or in person at the visitors center, Morefield Campground, or Far View Lodge.

SIGHTS NEARBY

Anasazi Heritage Center (27501 Hwy. 184, Dolores, 970/882-5600, www.blm. gov, 9am-5pm daily Mar.-Oct., 10am-4pm daily Nov.-Feb.), 10 miles north of Cortez, serves as an introduction to the region's archaeological attractions and an information center for Canyons of the Ancients National Monument.

Canyons of the Ancients National Monument (27501 Hwy. 184, Dolores, 970/882-5600, www.blm.gov, 9am-5pm daily Mar.-Oct., 10am-4pm daily Nov.-Feb., free), southwest of Cortez, is a relatively untouched wilderness of flat-topped mesas and twisting canyons whose sandstone walls harbor the largest concentration of archaeological sites in the country.

Four Corners Monument (U.S. 160, 38 miles south of Cortez, 928/206-2540, www.navajonationparks.org, 8am-8pm daily late May-mid-Sept.) marks the only spot in the United States where four states—Colorado, New Mexico, Arizona, and Utah—meet.

GREAT SAND DUNES NATIONAL PARK AND PRESERVE

Colorado

WEBSITE:
www.nps.gov/grsa

PHONE NUMBER:
719/378-6395

VISITATION RANK:
38

WHY GO:
Slide down the
tallest sand dunes
in North America.

▲ GREAT SAND DUNES
NATIONAL PARK

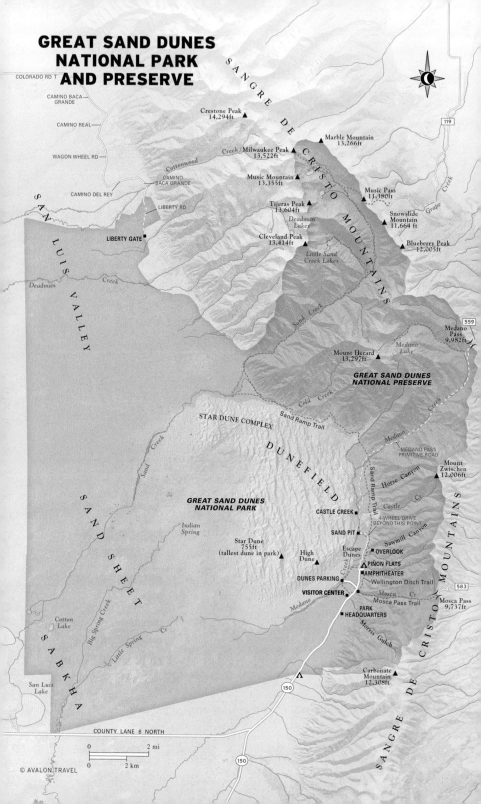

Along the eastern edge of Colorado's San Luis Valley is a vast, high-elevation basin almost as large as the state of New Jersey. Tucked into this valley, **GREAT SAND DUNES NATIONAL PARK AND PRESERVE** holds a remarkable dune field with mounds of sand up to 750 feet high. While these are the tallest dunes in North America, they are utterly dwarfed by their incredible backdrop—the long line of the jagged Sangre de Cristo mountain range. Water flowing from the mountains surrounds the dunes with braided streams. Contrary to other geological formations that alter more slowly with time, the dunes change daily. Shifting sands move with wind, water, and gravity, creating a fluid landscape that almost appears in motion.

PLANNING YOUR TIME

Great Sand Dunes National Park is located in southern Colorado, less than 65 miles north of the state border with New Mexico. This is the arid Southwest, far from the jutting peaks of Rocky Mountain National Park—although the Sangre de Cristos form a nearby reminder of Colorado's high mountains.

Elevations in the park span 7,515-13,604 feet, which keep temperatures in the 50-80°F range during the day **spring through fall** (May-Sept.). Winter temperatures range 30-45°F, sometimes with a few inches of snowfall. Year-round, the arid desert weather often has blue skies, but nighttime temperatures can plunge to cool and even frigid zones, while summer can produce afternoon lightning storms.

Despite the temperature, the surface of the sand heats up in summer; during midday, the sand can exceed 150°F. Plan for an early-morning or evening excursion on foot. During windstorms, which are frequent in spring, wear protective glasses.

ENTRANCE AND FEES

The entrance fee is $25 per vehicle ($20 motorcycle and bicycle, $15 individual) and is good for seven days. The entrance station is on Highway 150 at the park headquarters.

VISITORS CENTER

Located 0.7 mile beyond the entrance station, the **Great Sand Dunes Visitor Center** (11999 Hwy. 150, Mosca, 8:30am-5pm daily summer, 9am-4:30pm daily fall-spring) has interactive exhibits, park information, a bookstore, and a Junior Ranger Program. View the dunes through spotting scopes on the back porch. Ranger programs (May-fall, schedules vary weekly) are held at the visitors center or campground amphitheater and guided hikes are also offered. Several nighttime programs include unique experiences: full moon dune walks, stargazing, and viewing nocturnal migrations of salamanders and frogs. Special wheelchairs are also available for visitors with disabilities.

HIKING

From Loop 2 in Piñon Flats Campground, a trail goes to **Dunes Overlook** (2.3 mi. rt., 2-2.5 hrs.) with a 450-foot ascent occurring in switchbacks at the end where you can take in the dune field across the Medano Creek drainage.

Near the visitors center at the Montville-Mosca Pass Trailhead, hikers have the option of a short forest trail with views of the first dune ridge on the **Montville Loop** (0.5 mi. rt., 30 min.) or the tougher **Mosca Pass Trail** (7 mi. rt., 3-4 hrs.), which climbs 1,400 feet in elevation along the trickling Mosca Creek through the forest to 9,737-foot Mosca Pass in the Sangre de Cristo Mountains.

Top ③

STAR DUNE

① DRIVE TO SCENIC VIEWPOINTS

Bordered on the north by Sand Creek and to the east and south by Medano Creek, the **dune field** resembles a sea of sand waves. The tallest dune is 755-foot **Star Dune;** the second tallest is 699-foot **High Dune.** For the closest views, drive to the Dunes Parking Lot at the end of a spur road just past the parking lot. The shifting back and forth of the wind keeps the dunes relatively in place. Though the dune field covers 30 square miles—an area estimated to contain five billion cubic meters of sand—it is only 10 percent of the total sand in the area.

② GO SAND SLEDDING AND BOARDING

Specifically designed gear is used for sledding or boarding on the sand dunes. Near the park entrance, the **Oasis Restaurant and Store** (7800 Hwy. 150 N., Mosca, 719/378-2222, www.greatdunes.com, May-mid-Oct., $20) rents sandboards and sand sleds. From the Dunes Parking Lot, wade Medano Creek to access the closest slopes with a good pitch for sliding.

③ SCALE THE HIGH DUNE

From the Dunes Parking Lot, hiking the **High Dune on First Ridge** (2.5 mi. rt., 2-3 hrs.) is a grunt: each footstep sinks into the sand. You'll slog 699 feet in elevation, but it will feel like much more as you make a little headway step by step. The view from the top of the dune spreads across the entire dune field with the Sangre de Cristos rising above.

SOLITARY HIKER ON THE DUNES

ONE DAY IN GREAT SAND DUNES

A visit to Great Sande Dunes is all about the dunes. If you only have one day to explore its wonders, head for the sand dunes to enjoy their uniqueness. Choose from a quick cruise to **scenic viewpoints,** a longer **hike** to the tip of the dunes themselves, or rent a **sand board** and ride down the slopes for a speedy rush.

From the Point of No Return parking area, a trail climbs to two picnic areas on Medano Creek on the edge of the dunes. These are prime destinations for families where kids can frolic in the creek and play on the sand. The **Sand Pit** (1.5 mi. rt., 1 hr.) has gentle sand slopes, while **Castle Creek** (3 mi. rt., 1.5-2 hrs.) has a 400-foot dune that you can slide down and into a creek.

WHERE TO STAY

INSIDE THE PARK

Some of the 88 sites at the park's **Piñon Flats Campground** (877/444-6777, www.recreation.gov, Apr.-Oct., $20) can be reserved up to six months in advance. The remaining 44 sites are first come, first served. Amenities include flush toilets and drinking water.

OUTSIDE THE PARK

The **Oasis Restaurant and Store** (7800 Hwy. 150 N., Mosca, 719/378-2222, www.greatdunes.com, May-mid-Oct.) has a restaurant, convenience store, motel, campground, and gas station just outside the park entrance. The

town of **Alamosa,** 38 miles south, has limited services. Nearby lodging options include the primitive **Zapata Falls Campground** (BLM Monte Vista office, 719/852-7074) and motel rooms at **Great Sand Dunes Lodge** (719/378-2900, www.gsdlodge.com, Mar.-Oct.).

GETTING THERE AND AROUND

AIR

The closest airports are **Denver International Airport** (DEN, 8500 Peña Blvd., 303/342-2000, www.flydenver.com) and the smaller **Colorado Springs Airport** (COS, 7770 Milton E. Proby Pkwy., 719/550-1900, https://coloradosprings.gov/flycos). Car rentals are available at both.

CAR

Great Sand Dunes National Park is located 175 miles south of Colorado Springs via I-25 south and U.S. 160 west. From U.S. 160 near Alamosa, take Highway 150 north for 20 miles to the visitors center. There is no public transportation to or within the park.

TUBING MEDANO CREEK

COTTONWOODS ALONG MEDANO CREEK

HOW THE SAND DUNES FORM

The formula for creating the sand dunes is simple: wind and water deposit the sand in piles. It's an ongoing process that forms and reshapes the dunes, causing some to shift several feet in a week. The sand comes from surrounding mountains—the San Juan Mountains located 65 miles west and the Sangre de Cristo Mountains flanking the dunes on the east. Originally, a lake on the valley floor trapped sand blowing in from the San Juans and washing down the creeks that flow from the Sangre de Cristos. The lake has long since dried up, but the dunes continue to grow. Winds and water also recycle escaping sands back into the dunes.

The **sabkha** are wetlands of dried white mineral beds that flank the western portion of the dunes. The dunes' midsection contains 90 percent of the sand. The large **sand sheet** is mostly covered by grassland and swept over by prevailing winds that are responsible for building the dunes. Fields of yellow sunflowers show up in August. You can view both of these features while driving along the park's south boundary on County Lane 6 (between Mosca and Hwy. 150) and at several pullouts along the park entrance road.

SIGHTS NEARBY

San Luis Lakes State Wildlife Area (16399 Lane 6 N., Mosca, 719/587-6900, http://cpw.state.co.us) has wildlife-watching, birding, hunting, hiking, biking, and primitive camping in the desert near Great Sand Dunes.

Blanca Wetlands (BLM, Alamosa) is a collection of 200 ponds of prime wildlife habitat for fishing, birding, and wildlife-watching.

Zapata Falls Recreation Area (5415 BLM Road, Blanca, 719/852-7074, www. fs.usda.gov), seven miles southwest of the park, has primitive camping and hiking, wading, and slick bouldering to reach the chasm containing Zapata Falls.

Baca National Wildlife Refuge (719/589-4201, www.fws.gov/refuge/baca) gives tours one day weekly in summer by reservation. Topics include elk, migratory birds, historical homesteads, and refuge management.

▼ ASPEN ABOVE THE DUNES

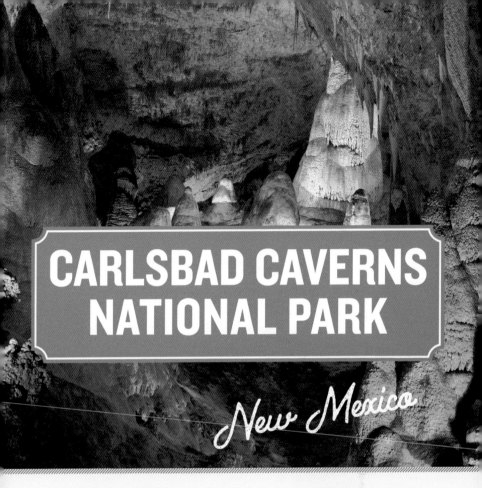

CARLSBAD CAVERNS NATIONAL PARK

New Mexico

PASSPORT STAMPS ▼▼▼

WEBSITE:
www.nos.gov/cave

PHONE NUMBER:
575/785-2232

VISITATION RANK:
36

WHY GO:
Tour underground
limestone caves.

▲ CARLSBAD CAVERNS
NATIONAL PARK

CARLSBAD CAVERNS NATIONAL PARK

VISITOR CENTER

ENTRANCE

SURFACE ELEVATION 4,406FT

BAT CAVE
200 FT BELOW SURFACE

DEVILS DEN
500 FT BELOW SURFACE

MAIN CORRIDOR

WITCHES FINGER

ELEVATOR SHAFT

SCENIC ROOMS

GREEN LAKE ROOM

ICEBERG ROCK

KINGS PALACE
829 FT BELOW SURFACE

QUEENS CHAMBER

REST AREA AND LUNCHROOM
755 FT BELOW SURFACE

BONEYARD

PAPOOSE ROOM

HALL OF GIANTS

GIANT DOME

PAINTED GROTTO

TWIN DOME

TEMPLE OF THE SUN

ROCK OF AGES

CRYSTAL SPRING DOME

TOTEM POLE

BIG ROOM

TOP OF THE CROSS

MIRROR LAKE

BOTTOMLESS PIT

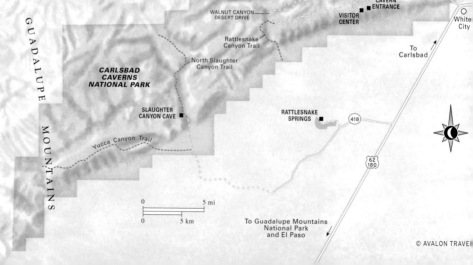

GUADALUPE MOUNTAINS

CAVERN ENTRANCE

WALNUT CANYON DESERT DRIVE

VISITOR CENTER

White City

Rattlesnake Canyon Trail

To Carlsbad

North Slaughter Canyon Trail

CARLSBAD CAVERNS NATIONAL PARK

SLAUGHTER CANYON CAVE

RATTLESNAKE SPRINGS

418

Yucca Canyon Trail

62 180

0   5 mi

0   5 km

To Guadalupe Mountains National Park and El Paso

One of the country's most awesome natural marvels, **CARLSBAD CAVERNS NATIONAL PARK** is mesmerizing. Scientists theorize that the Big Room—and many of the other caverns here—began to form more than 20 million years ago, as the petroleum deposits under the Guadalupe Mountains reacted with groundwater to create sulfuric acid, which ate through the stone to form vast hollow spots under the ground. These spaces started to fill with stalagmites and stalactites about 500,000 years ago, and now the intricate formations—still growing in some spots—range from hulking towers that ripple like clay to delicate needles that look more like icicles than stone.

Today, you can enjoy the park's wonders via a two-hour stroll around the aptly named Big Room—a vast cavern dripping with stalactites—or by spending several days visiting the park's more obscure underground worlds. For a taste of some of the 119 caves in the park, explore Lechuguilla Cave. At 136 miles, it is the longest cave in the park, loaded with rare gypsum and sulfur formations. Aboveground, the Chihuahuan Desert is especially scenic, studded with spiky plants and flowering cacti tucked into rugged canyons.

PLANNING YOUR TIME

Reaching Carlsbad Caverns requires a long drive to the southern border of New Mexico. Plan at least one day to explore the caverns, though the smaller, more adventurous group tours are worth a second day. **May-September** is high season with a full tour schedule, and lines inside and outside the cave may mean a long wait. For greater solitude, visit in **December** (before the holidays) or **January-February.** Though not all tours operate in winter, you'll have the place to yourself in near ghostly silence.

While temperatures may soar into triple digits aboveground in summer, cave temperatures hover at 56°F year-round. Bring a sweater or warm coat

THE NATURAL ENTRANCE AT CARLSBAD CAVERNS

Top ③

CHANDELIER DRAPERIES IN THE BIG ROOM

① ZOOM DOWN INTO THE BIG ROOM

The **Big Room** (entry/exit 8:30am-6:30pm daily late May-early Sept., 8:30am-4:30pm daily early Sept.-late May) is the largest cave in the Carlsbad complex. An elevator whisks visitors 754 feet down to the cavern floor. Lit with tasteful white lights, the Big Room glows like a natural cathedral: The ceiling soars into darkness within the 8.2-acre chamber. Along the 1.25-mile path, look for features such as the **Hall of Giants** and the **Bottomless Pit.** Plan 1.5 hours to complete the **Big Room Self-Guided Trail.**

② HIKE DOWN THE NATURAL ENTRANCE

Descend into the cavern on foot instead via the **Natural Entrance** (entry/exit 8:30am-6pm daily late May-early Sept., 8:30am-4pm daily Sept.-late May), which drops about 800 feet through the **Main Corridor** along a strenuous 1.25-mile trail dense with switchbacks. Walking down the Natural Entrance conveys the scale of this underground cave system: At one point, you have to hike for about 30 minutes around **Iceberg Rock,** a 200,000-ton boulder. The paved route has several steep sections with handrails and the path may be slippery. Plan one hour to complete the **Natural Entrance Self-Guided Trail.** The path ends at the elevators and the entrance to the Big Room.

③ MARVEL AT BATS IN FLIGHT

Late May-mid-October, hundreds of thousands of bats rush out from the depths of the caverns and into the bug-filled twilight. Half an hour before sunset at an amphitheater at the top of the Natural Entrance Trail, rangers give a short talk about the bats (ask at the visitors center for times). When the **Bat Flight** begins, you hear the soft flapping of their wings and feel the rush of air as they pass overhead.

AN OUTDOOR AMPHITHEATER PROVIDES SEATING FOR THE BAT FLIGHT.

and pack a lunch too, as the park cafeteria is pretty institutional.

Due to the park's proximity to **Guadalupe Mountains National Park** (about 40 min.), many visitors link a trip to the caverns with a visit to Guadalupe.

ENTRANCE AND FEES

The park entrance is via Carlsbad Caverns Highway, seven miles west of Whites City. In prime conditions, it takes about 45 minutes to reach the visitors center. In the summer months, allow an extra hour's wait at the visitors center. The entrance ticket is $15 per adult (age 16 and older) and is good for three days.

VISITORS CENTER

The **visitors center** (727 Carlsbad Caverns Hwy., 8am-7pm daily late May-early Sept., 8am-5pm daily early Sept.-late May) is located at the end of Carlsbad Caverns Highway, the park entrance road. This is where you can pick up cave tour tickets and park information.

For both of the self-guided trails, you can rent an **audio tour** ($5). The cave floor has a snack bar and restrooms hidden behind rock formations.

RANGER-GUIDED TOURS

Small-group tours offer an alternative to the crowds in the Big Room: It's quieter and you'll see a lot more of the caverns. **Reservations** (877/444-6777, www.recreation.gov) are required and can be booked up to six months in advance (at least 48 hours in advance). When available, first-come, first-served tickets are sold on the day of tours at the visitors center. Be sure to ask what time to arrive; some tours require hour-long hikes to the departure point.

For those who aren't afraid of tight spaces, the **Hall of the White Giant** and **Spider Cave** (once weekly in summer, 1 mi., 4 hrs., adults $20, children age 12 and older $10) are strenuous but rewarding trips. Expect to wiggle through some very narrow tunnels and to get muddy in the process.

KING'S PALACE

King's Palace (daily year-round, 1 mi., 1.5 hrs., adults $8, children age 4 and older $4) is the deepest part of the caves open to the public. Limited to 75 participants, the tour passes giant formations as well as tiny details such as a bat's skeleton grown into a stalagmite. Best of all, it includes a few minutes with the lights turned off, when you get to stand in the cool, smothering black. Unlike the other ranger-led tours, the paved trail is only steep at the entrance and exit.

LEFT HAND TUNNEL

Left Hand Tunnel (daily year-round, 0.5 mi., 2 hrs., adults $7, children age 6 and older $3.50) is best for a sheer sense of discovery. A small group of 15 visitors carries flickering lanterns through fantastic rock formations—made all the more bizarre as they loom out of the darkness.

LOWER CAVE

Lower Cave (weekly in summer, 1 mi., 3 hrs., adults $20, children age 12 and older $10) requires some exertion, as the path starts with a clamber down 50 feet of rope and narrow ladders. Formations include toothpick-like stalactites and the perfectly round and white formations called "cave pearls."

THE BIG ROOM

WHITE SANDS NATIONAL MONUMENT

White Sands, 275 square miles of blinding, shimmery gypsum, is a surreal and magnificent place. At every turn, you have to remind yourself what you're really looking at. In the summer, temperatures exceed 100°F, but the sand looks like no desert you've ever seen. On a cool winter day, especially after rainwater has pooled along the road, your brain can't stop thinking snow and ice. For the best photography, as well as a break from the heat, you'll probably want to visit either early or late in the day—but there is also something appropriately overwhelming about this featureless landscape at high noon.

Stop in at the **visitors center** (575/479-6124, www.nps.gov/whsa, 9am-5pm daily year-round, $5) for a schedule of ranger tours and to pick up a plastic sled for sliding down the dunes. Among the ranger tours (fee) is a trip to **Lake Lucero**, the crystal-filled lakebed that's the source of the sands, as well as occasional full-moon hikes, bicycle tours, and outings for sunrise photography.

The barren **Heart of the Sands** dunes at the core of the park form the most popular image of the place. You can set up camp in one of the mod metal picnic shelters (which include grills), and then go out to clamber, slip, and slide down the pristine white hills. A number of nature trails lead off the eight-mile-long **Dunes Drive**, such as the **Playa Trail,** the **Dune Life Nature Trail,** and the **Interdune Boardwalk.**

There's only one designated hike-in camping area (permit required, fee), about a mile from the road. Check ahead for periodic closures due to testing at the nearby White Sands Missile Range.

SLAUGHTER CANYON CAVE

Slaughter Canyon Cave (once weekly in summer, 1 mi., 5.5 hrs., adults $15, children age 8 and older $7.50) is located five miles south of Whites City off a well-signed county road. After a steep 0.5-mile hike to the cave entrance, the walk inside isn't too difficult. Look for formations like the glittering, crystal-covered column dubbed the Christmas Tree.

WHERE TO STAY

INSIDE THE PARK

There are no accommodations or campgrounds inside the park. **Primitive backcountry camping** is allowed with a permit (free) available at the visitors center. Inside the visitors center, the **Carlsbad Cavern Trading Company** sells a limited menu of to-go snacks and drinks.

OUTSIDE THE PARK

Guadalupe Mountains National Park (915/828-3251, www.nps.gov/gumo) is where people usually camp when visiting Carlsbad Caverns. It's located 35 miles south of Whites City on U.S. 62/180. **Carlsbad,** 30 miles north of the park on U.S. 62/180, has accommodations, though they are often overpriced. **Roswell** has a selection of national chain hotels.

GETTING THERE AND AROUND

AIR

The closest airport is **El Paso International Airport** (6701 Convair Rd., 915/212-0330, www.elpasointernationalairport.com) in Texas. From there, drive east on U.S. 62/180 to Highway 7 to reach Whites City, New Mexico (150 miles, 2.5 hrs.).

CAR

From Carlsbad, New Mexico, drive 19 miles south on U.S. 62/180 to reach Whites City. Fill your gas tank in Carlsbad to avoid being at the mercy of the one pricey station in Whites City.

From Whites City, drive 7 miles west on winding Carlsbad Caverns Highway. Plan 45 minutes to reach the visitors center, due to the curvy road and slow vehicles. Watch for wildlife darting onto the road.

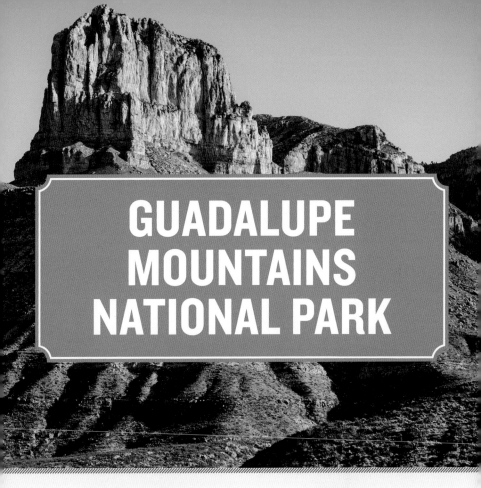

GUADALUPE MOUNTAINS NATIONAL PARK

WEBSITE:
www.nps.gov/gumo

PHONE NUMBER:
915/828-3251

VISITATION RANK:
48

WHY GO:
Hike ancient
fossil reefs.

▲ GUADALUPE MOUNTAINS
NATIONAL PARK

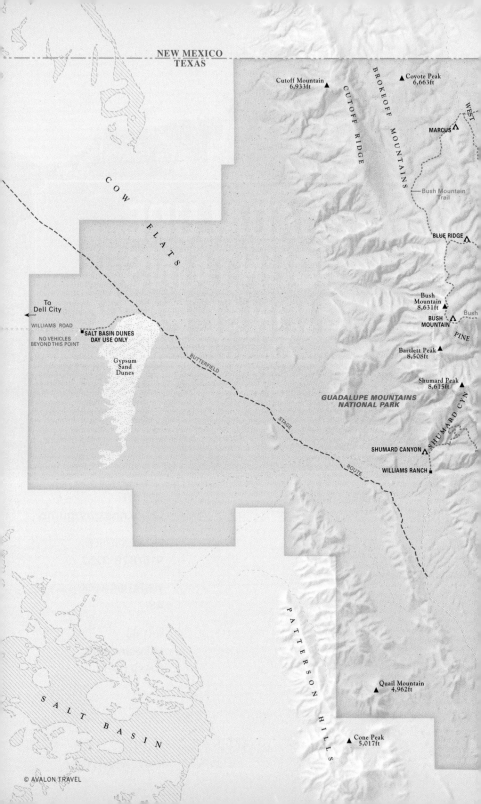

NEW MEXICO
TEXAS

Cutoff Mountain
6,933ft ▲

BROKEOFF MOUNTAINS

Coyote Peak
6,663ft ▲

WEST

MARCUS ⋀

CUTOFF RIDGE

Bush Mountain
Trail

BLUE RIDGE ⋀

COW FLATS

Bush
Mountain
8,631ft ▲

BUSH
MOUNTAIN ⋀

Bush

PINE

To
Dell City ←

WILLIAMS ROAD

NO VEHICLES
BEYOND THIS POINT

■ SALT BASIN DUNES
DAY USE ONLY

Gypsum
Sand
Dunes

BUTTERFIELD

Bartlett Peak
8,508ft ▲

Shumard Peak
8,615ft ▲

GUADALUPE MOUNTAINS
NATIONAL PARK

STAGE

SHUMARD CYN

SHUMARD CANYON ⋀

WILLIAMS RANCH ■

ROUTE

PATTERSON HILLS

SALT BASIN

Quail Mountain
4,962ft ▲

Cone Peak
5,017ft ▲

© AVALON TRAVEL

To Carlsbad
137

DOG CANYON
Indian Meadow Nature Trail

Bush Mountain Trail

NEW MEXICO
TEXAS

WILDERNESS RIDGE

Permian Reef Geology Trail

McKITTRICK CANYON

PRATT CABIN

UPPER DOG CANYON

Lost Peak 7,830ft

McKITTRICK RIDGE

McKittrick Canyon Trail

McKITTRICK CANYON

McKittrick Nature Trail

Tejas Trail

McKittrick Canyon Trail

SOUTH McKITTRICK CANYON

GROTTO

HUNTER LINE SHACK

The Notch 6,045ft

CANYON

SERVICE RD

MESCALERO

WILDERNESS AREA

FRIJOLE RIDGE

Tejas Trail

62 180

To Whites City and Carlsbad

TEJAS

NICKEL CREEK

SPRING CANYON

PINE TOP

Bowl Trail

Mountain Trail

Bear Canyon Trail

Hunter Peak 8,368ft

Tejas Trail

FRIJOLE RANCH HISTORY MUSEUM

Devil's Hell Trail

Foothills Trail

Guadalupe Peak (highest peak in Texas) 8,751ft

PINE SPRINGS VISITOR CENTER

GUADALUPE PEAK BACKCOUNTRY CAMPGROUND

THE PINERY BUTTERFIELD STAGE STATION RUINS

El Capitan Trail

El Capitan 8,085ft

Salt Basin Trail

ALT BASIN OVERLOOK

62 180

DELAWARE MOUNTAINS

Guadalupe

Arroyo

BUTTERFIELD

STAGE

ROUTE

To Dell City and El Paso

To Van Horn

54

0   1 mi

0   1 km

GUADALUPE MOUNTAINS
NATIONAL PARK

Beckoning high in the distance to a surprisingly low number of travelers, the **GUADALUPE MOUNTAINS** are an underappreciated natural wonder straddling the Texas-New Mexico border. They are built from an ancient exposed fossil reef and extend from desert floor to craggy summits. Guadalupe Mountains National Park climbs to the summit of Guadalupe Peak, the highest point in Texas. The diverse park is a compelling destination for hikers, backpackers, and campers who appreciate solitude and a challenging terrain that ranges from jagged peaks to smooth sand dunes, from deep canyons to sparkling springs.

PLANNING YOUR TIME

Guadalupe Mountains National Park is located in far West Texas, 110 miles east of El Paso and 56 miles south of Carlsbad, New Mexico. While you can drop in for a single day, you'll be able to explore more on a multi-night camping excursion. No paved roads penetrate the park; hiking is the only way to explore the interior. U.S. 62/180 provides access to the Pine Springs Visitor Center in the south, while Highway 137 accesses the Dog Canyon campground area in the north.

Spring (Mar.-May) and **summer** (June-Sept.) see mild, warm temperatures, while fall (Oct.-Nov.) and winter (Dec.-Feb.) are cooler and windy. The park, visitors center, and campground are open year-round, but some higher elevations can see snow on the trails in winter.

Due to the park's proximity (a 40-min. drive) to **Carlsbad Caverns National Park** in New Mexico, many visitors combine a tour of this park with a trip to the caverns.

ENTRANCE AND FEES

The entrance fee is $7-10 per person and is valid for seven days. There are no entrance stations; pay the fee at trailhead kiosks or in the visitors center.

VISITORS CENTER

Drop by the park's visitors center at **Pine Springs** (U.S. Hwy. 62/180 915/828-3251, 8am-4:30pm daily winter, 8am-6pm daily Apr.-Oct.) to pick up maps and brochures, find out the current weather forecast, view interpretive exhibits, browse the bookstore, and talk to the knowledgeable park staff. Adjacent to the center is the **Pinery Trail,** a paved pathway with scenic views, educational panels about the native plants, and the ruins of the Butterfield Overland Mail stage station.

RECREATION

HIKING

The best way to appreciate the park is by putting boot to rocky terrain on one of its hiking trails. More than a dozen options are available. To walk smaller self-guided nature trails, go to the park's headquarters, McKittrick Canyon, and Dog Canyon.

OVERLOOKING PINE SPRINGS

CLIMBING GUADALUPE PEAK

To fully experience the majesty of McKittrick Canyon, allow most of the day to reach the high ridges. Start at the McKittrick Canyon contact station to descend the **McKittrick Canyon Trail** (2.4-7.6 mi. one-way) before reaching the first milestone—Pratt Cabin, the 1929 structure of geologist and land donator Wallace Pratt. Another 1.1 miles leads to Grotto Picnic Area, one of the canyon's most scenic areas. With enough time and stamina, continue 4.1 more miles to McKittrick Ridge for views of colorful canyon walls and rugged outcroppings.

Accessed from Pine Springs Campground, the **Guadalupe Peak Trail** (4.1 mi. one-way) leads to stunning views atop the highest point in Texas. Despite the 2,906-foot ascent, the trek climbs at a moderate clip to 8,751 feet, where huge views take in the expansive desert and mountain surroundings.

The summit contains a large obelisk installed by American Airlines. One mile before the summit is a backcountry campsite.

THE TRAIL UP GUADALUPE PEAK

THE TRAIL THROUGH DEVIL'S HALL

Beginning at Pine Springs Campground, the **Devil's Hall Trail** (1.9 mi. one-way) follows a maintained path for one mile before the fun begins. Hikers must navigate the trail by following cairns, scrambling over boulders, and climbing a pour-over natural staircase to squeeze into a narrow, steep-walled slot canyon.

DEVIL'S HALL TRAIL

BACKPACKING

There are nine remote **wilderness sites** (backcountry permit required, free). Due to the isolated nature of these sites, it's essential to bring at least a gallon of water per person per day, ample food (open fires are prohibited), and emergency gear. First-come, first-served permits are available from the Pine Springs Visitor Center or Dog Canyon Campground.

WHERE TO STAY

The park's two campgrounds ($8) are first come, first served. Both have drinking water and flush toilets (no showers). Near the park's headquarters and visitors center, **Pine Springs** is the larger of the two, with 20 graveled tent sites among junipers and 19 RV sites in a big ol' paved parking lot. The nearby trailhead goes to Guadalupe Peak and Devil's Hall.

Sitting at 6,280 feet, **Dog Canyon Campground** is in a secluded, tree-filled canyon on the north side of the park. Its higher elevation and sheltered location beneath steep cliff walls result in cooler temperatures than Pine Springs. The canyon also protects the area from strong winds that blast through in winter and spring. The campground has nine tent sites and four RV sites. Cooking grills are available for charcoal fires.

GETTING THERE AND AROUND

The nearest international airport is in **El Paso** (ELP, 6701 Convair Rd., 915/212-0330, www.elpasointernationalairport.com), 110 miles west of the Guadalupe Mountains via U.S. Highway 62/180.

For those arriving from the east, take either I-20 or I-10 to Van Horn. Then, head north for about an hour on Highway 54, one of the most scenic drives in the state, to reach the park.

There is no public transportation into or within the park.

BIG BEND
NATIONAL PARK

Texas

PASSPORT STAMPS ▼▼▼

WEBSITE:
www.nps.gov/bibe

PHONE NUMBER:
432/477-2251

VISITATION RANK:
41

WHY GO:
See the Rio Grande.

▲ SOUTHWEST RIM OF
CHISOS MOUNTAINS

BIG BEND
NATIONAL PARK

To Alpine

▲ Graytop
5,502ft

118

Aqua Fria
Mountain ▲
Packsaddle
Mountain ▲

Corazones
Peaks ▲

Hen Egg Mountain ▲
4,963ft

CHRISTMAS MOUNTAINS

TERLINGUA
RANCH ■

118

Slickrock
Mountain ▲
▲ Croton Peak

Dogie
Mountain ▲

BLACK MESA

Terlingua Ghost Town
(Historic District)
Study Butte/
Terlingua

To
Presidio

170

ENTRANCE
STATION ■

Tule
Mountain ▲

The Window
4,600ft
CHISOS
BASIN

Lajitas ●

118

BURRO MESA

VISITOR CENTER ◆
CHISOS MOUNTAINS
LODGE

BURRO MESA
POUROFF ●

Emory Peak ▲
7,832ft

MESA DE ANGUILA

Terlingua Cr.

Old Maverick Road

Chimneys Trail

SOTOL VISTA ●

HOMER
WILSON
RANCH ■

Rio Grande

UNITED STATES
MEXICO

(RUINS) ▲▲✕✕▲

SANTA ELENA
CANYON OVERLOOK
DORGAN HOUSE (RUIN) ✦

Alamo Cr.

Blue Cr.

Dodson
Trail

Goat
Mountain ▲

CHISOS

MULE EARS
VIEW POINT ●

Smoky Cr. Trail

SANTA ELENA
CANYON

Dorgan House
Trail

COTTONWOOD ▲
CASTOLON
VISITOR CENTER

Cerro
Castellan
3,293ft ▲

Mule Ears Peaks ▲
3,881ft

Dominguez
Mountain ▲
5,156ft

SANTA ELENA
CANYON
PROTECTED AREA

Santa Elena ●

Triangulation
Station
Mountain ▲
3,143ft

Smoky Creek

RIVER ROAD WEST

CHIHUAHUA

0   5 mi
0   5 km

© AVALON TRAVEL

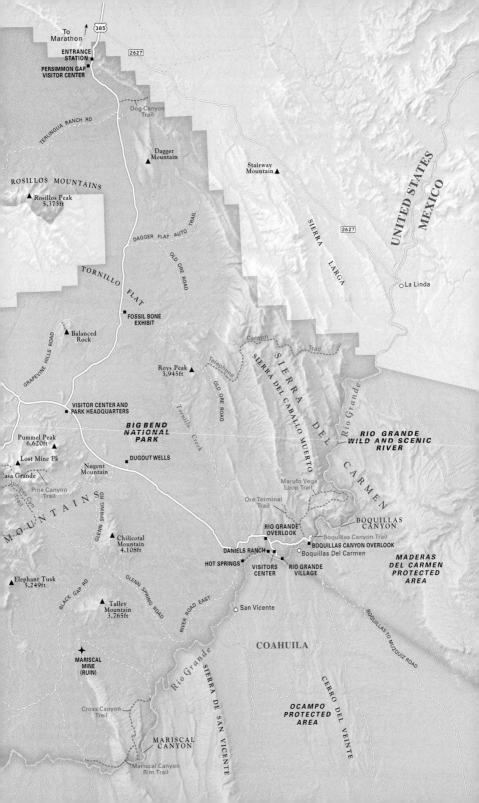

The namesake bend in the Rio Grande isn't the only enormous thing around here. **BIG BEND** encompasses more than 800,000 acres of spectacular canyons, mesmerizing Chihuahuan Desert, awe-inspiring Chisos Mountains, and unexpectedly temperate woodlands teeming with birdsong. The park is a birding mecca where high mountain cliffs house peregrine falcons, colorful tropical birds nest in spring, and migrating birds from the Northern Rockies fly south to winter in its warm climate.

Ancient limestone cliffs flank steep-walled Santa Elena Canyon, formations that lend a sacred aura to the slot where the Rio Grande slices its way toward the Gulf of Mexico. Downstream, the Chisos Mountains rise and views extend across the river into Mexico. Between the canyon and the mountains, a vast desert landscape blooms with ocotillo, yucca, and prickly pear cactus. Once the sun sets, dark skies yield a brilliant Milky Way.

PLANNING YOUR TIME

Big Bend National Park sits in an isolated pocket of southwest Texas. A car is the only means of access and driving times and distances are considerable. Advanced planning is required. Make reservations for lodging and camping six months in advance for visits in peak season—**mid-November-April.** Holiday lodging reservations should be made one year in advance.

Depending on your comfort level and tolerance for extreme topographical and climatic conditions, plan to spend 2-4 days in Big Bend National Park. Some visitors never leave the car, choosing instead to soak up the park's natural beauty on scenic drives, but hiking or camping is the best way to appreciate the varied ecosystems in this treasure.

The weather in Big Bend is only comfortable October-April. Summer is ridiculously hot—this *is* the Chihuahuan Desert—and despite the increased elevation and low humidity, triple-digit temperatures are brutal. May and June are the hottest months; periodic rainstorms later in the summer help ease the intensity and pain of the heat. Big Bend's rainy season even brings occasional heavy thunderstorms and flash flooding. Winter is the most volatile season in Big Bend, with generally mild temperatures, though extremes are possible, from 85°F scorchers to periods of light snow.

ENTRANCES AND FEES

The park has two entrance stations: The **North Entrance Station** (via U.S. 385 from Marathon) and the western gate at **Maverick Junction Entrance Station** (Hwy. 118). The entrance fee is $30 per vehicle ($25 motorcycle, $15 individual) and is good for seven days.

VISITORS CENTERS

Big Bend National Park has several visitors centers. The main visitors center is the park headquarters at **Panther Junction** (9am-5pm daily), 26 miles from the North Entrance Station and 25 miles from the Maverick Junction Entrance Station. This visitors center offers interpretive exhibits and scores of books, brochures, and maps. You can also get schedules for **free ranger-led programs** (varies weekly) that include guided walks and evening amphitheater programs. If you can catch a night-sky telescope program, you'll be treated to brilliant sights unseen around city lights.

Entering from the North Entrance Station, you will first pass through the seasonal visitors center at **Persimmon**

Top ③

1 TOUR CHISOS BASIN ROAD

For unbelievably dramatic mountain scenery, it's imperative to make the drive on the **Chisos Basin Road** (6 mi. one-way) to **Chisos Mountains Lodge.**

CHISOS VILLAGE IN THE CHISOS MOUNTAINS

Your ears will pop and your jaw will drop as you ascend the road into the mountain range, with the famous formations of **Casa Grande** and **Emory Peak** acting as a beacon to the basin. Keep an eye on the road as you navigate the switchbacks to the lodge; the dramatic hairpin turns have a 10 mph speed limit. Locate the turnoff to Chisos Basin Road three miles west of Panther Junction.

2 CRUISE ALONG ROSS MAXWELL SCENIC DRIVE

An ideal introduction to the complex range of natural wonders is a jaunt along **Ross Maxwell Scenic Drive** in the western portion of the park. The vast vistas slowly transform to striking views of volcanic rock formations reminiscent of an otherworldly scene straight out of a *Star Trek* episode. Drop by the historic village of **Castolon** (22 miles one-way) and set aside an hour to explore the small museum exhibits in the charming century-old military structures. This is a good place to grab a snack and a cold drink at the old general store. Sit on picnic tables out front to soak up the views of the cliffs of Mexico across the river. Walk down the hill to admire a nearby historic adobe house; step inside the small structures near the general store for interesting heritage exhibits.

Eight miles farther down the road is the must-see **Santa Elena Canyon Overlook** (30 mi. one-way) where immense cliffs pinch the Rio Grande. Find the turnoff to the scenic drive at the Castolon/Santa Elena Junction 13 miles west of Panther Junction.

SANTA ELENA CANYON

3 RAFT THE RIO GRANDE

The Rio Grande has two claims to fame that make floating the river a unique experience: its steep, tall canyon walls and its designation as the international boundary between the United States and Mexico. Depending on your skill level and sense of adventure, you can tackle frothing big Class IV rapids in a raft or paddle quieter waters in a canoe.

From Lajitas, **Santa Elena Canyon** (20 miles) features 13 miles of easy desert paddling and 7 miles of navigating severe rapids. The canyon stretch of the river funnels through enormous 1,500-foot-tall cliffs that tower overhead, and it hits the largest rapid, a Class IV run known as Rock Slide. For an easier day trip, opt for the "boomerang" paddle upstream and then float back to the put-in.

RIVER RAFTING ON THE RIO GRANDE.

A portion of the river designated as the **Rio Grande Wild and Scenic River** offers several trips appealing to beginner and intermediate boaters. The 10-mile-long Mariscal Canyon trek provides stunning scenery with 1,400-foot-tall limestone cliffs and some exciting Class II-III rapids. For a longer excursion (2-3 days), the 33-mile trip through Boquillas Canyon is an ideal choice for beginners, since there aren't any rapids higher than Class II. Even longer (up to 10 days) is a trek through the lower canyons, where paddlers can experience true solitude in the wilderness without encountering another human being for days at a time.

Gap (9am-4pm Sat.-Sun. summer). The park's smaller visitors centers include **Chisos Basin** (8:30am-4pm daily year-round), **Castolon** (10am-4pm daily Nov.-Apr.), and **Rio Grande Village** (8:30am-4pm daily Nov.-Apr.).

SCENIC DRIVES

Big Bend is the kind of place where you feel compelled to pull your car over every half mile to snap a photo of the endless succession of stunning scenes. Avoid the temptation—you can return to the spots later once you've processed their context—and just soak up the natural beauty through your own eyes rather than a viewfinder. Play some appropriate West Texas soundtrack music (Willie Nelson complements the scenery quite nicely) and marvel at the jagged peaks, desert cacti, and sweeping vistas. A word of advice: Finish your drive before sundown. Driving on park roads at night can be somewhat treacherous—especially when critters are out grazing on the roadside. Deer, javelina, and jackrabbits can jump out in front of your car at any time.

ONE DAY IN BIG BEND

If you only have one day to spend in the park, stop at **Panther Junction Visitor Center** before taking a scenic drive into the **Chisos Mountains** to **Chisos Basin Visitor Center**. Follow that with the **Ross Maxwell Scenic Drive** out to **Santa Elena Canyon Overlook** to see the **Rio Grande** spilling from the huge slot. If you have time, hike the short trail into the canyon.

Best Hike

LOST MINE TRAIL

DISTANCE: 4.8 miles round-trip
DURATION: 4 hours
EFFORT: moderate
TRAILHEAD: Basin Road, mile 5.1

Considered one of the ultimate Big Bend hikes, the **Lost Mine Trail** offers an ideal combination of moderate grades, a wide range of vegetation, extraordinary vantage points, and a handy interpretive brochure at the trailhead. Views include the Sierra del Carmen in Mexico.

OLD MAVERICK ROAD

If you're driving a high-clearance vehicle, tackle the **Old Maverick Road** (14 mi. one-way) for the rare chance to experience the invigorating sensation of plowing through rugged terrain just like they do in SUV ads. The dirt-and-gravel road completes the loop between Ross Maxwell Scenic Drive, Santa Elena Canyon Overlook, and Maverick Junction. Speckled with historical sites, it then slices across the Terlingua Creek Badlands. Plan one hour for the washboard drive.

RIO GRANDE VILLAGE ROAD

Not quite as dramatic, yet certainly worth experiencing, is the drive to **Rio Grande Village** (20 mi. one-way). The terrain slowly descends as you approach the river, and the charms of the Chihuahuan Desert are in full effect in the blooming cacti, gentle mesas, and the occasional javelina. For a little more excitement, take on the narrow mini overhangs along the short road to the hot springs (1.5 mi. one-way). Shortly before reaching Rio Grand Village, stop at the overlook past the tunnel for a view of the river.

RECREATION

HIKING

Big Bend offers more than 200 miles of hiking trails ranging from short, easy nature walks to primitive mountain trails for experienced hikers.

The short **Rio Grande Village Nature Trail** (1 mi. rt., 1 hr.) will introduce you to Big Bend's dramatic vistas and desert intricacies. The trail starts with a boardwalk crossing over a body of water originating from the wetland natural spring, immediately followed

RUINS OFF OLD MAVERICK ROAD

by a hot and hardscrabble trek across rocky terrain among myriad cacti and desert scrub. The highlight is the view from the top of the moderately sloped hill, where you'll find sweeping vistas of the Rio Grande and Mexico.

You can see the massive walls of **Santa Elena Canyon** (1.7 mi. rt., 2 hrs.) from miles away, but the effect of witnessing these sheer cliffs—more than 1,500 feet high on each side of the surprisingly narrow gap forged by the Rio Grande—is utterly mesmerizing up close. Across the shallow creek bed, look for a crude stone pathway, which leads to the trailhead. You'll encounter a series of tight switchbacks and concrete steps before ascending a rocky trail that eventually descends into the canyon. When you reach the end of the trail, you'll be surrounded by the stunning vertical cliff walls, which echo with the sounds of birds playing in the water.

The **Grapevine Hills Trail** (1.1 mi. one-way, 1.5 hrs.) trots through a desert gravel wash before finishing with a steep climb. The destination is the Balanced Rock, a large boulder wedged between two towering rocks.

BACKPACKING

Almost 20 miles of trails loop through the **Chisos Mountains** and offer prime backpacking routes. Forested canyons with colorful birds warbling in song lead to high scenic rim walks overlooking the Rio Grande thousands of feet below. Spread throughout the loops are 42 designated campsites with food storage lockers; four junctions include compost toilets.

Most hikers limit trips to 2-3 days due to unreliable water sources. **Permits** ($10) are required and are available first come, first served up to 24 hours in advance from Chisos Basin Visitor Center.

RAFTING

First-come, first-served **backcountry permits** ($12) are required for overnight rafting trips, available in person at Panther Junction Visitor Center. If you have the skills, you can bring your own gear or rent equipment locally; if you don't, hire a guide service.

▼ BALANCED ROCK ON THE GRAPEVINE HILLS TRAIL

To book guided river trips, rent gear, or hire shuttles, contact **Big Bend River Tours** (800/545-4240, www.bigbendrivertours.com), **Desert Sports** (888/989-6900, www.desertsportstx.com), or **Far Flung Outdoor Center** (432/371-2633, www.bigbendfarflung.com).

WHERE TO STAY

INSIDE THE PARK

The only accommodations in the park are at **Chisos Mountains Lodge** (432/477-2291 or 877/386-4383, www.chisosmountainslodge.com, from $145). Situated nearly a mile high in a cozy basin surrounded by mountain peaks, the complex offers a no-frills experience befitting its remote and rugged location. A variety of sleeping accommodations are spread across a series of hotel, motel, and lodge rooms, including the coveted Roosevelt Stone Cottages (book one year in advance). These five historic cottages ooze mountain character, with welcoming porches, regional decor, and big windows that capture the gentle breeze. Each features stone floors, double beds, showers, coffeepots, refrigerators, microwaves, and ceiling fans (no air-conditioning).

The **Chisos Mountains Lodge Restaurant** (7am-10am, 11am-4pm, and 5pm-8pm daily, $8-20) serves a surprisingly varied menu of regional Tex-Mex fare, standard dishes, and hearty breakfasts. "Hikers lunches" are available to go.

Three developed campgrounds (with drinking water and flush toilets) are open year-round. Located in the mountains, **Chisos Basin** (60 sites, 26 reservable) is the most scenic and is closest to the lodge restaurant. Sites are too small for RVs and the access road has sharp hairpin turns. **Rio Grande Village** (100 sites, 43 reservable) is on the river in the eastern edge of the park and can accommodate RVs. Some campsites at Rio Grande Village and Chisos Basin are available by **reservation** (877/444-6777, www.recreation.gov, $14) up to six months in advance.

Cottonwood Campground (24 sites, first come, first served, $14), on the west side, is appealing for its namesake cottonwood trees and proximity to the historic Castolon village and Santa Elena Canyon.

Rio Grande Village RV Campground (877/386-4383, $35) accepts reservations for its 25 sites, all with full hookups for RVs.

Big Bend has dozens of primitive **backcountry campsites** ($12), typically consisting of only a flat gravel pad; many are only accessible by high-clearance vehicles or four-wheel drives. A backcountry permit (first come, first served) is required from Panther Junction Visitor Center.

OUTSIDE THE PARK

There are a few motels and campgrounds outside the park in **Terlingua/Study Butte.** For a broader selection of choices, stay in **Midland.**

GETTING THERE AND AROUND

AIR

The closest airport is **Midland International Air & Space Port** (MAF, 9506 Laforce Blvd., 432/560-2200, www.flymaf.com), where you can rent a car and be in Marfa within three hours and Big Bend within four.

An alternative is **El Paso International Airport** (ELP, 6701 Convair Rd., 915/212-0330, www.elpasointernationalairport.com), which offers a few more flights. Unfortunately, it takes nearly five hours to drive to Big Bend.

CAR

From Midland, drive south on U.S. 385 for 225 miles (3.5 hours) to the park visitors center. There is no public transportation available to Big Bend or inside the national park.

SIGHTS NEARBY

Big Bend Ranch State Park (1900 Sauceda Ranch Rd., 432/358-4444, https://tpwd.texas.gov/state-parks) is the largest state park in Texas and is quite popular with those in search of a genuinely remote natural experience.

ROCKY MOUNTAINS

The Rocky Mountains climb along the backbone of the Continental Divide. In Rocky Mountain National Park, the hairpin bends of Trail Ridge Road reveal snowcapped peaks and alpine tundra. Farther south, the Black Canyon of the Gunnison squeezes through a narrow fissure.

Yellowstone sputters with geysers, mud pots, and hot springs. To its south, Grand Teton struts a line of sawtooth peaks in a landscape filled with bison.

Glacier's jagged arêtes and glacier-carved basins are sliced through by Going-to-the-Sun Road.

This rugged landscape gives way to the Great Plains. Grasslands and prairies are evident in the colorful Badlands and Theodore Roosevelt National Parks, while Wind Cave hides underground.

◄ ROCKY MOUNTAINS

ROCKY MOUNTAINS

Glacier NP

MONTANA

Helena

Billings

Theodore Roosevelt NP

NORTH DAKOTA

Yellowstone NP

Grand Teton NP

IDAHO

SOUTH DAKOTA

Wind Cave NP

WYOMING

Badlands NP

NEBRASKA

Salt Lake City

Cheyenne

UTAH

Rocky Mountain NP

Denver

COLORADO

Black Canyon of the Gunnison NP

0   100 mi
0   100 km

The National Parks of
THE ROCKY MOUNTAINS

ROCKY MOUNTAIN, CO

Alpine lakes, lush meadows teeming with elk, and a glaciated landscape of deep valleys beneath soaring summits creates awe-inspiring splendor (page 409).

BLACK CANYON OF THE GUNNISON, CO

Pitch a tent, search for great horned owls, and enjoy views of this narrow, deep chasm (page 428).

YELLOWSTONE, WY

Our first national park remains one of the finest, with gushing geysers, thundering waterfalls, and epic wildlife (page 435).

GRAND TETON, WY

A craggy spine of peaks laced with hiking trails spills into glacial lakes and historic Jackson Hole ranches (page 460).

GLACIER, MT

Captivating scenery, epic trails, huge lakes, and scenic drives fill this park's one million acres (page 482).

BADLANDS, SD

A wall of tall spires, grassy buttes, and colorful eroding cliffs present an otherworldly landscape (page 504).

WIND CAVE, SD

Beneath the ground's surface is the fifth-longest cave in the world (page 514).

THEODORE ROOSEVELT, ND

This badland and grassland landscape projects a raw beauty favored by Theodore Roosevelt (page 521).

1: THE BLACK CANYON OF THE GUNNISON
2: GRAND TETON
3: WIND CANYON TRAIL IN THE SOUTH UNIT OF THEODORE ROOSEVELT

Best OF THE PARKS

Going-to-the-Sun Road: Drive the only road bisecting Glacier on a skinny cliff shimmy to Logan Pass (page 487).

Old Faithful Geyser: Watch one of the most regular geysers erupt (page 441).

Wildlife-Watching: Pull out binoculars in Lamar Valley in Yellowstone, on Moose-Wilson Road in Grand Teton, and throughout Rocky Mountain National Park (pages 441, 465, and 413).

Trail Ridge Road: Drive the winding, hairpin curves on this scenic traverse across the Continental Divide in Rocky Mountain (page 413).

Badlands Loop Road: Tour this road through South Dakota's Badlands, dotted with scenic turnouts and dramatic vistas (page 508).

PLANNING YOUR TRIP

Plan at least **two weeks** to tour the national parks of the Rockies. Make lodging and campground **reservations** for in-park accommodations in Glacier, Yellowstone, Grand Teton, and Rocky Mountain up to 13 months in advance. Plan your trip for **summer** when visitors centers and services are open and the weather is pleasantly warm.

High Season

Summer (May-October) is high season in the Rockies, when the parks see the most visitors. July and August see peak visitation and the best weather. Summer heralds the opening of the high-elevation scenic drives—pending weather conditions and snow removal—such as Trail Ridge Road in Rocky Mountain and Going-to-the-Sun Road in Glacier.

Low Season

In **winter** (Nov.-Apr.), deep snows turn the parks white, and many park roads close for the season. Even though winter sees fewer people, it's the time for snow sports. In Yellowstone, visitors tour Old Faithful via guided snowcoaches or snowmobiles, while roads in Glacier and Grand Teton become snowshoeing and cross-country skiing paths.

▲ GOING-TO-THE-SUN ROAD, GLACIER

Road Trip

MAMMOTH TERRACES, YELLOWSTONE

YELLOWSTONE, GRAND TETON, AND GLACIER

String together these three iconic parks in a **one-week** road trip. Fly into **Bozeman Yellowstone International Airport, Montana,** to start the loop. With its proximity to Yellowstone, you can rent a car and be in the park on the same day. Make reservations for in-park lodging or camping up to 13 months in advance.

Yellowstone

88 miles / 1.5 hours

From Bozeman, drive to the North Entrance at Gardiner and park at **Mammoth Hot Springs** to tour the travertine terraces before overnighting at **Mammoth Hot Springs Hotel.** Get a predawn start to go wildlife-watching in **Lamar Valley**, hike the rim of the **Grand Canyon of the Yellowstone,** and watch **Old Faithful Geyser** erupt. Spend the night at historic **Old Faithful Inn** before driving to **West Thumb**

Geyser Basin on **Yellowstone Lake.** From here, head south to enter Grand Teton.

Grand Teton

7 miles / 15 minutes

You'll enter Grand Teton on the John D. Rockefeller Jr. Parkway and enjoy your first views of the **Tetons** across **Jackson Lake.** Stop at **Jackson Lake Lodge** where you can go **horseback riding,** dine in the **Mural Room,** and spend the

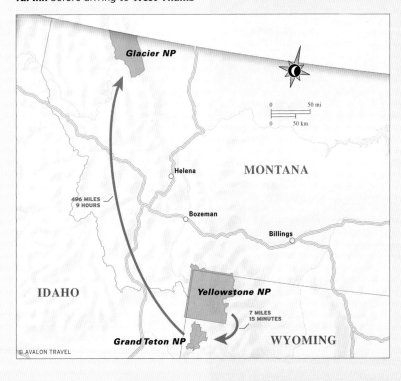

Glacier NP

0   50 mi
0   50 km

Helena

MONTANA

496 MILES
9 HOURS

Bozeman

Billings

IDAHO

Yellowstone NP

7 MILES
15 MINUTES

Grand Teton NP

WYOMING

© AVALON TRAVEL

night. In the morning, drive south along **Teton Park Road,** stopping at **Jenny Lake.** Take the boat shuttle to hike to **Hidden Falls** and **Inspiration Point.** Continue driving south on **Moose-Wilson Road** for wildlife-watching. Aim to spend the night in **Jackson.**

Glacier

496 miles / 9 hours

Hit the road by 8am for this long haul from Jackson, Wyoming, over Teton Pass and up the Rocky Mountains to **Many Glacier Valley** in **Glacier National Park.** You should arrive just in time to put your feet up on the back deck of **Many Glacier Hotel,** where you can dine amid mountain scenery and watch the sun set over the Continental Divide. In the morning, take a boat ride on **Swiftcurrent** and **Josephine Lakes** to stretch your legs on the **Grinnell Lake Trail.** The following day, finish your road trip with a cliff-side drive on the **Going-to-the-Sun Road,** stopping at **Logan Pass** to soak up the splendor.

1: LOWER FALLS OF THE GRAND CANYON
  OF THE YELLOWSTONE
1: INSPIRATION POINT, GRAND TETON
2: SWIFTCURRENT LAKE, MANY GLACIER

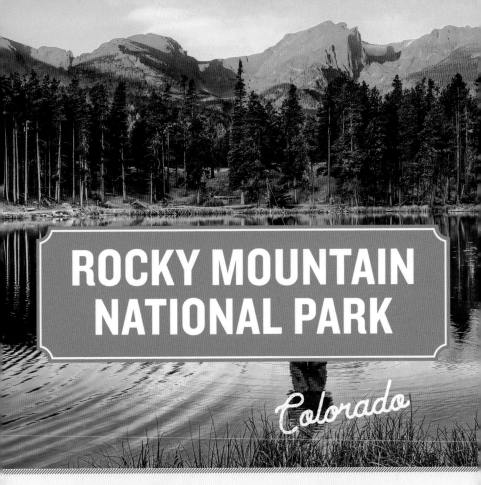

ROCKY MOUNTAIN NATIONAL PARK

Colorado

PASSPORT STAMPS ▼▼▼

WEBSITE:
www.nps.gov/romo

PHONE NUMBER:
970/586-1206

VISITATION RANK:
4

WHY GO:
Explore high peaks
and watch wildlife.

▲ SPRAGUE LAKE

ROCKY MOUNTAIN NATIONAL PARK protects a dramatic, wild landscape. Meadows, forests, and lakes butt up against a backdrop of sheer cliffs and soaring peaks. These peaks dominate the Continental Divide with some of the highest summits in the Lower 48 and the highest paved road in the United States. Rugged scenery is a guarantee.

From the lowest valley to the top of 14,259-foot-high Longs Peak, the enormous changes in elevation create a mosaic of interconnected ecosystems that top out in alpine tundra. While the west winds howl and a thick blanket of snow drapes the mountains, you can drive to Bear Lake, whose azure waters are even more stunning against the backdrop of evergreen forest and freshly fallen snow. Each spring, the cycle of life begins anew as the sun climbs higher in the sky, the birds return, the meadows turn green, and mule deer and other mammals give birth. Summer heralds the opening of Trail Ridge Road, the park's signature scenic drive, a winding ribbon of hairpin bends, each with a new vista of snowcapped peaks and windswept alpine tundra. In fall, aspen change to bright gold, and the air resounds with elk bugles and bighorn rams banging horns during the rut. The changeable scenery makes you want to return again and again to experience all of the park's moods.

PLANNING YOUR TIME

Rocky Mountain National Park is separated by the Continental Divide into east and west sides. These sides are only connected when **Trail Ridge Road** (U.S. 34, Memorial Day-mid-Oct.) is open. From mid-October through Memorial Day, **Estes Park** offers the main driving access into the park. In late spring, U.S. 34 reopens, connecting both halves of the park.

Rocky Mountain is one of the country's busiest national parks, and **summer** (May-Sept.) is its busiest season. Due to extreme elevation differences, the weather is changeable and unpredictable—even in summer. You might leave Denver's lowland heat to arrive in chilling winds at 12,000 feet. Summer afternoons frequently bring thunderstorms. Spring and fall offer a mix of warm sun, rain, or snow; fall tends toward blue skies. For elk calving season, visit late May-early June. To listen to bugling bull elk, go in fall. Winter (Dec.-Mar.) pummels the mountains with snow.

ENTRANCES AND FEES

The bustling east side has two entrances: the **Fall River Entrance Station** (U.S. 34) and the **Beaver Meadows Entrance Station** (U.S. 36). The gateway town of Estes Park is open year-round and provides access to both roads. Access the west side through the **Grand Lake Entrance Station** (U.S. 34, year-round), north of the town of Grand Lake.

The entrance fee is $35 per vehicle ($30 motorcycle, $20 individual) and is good for seven days.

VISITORS CENTERS
Beaver Meadows Visitor Center

The **Beaver Meadows Visitor Center** (U.S. 36, 8am-5pm daily in summer, 8am-4:30pm daily in winter) is the park's primary access point. In addition to an information desk, bookstore, and nature exhibits, the center houses one of the park's two **Backcountry Permit Offices** (970/586-1242), where you can obtain backcountry permits on a

Top **3**

1 WATCH WILDLIFE

BULL ELK

Hearing the eerie sounds of 1,100-pound **bull elk** echoing through the air is a quintessential Rocky Mountain experience, especially in the early morning, when the crowds are minimal and the rising rays cast a magical glow across the vibrant autumn landscape. The fall breeding season occurs **mid-September to mid-October.** During this time, anxious males round up their harems and bugle, issuing a loud and peculiar noise that begins at a deep, resonant sound, then rises to a high-pitched squeal, before ending in a series of grunts. Elk typically bugle between dusk and dawn, the best times for visitors to both see and hear the rutting ritual. **Dusk** is the most popular time, so the roads around **Moraine** and **Horseshoe Parks** and **Upper Beaver Meadows** are typically very crowded. To avoid the masses, try these areas at dawn instead or head to the Kawuneeche Valley on the west side.

The west side of Trail Ridge Road is a great place to spot **moose,** the largest members of the deer family. When in the **Kawuneeche Valley**, look for munching moose, as well as coyotes, elk, and mule deer.

West of the Fall River Visitor Center, the **Sheep Lakes** (U.S. 34) are the best place to look for the graceful **bighorn sheep,** the nimble symbol of this wildlife-rich national park. Bighorn sheep overwinter at high elevations and descend to the montane valleys in late spring, when they visit Sheep Lakes to graze on the lush grass. Bighorn sheep are typically in this area between 9am and 3pm. At the **Bighorn Crossing Zone** in Horseshoe Park, rangers toting stop signs control automobile traffic to allow the sheep to move peacefully in and out of the meadow, while also providing great photo ops for visitors caught in the "sheep jam."

2 DRIVE TRAIL RIDGE ROAD

Trail Ridge Road (U.S. 34, May-mid-Oct.), the 48-mile paved road between Estes Park and Grand Lake, is the only road that crosses Rocky Mountain National Park. The country's highest continuous paved road, Trail Ridge tops out at an impressive 12,183 feet. Although the whole route proffers great views, the best scenery is found in the 11-mile section above tree line, where you are surrounded by windswept tundra stretching in every direction toward snowcapped peaks, dramatic steep-walled cirques, and deep valleys.

Driving it is an awe-inspiring adventure with stunning views. From the lush montane forests and fertile lowlands at either end, the road quickly climbs to the tundra, a harsh environment home to tiny wildflowers, alpine lakes, and wildlife.

Pullouts along the way offer safe places to stop for photos and enjoy the forever views. From east to west, great viewpoints include **Hidden Valley, Many Parks Curve,** and **Rainbow**

TRAIL RIDGE ROAD

Curve. Farther west, learn about the tundra at the **Tundra World Nature Trail,** an easy half-hour walk from the **Rock Cut.** Two miles west of the road's unmarked high point is the **Alpine Visitor Center.**

Continuing west on Trail Ridge Road, you cross the **Continental Divide** at 10,758-foot **Milner Pass** and have stunning views into the upper Colorado River valley from the aptly named **Farview Curve,** a short distance above the gate that closes the road in winter.

3 CLIMB LONGS PEAK

CLIMBING LONGS PEAK

The 14,259-foot **Longs Peak** is the highest and most distinctive peak in Rocky Mountain National Park. Along with its flat-topped summit, Longs' east face (the Diamond) comprises one of the most iconic sights in the park.

Longs Peak is a very popular (and very difficult) challenge for mountaineers and technical rock climbers, with about 30,000 people attempting to climb it each summer. The **Keyhole Route** (15 mi. rt., 10-15 hrs., strenuous) climbs nearly 5,000 vertical feet and involves scrambling, steep drop-offs, and extreme exposure to the highly changeable alpine weather. A predawn start is essential, as is a detailed route description, a map, and appropriate safety gear. The Longs Peak trailhead and campground are located south of Estes Park via Highway 7.

Fortunately, you don't *have* to climb Longs Peak to admire it. Capture the stunning view of Longs Peak from **Bear Lake**'s easily accessible northern shore. It's so iconic that the scene is displayed on the back of the state quarter.

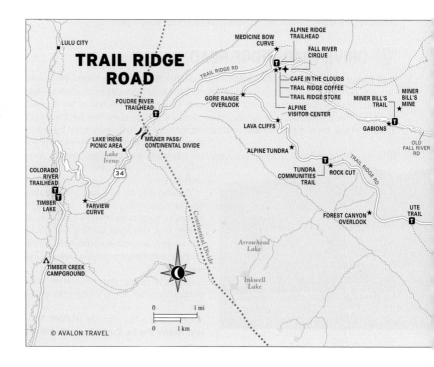

AVOID THE CROWDS

To avoid the crowds, hit the trails close to **sunrise** or later in the **evening.** Visit the **west side** midday, when most people are on the east side. Take the free **shuttle buses** whenever possible to avoid traffic during one of the inevitable "elk jams."

space-available basis. Beginning in mid-April, this visitors center also offers a variety of **ranger-led programs**.

Fall River Visitor Center

Just east of the Fall River Entrance Station is the **Fall River Visitor Center** (U.S. 34, 9am-4pm Fri.-Sat. mid-May, 9am-5pm daily late May-mid-Oct., limited hours Nov.-Dec.), with brochures, maps, and a bookstore.

Alpine Visitor Center

The **Alpine Visitor Center** (Trail Ridge Rd., 970/586-1222, 10:30am-4:30pm daily late May-mid-Oct.) has one of the best views in Colorado, a panorama looking down Fall River Canyon toward

Longs Peak and Estes Park far below. The center has exhibits, restrooms, and the **Trail Ridge Store,** the only place in the park where you can grab food or snacks.

Kawuneeche Visitor Center

The west side of Rocky Mountain National Park has just one entrance. It leads to the **Kawuneeche Visitor Center** (16018 U.S. 34, Grand Lake, 970/627-3471, 8am-5pm daily in summer, 8am-4:30pm daily in winter), where you can pick up maps and reserve backcountry campsites.

SIGHTS

MORAINE PARK

The large meadow west of the Beaver Meadows Entrance Station is **Moraine Park** (U.S. 36), one of the best places to spot wildlife, especially **elk.** Moraine Park stretches from **Bear Lake Road** to **Deer Ridge Junction** (U.S. 36/34). You can obtain great views of the meadow from both roads, as well as from the two side roads that pierce the meadow's eastern side to access several trailheads, picnic areas, and the Moraine Park Stables.

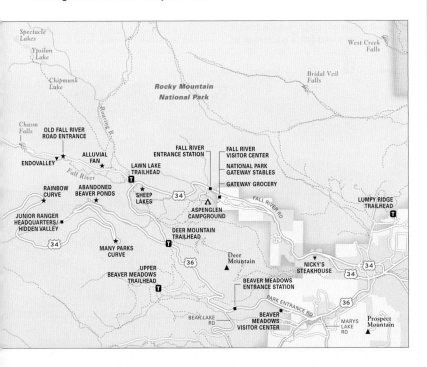

ONE DAY IN ROCKY MOUNTAIN

Visit **Bear Lake** and stroll around its turquoise waters, enjoy a picnic lunch, and then drive **Trail Ridge Road,** lingering at the **Alpine Visitor Center**, Many Parks Curve, and other stops for short hikes, wildlife sightings, photo ops, and phenomenal panoramic views.

If you have an extra day, add a morning hike up the **Twin Sisters Peaks** or to Wild Basin's rushing waterfalls, and then stop in Estes Park for a refreshing lunch and a visit to the **Stanley Hotel** before heading to **Horseshoe Park** and **Sheep Lakes** to search for bighorn sheep and grazing elk silhouetted in the twilight's golden glow.

Housed in a historic log and stone building, the seasonal **Moraine Park Discovery Center** (Bear Lake Rd., 970/586-1242, 9am-4:30pm daily late May-mid-Oct.) has a natural history exhibit describing how the park's distinctive landscape formed, a half-mile nature trail, and a gift shop and bookstore.

BEAR LAKE

The shimmering, cobalt-blue waters of **Bear Lake** are nestled beneath the soaring summit of Hallett Peak, with many impressive mountains, including Longs Peak, rising to the south and east. The best way to experience its beauty is by strolling the undulating, 0.5-mile-long **walking path**. From the shore, you'll enjoy great views of Longs Peak and other towering peaks and get a good look at

the mix of spruce, lodgepole pine, and fir trees. Bear Lake is also a great place to begin more extended hikes as well as relax and enjoy a delicious picnic along with the stunning views.

ALLUVIAL FAN

The prominent, treeless scar on the northern flank of **Horseshoe Park** was created in just a few hours when, on July 15, 1982, the Lawn Lake Dam collapsed, sending 129 million gallons of water racing down Roaring River and knocking down every tree in its path. After this wall of water reached flat Horseshoe Park, it slowed dramatically and dropped the boulders it was carrying, creating a distinct cone of sand,

▼ ROCKY MOUNTAIN NATIONAL PARK

LILY LAKE

gravel, and boulders called an alluvial fan. It's still visible from the **Alluvial Fan Parking Area** (Endovalley Rd. off Old Fall River Rd.).

LUMPY RIDGE

East of U.S. 34 and north of Estes Park, a dramatic line of rocky cliffs known as **Lumpy Ridge** rises high above the town. One of the ridge's most distinctive features is the **Twin Owls,** a rock formation that, from the proper angle, really looks like two owls perched on a slab known as the **Roosting Ramp.** No roads cross the ridge, which is a well-known destination for hiking and technical rock climbing. The ridge is accessed from a trailhead on Devils Gulch Road, a continuation of MacGregor Avenue, which heads north from the stretch of U.S. 34 between the junction with U.S. 36 and the national park.

LILY LAKE

Located at the toe of the Twin Sisters Peaks, **Lily Lake** is one of Rocky Mountain's most accessible alpine lakes. Lying just feet from Highway 7 about six miles south of Estes Park, this turquoise lake is a popular place to picnic and stroll along the shoreline. The 0.8-mile-long, **wheelchair-accessible trail** is completely flat, making it an excellent outing for families and visitors not yet acclimated to the elevation.

ENOS MILLS CABIN MUSEUM

Housed in a wooden cabin built in 1885, the small **Enos Mills Cabin Museum** (6760 Hwy. 7, 970/586-4706, www. enosmills.com, tour reservations required) has old photographs, letters, and other artifacts that help visitors appreciate the achievements of the "Father of Rocky Mountain National Park." The highlights are the gorgeous scenery and the opportunity to learn about the family's history from one of Mills's relatives.

WILD BASIN

Tucked into the park's southeastern corner, beautiful **Wild Basin** is home to a series of waterfalls and gorgeous wildflowers, including vivid clusters of delicate Colorado blue columbine (Colorado's state flower). Due to its outlying location, the crowds are often smaller than in the main park. Wild Basin is primarily a hiking destination, but **Lower Copeland Falls** lies just 0.3 mile from the Wild Basin trailhead, making it accessible to most visitors.

KAWUNEECHE VALLEY

The main entrance to the park's west side is through **Trail Ridge Road** (open May-mid-Oct.). Descending the western side of Trail Ridge Road, you're treated to spectacular views of snow-capped peaks, the upper Colorado River valley, lush meadows, dense pine forests, and glimpses of the shimmering blue waters of Grand Lake and several other lakes far below. The descent yields great views of the craggy peaks of the Never Summer Range, particularly from **Farview Curve,** a large pullout just above the seasonal closure gate and due east of the heavenly peaks.

The **Holzwarth Historic Site** (U.S. 36, mid-June-Labor Day) is the site homesteaded by German immigrant John Holzwarth Sr. From the parking area, walk a short, smooth **trail** that crosses the Colorado River before looping through the historic buildings, a series of rustic, hand-hewn wooden cabins. Although the buildings are only open to visitors from mid-June through Labor Day, you can walk around the site any time of year.

WILDFLOWERS ON TRAIL RIDGE ROAD

SPRAGUE LAKE

Harbison Meadows is the former site of two more homesteads belonging to sisters Annie and Kitty Harbison, who along with their family migrated here from Kansas in the late 1800s. Today, the empty grass meadows are a beautiful spot to enjoy a picnic lunch and watch for wildlife.

SCENIC DRIVES
OLD FALL RIVER ROAD

Built between 1913 and 1920, **Old Fall River Road** (July-Oct., closed in winter) is one of the park's signature scenic drives. From U.S. 34, at the bend between Sheep Lakes and Horseshoe Park, the road heads northwest from the Endovalley to the Alpine Visitor Center on Trail Ridge Road. After leaving the valley, the road climbs steadily through thick evergreen forest. About a mile from its start, there's a short excursion from a small pullout on the left side down a stone pathway to **Chasm Falls.** From this stop, the road continues beneath the looming hulk of 12,454-foot Mount Chapin. After passing **Willow Park,** where you can often spot elk, Old

Fall River Road crosses into the treeless alpine tundra. Near the crest at **Fall River Pass,** the road contours around the **Fall River Cirque,** a giant cookie bite that a glacier sculpted out of the hard rock, before joining Trail Ridge Road at the Alpine Visitor Center.

Although the dirt surface is frequently graded and accessible to regular passenger vehicles, it's intended as a leisurely scenic drive, with a **15 mph** speed limit, no guardrails, and 16 tight switchbacks. Because it's too narrow and winding for cars to safely pass, the **11-mile route** is a **one-way drive.**

BEAR LAKE

The paved Bear Lake Road climbs nine miles through the forest before ending at beautiful **Bear Lake,** one of the park's well-known destinations. Along the way, the road passes a large **Park & Ride,** from which you can catch any of the free seasonal shuttles, including the orange line to Bear Lake. The road also passes the **Glacier Basin Campground** and several picnic areas and trailheads, including those at **Sprague Lake.**

Best Hike

LUMPY RIDGE

DISTANCE: 3.2 miles round-trip
DURATION: 1.75 hours
ELEVATION CHANGE: 1,000 feet
DIFFICULTY: moderate
TRAILHEAD: Lumpy Ridge/ Gem Lake

One of the best moderate trails in the park is the classic route to **Gem Lake** on Lumpy Ridge. This route climbs steadily from the **Lumpy Ridge Trailhead** through evergreen forest and sparkling ancient granite, which ice, wind, and rain have sculpted over millions of years into the ridge's distinctive knobs. At the junction with the Black Canyon Trail about half a mile from the trailhead, veer to the right (east) to head toward the lake. This section has many aspen trees, making it a great place to visit in early autumn when the leaves slowly turn to gold. About 1.5 miles from the trailhead, after ascending several small switchbacks, you'll reach a distinctive rock formation creatively called **Paul Bunyan's Boot** (note the hole in the "sole"). From here, the final climb up to Gem Lake is steep, but the views along the way of Longs Peak, Mount Meeker, and Estes Park are well worth the effort. There are great places to rest along the lake, including several rocky outcrops and a small, sandy beach ideal for a well-deserved picnic.

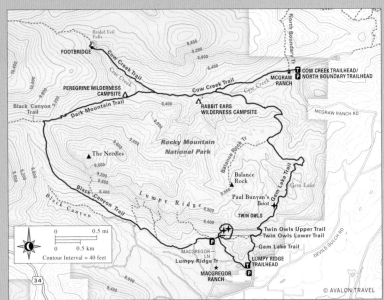

DREAM LAKE

HIKING

Plan to arrive at the trailhead around 6am to get a parking spot, as popular trailheads tend to fill. Or use the park shuttle bus to avoid the anxiety of parking. You'll want to return from your destination before the afternoon thunderstorms begin to hurtle lightning, especially at hikes above tree line.

EAST SIDE

Lawn Lake

A great path for exploring some of the extensive wilderness in the park's northeastern corner is the **Lawn Lake Trail** (Lawn Lake Trailhead, Endovalley Rd., 12.4 mi. rt., 6-7 hrs., moderate) near the start of Fall River Road. The trail follows the path of the Roaring River en route to Lawn and Crystal Lakes.

Deer Mountain

At the start of Trail Ridge Road, the 10,013-foot **Deer Mountain** (Deer Ridge Junction, U.S. 34/36, 6 mi. rt., 3-4 hrs., strenuous) has a modest 1,083-foot elevation gain on a straightforward trail. This makes a great first summit and one that is usually accessible by late spring.

Fern Lake

The **Fern Lake Trail** (Bear Lake Rd., 7.6 mi. rt., 5 hrs., easy) follows an easy route along a creek through a deep and shady valley and past several pretty waterfalls along a fern-draped path to beautiful Fern Lake.

Bear Lake

Bear Lake is the start of many fabulous walks, most of which follow a string of gorgeous, deep-blue lakes. The easy 0.5-mile stroll around the shoreline suits most visitors. Hardier hikers can use the Emerald Lake Trailhead to follow the **Bear Lake Trail** to spritely Nymph Lake (1 mi. rt., 30 min., easy), after which it climbs 425 feet to celestial **Dream Lake** (2.2 mi. rt., 1.5 hrs., moderate), and sparkling **Lake Haiyaha** (4.2 mi. rt., 2.5 hrs., moderate). Alternatively, above Nymph Lake you can branch off to the west to reach **Emerald Lake** (3.6 mi. rt., 2 hrs., moderate).

Flattop Mountain

The **Flattop Mountain Trail** (8.8 mi. rt., 5 hrs., strenuous) ascends 12,324-foot Flattop Mountain, located right on the Continental Divide. This historical route begins at the Bear Lake Trailhead at the very end of Bear Lake Road (9 miles west of the U.S. 36 turnoff). About 1.75 miles from the trailhead, the **Dream Lake Overlook** is a scenic spot

ALBERTA FALLS

HIKING TRAILS CURVE AROUND ROCKY PEAKS.

to rest, with great views of Longs Peak. At about 2.4 miles, the trail passes tree line, and about 3 miles from the trailhead, the **Emerald Lake Overlook** has great views of the lake and Hallett Peak. The trail ends at the junction with the North Inlet and Tonahutu Creek/Continental Divide National Scenic Trails.

Glacier Gorge

The **Glacier Gorge Trailhead** (east of Bear Lake) is the starting point for the short hike to the 30-foot-tall **Alberta Falls** (1.6 mi. rt., 1 hr., easy). From here you can climb 750 feet to **Mills Lake** (5.6 mi. rt., 3 hrs., moderate), **Black Lake** (10 mi. rt., 5 hrs., strenuous), or **Sky Pond** (9.8 mi. rt., 5 hrs., strenuous), with its stunning backdrop and crystal-clear waters. Some scrambling is required.

Twin Sisters

The stunning 360-degree views of Estes Park, the national park, and the Great Plains from the top of the **Twin Sisters Peaks** (4 mi. rt., 4 hrs., strenuous) are breathtaking. The trail leads through the forest, past a landslide, and up switchbacks to 11,000 feet. A long, straight slope through granite slabs reaches the saddle between the Twin Sisters Peaks, the higher of which is the 11,428-foot eastern peak. Access the gravel road off Highway 7.

Wild Basin

In the southeastern corner of the park, the **Wild Basin Trailhead** (Wild Basin Rd. via Hwy. 7) accesses an extensive trail system. One of the best day hikes follows a string of waterfalls, beginning with **Copeland Falls** (0.6 mi. rt., 20 min., easy) and then leading past an unnamed waterfall to the 200-foot-long **Calypso Cascades** (3.6 mi. rt., 2 hrs., moderate) and 40-foot-high **Ouzel Falls** (5.4 mi. rt., 3 hrs., moderate).

WEST SIDE

Colorado River to Lulu City

The **Colorado River Trail** (Colorado River Trailhead, Trail Ridge Rd., 7 4 mi. rt., 4 hrs., easy) wanders through Shipler Park at the base of the Never Summer Range to **Lulu City,** a mining town built in 1879 that, at its peak, had about 200 residents. Only the foundations from a couple of cabins remain.

North Inlet Trail

North of Grand Lake, the **North Inlet Trail** (Road 663) offers several hiking options, including the gushing **Cascade Falls** (6.8 mi. rt., 3.5 hrs., moderate) and the Big Pool (9.6 mi. rt., 5 hrs., moderate), a swimming hole.

East Inlet Trail

On Grand Lake's east side, the **East Inlet Trail** leads to pretty **Adams Falls** (West Portal Rd., 0.6 mi. rt., 20 min. easy), a short stroll that showcases a pretty cascade of water tumbling down the final steep pitch before mixing with the smooth waters of Grand Lake.

RECREATION

BACKPACKING

The east side of Rocky Mountain National Park has many backpacking options ranging from single-night stays to demanding multiday routes across the Continental Divide. Many of the day hikes can be extended overnight, such as the hike to **Fern Lake** (7.6 mi. rt.).

On the west side of the park, the **East Inlet Trailhead** leads to **Lone Pine Lake** (11 mi. rt., 2 days) and **Lake Verna** (27.6 mi. rt., 2-3 days).

You can tackle a portion of the 3,100-mile **Continental Divide Scenic Trail** (30 mi. one-way, 2-3 days). Start in the Arapaho National Forest on the Bowen Pass Spur Trail and hike through the Never Summer Wilderness before entering the park to loop with the Tonuhutu Creek Trail and finish at North Inlet Trailhead. From the North Inlet Trailhead, you can hike point-to-point over the Continental Divide to Flattop Mountain (12 mi. one-way) and Bear Lake (17 mi. one-way).

Backpackers must obtain a **permit** (970/586-1242, www.pay.gov, $26) for designated campsites in advance or in person from one of the **Backcountry Permit Offices**. Applications begin March 1 for the upcoming season.

ROCK CLIMBING

Rocky Mountain National Park is well known for its world-class technical rock climbing and mountaineering. **Lumpy Ridge**'s granite walls feature almost 400 trad routes, but the park's most famous multi-pitch technical route ascends the Diamond, the sheer, diamond-shaped alpine wall on **Longs Peak**'s upper east face. The **Colorado Mountain School** (341 Moraine Ave., Estes Park, 800/836-4008, http://coloradomountainschool.com) offers classes and guided rock climbing trips.

HORSEBACK RIDING

Two stables within the park offer more than a dozen rides daily: **Moraine Park Stable** (970/586-2327, www.sombrero.com) and **Glacier Creek Stable** (970/586-3244, www.sombrero.com).

▼ THE TRAIL TO LONGS PEAK

ASPEN

FISHING

Sportfishing is popular within the park and surrounding lakes and streams. Two great locations for catch-and-release fishing are **Fern Lake** and **Lawn Lake,** both of which host native greenback cutthroat trout. The clear, rushing **Colorado River** is a great place for fly-fishing, especially for brown and cutthroat trout. There are several access points along lower Trail Ridge Road, including the Holzwarth Historic Site.

WHERE TO STAY

INSIDE THE PARK

There is no lodging available within Rocky Mountain National Park; camping is the only overnight option and it's very popular, with only a small number of sites available. Make **reservations** (877/444-6777, www.recreation. gov) well in advance; reservations open on December 1 for the following year. The park's east side has several choices; three campgrounds accept reservations.

Moraine Park Campground (year-round) sits about 2.5 miles south of the Beaver Meadows Entrance Station with tent and RV sites. Facilities include vault and flush toilets, drinking water, a dump station, and access to park shuttles. In winter, toilets and drinking water are not available; sites are first come, first served.

Glacier Basin Campground (June-Sept.) is about six miles south of the Beaver Meadows Entrance Station with tent and RV sites. Facilities include drinking water, flush toilets, and food storage lockers; there is a park shuttle stop nearby.

Aspenglen Campground (late May-late Sept.) is located near the Fall River Visitor Center with tent and RV sites. Facilities include drinking water, flush toilets, and food storage lockers.

Longs Peak Campground (June-Sept.) is the best place to stay if you're planning on an early start to climb Longs Peak. Sites are tent-only; vault toilets are available.

THE STANLEY HOTEL

As you drive into **Estes Park,** you can't help but notice the enormous, gleaming-white building with the bright red roof perched high on a hill in front of the dramatic granite outcrops of Lumpy Ridge. This is **The Stanley Hotel** (333 Wonderview Ave., 800/976-1377, tours 970/577-4111, www.stanleyhotel. com), the most distinctive building in Estes Park and one of the oldest. It was built in 1909 by F. O. Stanley, who, along with his twin, was the co-owner of the company that built the famous Stanley Steamers. After being diagnosed with tuberculosis at the age of 54, Stanley moved to Estes Park to take advantage of its fresh air and copious sunshine. During the course of his first summer here, Stanley's health rebounded and he purchased some property with the intent of returning every summer. But Stanley and his wife, Flora, craved the more refined accommodations and social scene they were used to on the East Coast. They decided to build a grand Colonial Revival-style hotel with innovations like electricity throughout the building. Completion of the original 48-room Stanley Hotel in 1909 spurred the local economy, as did Stanley's efforts to improve and pave the roads from the Front Range up to Estes Park.

Today, the 140-room hotel is known for its amazing views from every window and for hosting horror writer Stephen King and serving as the inspiration for the terrifying Overlook Hotel in his best-selling novel *The Shining*. Reputedly one of the nation's most active sites for paranormal activity, the hotel is infamous for its ghostly guests, including Stanley and his wife, Flora, who apparently enjoys playing her antique piano in the middle of the night.

STANLEY HOTEL, ESTES PARK

Take a **Night Ghost Tour** through the hotel's most haunted areas. To learn more about its history, architecture, and famous (live) guests, sign up for **The Stanley Tour.** Each spring, the hotel sponsors the four-day **Stanley Film Festival** (www.stanleyfilmfest.com, Apr.), a ghoulish mixture of classic and modern horror flicks, workshops, and a student film competition. Buy tickets and book accommodations well in advance.

The only campground on the park's west side is **Timber Creek** (late May-early Nov.), just west of U.S. 34. Sites accommodate tents and RVs, but services are limited to flush toilets and drinking water.

OUTSIDE THE PARK

Estes Park serves as the gateway to the park's east side, providing easy access to Bear Lake and Moraine Park. Most restaurants and accommodations surround the junction of U.S. 34 and U.S. 36. **Grand Lake** is the west side's tourist hub, but accommodations are limited.

Book ahead May-September, the busiest season.

GETTING THERE
AIR

Denver International Airport (DEN, 8500 Peña Blvd., 303/342-2000, www. flydenver.com) is the nearest commercial airport and is serviced by all major American airlines. **Estes Park Shuttle** (1805 Cherokee Dr., 970/586-5151, www.estesparkshuttle.com) offers year-round, scheduled, door-to-door service from the Denver airport to all Estes Park venues.

LONGS PEAK FROM TRAIL RIDGE ROAD

CAR

To reach Estes Park from Denver, take I-25 north to U.S. 36 west, following signs for Boulder. Continue west on U.S. 36 for about 32 miles. At the junction with U.S. 34, turn left to remain on U.S. 36 (called Moraine Ave.), which passes through Estes Park before arriving at the Beaver Meadows Entrance Station. In good weather and traffic conditions, this trip typically takes about two hours.

GETTING AROUND

DRIVING

From Beaver Meadows, U.S. 36 continues west and then north, passing Bear Lake Road to the south (which connects to Moraine Park and Bear Lake). At the Deer Mountain Junction, the road splits: Trail Ridge Road heads west, while U.S. 34 continues north to meet Old Fall River Road before veering west to the Fall River Visitor Center.

Trail Ridge Road

The Fall River Visitor Center on U.S. 34 offers convenient access to both Trail Ridge and Fall River Roads (open seasonally). In summer, Trail Ridge Road is accessible from the east side at the junction of U.S. 34 and U.S. 36. Trail Ridge Road (U.S. 34, open May-mid-Oct.) is the only road into the park's west side. In winter, the road closes and the west side must be accessed through the Grand Lake Entrance Station.

SHUTTLES

Both Estes Park and the national park run free summer shuttles. From the Estes Park Visitor Center (500 Big Thompson Ave.), the park's **Hiker Shuttle Route** (7:30am-8pm daily late June-mid-Sept., 7:30am-8pm Sat.-Sun. mid-Sept.-mid-Oct., free) runs to the large **Park & Ride** (Bear Lake Rd.), with one stop at the Beaver Meadows Visitor Center. The park has two additional shuttles: The orange **Bear Lake Route** (7am-7pm daily, early May-mid-Oct.) runs every 10-15 minutes along Bear Lake Road; the green **Moraine Park Route** (7am-7pm daily, late May-mid-Oct.) runs every 30 minutes between Bear Lake Road and Fern Lake.

There is no public transport or shuttle service to the west side of Rocky Mountain National Park.

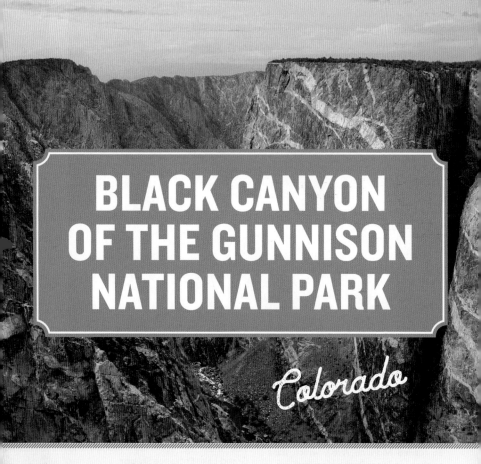

BLACK CANYON OF THE GUNNISON NATIONAL PARK

Colorado

WEBSITE:
www.nps.gov/blca

PHONE NUMBER:
970/641-2337, ext. 205

VISITATION RANK:
43

WHY GO:
Peer down into the thin slice of this deep, steep-walled gorge.

PASSPORT STAMPS ▼▼▼

▲ THE BLACK CANYON OF THE GUNNISON

"No other canyon in North America combines the depth, narrowness, sheerness, and somber countenance of the Black Canyon of the Gunnison," wrote noted geologist Wallace Hansen.

The **BLACK CANYON OF THE GUNNISON** was carved by the powerful Gunnison River, which first chewed through soft volcanic rock like a saw blade in a wooden groove. Once the river had carved this initial channel it remained there, chipping away at the hard metamorphic rock below. Over millions of years, the river excavated this gorge, whose walls are so tough that they barely retreated from the river. The canyon's sheer walls are higher than Chicago's Willis Tower and its inner gorge is so narrow that it receives only minutes of sunlight each day.

Along the South and North Rims, varied viewpoints overlook the gorge. The total canyon is 48 miles long, with 14 miles inside the national park. The canyon's deepest point plunges 2,722 feet. At its narrowest point on the rim, the canyon is only 1,100 feet across. Below Chasm Overlook at the Gunnison River, the canyon shrinks to a narrow slot of only 40 feet.

PLANNING YOUR TIME

In western Colorado, the Black Canyon of the Gunnison sits southeast of Grand Junction between Montrose and Gunnison. The park's North and South Rims are only 0.25 mile apart in places; however, to get from one rim to the other takes 2-3 hours of driving. The park is open year-round, with all roads open mid-April to mid-November. In winter, roads close with the exception of the South Rim Road to Gunnison Point. Due to more difficult accesses for the North Rim and East Portal Roads, most visitors only go to the **South Rim.**

Peak visitation is in **summer** (May-Sept.) when days range 55-90°F and frequent afternoon thunderstorms appear. Winter days see 15-40°F as the norm, with varied snow depths on the ground. Temperatures can fluctuate radically in one day; bring layers of clothing.

ENTRANCES AND FEES

The main entrance to the park is through the South Rim via **Highway 347.** The North Rim entrance is south of Crawford, where you can pay fees at the ranger station or a self-pay kiosk. The entrance fee is $25-30 per vehicle ($15-25 motorcycle, $12-15 individual) and is valid for seven days.

VISITORS CENTER

Located at Gunnison Point, the **South Rim Visitor Center** (Hwy. 347, 8am-6pm daily late May-early Sept., reduced hours off-season) has exhibits, a film, maps, a bookstore, backcountry permits, and Junior Ranger Programs.

SCENIC DRIVES
SOUTH RIM ROAD

From the park entrance, the paved **South Rim Road** (14 mi. rt., Apr.-mid-Nov.) has a dozen overlooks between the visitors center and **High Point**, the road's end. The following four overlooks are the best: From two viewpoints at **Gunnison Point**, orange lichen cliffs plunge down to the Gunnison River while vertical light-colored dikes slice the broken North Rim wall. At **Chasm View,** the depth drops by 1,820 feet to the river in one of the narrowest sections, making ultra-steep walls on which you might spot expert rock

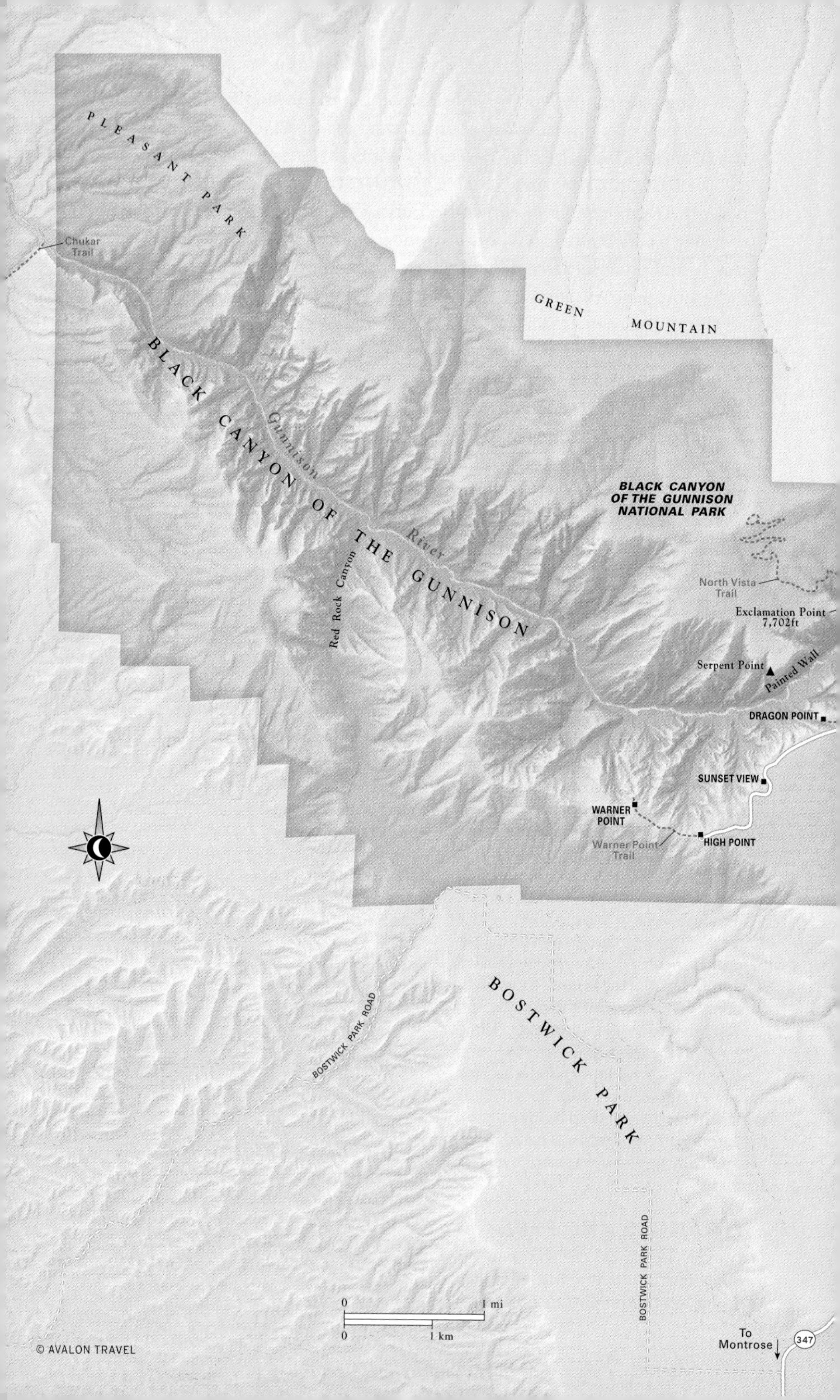

PLEASANT PARK

Chukar
Trail

GREEN   MOUNTAIN

BLACK CANYON OF THE GUNNISON

Gunnison

River

Red Rock Canyon

BLACK CANYON
OF THE GUNNISON
NATIONAL PARK

North Vista
Trail

Exclamation Point
7,702ft

Serpent Point   ▲ Painted Wall

DRAGON POINT ■

SUNSET VIEW ■

WARNER ■
POINT
Warner Point
Trail   ■ HIGH POINT

BOSTWICK   PARK

BOSTWICK PARK ROAD

BOSTWICK PARK ROAD

0 _____ 1 mi
0 _____ 1 km

To
Montrose   347

© AVALON TRAVEL

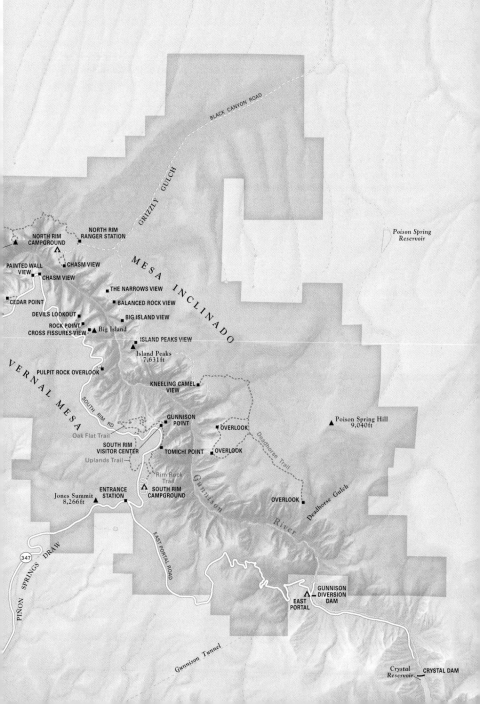

BLACK CANYON
OF THE GUNNISON
NATIONAL PARK

BLACK CANYON ROAD

GRIZZLY GULCH

Poison Spring
Reservoir

NORTH RIM
RANGER STATION

NORTH RIM
CAMPGROUND

MESA INCLINADO

PAINTED WALL
VIEW   CHASM VIEW

CHASM VIEW

THE NARROWS VIEW

CEDAR POINT

BALANCED ROCK VIEW

DEVILS LOOKOUT

BIG ISLAND VIEW

ROCK POINT
CROSS FISSURES VIEW   Big Island

ISLAND PEAKS VIEW

Island Peaks
7,631ft

PULPIT ROCK OVERLOOK

VERNAL MESA

KNEELING CAMEL
VIEW

Poison Spring Hill
9,040ft

SOUTH RIM RD

GUNNISON
POINT

Oak Flat Trail

OVERLOOK

SOUTH RIM
VISITOR CENTER

TOMICHI POINT

OVERLOOK

Uplands Trail

Deadhorse Trail

Rim Rock
Trail

Gunnison

OVERLOOK

Jones Summit
8,266ft

ENTRANCE
STATION

SOUTH RIM
CAMPGROUND

River

Deadhorse Gulch

EAST PORTAL ROAD

347

PIÑON SPRINGS DRAW

GUNNISON
DIVERSION
DAM

EAST PORTAL

Gunnison Tunnel

Crystal
Reservoir   CRYSTAL DAM

ONE DAY IN BLACK CANYON OF THE GUNNISON

Spend your time visiting the busy South Rim. Cruise the paved **South Rim Road,** stopping at the overlooks between the visitors center and High Point, the road's end. Park at the South Rim Visitor Center to stretch your legs on the **Rim Rock Nature Trail** and gaze into the canyon's abyss.

climbers. You can walk from Chasm View to **Painted Wall View,** which gets its name from layers of lighter rock amid the black across Colorado's highest cliff. With picnic tables, **Sunset View** is a good place to eat while taking in the immense canyon downstream.

NORTH RIM ROAD

From the park entrance for the North Rim, take the gravel **North Rim Road** (14 mi. rt., mid-Apr.-mid-Nov.) to six viewpoints, including **The Narrows View,** which overlooks the canyon's narrowest point (40 feet wide at river level).

EAST PORTAL ROAD

Between the South Rim entrance and campground, the **East Portal Road** (14 mi rt., mid-Apr.-mid-Nov.) begins a steep descent to the river. It plunges with a 16 percent grade and tight, sharp switchbacks to the **bottom of the Black Canyon of the Gunnison** and into Curecanti National Recreation Area at **Crystal Dam**.

RECREATION

Visitors bike the rim roads in spring and summer or **cross-country ski** and **snowshoe** in winter. On the North Rim, the Deadhorse Trail allows **horseback riding**. The park's sheer vertical walls attract expert **rock climbers** for about 145 climbs, most rated above 5.10. The East Portal Road provides access to the Gunnison River, where anglers can **fish** the Gold Medal Water and Wild Trout Water (200 yards downstream from Crystal Dam to the North Fork of the Gunnison River) within the steep canyon walls.

▼ THE GUNNISON RIVER

CLIFF-SIDE VIEW INTO THE CANYON

HIKING

From South Rim Visitor Center, the sunny **Rim Rock Nature Trail** (1 mi. rt., 30 min., easy) is a level, self-guided interpretive path. The steep **Oak Flat Loop Trail** (2 mi. rt., 1 hr., strenuous) drops below the rim inside the canyon, but not to the river. From this loop, strong scramblers can add on the unmaintained **Gunnison Route** (2 mi. rt., 3.5 hrs., strenuous, permit required), which plunges down a Class III gully (assisted by an 80-foot chain in one spot) to the river and crawls 1,800 feet straight back up.

At South Rim Road's terminus, the **Warner Point Nature Trail** (1.5 mi. rt., 45 min., moderate) wanders through pinyon-juniper forest with views of the San Juan Mountains. Pick up a guide to the trail's flora at the visitors center.

On the North Rim, walk from the trailhead near the ranger station along the **North Vista Trail** (3 mi. rt., 1.5 hrs., moderate) to Exclamation Point, a fitting name for the fabulous inner-canyon views. The route continues to **Green Mountain** (7 mi. rt., 3.5 hrs., strenuous) for 360-degree views of Grand Mesa, the Uncompahgre Plateau, and a different perspective peering down into the canyon.

WHERE TO STAY
INSIDE THE PARK

There is no lodging inside the park. Camping is your only option. Drinking water is trucked in during summer; off-season, campers should bring their own. On South Rim Road, **reservations** (877/444-6777, www.recreation.gov) are accepted in summer for 88 sites at the **South Rim Campground** (year-round, $16-22). Sites are first come, first served outside the summer season. On the North Rim Road, the smaller **North Rim Campground** (mid-Apr.-mid-Nov., $16) has 13 seasonal campsites. The **East Portal Campground** (mid-Apr.-mid.-Nov., $16) has 15 campsites located five miles down the steep and hairpin East Portal Road.

OUTSIDE THE PARK

Accommodations and food are available in the towns of **Gunnison, Grand Junction,** and **Montrose.**

CURECANTI NATIONAL RECREATION AREA

Upstream of the Black Canyon of the Gunnison National Park, **Curecanti National Recreation Area** (www.nps.gov/cure) is a series of three dam reservoirs that tame the Gunnison River. Farthest east and close to the town of Gunnison, **Blue Mesa Reservoir** is Colorado's largest body of water as well as the nation's largest kokanee salmon fishery. Downstream, the **Morrow Point Dam** and reservoir were primarily built to generate hydropower, whereas **Crystal Reservoir** maintains steady flows through the Black Canyon.

Blue Mesa Reservoir is the main destination for anglers and boaters, as well as hikers, campers, and bird-watchers. U.S. 50 parallels the reservoir's northern shore for about 16 miles before crossing the reservoir on **Middle Bridge** to the southern shoreline that has campgrounds, picnic areas, and boat launches. **Boating** and year-round **angling,** especially for trout and salmon, are the most popular activities.

The Gunnison and nearby rivers offer outstanding wade- and float-fishing. **Gunnison River Guides** (970/596-3054, http://gunnisonriverguides.com) offers guided trips.

The ranger-led, 1.5-hour **Morrow Point Boat Tour** (10am and 12:30pm Wed.-Mon. early June-early Sept., reservations required) tours the long, narrow upper reaches of the Black Canyon.

For boat permits and tour boat reservations, stop by **Elk Creek Visitor Center** (102 Elk Creek, Gunnison, 970/641-2337, 8am-6pm daily summer, reduced hours in fall-spring), 16 miles west of Gunnison.

GETTING THERE AND AROUND

AIR

Small regional airports include the **Montrose Regional Airport** (MTJ, 2100 Airport Rd., Montrose, 970/249-3203, wwwflymontrose.com), the **Gunnison-Crested Butte Airport** (GUC, 711 Rio Grande Ave., Crested Butte, 970/641-2304, www.gunnisoncounty.org), and the **Grand Junction Regional Airport** (GJT, 2828 Walker Field Dr., Grand Junction, 970/244-9100, www.gjairport.com). The largest international airport is **Denver International Airport** (DEN, 8500 Peña Blvd., Denver, 303/342-2000, www.flydenver.com).

CAR

To reach the South Rim, take U.S. 50 west from Gunnison for about 57 miles or east from Montrose for 15 miles. Turn onto Highway 347, which becomes the paved South Rim Road.

To access the North Rim, follow U.S. 50 east to the junction with Highway 92. Turn left onto Highway 92 and drive west and then north until just before the Crawford State Park entrance.

Turn left onto Black Canyon Road and follow signs for the next 12 miles to reach the park's North Rim. The paved road becomes gravel for seven miles in the park. Plan at least 2-3 hours to drive from rim to rim.

In winter (mid-Nov.-mid-Apr) the park roads close except for South Rim Road, which remains open from the visitors center to Gunnison Point. There is no public transit in the park.

SIDE TRIP TO GREAT SAND DUNES

230 miles / 4.5 hours

It's possible to link a visit to Black Canyon of the Gunnison with a side trip to Great Sand Dunes. Drive east on U.S. 50 for about 100 miles (2 hrs.) to the town of Gunnison. In Gunnison, follow Highway 144 south, turning east onto U.S. 285. At the T-junction with Highway 17, turn south to Lane 6 N. and head east to enter **Great Sand Dunes National Park.** Stop at the visitors center to check out the dunes through scopes on the back deck, and then walk the dunes or rent a sandboard to slide down their epic slopes.

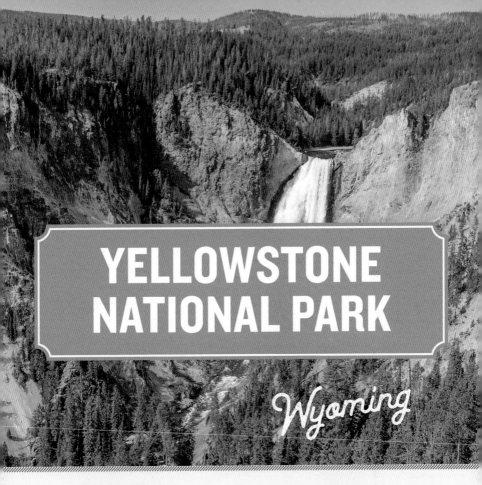

YELLOWSTONE NATIONAL PARK

Wyoming

PASSPORT STAMPS ▼▼▼

WEBSITE:
www.nps.gov/yell

PHONE NUMBER:
307/344-7381

VISITATION RANK:
6

WHY GO:
Watch wildlife, geysers, and volcanic wonders.

▲ LOWER FALLS

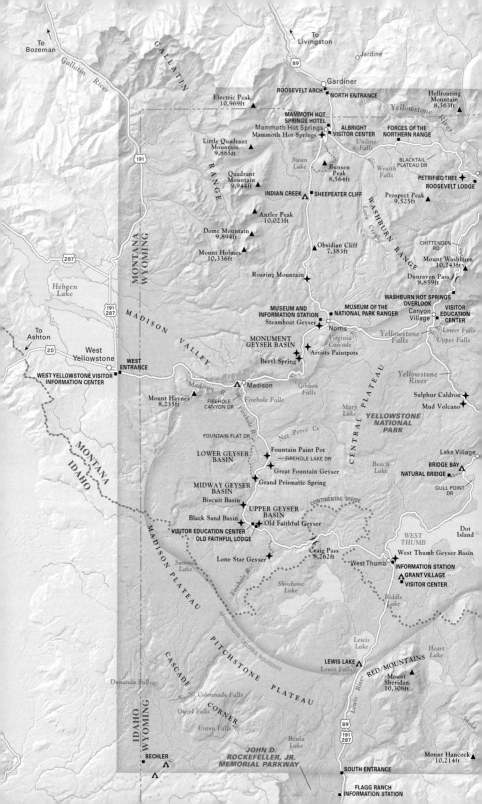

YELLOWSTONE
NATIONAL PARK

Buffalo Plateau

Cooke City

Silver Gate

Colter Pass
8,048ft

NORTHEAST ENTRANCE

To
Red Lodge

MONTANA
WYOMING

212

SLOUGH CREEK

Tower-
Roosevelt

Barronette
Peak
10,404ft

Abiathar
Peak
10,928ft

296

PEBBLE CREEK

Druid Peak
9,583ft

The Thunderer
10,554ft

Tower
Fall

TOWER FALL

YELLOWSTONE
ASSOCIATION
INSTITUTE

Mount
Norris
9,936ft

Cache
Mountain
9,596ft

A   B   S   A   R   O   K   A

LAMAR VALLEY

Soda Butte Creek

GRAND CANYON
OF THE YELLOWSTONE

APPROXIMATE CALDERA BOUNDARY

Lamar River

Parker Peak
10,203ft

R   A   N   G   E

White
Lake

Saddle
Mountain
10,670ft

Pollux Peak
11,067ft

Pelican Cone
9,643ft

Castor Peak
10,854ft

FISHING BRIDGE

LeHardys
Rapids

Pyramid Peak
10,497ft

MUSEUM AND
VISITOR CENTER

Steamboat
Point

Stevenson
Island

LAKE BUTTE
OVERLOOK

Cody Peak
10,267ft

Avalanche Peak
10,566ft

YELLOWSTONE
LAKE
surface elevation
7,733ft

Grizzly Peak
9,948ft

EAST ENTRANCE

To
Cody

20 14
16

Top Notch Peak
10,238ft

Sylvan Pass
8,530ft

Frank
Island

Mount Doane
10,656ft

Reservation
Peak
10,629ft

SOUTHEAST ARM

Mount
Stevenson
10,352ft

Mount
Langford
10,774ft

The Promontory

SOUTH ARM

Mount Schurz
11,139ft

Eagle Peak
11,358ft
(highest point
in the park)

Colter
Peak
10,683ft

Trail
Lake

TWO OCEAN PLATEAU

Table
Mountain
11,063ft

Yellowstone   River

Turret
Mountain
10,995ft

A   B   S   A   R   O   K   A

Overlook
Mountain
9,321ft

Mountain   Creek

CONTINENTAL DIVIDE

R   A   N   G   E

River

THOROFARE

0   5 mi

0   5 km

© AVALON TRAVEL

In **YELLOWSTONE NATIONAL PARK**, rumblings of a super-volcano boil to the surface—spewing, spitting, oozing, and bubbling. Steam rolls from vividly colored pools, muddy cauldrons burp smelly gases, and blasts of hot water shoot high into the air. This cantankerous landscape contains some of the world's most active hydrothermal features, gushing from spouters like iconic Old Faithful, while minerals create artsy travertine terraces at Mammoth Hot Springs.

Yellowstone resembles the early West, with herds of bison, elk, pronghorn, and bighorn sheep. Bear and bison jams on the roads are common—so many wild animals cluster in Lamar Valley that it has gained the nickname of "America's Serengeti." It's the place to hear the squawk of sandhill cranes and watch wolf pups tumble in play.

Even with its volcanic caldera and wildlife, Yellowstone has no better claim than America's first national park—except perhaps that it is also the world's first national park.

PLANNING YOUR TIME

Yellowstone National Park tucks into the northwest corner of Wyoming, its north and west borders spilling over into Montana and Idaho.

Summer (June-Aug.) and **winter** (Dec.-mid-Mar.) are high seasons in the park. Summer sees the most visitors, with July and August luring the biggest crowds. All park lodges, campgrounds, and visitors centers are open, as are most park roads. Temperatures range 60-80°F, depending on elevation, and afternoon thundershowers are common.

In **winter,** deep snows turn the park white. Park roads close (early Nov.-late Apr.), except for the road between Yellowstone's North and Northeast Entrances. Tours are via guided snowcoaches or snowmobiles (mid-Dec.-early Mar.). Lodging is available at Mammoth Hot Springs and Old Faithful.

Spring (Mar.-May) offers car-free bicycling on park roads that won't open to vehicles until late April or May. Come in May for bison calving season, or in June to spot bighorn sheep ewes with newborn lambs and grizzly bears foraging along Yellowstone Lake. By May, most park roads start to open and visitor services return. Weather bounces between blue skies, rain, and snow.

In **fall** (Sept.-Nov.), cooler days yield pleasant hiking with fewer crowds. Sporadic snowstorms can temporarily close park roads until winter descends in early November. Services are limited.

To guarantee lodging, camping, tour, or dinner reservations any time of year, make reservations **13 months in advance.**

ENTRANCES AND FEES

The entrance fee is $35 per vehicle ($30 motorcycle, $20 individual; Grand Teton joint pass: $70 per vehicle) and is good for seven days. Yellowstone has five entrance stations; several are closed in winter. Drive times between entrances can take several hours.

North Entrance (U.S. 89, near Gardiner, MT) is open year-round and provides the closest access to Mammoth Hot Springs.

Northeast Entrance (Hwy. 212, west of Silver Gate, MT) is open year-round and links the Beartooth Highway with the Lamar Valley. Winter snow shuts the roads east of Cooke City, but access remains open between the park entrance and Cooke City.

ONE DAY IN YELLOWSTONE

With 2.2 million acres and half of the world's geothermal features, where should you focus your limited time in Yellowstone? Drive the Grand Loop Road and watch for geysers, wildlife, and waterfalls. Stop to walk the boardwalks in **Midway Geyser Basin** and **Upper Geyser Basin** before catching **Old Faithful** as it erupts. Then cruise across the Continental Divide to drive along the shore of **Lake Yellowstone** into **Hayden Valley** to see bison and elk. Stop at **Artist Point** to peer into the **Grand Canyon of the Yellowstone** from its South Rim or **Lookout Point** on the North Rim.

West Entrance (Hwy. 20, West Yellowstone, MT), the busiest entrance in the park, is open mid-April to early November. In winter, it admits only snowcoaches and snowmobiles.

East Entrance (U.S. 20), between Fishing Bridge and Cody, Wyoming, is open mid-May to early November.

South Entrance (U.S. 89/191/287), on the border between Yellowstone and Grand Teton, is open mid-May to early November. In winter, it admits only snowcoaches and snowmobiles.

VISITORS CENTERS

The **West Yellowstone Visitor Information Center** (30 Yellowstone Ave., West Yellowstone, 307/344-2876, 8am-8pm daily late May-early Sept., 8am-4pm daily mid-Dec.-late Apr., spring, and fall) has information and **backcountry permits** (8am-4:30pm daily

June-Aug.). Inside the park, four visitors centers offer exhibits, park maps, bookstores, road conditions, trail information, Junior Ranger Program booklets, and naturalist talks and walks.

Old Faithful Visitor Center

Stop at the **Old Faithful Visitor Education Center** (307/344-2751, 8am-8pm daily late Apr.-early Nov., 9am-5pm daily mid-Dec.-Feb., hours vary in spring and fall) to learn about geysers, hot springs, mud pots, and fumaroles. Geyser eruption predictions are available, and the theater rotates park films.

Two information stations are located on the park road between Mammoth Hot Springs and Old Faithful:

Madison Information Station (307/344-2821, 9am-6pm daily late May-early Sept.) is in a historic cabin overlooking the Madison River. It hosts Junior Ranger programs.

OLD FAITHFUL VISITOR EDUCATION CENTER

AVOID THE CROWDS

Avoid July, which sees the heaviest visitation.

Visit in **June** or **September** when crowds thin in comparison to midsummer, in **May** for newborn bison and elk calves, or in **October** for fall colors, bear activity, and elk bugling.

Go in **winter** for the beauty of the icy landscape and prolific steam in geyser basins.

Avoid midday (10am-4pm), when most of the crowds are out in force. Utilize the **early morning** and **late afternoon-evening** hours instead.

Hit **Midway** and the **Lower Geyser Basins** in early morning en route to Norris Geyser Basin **by 10am.**

Visit the **Upper Geyser Basin** (Old Faithful, Black Sands, Biscuit) at **sunset** (8pm-9:30pm in summer).

Visit Old Faithful at sunrise (5am-6:30am in summer).

Go wildlife-watching in the **morning** and **evening,** when animals are more active.

Park early. Plan to be at your trailhead parking lot by **8am-9am** or earlier.

Stop at picnic areas for restroom breaks; geyser basins and Canyon Village restrooms usually have lengthy lines.

Norris Geyser Basin Museum & Information Station (307/344-2812, 9am-6pm daily late May-Sept., spring, and fall) has exhibits and ranger-led walks into the nearby geyser basin.

Mammoth Visitor Center

Built as the bachelor officers' quarters by the U.S. Army in 1909, the **Albright (Mammoth) Visitor Center** (Mammoth Hot Springs, 307/344-2263, 8am-7pm daily June-Sept., 9am-5pm daily Oct.-May) has exhibits on historic Fort Yellowstone. It also has a **backcountry office** (8am-4:30pm daily June-Aug.) with permits for backcountry camping, boating, and fishing.

Canyon Visitor Education Center

Canyon Visitor Education Center (Canyon Village, 307/344-2550, 8am-8pm daily May-mid-Oct.) features films, murals, and exhibits and contains a **backcountry office** (8am-4:30pm daily June-Aug.).

Fishing Bridge Visitor Center

Fishing Bridge Visitor Center (Yellowstone Lake, 307/344-2450, 8am-7pm daily late May-early Oct.) showcases bird and waterfowl specimens and has an outdoor amphitheater for naturalist presentations.

Grant Visitor Center

Grant Visitor Center (Grant Village, 307/344-2650, 8am-7pm daily late May-early Oct.) has exhibits and a park film. Just north of Grant Village is the tiny **West Thumb Information Center** (307/344-2876, 9am-5pm daily late May-early Oct.), which has a few exhibits about the geyser basin.

FISHING BRIDGE

Top ❸

① MARVEL AT OLD FAITHFUL

When **Old Faithful Geyser** erupts, it shoots up to 8,400 gallons of hot water as high as 185 feet. It's one of the most regular geysers in the park, erupting every 90 minutes. Often the geyser sputters for 20 minutes before each eruption, which lasts a few minutes. In summer, massive crowds fill the benches surrounding the geyser 30 minutes in advance.

OLD FAITHFUL GEYSER

Old Faithful is located behind the Old Faithful Visitor Education Center, which has exhibits that explain the geyser's inner workings. Eruption times are posted at the visitors center or on the park's geyser app.

② WATCH WILDLIFE

Wildlife-watching is equally as captivating as watching geysers blow. The massive **Lamar Valley** is America's Serengeti thanks to its hefty numbers of abundant wildlife. The Lamar River flows through the sagebrush valley where immense herds of **bison** feed. Between herds, look for **pronghorn, bighorn sheep, elk, bears, coyotes,** and **wolves.** In late fall, listen for bighorn sheep butting heads or elk bugling.

Sliced by the Yellowstone River, the bucolic **Hayden Valley** contains prime wildlife-watching. Look for **coyotes, moose, elk, raptors, grizzly bears, trumpeter swans, wolves,** and hordes of **Canada geese.**

Along the **Madison River,** pullouts permit viewing of **bison, elk, deer,** and **raptors.** In fall, bull elk often round up harems along the river, with the bulls' bugling echoing across the valley.

③ GAZE INTO THE GRAND CANYON OF THE YELLOWSTONE

The Yellowstone River cuts a colorful swath 1,000 feet deep and 0.75 mile wide through the **Grand Canyon of the Yellowstone.** The river crashes over the **Upper Falls** before thundering down the **Lower Falls,** the park's tallest and most famous waterfall. Three roads access overlooks surrounding the 20-mile-long canyon. Trails and stairways plunge into the canyon for closer views (but can require strenuous return climbs).

GRAND CANYON OF THE YELLOWSTONE

SIGHTS

MAMMOTH HOT SPRINGS

Raised boardwalks and stairways loop through the Mammoth Hot Springs, where sulfur fills the air and limestone creates travertine terraces and calcium carbonate sculptures.

To explore the **Lower Terraces**, park and stroll the boardwalk to **Liberty Cap,** a 37-foot-tall dormant hot springs cone, then visit **Palette Spring,** where orange and brown thermophiles color the sinter. The main boardwalk circles the striking travertine sculptures of **Minerva Terrace. Cleopatra, Mound,** and **Jupiter Terraces** flank the stairs to the overlook at the Upper Terrace Drive parking lot. To the left, a boardwalk leads to brilliant orange and white **Canary Spring.** You can continue exploring the Upper Terrace on foot or return to your car to drive the loop road.

Mammoth's Upper Terraces can be toured along the one-way **Upper Terrace Drive** (0.75 mile, mid-May-early Nov.). The road snakes through unique formations created from once-active hydrothermal features, such as **Orange Spring Mound.**

Three parking lots access the lower terraces south of Mammoth Village. The entrance to Upper Terrace Drive is

LIBERTY CAP

two miles south of Mammoth Village on the road toward Norris.

Fort Yellowstone

In the pre-National Park Service decades, the village of Mammoth was **Fort Yellowstone**, which housed the

▼ MAMMOTH TERRACES

ROOSEVELT ARCH

U.S. Army unit that managed the park. A self-guided walking tour visits the streets lined with buildings erected by the army in 1891-1916. The Albright Visitor Center was once the **Bachelor Officers' Quarters.** Across the way, the sagebrush-covered **parade ground** often contains bison or elk. The tour takes in the row of red-roofed **officers' quarters,** as well as a **granary, chapel, hospital, blacksmith shop,** and **stables.**

Roosevelt Arch

In Gardiner, the original park entrance road crosses under the stone-and-mortar **Roosevelt Arch** dedicated to President Theodore Roosevelt, who laid the cornerstone in 1903. Passenger vehicles can drive through the narrow entrance, or you can park your car on Park Street to walk through the arch and **Arch Park.**

TOWER FALL

Tower Fall (2.3 miles south of Roosevelt Jct.) plunges 132 feet from its brink between rhyolite spires, dropping from a hanging valley into a ribbon that spews in a long freefall. An overlook near the Tower Fall parking lot offers the best view.

NORRIS GEYSER BASIN

Norris Geyser Basin is the hottest basin, measuring 459°F at 1,087 feet below the surface. With features 115,000 years old, it is also the oldest geothermal basin. Interpretive boardwalks and paths tour two hydrothermal basins.

TOWER FALL

Back Basin

Back Basin (1.5 mi. rt.) houses **Emerald Spring,** its blue color the product of yellow sulfur minerals, near-boiling water, and colorful thermophiles. Unpredictable **Steamboat Geyser** shoots small bursts of water up to 40 feet in the air. The geyser links underground to the blue-green **Cistern Spring.** After the red-orange-rimmed pool of **Echinus Geyser,** the world's largest acidic geyser, the loop passes fumaroles, hot springs, mud pots, and roiling **Porkchop Geyser** to finish near **Palpitator Spring.** Continue north past **Minute** and **Monarch Geysers** to connect with the Porcelain Basin.

Porcelain Basin

The acidic **Porcelain Basin,** which contains the park's highest concentration of silica, has turquoise **Crackling Lake** bubbling along its edges. While **Pinwheel Geyser** is defunct, active **Whirligig Geyser** spills into a stream of orange iron oxide and green thermophiles. **Hurricane Vent** roars steam, and **Porcelain Springs** contains blue pools.

Museum of the National Park Ranger

Volunteer retired rangers staff the tiny **Museum of the National Park Ranger** (Norris Campground, 307/344-7353, 9am-5pm daily late May-Sept., free). It houses a historical photo collection of park rangers and shows a movie about the National Park Service.

GEYSER BASINS

South of Madison Junction, the Lower and Midway Geyser Basins hold a wide variety of geothermal sights.

A 0.5-mile interpretive boardwalk loops around **Fountain Paint Pot** (8 mi. south of Madison Jct.) in the Lower Geyser Basin. It includes all four hydrothermal features: geysers, mud pots, hot springs, and fumaroles.

The one-way **Firehole Lake Drive** (9.3 mi. south of Madison Jct.) passes eight thermal features. Brown **Firehole Lake** is the road's largest hot spring. **Great Fountain Geyser** shoots 75-220 feet high every 10-14 hours.

A 0.7-mile boardwalk loop tours **Midway Geyser Basin** (10 mi. south of Madison Jct.). The basin has four hydrothermal features, including the two largest hot springs in Yellowstone. The dormant crater of **Excelsior Geyser** contains a steaming turquoise pool spilling 4,050 gallons of water per minute into the Firehole River.

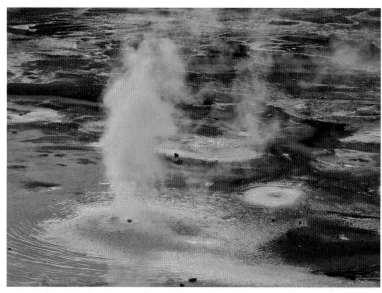

PORCELAIN SPRINGS, NORRIS GEYSER BASIN

GRAND PRISMATIC SPRING

Grand Prismatic Spring

At 370 feet across and 121 feet deep, **Grand Prismatic Spring** is the third-largest hot spring in the world. Sit on the benches to enjoy the glorious hues: fiery arms of orange, gold, and brown thermophiles radiate in a full circle from the yellow-rimmed, blue hot pool.

OLD FAITHFUL AREA

Old Faithful Inn

Built in 1903-1904, **Old Faithful Inn** is worthy of wows. With a steep-pitched roof and gabled dormers, the lobby vaults five stories high. It centers on an 85-foot-tall stone fireplace and hand-crafted clock built from wood, copper, and iron. Walk around the lobby balcony to absorb the historical intricacies, and watch Old Faithful Geyser erupt from the deck. Daily **tours** (hours vary, daily early May-early Oct., free) are available.

Upper Geyser Basin

The Upper Geyser Basin draws thousands of visitors each summer day. Maps at the visitors center aid in navigating its loops.

From the Old Faithful viewing area behind the visitors center, cross the Firehole River to reach **Geyser Hill,** where **Beehive Geyser** shoots 200 feet. The smaller **Anemone** and **Plume Geysers** erupt regularly, the first about every 10 minutes and the second hourly. Clear-blue **Heart Spring** sits near the **Lion Geyser Group,** a family of sputtering geysers: Little Cub, Big Cub, Lioness, and Lion. Turn right to admire the radiant color and ledges of **Doublet Pool,** while **Solitary Geyser** surges with short, six-foot bursts every 4-8 minutes.

The Firehole River Loop crosses two bridges to see famous hot pools. Start at **Castle Geyser,** a cone geyser built into the largest sinter formation in the world. Continue north to reach **Grand Geyser,** a fountain geyser that throws water 200 feet skyward. Just north are a pair of interconnected hot springs, **Beauty Pool** and **Chromatic Pool.**

As the boardwalk crosses the river again, erratic **Giant Geyser** might throw water up 300 feet. At the junction with the paved trail, **Grotto Geyser** squirts water from its odd-shaped cone. Continue north to **Riverside**

MORNING GLORY POOL, UPPER GEYSER BASIN

Geyser, which shoots an arc of water over the river at six-hour intervals. The striking green, orange, and yellow **Morning Glory Pool** marks the turnaround point.

Daisy Geyser Basin loops through unique features. **Daisy Geyser** erupts every 2-3 hours with water spewing out to 75 feet, and **Punch Bowl** boils in its 12-foot-diameter raised sinter bowl.

Biscuit Basin

Biscuit Basin (2 mi. north of Old Faithful) holds a collection of smaller geothermal features, accessed by a 0.7-mile boardwalk. The boardwalk tours past **Black Opal Pool, Wall Pool,** and **Sapphire Pool.** The last of these transformed from a geyser into a hot pool of crystal-clear 200-degree blue water.

Highlights on the upper loop include the yellow **Mustard Spring** and **Jewel Geyser,** which shoots water up to 20 feet in the air about every 10 minutes.

Black Sand Basin

Black Sand Basin (0.5 mi. northwest of Old Faithful) has a 0.6-mile boardwalk for viewing **Cliff Geyser** blowing water up to 40 feet from a small crater. One spur goes to **Sunset Lake,** named for its yellow-orange rim, and the other to see **Emerald Pool,** colored from algae. Walk a tiny spur off the north corner of the parking lot to see **Opalescent Pool,** fed by the almost constantly erupting **Spouter Geyser**.

▼ PUNCH BOWL, UPPER GEYSER BASIN

BISCUIT BASIN

GRAND CANYON OF THE YELLOWSTONE

North Rim

The one-way **North Rim Drive** (1.2 mi. south of Canyon Jct.) visits four signed overlooks of the canyon and Yellowstone River. The first stop is **Brink of the Lower Falls,** where a paved walkway with stairs leads to an overlook. The trail plummets 357 feet down switchbacks to a platform at the lip where you can feel the pounding water underfoot. Next, stop at **Lookout Point** via a quick ascent to an overlook of the falls, the canyon, and an osprey nest. Just before the overlook, a 0.4-mile trail and wood stairway drops 315 feet to **Red Rock Point,** a perch closer to the Lower Falls. The third stop on North Rim Drive is **Grand View Overlook,** accessed by a paved descent of 127 feet. Near the end of North Rim Drive, turn right onto the two-lane road to reach **Inspiration Point** for a more distant view up the canyon.

From the **Brink of the Upper Falls Road** (0.4 mi. south of North Rim Dr.), a short walk follows the river upstream. Turn left for a short descent to a viewing platform. The Upper Falls mesmerizes with a powerful 109-foot hurtle downstream.

South Rim

From **South Rim Drive** (1 mi. south of Canyon Jct.), cross the Chittenden Bridge to two parking areas. At **Uncle Tom's Point,** follow the paved walkway to the **Upper Falls** viewpoint as it faces the tall waterfall. North of the parking lot, a trail drops 385 feet of switchbacks and 328 steel stairs to **Uncle Tom's Overlook,** a small platform yielding the closest view of the **Lower Falls.** South Rim Drive terminates at the parking lot for **Artist Point.** An easy paved walkway leads to the classic view of the canyon and Lower Falls.

YELLOWSTONE LAKE

Yellowstone Lake is the largest water body in Yellowstone National Park and the largest high-elevation freshwater lake in North America. Located partly inside the Yellowstone Caldera, the northern section of the lake has its origins in volcanic activity and lava flows—hence **Steamboat Springs**—while the southern arms formed from glaciation. The lake's thermal activity includes geysers, fumaroles, and hot springs. Roads tour the western and northern shores, with multiple picnic areas for access.

LOWER FALLS, GRAND CANYON OF THE YELLOWSTONE

WEST THUMB GEYSER BASIN

Fishing Bridge

Where the Yellowstone River exits Yellowstone Lake, the original log **Fishing Bridge** was erected over the waterway in 1902. The current bridge replaced it in 1937 with walkways on both sides for seeing spawning cutthroat trout.

West Thumb Geyser Basin

On Yellowstone Lake, **West Thumb Geyser Basin** (northeast of West Thumb Jct.) is a smaller caldera within the larger Yellowstone Caldera. The geyser basin dumps more than 3,100 gallons of hot water daily into the lake and contains three geysers and 11 hot springs, plus fumaroles and mud pots. Two boardwalk loops (0.8 mi.) go to see **Fishing Cone**, where visitors once cooked their fish, and **Twin Geyser**, whose two vents shoot water up to 75 feet. The turquoise and emerald **Abyss Pool** may be one of the deepest in the park.

SCENIC DRIVES
GRAND LOOP ROAD

Most drivers split the 142-mile **Grand Loop Road** into 2-3 days, as a one-day push (5-8 hrs.) limits the amount of time to stop at sights. Different segments open annually late April through late May. Access the loop from the North Entrance road at Gardiner, Montana, and begin by driving through the historic **Roosevelt Arch** to enter Yellowstone.

At **Mammoth Hot Springs**, join the Grand Loop Road (U.S. 89) heading south toward **Norris, Madison Junction,** and **Old Faithful** (51 mi., 2 hrs., late Apr.-early Nov.). The road climbs south through hoodoos and crawls along the cliffs of **Golden Gate** before topping out at **Swan Lake Flat**. It passes **Obsidian Cliff,** a site of geological and Native American significance, and hissing **Roaring Mountain**, pumping out steam. After passing **Norris Geyser Basin**, a hotbed of geothermal activity, the road drops into the supervolcano caldera, passing blue **Beryl Springs** and **Gibbon Falls** to reach Madison Junction. From this low point in the caldera, begin climbing along the **Firehole River** toward the geyser basins. You'll reach **Lower Geyser Basin** first, followed by **Midway**, and then the **Upper Geyser Basin**, home to **Old Faithful Geyser** and the historic **Old Faithful Inn**.

From the geyser basins, the road bounces eastward twice over the Continental Divide to **West Thumb Junction** (17 mi., 45 min., mid-May-early Nov.). Turn left to stop at **West Thumb Geyser Basin**.

After West Thumb, aim north toward **Canyon Village** (37 mi., 1.5 hrs., mid-May-early Nov.). Follow the shoreline of **Lake Yellowstone**, passing **Bridge Bay** and **Lake Village**, which houses the historic **Lake Yellowstone Hotel**. After the junction at **Fishing Bridge**, the road hugs the **Yellowstone River** flowing north to sulfur-smelling **Mud Volcano** and wildlife-rich **Hayden Valley**, where you may get caught in a bison jam. At **Grand Canyon of the Yellowstone**, turn off on the South Rim Drive to stop at **Artist Point** before continuing to Canyon Junction.

At Canyon Junction, climb north over **Dunraven Pass** and drop through curves down to **Tower Fall** and **Tower-Roosevelt Junction** (19 mi., 45 min., late May-early Nov.). You can add on a spur out to Lamar Valley for wildlife-watching. Then, continue west to return to **Mammoth Hot Springs** (18 mi., 45 min., year-round). Take in **Petrified Tree** and **Undine Falls** before closing the loop.

WRAITH FALLS

FIREHOLE CANYON DRIVE

Firehole Canyon Drive (0.5 mi. south of Madison Jct., open mid-Apr.-early Nov.) cuts off on the west side of the Grand Loop Road. This steep and narrow one-way road goes to a scenic overlook of the 40-foot **Firehole Falls** and the area's 800-foot-thick lava flows.

FOUNTAIN FLAT DRIVE

Fountain Flat Drive (10.4 mi. south of Madison Jct., open late May-early Nov.) is a good place for **wildlife-watching**, particularly for elk and bison in June. Enjoy the Firehole River from the **Nez Perce Picnic Area**.

HIKING
MAMMOTH HOT SPRINGS
Bunsen Peak and Osprey Falls

From the Old Bunsen Peak Road Trailhead (4.8 mi. south of Mammoth) the trail to **Bunsen Peak** (4.2 mi. rt., 3 hrs., strenuous) winds back and forth up the mountain, passing Cathedral Rock en route. Steep switchbacks lead across talus slopes to the 8,564-foot summit. Return the way you came, or drop eastward 1.4 steep miles to the Old Bunsen Peak Road, turning right to circle three gentle miles around the peak's base (6.6 mi. rt., 4 hrs.). Lengthen the loop with a descent and return climb to 150-foot **Osprey Falls** (11.6 mi. rt., 7 hrs.) on the Gardner River.

Wraith Falls

The trail to **Wraith Falls** (0.8 mi. rt., 1 hr., easy) travels through a sagebrush-scented meadow to 79-foot Wraith Falls as it cascades down a wide-angled rock face squeezed into a canyon.

TOWER-ROOSEVELT
Lost Lake Loop

Hikers have plenty of things to see on the **Lost Lake Loop** (4 mi. rt., 2 hrs., moderate): a waterfall, the small lake, Petrified Tree, and views of the Absaroka Mountains. From Roosevelt Lodge, take the left spur to the **Lost Creek Falls Trail** to climb a pine-shaded ravine to the 40-foot falls. Return to the junction and continue on **Lost Lake Trail**

Best Hike

GRAND PRISMATIC OVERLOOK AND FAIRY FALLS

DISTANCE: 1.5 or 6.8 miles round-trip
DURATION: 1 or 3 hours
ELEVATION CHANGE: 52 or 129 feet
EFFORT: easy
TRAILHEAD: Fairy Falls parking area

At 197 feet, Fairy Falls is the park's fourth-highest waterfall, and it provides a scenic year-round destination for hikers, bikers, and skiers. In 2017, a spur trail added an overlook of Grand Prismatic Spring to see the cobalt hot spring and fiery arms of thermophiles. The trail is closed in spring until late May because of bear activity.

From **Fairy Falls Trailhead,** cross the Firehole River and hike the abandoned road. To climb to the new overlook of **Grand Prismatic Spring** (1.5 mi. rt.), take the signed 0.5-mile spur to ascend 105 feet in elevation to the platform. After returning to the trail, the route westward reaches the junction with the **Fairy Falls Trail** at 1.4 miles. Turning west, hike 1.5 miles through a young lodgepole forest to the base of the falls. In summer, the falls plunge ribbon-like into a pool; in winter, it's an ice sculpture. With the spur to Grand Prismatic Overlook, the round-trip distance is 6.8 miles to the falls.

▲ FAIRY FALLS

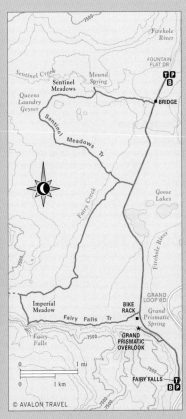

TROUT LAKE TRAIL

to reach the bridge at the lake's outlet. The trail rims the lake until it heads west through another ravine to **Petrified Tree.** From the Petrified Tree parking lot, the trail mounts a hill to the east before dropping behind Tower Ranger Station and back to Roosevelt Lodge.

Trout Lake

Trout Lake (1.2 mi. rt., 1.5 hrs., strenuous) is an idyllic little lake sitting at about 7,000 feet in elevation in the Absaroka Mountains. From the trailhead (Northeast Entrance Rd.) the path catapults vertically through a Douglas fir forest to circle the lake.

OLD FAITHFUL AREA

For a different vantage point of Old Faithful, circle the 0.7-mile loop around the geyser or climb to **Observation Point** (1.2 mi. rt.).

Lone Star Geyser

Lone Star Geyser (4.8 mi. rt., 3 hrs., easy) is tucked away from the busy Upper Geyser Basin. The 12-foot-tall pink and gray sinter cone spouts up to 40 feet in the air, erupting about every three hours with spurts lasting 30 minutes. From the Lone Star Geyser Trailhead (2.5 miles east of Old Faithful), walk south along the old asphalt service road through conifers along the meandering Firehole River. After a large meadow (scout for wildlife), ascend a gentle hill to the geyser basin.

Mystic Falls

From the Biscuit Basin parking lot, a boardwalk loop provides access to the trailhead for **Mystic Falls** (2 mi. rt., 1 hr., moderate). Turn right and hike 0.4 mile to a junction. Take the left fork and ascend 0.5 mile to Mystic Falls, a 70-foot waterfall that feeds a series of cascades.

MYSTIC FALLS

LONE STAR GEYSER

BIKING GRAND LOOP ROAD

GRAND CANYON OF THE YELLOWSTONE

Mount Washburn Lookout

At 10,243 feet, the **Mount Washburn Lookout** yields a panoramic 360-degree view from the highest peak in Yellowstone. Two strenuous trails climb in a steady plod on former roads to the summit. From Dunraven Pass (5.4 mi. north of Canyon Jct.), the **Dunraven Pass Trail** (6.4 mi. rt., 4 hrs.) traverses meadows and forest to crest a ridge, where a scenic walk finishes with a 360-degree circle to Mount Washburn Lookout. From the end of Chittenden Road (10.3 mi. north of Canyon Jct.), the steeper **Chittenden Trail** (5.4 mi. rt., 4 hrs., bikes permitted) has a bit more elevation gain in its meadowed switchbacks up the slope to the summit.

RECREATION

BACKPACKING

Backpackers must obtain **permits** ($3 pp) in person 48 hours in advance from the backcountry offices. To guarantee a trip, use the advanced reservation application online (submit starting Jan. 1, $25).

Black Canyon of the Yellowstone

Point-to-point backpacking trips in the **Black Canyon of the Yellowstone** (16.5 mi., 3 days) go from **Hellroaring Creek Trailhead** to **Blacktail Creek Trailhead.** Choose from 19 campsites on the route; the best flank the Yellowstone River. With lower elevation, this backpack trip is usually viable early May-early November.

Bechler River Trail

In the park's remote southwest, the **Bechler River Trail** (30 mi., 3-5 days) descends into Bechler River Canyon and the land of waterfalls. The point-to-point trail leads from the Lone Star Geyser Trailhead to the Bechler Ranger Station, with the core canyon campsites at Ouzel, Colonnade, and Albright Falls. Due to annual flooding, permit reservations are only available from July 15 onward. In addition to the hike, plan eight hours for the shuttle to the trailhead and back.

BIKING

In spring (late Mar.-mid-Apr.), roads between Mammoth and West Yellowstone open to bicyclists but remain closed to vehicles for quiet, car-free cycling. Bring your own bike, as rentals are not available.

Several side roads permit bikes in both directions while cars are limited to one-way travel. The **Old Gardiner Road** (10 mi. rt.) connects Gardiner with Mammoth Hot Springs. **Blacktail Plateau Drive** (12 mi. rt.) rolls through higher-elevation terrain with wildlife.

Only a handful of trails allow bikes, including Lone Star Geyser, Fountain Freight Road, and Old Faithful to Morning Glory Pool. In Gardiner, the level, kid-friendly **old rail trail** (10 mi. rt.) parallels the Yellowstone River. More challenging, the **Chittenden Trail** (5.4 mi. rt.) climbs to Mount Washburn Lookout.

HORSEBACK RIDING

Wranglers lead one-hour and two-hour **Saddle Up** (Xanterra, 307/344-7311, www.yellowstonenationalparklodges. com, daily June-early Sept.) horseback tours from the corrals at Roosevelt and Canyon.

BOATING AND FISHING

Yellowstone Lake attracts boaters for sightseeing, cruising, angling, sailing, and paddling. **Bridge Bay Marina** (Xanterra, 307/344-7311, www.yellowstonenationalparklodges.com, late May-Oct. for boat launch, daily mid-June-early Sept.) has a boat launch, marina services, and rentals. Located on the West Thumb, **Grant Village Marina** (mid-June-Oct.) has a boat launch, but no services.

In Yellowstone, fly-fishing is the epitome of fishing. Inside the park, the **Firehole, Madison,** and lower **Gibbon Rivers** offer prime fly-fishing for rainbow and brown trout. Portions of the **Yellowstone River** offer an outstanding trout fly-fishery with parts accessible from Grand Loop Road. **Yellowstone Lake** and **Lewis Lake** work for shoreline fishing, float-tube fishing, spin-casting, fly-fishing, and fishing from motorboats or rowboats.

WINTER SPORTS

In winter (mid-Dec.-early Mar.), visitors can explore groomed trails on snowshoes or cross-country skis and tour the snow-buried roads of Yellowstone in heated snowcoaches. Led by interpretive guides, snowcoaches stop at sights for photos and wildlife. Tours depart from **Mammoth Hot Springs** and **Old Faithful Snow Lodge** (reservations 307/344-7311, www.yellowstonenationalparklodges.com) and from companies in West Yellowstone, Gardiner, and Flagg Ranch. Reservations are required. Guided snowmobile tours are also available.

ROOSEVELT CORRALS

OLD FAITHFUL INN

WHERE TO STAY
INSIDE THE PARK

Make **reservations** (Xanterra, 307/344-7311, www.yellowstonenationalparklodges.com) for lodges, restaurants, and campgrounds **13 months in advance**. In winter, **dinner reservations** are required at Mammoth Hotel Dining Room and Snow Lodge.

In summer, reservations are mandatory for the Old West Dinner Cookout and are highly recommended for Old Faithful Inn, M66 Grill at Canyon Village, Grant Village Dining Room, and Lake Hotel Dining Room.

Mammoth Hot Springs

Mammoth Hot Springs Hotel (1 Grand Loop Rd., late Apr.-mid-Oct. and mid-Dec.-early Mar., from $100) is a large complex with almost 100 hotel rooms and 125 cabins. In winter, Mammoth is the only hotel in the park accessible by private vehicle. Nearby eateries include the **Mammoth Hotel Dining Room** (breakfast 6:30am-10am, lunch 11:30am-2:30pm early May-early Oct. and late Dec.-early Mar., dinner 5pm-10pm early May-early Oct., 5:30pm-8pm or 9pm

daily late Dec.-early Mar.) and **Mammoth Terrace Grill** (7am-9pm daily late Apr.-mid-Oct., hours vary seasonally).

Tower-Roosevelt

Roosevelt Lodge and Cabins (Grand Loop Rd., early June-early Sept., from $100) has simple Roughrider cabins with wood-burning stoves for heat, but no bathrooms. Frontier cabins come with an en suite toilet and shower. The 1920s lodge has a **dining room** (7am-10am and 11:30am-9:30pm daily early June-Sept.).

At the **Old West Dinner Cookout** (early June-mid-Sept.), guests saddle up or ride a wagon from the Roosevelt Corrals to the cookout at Yancy's Hole. Reservations are required.

Old Faithful Area

The most requested lodge in the park, **Old Faithful Inn** (early May-mid-Oct., from $150) is a National Historic Landmark. The main log lodge was built in 1903-1904, with the east wing added in 1913-1914 and west wing in 1927-1928. The 327-room inn has 10 room styles ranging from historic to modern. The main log lodge contains an immense lobby, the **Dining Room** (6:30am-10am, 11:30am-2:30pm, and 4:30pm-10pm daily in summer), the **Bear Pit Lounge** (11:30am-11pm), and the **Bear Paw Deli** (6:30am-6pm).

Old Faithful Lodge (mid-May-early Oct., from $100) is closest to Old Faithful Geyser, but in a quieter location. There are 96 simple and small motel-style rooms in rustic duplex or fourplex cabins with tiny windows and no porches. Some rooms have private baths; others share a communal bathroom and shower cabin. Inside, the huge stone-and-log lodge has a **Bake Shop** (6:30am-10pm daily May-Sept., 6:30am-8pm daily mid-late Sept.) and a **cafeteria** (11am-9pm daily, shorter hours in spring and fall).

Snow Lodge (late Apr.-mid-Oct. from $123, mid-Dec.-Feb. from $150) is the most modern hotel; the 134 rooms are larger and have modern-style bathrooms and furnishings. Cabins are located a short walk from the lodge. Restaurants include the **Obsidian Dining Room** (breakfast 6:30am-10:30am daily early May-mid-Oct., 6:30am-10am daily mid-Dec.-Feb., lunch 11:30am-3pm mid-Dec.-Feb., dinner 5pm-10:30pm daily May-mid-Oct., 5pm-9:30pm daily mid-Dec.-Feb.) and the **Geyser Grill** (8am-9pm daily in summer, shorter hours spring and fall, 10:30am-3:30pm daily in winter), plus a lounge.

PRONGHORN

Canyon Village

Canyon Lodge and Cabins (late May-late Sept., from $175) is the largest facility in the park and has the newest lodgings. Accommodations include hotel rooms in multistory lodges and motel-style rooms in cabins. The complex includes the **Canyon Lodge M66 Bar and Grill** (6:30am-10am, 11:30am-2pm, and 4:30pm-10pm daily early June-late Sept.), **Canyon Lodge Eatery** (6:30am-10:30am and 11:30am-9:30pm daily early June-early Oct.), the **Canyon Lodge Cafe** (6am-10pm daily June-early Sept.), and a visitors center.

Yellowstone Lake

Built in 1891, **Lake Yellowstone Hotel and Cabins** (mid-May-early Oct., from $190) is a striking Colonial-style structure facing the lake. A National Historic Landmark, the complex has three accommodations types: hotel rooms and suites in the historic lodge, hotel rooms in an older lodge, and cabins. Restaurants include a **Dining Room** (6:30am-10:30am, 11:30am-2:30pm, and 5pm-10pm daily), a bar, and a deli.

Set back from the shore of Yellowstone Lake, **Lake Lodge Cabins** (early June-late Sept., from $95) is a complex of rustic buildings. The single-floor, log Lake Lodge houses a lobby with two stonework fireplaces, a **cafeteria** (6:30am-9:30pm daily early June-late Sept.), and a bar. Behind the lodge, 186 heated cabins come in three styles, all with private baths.

At the southern end of West Thumb, **Grant Village Lodge** (Grant Village, late May-late Sept., from $255) is a collection of six buildings with hotel rooms. Built in 1984, each two-story building contains 50 rooms in two styles and with private baths. The **Dining Room** (6:30am-10am, 11:30am-2:30pm, and 5pm-10pm daily late May-Sept.) overlooks the lake. A short walk leads to the **Grant Village Lake House Restaurant** (7am-9am and 5pm-9pm daily late May-early Sept.).

Camping

Of the 12 campgrounds in Yellowstone, the largest 5 accept **reservations** (Xanterra, 307/344-7311, www.yellowstonenationalparklodges.com, $15-50) one year in advance: **Madison**

NAME	LOCATION	PRICE	SEASON	AMENITIES
Mammoth Campground	Mammoth Hot Springs	$20	year-round	campsites
Mammoth Hot Springs Hotel	Mammoth Hot Springs	$100-290	Apr.-Oct., Dec.-Mar.	hotel rooms, cabins, dining
Tower Fall Campground	Tower-Roosevelt	$15	late May-late Sept.	campsites
Roosevelt Lodge and Cabins	Tower-Roosevelt	$96-155	early June-early Sept.	cabins, dining
Slough Creek Campground	Northeast Entrance	$15	mid-June-early Sept.	campsites
Pebble Creek Campground	Northeast Entrance	$15	mid-June-late Sept.	campsites
Madison Campground	Madison	$25	May-mid-Oct.	campsites
Indian Creek Campground	Mammoth/Norris	$15	June- Sept	campsites
Norris Campground	Norris	$20	May-Sept.	campsites
Old Faithful Lodge	Old Faithful	$96-160	May-Oct.	cabins, dining
Snow Lodge	Old Faithful	$123-325	Apr.-Oct., Dec.-Feb.	hotel rooms, cabins, dining
Old Faithful Inn	Old Faithful	$150-335	May-Oct.	hotel rooms, dining
Canyon Campground	Canyon Village	$30	May-Sept.	campsites, showers
Canyon Lodge and Cabins	Canyon Village	$175-330	May-Sept.	hotel rooms, cabins, dining
Fishing Bridge RV Park	Fishing Bridge	$50	May-Sept.	RV hookups
Bridge Bay Campground	Lake Village	$25	May-Sept.	campsites, marina
Lake Lodge Cabins	Lake Village	$95-235	June-Sept.	motel rooms, cabins, dining
Lake Yellowstone Hotel and Cabins	Lake Village	$190-550	May-Oct.	hotel rooms, cabins, dining
Grant Village Campground	Grant Village	$30	June-Sept.	campsites
Grant Village Lodge	Grant Village	$255	May-Sept.	hotel rooms, dining
Lewis Lake Campground	South Entrance Road	$15	June-Oct.	campsites

(278 sites), **Canyon** (270 sites), **Fishing Bridge RV Park** (340 sites), **Bridge Bay** (432 sites), and **Grant Village** (430 sites).

Campers without reservations should head to the park's **first-come, first-served** campgrounds: Mammoth (85 sites, year-round, $20), Indian Creek (70 sites), Norris (100 sites), Tower Fall (31 sites), Slough Creek (23 sites), Pebble Creek (27 sites), or Lewis Lake (85 sites).

OUTSIDE THE PARK

Find lodging, restaurants, and services in **West Yellowstone, Gardiner**, and **Silver Gate-Cooke City**.

GETTING THERE

AIR

Bozeman Yellowstone International Airport (BZN, 406/388-8321, 850 Gallatin Field Rd., Belgrade, MT, www.bozemanairport.com) is closest to the park entrances at West Yellowstone and Gardiner. **Jackson Hole Airport** (JAC, 1250 E. Airport Rd., Jackson, 307/733-7682, www.jacksonholeairport.com) is closest to the south entrance. **Billings Logan International Airport** (BIL, 1901 Terminal Circle, Billings, MT, 406/247-8609, www.flybillings.com) works for summer access (late May-mid-Oct.) to the park's north and east roads. All airports have rental cars.

CAR

I-90 crosses east-west through Montana north of Yellowstone. Between Billings and Butte, multiple routes drop south to reach the park's **West, North,** and **Northeast Entrances.** East of Bozeman, drivers can take Highway 89 south through Gardiner to the North Entrance. West of Bozeman, Highway 191 drops south to the park entrance at West Yellowstone.

The most scenic approach is the **Beartooth Highway** (Hwy. 212, late May-mid-Oct., weather depending), which travels 111 miles from Red Lodge, Montana, to the Northeast Entrance. Plan three hours for the drive and check road and weather conditions.

From the west, Highway 14 enters the park's East Entrance via **Cody,**

Wyoming. Yellowstone's **South Entrance** straddles the border with Grand Teton National Park on Highway 89.

GETTING AROUND

There is no park shuttle. In summer, you'll need a vehicle to get around. In winter, visitors can ride snowcoaches or snowmobiles from West Yellowstone or Mammoth to Old Faithful or Grand Canyon of the Yellowstone.

DRIVING

Two-lane roads are the standard in Yellowstone. Throw in curves, wildlife, and scenery, and drivers need to pay attention—use pullouts for sightseeing and wildlife-watching. Driving between park areas can take 35-45 minutes due to wildlife jams and crowds. On summer afternoons, traffic gets extremely congested on the North Rim and South Rim Drives of the Grand Canyon of the Yellowstone. To avoid the mayhem, visit earlier or later in the day.

The Grand Loop Road from Mammoth Village east to Tower Junction and the Northeast Entrance Road are the only roads that are open year-round. All other roads close in winter.

PARKING

Parking lots in the park fill 10am-5pm (and restroom lines are long, too). RVs will find limited parking. At trailheads, claim a parking spot before 10am.

Two giant parking lots are available at Old Faithful and they pack out in summer. The smaller parking lot is between Snow Lodge and Old Faithful Inn. The larger parking lot is southwest of Old Faithful Lodge.

TOURS

Xanterra (307/344-7311, www.yellowstonenationalparklodges.com) operates wildlife-watching, geyser basin, and winter snowcoach tours. Reservations are required. **Yellowstone Forever Institute** (406/848-2400, www.yellowstone.org) offers expert-led educational tours year-round. Multiple companies in West Yellowstone, Gardiner, and Jackson also run full-day sightseeing tours.

GRAND TETON NATIONAL PARK

Wyoming

WEBSITE:
www.nps.gov/grte

PHONE NUMBER:
307/739-3399

VISITATION RANK:
9

WHY GO:
Bask in the beauty
of the Tetons.

PASSPORT STAMPS ▼▼▼

In **GRAND TETON NATIONAL PARK**, sawtooth spires claw the sky in one of the youngest mountain ranges in the Rockies. Towering thousands of feet high to culminate in the Grand Teton, these mountains dwarf all wildlife that roams across the floor of Jackson Hole. Gentle trails traipse through the valley, while almost every canyon contains a path grunting up to tiptoe across the Teton Crest.

Snuggled at the base of the peaks, glacial lakes string along the valley floor offering picturesque places to fish, paddle, and hike. In the foreground sits Jackson Lake, with marinas, campgrounds, lodges, and trails. Boaters ply the waters, and anglers go after trout. Rafters float the Wild and Scenic Snake River as it zigzags through Jackson Hole with changing views of the peaks. In summer, bicyclists pedal paved pathways, while in winter, skiers glide through dry powder under the skyscraping grandeur.

PLANNING YOUR TIME

Grand Teton National Park is in Wyoming, sandwiched between the town of Jackson in the south and Yellowstone National Park to the north. **Summer** (June-early September) is high season when visitors centers, campgrounds, lodges, marinas, and services are open; most **roads are open May-mid-November**. Lower-elevation trails are snow-free in June, while higher-elevation trails may not melt out until mid-July. **U.S. 26/89/191** provides year-round access to the park.

Most visitor services **close in winter,** when Grand Teton becomes a place of snowy fun. Teton Park Road closes **November-April,** from Signal Mountain Lodge to Taggart Lake Trailhead, and is groomed for cross-country skiing and snowshoeing.

To guarantee lodging, camping, tours, or dinner reservations for **summer,** make reservations at least **one year in advance.** For **winter** travel plans, make reservations **6-12 months in advance.**

In summer, warm days in the 70s-80s can evolve into afternoon thunderstorms, especially in the mountains. Spring and fall yo-yo between sunny days and rain or high-elevation snow. Winter snows blanket the ground late November through April.

ENTRANCES AND FEES

Grand Teton has three entrance stations that are open year-round. The **Moran Entrance** (U.S. 26/89/191 and U.S. 26/287) offers access from the east. The **Granite Canyon Entrance** is the south entrance to the Moose-Wilson Road, north of Teton Village. The **Moose Entrance** (Teton Park Rd.) accesses Teton Park Road.

The entrance fee is $35 per vehicle ($30 motorcycle, $20 individual; Yellowstone joint pass: $70 per vehicle) and is valid for seven days.

VISITORS CENTERS

Craig Thomas Discovery and Visitor Center

Craig Thomas Discovery and Visitor Center (Moose, 307/739-3399, 8am-7pm daily June-Sept., shorter hours spring and fall) has natural history exhibits, wildlife sculptures, a 30-foot climbing wall, kids' exhibits, and a topographic map that shows wildlife migration and glacier progression. The information desk has maps, schedules of ranger programs and hikes, current weather, and permits for backcountry camping and boating. A large bookstore sells field guides and books on wildlife, human history, and geology.

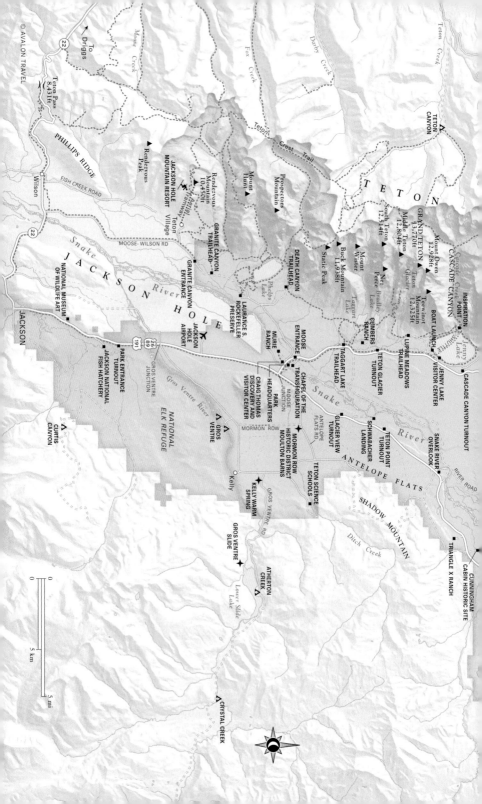

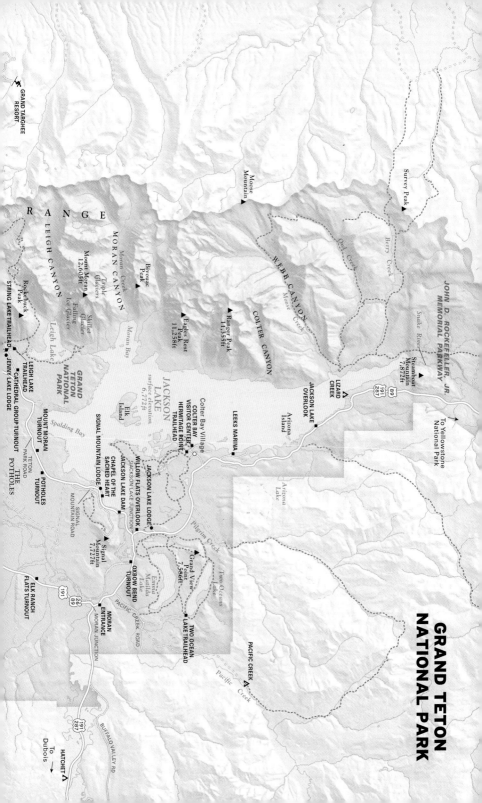

ONE DAY IN GRAND TETON

Begin by heading to Moose to orient yourself at the **Craig Thomas Discovery and Visitor Center**. Then, pop across the road to meet your guide for a float trip on the **Snake River**. While floating, you'll see **bald eagles** as the twisting river shifts your viewpoint of the sky-scraping **Teton Mountains**.

After floating back to Moose, drive north on the **Teton Park Road**, stopping at the **Teton Glacier** interpretive site to gaze on the **Grand Teton**. Then, drive to **Jenny Lake** and walk from the interpretive plaza to the lake overlooks to soak up the views.

Then, aim northward for **Signal Mountain**, driving to the two overlooks at the summit. One yields big views of **Jackson Lake** and the **Teton Mountains,** while the other looks northward toward the **Two Oceans Plateau** and **Teton Wilderness**.

Jenny Lake Visitor Center

At South Jenny Lake, **Jenny Lake Visitor Center** (307/739-3392, 8am-7pm daily June-early Sept., 8am-5pm mid-May-early June and Sept.) has activity schedules, ranger program information, maps, and a small bookstore. Also in the complex is **Jenny Lake Ranger Station** (307/739-3343, 8am-5pm daily early June-early Sept.), which has backcountry camping and boating permits and information on mountain climbing routes and conditions.

Colter Bay Visitor Center

Colter Bay Visitor Center (Colter Bay Village, 307/739-3594, 8am-7pm daily June-early Sept., 8am-5pm daily May-early June and Sept.-Oct.) has maps and information on hiking, boating, weather, backcountry permits, and activities. In summer, join in interpretive programs, see craft demonstrations,

and tour the Indian Arts Museum. A Grand Teton Association store carries books.

North of Colter Bay, tiny **Flagg Ranch Information Station** (John D. Rockefeller Jr. Memorial Parkway, U.S. 89/191/287, 307/543-2372, 9am-4pm daily early June-early Sept.) has information on trails, road conditions, and weather, and sells maps and books.

SIGHTS
MORMON ROW

Mormon Row is a treat for history buffs, photographers, and wildlife lovers. Originally a Mormon ranch settlement that started in the 1890s, the tract grew to 27 homesteads. Today, its six clusters of buildings are in the National Register of Historic Places, including the famous **Moulton Barn** that appears in the foreground of so many photos of Grand Teton. Even amateur photographers can capture impressive images of historic buildings backdropped by the Teton Range. Mormon Row is located in the southeast corner of the park, off Antelope Flats Road.

LAURANCE S. ROCKEFELLER PRESERVE CENTER

The **Laurance S. Rockefeller Preserve Center** (Moose-Wilson Rd., 307/739-3654, 9am-5pm daily early June-late Sept.) is located on a 1,000-acre preserve that was once a ranch owned by the Rockefeller family. The preserve's LEED-certified building contains

MORMON ROW

Top ❸

GRAND TETON

1 GAZE AT GRAND TETON

The Teton Mountains are dominated by their highest peak—the 13,770-foot **Grand Teton**. Carved by erosion from ice, water, and wind, the Grand Teton spirals into a pinnacle. A lure for climbers, the Grand serves as a notch in the belts of mountaineers who summit its vertical cliffs. The best way to enjoy the peak is by hiking to **Bradley Lake, Amphitheater Lake**, **Hurricane Pass**, or **Lake Solitude.** For the best car-accessible peeks at the peak, eyeball its crags through binoculars at the **Teton Glacier Turnout** on Teton Park Road. For photo ops, head to the **Chapel of Transfiguration** or **Mormon Row.**

2 CRUISE TETON PARK ROAD

Teton Park Road (24 miles, May-Oct.) is all about getting views of the Tetons. From Craig Thomas Discovery and Visitor Center in Moose, drive north through the Moose Entrance Station and turn right to see the **Menor's Ferry Historic District** and the small log **Chapel of the Transfiguration.** Continue north to **Teton Glacier Turnout,** where you can spot small **Teton Glacier** and towering **Grand Teton.** In about three miles, stop at **South Jenny Lake** to walk from the visitors center to overlooks of the idyllic waters.

From North Jenny Lake, turn left for a detour on **Jenny Lake Road** (4 mi. one-way). Stop at the **Cathedral Group Pullout** for views of three peaks: the Grand, Owen, and Teewinot. Past the String Lake Junction, Jenny Lake Road becomes one-way to **Jenny Lake Overlook,** which offers a different view of the peaks before looping back to Teton Park Road.

Continue north on Teton Park Road, stopping at the **Mount Moran turnout** to examine the black dike and small glaciers in the mountain's upper cliffs. The road continues north to **Signal Mountain Summit Road** (10 mi. rt.), where you can drive to Jackson Overlook for sweeping Teton views.

From the south side of Jackson Lake Dam, walk the paved path to the shore of **Jackson Lake.** At the **Jackson Lake Junction,** turn left to visit **Jackson Lake Lodge,** which has a historic mural and outstanding views.

3 WATCH WILDLIFE

Wildlife abounds in Grand Teton. **Bison, grizzlies, elk, moose, pronghorn,** and **deer** populate the fields of Jackson Hole. **Bald eagles** and **great blue herons** fish the Snake River, also home to river otters and muskrats. Morning and evening are the best times for watching wildlife; take along binoculars or a spotting scope. The best spots for viewing wildlife are along **Moose-Wilson Road, Antelope Flats Road,** and **Blacktail Ponds Overlook.**

BISON

AVOID THE CROWDS

To avoid the crowds of summer, visit in the quieter **spring** and **fall,** although weather can be erratic. If lower-elevation hiking and sightseeing is on your agenda, the shoulder seasons are the perfect time, with snow-clad peaks standing out against a blue sky. Most roads are open, and wildlife is active. **Spring** brings the chance to see bison and pronghorn newborns, and during fall, the air fills with the sound of elk bugling. **Fall** also brings outstanding hiking, with warm bug-free days and cool nights. During early spring or late fall, you may need to stay in Jackson or Teton Village when in-park facilities are closed.

exhibits, nature videos, and natural soundscapes. Rangers lead daily programs, talks, hikes, sunrise strolls, and evening walks. Kids can check out a backpack for a journaling experience while hiking the preserve's trails. The parking lot usually fills 9am-4pm; visit early in the morning or late in the afternoon.

MENOR'S FERRY HISTORIC DISTRICT

North of the Moose Entrance, **Menor's Ferry Historic District** (Teton Park Rd., Moose) preserves buildings from the 1890s. In summer, rangers guide afternoon walks or you can take a self-guided tour of the site's cabins, barns, smokehouse, farm implements,

MENOR'S FERRY HISTORIC DISTRICT

wagons, replica ferry, and **general store** (9am-4:30pm daily late May-late Sept.). The **Maud Noble Cabin** hosted some of the 1923 talks to create Grand Teton National Park.

CHAPEL OF THE TRANSFIGURATION

On the road to Menor's Ferry, a small log chapel was built in 1925 to frame a view of the Cathedral Group of the Teton Mountains. The **Chapel of the Transfiguration** substituted one of its stained glass windows for a clear window over the altar that looks squarely at the Grand Teton. **St. John's Episcopal Church** (www.stjohnsjackson. org) in Jackson owns the building, and services are held Sunday mornings in summer.

THE MURIE RANCH

At the north end of Moose-Wilson Road, the **Murie Center** (1 Murie Ranch Rd., Moose, 307/732-7752, www.tetonscience.org, 9am-5pm daily mid-May-mid-Oct., free) is a National Historic Landmark where the Murie family had their 77-acre ranch. Today, it serves as a learning center for **Teton Science School.** Visitors can pick up a self-guided walking tour guide on the Muries' front porch or take a docent-led **tour** (2:30pm Mon.-Fri. in summer) inside one of the ranch cabins.

JENNY LAKE

Tucked below the Grand Teton, **Jenny Lake** beckons photographers to capture its grandeur. It's also a place where visitors can lodge, camp, and spend days hiking, biking, boating, paddling, fishing, swimming, climbing,

JENNY LAKE AND MT. MORAN

JACKSON POINT OVERLOOK ON SIGNAL MOUNTAIN

backpacking, and wildlife-watching. South Jenny Lake houses a small visitors center, ranger station, store, scenic boat tours, and campground. To see the lake, walk the 0.5-mile, wheelchair-accessible **Discovery Loop** from the interpretive plaza.

SIGNAL MOUNTAIN

At 7,720 feet high, **Signal Mountain** (Signal Mountain Summit Rd.) cowers below the massive Tetons. Two forested routes climb 800 feet to reach the summit. Drive or bike the 5-mile paved road (May-Oct.), or hike the 6.8-mile trail from Signal Mountain Lodge. The summit has two overlooks: **Jackson Point Overlook** on the south with majestic Teton Mountain views and **Emma Matilda Overlook** on the north facing the Absarokas.

JACKSON LAKE LODGE

With views of Mount Moran and Jackson Lake, **Jackson Lake Lodge** (307/543-3100, www.gtlc.com, late May-early Oct.) is a National Historic Landmark. Windows frame the Teton Mountains, which compete for attention with the 10 "Rendezvous Murals" by Carl Roters, a late-20th-century American artist. John D. Rockefeller Jr. hand-selected the location on **Lunch Tree Hill** for its unobstructed mountain views. Commissioned by Rockefeller and built in 1955, the three-story lodge blends modern international architecture with artful takes on western and Native American elements. It also houses a small selection of Native American artifacts.

COLTER BAY

Colter Bay (U.S. 89/191/287) is one of those do-everything places with sights galore. To see the offshore islands, take a scenic cruise or rent a boat, canoe, or kayak. A maze of hiking trails loops the peninsulas, passing tiny lakes. Bikes can go on the trail to the jetty. Around Colter Bay, Jackson Lake often reflects Mount Moran and the Teton Mountains at sunrise or sunset.

MOOSE COW AND CALF

WILDLIFE-WATCHING

Moose-Wilson Road

Moose-Wilson Road (8 miles, mid-May-Oct.), a shoulderless, bumpy shortcut between Teton Village and Jenny Lake, snuggles into the southern base of the Teton Mountains. This narrow paved and gravel road weaves through beaver, porcupine, bear, and moose habitat, especially at **Sawmill Ponds** and the **Laurance S. Rockefeller Preserve**.

Antelope Flats Road

Antelope Flats Road (U.S. 89/191/287, 1.1 miles north of Moose Junction) is a habitat for bison, pronghorn, moose, coyote, and raptors such as northern harriers or American kestrels. In spring, look for migrating elk and newborns of bison and pronghorn.

Blacktail Ponds Overlook

Stop at **Blacktail Ponds Overlook** (U.S. 89/191/287, 1.3 miles north of Moose Junction) to see moose that often feed here. The habitat also attracts ospreys, waterfowl, and songbirds. Active beavers maintain the dams that keep the ponds in water.

Oxbow Bend

With slow-moving convolutions of water, **Oxbow Bend** (U.S. 89/191/287, one mile east of Jackson Lake Junction) has river otters, beavers, and muskrats. Look for moose foraging on willows. Squawking American pelicans add to the cacophony from songbirds, and ospreys and bald eagles hunt for fish.

HIKING
MOOSE

Phelps Lake

A maze of trails surrounds **Phelps Lake** in the Laurance S. Rockefeller Preserve and rewards hikers with stunning views of the Tetons. The most direct route to Phelps Lake is the **Lake Creek-Woodland Trail Loop** (3.4 mi. rt., 2 hrs., moderate), which tours both sides of a creek with opportunities to watch moose.

Phelps Lake Loop (6.6 mi. rt., 3.5 hrs., moderate) climbs via Lake Creek to circle the lake for a changing perspective on the Teton Mountains. Park at the Laurance S. Rockefeller Preserve Center before 9am to claim a parking spot at the trailhead.

Static Peak Divide

Static Peak Divide (16 mi. rt., 9 hrs., strenuous) demands a 5,000-foot grunt up a 10,790-foot Teton peak. From Death Canyon Trailhead (Moose-Wilson Rd.), take the trail to **Phelps Lake Overlook** and drop three switchbacks

HIKING STATIC PEAK FROM STATIC PEAK DIVIDE

to reach a junction. From here, the trail squeezes through steep-walled Death Canyon to a patrol cabin, where the north fork climbs a rocky scree and cliff ridge to the divide. A short path shoots up the remaining route to the summit for a view straight north to Grand Teton.

JENNY LAKE

Taggart and Bradley Lakes

Two lower-elevation lakes cower around 7,000 feet at the base of Avalanche and Garnet Canyons. For a shorter hike, head to **Taggart Lake** (3 mi. rt., 2 hrs., moderate). The longer loop adds on **Bradley Lake** (5.9 mi. rt., 4 hrs.), where you can stare straight up at the Grand Teton. Get an early start in order to claim a parking spot at the popular Taggart Lake Trailhead (Teton Park Rd.) between Jenny Lake and Moose.

Surprise and Amphitheater Lakes

At 9,714 feet, **Surprise and Amphitheater Lakes** (10.1 mi. rt., 6 hrs., strenuous) cluster 0.2 mile apart in a high, narrow subalpine basin extending from Grand Teton. From the Lupine Meadows Trailhead (Teton Park Rd.), hike 1.7 miles to a junction with the Taggart Lake Trail. Climb steep switchbacks on an open slope and then through a forest of whitebark pines and whortleberry to Surprise Lake. The main trail passes Surprise Lake and heads into the small hanging valley housing Amphitheater Lake, tucked at the base of Disappointment Peak.

AMPHITHEATER LAKE

LAKE SOLITUDE

Lake Solitude

Ride the Jenny Lake shuttle boat (fee) to the trailhead for **Lake Solitude** (14.8 mi. rt., 8 hrs., strenuous). From the west shore boat dock, follow the trail to Hidden Falls and Inspiration Point before connecting with Cascade Canyon Trail to climb west up to the Forks of Cascade Canyon. Turn right to break out of the forest into vast wildflower meadows surrounding blue Lake Solitude.

Holly Lake

Stunning **Holly Lake** (13 mi. rt., 6.5 hrs., strenuous) sits in an alpine cirque in Paintbrush Canyon that is populated by pikas. From the String Lake Trailhead, cross the outlet and hike north along the base of Rockchuck Peak. At the north trail junction, turn left to ascend Paintbrush Canyon through forest, avalanche slopes, and huge boulders into a hanging basin. At a junction, turn right to reach the lake.

Paintbrush-Cascade Canyon Loop

The **Paintbrush-Cascade Canyon Loop** (19 mi. rt., 10-12 hrs., strenuous) tops many bucket lists, but its distance and 4,100-foot gain makes it fit only for strong day hikers. From the String Lake Trailhead, approach Holly Lake, but in the hanging basin continue straight at the junction. The trail climbs through scree and across steep snowfields to cross 10,700-foot Paintbrush Divide before switchbacking down to Lake

HOLLY LAKE

Best Hike

HIDDEN FALLS AND INSPIRATION POINT

DISTANCE: 2.4-7.2 miles round-trip
DURATION: 1.5-4 hours
ELEVATION CHANGE: 1,250 feet
EFFORT: moderately strenuous
TRAILHEAD: Jenny Lake Visitor Center

Hidden Falls, a 200-foot tumbler in Cascade Canyon, and Inspiration Point, a rocky knoll at 7,257 feet, squeeze between Mount Tee-winot and Mount St. John. The views from the point's summit live up to its name. You'll look straight down on the blue waters of Jenny Lake, up to the peaks on both sides, and across Jackson Hole to the Gros Ventre Mountains. Hordes of hikers clog this trail, except in early morning or late in the day. The boat shuttle (fee) reduces this hike to a 2.4-mile loop from the west boat dock.

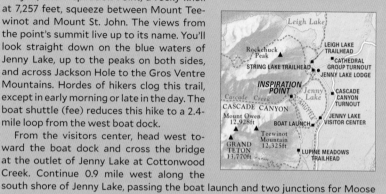

From the visitors center, head west toward the boat dock and cross the bridge at the outlet of Jenny Lake at Cottonwood Creek. Continue 0.9 mile west along the south shore of Jenny Lake, passing the boat launch and two junctions for Moose Pond Loop. At the second Moose Pond Loop junction, take either the upper or lower trail to reach Hidden Falls Trail; the lower trail walks 1.5 mile along the scenic lakeshore. Before Chasm Bridge over Cascade Creek, turn left at the junction for **Hidden Falls**, ascending the south side of Cascade Creek, passing one of the oldest trees in the park. At the next junction, continue straight to reach the spur that goes to Hidden Falls Overlook. To continue to Inspiration Point, cross the two upper bridges below the falls for more views, then climb four south-facing switchbacks to **Inspiration Point**. From the point, retrace your steps back to the visitors center.

Solitude. Use Cascade Canyon to connect with the Jenny Lake Trail back to the trailhead.

Leigh Lake-Rockchuck Loop

Walk the **Leigh Lake-Rockchuck Loop** (3.7 mi. rt., 2 hrs., moderate) counterclockwise for big views of Jenny Lake and the Tetons. From the Leigh Lake Trailhead, hike along String Lake and the creek to a junction. Continue straight on a short spur to the edge of Leigh Lake for pretty views. Turn around here for a short, gentle walk or hike farther west, crossing a bridge over a rocky creek. Climb 0.7 mile to a second junction, where a left turn breaks you out of the woods and onto the open slopes of Rockchuck Peak. You'll gradually descend to the foot of String Lake. Turn left onto the Jenny Lake Trail and cross the bridge at the outlet of String Lake to return to the trailhead.

JACKSON LAKE

Heron Pond and Hermitage Point

The **Heron Pond and Hermitage Point** (2.6 or 9.2 mi. rt., 2 or 5 hrs., moderate) hike takes in a variety of views on a gently rolling trail. Start at the Hermitage Point Trailhead at Colter Bay Village. At each junction, turn right to reach Jackson Lake Overlook and lily-padded **Heron Pond** with the Tetons reflected in the water. Cut left at the next junction to Swan Lake for the return to the trailhead.

To reach **Hermitage Point**, turn right at all junctions along the peninsula's west side where views span Jackson Lake and Mount Moran. At the

HERON POND AT COLTER BAY

point, continue up the east side of the peninsula to see the Absaroka Mountains. At the next junction, turn left to return to the trailhead via Swan Lake.

Emma Matilda and Two Ocean Lakes

Two glacially carved lakes are located one mile apart in a mix of forest and meadows on the 6,800-foot flanks of the Absaroka Mountains. While you can only reach **Emma Matilda Lake** (9.9-10.7 mi. rt., 5-6 hrs.) via hiking trails, vehicles can drive to **Two Ocean Lake** for hiking a loop (6.4-mi. rt., 3 hrs.) to both. The 7,586-foot **Grand View Point** (2.2-8.8 mi. rt., 3-5 hrs., strenuous) lies between the lakes and has the best views of the Tetons.

RECREATION
BACKPACKING

The king of backpacking trips is the **Teton Crest Trail** (34-58 mi.), a high-elevation romp with major elevation gains and descents. The route crosses Fox Creek Pass, Death Canyon Shelf, Mount Meek Pass, Alaska Basin, Hurricane Pass, and Paintbrush Divide at 9,600-10,720 feet. The **38-mile point-to-point** route requires a shuttle between trailheads, or you can complete the loop by adding 20 miles on the Valley Trail (**58-mile loop**). Jackson Hole Mountain Resort's aerial tram (fee) joins the Teton Crest Trail 3.8 miles from Rendezvous Mountain, reducing the total distance to 34 miles. Along the Teton Crest, you can camp at Marian Lake, Death Canyon Shelf, South Fork Cascade, and Upper Paintbrush.

Bear canisters and backcountry **permits** ($35) are required. They are available from **Jenny Lake Ranger Station** (307/739-3343, 8am-5pm June-mid-Sept.) or Craig Thomas Discovery and Visitor Center. Apply online (www.recreation.gov, early Jan.-mid-May, $45/trip) to guarantee your permit in advance.

▼ GRAND VIEW POINT

CLIMBING PAINTBRUSH DIVIDE ON PAINTBRUSH-CASCADE CANYON LOOP

BIKING

The **Multi-Use Pathway** (29 miles, dawn-dusk) is a mostly level, paved cycling and walking path that parallels the roads between Jenny Lake, Moose, Antelope Flats Road, and Jackson. For the most scenic ride, the Moose-Jenny Lake segment (7.7 miles) saunters just below the Tetons. The section from Jackson to Gros Ventre Junction closes November-April for migrating elk. Rent bikes from Dornan's **Adventure Sports** (12170 Dornan Rd., Moose, 307/733-2415, http://dornans.com, 8am-6pm daily early May-late Sept.).

ROCK CLIMBING

To reach Teton summits demands technical climbing skills and the gear for rock or ice routes. Climbing the **Grand Teton** involves 14 miles of hiking and 6,545 feet of ascent and descent. More than 35 climbing routes lead to its summit, with countless variations. The most popular and famous route for climbing the Grand is the exposed Upper Exum Ridge. Mid-July-August offers the best weather.

Exum Mountain Guides (South Jenny Lake, 307/733-2297, http://exumguides.com) leads individual and group climbs, plus offers climbing instruction and camps. **Jenny Lake Ranger Station** (307/739-3343, 8am-5pm June-mid-Sept.) is the only place for current climbing conditions and information and to pick up a backcountry camping **permit**.

HORSEBACK RIDING

Grand Teton Lodging Company (reservations 307/543-2811, www.gtlc.com, daily June-early Sept., $43-80) offers one- and two-hour horseback rides from corrals at Colter Bay, Jackson Lake Lodge, and Flagg Ranch.

BOATING AND FISHING

Jenny Lake

Boating on **Jenny Lake** (boat launch on Lupine Meadows Rd.) is a quiet, idyllic experience; only hand-propelled boats or motorboats with 10 horsepower or less are permitted. North of Jenny Lake, **String Lake** connects via a 600-foot portage to **Leigh Lake**, where paddlers can overnight in solitude at eight prime backcountry campsites. String Lake has a canoe and kayak launch site (North Jenny Lake Rd.).

Jenny Lake Boating (Jenny Lake boathouse, 307/734-9227, www.jennylakeboating.com, 7am-7pm daily mid-June-mid-Sept., shorter hours in fall) rents kayaks and canoes. Dornan's **Adventure Sports** (12170 Dornan Rd., Moose, 307/733-2415, http://dornans.

BOATING IN JENNY LAKE

com, 8am-6pm daily early May-late Sept.) rents canoes, kayaks, and paddleboards. Acquire boating permits and fishing licenses at **Colter Bay Visitor Center** (307/739-3594, 8am-7pm daily early June-early Sept).

Jackson Lake

Fifteen islands inhabit **Jackson Lake,** and their boat-accessible backcountry campsites are perfect destinations for boaters and paddlers. Three marinas offer launch sites late May-late September: **Leek's Marina** and **Signal Mountain Lodge** (307/543-2831, www.signalmountainlodge.com), and **Colter Bay Marina** (Grand Teton Lodging Company, 307/543-2811, www.gtlc.com). Rent motorboats, canoes, and kayaks from Colter Bay Marina and Signal Mountain Lodge.

▼ LEEK'S MARINA

Rafting the Snake River

Rafts, kayaks, and canoes can float the **Wild and Scenic Snake River** below Jackson Lake Dam. Start at Jackson Lake Dam or Cattleman's Bridge Site to take out at Pacific Creek. Only experienced paddlers should put in at Deadman's Bar and take out at Moose Landing (10 miles, two hours), an advanced section with strong currents, waves, logjams, and a maze of braided streams.

Guided scenic float trips (mid-May-Sept.) on the Snake River depart from **Jackson Lake Lodge** (Grand Teton Lodging Company, 307/543-2811, www.gtlc.com), **Signal Mountain Lodge** (307/543-2831, www.signalmountain-lodge.com), and Moose through **Barker-Ewing Scenic Float Trips** (Dornan's, 307/733-1800 or 800/365-1800, www.barkerewing.com) or **Triangle X-National Park Float Trips** (307/733-5500, http://nationalparkfloattrips.com). Guided Snake River fishing trips are offered through **Snake River Angler** (10 Moose St., Moose, 307/733-3699, www.snakeriverangler.com) and **Triangle X** (307/733-5500, www.trianglex.com).

WHERE TO STAY

INSIDE THE PARK

Reservations (Grand Teton Lodging Company, 307/543-2811, www.gtlc.com) for the park's four summer lodges and two RV campgrounds should be made 11 months in advance.

Moose

Located on the Snake River, **Dornan's Spur Ranch Cabins** (307/733-2415, www.dornans.com, May-Oct. and Dec.-Mar., from $200) have full kitchens. Their **Pizza Pasta Company** (11:30am-9:30pm daily, shorter hours in winter) serves pasta, pizza, calzones, hot subs, panini, soups, and salads. The **Chuckwagon** (307/733-2415, hours and days vary, mid-June-early Sept.) serves cowboy fare in a covered outdoor pavilion with picnic tables and mountain views. The **Moose Trading Post & Deli** (9am-5pm daily winter, 8am-8pm daily summer) makes made-to-order deli sandwiches.

Jenny Lake

Built in 1920, **Jenny Lake Lodge** (400 Jenny Lake Loop, 307/543-3100, www.gtlc.com, June-early Oct., from $758) offers rustic luxury in 37 log cabins. The complex includes an intimate restaurant with views of the Teton peaks. **Reservations** (307/543-3351) are recommended for breakfast and lunch and are required for dinner, when there is a dress code.

The **Grand Teton Climber's Ranch** (Teton Park Rd., 307/733-7271 summer, 303/384-0110 fall-spring, http://americanalpineclub.org, early June-mid-Sept.) offers small, hostel-style coed log cabins with wooden bunks. Facilities include sex-separated bathrooms and shower houses and an outdoor cook shelter. Bring your own sleeping bag, pad, cooking gear, food, and towels.

Jackson Lake

Jackson Lake Lodge (307/543-3100, www.gtlc.com, mid-May-early Oct., from $320) is a National Historic Landmark built in 1955 with a commanding panoramic view of the Tetons, an outdoor swimming pool, and horseback riding. Rooms are in the main lodge, separate two-story lodges, or in cabins. The complex includes four restaurants:

VIEW FROM JACKSON LAKE LODGE

NAME	LOCATION	PRICE	SEASON	AMENITIES
Grassy Lake Road	John D. Rockefeller, Jr. Memorial Parkway	free	June-Sept.	tent sites
Lizard Creek	John D. Rockefeller, Jr. Memorial Parkway	$23	June-Sept.	tent sites
Headwaters Campground & RV	John D. Rockefeller, Jr. Memorial Parkway	$38-75	June-Sept.	tent and RV sites, camping cabins
Headwaters Lodge & Cabins at Flagg Ranch	John D. Rockefeller, Jr. Memorial Parkway	$227-330	June-Sept.	motel rooms, cabins, camper cabins, dining
Colter Bay	Colter Bay	$30-75	mid-May-Oct.	tent and RV sites
Colter Bay RV Park	Colter Bay	$61-71		RV sites
Colter Bay Tent Village	Colter Bay	$72-75	May-Sept.	tent cabins
Colter Bay Cabins	Colter Bay	$175-280	May-Oct.	cabins
Jackson Lake Lodge	Jackson Lake	$320-835	May-Oct	hotel rooms, cottages, dining
Signal Mountain	Signal Mountain	$31-52	May-Oct.	tent sites
Signal Mountain Lodge	Signal Mountain	$211-430	May-Oct.	motel rooms, cabins, dining
Jenny Lake	Jenny Lake	$28	May-Sept	tent sites
Jenny Lake Lodge	Jenny Lake	$758-1,050	June-Oct.	cabins, dining
Grand Teton Climber's Ranch	Teton Park Road	$27		dorm bunks
Gros Ventre	Moose	$28-52	May-Oct.	tent and RV sites
Dornan's Spur Ranch Cabins	Moose	$200-360	May-Oct., Dec.-Mar.	cabins, dining
Triangle X Ranch	Moose/ Moran	rates vary	May-Oct., Dec.-Mar.	dude ranch

the upscale **Mural Room** (7am-9:30am, 11:30am-1:30pm, and 5:30pm-9:30pm daily), the café-style **Pioneer Grill** (6am-10pm daily), the **Blue Heron Lounge** (11am-midnight daily), with back patio service, and the **Poolside BBQ** (5:30pm-8pm daily mid-June-mid-Aug.). **Reservations** (307/543-3463) for the Mural Room and Poolside BBQ are accepted starting in late May.

Signal Mountain Lodge (1 Inner Park Rd., 307/543-2831, www.signal-mountainlodge.com, mid-May-mid-Oct., from $211) sits on Jackson Lake. The lodge has a variety of different room options and is so popular that it takes **reservations 16 months out.**

SUNSET OVER THE TETONS

The complex has two restaurants: the **Peaks Restaurant** (5:30pm-10pm daily) and the **Trapper Grill** (7am-10pm daily). Up the road at Leek's Marina, **Leek's Pizzeria** (307/543-2494, 11am-10pm daily late May-mid-Sept.) serves pizza and pasta.

Colter Bay Cabins (Colter Bay Village, 307/543-3100, www.gtlc.com, late May-early Oct., from $175) come in three sizes. **Colter Bay Tent Village** (late May-early Sept., from $72) has partial log and canvas cabins with communal bathrooms. **John Colter Café Court** (11am-10pm daily late May-early Sept.) has quick-order, and the **Ranch House** (6:30am-9pm daily late May-Sept.) plates western food. **Colter Bay Cookouts** (reservations required) offer outdoor dining around a western-style campfire via **Cookout boat cruises** (307/543-2811, June-mid-Sept.) and **Cookout horseback** or **wagon rides** (307/543-3100, Sun.-Fri. early June-early Sept.).

Flagg Ranch

Headwaters Lodge & Cabins at Flagg Ranch (John D. Rockefeller Jr. Memorial Parkway, 307/543-2861, www.gtlc.com, June-Sept., from $227) has three room types with en suite baths. The on-site **Sheffields Restaurant & Bar** (6:30am-9:30pm daily June-Sept.) offers dining in the restaurant or bar. In the adjacent campground, tiny **camper cabins** ($78) help those on a budget.

Triangle X Ranch

Triangle X Ranch (2 Triangle X Ranch Rd., 307/733-2183, http://trianglex.com, mid-May-mid-Oct. and late Dec.-mid-Mar.) is a dude ranch with lodging in cabins with private bathrooms. Early June-late August is peak season (from $1,865 per person weekly), with shorter stays possible in the off-season (mid-May-early June and Sept.-Oct., from $266 per person per day).

Camping

Grand Teton's five campgrounds are all first come, first served: **Lizard Creek** (60 sites), **Signal Mountain** (81 sites), popular **Jenny Lake** (49 tent-only sites), **Gros Ventre** (350 sites), and **Colter Bay** (335 sites). Most campgrounds fill by noon in summer.

Colter Bay RV Park (Colter Bay Village, 307/543-3100, www.gtlc.com) and **Headwaters Campground & RV Park** (Flagg Ranch, 307/543-2861, www.gtlc.com) accommodate RV campers and accept reservations 6-9 months in advance.

OUTSIDE THE PARK

Jackson and **Teton Village** offer lodging, restaurants, and amenities.

GETTING THERE

AIR

Jackson Hole Airport (JAC, 1250 E. Airport Rd., Jackson, 307/733-7682, www.jacksonholeairport.com) is actually inside Grand Teton National Park, just north of Jackson. It's a 10-minute drive north to the park's main visitors center and the Moose Entrance. Some visitors prefer flying into **Idaho Falls Regional Airport** (IDA, 2140 N. Skyline Dr., Idaho Falls, 208/612-8221, www.idahofallsidaho.gov) because the flights are often cheaper. It's more than a two-hour drive to the park. Both airports have rental cars.

CAR

U.S. 89/191/287 (open year-round) exits Yellowstone south to immediately enter John D. Rockefeller Memorial Parkway and Grand Teton National Park. The road stretches south to Moran Junction, the park's east entrance, and links with the Outside Road (U.S. 26/89/191).

From the south, **U.S. 26/89/191** leads north from the town of Jackson to the park's Moose Entrance.

From Idaho, Highway 33/22 crosses over Teton Pass to Jackson, Wyoming, connecting with U.S. 89/191/287 north into the park. Drivers from I-80 can take Highway 189 or 191 toward Jackson.

From I-25 east, you'll reach Dubois before traversing Togwotee Pass for a stunning descent to Moran Junction.

Winter weather can make for whiteouts and roads can be icy. Check conditions for park roads by calling 307/739-3682.

GETTING AROUND

DRIVING

U.S. 26/89/191 (known as the "Outside Road") is open year-round. From Moran, the road heads south along the Snake River to Moose and Jackson.

Teton Park Road (known as the "Inside Road") is open May-November.

▼ TETON PARK ROAD

JENNY LAKE BOATING

The segment from Taggart Lake Trailhead to Signal Mountain Lodge closes in winter. **Moose-Wilson Road** is a narrow paved and seasonal dirt road that closes in winter.

During July and August, **parking** lots at trailheads pack out. Plan to arrive before 9am to claim a spot.

SHUTTLES

Jenny Lake Boating (307/734-9227, www.jennylakeboating.com, 7am-7pm daily early June-early Sept., 10am-4pm daily mid-May-early June and mid-late Sept.) runs shuttles from the boat dock on Jenny Lake near the visitors center across the lake to trailheads.

TOURS

Scenic **bus tours** (Grand Teton Lodging Company, 307/543-2811, www.gtlc. com, 8:30am Mon., Wed., and Fri., late May-early Oct.) offer guided narration and travel to the Tetons, Jenny Lake Overlook, the Chapel of Transfiguration, and Oxbow Bend.

A **Jackson Lake boat tour** (Grand Teton Lodging Company, 307/543-2811, www.gtlc.com, daily late May-Sept., $32-70 adults, $14-40 kids) soaks up the lustrous views of Mount Moran on daytime and campfire meal cruises.

Reservations are required; hours and times vary.

Jenny Lake Boating (South Jenny Lake, 307/734-9227, www.jennylakeboating.com, daily mid-May-late Sept.) guides one-hour interpretive tours on Jenny Lake. Reservations by credit card are highly recommended.

The **Teton Science School** (700 Coyote Canyon Rd., Jackson, 307/733-1313, www.tetonscience.org, daily year-round) leads educational wildlife-watching expeditions.

Alltrans (307/733-3135 or 800/443-6133, www.jacksonholealltrans.com, June-Sept.) offers bus tours.

SIGHTS NEARBY

Jackson Hole Mountain Resort (3265 W. Village Dr., Teton Village, 307/733-2292 or 888/333-7766, www.jacksonhole.com, daily late May-early Oct. and late Nov.-early Apr.) has summer activities, including an ultra-scenic ride to the 10,450-foot summit of Rendezvous Mountain via their Aerial Tram, and skiing and snowboarding in winter.

GLACIER NATIONAL PARK

Montana

WEBSITE:
www.nps.gov/glac

PHONE NUMBER:
406/888-7800

VISITATION RANK:
10

WHY GO:
See glaciers and
wildlife along
scenic drives.

PASSPORT STAMPS ▼▼▼

▲ THE HIGHLINE TRAIL

GLACIER NATIONAL PARK is the undisputed "Crown of the Continent." It's a place where the earth's forces have left their imprints on the landscape with jagged arêtes, red pinnacles, and glacier-carved basins. The Continental Divide splits Glacier into west and east sides. Slicing through the park's heart, the historic Going-to-the-Sun Road twists and turns on a narrow cliff climb. Tunnels, arches, and bridges lead sightseers over precipices where seemingly no road could go.

More than 700 miles of trails wind through Glacier's remote wilderness, home to grizzly bears, wolves, mountain goats, wolverines, and bighorn sheep. Routes wind through some of the oldest rock in North America and sacred Native American land. Amid it all, a handful of glaciers cling to high elevations, struggling to survive in their last decade or so of life. Glacier preserves one of the nation's most intact ecosystems, a place to visit before the warming climate further alters the landscape.

PLANNING YOUR TIME

Located in northwest Montana on the Canadian border, Glacier is a remote park, but popular enough to clog during its short summer season. Make **reservations 13 months in advance** for in-park lodgings and **6 months** for camping. Only one route bisects the entire park: Going-to-the-Sun Road. Rush hour on this road is 8am-5pm seven days a week July-August. Plan for an early start, as the Logan Pass parking lot fills by 8:30am.

Summer (June-Sept.) attracts crowds when lodges, campgrounds, and trails are open. Barring deep snows, Going-to-the-Sun Road is open **mid-June-mid-October,** with peak visitation and the best weather in July-August. Snow buries some trails into July.

Although saddled with unpredictable weather, the off-season **fall, winter,** and **spring** offer less-hectic visits. Low-elevation trails are usually snow-free, but **minimal commercial services** are **open.** Peak-top snows descend in September. **Going-to-the-Sun Road** is **closed to vehicles** in spring and fall. In winter, snow closes most park roads, which become quiet snowshoeing and cross-country ski trails.

ENTRANCES AND FEES

Glacier National Park is split along the Continental Divide, with several entrances on each side. On the east side are **Two Medicine, St. Mary,** and **Many Glacier. Lake McDonald** and the **North Fork** cover the west side. The entrance fee is $35 per vehicle ($30 motorcycle, $20 individual) and is good for seven days.

Two Medicine (Hwy. 49, open late May-Oct.) leads to Two Medicine Lake on the east side.

BIGHORN SHEEP

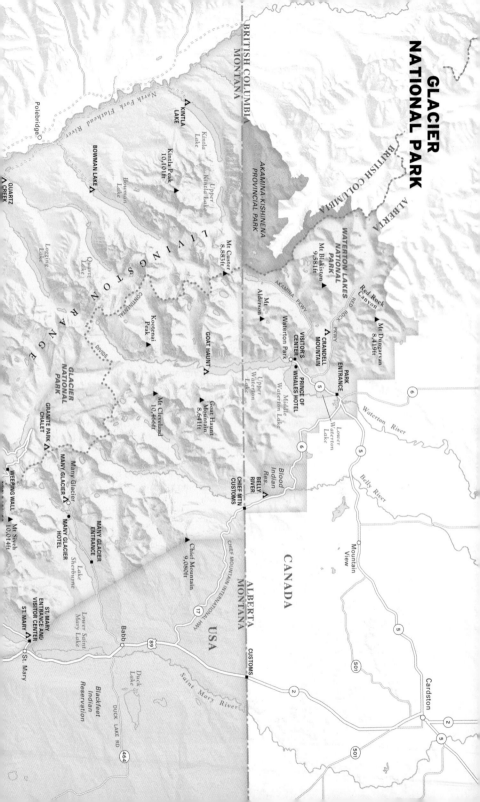

GLACIER
NATIONAL PARK

BRITISH COLUMBIA
MONTANA

ALBERTA
BRITISH COLUMBIA

Polebridge ○

North Fork Flathead River

▲ KINTLA LAKE

Kintla Lake

Kintla Peak 10,101ft ▲

Upper Kintla Lake

▲ BOWMAN LAKE

Bowman Lake

AKAMINA-KISHINENA PROVINCIAL PARK

WATERTON LAKES NATIONAL PARK

Mt Blakiston 9,581ft ▲

Red Rock Canyon

○ QUARTZ CREEK

Logging Lake

Quartz Lake

L I V I N G S T O N

Mt Custer 8,883ft ▲

Mt Alderson ▲

AKAMINA PKWY

Waterton Park ●

VISITOR'S CENTER ✕

CRANDELL MOUNTAIN ▲

PRINCE OF WHALES HOTEL ●

PARK ENTRANCE

RED ROCK PKWY

Mt Dungarvan 8,419ft ▲

Kootenai Peak ▲

GOAT HAUNT ▲

R A N G E

Upper Waterton Lake

Middle Waterton Lake

5

Waterton River

6

CONTINENTAL

DIVIDE

GLACIER NATIONAL PARK

Mt Cleveland 10,466ft ▲

Goat Haunt Mountain 8,641ft ▲

Blood Indian Res.

BELLY RIVER

Lower Waterton Lake

6

5

Belly River

▲ GRANITE PARK CHALET

Many Glacier

MANY GLACIER ✕

CHIEF MTN CUSTOMS ✕

8

● WEEPING WALL

MANY GLACIER HOTEL ●

MANY GLACIER ENTRANCE

Chief Mountain 9,080ft ▲

CHIEF MOUNTAIN INTERNATIONAL HWY

Mountain View

Mt Siveh 10,014ft ▲

Lake Sherburne

ALBERTA
MONTANA

CANADA

5

▲ ST. MARY

ST MARY ENTRANCE AND VISITOR CENTER

Lower Saint Mary Lake

17

Babb ○

89

CUSTOMS ✕

USA

501

Cardston

○ St. Mary

Duck Lake

Blackfeet Indian Reservation

DUCK LAKE RD

464

Saint Mary River

2

2

501

5

ONE DAY IN GLACIER

Glacier's biggest attraction is the 50-mile **Going-to-the-Sun Road.** A tour of the road over Logan Pass yields a small taste of the park's grandeur, with waterfalls, immense glacier-carved valleys, and serrated peaks. Plan to drive the road to **Logan Pass** and hike to **Hidden Lake Overlook, Avalanche Lake,** or **St. Mary Falls.** If you can, squeeze in a **boat tour** on St. Mary Lake.

St. Mary (U.S. 89, open May-Oct.) is the east portal for Going-to-the-Sun Road.

Many Glacier (U.S. 89, open mid-May-early Nov.) leads to Many Glacier and Swiftcurrent on the east side.

West Glacier (U.S. 2, open year-round) is the west portal for Going-to-the-Sun Road and Lake McDonald.

Polebridge (Outside North Fork Rd., open late May-Oct.) accesses Bowman and Kintla Lakes.

Camas (Outside North Fork Rd., open mid-May-Oct.) connects to Apgar and West Glacier.

Cut Bank (U.S. 89, open June-Sept.) has a dirt road that leads to Cut Bank Campground and trailheads.

Goat Haunt (open late May-mid-Sept.) is accessed by boat or trail from Waterton Lakes National Park in Canada.

VISITORS CENTERS

Glacier National Park has a few tiny visitors centers lining Going-to-the-Sun Road. All three visitors centers have maps, information, and backcountry desks for permits, and they offer night sky-watching programs.

The small **Many Glacier Ranger Station** (milepost 12.4, Many Glacier Rd., 406/888-7800, 8am-5pm daily late May-mid-Sept.) has hiking info and backcountry permits. The **Two Medicine Ranger Station** (Two Medicine Rd., 406/888-7800, 7am-5pm daily summer) issues backcountry permits and Blackfeet conservation permits ($10 pp).

Apgar Visitor Center

Apgar Visitor Center (406/888-7800, daily mid-May-mid-Oct., Sat.-Sun. fall, spring, and winter) sits at the west entrance. The **Apgar Backcountry Permit Office** (Apgar, 406/888-7859 May-Oct., 406/888-7800 Nov.-Apr., 7am-4:30pm daily May-Sept., 8am-4pm daily Oct.) is the main office for overnight backpacking or boating permits. Rush hour is the first 2-3 hours of each morning in July and August; lines begin forming at 6am.

▼ ST. MARY LAKE

Top 3

1 TOUR GOING-TO-THE-SUN ROAD

Going-to-the-Sun Road (mid-June-mid-Oct.) stands in a class by itself. The 50-mile historic transmountain highway bisects Glacier's heart, with tight curves that hug cliff walls producing scary, white-knuckle driving. Yet its beauty, diversity, color, flora, fauna, and raw wildness will leave an impression like no other. Although you can drive its length in less than two hours, most visitors take all day, driving over and back for different views. Early mornings and early evenings offer less-crowded times for driving. Better yet, ride the free park shuttle instead.

GOING-TO-THE-SUN ROAD

2 GAZE AT GLACIERS

Glacier National Park's glaciers will melt into static snowfields by 2030. So where can you see them while they last? From Going-to-the-Sun Road, **Jackson Glacier Overlook** offers the best views of Jackson and Blackfoot Glaciers. In Many Glacier, hike to **Grinnell Glacier** (11 mi. rt.), the most accessible glacier. On the jagged wall above the lake perch the tiny **Salamander Glacier** and **Gem Glacier,** both shrunken to static snow-

SPERRY GLACIER

fields. From Siyeh Bend on Going-to-the-Sun Road, hike the Siyeh Pass Trail (10 mi. one-way). The route offers views of **Piegan Glacier** while climbing to the pass and **Sexton Glacier** while descending to Sunrift Gorge. A strenuous climb (20 mi. rt., 10 hrs.) to Comeau Pass accesses the scoured basin that cradles **Sperry Glacier.** Follow rock cairns to an overlook of the ice, now reduced to less than 200 acres.

3 STROLL AROUND MANY GLACIER

Jagged parapets rim **Many Glacier**, where you can park the car and hike for days. Five valleys loaded with hiking trails and scenic lakes radiate from the core, which holds a campground, picnic area, cabins, and idyllic **Many Glacier Hotel**, a National Historic Landmark. Tour the restored hotel and sit on the deck to watch bears and bighorn sheep through binoculars.

An easy walking trail circles **Swiftcurrent Lake**, a mountain-rimmed pool preferred by moose. Paddlers can rent kayaks and rowboats or ride a **tour boat** on Swiftcurrent and Josephine Lakes, which shortens the walk to milky turquoise **Grinnell Lake**. At the end of the day, take in the sunset over the Continental Divide and watch on moonless nights for a sky full of stars and the northern lights.

HISTORIC MANY GLACIER HOTEL

Logan Pass Visitor Center

Logan Pass Visitor Center (406/888-7800, daily mid-June-mid-Sept.) perches at the apex of Going-to-the-Sun Road. It's a seasonal outpost with an information desk, a few displays, and a tiny Glacier National Park Conservancy bookstore (406/888-5756, http://glacier.org). The parking lot crowds by 8:30am.

St. Mary Visitor Center

St. Mary Visitor Center (406/888-7800, daily late May-early Oct.), at the east entrance, has the most exhibits, shows films, and has Native American programs. The visitors center is also a shuttle stop: To avoid parking hassles at Logan Pass, park your car here all day for free and catch the free shuttle up Going-to-the-Sun Road.

SIGHTS

APGAR

On the park's west end, **Apgar** crowds in summer as a tiny park hub. A restaurant, camp store, two inns, the lake's only boat ramp, swimming beaches, a visitors center, campground, and picnic area all cluster here at the lake's foot.

NORTH FORK

Outside the park, **Polebridge** is the hub of the remote North Fork—a backwoods place lacking modern amenities, including electricity, flush toilets, and cell service. The historic, red-planked **Polebridge Mercantile** (265 Polebridge Loop, 406/888-5105, http://polebridge-merc.com, daily Apr.-Oct., Sat.-Sun. winter) sells bakery goods. Next door, the tiny log **Northern Lights Saloon** (255 Polebridge Loop, 406/888-9963, 4pm-midnight daily late May-mid-Sept.) packs in diners, with extras spilling outside onto picnic tables.

From Polebridge, potholed dirt roads with bouncing rides launch into the park to two remote lakes with campgrounds and trails. **Bowman Lake** sits in a narrow, glacier-scoured trough. Secluded **Kintla Lake** tucks deep in the trees. Drop in a canoe, kayak, or paddleboard to tour the quiet shorelines.

LAKE MCDONALD

Catching water from Glacier's longest river, **Lake McDonald** stretches 10 miles long, 1.5 miles wide, and 472 feet deep to be the park's largest and deepest lake. Visitors fish, boat, paddle, and swim in its cold blue water. Access the lakeshore via three picnic areas, many pullouts along Going-to-the-Sun Road, or historic **Lake McDonald Lodge**, where scenic **boat tours** launch daily. Hikers can walk the lakeshore from Fish Creek Campground to **Rocky Point**. Those up for a climb can see the lake from above at **Apgar Lookout**.

▼ BOWMAN LAKE

AVOID THE CROWDS

Glacier sees record-breaking crowds in summer. Parking fills up at Logan Pass and some trailheads, a few overcrowded trails see long lines of hikers, and shuttles pack out with riders. So what can you do to have a more enjoyable trip?

Visit in June or September. Avoid the crowd season between July 4 and Labor Day. Because June still has snow in the high country, precluding access to Logan Pass and some trails, plan for potential limitations pending road plowing and weather. September brings more breathing space with access to Logan Pass and high-elevation trails. But be ready for schizophrenic weather bouncing between warm temperatures and snow.

Drive Going-to-the-Sun Road early or late. Once open for the season, you can drive Going-to-the-Sun Road 24/7. Drive it to catch the sunrise or sunset, and you'll encounter fewer people. Plus, early morning and evening yield better lighting for photography.

Spend the Evening at Logan Pass. Instead of spending the day at Logan Pass, arrive around 5pm to hike Hidden Lake Overlook with a picnic dinner. Because of bears, it's best to be off the trail by dusk. Then, stay in the parking lot after dark to soak up the Milky Way from this location with minimal light pollution.

Hike off the beaten path. Avoid the heavily used trails along the Going-to-the-Sun Road corridor and in Many Glacier. Instead, hike trails in Two Medicine (Scenic Point, Cobalt Lake, Dawson-Pitamakin), Cut Bank (Triple Divide, Medicine Grizzly Lake), or the North Fork (Quartz Lake Loop, Numa Lookout).

Plan ahead for backpacking. Apply in mid-March for an advance reservation for a summer backpacking permit to get to those idyllic backcountry havens.

Camp and stay put. Rather than fighting for a new campsite in a new campground every morning, select a campground to use as home base. Then, drive to other locations as day trips. Make reservations six months ahead for campgrounds at St. Mary, Fish Creek, and Many Glacier.

GOING-TO-THE-SUN ROAD

Rush hour on Going-to-the-Sun Road is 8am-5pm seven days a week July-August; plan for an early start, as the Logan Pass parking lot fills by 8:30am during those months. Early mornings and early evenings offer less-crowded times for driving. Better yet, ride the free park shuttle (goes to trailheads, but no time to get off at sightseeing stops) or take an interpretive bus tour (stops at sights). For route details, pick up the *Going-to-the-Sun Road Driving Guide* (406/892-3250, http://glacier.org, $10) from Glacier Conservancy bookstores.

West Side

From Apgar, the Going-to-the-Sun Road cruises along **Lake McDonald**, the largest lake in the park, which has the historic **Lake McDonald Lodge** at its upper end. The road follows **McDonald Creek**, the longest river in the park, with stops to see its tumbling rapids and waterfalls before reaching Avalanche, where the **Trail of the Cedars** runs through a rain forest, the easternmost in the country.

When the road swings north, the climbing begins through engineering feats that garnered the road's designation as a National Civil Engineering Landmark. Its 192-foot-long **West Tunnel** has two stunning alcoves framing Heavens Peak, and **The Loop** is the only hairpin.

Above the Loop, the road cuts through cliffs with views of the ribbon-like **Bird Woman Falls** and stair-step **Haystack Falls**. The **Weeping Wall** wails profusely in summer, enough to douse cars driving the inside lane, but in August, drips to a slow trickle.

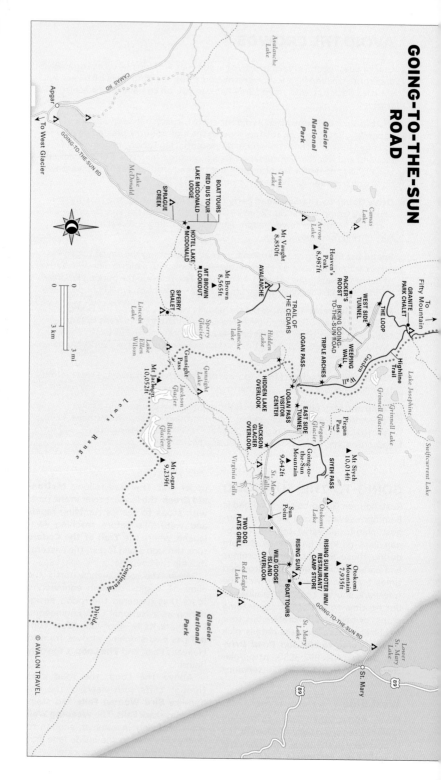

GOING-TO-THE-SUN ROAD

© AVALON TRAVEL

HAYSTACK FALLS

After **Big Bend,** drive slowly uphill to see **Triple Arches** (no pullout) at the very narrow S-turns. As the road swoops through the final mile to the pass, a wheelchair-accessible path goes to **Oberlin Bend Overlook,** the best spot for photographing the road's west side and the knife-like **Garden Wall** on the Continental Divide.

Logan Pass

Sitting atop the Continental Divide at 6,646 feet, **Logan Pass** rules an alpine wonderland of wildflower meadows, snowfields, and mountain goats. In June, high walls of snow rim the parking lot; July brings on wildflowers, and late summer turns meadows golden. Explore the small **visitors center** and scan surrounding slopes for goats, big-horn sheep, and bears. A boardwalk climbs toward **Hidden Lake Overlook,** tucked between two peaks and over-looking a brilliant blue lake.

The parking lot packs out 8:30am-4pm. If the lot is full, you may need to drive to other sights and return at a later time. Moonless nighttime visits to the pass yield ultra-clear skies full of stars.

East Side

From Logan Pass, the road drops by the cascades of **Lunch Creek,** a good place to sit on the rock wall to look up at **Pie-gan Mountain**. Below, the 408-foot **East Side Tunnel**, dug out entirely by hand, pops with a downhill view of **Go-ing-to-the-Sun Mountain**.

After **Siyeh Bend**, the route drops into the trees for a peekaboo look through binoculars at **Jackson Glacier** six miles away.

Along **St. Mary Lake**, a short up-hill stroll goes to **Sunrift Gorge**, a nar-row canyon cut by Baring Creek. **Sun Point** (5 min. walk) marks the site of the park's Going-to-the-Sun Chalets atop the rock promontory jutting into St. Mary Lake. As the road curves around the lake, it arrives at one of the most photographed spots, where giant sharp peaks dwarf tiny **Wild Goose Island**.

Around a bluff, **Rising Sun** has visi-tor services, including a boat tour, while **Two Dog Flats** lures elk, coyote, and bears to grassland meadows bordered by aspen groves. The Going-to-the-Sun Road terminates in the town of **St. Mary**.

ST. MARY

Turquoise **St. Mary Lake**, at nine miles long the second-largest lake in the park, flanks the east side of Going-to-the-Sun Road. Often windy, peaks pinch its upper end, while the small season-al town of **St. Mary** anchors its east end with visitor services. Midway, **Ris-ing Sun** has a campground, motel, pic-nic area, boat launch, and scenic **boat tours**. The best hiking trail goes above the shoreline from **Sun Point to Baring Falls** (1.6 mi rt., 1 hr., easy).

MOUNTAIN GOAT

TWO MEDICINE

Two Medicine Lake is the highest road-accessible lake in Glacier at almost a mile high. Peaks rich in Blackfeet history flank the lake. En route to the lake, a trail goes to **Running Eagle Falls** (0.6 mi. rt., 20 min., easy), where part of the falls runs underground and spits out through a cavern halfway down the cliff face. At the lake, jump on the historic **Sinopah tour boat** or rent a kayak or small motorboat to go fishing. The National Historic Landmark dining hall now operates as the **Two Medicine Campstore**. Two Medicine has trails to lakes, passes, and scenic overlooks.

RUNNING EAGLE FALLS

WATERTON LAKES NATIONAL PARK

Bordering Glacier in Canada, Waterton Lakes National Park serves as the entrance to Glacier's remote north country. Together, the two national parks are the world's first International Peace Park and International Dark Skies Park. They are also a Biosphere Reserve and World Heritage Site. In summer 2017, the Kenow Fire burned 94,000 acres of the park, which included many trails, a campground, backcountry campsites, picnic areas, and roads, but not Waterton Townsite, which houses motels, restaurants, a campground, boat tours, and visitor services.

The **Waterton Lakes Visitor Information Centre** (403/859-5133, www.pc.gc.ca) provides information, maps, permits, and licenses. The entrance gate is open 24-7 year-round (staffed early May-early Oct.). To enter, purchase a **Parks Canada day pass** (C$15-20, May-Oct.).

Sights and Activities

Chief Mountain International Highway: This two-nation scenic road circles Chief Mountain, sacred to the Blackfeet, and crosses through Glacier and Waterton.

Boat Tour: Hop aboard the historic *MV International* for a ride on the deepest lake in the Canadian Rockies. You'll float across the international boundary to Goat Haunt, USA, in Glacier.

Goat Haunt, USA: Accessible only by boat or on foot, Goat Haunt is a launchpad onto Glacier's remote northern trails.

Prince of Wales Hotel: This 1927 hotel maintains British ambience thanks to kilt-wearing bellhops and afternoon high tea.

Bison Paddock: In a tribute to the great wild herds that once roamed the prairies, Parks Canada maintains a small herd of bison.

Crypt Lake: A boat ride leads to the trailhead, where switchbacks ascend to what looks like impassable cliffs. A hidden tunnel curls into a hanging valley holding an alpine lake cowering below peaks in Glacier.

Getting There

North of Babb, Montana, **Chief Mountain International Highway** (30 miles) connects Glacier with Waterton. Its season and hours are linked to the Canadian and U.S. immigration and customs stations at the border (open daily mid-May-Sept., 7am-10pm June-Labor Day, 9am-6pm May and Sept.). At the north terminus, turn west onto Highway 5 and south into Waterton.

TRAIL OF THE CEDARS

HIKING

Ranger-led hikes go to multiple destinations; check at visitors centers or online for schedules. **Glacier Guides** (11970 U.S. 2 E., West Glacier, 406/387-5555 or 800/521-7238, www.glacierguides.com, mid-May-Sept.) leads day hikes and backpacking trips.

LAKE MCDONALD
Trail of the Cedars and Avalanche Lake

From the trailhead near Avalanche Campground, a boardwalk loops through a lush rain forest of cedars, hemlocks, and cottonwoods on the **Trail of the Cedars** (1 mi. rt., 1 hr., easy). Departing from the southeast end of the Trail of the Cedars, the trail to **Avalanche Lake** (4.6 mi. rt., 3 hrs., moderate) turns uphill for a short grunt to the top of the water-carved Avalanche Gorge. From the gorge, the trail climbs steadily through woods littered with glacial erratics and into a cliff-rimmed cirque with waterfalls.

LOGAN PASS
Hidden Lake Overlook

From Logan Pass Visitor Center, the first half of the trail to **Hidden Lake Overlook** (2.6 mi. rt., 2 hrs., moderate) climbs through alpine meadows. Then it passes moraines, waterfalls, mountain goats, and bighorn sheep to top out on the Continental Divide overlooking blue Hidden Lake, which is tucked below steep peaks.

ST. MARY
Piegan and Siyeh Pass

From Siyeh Bend on Going-to-the-Sun Road, a trail goes to **Piegan Pass** (8.8 mi. rt., 4-5 hrs., moderate) and **Siyeh Pass** (10 mi. point-to-point, 6 hrs., strenuous). The routes start together

HIDDEN LAKE OVERLOOK TRAIL

Best Hike

HIGHLINE TRAIL AND GRANITE PARK CHALET

DISTANCE: 11.4 miles point-to-point
DURATION: 5-6 hours
ELEVATION CHANGE: 1,300 feet up; 3,700 feet down
EFFORT: strenuous
TRAILHEADS: Logan Pass and the Loop

Beginning at **Logan Pass,** this point-to-point walk along the **Highline Trail** (mid-July-mid-Oct.) tiptoes along the Continental Divide to historic **Granite Park Chalet** before dropping to the **Loop**. Wildflowers peak mid-July-early August.

The trail drops from Logan Pass through a cliff walk above the Going-to-the-Sun Road before crossing a flower land that gave the Garden Wall arête its name. At three miles, more than half the total elevation gain is packed into one climb interrupted with a break at the saddle below Haystack Butte. After the high point, the trail drops and swings through several large bowls before passing Bear Valley to reach Granite Park Chalet atop a knoll at 6,680 feet.

At the rustic stone-and-log **Granite Park Chalet**, hikers cuddle up to the fire on cold days or picnic outside to take in the panoramic view. Overnighting at the chalet (Belton Chalets, 406/387-5654 or 888/345-2649, www.graniteparkchalet.com, July-early Sept.) requires reservations. **Online bookings for the upcoming summer go fast, starting in early January.** Overnighting offers time to climb to Swiftcurrent Lookout, Grinnell Glacier Overlook, or Ahern Pass.

Most day hikers go down the Loop Trail to catch a shuttle. Some opt instead to hike over **Swiftcurrent Pass to Many Glacier** (15 mi. from Logan Pass, shuttle available). Most backpackers spend a night at **Granite Park Backcountry Campsites** (permit required) before going north to Fifty Mountain. Before the Highline opens, hikers access the chalet from the **Loop** (8 mi. rt.).

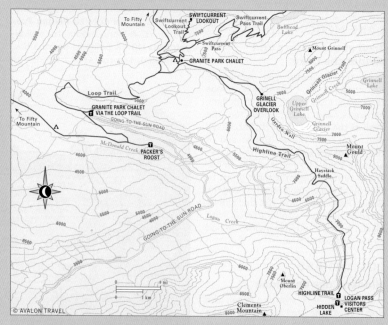

HEAVENS PEAK FROM THE HIGHLINE TRAIL

and climb to **Preston Park,** bursting with wildflowers. There a junction separates the trails. Go left above tree line to swing around a basin to Piegan Pass and come back on the same trail. Go right to circle Going-to-the-Sun Mountain on switchbacks to summit the pass, and then drop down Baring Creek to Sunrift Gorge. Use the shuttle to return to your vehicle.

St. Mary and Virginia Falls

From Going-to-the-Sun Road's east side, the trail to **St. Mary Falls** (2 mi. rt., 1 hr., easy) and **Virginia Falls** (3.4 mi. rt., 2 hrs., moderate) sees a constant stream of people. The west trailhead descends from the shuttle stop while the east trailhead launches from the vehicle parking lot. Both trails connect with the St. Mary Lake Trail leading to St. Mary Falls, where a wooden bridge crosses blue-green pools. From here, the trail switchbacks up to Virginia Falls, a broad waterfall spewing mist.

MANY GLACIER

Grinnell Glacier

The path to **Grinnell Glacier** (11 mi. rt., 6 hrs., strenuous) delights with wildflowers, bighorn sheep, and waterfalls. From the Swiftcurrent Picnic Area or Many Glacier Hotel, circle Swiftcurrent Lake to the west boat dock (taking the boat shuttle cuts the length to 7.8 mi. rt., or trims 2.5 miles off the return). Bop over the hill to Lake Josephine and go west until the Grinnell Glacier Trail diverges uphill. The trail climbs through multicolored rock strata overlooking milky turquoise Grinnell Lake and ascends a cliff stairway where a waterfall douses hikers. A steep grunt up the moraine leads to the glacier and glacial lake.

GRINNELL GLACIER

ICEBERG LAKE

Iceberg Lake and Ptarmigan Tunnel

From behind Swiftcurrent Motel, the trail to **Iceberg Lake** (10.4 mi. rt., 5 hrs., moderate) leads to a lake tucked into a toothy cirque. The route begins with a short, steep jaunt uphill, then maintains an easy railroad grade toward the lake. After crossing Ptarmigan Falls, stay straight at the marked junction to swing west through avalanche paths before crossing a creek, climbing the final bluff, and seeing stark icebergs against blue water. Going right at the junction climbs past Ptarmigan Lake to historic **Ptarmigan Tunnel** (11.4 mi. rt., 6 hrs., strenuous).

TWO MEDICINE
Scenic Point

From Two Medicine Road, **Scenic Point** (7.4 mi. rt., 4 hrs., strenuous) is a short climb with big scenery. As switchbacks line up like dominoes, stunted firs give way to silvery dead and twisted limber pines. Broaching the ridge, the trail enters seemingly barren alpine tundra and traverses a talus slope before descending to Scenic Point and views of the plains.

▼ SCENIC POINT TRAIL OVERLOOKS TWO MEDICINE LAKE.

CLIMBING TO GUNSIGHT PASS ABOVE GUNSIGHT LAKE

RECREATION

BACKPACKING

Glacier National Park's backpacking is unrivaled, with miles of well-marked scenic trails. Sixty-six designated backcountry campgrounds spread campers out to avoid crowds, and **permits** ($7 pp per night) guarantee solitude. Pick up permits 24 hours in advance at Apgar Backcountry Office or other permit locations; submit advance reservations online starting March 15 ($40). Go for popular trails such as **Gunsight Pass** (28 mi., including Sperry Glacier), or head for something remote like **Boulder Pass** (33 mi.). Bring rope for hanging food.

BIKING

Going-to-the-Sun Road is an unforgettable bicycle trip. While the 3,500-foot climb up the west side seems intimidating, it's not steep . . . just a constant uphill grind amid stunning scenery. Cycling begins in early April as snowplows free the pavement. Without cars on the road, riders climb as far as plowing permits. By May, free bicycle-carrying shuttles run from Lake McDonald Lodge to Avalanche. After the road opens to cars, cyclists may continue to ride, but due to heavy traffic, the west side closes to bikes 11am-4pm.

BOATING

Glacier's lakes provide stunning backdrops, but the threat to the pristine lakes posed by invasive species has forced the park to adopt stringent boating guidelines. Check with the park on current regulations.

On the west side, paddlers can ply the waters of **Lake McDonald, Bowman Lake**, and **Kintla Lake**. On the east

ALDER CREEK ON GOING-TO-THE-SUN ROAD.

TWO MEDICINE LAKE

side, **Two Medicine Lake**, **St. Mary Lake**, and **Swiftcurrent Lake** also attract paddlers. All have boat launches. Lake McDonald also permits launching from pullouts along Going-to-the-Sun Road. Use caution on St. Mary Lake, as winds there kick up fast.

Glacier Park Boat Company (406/257-2426, www.glacierparkboats. com, daily mid-June-mid-Sept.) rents

MANY GLACIER

canoes, kayaks, small motorboats, and rowboats at Apgar, Lake McDonald Lodge, Many Glacier, and Two Medicine. **North Fork Recreation** (80 Beaver Dr., Polebridge, 206/253-3374 or 406/888-9953, http://northforkrecmt. com) rents paddleboards, kayaks, and canoes for Bowman and Kintla.

FISHING

Wild westslope cutthroat trout attract anglers to **Kintla** and **Bowman Lakes;** those going after large lake trout head to **Lake McDonald**, although it is heavily fished.

Anglers in **Two Medicine Lake** have more success tossing in a line from a boat rather than fishing from the brushy shore. **Many Glacier Valley** has lots of fishing holes: Grinnell, Josephine, Swiftcurrent, Red Rock, and Bullhead Lakes support trout populations.

Rent fishing gear at **Glacier Outfitters** (196 Apgar Loop Rd., Apgar, 406/219-7466, www.goglacieroutfitters.com, 9am-8pm daily mid-May-late Sept., shorter hours in shoulder seasons).

RAFTING

Glacier has two boundary rivers for rafting—the Wild and Scenic **Middle Fork** and **North Fork of the Flathead River**. The rafting season runs

LAKE MCDONALD

May-September, with water levels usually peaking in late May. By late August, both rivers are at their lowest levels.

West Glacier houses four rafting companies that offer both scenic floats and white-water thrills. Contact **Glacier Raft Company** (6 Going-to-the-Sun Rd., 406/888-5454 or 800/235-6781, www.glacierraftco.com), **Great Northern Whitewater** (12127 U.S. 2 E., 406/387-5340 or 800/735-7897, www.greatnorthernresort.com), **Montana Raft Company** (11970 U.S. 2 E., 406/387-5555 or 800/521-7238, www.glacierguides.com), or **Wild River Adventures** (11900 U.S. 2 E., 406/387-9453 or 800/700-7056, www.riverwild.com).

North Fork Recreation (80 Beaver Dr., Polebridge, 406/888-9953, http://northforkrecmt.com) rents catarafts and inflatable kayaks. **Glacier Outdoor Center** (406/888-5454 or 800/235-6781, www.glacierraftco.com) offers vehicle shuttle services.

WHERE TO STAY

INSIDE THE PARK

Advance **reservations** for all in-park lodgings are imperative, especially July-August. Book **13 months in advance** (Xanterra, 855/733-4522, www.glaciernationalparklodges.com) for Many Glacier Hotel, Lake McDonald Lodge, Rising Sun Motor Inn, Swiftcurrent Motor Inn, and Village Inn Motel.

For Apgar Village Lodge and Motel Lake McDonald, make **reservations** (Pursuit Glacier Park Collection, 844/868-7474, www.glacierparkcollection.com) **one year in advance**.

Apgar

Apgar Village Lodge (33 Apgar Loop Rd., late May-late Sept.) clusters small motel rooms and rustic cabins within a few steps of Lake McDonald. On Lake McDonald's beach, every one of the 36 guest rooms in the **Village Inn Motel** (62 Apgar Loop Rd., late May-mid-Sept., from $160) wakes up to an unobstructed million-dollar view.

Lake McDonald

Historic **Lake McDonald Lodge** (288 Lake McDonald Lodge Loop, late May-late Sept., from $105) graces the southeast lakeshore with four types of accommodations: main lodge rooms, cabin rooms, suites, and budget rooms with shared bathrooms. The on-site **Russell's Fireside Dining Room** (6:30am-10am, 11:30am-2pm, and 5pm-9:30pm daily) offers breakfast, lunch, and dinner with no reservations. The cozy **Lucke's Lounge** (11:30am-10pm daily) serves a limited menu and local microbrews, wine, and cocktails. The cafeteria-style **Jammer Joe's Grill and**

NAME	LOCATION	PRICE	SEASON	AMENITIES
Apgar	Apgar	$20	Apr.-Oct.	tent and RV sites
Fish Creek	Apgar	$23	June-Sept.	tent and RV sites
Apgar Village Lodge	Apgar	$100-400	May-Sept.	motel rooms, cabins
Village Inn Motel	Apgar	$160-290	May-Sept.	motel rooms
Logging Creek	North Fork	$10	July-Sept.	tent sites
Quartz Creek	North Fork	$10	July-Oct.	tent sites
Bowman Lake	North Fork	$15	May-Oct.	tent sites
Kintla Lake	North Fork	$15	June-Oct.	tent sites
Avalanche Campground	Going-to-the-Sun Road	$20	June-Sept.	tent and RV sites
Rising Sun	Going-to-the-Sun Road	$20	June-Sept.	tent and RV sites
Sprague Creek	Going-to-the-Sun Road	$20	May-Sept.	tent and RV sites
Lake McDonald Lodge	Going-to-the-Sun Road	$105-360	May-Sept.	hostel, lodge, cottage rooms, dining
Motel Lake McDonald	Going-to-the-Sun Road	$130-170	June-Sept.	motel rooms
Rising Sun Motor Inn	Going-to-the-Sun Road	$155-175	June-Sept.	cabins, motel rooms, dining
Granite Park Chalet	Going-to-the-Sun Road	$80-105 pp	July-Sept.	backcountry hostel
St. Mary	St. Mary	$23	Apr.-Oct.	tent and RV sites
Many Glacier	Many Glacier	$23	May-Oct.	tent and RV sites
Swiftcurrent Motor Inn	Many Glacier	$95-175	June-Sept.	cabins, motel rooms, dining
Many Glacier Hotel	Many Glacier	$186-528	June-Sept.	hotel rooms, dining
Cut Bank	Two Medicine	$10	June-Sept.	tent and RV sites
Two Medicine	Two Medicine	$20	May-Oct.	tent and RV sites

Pizzeria (11am-9pm daily) serves pizza, pasta, wraps, burgers, and salads.

Motel Lake McDonald (3 Lake McDonald Lodge Loop, mid-June-mid-Sept., from $130) is an old 1950s-style two-story motel behind the camp store in the Lake McDonald Lodge complex.

St. Mary

On the east side of Going-to-the-Sun Road, **Rising Sun Motor Inn** (2 Going-to-the-Sun Rd., mid-June-mid-Sept., from $155) has cabin rooms and motel units, the **Two Dog Flats Grill** (6:30am-10pm daily), a store, and a hiker shuttle stop.

Many Glacier

In Many Glacier, **Many Glacier Hotel** (milepost 11.5, Many Glacier Rd., mid-June-mid-Sept., from $186) is the largest and most popular of the park's historic lodges due to its stunning location on Swiftcurrent Lake. Rooms and suites facing the lake have outstanding peak views. The on-site **Ptarmigan Dining Room** (6:30am-10am, 11:30am-3pm, and 5pm-9:30pm daily) serves breakfast, lunch, and dinner. The adjacent **Swiss Room** (11:30am-10pm daily) offers small bites.

At Many Glacier Road's terminus, **Swiftcurrent Motor Inn** (2 Many Glacier Rd., mid-June-mid-Sept., from $95) has cabins and simple motel rooms. **Nell's** (6:30am-10pm daily) crowds at mealtimes.

Camping

Most of Glacier's 13 campgrounds are first come, first served. **Make reservations six months in advance** (877/444-6777, www.recreation.gov) for Fish Creek, St. Mary, and Many Glacier.

Apgar (194 sites, Apgar Loop Rd., Apr.-Nov., $20), **Fish Creek** (178 sites, Fish Creek Rd., June-early Sept., $23), **Sprague Creek** (25 sites, Going-to-the-Sun Rd., mid-May-mid-Sept., $20), and **Avalanche** (87 sites, Going-to-the-Sun Rd., mid-June-early Sept., $20) flank the Lake McDonald valley on the west side of Going-to-the-Sun Road.

Rising Sun (83 sites, Going-to-the-Sun Rd., late May-mid-Sept., $20) and **St. Mary** (183 sites, Going-to-the-Sun Rd., mid-May-mid-Sept., $20-23) anchor the east side.

On the park's east side, three separate entrance roads terminate at **Two**

BLACK BEAR CUB

Medicine (99 sites, late May-late Sept., $20), **Cut Bank** (off Hwy. 49 and U.S. 89, 14 sites, early June-early Sept., $10), and **Many Glacier** (110 sites, Many Glacier Rd., late May-mid-Sept., $20-23).

In the remote North Fork Valley, small campgrounds are accessible only via rough dirt roads: **Kintla Lake** (June-mid-Sept., $15), **Bowman Lake** (late May-early Sept., $15), **Quartz Creek** (July-Nov., $10), and **Logging Creek** (July-Sept., $10).

OUTSIDE THE PARK

On the west side of Glacier, lodging, camping, and services are in **West Glacier, Coram, Hungry Horse,** and the **Flathead Valley** (Columbia Falls, Whitefish, Kalispell). On the east side, **St. Mary** and **East Glacier** have visitor services.

GETTING THERE

AIR

The closest airport to Glacier National Park is **Glacier Park International Airport** (FCA, www.iflyglacier.com). Some routes are open winter or summer only. Because Glacier is so close to Glacier Park International Airport, many travelers go directly into the park the day they arrive. The airport has car rentals.

TRAIN

Amtrak's daily **Empire Builder** (800/872-7245, www.amtrak.com) stops at several locations at Glacier National Park. High summer travel volumes make reservations imperative, and riders may need to contend with delays.

CAR

From I-90 just west of Missoula, Montana, take exit 96 onto U.S. 93 north, which leads 145 miles to Flathead Valley and West Glacier (3-4 hrs.).

GETTING AROUND

DRIVING

Driving in Glacier National Park is not easy. Narrow roads built for cars in the 1930s barely fit today's SUVs, much less RVs and trailers. With no shoulders and

THE EXTINCTION OF GLACIERS

Glaciers are moving ice. A glacier's upper end, called the accumulation zone, piles with snow, compressing into the ice's mass. With a mass at least 100 feet deep and 25 acres of surface area, glaciers move inches per day here. Due to climate change, scientists from the U.S. Geological Survey (USGS) estimate the park's glaciers will cease moving by 2030.

How Many Glaciers Remain?

Once glamorous diamonds, the park's current glaciers are relics from a mini ice age that peaked around 1850 with more than 150 glaciers. Since then, the glaciers have thinned, shrunk, broken into pieces, or melted entirely. A glacier shrinks when the math doesn't add up—when more ice melts annually than it makes. While early melt rates tended to be slow, the last century saw warmer summers and less snow, which triggered rapid melting that sped up with each decade. Fewer than 25 glaciers remain.

Why Are the Glaciers Melting?

Glacier National Park is a laboratory for studying climate change because the park's higher elevations have warmed at three times the rate of the overall planet. Average temperatures in Glacier now run 2°F hotter than they did in the mid-1900s, and the park now sees 30 fewer days with below-freezing temperatures. Warmer summers with more days above 90°F and shorter snowpack seasons are the norm. The USGS monitors the park's glaciers as climate barometers, using surface measurements, aerial photography, and repeat photography for comparisons between years.

How Are the Glaciers Melting?

As glaciers retreat, they fracture into patches, form lakes at their snouts, or split in two—all actions that speed up melting. In the Mount Jackson area, 27 glaciers once clustered over 5,300 acres; now 15 of those glaciers have disappeared, and those remaining have broken into multiple pieces. The warming climate caused Grinnell and Salamander Glaciers, once joined, to split into two separate glaciers, and since the 1930s, Grinnell Glacier shrinks every year, while Upper Grinnell Lake, at its snout, grows larger.

What Will Happen When the Glaciers Melt?

Glacier National Park's ecosystem will change; the most obvious will be an increase in forest elevations. More trees aren't necessarily disastrous, but with more forests eventually come more fires. Animals and birds, especially those living on the fringes of their habitat, may seek a food base elsewhere. Heat-intolerant pikas, for instance, may not survive warmer temperatures. Water, now seemingly so abundant, may not shed from the mountains in the sustained runoff from glaciers or at temperatures kept cool by the ice, threatening the survival of cold-loving bull trout and affecting irrigation and salmon runs.

Follow the ongoing study of Glacier National Park's glaciers and see comparative photography at www.usgs.gov. Pick up the *Climate Change* flier at visitors centers and ranger stations for more information.

HISTORIC RED BUS ON GOING-TO-THE-SUN ROAD

sharp curves, roads require reduced speeds and shifting into second gear on extended descents to avoid burning brakes.

Two roads cross the Continental Divide: **Going-to-the-Sun Road** (mid-June-mid-Oct.) bisects the park, while **U.S. 2** (open year-round) hugs Glacier's southern border. Both are two-lane roads. The Going-to-the-Sun Road is the more difficult drive, climbing 1,500 feet higher on a skinnier, snakier road than U.S. 2.

BUS SHUTTLES

The **Going-to-the-Sun Road shuttles** (July-Labor Day, free) stop at 17 points between Apgar and St. Mary, including Logan Pass and trailheads. No tickets are needed, and no reservations are taken. Departing every 15-30 minutes, these extremely popular shuttles enable point-to-point hiking on some of Glacier's most spectacular trails. Routes begin uphill service at 7am daily, with the last departures from Logan Pass at 7pm.

Xanterra (855/733-4522, www.glaciernationalparklodges.com, July-Labor Day) operates shuttles from Many Glacier to St. Mary.

BUS TOURS

Departing from all park lodges for Going-to-the-Sun Road, historic **red jammer buses** with rollback canvas tops are operated by **Xanterra** (855/733-4522, www.glaciernationalparklodges.com, daily late May-Sept.).

Launching from East Glacier, St. Mary, and West Glacier, **Sun Tours** (406/732-9220 or 800/786-9220, www.glaciersuntours.com, daily mid-June-mid-Sept.) leads four- and seven-hour tours over Going-to-the-Sun Road. Interpretation is steeped in Blackfeet cultural history.

BOAT TOURS

Glacier Park Boat Company (406/257-2426, www.glacierparkboats.com) runs tours from four locations on historic wooden boats. Buy tickets at the boat docks or make advance reservations by phone, especially for July-August. Tours depart from **Lake McDonald Lodge** (late May-late Sept), **Rising Sun** (mid-June-early Sept.) on St. Mary Lake, **Two Medicine Lake** (early June-mid-Sept.), and **Many Glacier Hotel** (mid-June-mid-Sept.) for a two-boat tour on Swiftcurrent Lake and Josephine Lake.

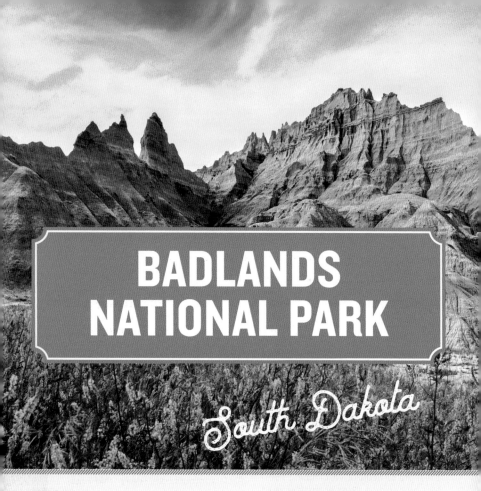

BADLANDS NATIONAL PARK

South Dakota

WEBSITE:
www.nps.gov/badl

PHONE NUMBER:
605/433-5361

VISITATION RANK:
23

WHY GO:
Experience the
prairie badlands.

PASSPORT STAMPS ▼▼▼

▲ BADLANDS NATIONAL PARK

THE BADLANDS are an eerie place. In daylight, the twisted spires and pinnacles look gray and faded, but at early light or at dusk, pale yellow, deep burgundy, and light pinks emerge. A visit to the Badlands is like a visit to another planet, one that is starkly forbidding and strikingly beautiful. Gazing over the plains from the high ridges of the park is not unlike the sense you get while gazing out to sea. Miles and miles of open plain lie before you, with little evidence of humankind. Though the dusty gray guise gives the landscape a barren appearance, the Badlands are filled with life. Host to bison, pronghorn, bighorn sheep, deer, fox, coyotes, prairie dogs, burrowing owls, and other prairie animals, including the rare black-footed ferret, the Badlands are a wildlife wonderland.

PLANNING YOUR TIME

The best time to visit is in the **spring** or **early summer** (April-June). The grasses are still a luscious green early in the year and the daytime temperatures are milder than the very hot days that occur more frequently in July and August. By the end of summer, the grasses are brown, removing a bit of color from the view, but the spires, buttes, and tables of the area are no less beautiful. If you are not staying overnight, try to spend at least **3-4 hours** in the park. Viewing a **sunset** or **sunrise** is one of the peak experiences of a visit.

ENTRANCES AND FEES

Badlands National Park is divided into two units. The **North Unit** is an easy day trip from Rapid City and has three year-round entrances: Pinnacles Entrance (Hwy. 240, south of Wall), Interior Entrance (Hwy. 44/377, north of Interior), and Northeast Entrance (Hwy. 240, south of I-90). The more remote **South Unit,** or the Stronghold District, has one road and no hiking trails.

The entrance fee is $25-30 per vehicle ($15-25 motorcycle, $12-15 individual) and is good for seven days.

VISITORS CENTERS

The **Ben Reifel Visitor Center** (25216 Ben Reifel Rd., Hwy. 240, 8am-5pm daily mid-Apr.-May, 8am-7pm daily June-mid-Aug., 8am-5pm daily Sept.-late Oct., 8am-4pm daily Nov.-mid-Apr.) is located at Park Headquarters on the south edge of the Badlands Loop Road. Paleontologists are on-site June-August working to uncover additional fossils. Visitors can tour the **Paleontology Prep Lab** (9am-4:30pm daily late May-mid-Sept.), which is used to prepare fossils for display.

The remote **White River Visitor Center** (Hwy. 27, Pine Ridge, 605/455-2878, 10am-3pm daily June-Aug.) is located 20 miles south of the town of Scenic, off Bombing Range Road (Hwy. 27) on the Pine Ridge Reservation. The visitors center serves those interested in visiting Pine Ridge or backcountry camping and hiking.

The park newspaper lists **ranger-guided programs** (late May-mid-Aug., free). Thanks to its dark skies, Badlands offers excellent stargazing through telescopes at **Cedar Pass Campground Amphitheater** (Fri.-Mon. nights in summer) and the annual **Badlands Astronomy Festival** (three days, June).

RECREATION
HIKING

The **Castle Trail** (10 mi. rt., 5 hr.) is the longest marked trail in the park. On the north end, the moderate trail winds down through some of the park spires and mounds. Most of the trail is level and crosses the grasslands with views of the Badlands formations to the west and south. Watch for cactus and

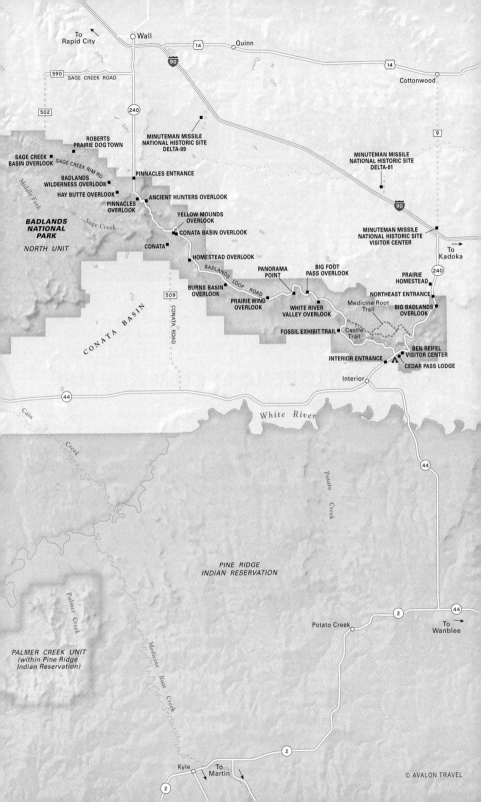

Top ③

① TAKE A SCENIC DRIVE OF THE BADLANDS

The **Badlands Loop Road** (23 miles, Hwy. 240) is the only paved road through the Badlands. From the **Pinnacles Entrance** in the north to the Ben Reifel Visitor Center in the southeast, the road winds between the ridges of the Badlands Wall—literally a wall of spires and pinnacles that was once the northern bank of the White River. Scenic turnouts along the road provide dramatic vistas of the Badlands and of the **Buffalo Gap National Grassland,**

CRUISE THROUGH THE BADLANDS.

which borders the park. Stop at the **Pinnacles Overlook,** the **Ancient Hunters Overlook,** and **Big Foot Pass Overlook** and walk the **Fossil Exhibit Trail** (20 min., easy), enjoying its interpretive signs and fossil displays.

② VIEW WILDLIFE ALONG SAGE CREEK RIM ROAD

South of the Pinnacles Entrance, the gravel **Sage Creek Rim Road** (22 miles) travels north and west to circle the Badlands Wilderness Area. Look for the **Hay Butte Overlook** and the **Badlands Wilderness Overlook.** The formations here are a little softer and less craggy than the spires along the Badlands Loop Road, but the wildlife is more abundant. The park's bison herd is usually seen in this area. Look for the **Roberts Prairie Dog Town,** where a large colony of black-tailed prairie dogs entertain with barking and social antics. At dusk, keep an eye out for the rare black-footed ferret. Just past Roberts Prairie Dog Town is the **Sage Creek Basin Overlook.** Head south and cross a bridge over Sage Creek where you can examine the riverbank to see the Pierre Shale—the oldest visible sedimentary layer in the park, dating back more than 70 million years. Seven miles past Roberts Prairie Dog Town, a left-hand turn on a gravel road brings you to **Sage Creek Campground.**

③ STRETCH YOUR LEGS ON THE DOOR AND WINDOW TRAILS

Three scenic trails depart from the Door and Window parking lot. The first 150 yards of the **Door Trail** (0.75 mi. rt., 30 min., easy) are a wheelchair-accessible boardwalk. At the end, the trail slopes upward and travels through a "door" in the Badlands Wall to great views of the grasslands and the outer wall of the Badlands. The **Window Trail** (0.25 mi. rt., 20 min., easy) is a wheelchair-accessible boardwalk that leads to a window in the Badlands Wall. Views of the grasslands, an erosion-carved canyon, and spires of the Badlands Wall abound. The **Notch Trail** (1.5 mi. rt., 2 hr., moderately strenuous) starts in a canyon, climbs a rope-and-log ladder, and follows a narrow ledge to the "notch," through which a sweeping view of the White River valley is revealed.

ONE DAY IN THE BADLANDS

Spend your one day in the park by entering through the North Unit **Interior Entrance.** Stop at the visitors center to get oriented and to pick up a schedule of park-sponsored events. Take a drive north along the **Badlands Loop Road** and hike the short **Fossil Exhibit Trail.** Finish your day trip by exiting via the **Pinnacles Entrance** on the north side of the park.

rattlesnakes. The trail ends on Highway 240, on the west side across from the Door and Window parking lot. Access the trailhead across the road from the Fossil Exhibit Trail, five miles northwest of the Ben Reifel Visitor Center on Badlands Loop Road.

BIKING

Bring your bicycles to travel the paved and gravel roads in the park. A brochure detailing loop trips on combined park and county roads is available at the visitors center.

During summer, the **Badlands Loop Road** (23 miles) can be an exhilarating, downhill ride from the Pinnacles Overlook to the visitors center. Slightly off the beaten path is the gravel **Sage Creek Rim Road** (22 miles). It skirts the northern edge of the wilderness area, runs past Roberts Prairie Dog Town, and passes though the lowest and oldest layers of the Badlands formations.

Sheep Mountain Table Road is located about four miles south of the town of Scenic off BIA 27/County Road

589. It is a seven-mile-long, dead-end dirt road with spectacular views of the South Unit of the park and of the Black Hills, 70 miles to the west. It is a moderately strenuous ride with a total elevation gain of about 400 feet.

HORSEBACK RIDING

Although there are no commercial horse-rental facilities in the park, the Sage Creek Wilderness offers prime horseback riding country. The **Sage Creek Campground** has a section designated for horse use, and a watering hole is located about a half mile southwest of the campground.

WHERE TO STAY

INSIDE THE PARK

If you're looking to experience a park sunrise or sunset, stay at **Cedar Pass Lodge** (20681 Hwy. 240, 605/433-5460 or 877/386-4383, www.cedarpasslodge. com, mid-Apr.-mid-Oct., from $173). The cabins have air-conditioning,

ROAD DOWN SHEEP MOUNTAIN TABLE

SAGE CREEK WILDERNESS AREA

modern amenities, small decks, and lodgepole pine furnishings. The **lodge restaurant** (mid-Apr.-Sept. daily 8am-7pm, Oct. 1-Oct. 14 8am-5pm) has a soup and salad bar, some vegetarian selections, and a limited dinner menu.

With 96 first-come, first-served sites, **Cedar Pass Campground** (20681 Hwy. 240, 605/433-5460 or 877/386-4383, www.cedarpasslodge.com, $25-40 Apr.-Oct., $10 in winter with no services) is located near the Ben Reifel Visitor Center. In summer, the campground has cold running water, flush toilets, and pay showers.

The **Sage Creek Wilderness Campground** (Sage Creek Rim Rd., North Unit, year-round, free) offers primitive camping with pit toilets (but no water) and equestrian facilities.

OUTSIDE THE PARK

The town of **Interior,** located at the southern edge of the North Unit of the park, has limited accommodations. The town of **Wall,** located eight miles north of the Pinnacles Entrance on the north side of the park, has several accommodations and restaurants.

GETTING THERE AND AROUND

Badlands has no park shuttles or public transportation. You'll need to take a tour, drive, hike, or bicycle to see the park. In winter, check road conditions because severe snowstorms may close roads.

AIR

The nearest airport is **Rapid City Regional Airport** (4550 Terminal Rd., Rapid City, SD, 605/394-4195, www.rcgov.org/airport), 11 miles from downtown Rapid City off Highway 44. Shuttle service between the airport and downtown is provided by Airport Express Shuttle (605/399-9999 or 800/357-9998). Car rental companies are at the airport.

CAR

From Rapid City, two routes go to Badlands National Park. Highway 44 skirts the southern edge of the North Unit, entering through the **Interior Entrance.** It's about a 75-mile drive (1.5 hrs.).

The second route to the park is I-90. It is the fastest route between Rapid City and the park: just 63 miles of 80 mph driving. If you are planning on spending the night in or near the park, this is the best route. Travelers headed west on I-90 will take exit 131 at Cactus Flat and head south on Highway 240 to the **Northeast Entrance.** It is about 10 miles from the Northeast Entrance to the Ben Reifel Visitor Center. If traveling east on I-90, take exit 110 for Wall and drive seven miles south to the **Pinnacles Entrance.**

TOURS

Several tour companies make day trips to the Badlands from Rapid City. **Affordable Adventures** (5542 Meteor St., Rapid City, 888/888-8249, www.affordableadventuresbh.com) provides narrated seven-hour tours.

Black Hills Adventure Tours (4131 Pleasant Dr., Rapid City, 605/209-7817, www.blackhillsadventuretours.com) has narrated driving tours of the Badlands and hiking tours in the park.

GeoFunTrek (605/923-8386, www.geofuntrek.com) has two tours to the Badlands: one classic and one that includes a daylight/sunset/stargazing tour.

Black Hills Aerial Adventures (21020 Hwy. 240, Interior, 605/673-2163, www.coptertours.com, May-Sept.) offers five different flying tours over the Badlands.

SIDE TRIP

Use Rapid City as your base to link a visit to **Wind Cave** and **Theodore Roosevelt National Parks**.

131 miles / 3 hours

Depart Rapid City by 8am and drive south to **Wind Cave National Park** to take a **cave tour**. Then loop north to **Mount Rushmore** and walk the **Avenue of Flags** to see the famous faces of four presidents carved into the mountain. Return to Rapid City to overnight.

239 miles / 4 hours

From Rapid City, drive north to **Theodore Roosevelt National Park**. Stop at the **South Unit** and tour the visitors center in Medora. Drive a loop through the South Unit, stopping at scenic overlooks of the badlands and prairie dog towns. Overnight in Medora, then drive 70 miles (1.5 hrs.) north to reach the **North Unit** for its scenic drive offering views of the **Little Missouri.**

SIGHTS NEARBY

The **Minuteman Missile National Historic Site** (I-90, exit 131, on the north side of the highway, 605/433-5552, www.nps.gov/mimi, Apr.-Oct. daily 8am-4:30pm, Nov.-Mar. Mon.-Fri. 8am-4:30pm, Sat.-Sun. 9am-4pm) outlines the history of the Cold War and the Minuteman missile program.

The **Wounded Knee Museum** (600 Main St., Wall, 605/279-2573, www.woundedkneemuseum.org, mid-May-mid-Oct. daily 9am-5:30pm) has maps for self-guided tours of the Wounded Knee massacre site, located on the Pine Ridge Reservation.

National Grasslands Visitor Center (708 Main St., Wall, 605/279-2125, summer daily 8am-8pm, off-season Mon.-Fri. 8am-4:30pm) highlights the history of the Great Plains, prairie plants, and animals.

▼ THE WIND-CARVED BADLANDS

MOUNT RUSHMORE

Four hundred people toiled for 14 years to create the monument we see today. Mount Rushmore is huge. It is hard to get a feel for the sheer size of the monument from the various viewing platforms available at the base of the mountain. George Washington's head is six stories tall; the distance from his forehead to his chin is 60 feet. His eye alone is 11 feet wide, and his mouth is 18 feet wide. If his entire body were carved proportionately, he would be around 465 feet tall. Add to those dimensions another three heads, making the monument approximately 60 feet high and 185 feet wide, and you have some insight into the project's size. The tools used to carve the mountain included pneumatic drills, jackhammers, chisels, and dynamite. The workers would hike the 700 stairs to the top of the mountain every morning, climb into sling chairs (called bosun chairs), and be lowered down the face of the mountain to their carving position for the day. The chairs were affixed to the top of the mountain by ⅜-inch steel cable, and workers were lowered with winches. This was not a job for someone afraid of heights. Dangerous as it was, there were no fatalities and only a few minor injuries were incurred at the monument over the 14 years of the carving project.

MOUNT RUSHMORE

Gutzon Borglum was the designer and director of the project, but he was not always on-site. While he was gone in search of additional funding for the project or working on other commissions, he left his assistants, including his son, Lincoln Borglum, in charge of the project. He would return on a regular basis to inspect the progress of the carving, making corrections and changes to the design as needed in order to work with the rock structure of the mountain.

In March 1941, Gutzon Borglum died. With the death of the artist, and at a time when America was facing involvement in World War II, the decision was made to discontinue work on the monument. With the faces of Mount Rushmore virtually complete, Lincoln Borglum supervised the final touches and cleanup of the monument site. In October 1941, the monument was declared complete.

Sights

At the **Information Center,** find maps to the grounds, schedules for ranger-guided programs, and a park newspaper. The *Mount Rushmore Audio Tour: Living Memorial* (2 hours), available at the **Audio Tour Building,** includes historical recordings of Gutzon Borglum, Lincoln Borglum, and Mary Borglum Vhay.

The **Avenue of Flags** lines the pedestrian walkway and forms a colorful frame for the majestic presidential faces straight ahead. The 56 flags on display represent each state, district, commonwealth, and territory of the United States. Each flagpole also reveals the date that statehood was attained.

The pedestrian walkway that begins at the entrance to the monument and passes through the Avenue of Flags terminates at the **Grand View Terrace.** The terrace, which looks straight across at Mount Rushmore, is one of the best locations for photographs.

AVENUE OF FLAGS

The **Lincoln Borglum Visitor Center & Museum,** the main visitors center in the park, is located on the lower level of the Grand View Terrace. The interactive exhibits include a timeline of American history, information about Mount Rushmore's sculptor, Gutzon Borglum, and about the workers who carved a mountain. Two small theaters show two short films continuously.

From the Grand View Terrace, follow the concrete pathway located on the Lincoln side of the monument to the **Borglum Viewing Terrace,** the site of Borglum's first temporary studio, where he worked before a more spacious studio was built closer to the mountain.

The **Sculptor's Studio** (June-Aug. daily 8am-7pm, Sept. daily 9am-5pm), Borglum's second studio on-site, contains the working model for Mount Rushmore. It also displays a collection of tools and several early photographs of Mount Rushmore before and after the carving, and hosts ranger talks (15 min., summer).

The **Presidential Loop** (0.5 mi. rt., easy) brings visitors to the closest viewing points of the monument. The trail is wheelchair-accessible from the Washington side of the Grand View Terrace to the base of the mountain. From that point, 450 wooden stairs climb partially up the mountain and then continue down to the Sculptor's Studio.

The **Lakota, Nakota, and Dakota Heritage Village** began with one tepee just off the Presidential Trail. Over the years, the program added more tepees. During the summer, volunteer interpreters are on-site to talk about the traditional lifestyle and customs of the Native Americans.

GUTZON BORGLUM

Getting There

Mount Rushmore National Memorial (13000 Hwy. 244, Bldg. 31, Ste. 1, 605/574-2523, www.nps.gov/moru, $11 parking) is an 80-mile drive (1.5 hrs.) west of Badlands National Park. During summer (late May-mid-Aug.) the park buildings are open daily 8am-10pm. The grounds at Mount Rushmore are open 5am-11:30pm daily mid-March-October and 5am-9:30pm November-mid-March. A café near the monument entrance is the only dining facility on-site.

From Rapid City Airport, the fastest road to Mount Rushmore (32 miles) is U.S. 16, also called Mount Rushmore Road. The grounds of Mount Rushmore are relatively small. Once there, moving from site to site is all by foot. No shuttles are available.

Several companies lead tours. **Mount Rushmore Tours** (2255 Fort Hayes Dr., Rapid City, 888/343-3113, www.mountrushmoretours.com) offers two narrated tours on a good-sized charter bus. **ABS Travel Group** (945 Enchantment Rd., Rapid City, 888/788-6777, www.abstravelgroup.com) specializes in short-duration, small-group tours of Mount Rushmore. Pickup is in Rapid City. **Golden Circle Tours** (12021 U.S. 16, 605/673-4349, www.goldencircletours.com) offers free pickup in Custer, Hill City, and Hot Springs.

Black Hills Aerial Adventures (313 Speck Center Rd., Keystone, 605/673-2163, http://coptertours.com, daily 9am-7pm) has six different flight tours, including a short introductory ride; tours feature Mount Rushmore, the Crazy Horse Memorial, Harney Peak, and Custer State Park.

WIND CAVE NATIONAL PARK

South Dakota

WEBSITE:
www.nps.gov/wica

PHONE NUMBER:
605/745-4600

VISITATION RANK:
32

WHY GO:
Explore underground
caves.

PASSPORT STAMPS ▼▼▼

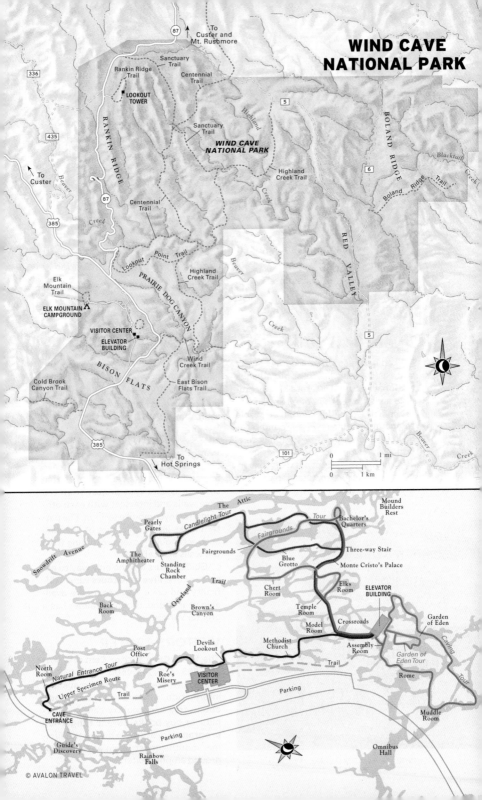

Wind Cave is one of the longest caves in the world. Considered sacred by Native Americans, the cave was discovered by Europeans in 1881 when two brothers, Jesse and Tom Bingham, heard a loud whistling noise while passing through the region. Upon investigation, they discovered a small hole in the ground from which a strong gust of wind emanated. This small hole is the only natural entrance to the cave that has ever been found. Below the surface, beneath just one square mile of the park, a maze winds through 143 miles of explored cave passages.

On the surface, **WIND CAVE NATIONAL PARK** is where East meets West—where the Great Plains prairie meets the ponderosa pine forest. Its mixed-grass prairie ecosystem supports abundant wildlife, including bison, mule deer, white-tailed deer, prairie dogs, pronghorn, wild turkeys, and elk. Hiking trails tour eroded, rounded hills that provide scenic views as far as the eye can see.

PLANNING YOUR TIME

Tucked in the southwest corner of the state, Wind Cave lies west of Badlands National Park, and it's possible to combine a visit to both in one trip. Underground, the caves maintain a stable temperature that hovers around 53°F, despite summer heat or frigid winters. Bring a sweatshirt or sweater.

Summer (May-Sept.) is high season, with the most cave tour choices and the most visitors.

WIND CAVE NATIONAL PARK

ENTRANCES AND FEES

Wind Cave has three entrances: **north** (Route 87 from Custer State Park), **south** (U.S. 385 from Hot Springs), and **west** (U.S. 385 from Pringle). There is no entrance fee; however, guided cave tours range $10-30 per person.

Cave Tours

Wind Cave is famous for its boxwork, an unusual type of speleothem (cave formation). Boxwork is made of thin slices of calcite that project from the cave walls and intersect with each other in a honeycomb-like fashion. The pattern looks like a collection of diamond and rectangular boxes protruding from the walls and ceilings.

Guided tours are the only way to enter the cave. **Five cave tours** vary in difficulty and price. Cave tours are available year-round, though summer has a greater variety.

VISITORS CENTER

The **Wind Cave Visitor Center** (26611 U.S. 385, 605/745-4600, 8am-4:30pm daily) is where you can find maps and information, arrange your **cave tour,** obtain free backcountry camping permits, or buy books. Several **ranger-led programs** are available during the summer months; most begin at the campground amphitheater.

Top ③

① TAKE IT EASY: GARDEN OF EDEN TOUR

The **Garden of Eden Tour** (3-4 tours daily year-round, adults $10, children ages 6-16 $5, children under 6 free) is the shortest and least strenuous of all the cave tours, with just 150 stairs to navigate. The tour takes about one

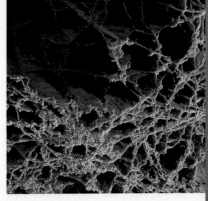

BOXWORK FORMATIONS

hour and requires about 0.25 mile of walking. Entry and exit to the cave is by elevator. Along the trail, you'll see small amounts of popcorn, boxwork, and flowstone (a calcite formation that looks as if it is flowing over the rocks).

② PICK UP THE PACE: NATURAL ENTRANCE TOUR

The **Natural Entrance Tour** (6-12 tours daily Apr.-Oct., adults $12, children 6-16 $6, children under 6 free) is a 1.25-hour tour that is moderately strenuous, requiring about 0.5 mile of hiking and walking 300 stairs along the route, most of which are downward climbs. (Exit from the cave is via elevator.) This tour brings visitors to the only natural entrance to the cave to discover why the cave got its name. Entry is via an artificially constructed entrance, and the tour takes visitors to the middle level of the cave, where the boxwork formation for which the cave is famous is abundant.

NATURAL ENTRANCE TO THE WIND CAVE

③ WORK UP A SWEAT: FAIRGROUNDS TOUR

The **Fairgrounds Tour** (3-8 tours daily Memorial Day-Labor Day, adults $12, children ages 6-16 $6, children under 6 free) takes about 1.5 hours to complete and requires about 0.5 mile of hiking. This tour is the most strenuous of the walking tours with more than 450 stairs to climb, including a single staircase of more than 90 stairs. The tour visits the upper and middle levels of the cave. Boxwork is abundant in the middle section, and the upper level of the cave features large rooms in which popcorn and frostwork are common.

SPECIALTY CAVE TOURS

HISTORIC CANDLELIGHT TOUR

The **Historic Candlelight Tour** (1-2 tours daily Memorial Day-Labor Day, adults $12, children ages 8-16 $6) is a strenuous, two-hour tour that requires about one mile of hiking. The tour takes place in a less-developed area of the cave along a fairly rugged trail and explores Wind Cave much the way early cavers did—without the benefit of electricity. Each participant carries a candle bucket, which is the only lighting for the tour. Cave walls loom into the light and shadows dance along the walls, heightening the sensation of visiting another world below the surface of our day-to-day lives.

Participation is limited to 10 people per tour and the minimum age is eight. Participants are required to wear shoes with nonslip soles; no sandals are permitted. Advance reservations are recommended.

WILD CAVE TOUR

For the adventurous soul, the **Wild Cave Tour** (Memorial Day-Labor Day, once daily, $30) is the tour of choice. Be prepared to get dirty, as this tour requires crawling through some very narrow spaces while learning the basics of safe caving. The four-hour

CAVE TOUR

tour covers about 0.5 mile, much of it spent crawling. This tour is not for the claustrophobic!

The park provides kneepads, hard hats, and lights; participants should wear long pants, long sleeves, and sturdy, lace-up boots or shoes with nonslip soles. Note that participants must be at least 16 years old (those age 16-17 must have a signed parental consent form). Advance reservations are required.

HIKING

On the surface, more than 30 miles of marked hiking trails range from easy to strenuous. For a short hike, try one of the three **nature trails**, marked with interpretive signage and displays; each is about one mile long. The **Elk Mountain Trail** begins at the end of the Elk Mountain Campground road and circles up through the forest near the park's boundary. The **Prairie Vista Trail** begins at the visitors center, and interpretive signage focuses on information about the prairie grasses. The **Rankin Ridge Trail** is located off Highway 87 in the northwestern corner of the park. The hike begins and ends at the parking lot of the Rankin Ridge Lookout Tower.

LOOKOUT POINT-CENTENNIAL TRAIL LOOP

The **Lookout Point-Centennial Trail Loop** (4.5 mi. rt., 3 hrs., moderate) exposes the hiker to all of the diversity of the park. From the trailhead, the hike begins in a stand of ridgetop pines and then descends rapidly to the valley floor. From there, it meanders along Beaver Creek, winding between the low hills of the park. About two miles in, the Centennial Trail takes a fairly sharp left. Continue straight at this point, and you will be on a short stretch of the Highland Creek Trail. This trail will loop around to join the Lookout Point Trail. Where the Highland Creek Trail veers south, continue heading west along the Lookout Point Trail; it will return you to the Centennial Trail trailhead. Throughout the hike, you will traverse a streambed, pass through prairie grasslands and rolling hills, and climb into some of the pine forests.

From the visitors center, head north on U.S. 385 and take an almost

BRIDGE IN WIND CAVE NATIONAL PARK

immediate right on Highway 87; the trailhead is 0.7 mile down on the east (right) side of the road.

WIND CAVE CANYON

Wind Cave Canyon (3.6 mi. rt., 1.5 hrs., easy) follows a former service road into Wind Cave Canyon at the park's boundary. This is one of the best places in the park for bird-watching; look along limestone walls to spot cliff swallows and great horned owls. Stands of dead trees make great nesting places for several varieties of woodpeckers.

The trailhead is on the east side of the road, one mile north of the junction of the south entrance and U.S. 385.

WHERE TO STAY

INSIDE THE PARK

The only in-park accommodation is **Elk Mountain Campground** ($18 in summer, $9 in winter), one mile north of the visitors center. The campground has 75 first-come, first-served sites. Facilities include restrooms with flush toilets and cold running water (in summer), but no hookups.

Backcountry camping is allowed in the northwestern part of the park. Campers must have a **permit,** which is free from the visitors center.

OUTSIDE THE PARK

Located 11 miles south of the park, the city of **Hot Springs** has accommodations for park visitors.

GETTING THERE AND AROUND

AIR

The **Rapid City Regional Airport** (RAP, 4550 Terminal Rd., 605/394-4195, www.rcgov.org/airport) is located about 11 miles from downtown Rapid City, off Highway 44 east. Car rental companies are at the airport.

For the most direct route from I-90 and Rapid City, take Route 79 south to U.S. 385, turning right to Hot Springs (57 miles, 1.2 hr.). The park entrance is six miles north on U.S. 385. To reach Wind Cave from the south, aim for Hot Springs on U.S. 385.

PRAIRIE DOG

CAR

For drivers coming from Mount Rushmore, drive 4.6 miles west to U.S. 385 to go south through Hill City, Custer, and Pringle to reach the west entrance of the park (57 mi., 1.2 hrs.).

Inside the park, the visitors center sits on a signed side road about 0.5 mile off U.S. 385. From the south entrance, go 4.5 miles to the turnoff on the left. From the north and west entrance roads, the visitors center turnoff is on the right just south of the junction of U.S. 385 and Route 87.

There is no public transit within the park. Driving or bicycling is the only way to travel the main paved road. Two dirt roads (#5 and #6) tour the eastern portion of the badlands.

SIGHTS NEARBY

Crazy Horse Memorial (12151 Avenue of the Chiefs, Crazy Horse, 605/673-4681, www.crazyhorsememorial.org, summer daily 7am until after the laser light show, winter daily 8am-5pm) is a mountainside sculpture still under construction.

Jewel Cave National Monument (13 miles west of Custer, 605/673-8300, www.nps.gov/jeca, April-Nov. daily, Dec.-Mar. Mon.-Fri., summer daily 8am-5:30pm, spring, winter, and fall daily 8:30am-4:30pm) has ranger-led tours through the third-longest cave in the world.

Custer State Park (13329 U.S. 16A, 605/255-4515, https://gfp.sd.gov) contains 1,300 free-roaming bison and other wildlife. The bison can often be seen from Wildlife Loop Road.

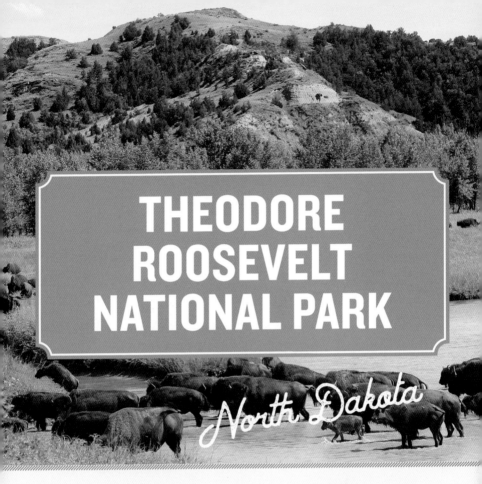

THEODORE ROOSEVELT NATIONAL PARK

North Dakota

PASSPORT STAMPS ▼▼▼

WEBSITE:
www.nps.gov/thro

PHONE NUMBER:
701/623-4466

VISITATION RANK:
28

WHY GO:
See wild horses, bison, and badlands.

▲ THEODORE ROOSEVELT
NATIONAL PARK

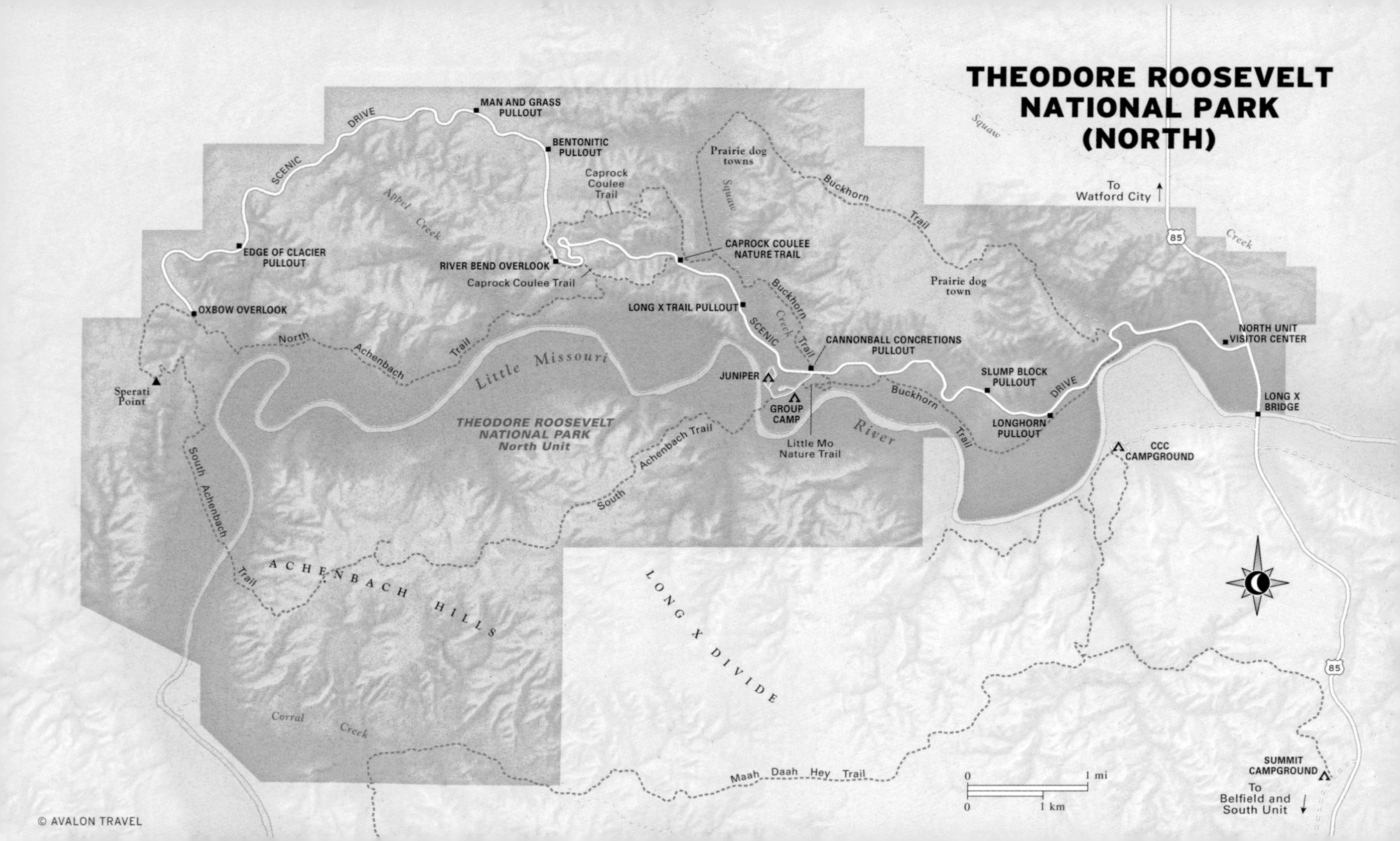

© AVALON TRAVEL

THEODORE ROOSEVELT NATIONAL PARK (NORTH)

Sperati Point

OXBOW OVERLOOK

EDGE OF GLACIER PULLOUT

SCENIC DRIVE

MAN AND GRASS PULLOUT

RIVER BEND OVERLOOK

BENTONITIC PULLOUT

Caprock Coulee Trail

Caprock Coulee Trail

LONG X TRAIL PULLOUT

CAPROCK COULEE NATURE TRAIL

Prairie dog towns

Squaw Creek

Buckhorn Trail

JUNIPER

GROUP CAMP

Little Mo Nature Trail

SCENIC DRIVE

CANNONBALL CONCRETIONS PULLOUT

Prairie dog town

Buckhorn Trail

Buckhorn Trail

LONGHORN PULLOUT

SLUMP BLOCK PULLOUT

River

SCENIC DRIVE

THEODORE ROOSEVELT NATIONAL PARK North Unit

ACHENBACH HILLS

Corral Creek

South Achenbach Trail

North Achenbach Trail

Achenbach Trail

Little Missouri

South Achenbach Trail

LONG X DIVIDE

Maah Daah Hey Trail

CCC CAMPGROUND

SUMMIT CAMPGROUND

To Belfield and South Unit

85

LONG X BRIDGE

NORTH UNIT VISITOR CENTER

Squaw Creek

To Watford City

85

0 1 km
0 1 mi

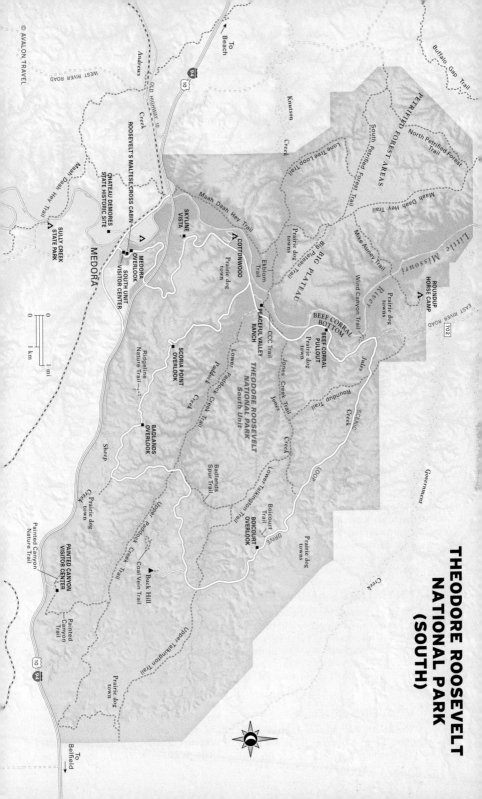

Grasslands and badlands collide around the Little Missouri River in **THEODORE ROOSEVELT NATIONAL PARK.** These wild lands of the Great Plains still harbor bison much like they did in the 1800s. Above the wind, alarm calls of prairie dogs resound and broken patches of junipers hide elk. These animals, along with feral horses, thrive on the land's native grasses. In these badlands, sandstone and soft clay erode into fantastical formations—hoodoos and pillars with capstones—while mud layers lend pastels to bluffs rising from the river. This otherworldly landscape may appear barren at first glance, but it contains a raw beauty favored by Theodore Roosevelt.

PLANNING YOUR TIME

Theodore Roosevelt National Park is part of the North Dakota badlands. Three separate parcels make up the park and are linked by the Little Missouri River and the Maah Daah Hey Trail.

The **South Unit** is the most visited and easily accessible, located adjacent to I-94 near the town of Medora. The North Unit is 70 miles north. The **Elkhorn Ranch Unit** sits between the North and South Units and requires a high-clearance vehicle for its remote access.

The North and South Units observe different time zones: the South Unit observes Mountain Standard Time, while the North Unit is in Central Time.

Summer (May-Sept.) is high season, when park services are open and temperatures are warm, though sudden thunderstorms can downpour. Winters are bitingly cold and snow can close park roads.

ENTRANCES AND FEES

The main entrance is in the **South Unit,** near the town of Medora and I-94. The **North Unit** entrance is on Highway 85 south of Watford City. The entrance fee is $30 per vehicle ($25 motorcycle, $15 individual) and is good for seven days.

VISITORS CENTERS

The **South Unit Visitor Center** (8am-6pm daily in summer, 8am-4:30pm daily fall-spring) has a museum with exhibits on geology and history, a bookstore, and restrooms. Ranger-led talks, walks, hikes, and campfire programs are scheduled in June-mid-September. Moved here from its original location is Theodore Roosevelt's **Maltese Cross Cabin**, a restored icon from his years in the badlands. Rangers lead tours of the cabin daily in summer. The **Dakota Nights Astronomy Festival** takes place in mid-September and offers stargazing with astronomers and rangers.

Farther east in the South Unit is the **Painted Canyon Visitor Center** (8:30am-4:30pm daily May-Oct.), which has indoor exhibits, a bookstore, hiking trails, and an outdoor overlook with panoramic views of the badlands. Bison frequent the area. The **Painted Canyon Nature Trail** (0.9 mi. rt., 45 min.) drops into the colorful canyon. The center is located off exit 32 of I-94.

The **North Unit Contact Station** (9am-5pm Fri.-Mon.) is housed in temporary trailers at the North Unit entrance. The information desk can advise on current trail conditions. Restrooms and a gift shop are available.

SCENIC DRIVES
SOUTH UNIT

A paved, 36-mile drive (2 hrs.) loops multiple interpretive stops through the park's South Unit. Several overlooks take in the badlands. **Peaceful Valley Ranch** is the only original remaining ranch house in the South Unit. At **Boicourt Overlook**, peer down on the Little Missouri River. The loop passes

THE NORTH UNIT

several **prairie dog towns** that can be noisy with alarm call barks. Watch for pronghorn, horses, and bison on the narrow road with steep, sharp curves.

ELKHORN RANCH

Theodore Roosevelt had the **Elkhorn Ranch** built in 1884-1885 on land sliced by the Little Missouri River. He abandoned the dwelling two years later after losing nearly all his livestock to brutal weather. Today, only stones marking the foundations remain, yet you can still get a sense of the quietude the president enjoyed while ranching in the Dakota Territory.

The Elkhorn Ranch Unit sits between the North and South Units. To get there, take exit 23 off I-94 and drive 35 miles (90 min.) along the rough gravel road. A high-clearance vehicle is required. Stop first at the visitors center for road conditions and directions.

NORTH UNIT

From the North Unit entrance station, cruise along the 28-mile paved and scenic drive with interpretive stops at several overlooks of the Little Missouri. **River Bend,** at the halfway point, and **Oxbow Overlook,** at the road's terminus, are the best places to soak in the views. En route, watch for the herd of **longhorn steers,** maintained by the park, and other wildlife. For a geologic oddity, stop at **Cannonball Concretions Pullout**, where large round rocks are exposed by erosion.

HIKING
SOUTH UNIT

Short but steep, the **Ridgeline Trail** (0.6 mi. rt., 30 min., moderate) takes in colorful badlands, grasslands, and bison, with birds and wildflowers in spring.

CANNONBALL FORMATIONS

The **Coal Vein Trail** (0.8 mi. rt., 30-45 min., moderate) is the best way to learn the geology of the badlands—you'll see clay layers, caprocks, slumping, and chimneys. Pick up an interpretive brochure at the trailhead.

The **Wind Canyon Trail** (0.4 mi. rt., 20 min., easy) ascends past a wind-sculpted canyon for views of the Little Missouri.

NORTH UNIT

Little Mo Nature Trail (0.7-1.1 mi., 30-45 min., easy) explores the river habitat along the Little Missouri River.

The **Caprock Coulee Nature Trail** (1.5 mi. rt., 1 hr., moderate) explores badlands features such as coulees, erosions, and petrified wood. Pick up an interpretive brochure at the trailhead. From the same trailhead, follow a portion of the **Buckhorn Trail** (1.5 mi. rt., 1 hr., moderate) to a prairie dog town where you can watch the antics of these furry ground dwellers.

WHERE TO STAY

INSIDE THE PARK

There are no accommodations or restaurants in the park. Camping is the only overnight option.

THE LITTLE MISSOURI

Reservations are accepted for half of the 66 sites at the South Unit's **Cottonwood Campground** (701/623-4466 or 877/444-6777, www.recreation.gov, year-round, $14). The North Unit's **Juniper Campground** (701/842-2333, year-round, $14) has 50 first-come, first-served sites. Both campgrounds have drinking water and flush toilets in summer with reduced services and fees in winter.

Backcountry camping is allowed with a free permit available from the visitors centers. There are no established backcountry campsites.

OUTSIDE THE PARK

The closest accommodations and services are located near the South Unit in **Medora**.

▼ WIND CANYON TRAIL IN THE SOUTH UNIT

THEODORE ROOSEVELT

Theodore Roosevelt came to the badlands to work as a cowboy almost two decades before becoming president of the United States. His experience here shaped him into one of the United States' earliest conservationists.

Roosevelt came to Dakota Territory in 1883 to hunt bison for two weeks. These rugged badlands took root in his mind and the landscape captivated him. Before returning to New York, he bought Chimney Butte Ranch (called the Maltese Cross Ranch) and a herd of cattle. The ponderosa-pine Maltese Cabin (reconstructed near the South Unit Visitor Center) was part of this ranch and was Roosevelt's part-time home as he bounced between New York and the Dakotas. After the death of Roosevelt's wife and mother, followed by a heavy political loss, he returned to the ranch intending to quit politics and become a cattle rancher.

Roosevelt then purchased Elkhorn Ranch, dubbed the "home ranch," to expand his cattle business. In 1884-1885, he hired two men to build the house, barn, and outbuildings. Within two years, a drought coupled with a wickedly cold winter nearly killed off his herd, prompting him to abandon the ranch and move back to New York and into politics.

Eleven years later, Roosevelt became the 26th president of the United States, attributing his election win to his experiences in North Dakota. He wrote three books on his cowboy life there, which formed the backbone for his push for conservation. Roosevelt's legacy includes the establishment of the U.S. Forest Service, the creation of five national parks, and numerous proclamations preserving wildlife reserves, national forests, national monuments, and antiquities.

This park honors Roosevelt for his vision and his efforts.

GETTING THERE AND AROUND

AIR

The nearest airport is in **Bismarck** (BIS, 2301 University Dr., 701/355-1800, www.bismarckairport.com), 140 miles east of the South Unit via I-94. The airport has rental cars.

CAR

There is no public transportation to or within the park. Visiting the park will require a car with long drives between the three units.

To reach the **South Unit,** take I-94 (exit 24 or 27) to the town of Medora and the South Unit Visitor Center. Use exit 32 (7 miles east of Medora) to reach the Painted Canyon Visitor Center.

From Medora, it's a 70-mile drive to the **North Unit**. From I-94 at Belfield, take exit 42 to Highway 85.

To reach the **Elkhorn Ranch Unit**, you'll need a high-clearance, four-wheel-drive vehicle for the rough gravel road. Obtain road conditions and directions from visitors centers. From Medora, the drive takes 1.5 hours.

SIGHTS NEARBY

Knife River Indian Villages National Historic Site (564 County Rd. 37, Stanton, 701/745-3300, www.nps.gov/knri, 9am-5pm daily late May-early Sept., 8am-4:30pm daily mid-Sept.-mid-May) is home to a reconstructed earthen lodge, with trails through the Mandan and Hidatsa village site.

Maah Daah Hey Trail (www.mdhta.com) is a 144-mile National Recreation Trail that links all three units of Theodore Roosevelt National Park.

The **Little Missouri River** (701/764-5256, www.parkrec.nd.gov) attracts canoeists and kayakers for a five-day, 108-mile float (May-June) between the South and North Units.

GREAT LAKES
AND
NORTHEAST

Along the boulder-strewn shores of Maine lies the only national park in the northeastern United States: Acadia National Park. Watch the sun rise from Cadillac Mountain, stroll the Park Loop Road, and ride the carriage roads at this East Coast gem.

The Great Lakes region is home to three national parks. In Ohio, Cuyahoga Valley National Park contains river canals of historical import. In Michigan, a cluster of islands in Lake Superior form Isle Royale National Park. Tucked into a corner of Minnesota is the remote Voyageurs National Park, a haven for kayakers and canoers.

◄ BLUE HEN FALLS,
CUYAHOGA NATIONAL PARK

The National Parks of
THE GREAT LAKES AND NORTHEAST

ACADIA, ME
Drama comes from mountains tumbling to the sea and ocean waves crashing upon granite ledges, while serene lakes provide pastoral alternatives (page 534).

CUYAHOGA VALLEY, OH
Canals and a scenic railway cut through a lush countryside of forests, wetlands, and prairies (page 550).

ISLE ROYALE, MI
Seasonal boat tours guide visitors around this isolated archipelago (page 559).

VOYAGEURS, MN
Remote forests, 655 miles of wild shoreline, and more than 500 islands are found in this this water-filled park (page 566).

1: JORDAN POND, ACADIA
2: SCHOODIC PENINSULA, ACADIA
3: VIRGINIA KENDALL LEDGES, CUYAHOGA VALLEY

Best OF THE PARKS

Jordan Pond House: Sip afternoon tea at this rustic 19th-century teahouse (page 539).

Kettle Falls Hotel: Grab a meal or a drink at this historic lodge 16 miles from the nearest road (page 570).

Canoeing and Kayaking: Paddle miles of shoreline waters at Voyageurs and Isle Royale (pages 571 and 563).

Wildlife-Watching: Spy moose at Hidden Lake (page 563).

Ohio & Erie Canal Towpath Trail: Bike along the Cuyahoga River on this historic path (page 553).

Everett Road Covered Bridge: Pose for pics on the only remaining covered bridge in Summit County, Ohio (page 554).

PLANNING YOUR TRIP

Plan at least **one weekend** in Acadia and **another week or two** to tour the national parks of the Great Lakes. Make lodging and campground **reservations** up to one year in advance.

September-mid-October is the best time to travel in Maine. Days are warm and mostly dry, nights are cool, fog is rare, bugs are gone, and crowds are few. Foliage turns by early October, usually reaching peak colors mid-month.

Summer (May-Oct.) is the most popular time to visit the Great Lakes,

when visitors centers and services are open and the weather is temperate with long, lingering evenings. July is typically the warmest month, but it's also the buggiest. Time a camping trip in mid-June or after mid-August, when the mosquitoes and blackflies are less bothersome.

Fall is the best time to visit Cuyahoga, when one can savor the vibrant fall foliage and crisp, dry air. But the park's hiking and biking trails are available spring through fall.

▲ PADDLE VOYAGEURS' WATERS.

Touring the Great Lakes

VOYAGEURS AND ISLE ROYALE

You can hit these two national parks in **one week.** Fly into **Minneapolis-St. Paul International Airport** and then rent a car for the drive to the parks. You will also need to travel by boat to explore these parks, which are prime destinations for paddlers.

Voyageurs

283 miles / 5 hours

From Minneapolis-St. Paul, drive north to the **Rainy Lake Visitor Center** in **Voyageurs National Park** and spend three days in the park. Take a boat tour to either **Little American Island** or **Kettle Falls,** then get out on the water yourself in a canoe or kayak.

Isle Royale

244 miles / 5 hours

From Voyageurs, drive east to **Grand Portage** on Lake Superior, the back door to **Isle Royale.** Catch the passenger ferry to **Rock Harbor** and rent a kayak to spend three days paddling the waters around Isle Royale.

After returning to Grand Portage, paddlers may want to extend their adventures by stopping to tour the **Boundary Waters Canoe Area Wilderness.** This paddling paradise sits 66 miles (1.75 hrs.) southwest from Grand Portage, en route back to Minneapolis-St. Paul.

LAKE, VOYAGEURS NATIONAL PARK

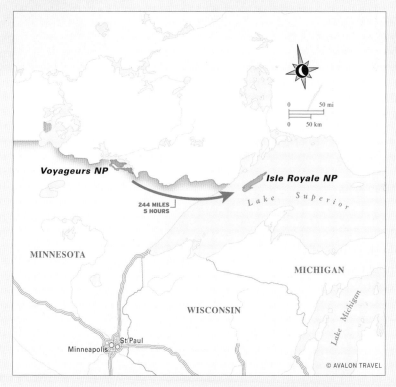

Voyageurs NP

Isle Royale NP

244 MILES
5 HOURS

Lake Superior

MINNESOTA

MICHIGAN

WISCONSIN

Lake Michigan

St Paul
Minneapolis

© AVALON TRAVEL

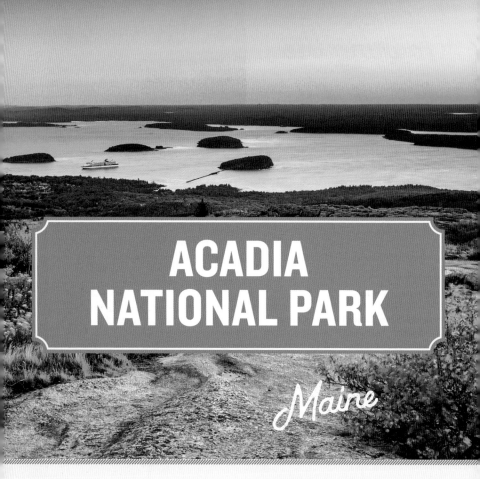

ACADIA
NATIONAL PARK

Maine

WEBSITE:
www.nps.gov/acad

PHONE NUMBER:
207/288-3338

VISITATION RANK:
7

WHY GO:
Travel the rugged
northeast island
seacoast.

PASSPORT STAMPS ▼▼▼

▲ SUNRISE VIEW FROM
CADILLAC MOUNTAIN

Rather like an octopus (or perhaps an amoeba), **ACADIA NATIONAL PARK** extends its reach here and there, sprawling over roughly half of Mount Desert Island. The first national park east of the Mississippi River, and the only national park in the northeastern United States, it was created from donated parcels—a big chunk here, a tiny piece there—and slowly fused into its present-day size of more than 50,000 acres. We can thank George B. Dorr, Charles W. Eliot, and John D. Rockefeller Jr. for the park we enjoy today.

Towering above rocky beaches, Acadia tops out at the pink granite of Cadillac Mountain, the highest point on the East Coast. Within its boundaries are mountains, lakes, ponds, trails, vistas, and campgrounds. Each year more than two million visitors come to drive the Park Loop Road, tour the horse-driven Carriage Roads, and hike the granite steps up the park's many trails. Yet even at the height of summer, when the whole world seems to have arrived, it's possible to find peaceful niches and less-trodden paths.

PLANNING YOUR TIME

Acadia National Park sits on the Maine coast south of Bangor. Mount Desert Island is the most accessible of the park's watery isles; the Schoodic Peninsula and Isle au Haut require time to explore and are best reached via boat or ferry.

You can circumnavigate Mount Desert Island in one day, hitting the highlights along the Park Loop Road with just enough time to *ooh* and *aah* at each. But to truly appreciate Acadia, you must hike the trails, ride the carriage roads, get afloat on a whale-watching cruise or a sea kayak, visit museums, and explore an offshore island or two. A week or longer is best, but you can get a taste of Acadia in 3-4 days.

The region is very seasonal, with most restaurants, accommodations, and shops open **mid-May-mid-October.** May and June bring spring, but also mosquitoes and blackflies, and weather is temperamental—sunny and hot one day, damp and cold the next. July and August are summer at its best, but also bring the biggest crowds. September is a gem of a time to visit: few bugs, fewer people, less fog, and autumn's golden light.

Foliage usually begins turning in **early October,** making it an especially beautiful time to visit (the Columbus Day holiday weekend brings a spike in visitors). Winter is Acadia's silent season, with several roads closed due to snow.

ENTRANCES AND FEES

The main park entrance is **Route 3** through Ellsworth to Mount Desert Island. Route 3 continues southeast, passing through the **Hull Cove Entrance** to the gateway town of Bar Harbor and the **Cadillac Mountain Entrance.**

The entrance fee is $30 per vehicle ($25 motorcycle, $15 individual) and is good for seven days.

VISITORS CENTERS

Acadia's **ranger programs** are wonderful opportunities to learn about the park's natural and cultural heritage. July-August, dozens of weekly programs are listed in the park handout. Most programs are free, though some require reservations. Park rangers also give evening lectures in the summer at the Blackwoods and Seawall campground amphitheaters.

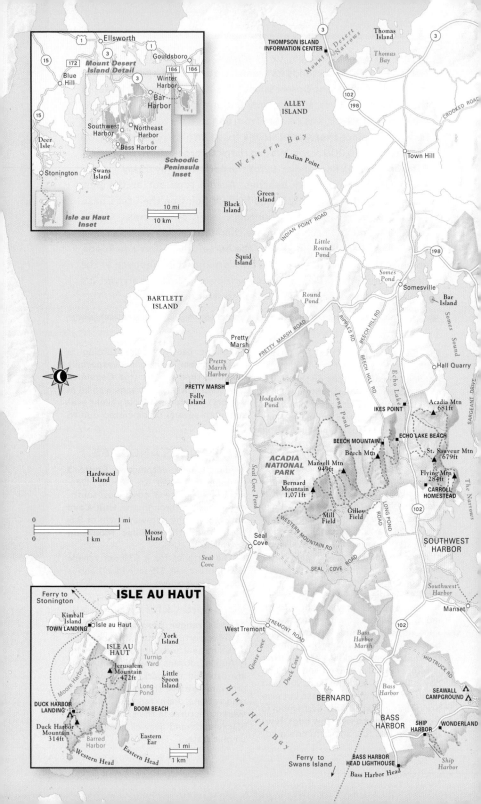

Ellsworth

Gouldsboro

3

1

1

15

172

186 186

Blue
Hill

3

Winter
Harbor

*Mount Desert
Island Detail*

**Bar
Harbor**

15

Southwest
Harbor

Northeast
Harbor

*Schoodic
Peninsula
Inset*

Deer
Isle

Stonington

Swans
Island

Bass Harbor

*Isle au Haut
Inset*

10 mi

10 km

THOMPSON ISLAND
INFORMATION CENTER

Thomas
Island

3

Mount Desert Narrows

Thomas
Bay

ALLEY
ISLAND

102

198

CROOKED ROAD

Western Bay

Indian Point

Town Hill

Black
Island

Green
Island

Squid
Island

INDIAN POINT ROAD

*Little
Round
Pond*

Somes
Pond

198

Somesville

Bar
Island

BARTLETT
ISLAND

*Round
Pond*

RIPPLES RD

BEECH HILL RD

Hall Quarry

Pretty
Marsh

PRETTY MARSH ROAD

*Pretty
Marsh
Harbor*

Echo Lake

Somes Sound

SARGEANT DRIVE

PRETTY MARSH

Folly
Island

*Hodgdon
Pond*

IKES POINT

Acadia Mtn
681ft ▲

BEECH MOUNTAIN

Beech Mtn ▲

ECHO LAKE BEACH

St. Sauveur Mtn
679ft ▲

Hardwood
Island

Long Pond

**ACADIA
NATIONAL
PARK**

Mansell Mtn
949ft ▲

Bernard
Mountain
1,071ft ▲

Flying Mtn
284ft ▲

**CARROLL
HOMESTEAD**

102

Seal Cove Pond

Mill
Field

Gilley
Field

LONG POND

WESTERN MOUNTAIN RD

SOUTHWEST
HARBOR

0   1 mi

0   1 km

Moose
Island

*Seal
Cove*

Seal
Cove

SEAL COVE ROAD

*Southwest
Harbor*

Manset

Ferry to
Stonington

Kimball
Island

TOWN LANDING

Isle au Haut

ISLE AU HAUT

York
Island

ISLE AU
HAUT

*Turnip
Yard*

West Tremont

TREMONT ROAD

*Bass
Harbor
Marsh*

102

HIO TRUCK RD

Jerusalem
Mountain
472ft ▲

Little
Spoon
Island

Moose Harbor

*Long
Pond*

**DUCK HARBOR
LANDING**

Duck Harbor
Mountain
314ft ▲

BOOM BEACH

*Barred
Harbor*

Eastern
Ear

Western Head

Eastern Head

1 mi

1 km

Goose Cove

Duck Cove

BERNARD

*Bass
Harbor*

**BASS
HARBOR**

Ship
Harbor

**SHIP
HARBOR**

WONDERLAND

**SEAWALL
CAMPGROUND** ▲

Blue Hill Bay

Ferry to
Swans Island

**BASS HARBOR
HEAD LIGHTHOUSE**

Bass Harbor Head

*Ship
Harbor*

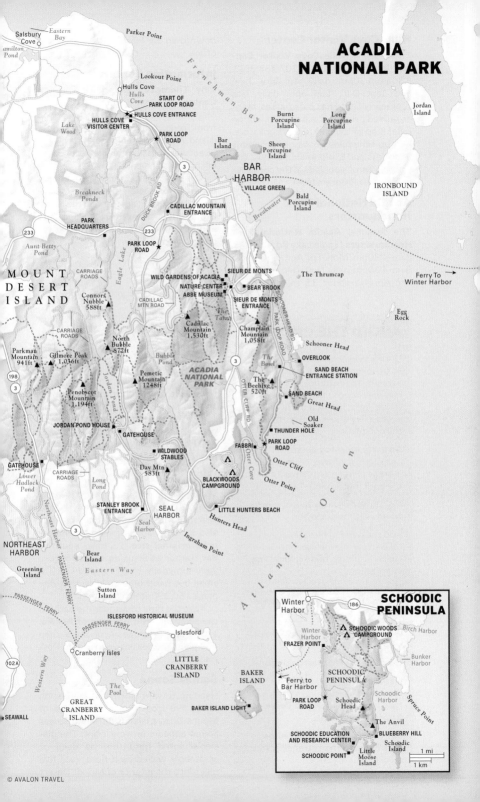

Hulls Cove Visitor Center

The modern **Hulls Cove Visitor Center** (Rte. 3, Hulls Cove, 207/288-3338, 8:30am-4:30pm daily Apr.-late June and Sept.-Oct., 8am-6pm daily late June-early Sept.) has park passes, ranger-guided programs, a park film, a large relief map of the park, and a bookstore. Pick up schedules for ranger programs and the Island Explorer shuttle bus. You can also enroll your kids in the park's Junior Ranger Program (fee).

Acadia National Park Headquarters

The seasonal **Acadia National Park Headquarters** (Eagle Lake Rd./Rte. 233, 8am-4:30pm Mon.-Fri. Apr. 15-Oct. 31, 8am-4:30pm daily Nov.-Dec. and Mar.-mid-Apr.) is about 3.5 miles west of downtown Bar Harbor. It has a ranger office.

Information Centers

Tiny **Thompson Island Information Center** (8:30am-5:30pm daily mid-May-mid-Oct.) sits across the bridge from Trenton en route to Mount Desert Island. A park ranger is usually available to answer questions and give advice on hiking trails and park activities.

The park maintains the small **Village Green Information Center** in downtown Bar Harbor, adjacent to the Island Explorer bus stop on Firefly Lane. Park and bus information, as well as visitor passes, are available.

SIGHTS

MOUNT DESERT ISLAND

Abbe Museum

The **Abbe Museum** (26 Mount Desert St., Bar Harbor, 207/288-3519, www.abbemuseum.org) is a superb introduction to prehistoric, historic, and contemporary Native American tools, crafts, and other cultural artifacts, with an emphasis on Maine's Micmac, Maliseet, Passamaquoddy, and Penobscot people.

It has two campuses: The **main campus** (26 Mount Desert St., Bar Harbor, 207/288-3519, www.abbemuseum.org, 10am-5pm daily May 1-Oct. 31, $8 adults, $4 children ages 11-17) is home to a collection spanning nearly 12,000 years. Admission to the main campus also includes admission to the **museum's original site** (2.5 miles south of Bar Harbor at Sieur de Monts Spring, 9am-4pm daily mid-May-mid-Oct.), a small but handsome building that displays a 50,000-item collection.

Take the time to wander the paths in the adjacent **Wild Gardens of Acadia,** a 0.75-acre microcosm of more than 400 plant species native to Mount Desert Island.

Somes Sound

Heading toward Northeast Harbor on Route 198 from the northern end of Mount Desert Island, cliff-lined Somes Sound appears on your right. The glacier-sculpted fjard (not as deep or as steeply walled as a fjord) juts five miles into the interior of Mount Desert

---

AVOID THE CROWDS

During midsummer, Acadia seems to be loved to death. Long lines of cars clog the entrances, and parking lots overflow. In fact, at congested times, rangers temporarily restrict access. Try these tactics to avoid the congestion:

Go early morning or late in the afternoon for fewer crowds and more enjoyment. Most visitors fill the park roads 10am-4pm.

Visit in **spring, late fall,** or **winter** when visitation is lower.

Skip the parking headache and take an off-the-beaten path adventure such as **hiking, bicycling,** or **paddling.**

Leave your vehicle behind and take the free **Island Explorer Shuttle Bus** into the park.

Bicycle the carriage roads, where cars are not permitted.

Go after-dark for **stargazing.**

Instead of going to Cadillac Mountain for sunrise or sunset, catch **sunrise on Ocean Drive** or sunset from a boat.

Buy your **entrance pass online** to pass through the entrance station quickly.

Top ③

1 DRIVE THE PARK LOOP ROAD

ACADIA'S PARK LOOP ROAD

The 27-mile **Park Loop Road** takes in most of the park's big-ticket sites. Part of the route is one-way, so you'll drive the loop clockwise. From the **Hulls Cove Visitor Center**, the road winds past several of the park's scenic highlights, ascending to the summit of **Cadillac Mountain** with overlooks to magnificent vistas. Along the way are trailheads and overlooks, **Sieur de Monts Spring, Sand Beach, Thunder Hole, Otter Cliff, Fabbri Picnic Area, Jordan Pond House, Bubble Pond,** and **Eagle Lake.**

2 SIP AFTERNOON TEA AT JORDAN POND HOUSE

The **Jordan Pond House** (Park Loop Rd., 207/276-3316, www.acadiajordanpond-house.com, 11am-9pm daily) is a modern facility in a spectacular waterside setting. Jordan Pond House began life as a rustic 19th-century teahouse; wonderful old photos still line the walls of the current incarnation, which was built after a disastrous fire in 1979. Afternoon tea is still a tradition, with tea, popovers, and strawberry jam served on the lawn until 5pm daily in summer, weather permitting. Jordan Pond is far from a secret, so expect to wait for seats at the height of summer. Jordan Pond House is on the Island Explorer's Route No. 5.

3 TOUR THE CARRIAGE ROADS ON MOUNT DESERT ISLAND

RIDE A HORSE-DRAWN CARRIAGE ON ACADIA'S CARRIAGE ROADS.

In 1913, John D. Rockefeller Jr. began laying out what eventually became a 57-mile carriage road system. Motorized vehicles have never been allowed on these lovely graded byways, making them real escapes from the auto world. Devoted now to multiple uses, the "Rockefeller roads" see hikers, bikers, baby strollers, wheelchairs, and even horse-drawn carriages.

To recapture the early carriage roads era, take one of the horse-drawn open-carriage tours run by **Carriages of Acadia** (Wildwood Stables, Park Loop Rd., Seal Harbor, 877/276-3622, www.acadiahorses.com), south of the Jordan Pond House. Four one- and two-hour tours run daily (mid-June-mid-Oct.). Make reservations, especially in summer.

ONE DAY IN ACADIA

Drive or take the Island Explorer to tour the **Park Loop Road.** To take in a broad view of the mountain-and-island environment, stop at the summit of **Cadillac Mountain.** Stroll the nature trail at **Jordan Pond,** and enjoy afternoon tea at **Jordan Pond House.** Then, tour the museum and paths at **Sieur de Monts Spring.**

With more time, you can hike the Beehive Trail or Precipice Trail, take a boat tour, bike the carriage roads, and explore remote Schoodic Point.

Island from its mouth between Northeast Harbor and Southwest Harbor. Watch for the right-hand turn for **Sargent Drive,** and follow the lovely, granite-lined route along the east side of the sound. Halfway along, a marker at one of the few pullouts explains the geology of this spectacular natural inlet. Traffic can be fairly thick in midsummer.

Suminsby Park, located off Sargent Drive (400 feet from Route 3), has rocky shore access, a hand-carry boat launch, picnic tables, grills, and a pit toilet. An ideal way to appreciate Somes Sound is from the water—sign up for an excursion out of Northeast Harbor or Southwest Harbor.

Southwest Harbor is the hub of Mount Desert Island's "quiet side." In summer, its tiny downtown district is probably the island's busiest spot west of Somes Sound.

Bass Harbor Head Lighthouse

At the southern end of Mount Desert, follow Route 102A to the turnoff toward Bass Harbor Head. Drive or bike to the end of Lighthouse Road, walk down a steep wooden stairway, and look up and to the right. Voilà! **Bass Harbor Head Lighthouse**—its red glow automated since 1974—stands sentinel at the eastern entrance to Blue Hill Bay. Built in 1858, the 26-foot tower and lightkeeper's house are privately owned, but the dramatic setting captivates photographers.

Cadillac Mountain

The sunrise awaits those who can drive predawn to the summit of **Cadillac Mountain**. It's a tradition, albeit an overcrowded one in summer, to catch the first rays to hit the eastern United

BASS HARBOR HEAD LIGHTHOUSE

SCHOODIC PENINSULA

States from Acadia's highest point. (You can also watch the sunrise from Ocean Drive and other locations.) Sunset aficionados also nab colors across the western horizon.

SCHOODIC PENINSULA

On the mainland, the **Schoodic Peninsula** is separated from Mount Desert Island by an almost two-hour drive. The lack of congestion, even at the height of summer, is the main appeal for a visit to the eastern side of Frenchman Bay. The Schoodic Peninsula also has abundant opportunities for outdoor recreation, two scenic byways, and dozens of artist and artisan studios. But the biggest attractions are the spectacular vignettes and vistas—of offshore lighthouses, distant mountains, and close-in islands—and the unchanged villages.

To reach the park boundary from Route 1 in Gouldsboro, take Route 186 south to Winter Harbor. Continue through town, heading east, and then turn right and continue to the park. The **Island Explorer bus** circulates through Winter Harbor, around the Schoodic Loop, and on to Prospect Harbor, with stops along the way.

Winter Harbor

Winter Harbor, known best as the gateway to Schoodic, is home to an old-money, low-profile, Philadelphia-linked summer colony on exclusive Grindstone Neck. The landscape of the smaller and far-less-touristed Schoodic isn't as awe-inspiring as that on Mount Desert, but it's no less powerful—and it has a more remote, raw edge. Too-frequent fog rolls in to shroud the stunted, scraggly spruce clinging to its pink granite shores. There's a **campground** and visitors center, along with eight miles of **carriage roads** for foot or bicycle exploration.

Scenic Drive

The **Schoodic Peninsula Loop** (6 mi. one-way) meanders counterclockwise around the tip of the Schoodic Peninsula. You'll discover picnic areas, trailheads, offshore lighthouses, a welcome center with exhibits, and turnouts with scenic vistas. Do this loop early in the morning or later in the afternoon. The gorgeous late September-early October foliage increases traffic. Small periodic pullouts can squeeze in a few cars. If you see a viewpoint you like with room to pull off, stop; it's a long way around to return.

Begin at the **Schoodic Woods Campground,** where you leave your car to explore via bicycle or the Island Explorer bus. At 2.2 miles past the picnic area, watch for a narrow, unpaved road on the left, across from an open beach vista. It winds for one mile (keep left at the fork) up to a tiny parking circle, from which you can follow the Schoodic Trails to the open ledges on 440-foot **Schoodic Head.**

A second spur hangs right onto a short, two-way road to **Schoodic Point.** The **Schoodic Institute** campus (207/288-1310, www.schoodicinstitute. org), on the site of a former top-secret U.S. Navy base, has a small info center staffed by volunteers and park rangers. The restored **Rockefeller Hall** has exhibits highlighting Schoodic's ecology and history, the former navy base's radio and cryptologic operations, and current research programs. The Schoodic Institute also offers ranger-led activities, lectures, and other programs and events. At **Schoodic Point,** the highlight of the drive, the surf crashes onto big slabs of pink granite.

Back on the Loop Road, you'll spot **Little Moose Island,** accessible at low tide. At **Blueberry Hill**, a moorlike setting with low growth allows almost 180-degree views of the bay and islands.

ISLE AU HAUT

The Isle au Haut section of the park sees maybe 5,000-7,500 visitors annually, with a daily cap of 128. The limited boat service, the remoteness of the island, and the scarcity of campsites contribute to the low count, leaving the trails and views for only a few hardy souls. The **ranger station** (207/335-5551) has trail maps, information, and the only public facilities.

HIKING
MOUNT DESERT ISLAND
Jordan Pond

The **Jordan Pond Nature Trail** (3.3 mi. rt., 1.5 hr., easy) starts from the Jordan Pond parking area and leads through woods and down to the pond to follow the shore before looping back.

Champlain Mountain

Near Sieur de Monts Spring, the **Champlain North Ridge Trail** (Bear Brook Trail, 2 mi. rt., 2-3 hr., strenuous) bolts 852 feet up a steep ascent through pines and granite to Champlain Mountain. The summit yields views of the ocean, islands, Schoodic Peninsula, and Bar Harbor. (Combine this trail with the Precipice and Beechcroft Trails for more distance.)

▼ VIEW OVER JORDAN POND

Best Hike

BEEHIVE LOOP TRAIL

DISTANCE: 1.6 miles round-trip
DURATION: 1-2 hours
ELEVATION CHANGE: 450 feet
DIFFICULTY: moderately strenuous
TRAILHEAD: Bowl Trailhead on Park Loop Road across from Sand Beach

The sometimes-crowded Beehive Trail starts and ends on the Bowl Trail, which those needing less of a challenge can use to reach the beehive-shaped summit, minus the climbing option. Not for acrophobes or tiny kids, the climbing option is a fun scramble (no technical rock climbing skills needed) with switchbacks, stone steps, handrails, and iron ladders. Ascending the Beehive's southern face, the exposed, steep route picks its way up smoothed granite to Beehive summit for views of beaches and bays. When the route crowds with hikers, you may have to wait at the obstacles. From the summit, return via the Bowl Trail, which descends past Bowl Lake.

From the Park Loop Road, the **Precipice Trail** (2.3-mi. loop, 3 hrs., strenuous, closed mid-Apr.-mid-Aug.) lures hordes of wannabe climbers to its steep but nontechnical 1,072-foot ascent of switchbacks, ladders, and exposed ledges to reach the summit. Return via the Champlain North Ridge Trail and Orange and Black Path.

The **Beachcroft Trail** (2.4 mi. rt., 2-3 hrs., moderately strenuous) is known for its 1,500 beautifully engineered granite steps. The route gains 1,100 feet over Huguenot Head to the summit of Champlain Mountain.

Sand Beach

From the east end of Sand Beach, the **Great Head Trail** (1.5-mi. loop, 1 hr., moderate) circles a headland with views of the ocean, tidepools, and the Beehive.

Gorham Mountain

Many of Acadia's trails shoot up mountainsides, climbing from the ocean to summits with scrambling on granite. From Gorham Mountain Trailhead, the **Gorham Mountain Trail** (1.8 mi. rt., 2 hrs., moderate) climbs 525 feet

to follow cairns across rock ledges to the summit of Acadia's third-highest mountain, with big terrestrial and ocean views.

For an added challenge, detour to **Cadillac Cliffs** to climb the granite stairs and walk under two rock slab tunnels. For a longer hike, combine this trail with the Bowl Trail and Ocean Path to return to your car.

Bass Harbor

From the Ship Harbor Trailhead, a figure-eight loop makes up the **Ship Harbor Nature Trail** (1.3 mi. rt., 1 hr., easy). The trail tours the forest to the ocean, where low tides beg exploring.

The **Wonderland Trail** (1.4 mi. rt., 45 min., easy) follows a fire road through a forest of mossy, wind-gnarled trees to a small cobble beach. The trailhead is one mile west of Seawall Campground.

Beech Mountain

From the end of Beech Hill Road, climb **Beech Mountain** (1.2 mi. rt., 1 hr., moderate) for 700 feet to a fire tower overlooking Echo Lake and the Blue Hill Peninsula.

ISLE AU HAUT

None of Isle au Haut's 18 miles of trails could be labeled "easy." The footing is rocky, rooted, and often squishy, but the park trails are well marked and the views—of islets, distant hills, and the ocean—make the effort worthwhile.

Duck Harbor Trail

The most-used park trail is **Duck Harbor Trail** (7.6 mi. rt., 4 hrs., moderate), which connects the town landing with Duck Harbor. Though the summit is only 314 feet, **Duck Harbor Mountain** (2.4 mi. rt., 3-4 hrs., strenuous) is the island's toughest trail, but rewards with a 360-degree view.

RECREATION

BICYCLING

The best choices for cycling on pavement are the 33-mile **Park Road Loop** on Mount Dessert Island and the 6-mile **Schoodic Loop.** Go early or late in the day to avoid the heaviest traffic. For car-free riding on crushed-rock roads, nearly 45 miles of **carriage roads** await. Some prohibit bikes, but most are multiuse with hikers, horses, and carriages. **SeaScape Kayak and Bike** (8 Duck Pond Rd., Winter Harbor, 207/963-5806, www.seascapekayaking.com) rents bicycles.

SWIMMING

Mount Desert Island

Sand Beach is Mount Desert Island's biggest sandy beach. Lifeguards are on duty during the summer—and even then, the biggest threat can be hypothermia. The saltwater is terminally glacial—in mid-July it still might not reach 60°F. Avoid the parking lot scramble by taking Island Explorer Route No. 3/Sand Beach.

The park's most popular freshwater swimming site is **Echo Lake,** south of Somesville on Route 102 (take Island Explorer Route No. 7/Southwest Harbor). The site is staffed with a lifeguard and can be crowded on hot days.

The eastern shore of **Hodgdon Pond** (also on the western side of the island) is accessible by car via Hodgdon Road and Long Pond Fire Road. **Lake Wood,** at the northern end of Mount Desert, has a tiny beach, restrooms, and auto access. To get to Lake Wood from Route 3, head west on Crooked Road to unpaved Park Road. Turn left and continue to the parking area, which will be crowded on a hot day. Arrive early.

Schoodic Peninsula

The best freshwater swimming on the Schoodic Peninsula is at **Jones Beach**

▼ SAND BEACH

EXPLORE LONG POND BY CANOE OR KAYAK.

(sunrise-sunset daily), a community-owned recreation area on Jones Pond in West Gouldsboro. Here you'll find restrooms, a nice playground, picnic facilities, a boat launch, a swim area with a float, and a small beach. The beach is located at the end of Recreation Road, off Route 195, which is 0.3 mile south of Route 1.

Isle au Haut

For freshwater swimming on Isle au Haut, head for **Long Pond,** a skinny, 1.5-mile-long swimming hole running north-south on the east side of the island, abutting national park land. There's a minuscule beach-like area on the southern end with a picnic table and a float.

CANOEING AND KAYAKING

Long Pond (Pretty Marsh Rd.) is the largest lake on Mount Desert Island. Bring a canoe or kayak to launch at **Pond's End**. It's four miles to the southern end of the lake. Another option is to launch your canoe on the quieter, cliff-lined southern end of the lake, much of which is in Acadia National Park. To find the put-in, take Seal Cove Road (on the east end of downtown Southwest Harbor) to Long Cove Road. Turn right to enter the small parking area near the

pumping station. Almost the entire west side of Long Pond is Acadia National Park property.

If you have a canoe, kayak, or rowboat, you can reach swimming holes in **Seal Cove Pond** and **Round Pond,** both on the western side of Mount Desert.

National Park Canoe & Kayak Rental (145 Pretty Marsh Rd./Rte. 102, Mount Desert, 207/244-5854, www.nationalparkcanoerental.com, mid-May-mid-Oct.) makes canoeing and kayaking a snap. Just rent the boat, carry it across the road to Pond's End, and launch it. Be sure to pack a picnic. Reservations are essential July-August.

Experienced sea kayakers can explore the coastline throughout the **Schoodic Peninsula,** while canoeists can paddle the placid waters of **Jones Pond**. **SeaScape Kayak and Bike** (8 Duck Pond Rd., Winter Harbor, 207/963-5806, www.seascapekayaking.com) has freshwater rental kayaks on Jones Pond.

ROCK CLIMBING

Acadia has splendid sites prized by technical rock climbers: the sea cliffs at Otter Cliff and Great Head, South Bubble Mountain, Canada Cliff (on the island's western side), and the South Wall and the Central Slabs on Champlain Mountain. If you haven't tried

CLIMBERS PREPARE TO SCALE ACADIA'S GRANITE CLIFFS.

climbing with ropes, harnesses, and protection, never do it yourself without instruction. **Acadia Mountain Guides Climbing School** (228 Main St., Bar Harbor, 207/288-8186 or 888/232-9559, www.acadiamountainguides.com) and **Atlantic Climbing School** (ACS, 67 Main St., 2nd fl., Bar Harbor, 207/288-2521, www.acadiaclimbing.com) both provide instruction and guided climbs.

WHERE TO STAY

INSIDE THE PARK

Mount Desert Island has at least a dozen commercial campgrounds, but only two are within park boundaries. There are no other accommodations inside the park.

Mount Desert Island

Reservations for **Blackwoods Campground** (877/444-6777, www.recreation.gov, year-round, $15-30) are recommended May-October and are a must in July-August. The campground's 306 sites are popular thanks to its location on the east side of the island. A trail connects the campground to the Ocean Drive trail system. The campground is located off Route 3, five miles south of Bar Harbor.

Half of the 214 sites at **Seawall Campground** (877/444-6777, www.recreation.gov, May-Sept., $22-30) are available by reservation; the remaining sites are first come, first served. In midsummer, arrive as early as 8:30am to secure a site. The campground is on Route 102A in Seawall, south of Southwest Harbor.

Schoodic Peninsula

The Schoodic Peninsula's **Schoodic Woods Campground** (Park Loop Rd., 877/444-6777, www.recreation.gov, $22-40) has 96 sites, including walk-in tent sites, drive-in sites, and RV sites. There is also a welcome center and an amphitheater. Hiking trails connect to Schoodic Head; nonmotorized paths link the east and west sides of the peninsula. The campground is located about a mile south of Route 186, north of the Frazer Point Picnic Area.

Isle au Haut

On Isle au Haut, you'll need to get your bid in early to reserve one of the five six-person lean-tos at **Duck Harbor Campground** (207/288-3338, May 15-Oct. 15, $25). The three-sided lean-tos are big enough (8 by 12 feet, 8 feet high) to hold a small (two-person) tent, or a tarp will do the trick. No camping is permitted outside of the lean-tos and nothing can be attached to trees. Contact Acadia National Park before April 1 for a reservation request form and call the Isle au Haut Company (207/367-5193) for the current ferry schedule before choosing reservation dates.

OUTSIDE THE PARK

Bar Harbor is the largest and best known of the park's communities. It offers lodging, restaurants, campgrounds, and services. **Ellsworth** and **Trenton** have inexpensive lodging.

GETTING THERE
AIR

Bangor International Airport (BIA, 287 Godfrey Blvd., Bangor, 207/992-4600, www.flybangor.com) is served by major U.S. carriers and is located one hour from the park. Flying into **Boston Logan International Airport** (BOS, Boston, MA, 800/235-6426, www.massport.com) puts you within a five-hour drive of the park.

For those without a rental car, **Cape Air** (866/227-3247, www.flycapeair.com) flies from Boston to **Hancock County Airport** (BHB, 207/667-7329, www.bhbairport.com), 10 miles from Acadia National Park. Route No. 1 of the free Island Explorer bus connects the Hancock County/Bar Harbor Airport in Trenton with downtown Bar Harbor.

CAR

You can't get to Acadia without going through Ellsworth and Trenton: The only way onto Mount Desert Island is **Route 3** (expect traffic 8am-9am and 3pm-4pm weekdays). **Bar Harbor** is about 20 miles (30-45 min.) via Route 3 from Ellsworth; about 45 miles (75 min.) via Routes 1A and 3 from Bangor; and about 275 miles (5 hrs.) via I-95 and Route 3 from Boston. It's about 12 miles (20 min.) via Routes 233 and 198 or 20 miles (35 min.) via Route 3 to Northeast Harbor.

BUS

If you're day-tripping to Mount Desert Island, you can leave your car in Trenton and hop aboard the free **Island Explorer** (www.exploreacadia.com) bus. Once on the island, continue to use the Island Explorer bus system to avoid parking hassles.

GETTING AROUND
DRIVING

Traffic gets heavy at midday in midsummer, so aim for an early-morning start if you can. The maximum speed limit on the Park Loop Road is 35 mph, but be alert for gawkers and photographers stopping without warning, and pedestrians dashing across the road from stopped cars or tour buses.

▼ VIEW FROM CADILLAC MOUNTAIN

SUNRISE WAVES ON OTTER CLIFF

SHUTTLE BUS

On Mount Desert Island, use the free **Island Explorer** (207/667-5796, www.exploreacadia.com, daily June-Oct.) bus system to avoid parking hassles. The shuttle bus has nine routes that link multiple destinations within the park. Although the Island Explorer buses do reach a number of key park sights, they are not tour buses. There is no narration, the bus cuts off the Park Loop Road at Otter Cliff, and it excludes the summit of Cadillac Mountain. But it is free, efficient, and environmentally friendly.

GETTING TO SCHOODIC PENINSULA

Winter Harbor is about 25 miles via Routes 1 and 186 from Ellsworth. Although Winter Harbor is roughly 43 miles (1.25 hours) from Bar Harbor by car, it's only 7 miles by water. You can get here by passenger ferry via **Bar Harbor Ferry** (207/288-4585, Bar Harbor, www.barharborferry.com, daily mid-June-late Sept.) or the bus from Ellsworth, but you'll need a vehicle or bicycle to explore beyond the part of the Schoodic Peninsula that's served by the Island Explorer bus.

GETTING TO ISLE AU HAUT

Two companies offer transportation to Isle au Haut's town landing. The **Isle au Haut Boat Company** (Seabreeze Ave., Stonington, 207/367-5193, www.isleauhaut.com) operates daily Monday-Saturday, with two trips on Sunday (mid-June-early Sept.). Use Isle au Haut Boat Company if your destination is the park, as its boat lands right at Duck Harbor twice daily during peak season.

Offering seasonal service to Isle au Haut is **Old Quarry Ocean Adventures** (Stonington, 207/367-8977, www.oldquarry.com), which transports passengers on the *Nigh Duck*. The boat usually leaves Old Quarry at 9am and arrives at the island's town landing at 9:45am, returning from the same point at 5pm.

TOURS

Bus Tours

Scenic **bus tours** (207/288-0300, www.acadiatours.com, daily mid-May-Oct., 2.5 hr.) soak up the sights of Park Loop Road while someone else does the driving. These narrated tours stop at Cadillac Mountain, Thunder Hole, and either Sieur de Monts Spring or Jordan Pond House for 15 minutes at each.

DAY TRIP TO FRENCHBORO, LONG ISLAND

The island officially known as Long Island, but more commonly known as Frenchboro, makes for a delightful day trip. One of only 15 Maine coastal islands that still support a year-round population, Frenchboro is a very quiet place where islanders live as islanders always have—making a living from the sea and being proud of it. A good way to get a sense of the place is to take the 3.5-hour lunch cruise run by Captain Kim Strauss of **Island Cruises** (Little Island Marine, Shore Rd., Bass Harbor, 207/244-5785, www.bassharborcruises.com). For an even longer day trip to Frenchboro, plan to take the passenger ferry *R. L. Gott* during her weekly run for the Maine State Ferry Service. Each Friday early April-late October, the *R. L. Gott* departs Bass Harbor at 8am, arriving in Frenchboro at 9am. The return trip to Bass Harbor is at 6pm, allowing nine hours on the island.

The **Frenchboro Historical Society Museum** (207/334-2924, www.frenchboro.lib.me.us, afternoons Memorial Day-Labor Day, free), just up from the dock, has interesting old tools, other local artifacts, and a small gift shop. The island has a network of easy and not-so-easy maintained trails through the woods and along the shore. The trails are rustic, and most are unmarked, so proceed carefully. In the center of the island is a beaver pond.

When you go, stop at **Lunt's Dockside Deli** (207/334-2902, http://luntsdeli.com, 11am-7:30pm Mon.-Sat. July-Aug.). Lobster rolls and fish chowder are the specialties, but there are sandwiches, hot dogs, and even vegetable wraps. The view is wonderful, and you might even get to watch lobsters being unloaded from a boat.

Oli's Trolley (866/987-6553, http://olistrolley.com, daily late Apr.-Oct., 1-4 hrs.) guides tours to various locations including Cadillac Mountain and downtown Bar Harbor.

Boat Cruises

Rangers join boat cruises offering interpretive details on the park sights. The **Baker Island Tour** is booked through Bar Harbor Whale Watch Co. (1 West St., Bar Harbor, 207/288-2386 or 888/942-5374, www.barharborwhales.com, mid-June-mid-Sept., 4.5 hrs.) and visits history-rich Baker Island. The tour includes skiff access to the 130-acre island's farmstead, lighthouse, and intriguing rock formations. The return trip provides a view from the water of Otter Cliff (bring binoculars), Thunder Hole, Sand Beach, and Great Head. Make reservations to guarantee a space.

Other tours include the **Frenchman Bay Cruise** (207/288-4585, www.downeastwindjammer.com, daily mid-May-early Oct., 2 hrs.), on a 151-foot, four-mast schooner; and the **Islesford Historical Cruise** (207/276-5352, www.cruiseacadia.com, daily mid-May-early Oct., 2.5 hrs.), which visits Little Cranberry Island to see the Islesford Historical Museum and Somes Sound.

SIGHTS NEARBY

Lamoine State Park (23 State Park Rd., Lamoine, 207/667-4778, www.maine.gov), eight miles southeast of Ellsworth, has camping, boating, kayaking, and fishing.

Holbrook Island Sanctuary (Brooksville, Lamoine, 207/326-4012, www.maine.gov) is a scenic day-use natural area with beaches, wildlife, and wildflowers that borders Penobscot Bay.

TAKE A BOAT TOUR TO BAKER ISLAND.

CUYAHOGA VALLEY NATIONAL PARK

Ohio

WEBSITE:
www.nps.gov/cuva

PHONE NUMBER:
330/657-2752

VISITATION RANK:
13

WHY GO:
Absorb nature with a slice of Midwest history.

PASSPORT STAMPS ▼▼▼

▲ CUYAHOGA VALLEY
NATIONAL PARK

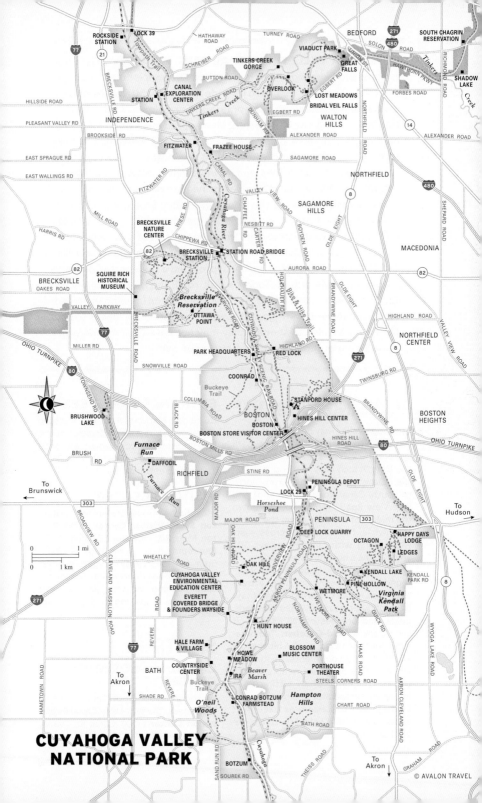

CUYAHOGA VALLEY
NATIONAL PARK

CUYAHOGA VALLEY NATIONAL PARK follows the twists and turns of the Cuyahoga River for 22 miles. The park is home to a great diversity of wildlife thanks to its wide range of habitats—from deep ravines and wetlands to open prairie and grasslands. Bird-watchers routinely spot great blue herons, short-eared owls, bobolinks, even bald eagles. Anglers pluck steelhead, bullhead, bluegill, and bass from the rushing waters. White-tailed deer seem to be everywhere, coyotes prowl the hillsides, and spring peepers provide the evening soundtrack. More than 125 miles of hiking trails weave their way through the park, while the Cuyahoga Valley Scenic Railroad provides a decidedly more passive park experience, giving riders an eagle's-eye view of the landscape from the comfort of a vintage railcar.

The Cuyahoga Valley preserves remains of the Ohio and Erie Canal. In the early 1800s, the canal provided a transportation route through the wilderness. Today, a trail, road, and railroad follow the Cuyahoga River where 15 locks once aided boats in going upstream and downstream. The adjacent towpath provided the means to haul the boats. While Cuyahoga Valley may not have the fame of larger national parks, it garners high numbers of visitors.

PLANNING YOUR TIME

Cuyahoga Valley may be one of the easiest parks to reach in the national park system. Tucked as a greenbelt in eastern Ohio, it's an easy day trip from either Cleveland or Akron. From north to south, Canal Road (north end) and Riverview Road (south end) cut down the middle of the park along the rivers; meanwhile, I-271 and I-80 cross east-west, along with Ohio Highways 303 and 82, plus a host of lesser roads.

While the park is open daily year-round, some seasons are more attractive than others. **Spring** (Mar.-May) is wildflower season, while the reds, golds, and oranges of fall usually hit their peak in **mid-October.** Temperatures for those seasons can hit the low 70s with very cool nights. In summer, the humidity and heat ramp up, with the thermometer often hitting 95°F. In winter, temperatures plunge, yo-yoing from 35°F to subzero, as lake-effect snow rolls in from Lake Erie to the delight of skiers.

ENTRANCES AND FEES

Cuyahoga National Park has multiple entrances. Start your exploration at the Boston Store Visitor Center, accessed via I-271 and I-80 on Boston Mills Road. There is no entrance fee.

VISITORS CENTER

Most first-time visitors aim for the **Boston Store Visitor Center** (5793 Boston Mills Rd., Peninsula, 330/657-2752, 8am-6pm daily June-Aug., 9:30am-5pm daily Sept.-May) to get oriented. The center has information, brochures, canal-building exhibits, and a short park video. Maps and field guides are available.

SIGHTS

CANAL EXPLORATION CENTER

At the intersection of Canal and Hillside Roads, the two-story **Canal Exploration Center** (7104 Canal Rd., Valley View, 216/524-1497, 10am-4:30pm daily June-Aug., shorter hours Sept.-May) once served as a tavern and a general

ONE DAY IN THE PARK

Start your visit by driving along the Ohio and Erie Canalway National Scenic Byway. Stop at the **Canal Exploration Center,** then continue south on Riverview Road to the **Boston Store Visitor Center.** Stretch your legs by walking a little of the **Towpath Trail** south to Lock 29. Continue south on Riverview Road to see the **Everett Road Covered Bridge** and sink into history at the **Hale Farm and Village.**

store. Today, the historic building hosts exhibits on the canal era with interactive displays that appeal to kids and adults.

HUNT HOUSE

Kids will love the nature exhibits at the **Hunt House** (2054 Bolanz Rd., Peninsula, 10am-4pm daily June-Aug., Sat.-Sun. Apr.-May and Sept.-Oct.), located between Riverview Road and Akron Peninsula Roads. Reach it via the Towpath Trail.

OHIO & ERIE CANAL TOWPATH TRAIL

The crushed-limestone **Ohio & Erie Canal Towpath Trail** follows the historic Ohio and Erie Canal for more than 80 miles, attracting hikers and cyclists. Pick up the trail in **Valley View** and follow it as it winds its way through beautiful Cuyahoga Valley National Park. The scenery along the path, which hugs

and at times crisscrosses the Cuyahoga River, is simply amazing. Old canal locks and mile markers can be spotted, as can dense forests, fertile wetlands, and varied wildlife. Stop off at numerous visitors centers and historical sites along the way to view exhibits. The 20 miles of trail inside the park are open to hikers, runners, bicycles, strollers, and wheelchairs. The complete route runs from Cleveland to Zoar.

CUYAHOGA VALLEY SCENIC RAILROAD

One of the longest scenic railroads in the nation, the **Cuyahoga Valley Scenic Railroad** (7900 Old Rockside Rd., 800/468-4070, www.cvsr.com, Tues.-Sun. Apr.-Oct., fee) stretches a full 51 miles, from just south of Cleveland all the way down to Canton—and "scenic" is the operative word. For much of the

▼ CUYAHOGA VALLEY SCENIC RAILROAD

COVERED BRIDGE

journey, the tracks bisect the majestic Cuyahoga Valley National Park while hugging the Cuyahoga River and paralleling the popular Towpath Trail. Passengers ride in authentic climate-controlled coaches built in the 1950s. More than just a tour train, the railroad is a key resource for visitors to the valley. A round-trip takes about three hours. First-class seats on the second level have more legroom and bigger windows.

BLOSSOM MUSIC CENTER

Built in the late 1960s as the summer home of the Cleveland Orchestra, **Blossom Music Center** (1145 W. Steels Corners Rd., Cuyahoga Falls, 888/225-6776, www.clevelandorchestra.com) sees a full range of live-music action from spring until fall. Tucked into Cuyahoga Valley National Park, its setting is one of dense forests, leafy hillsides, and wide-open skies. On a warm summer evening, there is no greater joy than tossing down a blanket and enjoying a picnic under the stars while the orchestra or your favorite band performs. Then again, that night can sour quickly if the clouds darken and the rain falls;

be prepared with tarps, rain gear, and an extra set of dry clothes for the long drive home. Or do what many regulars do: Spring for seats in the covered pavilion as insurance. Traffic in and out of the park can be brutal, so leave plenty of extra travel time.

HALE FARM & VILLAGE

Want to show your children what life was like before cell phones, computers, and refrigerators? **Hale Farm & Village** (2686 Oak Hill Rd., Bath, 330/666-3711, www.wrhs.org, 10am-5pm Wed.-Sun. May-Sept., Sat.-Sun. Sept.-Oct.) is a town trapped in the mid-1800s, when things like electricity, automobiles, and iPhones were still a few years down the road. This living-history museum employs historical interpreters dressed in period costume to recount the story of the Western Reserve, the Civil War years, and life in the middle of the 19th century.

EVERETT ROAD COVERED BRIDGE

The striking red **Everett Road Covered Bridge** (2370 Everett Rd., Peninsula) spans Furnace Run, which looks like a placid, rock-strewn stream much of the year. But in 1975, a torrent of water gushed through the ravine and destroyed the original bridge. Located 0.5 mile west of Riverview Road, the reconstructed one-lane bridge is one of the most photographed locations in Cuyahoga and a tribute to Ohio's legacy of 19th-century covered bridges. Cars can no longer drive on the bridge, but you can walk through it.

SCENIC DRIVE
OHIO AND ERIE CANALWAY NATIONAL SCENIC BYWAY

Paralleling the Cuyahoga River, the **Ohio and Erie Canalway National Scenic Byway** (www.ohioanderiecanalway. com) bisects Cuyahoga Valley National Park from the north end of the park at Rockside Road to the south. The route travels Canal Road, Chaffee Road, Chippewa Road, and Riverview Drive until it becomes Merriman Road after exiting the park's south boundary. This 20-mile segment of the byway is part of a larger 110-mile route that extends from Cleveland to Schoenbrunn Village, New Philadelphia. Inside the park, the road follows the same route as the Towpath Trail and Cuyahoga Valley Scenic Railroad. Stop to take a hike or visit the restored buildings and living museums that celebrate the canal era and its impact on Ohio's economy.

RECREATION
HIKING

Twenty miles of the **Towpath Trail** are within the park. With seven access points, you can hike up to 19.8 miles. For point-to-point hiking on the towpath, hop on the **Cuyahoga Valley Scenic Railroad** (7900 Old Rockside Rd., 800/468-4070, www.cvsr.com, Tues.-Sun. Apr.-Oct., fee) and hike back to your starting point.

The trail to **Brandywine Falls** (8176 Brandywine Rd., Sagamore Hills, 1.5 mi. rt., 1 hr., easy) follows a boardwalk through a mossy hemlock forest to reach a viewing platform facing the 65-foot veil-style falls. Fall colors come on strong in the gorge. Plan to go early or late in the day, as parking can fill 10am-2pm.

The **Blue Hen Falls** (2001 Boston Mills Rd., Peninsula, 0.5 mi. rt., 30 min., easy) trail crosses Spring Creek on a wooden bridge. At the junction, turn right to reach the 15-foot Blue Hen Falls. Plan to go early or late in the day, as parking can pack out 10am-2pm.

BLUE HEN FALLS

BRIDAL VEIL FALLS

Bridal Veil Falls (Gorge Pkwy., Walton Hills, 0.5 mi. rt., 30 min., easy) is accessed by a short boardwalk that leads to a viewing platform.

The **Ledges Loop** (701 Truxell Rd., Peninsula, 2.2 mi. rt., 1.5 hr., moderate) starts on a spur; at the loop, head in either direction. On the east side, Ice Box Cave is closed to protect bats; the west side includes an overlook of the area. Many hikers park at Kendall Lake instead of the Ledges Trailhead to add on a one-mile loop around the lake. After hiking around Kendall Lake, connect to the Ledges by crossing Kendall Park Road to the Pine Grove Trail and then heading west, after which you will link up with the Ledges Loop. Adding on the lake and connection via Pine Grove ups the distance to 4.8 miles round-trip.

From the Ira Trailhead, take the Towpath Trail to the **Beaver Marsh** (3801 Riverview Rd., Cuyahoga Falls, 0.8 mi. rt., 30 min., easy), which the National Audubon Society has designated an Important Bird Area.

BIKING

The **Towpath Trail** follows the Cuyahoga River. You can bicycle a total of 20 miles from north to south; seven access points allow you to shorten the distance. For one-way biking on the towpath, you and your bike can hop on the **Cuyahoga Valley Scenic Railroad** (7900 Old Rockside Rd., 800/468-4070, www.cvsr.com, Tues.-Sun. Apr.-Oct., fee) and then cycle back to your starting point. In addition to regular depot stops, the train has several bike-aboard pickup/drop-off stops. Simply flag down the train by waving both hands over your head (a one-hand wave just salutes the engineer). Pay the fee when you board.

WINTER RECREATION

Tucked deep within Cuyahoga Valley National Park, the cozy stone-and-chestnut **Winter Sports Center at Kendall Lake** (Truxell Rd., Peninsula, 330/657-2752, hours vary in winter) serves as the nucleus of winter activities in the park. In addition to the breathtaking scenery, the lodge offers cross-country ski instruction, equipment rental, and helpful information. Sign up for a weekend cross-country ski

VIRGINIA KENDALL LEDGES

lesson on your skis or theirs, followed by a vigorous miles-long expedition down the Towpath Trail. For a slower, simpler pace, don a pair of rented snowshoes and head into the backcountry. For sliding thrills, try the tubing hill. When nearby Kendall Lake is adequately frozen, take your ice-skating to the great outdoors. Don't have your own skates? No problem, the shelter rents them. Even if you prefer to pull on nothing more than a pair of hiking boots, come to this lodge for maps, hot chocolate, and like-minded companionship.

WHERE TO STAY

INSIDE THE PARK

The 165-year-old **Inn at Brandywine Falls** (8230 Brandywine Rd., Sagamore Hills, 330/467-1812, www.innatbrandywinefalls.com, open year-round, from $150) is a bed-and-breakfast tucked into Cuyahoga Valley National Park, literally steps from scenic Brandywine Falls. The inn contains six bedrooms furnished with antiques, plus a living room, dining room, and porches. The gourmet breakfast is a candlelit affair.

The historic **Stanford House** (6093 Stanford Rd., Peninsula, 330/657-2909, www.conservancyforcvnp.org, open year-round, from $600-900, two-night min.) has nine bedrooms, plus a dining room, living room, commercial kitchen, outdoor fire circle, and beautiful grounds. The entire house is available for rent.

For Towpath Trail users, the **Stanford Campsites** (near Stanford House, late May-Oct., $25) provide a place to camp on the route. Each of the five campsites can fit two tents and six campers and has picnic tables. Shared facilities include a portable toilet, potable water, and a communal fire pit (firewood provided). **Reservations** (www.reserveamerica.com) for the campsites are accepted on May 1 for the season. Campers without reservations can check with the Stanford House (4pm-7pm daily) for availability.

OUTSIDE THE PARK

Lodging is plentiful in the surrounding area, which includes **Independence, Akron,** and **Cleveland.**

GETTING THERE

AIR

Cleveland Hopkins International Airport (CLE, 5300 Riverside Dr., Cleveland, 216/265-6000, www.clevelandairport.com) is 25 miles northwest of the national park and has car rentals.

TRAIN AND BUS

Amtrak (www.amtrak.com) trains and **Greyhound** (www.greyhound.com) buses stop in Cleveland.

CAR

From Cleveland, take I-77 south for 15.5 miles to exit 147 and turn left onto Miller Road. Drive 0.6 mile and turn right onto Highway 21 (Brecksville Rd.) for 0.4 mile. Turn left onto Snowville Road and continue 2.8 miles. Turn right onto Riverview Road and drive 1.7 miles. Turn left onto Boston Mills Road to reach the visitors center. The drive should take about 30 minutes.

From Akron, drive north on I-77, then veer left onto exit 125A to join Highway 8 for 12.6 miles to Cuyahoga Falls. At exit 14A, turn right onto Boston Mills Road and drive 3.4 miles to the visitors center. The drive should take 25 minutes.

GETTING AROUND

The **Cuyahoga Valley Scenic Railroad** (7900 Old Rockside Rd., 800/468-4070, www.cvsr.com, Tues.-Sun. Apr.-Oct.) stops at two stations inside the park: Rockside and Peninsula. The train makes 2-3 round-trip journeys through the park with five flag stops where you can board or debark.

During weekends and in summer, **parking** can be difficult. The parking lots at popular trailheads fill 10am-2pm. To access the Towpath Trail, park at Canal Exploration Center, Station Road, or Rockside Rock rather than the busy locations of Boston Store, Hunt House, Ira Trailhead, and Lock 29 in Peninsula.

SIGHTS NEARBY

James A Garfield National Historic Site (8095 Mentor Ave., Mentor, 440/255-8722, www.nps.gov/jaga) offers tours of a restored 1832 farmhouse with the period antiques of James Garfield, 20th president of the United States.

First Ladies National Historic Site (205 S. Market Ave., Canton, 330/452-0876, www.nps.gov/fila) celebrates U.S. first ladies with tours by costumed guides of the restored 1841 Victorian mansion of Ida Saxton, wife of William McKinley, 25th president of the United States.

David Berger National Memorial (26001 S. Woodland Rd., Beachwood, 216/831-0700, www.nps.gov/dabe) features a sculpture of the broken Olympic rings to honor wrestler David Berger, one of 11 Israeli athletes killed at the 1972 Munich Olympic Games.

ISLE ROYALE
NATIONAL PARK

Michigan

PASSPORT STAMPS ▾▾▾

WEBSITE:
www.nps.gov/isro

PHONE NUMBER:
906/482-0984

VISITATION RANK:
56

WHY GO:
Explore a unique
freshwater island.

▲ LAKE SUPERIOR

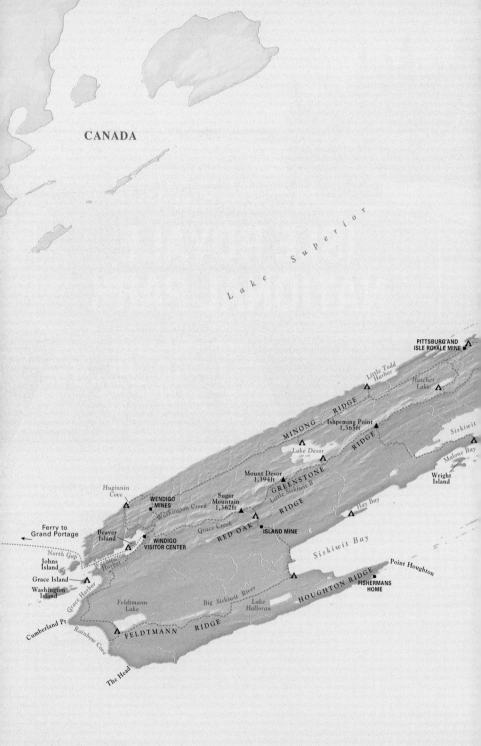

CANADA

Lake Superior

PITTSBURG AND
ISLE ROYALE MINE ▪

Little Todd
Harbor

Hatchet
Lake

MINONG RIDGE

Ishpeming Point
1,365ft ▲

RIDGE

Siskiwit

Lake Desor

Malone Bay

Mount Desor
1,394ft ▲

GREENSTONE

Wright
Island

Huginnin
Cove

WENDIGO
MINES ▪

Sugar
Mountain
1,362ft ▲

Little Siskiwit R.

RIDGE

Washington Creek

Ferry to
Grand Portage

Beaver
Island

WINDIGO
VISITOR CENTER

Grace Creek

RED OAK

ISLAND MINE ▪

Hay Bay

Siskiwit Bay

North Gap

Johns
Island

Point Houghton

Grace Island

Washington
Island

Grace Harbor

HOUGHTON RIDGE

FISHERMANS
HOME

Feldtmann
Lake

Big Siskiwit River

Lake
Halloran

Cumberland Pt

Rainbow Cove

FELDTMANN   RIDGE

The Head

© AVALON TRAVEL

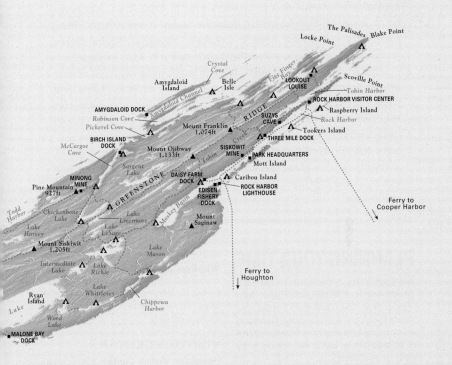

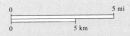

Established in 1940, **ISLE ROYALE NATIONAL PARK** may be one of the least visited units of the national park system. Centered on 45-mile-long Isle Royale, the largest island in Lake Superior, the park encompasses about 400 smaller islands as well as all submerged lands within a 4.5-mile radius of the archipelago. More than 80 percent of the national park lies underwater. In 1980, it was designated an International Biosphere Reserve. Today, it appeals to hikers, backpackers, boaters, anglers, kayakers, canoeists, scuba divers, and wildlife-watchers, especially those hoping to spot a moose.

Those who make the trek by boat or seaplane to Isle Royale come primarily to hike its 165 miles of trails, fish its 46 inland lakes, and paddle its saw-toothed shoreline. Wildlife viewing is popular, too, especially for the moose that swam across from Ontario several decades back. This land thrust up from folded rock layers now contains a rich mixed forest that provides habitat for beavers, foxes, and wolves. It's a place for those who like the feel of wilderness and water, where solitude offers a chance to soak up the sights, sounds, and smells.

PLANNING YOUR TIME

Isle Royale sits in the midst of Lake Superior, north of Michigan's Upper Peninsula near the Canadian border. No roads touch the 45-mile-long island and its only contact with the outside world is ship-to-shore radio. All access is by boat or seaplane.

Civilization on Isle Royale is concentrated in two small developments at opposite ends of the island. **Windigo,** on the south end, has a visitors center, grocery, and marina. **Rock Harbor,** on the north end, offers the same, plus a lodge, restaurant, and cabins. The rest of the island is 210 square miles of backcountry.

Isle Royale is open daily **mid-April-October** but closes November-mid-April due to extreme weather conditions. Summer is the warmest time to visit, but plan for it to be buggy June-July. The island bans dogs and wheeled vehicles (mountain bikes or canoe carts), except for wheelchairs.

ENTRANCES AND FEES

Most boats and seaplanes land in **Rock Harbor** at the northeast tip of the island. Boats from Minnesota dock in **Windigo,** at the southern tip. The entrance fee is $7 per person, which is collected by ferry or seaplane concessionaires. Private boaters can pay at the visitors centers.

VISITORS CENTERS

Houghton Visitor Center (800 E. Lakeshore Dr., 906/482-0984, 8am-6pm Mon.-Fri., 10am-6pm Sat. June-mid-Sept., 8am-4pm Mon.-Fri. mid-Sept.-May) is located on the mainland in Houghton, where the Ranger III passenger ferry docks. The visitors center has boating permits, a park orientation video, a Junior Ranger Program, and a park store.

The **Rock Harbor Visitor Center** (8am-6pm daily July-Aug., hours vary May-June and Sept.) is located on the northeast end of Isle Royale where ferries and seaplanes land from Houghton or Copper Harbor. The center has exhibits, backcountry permits, and ranger-led programs. Field guides and maps are available.

The **Windigo Visitor Center** (8am-6pm daily July-Aug., hours vary May-June and Sept.-Oct.) is on the

Top ❸

❶ GO FOR A HIKE

The islands' wildlife, especially the **moose** and **wolf** populations, are a draw for naturalists and tourists alike. Hikers have a decent chance of spotting moose in ponds, lowlands, or inland lakes. Moose particularly like the mineral licks at **Hidden Lake.**

East of Rock Harbor, the **Scoville Point Trail** (4.2 mi. rt., moderate) traces a rocky finger of forested land in a figure-eight loop to a point surrounded by Lake Superior. From the Rock Harbor Trail, interpretive signs lead to **Suzy's Cave** (3.8 mi. rt., moderate), formed by wave action of a once-deeper Lake Superior.

FOGGY TRAIL ON ISLE ROYALE

For big views, follow the Lake Superior shoreline to Daisy Farm campground and the **Ojibway Trail**, which heads north to the **Ojibway Tower** (3.5 mi. rt., moderate), an air-monitoring station. The tower marks the highest spot on the eastern end of the island. Climb its steps (but do not enter the tower room) for an unmatched view of the island's interior lakes and bays on both the north and south sides.

Pick up an interpretive trail guide from Windigo Visitor Center, then head uphill on the **Windigo Nature Trail** (1.2 mi. rt., easy) as it rolls through forests of cedar, maple, and birch. From the Feldtmann Lake Trailhead near the dock, **Grace Creek Overlook** (3.6 mi. rt., moderate) climbs to a rocky outcrop for views of the island.

❷ PADDLE THE ISLAND WATERS

For paddlers, Isle Royale is a dream destination, a nook-and-cranny wilderness of rocky islands, secluded coves, and quiet bays interrupted only by the low call of a loon. First-time visitors can't do better than the **Five Fingers,** the collection of fjord-like harbors and rocky promontories on the east end of the island. Not only is the area well protected (except from northeasterly winds), it offers some of the finest Isle Royale scenery and solitude. **Lookout Louise,** north of Tobin Harbor, has one of the island's most spectacular views of its ragged northeastern shoreline. With a canoe, it's a 20-minute paddle to the trailhead and a two-mile hike to the overlook. Rental kayaks and canoes are available in Windigo and Rock Harbor.

Isle Royale is generally better suited to **kayaks,** though open canoes can handle these waters in calm weather. The entire island offers paddling opportunities for kayaks, though shoreline access varies.

❸ BOAT IN THE BACKCOUNTRY

Isle Royale's scenic waterways beckon private boaters. Boats that dock overnight need a backcountry **permit** (even for anchoring). Pick up free backcountry permits at the island visitors centers or on board the Ranger III. The docks in **Rock Harbor** and **Windigo** have pump-out services, fuel, and potable water. Rock Harbor has seasonal dockage with power and water.

ONE DAY IN ISLE ROYALE

If you only have one day, take the **MV Isle Royale Queen** ferry from Copper Harbor to Rock Harbor, which gives you three hours to explore. Take a boat tour of Rock Harbor on the **MV Sandy,** hike to Suzy's Cave, or rent a canoe from **Rock Harbor Lodge** to explore the bay.

southwest end of the island where ferries arrive from Grand Portage, Minnesota. The center has exhibits, backcountry permits, and ranger programs, plus maps and field guides for sale.

WHERE TO STAY

INSIDE THE PARK

For a quiet island stay, set up at the **Rock Harbor Lodge** (906/337-4993 May-Sept. or 866/644-2003 Oct.-Apr., http://rockharborlodge.com, from $250). The 60 lodge rooms are basic motel-style, but they sit right at the water's edge with a glorious view of nearby islands and Lake Superior. Rates include one half-day use of a canoe and three meals at the lodge dining room. Nearby, 20 housekeeping cottages include small kitchens, one double bed, and one bunk bed. Reservations are a must.

Rock Harbor has two dining options: **Lighthouse Restaurant** (7am-8:30am, noon-1:30pm, and 5:30pm-7:30pm daily late May-early Sept.) and **Greenstone**

Grill (7am-7:30pm daily late May-early Sept.). The **Marina Store** (9am-5pm daily) carries food and camping supplies.

Two rustic, one-room **Windigo Camper Cabins** (906/337-4993 May-Sept. or 866/644-2003, http://rockharborlodge.com, available seasonally, from $50) are located in Washington Harbor, 45 miles from Rock Harbor. Amenities include a futon sofa, two bunk beds, and electrical outlets. There is a vault toilet nearby.

Isle Royale has 36 **campsites**, accessible either by foot or by boat; some sites are only reachable by canoe or kayak. It's possible to backpack from one campground to the next (6-8 miles per day); most sites have a maximum stay limit of 2-3 nights. These first-come, first-served sites include drinking water and vault toilets and accommodate up to six people. Group sites (7-10 people) require advance reservations. A free camping permit, available from the island visitors centers, is required for all overnight stays.

ROCK HARBOR

OUTSIDE THE PARK

Houghton and **Hancock** are the gateways to Isle Royale, with lodging and restaurants.

GETTING THERE

AIR

The closest international airports are **Thunder Bay International Airport** (100 Princess St., Thunder Bay, ON, Canada, 807/473-2600, www.tbairport.on.ca), which is located 50 miles northeast of Grand Portage, Minnesota; **Duluth International Airport** (4701 Grinden Dr., Duluth, MN, 216/727-2968, http://duluthairport.com), which is 150 miles south of Grand Portage, Minnesota; and **Green Bay-Austin Straubel International Airport** (GRB, 2077 Airport Dr., Green Bay, WI 920/498-4800, www.flygrb.com), which is 200 miles south of Houghton, Michigan. All three airports have rental cars.

Seaplane service from Houghton is expensive but is the quickest way to reach Isle Royale. **Isle Royale Seaplanes** (21125 Royce Rd., Hancock, 906/483-4991, https://isleroyaleseaplanes.com, mid-May-mid-Sept.) travel from Houghton County Memorial Airport to Windigo and Rock Harbor. Reservations are required. The 35-minute flight can be delayed by wind and fog.

BOAT AND FERRY

Boats and ferries are for passengers only; cars are not permitted. Make reservations for all ferries at least 2-3 months in advance, although last-minute spots can be available. Canoes and kayaks are allowed for a fee.

From Houghton, Michigan: The National Park Service operates the 165-foot **MV Ranger III** (800 E. Lakeshore Dr., 906/482-0984, late May-Sept.). The **Ranger III** departs Houghton at 9am on Tuesday and Friday; return trips from Rock Harbor are at 9am Wednesday and Saturday. The 73-mile passage to Rock Harbor takes six hours.

From Copper Harbor, Michigan: The **MV Isle Royale Queen IV** (14 Waterfront Landing, 906/289-4437, www.isleroyale.com, early May-Sept.) passenger ferry departs at 8am daily for the three-hour passage to Rock Harbor;

ISLE ROYALE COVE

the return trip departs Rock Harbor at 2:45pm.

From Grand Portage, Minnesota: **MV Voyageur II** (218/475-0024, www.grand-isle-royale.com, May-early Oct., schedule varies) travels to Windigo (2 hrs.) and Rock Harbor (8.5 hrs.) every other day and returns on opposite days. Other drop-off and pickup locations are available.

BUS

Indian Trails (800/292-3831, www.indiantrails.com) operates bus service from Green Bay, Wisconsin, to Houghton, Michigan.

GETTING AROUND

Hiking or kayaking are the best modes for getting around the islands. The park service offers boat tours on its 25-passenger **MV Sandy** (906/482-0984, June-early Sept., times and rates vary) from Rock Harbor. **MV Voyageur II** (4.5-5 hrs.) circles each half of the island on different days with additional stops.

SIGHTS NEARBY

Keweenaw National Historic Park (25970 Red Jacket Road, Calumet, MI, 906/337-3168, www.nps.gov/kewe) contains 21 heritage sites from the region's copper mining days.

Grand Portage National Monument (Grand Portage, MN, 218/475-0123, www.nps.gov/grpo) celebrates Ojibwe and fur trading heritage at a reconstructed depot and fort site.

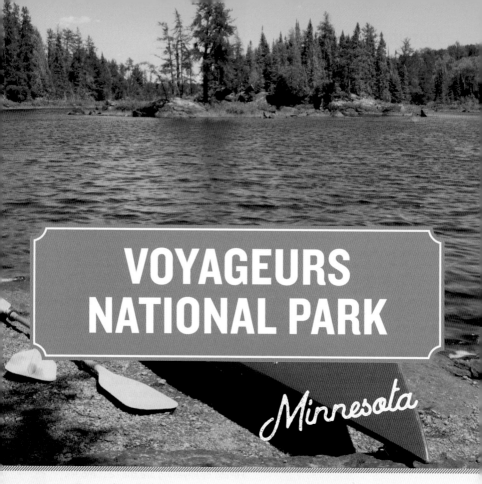

VOYAGEURS NATIONAL PARK

Minnesota

WEBSITE:
www.nps.gov/voya

PHONE NUMBER:
218/283-6600

VISITATION RANK:
46

WHY GO:
Soak up a watery
wilderness.

PASSPORT STAMPS ▼▼▼

Befitting the Land of 10,000 Lakes, **VOYAGEURS NATIONAL PARK** is dominated and defined by water. The park is centered on four large lakes—Rainy, Kabetogama, Namakan, and Sand Point—and water covers nearly 40 percent of its 218,200 acres. Water isn't just part of the scenery, it's the primary means of transportation, too. Most people enjoy the park from a fishing boat, houseboat, or pontoon. You'll have to travel by boat to witness the hundreds of lopsided islands and slender bays, or to explore the rugged 75,000-acre Kabetogama Peninsula at the heart of the park.

Named for French-Canadian fur traders, called *voyageurs*, the park shares its waters with Canada. Given the park's remote northern location and difficult access, Voyageurs is one of the least visited national parks. This makes it easy to commune with nature in peace, especially if you head out to the Kabetogama Peninsula or spend a night under the stars. This wilderness park, formed in the footprint of an ancient glacial lake, serves as a year-round playground with cross-country skiing, snowshoeing, and snowmobiling in winter.

PLANNING YOUR TIME

Voyageurs National Park follows the northern Minnesota-Ontario border for 55 meandering miles. Access for most visitors is through one of the four resort areas on the park's periphery. **Rainy Lake** is at the northwest corner, not far from International Falls, while **Crane Lake** is outside the park on the far southeast end. **Kabetogama** and **Ash River** sit in between. Each gateway offers lodging, food, fishing guides, water taxis, and just about anything else you could need during your trip.

Most visitors arrive in **summer** (May-Sept.) for the warmest weather, but prepare for mosquitoes June-July. Snow covers the park November-early April and lake ice usually lasts until early May.

ENTRANCES AND FEES

The park has three main entrances. East of International Falls, access **Rainy Lake** off Highway 11. **Kabetogama** is north of Highway 53. To reach **Ash River,** drive 12 miles northeast of Highway 53 on the Ash River Trail to Mead Wood Road. Except for roads leading to these entry points, there are no roads inside the park.

There is no entrance fee; however, all overnight visitors must have a **free permit,** available from the park visitors centers or self-registration stations at most boat launches.

VISITORS CENTERS

There are three visitors centers, all accessible by car. The **Rainy Lake Visitor Center** (1797 Town Rd. 342, 218/286-5258, 9am-5pm daily late May-Sept., 10am-5pm Wed.-Sun. Oct.-late May) offers boat tours and ranger-led programs. The **Ash River Visitor Center** (9899 Meadwood Rd., 218/374-3221, 9am-5pm daily late May-Sept.) is housed in the historic Meadwood Lodge, a 1935 log building. The **Kabetogama Lake Visitor Center** (9940 Cedar Ln., 218/875-2111, 9am-5pm daily late May-Sept.) has boat tours and ranger-led programs. All three visitors centers have exhibits, films, bookstores, and backcountry permits. Crane Lake has a ranger station, which may be unstaffed.

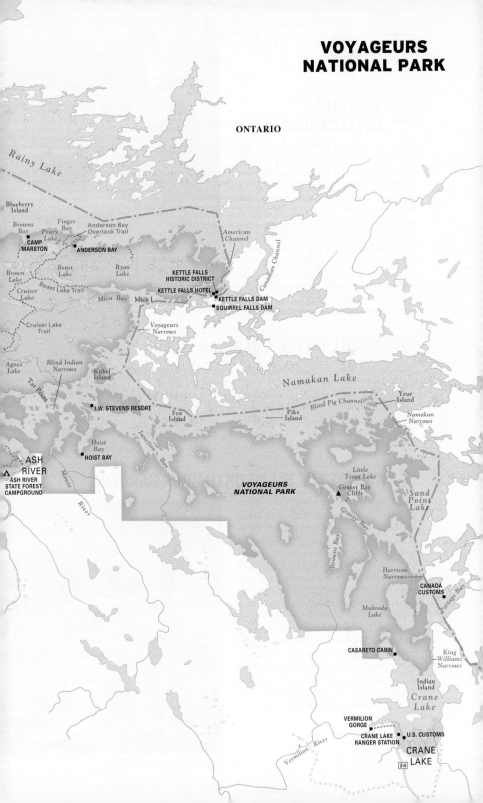

VOYAGEURS
NATIONAL PARK

ONTARIO

Rainy Lake

Blueberry Island

Browns Bay

Finger Bay

Peary Lake

Anderson Bay Overlook Trail

CAMP MARSTON

ANDERSON BAY

Brown Lake

Beast Lake

Ryan Lake

Cruiser Lake

Beast Lake Trail

American Channel

Canadian Channel

KETTLE FALLS HISTORIC DISTRICT

KETTLE FALLS HOTEL

KETTLE FALLS DAM

SQUIRREL FALLS DAM

Mica Bay

Mica I.

Cruiser Lake Trail

Voyageurs Narrows

Agnes Lake

Blind Indian Narrows

Kubel Island

Tar Point

Namakan Lake

Your Island

I.W. STEVENS RESORT

Fox Island

Pike Island

Blind Pig Channel

Namakan Narrows

Hoist Bay

HOIST BAY

Junction Bay

ASH RIVER

ASH RIVER STATE FOREST CAMPGROUND

Moose River

VOYAGEURS NATIONAL PARK

Little Trout Lake

Grassy Bay Cliffs

Sand Point Lake

Browns Bay

Grassy Bay

Harrison Narrows

CANADA CUSTOMS

Portage Bay

Mukooda Lake

CASARETO CABIN

King Williams Narrows

Indian Island

Crane Lake

VERMILION GORGE

CRANE LAKE RANGER STATION

U.S. CUSTOMS

CRANE LAKE

Vermilion River

24

Top ❸

❶ BOAT IN TO KETTLE FALLS

KETTLE FALLS HOTEL

The red-and-white **Kettle Falls Hotel** (12977 Chippewa Tr., 218/240-1724, www.kettlefallshotel.com) sits 16 miles from the nearest road. Visitors arrive by boat to stroll its grounds, enjoy a meal or a drink in the Lumberjack Saloon, or just relax on the endless veranda. The simple, antiques-filled lodge was erected on this remote border site around 1910. It is rumored to have started as a brothel, and did a thriving business during Prohibition, but soon it became a fashionable getaway for the rich and famous such as Charles Lindbergh and John D. Rockefeller. A short walk from the hotel is the **Dam Tender's Cabin,** a restored 1912 log home.

❷ STROLL LITTLE AMERICAN ISLAND

Gold fever struck Rainy Lake in July 1893 when prospector George Davis hit pay dirt on **Little American Island.** You'll learn the whole story of the Rainy Lake Gold Rush along a short wheelchair-accessible trail past a mineshaft, tailings piles, and other remnants from the only area mine that produced significant ore.

For a glimpse of another Rainy Lake industry, take a boat to **Oveson's Fish Camp** where an icehouse, fish processing house, and camp home were in use between 1958 and 1985. They still stand at the water's edge.

❸ ADMIRE THE ELLSWORTH ROCK GARDENS

Accessible by boat on the north shore of Kabetogama Lake, **Ellsworth Rock Gardens** features 52 terraced flower beds and more than 150 geometric and animal-themed sculptures assembled out of local granite. The sculptures were built by Chicago contractor and regular summer visitor Jack Ellsworth between 1944 and 1965 and make this singular spot an ideal picnic ground.

The cliffs on the Canadian side of **Namakan Narrows,** a channel at the southeast end of Namakan Lake, feature moose, human, canoe, and other ancient pictographs. A popular natural attraction near Crane Lake is the pinkish granite **Grassy Bay Cliffs.**

ELLSWORTH ROCK GARDENS

ONE DAY IN VOYAGEURS

If you only have one day in the park, take a narrated **boat tour** from Rainy Lake to **Little American Island** or **Kettle Falls.**

RECREATION

HIKING

Voyageurs may be all about the water, but hikers will not be disappointed. These trails do not require boat access.

Rainy Lake's **Oberholtzer Interpretive Trail** (1.5 mi. rt., easy) covers a cattail marsh, pine forest, and scenic views of Black Bay; the first half of the trail is wheelchair-accessible.

The Ash River's **Blind Ash Bay Trail** (2.5 mi. rt., moderate) is arguably Voyageurs' most beautiful short mainland path. The hilly path follows a rocky ridge—with great views of Kabetogama Lake from atop—and ends looking out over the narrow namesake bay.

A few miles northwest of the Kabetogama Lake Visitor Center, the slightly hilly **Echo Bay Trail** (2.5 mi. rt., moderate) loops through a mix of aspen and conifer stands. You'll pass many areas flooded by beavers and might spot wolf tracks.

The **Kab-Ash Trail** (27.9 mi. one-way) links the Kabetogama Lake and Ash River gateways. The path travels through a variety of forest types and wetland boardwalks for great wildlife-viewing.

CANOEING AND KAYAKING

Canoes and kayaks can navigate to 33 day-use sites. Most paddlers start at Ash River because it has the easiest access to quiet back bays, though the north end of Kabetogama Lake (accessible from the private Woodenfrog Campground) has lots of small islands and relatively few boaters. Canoe rentals are available at each of the four gateway towns.

Canoe tours (1.5-2 hr., summer only, call for reservations, free) launch from the visitors centers. From Rainy Lake (218/286-5258), the historic North Canoe tour is aboard a 26-foot canoe; the Beaver Lodge tour paddles through Black Bay. Kabetogama (218/875-2111) also paddles a 26-foot North Canoe. From Ash River (218/374-3221), paddle along Ash River to view wildlife.

SERENE LAKES AWAIT EXPLORATION.

WATER COVERS NEARLY 40 PERCENT OF THE PARK.

BOATING AND FISHING

Boaters can launch from all visitors centers as well as the Crane Lake Ranger Station. **Permits** (877/444-6777, www.recreation.gov) are required to overnight and a Minnesota fishing license (available in gateway towns) is needed for angling. The gateway towns have marinas, rentals, and free public boat ramps. Boaters should understand the U.S. Coast Guard buoy system and be able to read navigation maps, which are available at visitors centers.

WINTER RECREATION

Snow blankets Voyageurs in winter and the lakes freeze. That's when the groomed trails in the park call to snowmobilers, cross-country skiers, and snowshoers. Winter ice roads are maintained on frozen **Rainy Lake,** around the Kabetogama Peninsula's north end, and on **Kabetogama Lake.** It's the one season when you can drive a (snow) vehicle into the park! Accessed via an ice road, a sledding hill is on **Sphunge Island.**

WHERE TO STAY

INSIDE THE PARK

A night in the historic **Kettle Falls Hotel** (12977 Chippewa Tr., Kabetogama, 218/240-1724 or 218/875-2070 in winter, www.kettlefallshotel.com, May-Sept., from $90) is a highlight for many visitors. The 12 antiques-filled rooms in the main lodge share three baths; more modern cabins sleep up to six. The hotel rents canoes, kayaks, and boats and provides a shuttle service (fee) from the mainland.

There are more than 270 **boat-in campsites** (rates vary). Sites have fire rings, picnic tables, privies, tent pads, and bear-proof food lockers. Advance reservations (877/444-6777, www.recreation.gov, $10 fee) and a permit (free) are required.

LAKESIDE CAMPSITE

BOUNDARY WATERS OF MINNESOTA

HOUSEBOATS

A houseboat is popular for exploring Voyageurs—it lets you enjoy the wilderness with all the comforts of home. No experience (or license) is needed; rental companies set you up with everything from food to maps. The National Park Service maintains designated mooring sites ($10 per night) with fire rings throughout the park, or you can overnight at one of the resort areas. Overnight stays on a houseboat require a **permit reservation** (877/444-6777, www.recreation.gov). Park-authorized operators include **Northernaire Houseboats** (2690 County Rd. 94, 218/286-5221, www.northernaire-houseboats.com) and **Rainy Lake Houseboats** (800/554-9188, www.rainylakehouseboats.com) in the Rainy Lake area and **Ebel's Voyageur Houseboats** (888/883-2357, www.ebels.com) in Ash River.

OUTSIDE THE PARK

Dozens of lodging options sit on the periphery of the park in **International Falls, Rainy Lake, Ranier, Kabetogama Lake, Crane Lake, Ash River,** and **Orr.**

GETTING THERE AND AROUND

The park has no public transit. Most visitors get around in a motorboat, sailboat, canoe, or kayak.

AIR

The nearest airport is **Falls International Airport** (INL, 3214 2nd Ave. E., 218/283-4461, www.internationalfallsairport.com), which is served by **Delta Airlines** (800/221-1212) and has car rentals. From International Falls, the Rainy Lake Visitor Center is 12 miles east along Highway 11.

BOAT

Narrated **boat tours** (June-Sept., $30-50) go out on national park vessels from Rainy Lake, Kabetogama Lake, and Ash River. From Rainy Lake, the 2.5-hour Grand Tour aboard the *Voyageur* stops at Little American Island after viewing eagle nests. The 6.5-hour Kettle Falls Cruise travels to the Kettle Falls Hotel. From Kabetogama Lake, the *Amik* departs for a 5.5-hour cruise to Kettle Falls. Make **reservations** (877/444-6777, www.recreation.gov) for all boat tours.

SIGHTS NEARBY

Boundary Waters Canoe Area Wilderness (Superior National Forest, 218/626-4300, www.fs.usda.gov), which borders Voyageurs, contains more than 1,200 paddling routes with 2,000 backcountry campsites.

Woodenfrog State Forest (County Road 122, 218/235-2520, http://dnr.state.mn.us) has a campground, swimming beach, and boat launch on Kabetogama Lake.

THE SOUTH

Virginia's Shenandoah straddles the cultural border between East and South. The park's scenic Skyline Drive links to the Blue Ridge Parkway to reach the Smoky Mountains, home to Great Smoky Mountains National Park. Here, crystal-clear trout streams and white-water rivers cut through rounded peaks and jagged mountaintops.

Scattered throughout the South are a handful of tiny, singular national parks with homes in Kentucky, Arkansas, and South Carolina. Hot springs, underground caves, and ancient stands of old-growth cypress offer unique excursions for the adventurous visitor.

Florida's languid lushness is captured in Everglades National Park, home to birds, alligators, and crocodiles. Coral reefs surround the offshore islands of Biscayne and Dry Tortugas.

◄ GREAT SMOKY MOUNTAINS

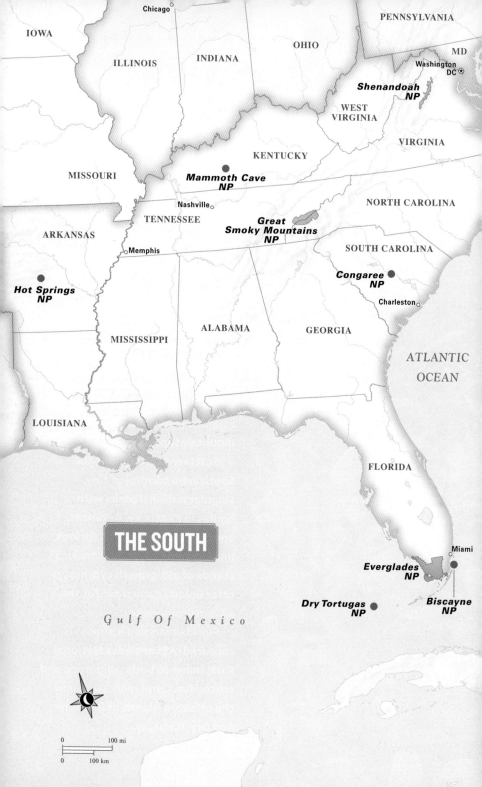

THE SOUTH

The National Parks of
THE SOUTH

GREAT SMOKY MOUNTAINS, NC/TN

The most visited national park has big reason for its popularity: scenic drives, historic early settlements, hikes to high viewpoints, and evening firefly shows (page 581).

SHENANDOAH, VA

This long, narrow park is home to Skyline Drive, hiking trails, and a hardwood forest that blazes with fall colors (page 600).

MAMMOTH CAVE, KY

The world's longest cave system features flowstones, columns, stalactites, and bottomless pits (page 610).

HOT SPRINGS, AK

This historic landmark houses one of the most sumptuous clusters of natural hot spring bathhouses in North America (page 616).

CONGAREE, SC

The ancient cypress swamp contains what may be the tallest old-growth canopy remaining on earth (page 625).

EVERGLADES, FL

Guided trams, bike routes, and water trails offer access to this fragile, swampy ecosystem where alligators and crocodiles coexist (page 630).

BISCAYNE, FL

This largely underwater park features coral reefs, shipwrecks, and mangrove forests on islands (page 644).

DRY TORTUGAS, FL

Reached by boat or seaplane, the park's seven islands combine diverse wildlife, remarkable coral reefs, shipwrecks, pirate legends, and a military fort (page 650).

1: ROARING FORK MOTOR NATURE TRAIL, GREAT SMOKY MOUNTAINS
2: STALACTITES, MAMMOTH CAVE
3: SUNSET OVER THE EVERGLADES

Best OF THE PARKS

Newfound Gap Road: Drive this scenic road through multiple types of forests and over the lowest pass in the Smokies (page 585).

Bathhouse Row: Soak in historic hot springs (page 620).

Skyline Drive: Cruise the curves on this scenic ridgetop road with 75 overlooks (page 604).

Mammoth Cave: Explore the most extensive cave system in the world (page 611).

PLANNING YOUR TRIP

Plan at least **two weeks** to tour the national parks of the South. Make lodging and campground **reservations** for Great Smoky Mountains, Shenandoah, and Everglades in advance. Tickets for tours of Mammoth Cave frequently sell out; make advance reservations to guarantee slots. Snow sometimes closes Newfound Gap Road in Great Smoky Mountains in winter.

May-October is high season in most of the southern U.S. parks, with July and August the busiest months. Expect peak-season rates, congested roads, and difficulty getting reservations. Although summer is the prime tourist season, unless your plans involve some beach time or a stay in a mountain retreat, the humidity in the southern parks can be oppressive.

Accompanied by pleasant weather and fewer tourists, late spring **(May-June)** and fall **(September-October)** are the best times to explore the parks of Virginia and Tennessee. Fall foliage in the region is some of the most spectacular in the country. South Carolina is best in spring, **mid-March to mid-May,** when natural beauty hits its apex and lodging is at a premium.

Late December-April is high season in Florida, when lodging rates are usually higher. Accommodations often cost less midseason (May-July, late Oct.-mid-Dec.). Summer is the least crowded time to visit Florida: temperatures and humidity are fairly high, and the Atlantic **hurricane season** (June-September) can bring storms.

1: SKYLINE DRIVE, SHENANDOAH
2: FROZEN NIAGARA FORMATION, MAMMOTH CAVE

Road Trip

GREAT SMOKY MOUNTAINS, SHENANDOAH, AND MAMMOTH CAVE

Connecting two Appalachian national parks, the **Blue Ridge Parkway** links Shenandoah with Great Smoky Mountains. Fly in to Dulles International Airport outside **Washington DC** and rent a car to start your journey.

Shenandoah

111 miles / 4 hours
From Dulles, drive 53 miles (1 hr.) to **Front Royal,** the north entrance to **Skyline Drive** and **Shenandoah National Park.** Go at a leisurely pace to enjoy the scenery, multiple overlooks, and spectacular fall colors on the 105-mile drive (3 hrs.). Spend the night at **Lewis Mountain Cabins,** 57.5 miles into the drive. The next morning continue south on Skyline Drive to exit the park at Rockfish Gap near **Waynesboro.**

SKYLINE DRIVE, SHENANDOAH

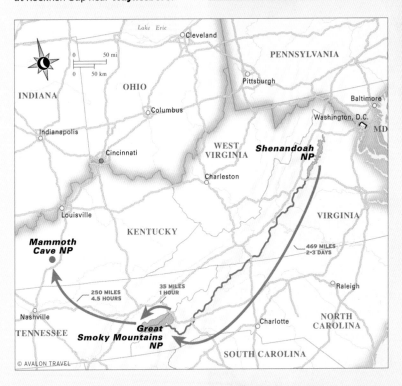

Blue Ridge Parkway

469 miles / 2-3 days

After crossing I-64, Skyline Drive continues south as the **Blue Ridge Parkway.** Follow the parkway for 469 winding miles from I-64 southwest to **Great Smoky Mountains National Park.** The drive from Floyd to the North Carolina state line is one of the most beautiful on the parkway. You'll want to break the drive into a couple of days to stop at parks, museums, and sights. Overnight in Roanoke, Virginia, or Asheville, North Carolina. The parkway ends at Newfound Gap Road near **Cherokee, North Carolina,** where your journey into the Smokies begins.

Great Smoky Mountains

35 miles / 1 hour

Begin your cross-park route heading north via **Newfound Gap Road** (35 mi., 1 hr.). The twisting road is popular for motorcycle touring, autumn foliage, and wildlife, such as black bears and white-tailed deer. Stop along the way at any of the multiple overlooks. Add on a detour to **Cades Cove** (68 mi. rt., 3 hrs.), a onetime mountain community where you might spy bears lounging in the remnants of an apple orchard. Wrap up this segment at **Gatlinburg, Tennessee.**

Mammoth Cave

250 miles / 4.5 hours

From Gatlinburg, go northwest to **Mammoth Cave National Park,** where you can spend the night in the **Lodge at Mammoth Cave.** The following day, go underground with a ranger-led tour, with options ranging from 1.25 to 6 hours.

1: LINN COVE VIADUCT ON THE BLUE RIDGE PARKWAY
2: CADES COVE ROAD, GREAT SMOKY MOUNTAINS
3: MAMMOTH CAVE NATIONAL PARK ENTRANCE

GREAT SMOKY MOUNTAINS NATIONAL PARK

Tennessee and North Carolina

PASSPORT STAMPS ▼▼▼

WEBSITE:
www.nps.gov/grsm

PHONE NUMBER:
865/436-1200

VISITATION RANK:
1

WHY GO:
See the country's
oldest mountains.

▲ GREAT SMOKY MOUNTAINS
NATIONAL PARK

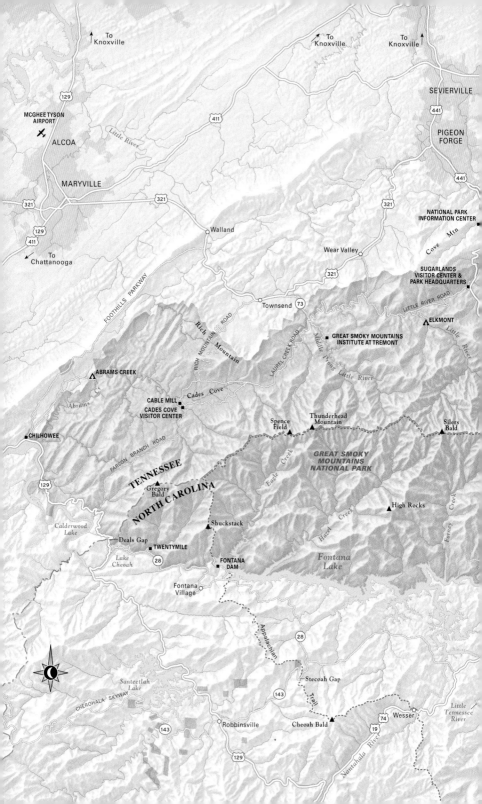

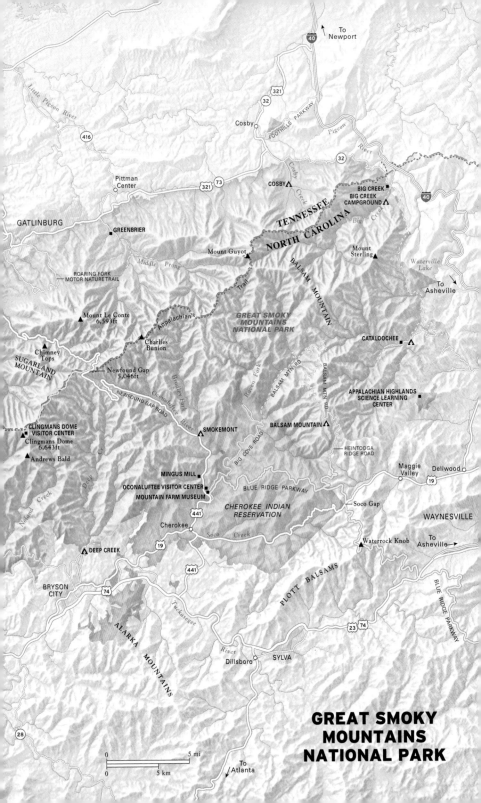

GREAT SMOKY MOUNTAINS NATIONAL PARK

GREAT SMOKY MOUNTAINS NATIONAL PARK is the most visited national park in the country, with visitor numbers topping 11 million annually. There are 850 miles of hiking trails, including 71 miles of the Appalachian Trail; 16 mountains of more than 6,000 feet elevation; 2,100 miles of mountain streams and rivers; and an astoundingly diverse set of flora and fauna. Straddling the North Carolina/Tennessee state line, Great Smoky Mountains National Park's 522,427 acres are nearly equally split between the two states. On the North Carolina side of the park, the mountains pile up against one another, making for tall peaks, steep slopes, and deep coves. It's wild here and more sparsely populated than the Tennessee side, but throughout the park you'll find places so remote and so isolated they've remained undisturbed by humans for impossible stretches of time—or at least they feel that way.

Today the remote places are still remote, requiring sometimes considerable effort to reach, but Cades Cove is a sightseer's delight with its preserved historic churches, schools, and homesteads. In the fall, droves of visitors come for one of the most impressive color shows in the eastern United States.

PLANNING YOUR TIME

Great Smoky Mountains National Park straddles the border between Tennessee and North Carolina. Most visitors devote a single day to the park, driving **Newfound Gap Road** from Gatlinburg, Tennessee, south to the North Carolina town of Cherokee. To give the park a fair shake, devote at least **three days** here.

Summer (mid-June-mid-Aug.) and **fall** (Oct.) constitute the park's high season and are the busiest times to visit. Seasonal considerations have a big influence on park visitation. Crowds arrive for the blooming of spring wildflowers. Each autumn the park is crawling with visitors for a look at the mountains blazing with red, yellow, and burgundy leaves. Summer brings hikers and that cool mountain air, while winter finds the park more empty than full, but no less beautiful.

Within the park, make **camping reservations** six months in advance and reservations at LeConte Lodge **one year in advance.**

Elevation in the park ranges from 900 feet at the lowest point to more than 6,600 feet at the highest, and weather can vary wildly. Clingmans Dome, the highest point in the park, has an average high temperature of only 65°F in July; the only time you're guaranteed *not* to see snow flurries is June-August. While it's in the upper 60s on Clingmans Dome, it can be in the low 90s in Cades Cove.

Park roads close in winter, though dates vary. **Newfound Gap Road** remains open in all but the most serious of weather. In winter, check current conditions (865/436-1200).

ENTRANCES AND FEES

Great Smoky Mountains National Park has three main entrances. **From Gatlinburg, Tennessee,** at the north end of Newfound Gap Road, U.S. 441 leads south two miles into the park. The southern entrance of Newfound Gap Road is in **Cherokee, North Carolina,** two miles north along U.S. 441. From **Townsend, Tennessee,** Highway 73 heads three miles east into the park at Cades Cove. There is no entrance fee.

Top ❸

❶ DRIVE NEWFOUND GAP ROAD

Easily the most heavily traveled route in the Smokies, **Newfound Gap Road** (U.S. 441) connects Cherokee with Gatlinburg. Newfound Gap Road is the perfect introduction to Great Smoky Mountains National Park: Contour-hugging curves, overlooks with million-dollar views, easy hikes right off the roadway, and a 3,000-foot elevation change give you a great overview of these mountains and this spectacular park. During peak times in the summer and fall, it's not uncommon to encounter a traffic jam or two along this 33-mile scenic route.

❷ TOUR CADES COVE

Fields, forests, high peaks, wildlife, and historic structures are just some of the highlights of the **Cades Cove Loop** (11 miles, closed to vehicles until 10am Wed.-Sat. May-Sept.). One of the most popular spots in the park in any season, expect crowds, especially in the fall, and plan to spend two hours or more on this one-way road through the valley floor. Wildlife is especially active in the hours around dawn and dusk.

In 1850, nearly 700 people called this valley home. Today, a number of historic structures remain standing along the valley floor. Among them is the most photographed structure in the park, the **Methodist Church.** From time to time a wedding is held here, though it's more common for visitors to leave handwritten prayers on scraps of paper at the altar. The **Cable Mill Area** is the busiest section of the loop. Here you can see an actual mill in operation, and can even buy cornmeal or flour ground on-site. In addition to the mill and Methodist Church, the area contains two other churches, a few barns, log houses, and a number of smaller structures.

Hikes include gentle strolls to homesteads, cabins, and churches, or longer hikes to **Abrams Falls.** The road is paved, and very well maintained. Though it's **one-way,** two shortcuts cross the valley to shorten the drive (or circle back for one more look, whichever strikes your fancy).

❸ TRAVEL BACK IN TIME AT CATALOOCHEE VALLEY

This isolated valley on the northeastern edge of Great Smoky Mountains National Park was home to two communities—Big and Little Cataloochee—and more than 1,200 people in 1910. By the 1940s all but a few were gone, having left the valley for hills and hollows nearby. Today, this is one of the more beautiful spots in the national park, and a few **historic structures** are all that remain of the communities that thrived here, save a few memories and stories written down.

The most prominent building is the **Palmer Chapel.** Built in 1898, it still sees sporadic use. Across the road is the **Beech Grove School,** the last of three schools to serve the children of the valley. Just up the road is the **Caldwell House,** a frame-built home with paneling on the interior walls. The final structure is the **Palmer House** (off Big Creek Rd.), an 1800s log home with a 20th-century addition.

THE PALMER CHAPEL, CATALOOCHEE VALLEY

ONE DAY IN GREAT SMOKY

From either entrance, drive the **Newfound Gap Road.** En route from Clingmans Dome, hike **Andrews Bald** to take in the 360-degree view of the Great Smokies. Finish by circling **Cades Cove** to soak up the pastoral countryside.

With more time, you can tack on the **Roaring Fork Motor Nature Trail,** stopping to hike to **Rainbow Falls** or explore the lowland scenery of Cataloochee Valley.

VISITORS CENTERS

Sugarlands Visitor Center

The first stop for visitors entering the park from Tennessee is **Sugarlands Visitor Center and Park Headquarters** (1420 Old TN-73 Scenic, Gatlinburg, TN, 865/436-1200, 8am-4:30pm daily Dec.-Feb., 8am-5pm daily Mar. and Nov., 8am-6pm daily Apr.-May, 8am-7:30pm daily June-Aug., 8am-6:30pm daily Sept.-Oct.), located just inside the park about two miles from Gatlinburg. Here you'll find information as well as a 20-minute film introducing the park.

Oconaluftee Visitor Center

If entering from the North Carolina side, **Oconaluftee Visitor Center** (1194 Newfound Gap Rd., Cherokee, NC, 828/497-1904, 8am-4:30pm daily Dec.-Feb., 8am-5pm daily Mar. and Nov., 8am-6pm daily Apr.-May, 8am-7:30pm daily June-Aug., 8am-6:30pm daily Sept.-Oct., closed Dec.-Mar.) is the best place to begin. It's two miles north of Cherokee on U.S. 441/Newfound Gap Road.

Clingmans Dome Visitor Contact Station

Along Newfound Gap Road is the turnoff to Clingmans Dome and the **Clingmans Dome Visitor Contact Station** (Clingmans Dome Rd., off Newfound Gap Rd., 25 miles from Cherokee, NC, and 23 miles from Gatlinburg, TN, 865/436-1200, 10am-6pm daily Apr.-June and Aug.-Oct., 10am-6:30pm daily July, 9:30am-5pm daily Nov.). You'll find information on the park, a bookstore operated by the Great Smoky Mountains Association (www.smokiesinformation.org), and restrooms.

Cades Cove Visitor Center

In Cades Cove is the **Cades Cove Visitor Center** (Cades Cove Loop Rd., 865/436-1200, 9am-4:30pm daily Dec.-Jan., except Christmas Day, 9am-5:30pm daily Feb. and Nov., 9am-6:30pm daily Mar. and Sept.-Oct., 9am-7pm daily Apr. and Aug., 9am-7:30pm daily May-July). Indoor and outdoor exhibits, including

▼ CLINGMANS DOME

historic structures, illustrate southern mountain life and culture. It also has a Great Smoky Mountains Association bookstore (www.smokiesinformation.org) and shop.

SIGHTS

NEWFOUND GAP ROAD

From Cherokee, North Carolina, this scenic road tours 33 miles north to exit the park at Gatlinburg, Tennessee. With year-round access, it offers overlooks, historic sites, and short trails to stretch your legs along the way.

Mountain Farm Museum

The **Mountain Farm Museum** (Oconaluftee Visitor Center, sunrise-sunset daily year-round, free) showcases some of the finest farm buildings in the park. Most date to the early 1900s. Among them are a barn, an apple house, and the Davis House, a log home built from chestnut wood and constructed before the American chestnut blight decimated the species. During peak times, costumed living-history interpreters demonstrate the day-to-day chores that would've occurred.

Mingus Mill

North of the Oconaluftee Visitor Center you'll find **Mingus Mill** (9am-5pm daily mid-Mar.-mid-Nov. and Thanksgiving weekend). This historic gristmill was built in 1886; rather than use a waterwheel to power the machinery and mill in the building, it uses a water-powered turbine to generate power. The cast-iron turbine still works!

Deep Creek Valley Overlook

The **Deep Creek Valley Overlook** is one of the most popular overlooks in the park for good reason. From here you'll have a long view of the mountains, which roll away from you for as far as you can see. It is 14 miles north of the Oconaluftee Visitor Center and 16 miles south of Sugarlands Visitor Center.

Oconaluftee River Valley Overlook

Midway along Newfound Gap Road is the **Oconaluftee River Valley Overlook,** where you can spy the deep cut of the valley formed by the Oconaluftee River.

Newfound Gap

One of the most visited overlooks is at **Newfound Gap.** This is the highest elevation on Newfound Gap Road, at 5,048 feet, and though the views here are fantastic, the first thing you'll probably notice is the Rockefeller Memorial, a simple stone terrace that straddles the Tennessee/North Carolina state line and commemorates a $5 million gift made by the Rockefeller Foundation to acquire land for the park. To avoid the crowds, go early in the morning or near sunset.

Clingmans Dome

At 6,643 feet, **Clingmans Dome** is the third-highest mountain in the eastern United States, and the highest in the Great Smoky Mountains. A flying saucer-like observation tower at the end of a long, steep walkway gives 360-degree views of the surrounding mountains. The road to the summit is closed December 1-March 31, but the observation tower remains open for those willing to make the hike. To get to Clingmans Dome, turn off Newfound Gap Road 0.1 mile south of Newfound Gap, and then take Clingmans Dome Road (closed

MINGUS MILL

in winter), which leads 7 miles to the parking lot. The peak is near the center of the park, due north from Bryson City, North Carolina.

Campbell Overlook

Named after one of the founding members of the Smoky Mountains Hiking Club, the **Carlos Campbell Overlook** is home to one of the best views of Mount LeConte you'll find: At 6,593 feet, LeConte is the third-highest peak in the Smokies. The overlook is two miles south of Sugarlands Visitor Center.

GREENBRIER COVE

Greenbrier Cove was once home to a mountain community. This area was settled in the early 1800s, and families farmed, trapped, and hunted the land until the establishment of the national park. This cove has an interesting footnote: Dolly Parton's ancestors, Benjamin C. and Margaret Parton, moved here in the 1850s and their descendants left when the park was formed. Greenbrier is stunning, especially in the spring. The cove is known as a wildflower hot spot, but don't underestimate the beauty of this place in any season.

COSBY

For the first half of the 20th century, **Cosby** was known as the moonshine capital of the world. Today, there isn't much by way of moonshine production in town, and most of the visitors come here for the national park. Cosby's present reputation is as a friendly town with one of the lesser-used park entrances. In town you'll find a few restaurants and a handful of cabin rentals, but the park is the real treasure.

ELKMONT

In 1908, the little logging town of Elkmont was born, and in 1912, the Wonderland Park Hotel was built. Cottages dotted the hillsides and bottoms. Once the park was established, cottage owners were granted lifetime leases on their property, and family members continued to renew the leases at 20-year intervals until the early 1990s. The Wonderland Park Hotel and the cottages were at one time slated for demolition, but the **Elkmont Historic District** is now listed in the National Register of Historic Places. The hotel collapsed in the early 2000s, and the Park Service has visions of restoring a few of the remaining cottages, but work has yet to begin in earnest.

Fireflies

The **synchronous fireflies** may have been one of the reasons the Wonderland Park Hotel was built in Elkmont. For a two-week window every summer (**early to mid-July**), their nightly light show delights crowds as drifts of male fireflies rise from the grass to flash their mating signal—blinking in coordinated ways that baffle researchers.

Viewing the synchronous fireflies is deservedly popular—a **lottery** (877/444-6777, www.recreation.gov) controls access and limits traffic congestion. Hopeful visitors can apply online during the three days the lottery is open; applicants will have two dates to choose from. Lottery results become available about a week later. The lucky winners will receive a parking pass for Sugarlands Visitor Center, where they will board the shuttle to Elkmont and back.

FONTANA LAKE

At the southern edge of Great Smoky Mountains National Park lies Fontana Lake, a 10,230-acre reservoir created in the 1940s. The 480-foot-tall, 2,365-foot-wide **Fontana Dam,** complete with three hydroelectric generators, was completed in 1944. It provided much-needed electricity to the factories churning out materials for World War II, including Oak Ridge, Tennessee, where research leading to the atomic bomb was conducted.

The exhibits at the **Fontana Dam Visitor Center** (Fontana Dam Rd., off NC-28 near the state line, www.tva.gov, 9am-6pm daily May-Oct., free) tell the story of the region and the construction of the dam. There's also a small gift shop, and a viewing platform overlooking the dam.

DEEP CREEK

Just south of Cherokee and just north of Bryson City, **Deep Creek** is a spot more popular with locals than tourists, but it's worth a stop. Deep Creek is relatively

ROARING FORK CREEK

placid, aside from a couple of water-falls upstream. If you're not into wad-ing or tubing, don't worry—this is a love-ly place to picnic and hike or even camp away from the crowds found in some of the more popular spots in the park.

SCENIC DRIVES

ROARING FORK

The **Roaring Fork Motor Nature Trail** (open Mar.-Nov., 5.5 miles) used to be one of the most beautiful drives in Great Smoky Mountains National Park. This one-way loop, which follows the old roadbed of the Roaring Fork Com-munity, passes through what were lush rhododendron thickets and dense hardwood forests. A 2016 wildfire left a landscape of charred tree stands and fewer rhodies and laurel, but the green-ery will flourish again in time.

To start, turn onto Historic Nature Trail (Old Airport Road) at traffic light #8 in Gatlinburg and follow the signs. Drive a short distance on Cherokee Or-chard Road, which runs through what was an 800-acre commercial orchard in the 1920s and 1930s. Shortly after the orchard, you'll be at the head of the trail.

RICH MOUNTAIN ROAD

Rich Mountain Road (open Apr.-Nov.) is a photographer's dream.

Running north from Cades Cove over Rich Mountain to **Tuckaleechee Cove** and **Townsend**, this **one-way grav-el road** provides a few stunning views of Cades Cove and Tuckaleechee Cove. You're likely to see bear, deer, turkeys, and other wildlife along the way. The road is typically in good condition and isn't too challenging as far as back roads go, but avoid tackling this drive in a low-clearance vehicle or your econo-my rental car; instead, go with a truck or SUV (no 4WD necessary). Know that the road gets a little steep once it passes outside park boundaries, but it's nothing too hair-raising.

BALSAM MOUNTAIN ROAD

Balsam Mountain Road (open May-Nov.) is a lovely drive where you may be lucky to see 10 other cars. Accessible only from the Blue Ridge Parkway near Soco Gap, the road traverses 14 miles of ridgeline. To reach Balsam Mountain Road, turn off the Parkway at Milepost 458 and follow Heintooga Ridge Road to the Heintooga Overlook and Picnic Area; here the road changes names to Balsam Mountain Road, and turns to gravel. As soon as it turns into Balsam Mountain Road it becomes one-way, so you're committed to follow it to its end—which will take about 1.5 hours.

Best Hike

ANDREWS BALD

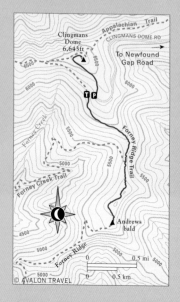

DISTANCE: 3.5 miles round-trip
DURATION: 3 hours
ELEVATION GAIN: 1,200 feet
DIFFICULTY: moderate
TRAILHEAD: Clingmans Dome parking area at the end of Clingmans Dome Road

The highest grassy bald in Great Smoky Mountains National Park, Andrews Bald is a beautiful sight at the end of a nearly two-mile hike from Clingmans Dome. Balds are meadows found higher up on the mountain, and this one is absolutely lousy with flame azalea and rhododendron blooms in the summer. Note that Clingmans Dome Road is closed in the winter.

The **Forney Ridge Trail** starts in a spruce-fir forest that was once beautiful, but is now unfortunately dead or dying. That's because the forest has been ravaged by a tiny bug—the balsam woolly adelgid—that devours Fraser firs. However, there is a certain beauty in the white bones of the tree trunks jutting up from the land. Don't worry though, the views get considerably better in a short time. Around 1.6 miles into the hike you'll reach the edge of **Andrews Bald,** where the forest opens up into a fantastic panorama. In spring and summer, there is a proliferation of wildflowers, flame azalea, and rhododendron.

PARSONS BRANCH ROAD

Parsons Branch Road (closed in winter) is a great drive. Take a right turn just beyond the Cades Cove Visitor Center parking area and you'll find yourself on a 10-mile long, one-way gravel road leading to U.S. 129 and Deals Gap on the extreme southwestern edge of the park. At times pothole riddled and crossing 18 or so small streams along the way, the road is a slow one, taking around an hour to drive. The road passes **Henry Whitehead Place,** an odd-looking pair of conjoined cabins. You'll cross the same stream several times before climbing to the crest of the drive. Here you'll find the trailhead for **Gregory Bald Trail.** This is the halfway mark of the road and it is, as they say, all downhill from here.

HIKING

NEWFOUND GAP ROAD

Kephart Prong Trail

Kephart Prong (4 mi. rt., 2 hrs., easy) offers an easy way to get more familiar with hiking in the Smokies. Begin by crossing the Oconaluftee River via a footbridge and follow the wide, nearly flat trail. At 0.25 mile into the hike, a Civilian Conservation Corps camp contains ruins such as foundations, chimneys, and other evidence of use in the 1930s. Continuing along the path, cross the stream of Kephart Prong, then begin to climb, passing the remains of a fish hatchery in 0.6 mile. Three more crossings of the Kephart Prong await. Soon, the trail passes narrow-gauge railroad tracks, evidence of a long-gone logging operation. The route

MOUNTAINS LINED WITH COLORFUL AUTUMN FOLIAGE

terminates at Kephart Shelter, where the trail meets Sweat Heifer Creek Trail and Grassy Branch Trail.

Charlies Bunion

From the Newfound Gap parking lot, the **Charlies Bunion Trail** (8.1 mi. rt., 7-8 hrs., strenuous) follows the Appalachian Trail and the Boulevard to Mount LeConte. The trail climbs for two miles, passing the junction with Sweat Heifer Creek Trail. At 2.8 miles, the Boulevard forks off to the left; continue straight to reach Charlies Bunion. In 0.25 mile, the Icewater Spring Shelter is a good spot to rest. From the spring, continue less than one mile to a short spur trail on the left that leads to the rock outcrop known as Charlies Bunion.

Alum Cave Bluff to Mount LeConte

One of the most popular hikes in the park, the **Alum Cave Bluff to Mount LeConte** (Alum Cave Trailhead, 5 mi. one-way, 3.5 hrs., moderate) trail starts off fairly gently as it climbs alongside Alum Cave Creek amid several cascades and beautiful rhododendron thickets. At 1.5 miles, you'll reach Arch Rock, a natural tunnel at the half-mile-long Alum Cave Bluffs. Pitching more steeply, a set of stone steps leads out of Arch Rock to Inspiration Point for a territorial view.

Most hikers turn around here, the halfway point to Mount LeConte. To forge on is more challenging, as the path steepens. The trail narrows to a set of rock ledges with steel cables bolted into the mountain for use as handholds. The drop may be precipitous, but the views are fantastic. Soon, the trail intersects with Rainbow Falls Trail, leading to the summit of Mount LeConte. Arrive early for a parking space at the trailhead.

Chimney Tops

The popular **Chimney Tops** (4 mi. rt., 3.5 hrs., strenuous) hike leads to an outstanding view from its namesake pinnacles. Many people explore the first few hundred yards of this trail because it's right off Newfound Gap Road. The cascades, pools, and boulders found along **Walker Camp Prong** are picturesque and good for wading and sunbathing. As you climb, you'll cross **Road Prong,** another stream, twice. Just after the second crossing the trail splits. Stay right to head to the chimneys. After a brief ascent, the trail steepens in a long, straight climb and narrows on the ridgeline. At the foot of the **Chimney Tops,** a sign warns you to proceed at your own risk. Heed this sign, as the last bit of "trail" to the summit is a **scramble.**

A SMALL WATERFALL IN THE SMOKIES

CADES COVE
Abrams Falls Trail

Abrams Falls (5 mi. rt., 3 hrs., moderate) is the destination for most hikers who set off from this lot. Only a few steps from the trailhead is a **kiosk** that will set you on the right path. The trail follows **Abrams Creek** all the way to the waterfall. The only real elevation gains come when you thrice leave the creek to climb up and around a ridge, crossing a feeder stream in the process. After you cross Wilson Branch on a **log bridge,** you'll follow the trail downstream, cross Wilson Branch once again, and arrive at the falls.

Rich Mountain Loop

The first part of the **Rich Mountain Loop** (Cades Cove, 8.5 mi. rt., 4.5 hrs., moderate) passes one of the meadows that makes Cades Cove such a fabulous place. For 1.4 miles, it goes through the woods and along the edge of the meadow to the **John Oliver Cabin.** The trail continues behind the cabin to meet up with **Martha's Branch** and begin climbing, crossing the branch a number of times. Mile 3 yields a tight view of Cades Cove. Continue 0.3 mile to **Indian Grave Gap Trail** and turn right. In 0.8 mile is **Campsite 5** (for backpackers). After the junction with Rich Mountain Trail,

BLACK BEAR IN CADES COVE

follow Indian Grave Gap Trail 0.3 mile to a side trail. This path is only about 100 yards long and takes you to the highest point on Rich Mountain, **Cerulean Knob,** and the foundation of the former fire tower. After a power-line clearance, the trail reaches **Scott Mountain Trail** and **Campsite 4.** From the junction of these trails, continue straight ahead on **Crooked Arm Ridge Trail** (it's what Indian Grave Gap Trail turns into). This trail is steep, rutted, and littered with the evidence of horses, but circles back to **Rich Mountain Loop Trail** 0.5 mile from the parking area.

CATALOOCHEE VALLEY
Boogerman Trail

Start the **Boogerman Trail** (Cataloochee Campground, 7.4 mi. rt., 3.5-4 hrs., moderate) by crossing **Palmer Creek.** Follow Caldwell Fork upstream for nearly a mile to reach **Boogerman Trail.** Turn left onto the trail and begin a gentle climb. At a lower ridgeline, the path levels out, and then descends through a grove of pine trees before ascending again. Soon, the trail makes a steep ascent to another level ridge with signs of human settlement, the first of which is a **stone wall.** Continue the descent and cross the stream a few times, passing more rock walls along the way. When you pass the decayed remains of a **cabin,** you're close to the junction with Caldwell Fork Trail. At **Caldwell Fork Trail,** turn right and cross Snake Branch stream and soon thereafter, Caldwell Fork. Cross Caldwell Fork several more times before reaching the junction with **Boogerman Trail** and the path back to the trailhead.

Laurel Falls Trail

As the shortest waterfall hike in the park, **Laurel Falls** (Little River Road, 2.5 mi. rt., 1.5-2 hrs., easy) lures scads of hikers. After a short, steep start, the paved trail has a gentle grade to the waterfall.

ROARING FORK
Rainbow Falls

The 80-foot-high **Rainbow Falls** (Rainbow Falls Trailhead, Cherokee Orchard Loop Road, 5.4 mi. rt., 3-4 hrs., moderate) is the most popular waterfall hike. Departing the parking area, cross

Trillium Gap Trail and climb alongside LeConte Creek. Follow the trail through a couple of switchbacks and then cross the creek on a **log bridge.** At another crossing, you can see **Rainbow Falls** above. Continue up the trail to a spot just below the falls.

GREENBRIER COVE AND COSBY

Ramsey Cascades Trail

Ramsey Cascades (Ramsey Cascades Trailhead, 8 mi. rt., 5.5 hrs., strenuous) is the tallest waterfall in Great Smoky Mountains National Park, spilling 100 feet in a series of steps before collecting in a pool at the base. The first portion of this trail is a continuation of the gravel road to the parking area. It crosses **Little Laurel Branch,** and, almost immediately after, the Middle Prong of Little Pigeon River via a long **footbridge.** If you've timed your hike with the wildflower bloom, the next half-mile will be a riot of color. Until the 1.5-mile mark, where the jeep trail ends, the hike is easy. Ignore a left spur trail and continue on through a thicket of rhododendron. The trail will turn steep and cross **Ramsey Prong** and a side stream. When you hear the waterfall, you're at the final rocky and slick approach. When scrambling, use caution.

Porters Creek Trail

From the traffic loop 0.9 mile up the road from the **Ramsey Cascades Trailhead,** begin hiking a gravel road along rock walls, evidence of homesites, and an old **cemetery.** Cross a stream by wading (if the water's not too high) or using the foot log. In one mile, an **old traffic turnaround** indicates the start of the trail. **Porters Creek Trail** (Greenbrier Road, 0.9 mile beyond the Ramsey Cascades Trailhead, 7.2 mi. rt., 4 hrs., moderate) is the trail to the far left. On the trail, cross Porters Creek in 0.5 mile. **Fern Branch Falls** awaits 0.4 mile farther, surprisingly high at 35 feet, and the surrounding area is thick with moss and wildflowers in the spring. Continue past the waterfall to the end of the hike and **Backcountry Campsite 31** at 3.6 miles.

Hen Wallow Falls Trail

From the outset, **Hen Wallow Falls Trail** (Gabes Mountain Trailhead, 4.4 mi. rt., 3.5 hrs., moderate) is a steady climb on a path that's at times rugged. Start on **Gabes Mountain Trail** for 2.1 miles until a signed, steep **side trail** leads 0.1 mile to the waterfall. **Hen Wallow Falls** tumbles 90 feet into a small pool that is full

▼ RAMSEY CASCADES

MIDDLE PRONG OF THE LITTLE RIVER

of salamanders. The falls are only 2 feet wide at the top, but fan out to 20 feet at the bottom. During dry months, they are still pretty, but less wow-inducing.

RECREATION

BACKPACKING

Backpacking to **Mount LeConte from Grotto Falls** (13.5 mi. rt., 2 days, strenuous) requires some preparation. Register with the **Backcountry Information Office** (Sugarlands Visitor Center, 865/436-1297, https://smokiespermits.nps.gov, 8am-5pm daily, $4 pp/night) for a permit, then make a site reservation. On Mount LeConte, you'll have only two options: LeConte Lodge, which is a hot ticket and books up early, and the LeConte Shelter, which is easier to secure. LeConte Lodge requires reservations one year in advance. The LeConte Shelter is reserved through the Backcountry Information Office; reservations may be made up to 30 days in advance.

BIKING

The park closes off the loop road through **Caves Cove** on Wednesday and Saturday mornings (sunrise-10am)

from the second week in May until the second-to-last Saturday in September, so that cyclists and hikers can enjoy the cove without having to worry about automobile traffic. The **Cades Cove Store** (near Cades Cove Campground, 865/448-9034) rents bicycles in summer and fall.

FISHING

Anglers go to **Cosby Creek** year-round. In the spring it's possible to catch fish along the creek, but in the summer it's best to venture into the headwaters. Fall fishing is spectacular, and you can even catch fish in winter except for the coldest days. Fishing is plentiful off **Cataloochee Creek** and its tributaries, with the main quarry being wild trout. Smallmouth bass and rock bass are fairly abundant in Smoky's waters. Look for smallmouth bass along the West Prong of the Little Pigeon River, near the park's western entrance, and in the Little Pigeon River near **Greenbrier.** Smallmouth and rock bass are found in the **Little River** on the way to Cades Cove and Abrams Creek, specifically the feeder creeks like Noland, Hazel, and Eagle Creek.

GROTTO FALLS

Trout love the feeder streams and headwaters that flow into **Fontana Lake**, which contains largemouth, smallmouth, and rock bass. Deep water has walleye and muskies (and it gets deeper than 400 feet deep in some points). Anglers use boats and kayaks on the lake, and you'll see more than a few fly rods strapped to the backpacks of hikers headed to the streams along the lake's north banks.

HORSEBACK RIDING

Three commercial stables in the park offer "rental" horses. **Smokemont** (828/497-2373, www.smokemontridingstable.com) is located in North Carolina near Cherokee. Two are in Tennessee: **Smoky Mountain** (865/436-5634, Gatlinburg, TN, www.smokymountainridingstables.com) and **Cades Cove** (10018 Campground Dr., Townsend, TN, 865/448-9009, http://cadescovestables.com).

WHERE TO STAY
INSIDE THE PARK

LeConte Lodge (865/429-5704, www.lecontelodge.com, Mar. 21-Nov. 22) is the only true lodging in the park, accessible via a 5-6.8-mile hike. Even though there is no running water or electricity, the lodge books quickly. Reservations are via lottery up to **one year in advance.**

NAME	LOCATION	PRICE	SEASON	SITES	AMENITIES
Abrams Creek	Foothills Pkwy.	$17.50	Apr.-Oct.	16	tent and RV sites
Balsam Mountain	Balsam Mountain Rd.	$17.50	May-Oct.	46	tent sites
Big Creek	off Hwy. 284	$17.50	Mar.-Oct.	12	tent, RV, group, and horse sites
Cades Cove	Cades Cove	$21-25	year-round	159	tent and RV sites; camp store
Cataloochee	Cataloochee	$25	Mar.-Oct	27	tent and RV sites
Cosby	Cosby	$17.50	Mar.-Oct	157	tent and RV sites
Deep Creek	north of Bryson City	$21	Apr.-Oct.	92	tent and RV sites; dump station
Elkmont	Sugarlands Visitor Center	$21-27	Mar.-Nov.	220	tents and RV sites; dump station
Smokemont	Newfound Gap Road	$21-25	year-round	142	tent and RV sites; dump station

The park has nine campgrounds. Campgrounds have restrooms with flush toilets and each site has a fire grate and picnic table. **Reservations** (877/444-6777, www.recreation.gov, $17-27) are accepted up to six months in advance at the following:

Elkmont (Gatlinburg, TN), located west of Sugarlands Visitor Center, is the largest of the campgrounds and one of the most visited.

Smokemont (Cherokee, NC) is just off Newfound Gap Road, 3.2 miles north of the Oconaluftee Visitor Center.

Cades Cove (Townsend, TN) is a popular spot on the east side off the Cades Cove Loop.

HISTORIC CABIN ON MOUNT LECONTE

EVENING LIGHT ON THE SMOKIES, SEEN FROM AN OVERLOOK ON NEWFOUND GAP ROAD

Cosby (Cosby, TN) is the park's third-largest campground, located in the quiet northwest corner of the park.

Reservations are **required** at Abrams Creek, Balsam Mountain, Big Creek, and Cataloochee.

OUTSIDE THE PARK

Most accommodations, dining options, and services are found in either **Gatlinburg, Tennessee,** or **Cherokee, North Carolina. Cosby, Tennessee,** has a few accommodations and dining options, but selections are limited. For spring, summer, and fall, make reservations at least six months in advance.

GETTING THERE

AIR

Asheville Regional Airport (61 Terminal Dr., Asheville, NC, 828/684-2226, www.flyavl.com) is located about one hour east of Cherokee. **McGhee Tyson Airport** (2055 Alcoa Hwy., Alcoa, TN, 865/342-3000, www.flyknoxville.com) is about one hour west of Gatlinburg. Car rentals are available at the airports.

CAR

There are three main entrances to Great Smoky Mountains National Park. From **Cherokee, North Carolina,** drive two miles north along U.S. 441 into the park on Newfound Gap Road.

From **Gatlinburg, Tennessee,** follow U.S. 441 south two miles into the park along Newfound Gap Road.

Townsend, Tennessee, provides access to Cades Cove via Highway 73, three miles east.

There are seventeen additional points of entry into the park via automobile. The majority are gravel roads in varying states of maintenance that require different degrees of driving confidence and skill. If you're up for an adventure, these roads can lead to some beautiful corners of the park that few others experience.

GETTING AROUND

The park has no park shuttles or public transportation—you will need **your own vehicle.** It also has **no gas stations**; fill up first in Cherokee, North Carolina, or in Tennessee in Gatlinburg or Townsend.

DRIVING

The 33-mile-long **Newfound Gap Road (U.S. 441)** bisects the park from north to south. It's the most heavily traveled route in the park and provides a good introduction for first-time visitors. Newfound Gap Road starts at the southern terminus of the Blue Ridge Parkway, just outside Cherokee, North Carolina, and ends in Knoxville, Tennessee, 70 miles to the northwest.

From Cherokee, you can head straight to the eastern entrance of Great Smoky Mountains National Park via Newfound Gap Road. Take U.S. 441/Highway 71 north through Great Smoky Mountains National Park and into Gatlinburg, Tennessee. It's easy to make the trip from one end to the other in an afternoon, though it may take a little longer in peak seasons. Knoxville, Tennessee, is 36 miles to the northwest of Great Smoky Mountains National Park along U.S. 441 and Highway 71.

To reach **Cataloochee Valley** from I-40, take exit 20 onto U.S. 276. Take an immediate right onto Cove Creek Road. Zigzag up the gravel and paved road following the narrow, winding route for about 12 miles. It will suddenly open up into the wide, grassy expanse that is Cataloochee Valley. The valley is open to vehicle traffic 8am-sunset.

SIGHTS NEARBY

The Blue Ridge Parkway (828/348-3400, www.nps.gov/blri) connects Great Smoky Mountains National Park in North Carolina with Shenandoah National Park in Virginia.

APPALACHIAN TRAIL

Cutting through the heart of Great Smoky Mountains National Park, the **Appalachian Trail** runs along the high ridgeline that forms the border between North Carolina and Tennessee. There are 71.6 miles of the Appalachian Trail in Great Smoky Mountains National Park, and it's a highlight for thru-hikers (those taking the Appalachian Trail north to Maine or south to Georgia, all in one enormous hike), segment hikers (those hiking the whole thing one piece at a time), and day hikers (the rest of us). For the lowdown on the Appalachian Trail, contact the **Appalachian Trail Conservancy** (www.appalachiantrail.org) or visit the **National Park Service** (www.nps.gov/appa), where you'll find trip-planning information, maps, trail reports, and more.

Permits

Though there are no fees required to hike the Appalachian Trail, there are requirements when hiking the Appalachian Trail in Great Smoky Mountains National Park. Thru-hikers are eligible for a **thru-hiker permit** (www.smokiespermits.nps.gov, $20); thru-hikers must begin and end their hike at least 50 miles from the border of the park and only travel on the Appalachian Trail while in the park. Segment hikers and backpackers need a permit from the **Backcountry Information Office** (Sugarlands Visitor Center, 865-436-1297, https://smokiespermits.nps.gov, 8am-5pm daily, $4 pp/night). A permit is not required for day hikers.

Trail Shelters

For AT thru-hikers there's only one choice for where to stay in Great Smoky Mountains National Park: **Appalachian Trail shelters.** Of the 12 sites at each shelter, four spots are reserved for thru-hikers only and they're first come, first served. If you're thru-hiking and find a shelter full, you are permitted to pitch your tent next to the shelters. Segment hikers and backpackers can reserve spots in these Appalachian Trail shelters, or at any of the numerous backcountry campsites along and near the Appalachian Trail. There are too many backcountry campsites near the Appalachian Trail, as well as other backcountry shelters, to list here. For a complete list, consult a park trail map (www.nps.gov/grsm).

Day Hikes

Day hikers are drawn to the Appalachian Trail's fantastic balds (high natural and agricultural meadows), like Andrews Bald and Silers Bald; peaks like Mount Cammerer and Rocky Top (yes, the one from the song); and just to say they've hiked part of the Appalachian Trail. The route through the park is always high and at times rocky, at other times steep (at other times both), but the views are worth it.

THE APPALACHIAN TRAIL

Day hikers who want to log a few miles of the Appalachian Trail will find a few opportunities to get their boots muddy. Notable day hikes include:

Charlies Bunion (8.1 mi. rt.): Access the Appalachian Trail north from the trailhead at the Newfound Gap Road Overlook.

Mount Cammerer (11.2 mi. rt.): Take the Low Gap Trail at the Cosby Campground to the Appalachian Trail, then proceed to the summit and a stone fire tower. Note: Only 4.2 miles are on the Appalachian Trail.

Rocky Top (13.9 mi. rt.): Follow the Anthony Creek Trailhead from the Cades Cove picnic area to Bote Mountain Trail. At Spence Field, you'll meet up with the Appalachian Trail; follow it to Rocky Top and spectacular views.

SHENANDOAH NATIONAL PARK

Virginia

WEBSITE:
www.nps.gov/shen

PHONE NUMBER:
540/999-3500

VISITATION RANK:
17

WHY GO:
Tour the Blue Ridge Mountains.

▲ SHENANDOAH NATIONAL PARK

Amid the thick forest of **SHENANDOAH NATIONAL PARK**, rare and common species of animals thrive. This 300-square-mile slice of nature holds black bears and big brown bats, white-tailed deer and bald eagles, and the endangered Shenandoah salamander. But it's the vast forests of Shenandoah that lend the park its beauty. About 95 percent of the park is covered in trees that change with seasonal color. Those trees emit organic compounds into the air that give the Blue Ridge Mountains their name.

More than 500 miles of trails, many accessible from Skyline Drive, wind through lush forests and across long ridgelines. On these hikes, you'll find more than a dozen waterfalls and plentiful wildflowers, and be granted the opportunity to see wildlife. Remnants of former homesites are visible in crumbling walls and chimneys and mossy cemeteries hidden in the underbrush. A 101-mile segment of the Appalachian Trail (AT) threads its way down Skyline Drive, making it ideal for short hikes as it crosses and recrosses the road.

PLANNING YOUR TIME

Located only 75 miles west of Washington DC, Shenandoah National Park is a popular escape. The park follows the ridge of Virginia's Blue Ridge Mountains for 105 miles and is divided into three sections, designated by roads bisecting Skyline Drive.

The **Northern District** stretches from Front Royal (U.S. 340, MP 0) to Thornton Gap (U.S. 211, MP 31.5).

The **Central District** continues south to Swift Run Gap (U.S. 33, MP 62.7).

Rockfish Gap (I-64, U.S. 250, MP 104.6) marks the southern boundary of the **Southern District.**

The most popular time to visit Shenandoah National Park and cruise along Skyline Drive is **autumn** (Sept.-Oct.), when the leaves turn and the broad, green valleys become a riot of color. This can mean long lines at entrance stations and slow traffic along Skyline Drive; expect a lot of leaf-peeping companions, especially on weekends.

Inclement weather can close the road any time of year, and spring and summer storms can bring heavy rain, lightning, fog, and hail to the area. During deer-hunting season (mid-Nov.-early Jan.), Skyline is closed at night to give the deer a break.

Though the park is open year-round, in **winter** sections of Skyline Drive close. However, many people hike in or drive a short way up Skyline to take in the snowy views.

ENTRANCES AND FEES

There are entrance stations at four points along Skyline Drive:

Front Royal (MP 0) off U.S. 340 near Front Royal

Thornton Gap (MP 31.5) off U.S. 211 east of Luray

Swift Run Gap (MP 62.7) off U.S. 33 east of Elkton

Rockfish Gap (MP 104.6) off U.S. 250 east of Waynesboro

The entrance fee is $30 per vehicle ($25 motorcycle, $15 individual) and is good for seven days.

VISITORS CENTERS

Shenandoah National Park has two visitors centers. The **Dickey Ridge Visitor Center** (MP 4.6, 8:30am-5pm daily Apr.-mid-Nov., 9am-5pm daily Apr.-Nov.) is the first stop when traveling southbound along Skyline Drive. There's a very nice view, as well as restrooms,

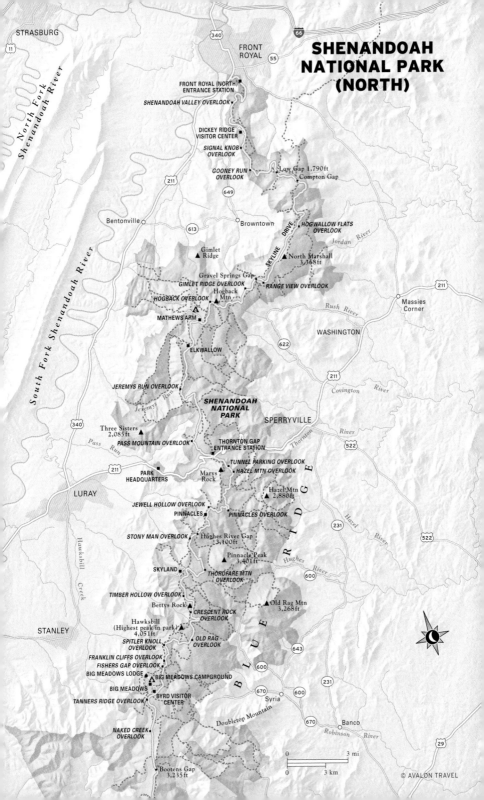

SHENANDOAH NATIONAL PARK (NORTH)

STRASBURG

11

340

66

FRONT ROYAL

55

FRONT ROYAL (NORTH) ENTRANCE STATION

SHENANDOAH VALLEY OVERLOOK

North Fork Shenandoah River

DICKEY RIDGE VISITOR CENTER

SIGNAL KNOB OVERLOOK

GOONEY RUN OVERLOOK

211

649

Low Gap 1,790ft
Compton Gap

Bentonville

613

Browntown

SKYLINE DRIVE

HOGWALLOW FLATS OVERLOOK

Jordan River

▲ Gimlet Ridge

▲ North Marshall 3,368ft

Gravel Springs Gap

GIMLET RIDGE OVERLOOK

Hogback Mtn

RANGE VIEW OVERLOOK

HOGBACK OVERLOOK

▲

MATHEWS ARM

Massies Corner

211

South Fork Shenandoah River

ELKWALLOW

Rush River

WASHINGTON

622

JEREMYS RUN OVERLOOK

Jeremys Run

SHENANDOAH NATIONAL PARK

SPERRYVILLE

211

Covington River

340

▲ Three Sisters 2,085ft

PASS MOUNTAIN OVERLOOK

THORNTON GAP ENTRANCE STATION

Thornton River

522

211

PARK HEADQUARTERS

Marys Rock

TUNNEL PARKING OVERLOOK
HAZEL MTN OVERLOOK

LURAY

Hazel Mtn ▲ 2,880ft

Hazel River

522

JEWELL HOLLOW OVERLOOK

PINNACLES

PINNACLES OVERLOOK

231

STONY MAN OVERLOOK

Hughes River Gap 3,100ft

Hawksbill Creek

▲ Pinnacle Peak 3,401ft

Hughes River

SKYLAND

THOROFARE MTN OVERLOOK

600

TIMBER HOLLOW OVERLOOK

Bettys Rock

▲ Old Rag Mtn 3,268ft

STANLEY

CRESCENT ROCK OVERLOOK

Hawksbill ▲
(Highest peak in park)
4,051ft

SPITLER KNOLL OVERLOOK

OLD RAG OVERLOOK

643

FRANKLIN CLIFFS OVERLOOK
FISHERS GAP OVERLOOK

600

BIG MEADOWS LODGE

▲ BIG MEADOWS CAMPGROUND

BLUE RIDGE

BIG MEADOWS

BYRD VISITOR CENTER

670

Syria

600

231

TANNERS RIDGE OVERLOOK

NAKED CREEK OVERLOOK

Doubletop Mountain

670

Banco

Robinson River

29

Bootens Gap 3,235ft

0   3 mi

0   3 km

© AVALON TRAVEL

ONE DAY IN SHENANDOAH

Skyline Drive traverses the entire length of the park from north to south. A scenic drive along its twisting corridor should be on your one-day agenda. If you have time, add a short day hike along the way.

brochures, backcountry permits, and a gift shop.

The **Harry F. Byrd Sr. Visitor Center** (MP 51, 9am-5pm daily late Mar.-Nov., 9:30am-4pm Fri.-Sun. Dec.-early Jan., hours vary mid-Jan.-late Mar.) has restrooms, an information desk, and a great exhibit that details the story of Shenandoah National Park.

SCENIC DRIVE
SKYLINE DRIVE

The 105-mile **Skyline Drive** carries you through Shenandoah National Park from Front Royal to Rockfish Gap, just outside of Waynesboro, where the drive continues via the Blue Ridge Parkway. Along the narrow, curvy ridgetop route, 75 overlooks offer views of the Shenandoah Valley to the west and the piedmont of Virginia to the east. The drive is lovely in any season but most colorful in the fall. Spring buds and wildflowers and jewel-green summer mountains are other seasonal attractions.

Stops along Skyline Drive are referred to by milepost (MP). The milepost markers make it easy to orient yourself in the park and give you an easy measure from place to place. Milepost 0 is at Front Royal, at the northern end of Skyline Drive. Milepost 104.6 is at Rockfish Gap at the southern end. It takes around three hours to drive from end to end.

Skyline Drive remains open year-round, except when winter snow accumulation outpaces the park's ability to maintain roadways. Along Skyline Drive, fog can pop up in any season.

(MP 4.6) Dickey Ridge Visitor Center: This is the first stop south along Skyline Drive.

(MP 6) Gooney Run Overlook: Looking out from the Gooney Run Overlook you can see Gooney Run, the stream that drains Browntown Valley. Several turns of the Shenandoah River are visible here as well, as are Signal Knob and Dickey Ridge.

▼ SKYLINE DRIVE

OLD RAG FROM PINNACLES OVERLOOK

(MP 9.2) Lands Run: A short wooded stroll on the **Lands Run Falls Trail** is perfect for those pressed for time but who want to see one of the park's waterfalls.

(MP 10.4) Fort Windham Rocks and Compton Gap: Carson Mountain (2,580 ft.) is unremarkable except for its summit, a geologic feature known as the Fort Windham Rocks. Geologists say the rocks are 600-800 million years old and are examples of the Catoctin lava formations.

(MP 20.8) Hogback Mountain Overlook: The largest overlook area in Shenandoah National Park, this is a popular stop.

(MP 22.1) Matthews Arm Campground: Matthews Arm is near Overall Run Falls, which has the highest drop of all the falls in the park.

(MP 24.1) Elkwallow Wayside: Stop for food or services.

(MP 32) Mary's Rock Tunnel and Trail: This 670-foot-long tunnel was cut through Mary's Rock in 1932. At only 12.66 feet in width, Mary's Rock Tunnel is a little tight, so be aware if you're driving an RV or trailer.

(MP 35.5) Pinnacles Overlook: From Pinnacles Overlook you have a great view of Old Rag Mountain.

(MP 41.7) Skyland Resort: The highest point along Skyline Drive is at the northern entrance to Skyland Resort, where the road reaches 3,680 feet in elevation.

(MP 45.6) Hawksbill Mountain: The highest peak in the park, 4,050-foot Hawksbill Mountain, is accessible only by a moderate hike.

(MP 50.7) Dark Hollow Falls: A short trail leads to a beautiful 70-foot waterfall.

(MP 51) Big Meadows: Big Meadows is home to the largest open meadow in Shenandoah National Park, **a lodge, a campground,** and a **dining room.** There's also a long hike to one of the highest waterfalls in the park.

(MP 52.8) Rapidan Camp: A moderate to difficult hike from Milam Gap will take you to a waterfall and the former retreat of President Herbert Hoover.

(MP 56.4) Bearfence Mountain: From the top of 3,640-foot Bearfence Mountain, you'll get a commanding, 360-degree view of Shenandoah National Park.

(MP 57.5) Lewis Mountain: At Lewis Mountain you'll find first-come, first-served **camping,** cute rustic cabins, and a camp store.

(MP 62.8) South River Falls: These 83-foot waterfalls are the third largest in Shenandoah National Park. You can only see them on a hike along the South River.

(MP 76.9) Brown Mountain Overlook: This overlook's ridges descend to the valley floor in stacked waves; at their head is a mountain that in autumn is ablaze with color, save the spots where rocky protrusions show through the trees.

(MP 79.5) Loft Mountain: Stop and grab a bite to eat from **Loft Mountain Wayside** or take the trail to the summit of Loft Mountain. The turnoff here ends at the **Loft Mountain Campground,** situated on top of Big Flat Mountain, the second-highest peak in the Southern District.

(MP 84.8) Blackrock Summit: This is a beautiful spot to stop and take in the scenery.

(MP 90) Riprap Overlook: The trailhead for the **Riprap Hollow Trail,** one of the best loop hikes in the Southern District.

(MP 92.6) Crimora Lake Overlook: This is one of the top vistas along Skyline Drive primarily because of the beautiful Crimora Lake forming the centerpiece of the view.

(MP 96.9) Calf Mountain Overlook: From an elevation of 2,485 feet, the Calf Mountain Overlook provides some dizzying views. As you round the bend, the road seems to continue right out into the air (but it really just makes a tight turn). The overlook is a long one, with near-360-degree views.

(MP 105) Rockfish Gap: The south entrance station marks the end of Skyline Drive and the beginning of the Blue Ridge Parkway.

RECREATION

HIKING

The **Lands Run Falls Trail** (MP 9.2; 1.2 mi. one-way, 1 hr., easy) is a short, pleasant hike down an old road to a small but pretty waterfall. Follow the fire road from Lands Run parking area as it descends immediately. At 0.6 mile in, you'll see a stream coming down the mountain from your left before passing through a culvert under the road. Look to the right and you'll see the falls. If you take a short spur trail, you can get some very good views.

Hiking **Old Rag Mountain** (exit MP 31.5; 5.6 mi. rt., 7-8 hrs., strenuous) is a rite of passage for many visitors. It's harsh, rocky, and exposed near the summit, so if there's the chance of bad weather (especially lightning), keep an eye on the sky. Find the trailhead on Route 707/Nethers Road, just over a mile from Nethers. From the parking

LANDS RUN FALLS

DARK HOLLOW FALLS

area, walk up Nethers Road about 0.8 mile to the trailhead. The blue-blazed trail climbs steadily for 0.75 mile, growing much steeper to the ridge. In another 0.5 mile, you'll reach the ridgetop and emerge onto the outcrop. This is where the scramble begins, climbing over granite boulders and multiple false summits. The real summit is marked with a concrete post.

At the **Hawksbill Summit** (MP 45.6; 2.8 mi. rt., 2-3 hrs., strenuous) trailhead, a spur trail leads about 100 yards to the Appalachian Trail, which you'll follow to your left. The rocky trail climbs through several talus slopes to a cement signpost noting the Appalachian Trail mileage. Make a hard left onto the Salamander Trail and keep climbing to a very rocky point. Near the top, the trail joins a fire road, making the rest of the route very easy. The summit contains the Byrds Nest, a shelter built for former U.S. senator and Virginia governor Harry F. Byrd Sr.

Dark Hollow Falls (MP 50.7; 1.4 mi. rt., 2 hrs., strenuous) is one of the most popular waterfall hikes in Shenandoah National Park thanks to its short distance and excellent view. From the parking area, the trail descends and follows Hogcamp Branch. You'll reach your first overlook of Dark Hollow Falls at 0.6 mile. Continue on the trail to the base of the falls at 0.7 mile.

Cross Skyline Drive to the trailhead for **Rapidan Camp** (MP 52.8; 4 mi. rt., 3 hrs., strenuous). You'll follow the Appalachian Trail a short way until it joins Mill Prong Trail. Turn left onto Mill Prong Trail, descending as you parallel the stream. At 1.5 miles, pass Big Rock Falls and continue downhill to a crossing of Mill Prong at 2.0 miles. Cross the bridge and climb up to Rapidan Camp. The camp's namesake river is just a few paces away. Retrace your steps back uphill to the parking area.

The **South River Falls** (MP 62.8; 4.4 mi. rt., 3 hrs., strenuous) descends 0.1 mile until it meets with the Appalachian Trail, marked by a cement post. Follow the blue blazes and descend a series of gradual switchbacks. You'll pass by several creeks as they flow out of the mountain to join with the South River. At 0.75 mile, you'll encounter a creek that's almost entirely hidden by the rocks, although you can hear it. It joins the South River, along with another stream before the river plunges over the falls and into a deep grotto. The overlook is at 1.3 miles. A circuitous route 1.5 miles farther joins an old

SUNSHINE FILTERS THROUGH THE FOREST.

road, which descends then turns back toward the falls and a cement post at 2.1 miles. A short spur trail goes to the base of the falls and its large pool.

One of the best loop hikes in the Southern District, **Riprap Hollow Trail** (MP 90; 9.8 mi. rt., 7 hrs., strenuous) leads to great views and swimming holes in a spring-fed stream. From the parking area, walk 50 yards along the blue-blazed trail to where it intersects with the white-blazed Appalachian Trail. Turn right and head uphill to the intersection with Riprap Hollow Trail, where a left turn leads to vistas, including Chimney Rock, before descending into Cold Springs Hollow. A stream cuts through a small gorge to a 20-foot waterfall followed by a large swimming hole. To continue the loop, follow the blue blazes to intersect with the Wildcat Ridge Trail. Turn left, cross the stream, and go through a small gorge to a steep set of switchbacks. Follow the trail for two miles to a four-way intersection with the Appalachian Trail. Turn left to hike back the final 2.8 miles to the parking area.

BACKPACKING

The **Appalachian Trail** passes 101 miles through Shenandoah, mostly paralleling Skyline Drive. Contrary to other wilderness sections of the trail outside the park, this portion of the trail crosses the road many times. The route has minimal water and a couple of shelters.

Backcountry camping **permits** (free) are required and are available from entrance stations, park headquarters, and visitors centers. **Appalachian Trail permits** (for long-distance AT hikers) are available by self-registration on the AT near Shenandoah National Park entry points.

RAPIDAN CAMP TOURS

Advance reservations are required for the ranger-led tour to **Rapidan Camp** (Thurs.-Sun. May-Oct., 2.5 hours, 877/444-6777, www.recreation.gov, $10), the former summer camp of President Herbert Hoover and a National Historic Landmark. Two restored cabins—the President's Cabin and the Prime Minister's Cabin—are included on the tour. Tours depart on national park vans from Harry F. Byrd Sr. Visitor Center.

WHERE TO STAY

INSIDE THE PARK

Two lodges and a set of cabins accept **reservations** (DNC Parks & Resorts, 877/847-1919, www.goshenandoah.com). None are luxurious by any stretch. They are built instead to facilitate the enjoyment of the park, so the beds will be passable and the showers hot, but don't expect plush robes and after-dinner cordials.

Skyland Resort (MP 41.7 and 42.5, 540/999-2212, from $128) has traditional rooms as well as cabins and a full-service dining room.

Big Meadows Lodge (MP 51.2, 540/999-2222, from $130) accommodations range from lodge rooms to small, rustic cabins. It also has dining available.

Lewis Mountain Cabins (MP 57.5, 540/999-2255, from $133) are cozy and quaint, with no phone or Internet. Each cabin has electricity, a private bathroom, linens, and an outdoor grill.

For a quick bite, stop by one of three Wayside Food Stops: the **Elkwallow Wayside** (MP 24.1), **Big Meadows Wayside** (MP 51.2), and **Loft Mountain Wayside** (MP 79.5). Camping supplies are also available.

Shenandoah also has four **campgrounds** (early spring-late fall) on Skyline Drive. Make **reservations** (877/444-6777, www.recreation.gov) six months in advance at all but Lewis Mountain Campground. Campgrounds have showers and potable water.

Matthews Arm Campground (MP 22.1, 540/999-3132, $15, groups $50)

Big Meadows Campground (MP 51.2, 540/999-3500, ext. 3231, $17-20, groups $45)

Loft Mountain Campground (MP 79.5, 540/999-2255, $15, groups $35-50)

Lewis Mountain Campground (MP 57.5, 540/999-2255, first come, first serve, $15)

OUTSIDE THE PARK

The northern gateway of **Front Royal** has accommodations and restaurants. The town of **Luray** is the western gateway to Shenandoah National Park and has rental cabins, a few inns and motels, and eateries. For the greatest variety and choices, stay in **Washington DC.**

GETTING THERE AND AROUND

Skyline Drive is the main access through the park. There is no public transit. Inside the park, gasoline is only available at the Big Meadows Wayside (MP 51.2).

AIR

Several major regional airports serve the region, but **Dulles International Airport** (IAD, 1 Saarinen Circle, Dulles, VA, 703/572-2700, www.metwashairports.com) has the most flights. Car rentals are available at the Washington DC airports.

CAR

Front Royal, Virginia, and the entrance to Shenandoah National Park is just a few miles east of where I-66 meets I-81 (18 miles west). U.S. 340 and U.S. 522 also go through Front Royal. On Skyline Drive, there are only two points where roads intersect the route. U.S. 211 crosses Skyline Drive at Thornton Gap (MP 31.5); from here, the town of **Luray** is less than 10 miles west. Farther south, U.S. 33 intersects Skyline at Swift Run Gap (MP 62.7); the town of **Elkton** is only seven miles west. There are entrance stations to Shenandoah National Park at both Thornton Gap and Swift Run Gap.

SIGHTS NEARBY

The **Blue Ridge Parkway** (828/348-3400, www.nps.gov/blri) connects Shenandoah with Great Smoky National Park.

Shenandoah River State Park (350 Daughter of Stars Dr., Bentonville, VA, 540/622-6840, www.dcr.virginia.gov/state-parks) has cabins, camping, fishing, hiking, biking, and paddling.

MAMMOTH CAVE NATIONAL PARK

Kentucky

WEBSITE:
www.nps.gov/maca

PHONE NUMBER:
270/758-2180

VISITATION RANK:
34

WHY GO:
Explore the world's longest cave system.

PASSPORT STAMPS ▼▼▼

▲ MAMMOTH CAVE NATIONAL PARK

Upon entering **MAMMOTH CAVE NATIONAL PARK**, visitors first see dense stands of eastern hardwood forest that are home to large populations of deer and wild turkeys. Beneath this forest lies the park's main attraction: the most extensive cave system in the world. With nearly 400 miles of mapped passageways and perhaps hundreds of miles of undiscovered routes, Mammoth Cave is so big that no known cave in the world is even half as long as Mammoth. It's also incredibly diverse, supporting approximately 130 life-forms. Evidence indicates that humans explored Mammoth Cave 4,000 years ago, although it wasn't until 1798 that the cave was rediscovered. Established as a national park in 1941, Mammoth Cave was a tourist attraction as early as 1816, making it the second-oldest tourist site in the United States after Niagara Falls.

PLANNING YOUR TIME

Mammoth Cave sits about 100 miles south of Louisville, close to the border with Tennessee. The national park is split into two regions: "above ground" and "below ground." Above ground you'll find hiking trails, campgrounds, and rivers for fishing, floating, and paddling. Below ground are the tours that enter the cave. Only one cave tour route is self-guided; all the other tours are guided. Tour reservations are accepted six months in advance.

The park is open year-round, with limited operation in winter. In **summer** (May-Sept.), temperatures warm into the 80s, while winters keep it cool in the 40s, with possible snow and ice. In spring, the national park receives the highest annual precipitation in the state. Underground, the cave stays a cool 54°F year-round.

ENTRANCES AND FEES

The park has multiple entrances; most visitors will enter via **Cave City** or **Park City** to reach the Historic Entrance and visitors center. There is no entrance fee to the park, but underground tours require fees.

VISITORS CENTER

Mammoth Cave National Park Visitor Center (8am-6:30pm daily May-Aug., 8am-6pm daily mid-Mar.-May and Aug.-Oct., 8:30am-4:30pm daily Nov.-mid-Mar.) is where to go for all park tours—options, schedules, tickets, and departures. The center has exhibits, permits, and information on ranger-led walks, evening presentations, and the Junior Ranger Program.

CAVE TOURS

There are more than a dozen **cave tours** (adults $7-55, seniors $3.50-26, children 6-12 $5-16) offered daily. Tours range in distance from 0.25 mile to 5.5 miles and from 1.25 hours to 6.5 hours. Introductory and general tours give an overview of the cave, its history, and its formation. Mammoth Cave also offers specialty tours, such as lantern-lit and photography- or geology-focused tours. Review tour details (distance, length, difficulty, and number of stairs) carefully—some tours depart multiple times daily, while others enter the cave elsewhere than the visitors center. **Tour reservations** (877/444-6777, www.recreation.gov) are highly recommended in summer.

The **Frozen Niagara Tour** (0.25 mi., 12 stairs with an optional 47 stairs, 75 min.) is best for families with kids. The tour visits Frozen Niagara Falls, one of the most artistic collections of dripstones and the most famous feature in the cave system. The feature is included on four longer and more difficult tours:

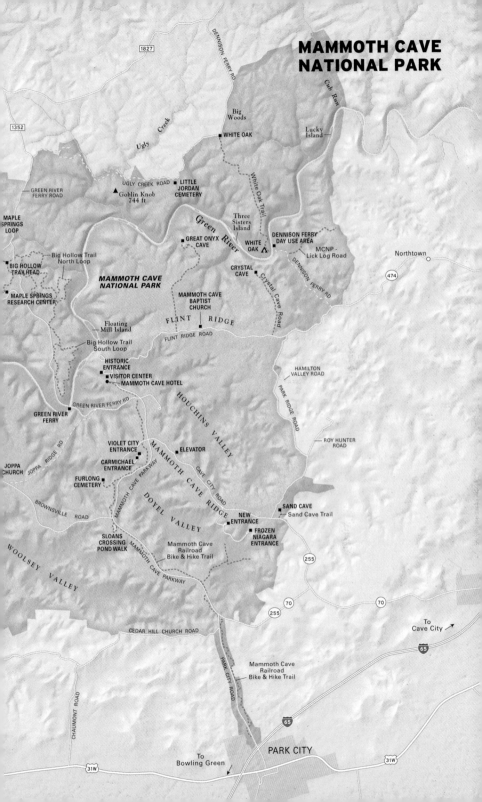

MAMMOTH CAVE NATIONAL PARK

CAVE TOUR

Domes and Dripstones, Grand Avenue, Introduction to Caving, and Wild Cave.

To be wowed by large cave rooms like the Rotunda, take the **Historic Cave Tour** (2 mi., 440 stairs, 2 hrs.). First though, you'll need to enter Fat Man's Misery, a serpentine slot that requires squeezing through sideways. You may need to stoop or squat to avoid bonking your head on Tall Man's Misery.

For a real spelunking adventure, sign up for **Introduction to Caving** (1 mi., 280 stairs, 3.5 hrs.) or the **Wild Cave Tour** (5 mi., strenuous, 5 hrs.). On the Introduction to Caving, you'll wriggle through holes and work your way up rock-littered slopes. The Wild Cave Tour takes participants to rarely visited areas of the cave—crawling, slithering, duck-walking, and navigating other physical challenges. Hiking boots with ankle support and shoelaces (no Velcro) are required on both tours.

The **Mammoth Cave Accessible Tour** (0.5 mi., no stairs) uses an elevator entrance to follow a wheelchair-accessible route into the cave. Guests pass through the Snowball Room and part of Cleaveland Avenue.

Only one tour is self-guided—the **Discovery Tour** (10am-2pm daily, 0.75 mi., 160 stairs). Stop at the visitors center for tickets the day of the tour (no reservations) and explore the cave at your own pace. Rangers are staged along the passageway to share interpretive tidbits.

RECREATION
HIKING AND BIKING

Nearly 84 miles of trails are open to hikers, with multiuse trails open to mountain bikers and horseback riders. (Three trails are wheelchair-accessible.) At the visitors center, short trails loop to the surface of cave features and overlooks of the Green River. The **Sinkhole Trail** (2 mi. rt., 1 hr.) starts from the paved Heritage Trail and descends to the Echo River Springs Trail. Along the way, the trail passes Mammoth Dome Sink, a huge sinkhole that created Mammoth Dome in the cave.

For multiuse backcountry trails, hikers and bikers can head out on the **Maple Springs Trail** (2 mi. rt.), **White Oak Trail** (5 mi. rt.), and **Big Hollow Trail** (9.1 mi. rt.).

The gravel **Mammoth Cave Railroad Bike and Hike Trail** (18 mi. rt.) follows parts of the original train route that once connected Park City with Mammoth Cave Visitor Center. The trailhead is at the visitors center and starts at Engine No. 4.

CANOEING AND KAYAKING

Mammoth Cave Canoe & Kayak (1240 Old Mammoth Cave Rd., 270/773-3366, http://mammothcave-adventures.com) and **Green River Canoeing** (3057 Mammoth Cave Rd., Cave City, 270/773-5712, www.mammothcavecanoe.com) can outfit you for an enjoyable paddling trip down the Green River in either a canoe or kayak. Beginners are encouraged to

HIKING TRAILS OFFER ABOVE-GROUND VIEWS.

try the 8-mile trip from Dennison Ferry to Green River Ferry, while more intermediate paddlers can choose from a 12-mile day trip or an overnight trip.

WHERE TO STAY

INSIDE THE PARK

Rooms at the **Lodge at Mammoth Cave** (171 Hotel Rd., 844/760-2283, http://mammothcavelodge.com, from $82) may be small and a bit dated, but they are clean with a central location near the visitors center. (Request a room on the ravine side to enjoy a view from your balcony.) Quaint cottages and cabins offer a more private retreat. Reservations are accepted one year in advance. Two on-site restaurants offer to-go fare and fine-dining options.

Campers will find 105 sites at the **Mammoth Cave Campground** (877/444-6777, www.recreation.gov, May-mid-Oct., $20-50), just 0.25 mile from the visitors center. Half the sites are available by reservation, while the remaining sites are first come, first served. Flush toilets and hot showers are available. **Maple Springs Group Campground** (Mar-Nov., $25-35) has seven group sites plus horse facilities. **Houchin Ferry Campground** (first come, first served, year-round, $12) has 12 primitive sites on the banks of the Green River.

OUTSIDE THE PARK

Cave City is the gateway to Mammoth Cave National Park and provides accommodations, dining, and services.

GETTING THERE AND AROUND

The park has no shuttle system or public transportation. Driving is the only way to get around. Do not rely on GPS mobile navigation systems—bring a map instead.

AIR

Two international airports sit within 100 miles of Mammoth Cave. To the north is **Louisville International Airport** (SDF, 600 Terminal Dr., Louisville, KY, www.flylouisville.com, 502/368-6524). To the south is **Nashville International Airport** (BNA, 1 Terminal Dr., Nashville, TN, 615/275-1675, www.fly-nashville.com). Car rentals are available at each airport.

CAR

Mammoth Cave National Park is west of I-65, between Elizabethtown and Bowling Green. From the north, take Exit 53 for Cave City and turn right onto Route 70 to reach the park entrance. From the south, take Exit 48 to Park City. Turn left onto Route 255 to the park entrance.

SIGHTS NEARBY

Nolin Lake State Park (2998 Brier Creek Rd., Mammoth Cave, 270/286-4240, http://parks.ky.gov) is north of the national park with camping, boating, and fishing on Nolin Lake.

HOT SPRINGS
NATIONAL PARK

Arkansas

WEBSITE:
www.nps.gov/hosp

PHONE NUMBER:
501/620-6715

VISITATION RANK:
15

WHY GO:
Soak in historic
hot springs.

▲ MAURICE BATHHOUSE

HOT SPRINGS NATIONAL PARK gushes with 700,000 gallons of hot water per day, making it unique in the eastern United States, where hot springs are rare. More than 4,400 years ago, rainwater soaked deep into the earth here, more than one mile down to a fault where it was then heated. The heated water is disgorged through the fault to the surface in downtown Hot Springs. Today, the area is a national park and houses one of the most sumptuous clusters of natural hot spring bathhouses in North America.

A leftover from the heyday of the Edwardian Era, this once-luxurious spot attracted the rich and famous with its buildings of marble surrounded by fountains. The historical architecture speaks to the affluence during its construction. (The springs also attracted the not-so-wealthy seeking to gain health benefits from its minerals.)

Hot Springs is the smallest park in the United States, yet the park receives an annual 1.5 million visitors. While its elegance pales under today's standards, it offers a visual and sensory glimpse into history.

PLANNING YOUR TIME

The park is easily accessible, just an hour's drive from Little Rock. The small park has two sections. **Bathhouse Row** covers a few downtown blocks at the base of Hot Springs Mountain and can be toured on foot. **Hot Springs Mountain** contains scenic drives, hiking trails, and a campground.

While the bathhouses are open year-round, soaking in the springs loses its appeal during the hot, humid summer when temperatures hover in triple digits. However, that is when visitor services are in full swing and outdoor tours are available.

September-May offers a more tempting time to plunge into the hot water. In winter, when the thermometer plummets below freezing, the baths offer a cozy respite.

ENTRANCE AND FEES

The national park is located in the town of **Hot Springs** and has no official entrance. There is no entrance fee.

VISITORS CENTER

Located on Bathhouse Row, **Fordyce Bathhouse Visitor Center** (369 Central Ave., 501/620-6715, 9am-5pm daily year-round, free) claims the most elegant bathhouse from the early 1900s. It even had a bowling alley in the basement and a third-floor music room with a grand piano and a gym.

Rangers lead **guided tours** (daily, free) of the restored building, pointing out stained glass ceilings and a ceramic fountain. The tour takes in 23 rooms replicated with furniture of the period, including treatment rooms that featured massage and electrotherapy. The historical museum has exhibits, films (one shows what the bathing routine entailed), and pictures of its operation from 1915 to 1962.

SIGHTS

The minerals in the hot springs were believed to have health benefits, thus many **drinking fountains** line Bathhouse Row and the Grand Promenade. Many visitors bring water bottles to fill and take home. **Whittington Spring** (Whittington Ave.) and **Happy Hollow Spring** (Fountain Ave.) are cold-water springs treated with ozone filtration.

HOT SPRINGS NATIONAL PARK

CEDAR GLADES ROAD

Sunset Trail

CEDAR GLADES ROAD

CEDAR STREET

Balanced Rock

HOT SPRINGS NATIONAL PARK

SUGARLOAF MOUNTAIN

Sunset Trail

CITY OF HOT SPRINGS

Linden Street Park

WHITTINGTON AVENUE

Creek

WHITTINGTON SPRING

Mountain Top Trail

SHELTER

WHITTINGTON AVENUE

Whittington

City Park

WEST MOUNTAIN DRIVE

West Mountain Trail

West Mountain Trail

WEST MOUNTAIN SUMMIT DR

HOT SPRINGS NATIONAL PARK

1,000ft

West Mountain Drive

Oak Trail

WEST MOUNTAIN

Sunset Trail

Mountain Top Trail

PROSPECT AVENUE

▲ 1,260ft

QUAPAW AVENUE

OUACHITA AVENUE

0   .25 mi

0   250 m

70B 270B

GRAND AVENUE

© AVALON TRAVEL

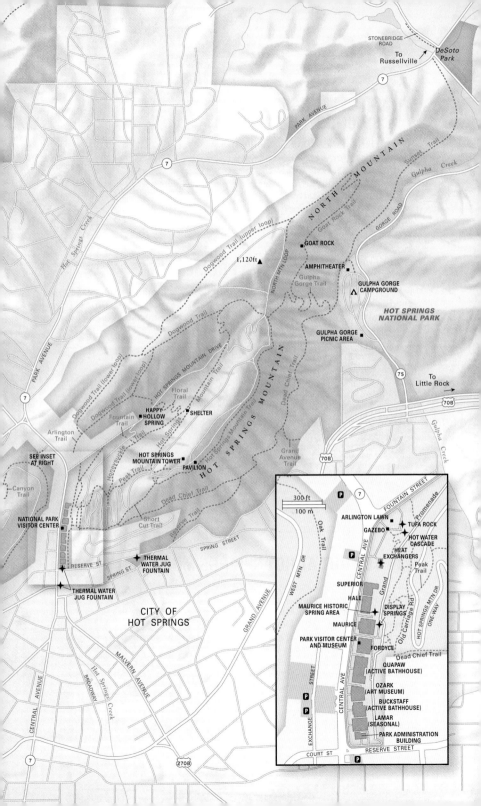

STONEBRIDGE ROAD

To Russellville

DeSoto Park

7

PARK AVENUE

NORTH MOUNTAIN

Sunset Trail

Gulpha Creek

Goat Rock Trail

GOAT ROCK

1,120ft

Dogwood Trail (upper loop)

NORTH MTN LOOP

AMPHITHEATER

Gulpha Gorge Trail

GULPHA GORGE CAMPGROUND

HOT SPRINGS NATIONAL PARK

Gorge Road

Dogwood Trail

GULPHA GORGE PICNIC AREA

Dead Chief Trail

Dogwood Trail (lower loop)

Dogwood Trail (lower loop)

Hot Springs Mountain Drive

Mountain Trail

Floral Trail

Fountain Trail

HOT SPRINGS MOUNTAIN

7S

To Little Rock

70B

Arlington Trail

HAPPY HOLLOW SPRING

SHELTER

Hot Springs Mountain Trail

SEE INSET AT RIGHT

Honeysuckle Trail

Hot Springs Peak Trail

HOT SPRINGS MOUNTAIN TOWER

PAVILION

Grand Avenue Trail

70B

Canyon Trail

Dead Chief Trail

Reserve Trail

Short Cut Trail

Gulpha Creek

NATIONAL PARK VISITOR CENTER

RESERVE ST

SPRING ST

SPRING STREET

THERMAL WATER JUG FOUNTAIN

THERMAL WATER JUG FOUNTAIN

CITY OF HOT SPRINGS

GRAND AVENUE

7

MALVERN AVENUE

BROADWAY

Hot Springs Creek

CENTRAL AVENUE

7

270B

Inset:

300 ft
100 m

P

7

FOUNTAIN STREET

Promenade

ARLINGTON LAWN

TUFA ROCK

GAZEBO

HOT WATER CASCADE

HEAT EXCHANGERS

P

Oak Trail

CENTRAL AVE

WEST MTN DR

Grand

Peak Trail

SUPERIOR

HALE

MAURICE HISTORIC SPRING AREA

DISPLAY SPRINGS

Old Carriage Rd

HOT SPRINGS MTN DR

ONE-WAY

MAURICE

PARK VISITOR CENTER AND MUSEUM

FORDYCE

Dead Chief Trail

QUAPAW (ACTIVE BATHHOUSE)

OZARK (ART MUSEUM)

EXCHANGE STREET

CENTRAL AVE

P

BUCKSTAFF (ACTIVE BATHHOUSE)

P

LAMAR (SEASONAL)

PARK ADMINISTRATION BUILDING

COURT ST

RESERVE STREET

P

Top ③

① SOAK IN THE HOT SPRINGS

Two of the historic Bathhouses still offer hot soaks for weary visitors. For a traditional soak, walk inside the 1912 **Buckstaff** for a dip in your own individual tub. **Quapaw Baths & Spa** offers a more modern spa experience with covered indoor thermal pools and a steam cave.

QUAPAW BATHHOUSE

② STROLL THE GRAND PROMENADE

Between Bathhouse Row and the base of Hot Springs Mountain, the **Grand Promenade** passes features fed by hot spring water: thermal fountains, drinking fountains, and display springs. It also has picnic tables and game tables (bring your own checkers or chess).

GRAND PROMENADE

③ TOP OUT AT HOT SPRINGS MOUNTAIN TOWER

Rising like a forested oasis in the middle of the town of Hot Springs, Hot Springs Mountain is topped by **Hot Springs Mountain Tower** (401 Hot Springs Mountain Dr., 501/881-4020, http://hotspringstower.com, 9am-9pm daily in summer, shorter hours Sept.-June, fee). An elevator whisks visitors to the top of the 216-foot-tall tower where observation decks yield 360-degree views of the town of Hot Springs and the Ouachita Mountains.

BEAUTIFUL VIEW FROM HOT SPRINGS MOUNTAIN TOWER

ONE DAY IN HOT SPRINGS

Thanks to its small size, you can easily experience the park in one day. Start at the **Fordyce Bathhouse Visitor Center** to get oriented and take a tour. Then walk the National Historic District of **Bathhouse Row** and the **Grand Promenade** and go for a soak in one of the bathhouses. Afterward, drive to the top of Hot Springs Mountain and climb the **Hot Springs Mountain Tower** to take in the views. Return to Bathhouse Row and relax at the **Superior Bathhouse Brewery**.

BATHHOUSE ROW

A National Historic Landmark, **Bathhouse Row** has eight bathhouses, leftover hallmarks of 20th-century opulence. The actual row is about 0.25 mile long, an easy walk along Central Avenue. Most buildings are open to the public, but even the closed ones are worth admiring for their architecture. From north to south, the bathhouses include:

Superior is the smallest bathhouse, built in 1916, with a sunporch and brick pilasters. Its services—massage, hydrotherapy, and mercury—were the least expensive. Today, **Superior Bathhouse Brewery** (www.superiorbathhouse.com, daily 11am-9pm Sun.-Thurs., 11am-11pm Fri.-Sat., reduced hours in winter) turns hot spring water into thirst-quenching adult beverages.

Hale, the oldest bathhouse on the row, was built in 1892. Two subsequent remodels changed its architecture to Mission Revival style, with its original red brick covered in white stucco.

Maurice opened in 1912 with a roof garden and basement pool. It is not open to the public.

Fordyce, the largest and most elegant bathhouse, opened in 1915 with the most services—from chiropody to ice thermal water and electrotherapy. It now serves as the visitors center.

Quapaw, which opened in 1922, is the longest bathhouse on the row. Topped with a mosaic tile dome, the Spanish Colonial Revival building now houses modern spa services where visitors can bathe in water from the hot springs.

BATHHOUSE ROW

OZARK BATHHOUSE

Ozark, built in Spanish Colonial Revival architecture, opened shortly after Quapaw with less extravagant services for the middle class.

Buckstaff is the best-preserved traditional bathhouse. Built in 1912 with a marble interior, it is fronted by Doric columns and classical architecture. Today, visitors soak in individual tubs and get massages.

Lamar, which opened in 1923, reflects Spanish-style architecture with stucco trimmed with brick and stone. It contains **Bathhouse Row Emporium** (501/620-6740, 9am-5pm daily Apr.-Sept., 10am-5pm Mon.-Fri. and 9am-5pm Sat.-Sun. Oct.-Mar.), which sells books, bath souvenirs, bottles to fill with water from the hot springs, and hot beverages made with spring water.

North of Bathhouse Row, a cluster of paths connects a gazebo and lawns. **Hot Water Cascade** tumbles into a collection pool, where you can dip your hand in to check the temperature. **Tufa Rock**, a large gray rock, was created from the buildup of minerals brought to the surface in thermal waters, which then evaporated to leave the hardened mass behind. **Tufa terraces** also line the hillside, where you can depart for a 0.2-mile side trail that takes off at Stevens Balustrade and returns to Grand Promenade at Hot Water Cascade.

SCENIC DRIVES
NORTH MOUNTAIN DRIVE

North of Bathhouse Row on Central Avenue, follow Fountain Street northeast for **North Mountain Drive.** The short yet scenic drive travels three miles to Hot Springs Mountain. In 0.25 mile, turn right to begin the one-way climb along seven hairpin switchbacks to reach the summit loop. A right turn immediately reveals a picnic area, restrooms, an overlook, and a pavilion. Turn left onto a side spur to the parking lot for **Hot Springs Mountain Tower,** the main attraction. To return to Fountain Drive, leave the summit loop at its northeast end and descend one mile (one-way) for fewer switchbacks.

WEST MOUNTAIN DRIVE

West Mountain Drive offers a scenic tour with access to nearby trails. From Bathhouse Row, drive north for 0.25 mile and turn left onto Whittington Avenue. A left turn follows West Mountain Drive along a one-way loop around the east flank of the mountain and past three overlooks to its tiny summit. Exit the loop by heading south on West Mountain Drive, which ends at Prospect Avenue, south of Bathhouse Row.

RECREATION

HIKING

Hot Springs National Park has 26 miles of hiking trails. The longest trail in the park is the **Sunset Trail** (10 mi. one-way, 4-5 hrs.), which leads from Gulpha Gorge Campground to the summit of West Mountain Summit Overlook. The trail crosses several roads that break it into shorter hiking segments and connect it with other hiking trails. The most popular section is the 2.9 miles from Black Snake Road to West Mountain Summit Overlook, which has the best sunset-viewing location.

On West Mountain, the **West Mountain Trail** (2.3 mi. rt., 1.5 hrs.) has interesting features—stone steps and a stone footbridge with ironwork—rather than a dramatic destination. Catch it from the Mountain Top Trailhead above Prospect Avenue to return on the Mountain Top Trail.

From the north overlook on Hot Springs Mountain, the **Goat Rock Trail** (2.2 mi. rt., 1.5 hrs.) drops down switchbacks to small meadows that lead to a stone stairway. The trail climbs 40 feet to the novaculite Goat Rock Overlook with views of Indian Mountain.

HOT SPRINGS

Quapaw Baths & Spa

For a modern-day spa experience, **Quapaw Baths & Spa** (413 Central Ave., 501/609-9822, http://quapawbaths.com, 10am-6pm Wed.-Mon.) offers four large indoor hot pools covered by a stained glass ceiling. Private baths (individuals or couples) include hydrotherapy plus a variety of herbal additions to enhance your relaxation. After soaking, unwind further in a small steam cave. The spa has a full menu of facials, massages, and body treatments. Proper swim attire is required, and visitors are provided with a robe and slippers. Reservations are requested; guests age 14-18 must be with an adult.

Buckstaff

For a traditional Hot Springs soak, **Buckstaff** (509 Central Ave., 501/623-2308, www.buckstaffbaths.com, 8am-11:45am and 1:30pm-3pm Mon.-Sat., 8am-11:45am Sun. Mar.-Nov.; 8am-11:45am and 1:30pm-3pm Mon.-Fri. and 8am-11:45am Sat. Dec.-Feb.) has individual tubs in separate men's and women's facilities. Add on a Swedish massage, loofah mitt, or paraffin hand treatment. Reservations are not accepted for the baths and massages. Manicures, pedicures, and facials require reservations. Kids must be at least 10 years old.

WHERE TO STAY

INSIDE THE PARK

Lodging inside the park consists of one campground. However, the National Park Service plan to have the

HOT SPRINGS NATIONAL PARK

THE TRADITIONAL BATHING ROUTINE

At Hot Springs, the traditional bathing routine followed the protocols of European spas.

1 In the bath hall, soak in a private tub for 20 minutes in 100°F water. Optionally, scrub with a loofah.

2 Climb into a steam cabinet, with head inside for two minutes or head outside for five minutes.

3 In a sitting tub, soak in a 108°F water for 10 minutes.

4 Apply heat packs for 4-20 minutes on any achy spots.

5 Cool down with a two-minute shower of cold water.

6 Finish with a full-body Swedish massage.

7 Leave refreshed.

historic Hale Bathhouse turned into a nine-room boutique hotel that will also house a restaurant.

Sites at **Gulpha Gorge Campground** (305 Gorge Rd., first come, first served, $30) can accommodate tents and RVs. All campsites have picnic tables, pedestal grills, and fire rings. Facilities include restrooms with flush toilets, potable water, and a dump station.

OUTSIDE THE PARK

The town of **Hot Springs** has chain and independent motels, B&Bs, and inns that surround the national park. The vicinity also has several campgrounds.

GETTING THERE

AIR

Six airlines service Little Rock National Airport, known as the **Bill and Hillary Clinton National Airport** (LIT, 1 Airport Dr., Little Rock, 501/372-3439, www.fly-lit.com). Car rentals are at the airport.

TRAIN

Amtrak (LRK, 1400 W. Markham St., 800/872-7245, www.amtrak.com) services Little Rock.

SHUTTLES AND BUSES

Greyhound Bus (800/231-2222, www.greyhound.com) connects with Hot Springs. The bus station (1001 Central

Ave., Hot Springs) sits 0.5 mile south of the visitors center. **Intercity Transportation** (501/960-5162, http://intercitytransportation.com) runs from the Little Rock airport to Hot Springs National Park.

City buses (fee) service the town and the national park of Hot Springs. Routes begin and end at the Transportation Plaza downtown.

CAR

From Little Rock, go west on I-30 to exit 111. Take U.S. 70 west to reach the town of Hot Springs. In town, U.S. 70 becomes East Grand Avenue. Turn right onto Spring Street, which becomes Reserve Street in about 0.5 mile. At Central Avenue, turn right to reach the visitors center. The total distance is 57 miles, and it takes one hour to drive.

GETTING AROUND

Parking is limited on Central Avenue along Bathhouse Row. You'll find easier parking for free in the city lot on Exchange Street. To get there, drive south on Central Avenue to Court Street (also called Reserve St.) and turn right. Continue one block west and turn right onto Exchange Street (one-way). Off-street parking is available on the right and in a parking garage on the left.

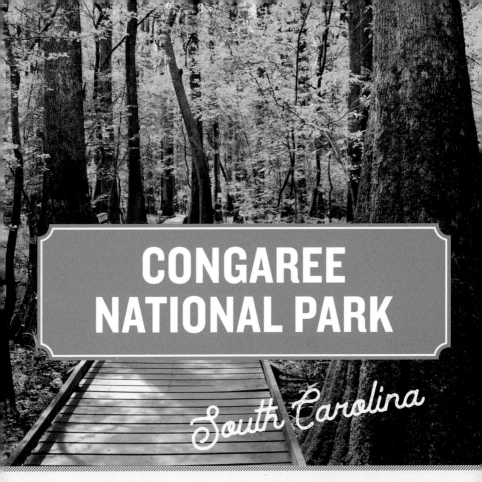

CONGAREE NATIONAL PARK

South Carolina

PASSPORT STAMPS ▼▼▼

WEBSITE:
www.nps.gov/cong

PHONE NUMBER:
803/776-4396

VISITATION RANK:
50

WHY GO:
See the largest intact old-growth hardwood forest.

▲ CONGAREE NATIONAL PARK

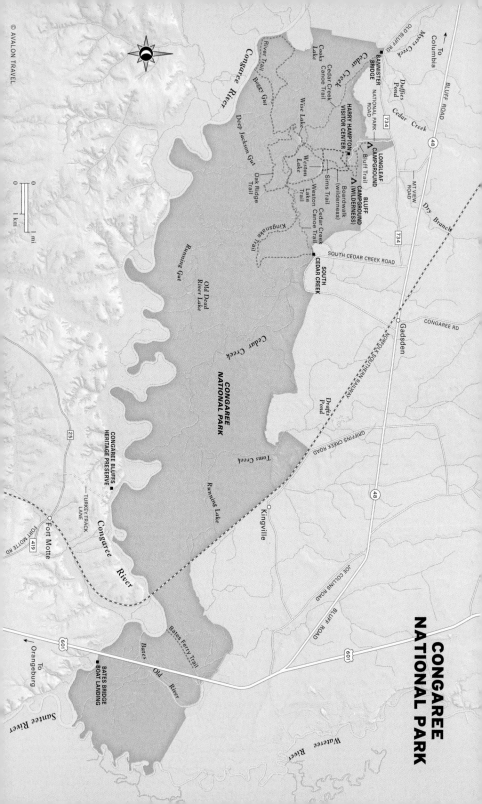

There's nothing like it on the planet. Set on a pristine tract close to Columbia's sprawl but seemingly a galaxy away, **CONGAREE NATIONAL PARK** contains the most ancient stands of old-growth cypress left in the world. The forest populates a floodplain of the Congaree and Wateree Rivers, which swell with water several times each year to overflow their banks. In doing so, they deposit a nutrient-rich silt that helps sustain the immensely tall trees—loblolly pine, tulip trees, sweet gum, bald cypress, white pine, sycamore, and laurel oak. The park contains the tallest of 15 species of trees, plus six national champion trees for their overall size. Only the redwoods stretch taller than Congaree's biggest trees.

Swamps are one of the hallmarks of the bottomlands that support the forest. The wetlands nurse birds galore, as well as snakes, turtles, frogs, alligators, catfish, and otters. It's the swamps that saved this habitat from several centuries of plundering the eastern forests for lumber. Due to the difficulty of navigating the forested wetlands, companies seeking timber profits ignored this landscape. So did farmers and ranchers. The result is a unique national park that is also an International Biosphere Reserve.

PLANNING YOUR TIME

Congaree sits smack in the middle of South Carolina, about a 30-minute drive south of Columbia. Despite its relatively urban locale, this park is wilderness—swamps mean no roads. To see the old-growth forest requires hiking or paddling. Flooding may occur without warning, especially in Cedar Creek and Congaree River. Check weather and conditions before entering the park.

While visitors come year-round, **spring** (Mar.-May) and **summer** (June-Aug.) see the most people. Spring can be wet, and summers are hot and humid, fraught with frequent thunderstorms, and a general bug-fest with swarms of 21 species of mosquitoes.

Fall (Sept.-Nov.) is a favorite time to visit—the air is crisp, and the foliage stunning. Autumn colors peak late October-early November. Winter (Nov.-Feb.) brings unpredictable floods that can submerge trails.

ENTRANCE AND FEES

The main entrance to the park is on Old Bluff Road, one mile before the visitors center. There is no entrance fee.

VISITORS CENTER

The **Harry Hampton Visitor Center** (Old Bluff Rd., 9am-5pm daily) is the place to get oriented in the park, with exhibits, a film, information, backcountry permits, and a great gift shop. Ranger-led programs depart from the visitors center.

RECREATION

HIKING

Congaree's 22,000 acres hold 20 miles of hiking trails. (Sorry, pedal-pushers—no bikes are allowed on the trails or boardwalks.)

Adjacent to the visitors center is a system of elevated boardwalks that loop through old-growth forest. The **Boardwalk Loop** (2.4 mi., 1.5 hrs.) offers the shortest tour; the flat trail is great for wheelchairs, strollers, and small kids. A well-done self-guided tour brochure explains the fascinating aspects of this unique environment. Along the trail, cypresses tower more than 130 feet into the air. At ground level, hundreds of cypress "knees" (parts of their root system) jut aboveground and you'll see unbelievably massive loblolly pines.

You'll have the rare experience of seeing what an old-growth forest actually looks like and why it's so peaceful: Because the canopy shuts off so much light, there is almost no understory. You can walk among the great trees as if you were in a scene from *Lord of the Rings*. Gorgeous Weston Lake is actually an oxbow lake that was once part of the Congaree River, isolated as the river changed course over time. You'll see—and more often, hear—a wide range of wildlife, including owls, waterfowl, and several species of woodpecker, including the rare red-cockaded woodpecker.

Serious hikers can enjoy an expansive series of trails (with brown blazes and numbers) that go even deeper into the wilderness:

Weston Lake Loop (4.4 mi. rt., 2-3 hrs.) passes cypress knees and waterbirds along Cedar Creek.

Oakridge Trail (6.6 mi. rt., 3-4 hrs.) travels through large oaks where you might see wild turkeys.

River Trail (10 mi. rt., 5 hrs.) goes to the Congaree River (check flood status).

Kingsnake Trail (11.7 mi. rt., 6 hrs.) attracts birders to habitat along Cedar Creek.

CANOEING AND KAYAKING

Paddlers can float the **Cedar Creek Canoe Trail** (15 miles) from Bannister's Bridge to the Congaree River. You must bring your own boat or rent gear in Columbia. Be aware of fluctuating water levels. In spring and fall, rangers guide **canoe tours** (4 hrs., limited schedule, free) with canoes, PFDs, and paddles provided. **Reservations** (www.recreation.gov, 877/444-6777) are required and open on the first day of the previous month.

The **Congaree River Blue Trail** (50 mi.) is a more ambitious paddling adventure that requires overnighting.

WHERE TO STAY

INSIDE THE PARK

There are no lodges or restaurants inside the park. The only accommodations are two tent-only campgrounds. **Longleaf Campground** (year-round, $10) has 14 walk-in campsites and a restroom. **Bluff Campground**

BALD CYPRESS KNEES

CYPRESS FOREST AND SWAMP

(year-round, $5) has six hike-in campsites that require a one-mile hike from the parking lot; there is no restroom.

Reservations (www.recreation.gov, 877/444-6777) are required up to six months in advance. Both campgrounds have picnic tables and fire rings, but no water (bring your own). Vehicles are not permitted inside the campgrounds.

Primitive camping is free with a permit from the visitors center.

OUTSIDE THE PARK

Twenty miles northwest, **Columbia** has the closest lodging and the most restaurants. A few dining options are nearby in **Gadsden,** but there is no lodging.

GETTING THERE AND AROUND

There is no public transportation that connects Columbia with the park. Rental cars and taxis are available in Columbia.

AIR

Two international airports provide access to the park. **Charlotte Douglas International Airport** (CLT, 5501 Josh Birmingham Pkwy, Charlotte, NC, 704/359-4013, www.cltairport.com) is located two hours north in North Carolina. **Charleston International Airport** (CHS, 5500 International Blvd., Charleston, SC, 843/767-7000, www.iflychs.com) is two hours southeast in South Carolina. Car rentals are available at each airport.

CAR

From Charlotte, drive south on I-77 for 95 miles to Columbia. Take exit 5 to Highway 48 east (Bluff Rd.) and continue eight miles. Veer right onto Old Bluff Road and go 4.5 miles to the park entrance.

From Charleston, drive northwest on I-26 to exit 145B. Continue north on U.S. 601 to Highway 48 (Bluff Rd.), where the road heads west. Turn left onto South Cedar Creek Road, then turn right onto Old Bluff Road to the park entrance.

SIGHTS NEARBY

Poinsett State Park (6660 Poinsett Park Rd., Wedgefield, SC, 803/494-8177, http://southcarolinaparks.com) is on Old Levi Mill Lake with camping, cabins, boating, paddling, and fishing.

EVERGLADES NATIONAL PARK

Florida

WEBSITE:
www.nps.gov/ever

PHONE NUMBER:
305/242-7700

VISITATION RANK:
24

WHY GO:
See the largest subtropical wilderness in the United States.

▲ EVERGLADES NATIONAL PARK

Shingle Creek, a small and inconspicuous stream behind an elementary school in Orlando, is the humble origin of one of the world's most treasured wetland ecosystems. Those headwaters merge into the Kissimmee River, which flows into Lake Okeechobee to discharge into the Everglades—a vast expanse of marshes, swamps, islands, forests, and waterways encompassing mainland Florida's southernmost points. Comprising essentially all of the wetlands and prairies south of Lake Okeechobee and sandwiched between Naples in the west and Miami in the east, the area covers nearly 4,000 square miles. Despite the best efforts of voracious real estate developers, most of the Everglades remain wild—although decades of agriculture, drainage, attempts at "taming" the land, and nearby population growth have dramatically (and in some cases, permanently) altered the ecosystems for the worse.

EVERGLADES NATIONAL PARK is huge. There's a whole lot of natural beauty to absorb here, and almost all of it can be explored and enjoyed in relative peace and quiet. The swamps, forests, and waterways teem with diversity, which is one of the reasons it's been named an International Biosphere Reserve and World Heritage Site. But rising sea levels associated with climate change are already submerging the glades.

PLANNING YOUR TIME

The Everglades are a relatively undisturbed swamp that sprawls across three counties at the southern tip of Florida, with three entrances in three different cities. You'll need a car for the long drives between, as no roads connect the enntrances, and facilities are few and far between.

Miami: Accesses the east part of the Everglades and is often the only part of the region that many visitors see. The airboat operators and kitschy "alligator wrestling" shows of the Miccosukee tribe are unique to the area and give a glimpse of the vast natural expanse.

Homestead: Accesses the southern portion of the Everglades. This area of the park is geared toward outdoor activities, with incredible opportunities for canoeing, kayaking, and camping. Visitors can fully immerse themselves in the wild expanses of the Everglades.

Everglades City: On the west coast, this is the gateway to the Ten Thousand Islands.

The best time to visit is **December-March** (the dry season). The weather is much more bearable with temperatures in the mid-70s, the bugs are less overwhelming, and the skies and trees are filled with scores of migratory bird species.

In summer, the heat amps up into the 90s with a sweltering humidity of 90 percent. Hurricane season is mid-May to November. July is peak season for voracious mosquitoes and biting flies; bring repellent, long-sleeve shirts and long pants. In winter, the bugs dwindle.

ENTRANCES AND FEES

The park's main entrance is the Ernest F. Coe Visitor Center near **Homestead** on the Main Park Road (State Road 9336). Shark Valley Visitor Center (Hwy. 41), west of **Miami,** serves as the park's north entrance. A remote

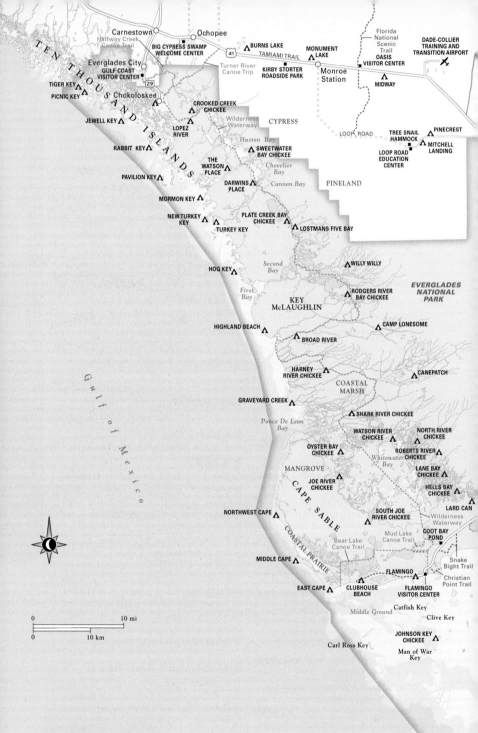

EVERGLADES
NATIONAL PARK

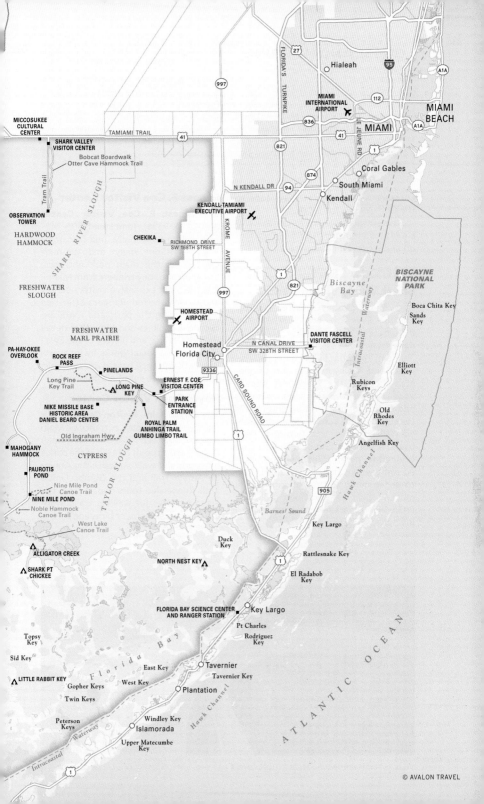

© AVALON TRAVEL

GO ISLAND HOPPING

Homestead makes a good base for further exploration of Dry Tortugas and Biscayne National Parks. From the south entrance of Everglades, drive southeast on the Overseas Highway to **Key West** (135 mi., 3 hrs.). Hop a boat to reach **Dry Tortugas National Park.** Camp overnight or stay in Key West.

From Key West, drive northeast to reach the Florida mainland and **Biscayne National Park,** where donning a snorkel and mask will let you see the colorful marinelife. Paddling can take you into mangrove swamps.

entrance at **Everglades City** leads to the Gulf Coast Visitor Center.

The entrance fee is $25-30 per vehicle ($20-25 motorcycle, $8-15 individual) and is good for seven days.

VISITORS CENTERS

Shark Valley Visitor Center

The **Shark Valley Visitor Center** (36000 SW 8th St., 305/221-8776, 8:30am-5pm daily Dec.-Apr., 9am-5pm daily May-Nov.) is right on the busy Tamiami Trail that links Miami and Naples. Shark Valley offers a sort of one-stop-shop for the Everglades experience. The visitors center has exhibits and films. Outside are two short trails (one accessible), boat cruises, guided walking tours, and two-hour tram tours. A popular 15-mile bike trail loop originates here; bikes can be rented right where the trams depart. Plan to arrive early, as the parking lots fill quickly. Make **reservations** (305/221-8455, www.sharkvalleytramtours.com) in advance for tram tours.

Ernest F. Coe Visitor Center

The **Ernest F. Coe Visitor Center** (40001 SR-9336, Homestead, 305/242-7700, 8am-5pm daily mid-Dec.-mid-Apr., 9am-5pm daily mid-Apr.-mid-Dec.) is at the main park entrance. Convenient to day trippers from Miami, it is the most expansive visitors center and is well staffed. Rangers offer tips on navigating the park, and there are excellent exhibits and films that detail the flora, fauna, and history of the Everglades, plus special works by local artists. Park entrance passes are available, and a bookstore sells field guides.

Royal Palm Visitor Center

The **Royal Palm Visitor Center** (four miles west of the park entrance on Main Park Rd., 305/242-7700, 8am-4pm daily) is the starting point for two of the park's most popular walking trails: the Anhinga Amble Trail and the Gumbo Limbo Trail. Ranger-led tours depart from the visitors center for walking trails, wading through sloughs, or bicycling.

VIEW FROM SHARK VALLEY OBSERVATION TOWER

Top ❸

1 WATCH WILDLIFE

AMERICAN CROCODILE

The main reason people set foot within the vast expanses of the Everglades is to get a look at wild, natural Florida. And the Glades do not disappoint. The one animal instantly associated with the area is the **American alligator,** a large beast (some grow to roughly 16 feet) and a stealthy predator. Backwater boaters are frequently surprised when they discover that they've paddled within inches of one of these prehistoric marvels. Gators tend to hug the shoreline and prefer the cover of mangroves—spotting them can be a challenge.

One can also see **American crocodiles**, which tend to be found in the park's southern area around Flamingo. These carnivorous relics headline the park's endangered species, along with manatees, Florida panthers, wood storks, and snail kites.

The most abundant wildlife are **birds.** Dozens of species call the Glades home, including **spoonbills, wood storks, egrets, flamingos,** and **bald eagles**. During migration season, dozens more nonnative species can be seen as well. Ranger-led bird-watching programs depart from Flamingo Visitor Center.

2 CANOE AND KAYAK THE GLADES

The best way to experience the Everglades is in a boat. Canoe and kayak rental opportunities abound, and there are several boat trails throughout the park—everything from hour-long paddles to 7-10-day wilderness adventures. Winter is the best time to canoe and kayak, when the waters are calmer and the weather mild.

Many rental agencies offer **guided tours,** but the quietude of solo exploration has its advantages. A kayak is better suited to the narrow waterways and you'll appreciate the navigational flexibility when making your way through a dense thicket of mangroves. Several Seminole-style **"chickees"** (backcountry permit required) are located throughout the park, providing an elevated and roofed camping area right on the water.

3 PADDLE THROUGH THE TEN THOUSAND ISLANDS

CANOE TRIPS

The massive **Ten Thousand Islands National Wildlife Refuge** covers more than 35,000 acres of mangrove swamps, tiny keys, grassy marshes, and tropical hardwood hammocks, nearly all of which are undeveloped. The only signs of human life here are a short, rough **hiking trail** and a two-story **observation tower** that provides stunning panoramas of the marshlands. The other, oh, 34,990 acres are best explored by hikers, hunters, anglers, and boaters.

The tower and trail are easily accessed via a parking lot right alongside the Tamiami Trail. Enter the wildlife refuge area east from Naples.

ONE DAY IN THE EVERGLADES

Drive the **Main Park Road** through the Everglades, taking in the sights and walking trails. Stop at the **Ernest F. Coe Visitor Center** to get oriented, and then cruise down to the **Flamingo Visitor Center** for a **boat tour** through the backwaters of Florida Bay.

With more time, you can hop on the tram tour in Shark Valley and rent a canoe to paddle the wildlife-rich waters.

Flamingo Visitor Center

The **Flamingo Visitor Center** (1 Flamingo Lodge Hwy., 239/695-2945, 8am-4:30pm daily mid-Nov.-mid-Apr., hours vary off-season) is located at the end of the park's main paved road, about an hour south of Ernest Coe. There's not much here for the casual visitor besides the imposing visitors center and the marina, but it feels like a bustling metropolis compared to the rest of the Everglades.

The center houses an educational area and a marina offers boat tours and rents canoes or kayaks. The short **Eco Pond Trail** (0.5 mi.) is pleasant and wheelchair-accessible. The visitors center also has backcountry permits, available by self-registration in the off-season.

Gulf Coast Visitor Center

On the park's remote northwest coast, the **Gulf Coast Visitor Center** (815 Oyster Bar Ln., Everglades City, 239/695-3311, 8am-4:30pm daily mid-Nov.-mid-Apr., 9am-4:30pm daily mid-Apr.-mid-Nov., free) gives visitors access to the waterways and tiny islands of the Ten Thousand Islands. The center's main building has nature exhibits, films, and backcountry permits.

SCENIC DRIVE
MAIN PARK ROAD

There's only one road in and out of Everglades National Park, so dedicate a full day to the journey from the park entrance to the far reaches of the **Flamingo Visitor Center**. A handful of minimally equipped pullovers along the 38-mile **Main Park Road** offer stops to walk along a boardwalk, have a picnic, or just stare off into the vast expanse of the Everglades.

▼ SUNSET OVER THE EVERGLADES

ANHINGA TRAIL

Long Pine Key

Long Pine Key (4 miles along Main Park Rd.) is a great stop for biking, hiking, and picnicking. It's also a very popular **campsite.** The unnamed 14-mile **bike trail** leads through slash pine and prairies, but there's not a whole lot of shade. Hikers and day-trippers should head for the (unnamed) 0.5-mile multipurpose trail, which offers a similarly diverse look at the area's ecology.

Rock Reef Pass

The sign just before **Rock Reef Pass** (11 miles along Main Park Rd.) reminds you just how flat and near-swampy this part of the state is. It states, "Elevation: Three Feet." This is practically mountainous for the Everglades, as much of the area is actually at or below sea level. The high altitude of Rock Reef Pass makes for a unique ecological combination of pine forest and marshes filled with dwarf cypress trees. There's a short **boardwalk** here that allows you to get out into areas that alternate between tinderbox trails in the dry winter and foot-deep swamp in the summer rainy season.

Pa-hay-okee Overlook

The elevated boardwalk at **Pa-hay-okee Overlook** (12.5 miles along Main Park Rd.) offers magnificent and expansive vistas onto the grassy infinity of the Everglades. It's also very popular: In the busy season, there is the distinct possibility of a packed parking lot and cattle-chute movement along the boardwalk. For the most quietude and the best chance of having these beautiful views to yourself, make sure to get here early in the day. This boardwalk is wheelchair-accessible.

Mahogany Hammock

Mahogany Hammock (20 miles along Main Park Rd.) is another boardwalk-through-the-Glades experience. Although this loop trail is quite short, the density of mahogany trees (and the shade they provide!) makes it unique and a nice place for a quick stop. Mahogany's boardwalk rewards visitors who look up into the mahogany canopy, where they're likely to see migratory birds.

RECREATION
HIKING

Everglades National Park offers a variety of hiking experiences, from easily accessed, elevated boardwalks and quick, shaded loops to more challenging and lengthy forays into the more ecologically imposing areas of the park.

The two trails at the Royal Palm Visitor Center, the **Anhinga Amble** (0.8

GUMBO LIMBO TRAIL

bird-watching is incredible. If you have to pick, take the Anhinga; even though this easy loop trail is just under a mile long, it provides an excellent (if quick) look at some great natural beauty.

Other quick and gorgeous trails include the mangrove-lined, waterfront **Bayshore Trail** (2 mi.), which starts at Flamingo Campground, and the **Eco-Pond Trail** (0.5 mi.), a loop of bird-watching heaven that starts from the Flamingo Visitor Center.

BIKING

Bicyclists can tour multiple areas, but two trails offer the best options. Rent bikes (first come, first serve) from **Shark Valley Tram Tour** (305/221-8455, www.sharkvalleytramtours.com, 8:30am-4pm daily) for a self-guided ride along the utterly flat paved route of the **Shark Valley Trail** (15 mi., 2-3 hrs.), or bring your own bikes to ride at Long Pine Key on the Main Park Road.

The **Long Pine Key Nature Trail** (13 mi., 2-3 hrs.) is a loop that goes on double-track through palmettos and pines from the campground to Pine Glades Lake. It connects with the paved (and trafficked) Main Park Road to return. Bring water for the heat, and bike in the morning to avoid afternoon lightning in summer.

mi.) and **Gumbo Limbo** (0.4 mi.), are by far the most popular non-boardwalk trails in Everglades National Park, and not just because they're the closest to the main entrance. Both trails manage to be easily navigable while taking hikers through the stunning variety of the Everglades' terrain. Even during the hottest summer months, you're likely to see a decent array of wildlife (especially alligators). During the winter months,

MANGROVE AT NINE MILE POND

KAYAK THE GULF COAST

CANOEING AND KAYAKING

Experienced boaters can explore the 3-6 miles of twists and turns of **Hell's Bay Canoe Trail,** a challenging run that announces its intentions with a comically difficult put-in and a trail that can take up to six hours to navigate completely—oddly enough, it's quite popular!

The challenging **West Lake Canoe Trail** (8 mi.) runs mainly through open waters but also takes boaters through some impressive (and occasionally claustrophobic) mangrove tunnels.

Easier options include the **Nine Mile Pond Trail** (the pond it's named after is nine miles from the former site of a visitors center). The well-marked trail is only 3.5 miles long, guiding paddlers through mangrove tunnels and several wider marshes. It's best explored during the summer when water levels are high. Even easier is the **Noble Hammock Canoe Trail** (2 mi.), which only takes about an hour to traverse. The **Mud Lake Canoe Trail** is also very popular. It is close to the Flamingo Visitor Center and is quite short. From Flamingo, boaters can also explore the waters of **Florida Bay** and its numerous keys.

Ten Thousand Islands

Serious canoers and kayakers go for the **Wilderness Waterway** (99 mi., 7-10 days), which gets boaters into some of the most isolated and beautiful areas of the Everglades. Running along Cape Sable and the western edge of the Glades, from Flamingo north to Chokoloskee, this region is known as the **Ten Thousand Islands** (239/657-8001, www.fws. gov/refuge/ten_thousand_islands). Some of the waterway is in Everglades National Park, while some of it traverses Ten Thousand Islands National Wildlife Refuge. Boats launch into the refuge's waterways from the tiny fishing village of **Goodland** (near Marco Island) and at the **Port-of-the-Islands Resort & Marina** (525 Newport Dr., Naples, 239/389-0367).

Rentals and Tours

Canoe rentals are available at the Gulf Coast Visitor Center, but you may have better luck at private operators, as these rentals run out quickly during peak season.

Everglades Adventures (107 Camellia St., Everglades City, 239/695-3229, http://www.iveyhouse.com) operates out of the Ivey House Inn. Its daytime, sunset, and overnight tours have a decidedly eco-friendly bent and can be done in either kayaks or canoes. Rentals are also available, and the company runs shuttle services for Wilderness Waterway route kayakers and their boats between Everglades City and Flamingo.

Shurr Adventures (32016 Tamiami Trail, Miami, 239/300-3004, www. schurradventures.com) focuses on kayak tours through the diverse ecosystems of the Ten Thousand Islands. It also offers a backcountry mangrove tour.

At Flamingo, **Everglades Flamingo** (305/501-2852, http://evergladesadventures.com) rents canoes and kayaks.

FISHING

Numerous fishing charters are available in the area. Most charters are essentially the same, offering anglers the opportunity to choose between flats and deepwater fishing excursions, and most are geared toward small groups (2-5 people).

Everglades Kayak Fishing (239/695-9107, www.evergladeskayakfishing.com), **Capt. Tony Polizos** (239/695-2608) and operate out of Everglades City. At Flamingo, **Everglades Flamingo** (305/501-2852, http://evergladesadventures.com) rents fishing skiffs.

WHERE TO STAY
INSIDE THE PARK

Camping is your only option within the park's boundaries. There are no accommodations or food. Two easily accessible campgrounds are on the Main Park Road. Both welcome tent campers and RVs. Facilities include solar-heated showers, RV dump stations, picnic tables, grills, drinking water, and amphitheaters for evening ranger programs.

Flamingo Campground

Flamingo Campground (877/444-6777, www.recreation.gov, year-round, $20-30) is the largest and most popular campground due to its proximity to the Flamingo Visitor Center and views of Florida Bay from quite a few sites. Its end-of-the-road isolation also has considerable appeal. There are 234 drive-up sites, 40 walk-in single sites, 41 RV sites, and 3 walk-in group sites. The campground may feel busy or even a little overcrowded (especially over the winter holidays), but a quick walk or bike ride puts you in pristine natural quietude. Reservations are accepted up to six months in advance for stays in November-April.

Long Pine Key Campground

Located near the Homestead entrance, **Long Pine Key Campground** (mid-Nov.-Apr., $20-30) has 108 drive-up sites and one group site. Sites are available first come, first served. The Anhinga and Long Pine Key Trails are nearby.

▼ TAYLOR SLOUGH

FLAMINGO AREA

Backcountry Camping

Backcountry campsites range from chickees along the Wilderness Waterway and in Florida Bay to "beach" sites in Cape Sable to standard ground sites. All are only accessible by boat. The three beach sites at **Cape Sable** are the largest, accommodating around 150 people. They're as beautiful as they are rustic and are often uncrowded.

Backcountry permits ($15 processing fee, $2 per person per day mid-Nov.-mid-Apr., free mid-Apr.-mid-Nov.) are required for overnight trips and are first come, first serve. Campsites that only fit 1-2 people go fast. Pick up permits at the Gulf Coast Visitor Center or Flamingo Visitor Center.

OUTSIDE THE PARK

Accommodations, restaurants, and services are located in **Miami, Homestead,** and **Everglades City**.

GETTING THERE

AIR

The nearest airport is **Miami International Airport** (MIA, 4200 NW 21st St., 305/876-7000, www.miami-airport.com), which is served by multiple daily flights and all major budget American carriers—including dozens of direct flights from around the country. It is

also the primary point of entry for travelers entering the United States from South America and the Caribbean. Car rentals are available at the airport.

CAR

From Miami, a 40-mile (45 min.) drive along the Tamiami Trail (U.S. 41) to the Shark Valley Visitor Center, a busy spot that's one of the main entry points to this part of the Everglades. About 35 miles (1 hr.) southwest of Naples via the Tamiami Trail (U.S. 41) is the town of Everglades City, home to the Gulf Coast Visitor Center. This visitors center is the best starting point for exploring the western half of the Everglades, including the Ten Thousand Islands area.

Ernest F. Coe Visitor Center lies at the southern entrance to Everglades National Park, 50 miles (1 hr.) south of Miami via Highway 997 or 821. From Miami, it's about 35 miles (30 min.) to get to Homestead and Florida City and then another 15 miles (30 min.) west into the park.

From Key West, take the Overseas Highway (U.S. 1) through Florida City before dropping into Homestead. The 130-mile drive takes three hours.

GETTING AROUND

There is no public transportation within the park. Boat rentals are available outside the park entrances.

TOURS

From Homestead, the **Homestead Trolley** (www.cityofhomestead.com, late Nov.-Apr., free) runs guided tours to the Everglades.

Tram Tours

The most popular tour is the **Shark Valley Tram Tour** (305/221-8455, www.sharkvalleytramtours.com, 9am-4pm daily mid-Dec.-Apr., 9:30am-4pm daily May-mid-Dec., fee) departing from the Shark Valley Visitor Center. Park naturalists guide two-hour tours in covered, open-air buses with pull-behind cars. Midway through the tour, you'll stop at a 45-foot-high observation platform to see the Everglades from above. Guides point out sharks and gators. Reservations are highly recommended in winter.

BIG CYPRESS NATIONAL PRESERVE

Big Cypress Swamp covers an impressive 720,000 acres, most of which are under the protection of the Big Cypress National Preserve. Access is limited by the terrain, but visitors will find that much of the park can be used for camping, hiking, and hunting. Ochopee is the only real town along this stretch of the Tamiami Trail.

The **Big Cypress Swamp Welcome Center** (33000 Tamiami Trail, Ochopee, 9am-4:30pm daily) is where to go for maps, ranger advice, or permits. The **Oasis Visitor Center** (52105 Tamiami Trail E., 239/695-1201, www.nps.gov/bicy, 9am-4:30pm daily) has sparkling-clean restrooms, helpful park rangers, and small educational and art exhibits inside the (blissfully) air-conditioned main building.

Sights

At only 61 square feet, the **Ochopee Post Office** (38000 Tamiami Trail E., 10am-4:15pm Mon.-Fri., 10:15am-11:30am Sat.) is the smallest post office in the United States. Although there's not much more inside than a desk, a scale, a computer, and a chair for the good-spirited clerk, that's enough for it to act as a fully functional post office for the few residents of Ochopee.

Brothers Dave and Jack Shealy head up the **Skunk Ape Research Headquarters** (40904 Tamiami Trail E., Ochopee, 239/695-2275, www.skunkape.info, 7am-7pm daily), gathering evidence about the legendary Skunk Ape (a Bigfoot-like creature) and presenting it to visitors in the form of T-shirts, bumper stickers, and other Skunk Ape-related memorabilia. A stop here is an essential voyage into classic, kitschy Floridiana.

The 0.5-mile Boardwalk Trail at **Kirby Storter Roadside Park** (U.S. 41/Tamiami Trail, sunrise-sunset daily, free) provides incredible views of

BIG CYPRESS NATIONAL PRESERVE

the cypress swamp and the vast expanses of marshlands that make up the Big Cypress Preserve. Bird-watching is excellent.

Located just a half mile west of the Big Cypress Visitor Center, **Clyde Butcher's Big Cypress Gallery** (52388 Tamiami Trail E., 239/695-2428, https://clydebutcher.com, 9:30am-4:30pm daily, free) displays stunning black-and-white photography and visual documentation of wild and natural Florida. The property is also home to Butcher's studio; every Saturday at 11am there are guided swamp walks on the property behind the gallery.

Ranger Tours

Ranger-led tours (daily, free) depart the visitors centers for short walks that vary from easy trails (some wheelchair-accessible) to "Slough Slogs," bird-watching, or nighttime starlight tours. Other tours travel by bicycle, canoe, or boat. Tour schedules change seasonally; winters run full schedules of programs while summers have reduced tours.

Boat Tours

Everglades National Park Boat Tours (www.evergladesnationalparkboattoursgulfcoast.com, daily year-round, rates and times vary) take in the Ten Thousand Islands, mangrove wilderness, and wildlife, with narration by national park-trained naturalists. Tours depart from the Gulf Coast marina. Purchase tickets at the Gulf Coast Visitor Center (905 S. Copeland Ave., 239/695-2591) in Everglades City.

Scenic Drives

One of the biggest draws in Big Cypress is a drive along the 27-mile **Loop Road** (off U.S. 41/Tamiami Trail at the Miami-Dade County line). The smooth, well-marked road makes its way through dense forests of dwarf cypress and slash pine. The pastoral setting is as relaxing as the frequent wildlife-spotting is invigorating. The drive along the shorter **Turner River Loop,** a 16-mile loop that starts at H. P. Williams Roadside Park (U.S. 41 and Turner River Rd.), is a great option for bird-watchers

Recreation

There are three well-marked hiking trails within the preserve, all of which are part of the **Florida Trail.** The most popular is the 6.5-mile trail that connects the Loop Road in the south and U.S. 41. There's a much longer and more challenging trail with a trailhead at the visitors center; it winds nearly 28 miles through slash pine copses, hardwood hammocks, and dry prairie land.

One of the best places to put in your canoe or kayak is the **Turner River Canoe Access** (entry point at U.S. 41 west of Turner River Rd., 239/695-2000, www.nps.gov/bicy). Non-boaters will also find this a good spot to stop thanks to the boardwalk nature trail.

Where to Stay

The **Skunk Ape Headquarters Campground** (40904 Tamiami Trail E., 239/695-2275, www.skunkape.info) is a typical roadside campground. For a slightly wilder experience, the **Burns Lake Campground & Backcountry Access** (Aug. 29-Jan. 6) has a dozen or so primitive campsites surrounding Burns Lake. **Monument Lake Campground** (Aug. 28-Apr. 15) offers a similar setup, with restrooms, a cold-water shower, and picnic/barbecue facilities.

Non-camping accommodations are limited to the **Swamp Cottage & Bungalow** (52388 Tamiami Trail E., 239/695-2428, www.clydebutcher.com) at Clyde Butcher's Big Cypress Gallery. Reservations can be something of a challenge.

There are two restaurants in Ochopee: **Joanie's Blue Crab Cafe** (39395 Tamiami Trail E., 239/695-2682, http://joaniesbluecrabcafe.com, 11am-5pm daily) and **Tippy's Big Cypress BBQ** (39025 SW 8th St./U.S. 41, 305/559-6080, www.tippysoutpost.com, 7am-11pm Mon.-Thurs., 6am-midnight Sat.-Sun.).

Getting There

Ochopee is on the Tamiami Trail (U.S. 41), about 35 miles (30 min.) east of Naples, 8 miles (about 10 min.) from Everglades City, and 10 miles (about 15 min.) from the eastern boundary of Big Cypress.

Airboat Tours

Airboat tours are an incredibly popular way to see the Everglades, zipping through a sea of grass. (However, given the delicate ecosystems, it's hard to recommend this method of touring because the boat noise can disturb wildlife.) Airboats are not allowed within the wilderness of Everglades National Park and the Ten Thousand Islands National Wildlife Refuge.

An exception is an area in the north near Everglades City. Airboat tours into this area are operated by **Coopertown** (305/226-6048, www.coopertownairboats.com), **Gator Park** (305/559-2255, www.gatorpark.com), and **Everglades Safari Park** (305/226-6923, www.evergladessafaripark.com). Plenty of other airboat tours go to locations outside the national park.

BISCAYNE NATIONAL PARK

Florida

WEBSITE:
www.nps.gov/bisc

PHONE NUMBER:
305/230-1144

VISITATION RANK:
39

WHY GO:
Explore a national
park that is
95 percent water.

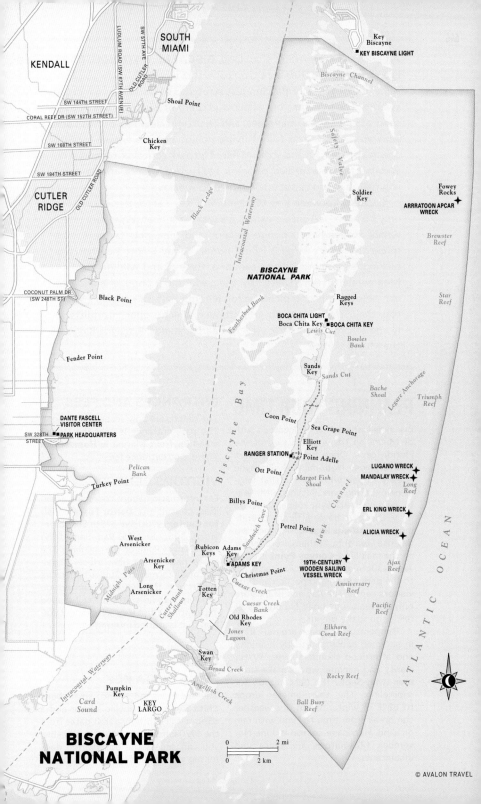

KENDALL

SOUTH
MIAMI

Key
Biscayne
■ KEY BISCAYNE LIGHT

LUDLUM ROAD (SW 67TH AVENUE)
SW 57TH AVE
OLD CUTLER ROAD

SW 144TH STREET

Shoal Point

Biscayne Channel

CORAL REEF DR (SW 152ND STREET)

SW 168TH STREET

Chicken
Key

Safety Valve

SW 184TH STREET

CUTLER
RIDGE

OLD CUTLER ROAD

Soldier
Key

Fowey
Rocks

ARRRATOON APCAR
WRECK

*Brewster
Reef*

COCONUT PALM DR
(SW 248TH ST)

Black Point

Black Ledge

Intracoastal Waterway

BISCAYNE
NATIONAL PARK

*Star
Reef*

Ragged
Keys

Fender Point

Featherbed Bank

BOCA CHITA LIGHT
Boca Chita Key ■ ■ BOCA CHITA KEY

Lewis Cut

*Bowles
Bank*

DANTE FASCELL
VISITOR CENTER
SW 328TH ■ ■ PARK HEADQUARTERS
STREET

Biscayne Bay

Sands
Key

Sands Cut

*Bache
Shoal*

Legare Anchorage

*Triumph
Reef*

Coon Point

Sea Grape Point

Elliott
Key

RANGER STATION ■ ■ Point Adelle

LUGANO WRECK ✦
MANDALAY WRECK ✦

*Long
Reef*

*Pelican
Bank*

Ott Point

*Margot Fish
Shoal*

Hawk Channel

ERL KING WRECK ✦

Turkey Point

Billys Point

ALICIA WRECK ✦

West
Arsenicker

Petrel Point

Rubicon
Keys

Adams
Key
■ ADAMS KEY

Sandwich Cove

19TH-CENTURY ✦
WOODEN SAILING
VESSEL WRECK

*Ajax
Reef*

Arsenicker
Key

Christmas Point

*Anniversary
Reef*

Long
Arsenicker

Midnight Pass

Totten
Key

Caesar Creek

*Pacific
Reef*

Cutler Bank Shallows

*Caesar Creek
Bank*

Old Rhodes
Key

*Jones
Lagoon*

*Elkhorn
Coral Reef*

Swan
Key

Broad Creek

A T L A N T I C   O C E A N

Rocky Reef

Intracoastal Waterway

Pumpkin
Key

KEY
LARGO

Angelfish Creek

*Card
Sound*

*Ball Buoy
Reef*

BISCAYNE
NATIONAL PARK

0   2 mi

0   2 km

© AVALON TRAVEL

A park with more water than land, **BISCAYNE NATIONAL PARK** is a stunning, 173,000-acre tropical water world. Its mainland contains one of east Florida's longest stretches of saltwater mangrove swamp. The immense but shallow estuary of Biscayne Bay houses seagrass meadows, manatees, and an utterly clear mix of fresh and seawater. Coral reefs full of living polyps provide a base for 500 species of colorful and striking fish. The park contains incredible diversity: cacti, butterflies, pelicans, sea turtles, sharks, upside-down jellyfish, ibis, and about 20 endangered species.

Located between Key Biscayne and Key Largo, the islands can only be accessed with a canoe, a kayak, or a boat. Wreckers (shipwreck scavengers), sponge makers, and pineapple farmers once made the park's largest island home. Today Elliott Key has picnicking, swimming, hiking, camping, fishing, and wildlife-viewing. Meanwhile, on Boca Chita Key, the park's most popular island, you can enjoy a relaxing picnic, stroll along a half-mile hiking trail, or tour the 65-foot ornamental lighthouse, which is open intermittently and affords a fantastic view of nearby islands, Biscayne Bay, and the Miami skyline.

PLANNING YOUR TIME

Biscayne National Park is located south of Miami on the Atlantic side of the Florida cape. Once proposed as part of Everglades National Park, Biscayne is easy to pair with visiting that larger neighboring park. Although the water portion of Biscayne is open 24 hours daily, the keys have different operating hours. **Adams Key,** for instance, is a day-use area only. At the visitors center on the mainland, **Convoy Point** is open 7am-5:30pm daily. While you can drive to the park's mainland portion and the visitors center, the bay and islands are only accessible by boat. No bridges or ferries go to the islands.

Temperatures float around 82°F in summer, accompanied by humidity and afternoon thunderstorms. Water clarity and minimal waves make **summer** (May-Sept.) the best season for snorkeling. The thermometer drops to 68°F in winter, when dry weather can break from time to time with rain or wind. Hurricane season is June-November. Mosquitoes are year-round inhabitants.

ENTRANCES AND FEES

The islands are only accessible by boat. The park entrance is near the Homestead Bayfront Marina in **Homestead.** There is no entrance fee.

VISITORS CENTER

For information about tours and activities, consult the **Dante Fascell Visitor Center** (9700 SW 328th St., Homestead, 305/230-7275, 9am-5pm daily) near Convoy Point on the mainland. The center has exhibits, films, a local art gallery, and information. Guided boat tours depart from the visitors center and you can rent paddle crafts for self-guided exploration. **Elliot Key** has a ranger station that is staffed intermittently.

SIGHTS
BOCA CHITA KEY

The most visited island, small **Boca Chita Key** has an idyllic harbor and a 65-foot-tall lighthouse that dates from the 1930s. If a park ranger is available, you can access the observation deck for big views full of water as far as the

BOCA CHITA KEY

eye can see. You'll also spot islands and Miami. Reach this island on the north end of the keys by boat.

ADAMS KEY

Close to the visitors center, tiny **Adams Key** (day use only) contains mangroves where you can swim, paddle, or snorkel. On land, there's a picnic area, a short trail, and a dock. The island once housed the Cocolobo Club, a getaway for the rich and famous. Reach this island on the south end of the keys by boat.

ELLIOT KEY

North of Key Largo, **Elliot Key** is the largest island at about seven miles long. It offers swimming, paddling, camping, picnicking, and a hiking trail. Historically, the Tequesta Indians used it periodically, but its early settlers grew pineapples, collected sponges, and sought spoils from wrecked ships.

RECREATION

HIKING

On Elliott Key, the **Spite Highway Nature Trail** (6 mi.) travels the length of the island, crossing through subtropical forest that harbors butterflies.

Access to the key is by boat; camping is available.

CANOEING, KAYAKING, AND PADDLEBOARDING

Beginner paddlers should stick to the mangrove fringes around Biscayne Bay, but experienced paddlers can tackle the seven-mile crossing to the keys. Camping is available on Boca Chita Key and Elliot Key.

Secluded **Jones Lagoon**, a shallow waterway with myriad islands between Totten and Old Rhodes Keys, offers outstanding sheltered paddling routes to see fish, sharks, and birds. **Hurricane Creek** is a paddling destination that offers snorkeling in mangroves on the north end of Old Rhodes Key. Consult with the visitors center on paddle routes before launching. Winter is the best time for these two trips.

Dante Fascell Visitor Center (9700 SW 328th St., Homestead, 305/230-7275) rents canoes, kayaks, and paddleboards. Rangers guide full-day paddling trips to Jones Lagoon, available by reservation only. **Biscayne National Park Institute** (786/335-3644, www.biscaynenationalparkinstitute.org, reservations recommended) also guides kayaking and paddleboarding trips.

TOTTEN KEY

DIVING AND SNORKELING

The keys of Biscayne proved deadly for many ships sailing these waters. Today, six shipwrecks line the **Maritime Heritage Trail**, an underwater sight for snorkelers on the Atlantic side of the park. The wrecks date mostly from the late 1800s and early 1900s and look more like skeletons than ships. Access is by boat only and there are mooring buoys at the wrecks. Maps and brochures are at the visitors center.

Shallow coral reefs and shipwrecks make perfect snorkeling locations; divers can explore deeper waters and wrecks. If you have a boat, you can explore on your own. Otherwise, board a guided half- or full-day snorkeling trip through **Biscayne National Park Institute** (786/335-3644, www.biscaynenationalparkinstitute.org, reservations recommended) around Biscayne Bay, the offshore coral reefs on the Atlantic side of the national park, and the shipwrecks. **Tropic Scuba** (305/669-1645, http://tropicscuba.com) has charter snorkeling and scuba diving trips.

BOATING AND FISHING

Anglers must bring their own boat into Biscayne National Park to go after tarpon, grouper, snapper, and bonefish. For boaters, **Miami County Parks** (www.miamidade.gov) operates two launching marinas that go directly into the park: **Homestead Bayfront Park** (9698 N. Canal Dr., Homestead, 305/230-3033) and **Black Point Marina** (24775 SW 87th Ave., Miami, 305/258-4092). A Florida fishing license is required.

SNORKELERS EXPLORE ELKHORN REEF.

WHERE TO STAY

INSIDE THE PARK

Camping (tents only, first come, first served, $25) is available on two islands. There are no other accommodations or services.

Popular **Boca Chita Key** features a grassy waterside camping area with picnic tables, grills, and toilets. Spacious **Elliott Key** offers waterside and forested camping areas, picnic tables, grills, drinking water, and restrooms with cold showers. Daily transportation to Elliot Key is available via the **Biscayne National Park Institute** (786/335-3644, www.biscaynenationalparkinstitute.org). Paddlers staying overnight can leave their cars at the visitors center with a parking permit (free). Group camping is also available.

Boaters can stay in either of the two island harbors for a fee. Any vessel still in the harbor after 5pm is presumed to be staying overnight and will be charged.

OUTSIDE THE PARK

The closest accommodations and restaurants are in **Homestead** and **Florida City.** Less than 30 miles away, **Miami** adds more options.

GETTING THERE AND AROUND

The nearest international airport is **Miami International Airport** (MIA, 2100 NW 42nd Ave., Miami, 305/876-7000, www.miami-airport.com), which also has car rentals.

To reach the Dante Fascell Visitor Center in Homestead, drivers have three options:

From the Florida Turnpike: Take exit 6 (Speedway Blvd.) and turn left onto SW 328th Street (North Canal Drive). Turn left and drive four miles to the park entrance.

From the north on U.S. 1: At Homestead, turn east onto SW 137th Avenue (Speedway Blvd.) and continue five miles. At SW 328th Street (North Canal Dr.), turn left and drive four miles to the park entrance.

From the south on U.S. 1: At Homestead, turn right onto SW 344th Street (Palm Dr.) and continue four miles. Turn right on SW 328th Street (North Canal Dr.) and drive east for four miles to the park entrance.

The **Homestead National Parks Trolley** (www.cityofhomestead.com, late Nov.-Apr., free) provides guided tours from Homestead to Biscayne and Everglades National Parks.

BOAT TOURS

Biscayne National Park Institute (786/335-3644, www.biscaynenationalparkinstitute.org, reservations recommended) guides interpretive boat or sailing tours. Three-hour trips go to Boca Chita Key. The institute also guides higher-activity, full-day tours that combine sightseeing the islands with snorkeling and paddling. Several other companies operate boat or sailing charters; consult with the visitors center for licensed concessionaires.

SIGHTS NEARBY

Bill Baggs Cape Florida State Park (1200 S. Crandon Blvd., Key Biscayne, 305/361-5811, www.floridastateparks.org) has a historic lighthouse, a beach for sunbathing and swimming, and kayaking, biking, and overnight boat camping.

Dagny Johnson Key Largo Hammock Botanical State Park (Mile 106, County Road 905, Key Largo, 305/451-1202, www.floridastateparks.org) houses a West Indian tropical hardwood hammock, one of the largest in the United States.

Florida Keys National Marine Sanctuary (https://floridakeys.noaa.gov), south of Biscayne and accessible by boat, attracts snorkelers and scuba divers with its coral reefs, exquisite fish (including dolphins), and shipwrecks.

DRY TORTUGAS NATIONAL PARK

Florida

WEBSITE:
www.nps.gov/drto

PHONE NUMBER:
305/242-7700

VISITATION RANK:
53

WHY GO:
Explore the underwater habitat of coral and sand islands.

PASSPORT STAMPS ▼▼▼

▲ DRY TORTUGAS NATIONAL PARK

DRY TORTUGAS NATIONAL PARK

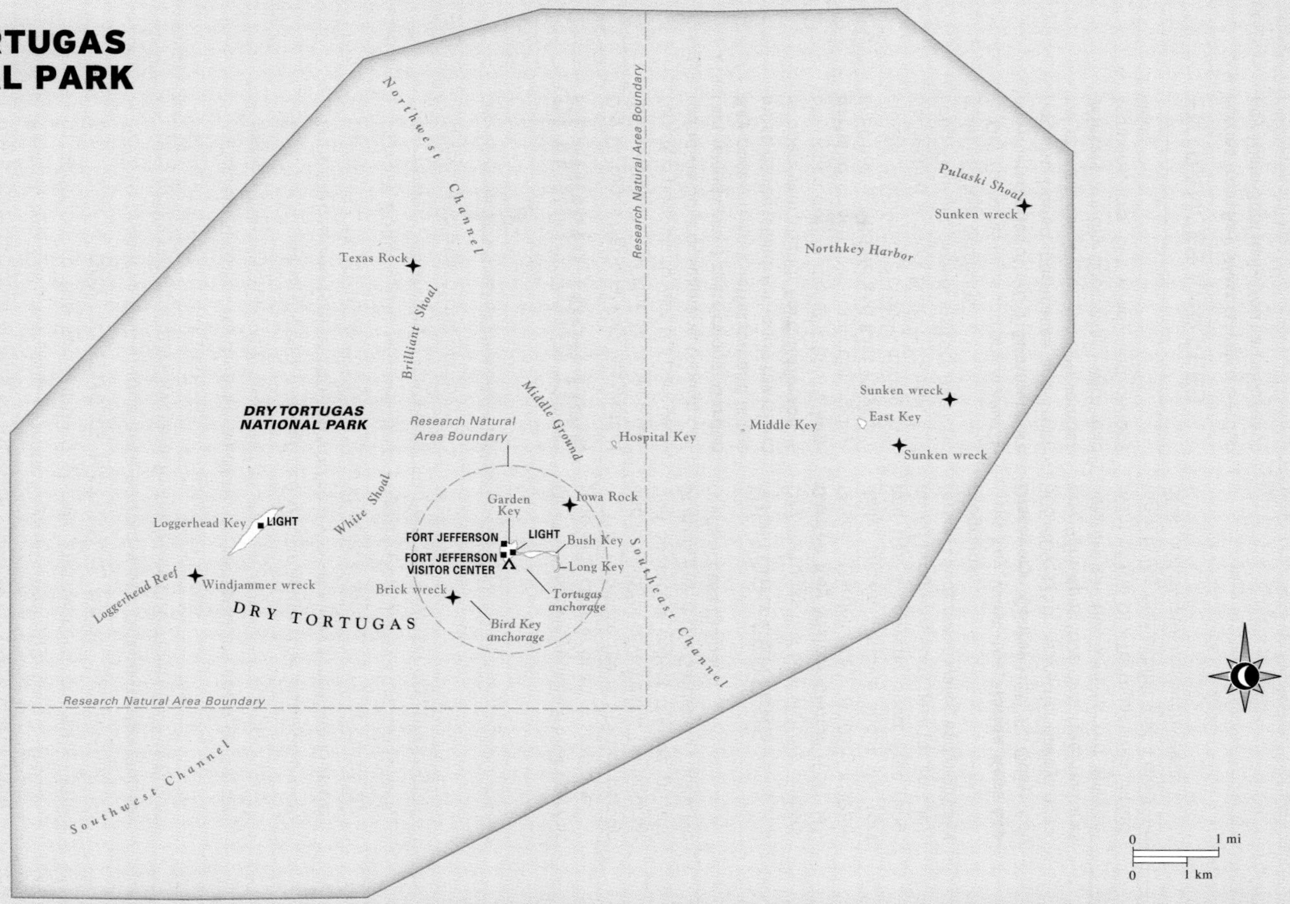

Southwest Channel

Research Natural Area Boundary

Loggerhead Reef

Loggerhead Key

Windjammer wreck

LIGHT

DRY TORTUGAS

DRY TORTUGAS
NATIONAL PARK

White Shoal

Research Natural
Area Boundary

Brick wreck

FORT JEFFERSON
VISITOR CENTER

Bird Key
anchorage

Garden
Key

LIGHT

Bush Key

Long Key

Tortugas
anchorage

Iowa Rock

Texas Rock

Brilliant Shoal

Northwest Channel

Middle Ground

Hospital Key

Research Natural Area Boundary

Southeast Channel

Middle Key

Sunken wreck

East Key

Sunken wreck

Northkey Harbor

Pulaski Shoal

Sunken wreck

0
1 km
0
1 mi

Roughly 68 miles west of Key West lies a cluster of seven islands, composed of coral and sand, that are collectively known as the Dry Tortugas. Originally named Las Tortugas (the Turtles) by Spanish explorers, the islands eventually became "Dry Tortugas" on mariners' navigational charts to indicate the lack of fresh water here. Part of the 220-mile-long Florida Keys archipelago, these islands, in addition to the surrounding shoals and waters, comprise the 64,657-acre **DRY TORTUGAS NATIONAL PARK**, established in 1992 to preserve this unique area and now one of the most remote units in the national park system. In addition, Dry Tortugas has been listed in the National Register of Historic Places.

Celebrated for its diverse wildlife, its remarkable coral reefs, its enthralling shipwrecks, and its pirate legends and military past, Dry Tortugas is indeed a must-see destination, the kind of place that makes you feel as though you're a world away from the Florida mainland. If you have the time, you should board a ferry or come by private boat to this unique destination—popular with sunbathers, swimmers, snorkelers, kayakers, anglers, bird-watchers, photographers, and overnight campers.

PLANNING YOUR TIME

Dry Tortugas National Park lies west of the southern tip of Florida in open waters. It is possible to visit the park year-round via boat or seaplane, though certain islands have restrictions. **Garden Key** contains Fort Jefferson and is the most visited island. Although the island is open year-round, **Fort Jefferson** is only open during daylight hours. **Loggerhead** is open year-round during daylight hours. **Middle and East Keys** are closed April-mid-October during turtle nesting season. Bush, Hospital, and Long Keys are closed; visitors must remain 100 feet offshore.

Dry Tortugas has subtropical weather, which ranges 60-90°F. **Summers** are hot and humid; hurricanes and tropical storms can occur June-November. **Winters** are dry (Dec.-Mar.) with mild temperatures, but windy and choppy seas.

ENTRANCES AND FEES

Ferries from **Key West** travel to Garden Key 10am-3pm daily. You can also reach Dry Tortugas via your own boat (permit required), charter boat, or seaplane.

The entrance fee is $15 per person and is valid for seven days. Transportation operators collect the fee; private boaters pay at the Garden Key dock. No roads access the park.

VISITORS CENTERS

Dry Tortugas has two visitors centers. **Garden Key Visitor Center** (Fort Jefferson, Garden Key, 8:30am-4:30pm daily) shows a movie about the fort and has a souvenir shop. Free ranger-led programs start here for Fort Jefferson tours, moat walks, and night sky programs.

In Key West, the **Florida Keys Eco Discovery Center** (35 E. Quay Rd., 305/809-4750, www.floridakeys.noaa. gov, 9am-4pm Tues.-Sat., free) features exhibits on the wildlife and environment of the Dry Tortugas area, including a living reef exhibit and a mock-up of an underwater research vessel.

FORT JEFFERSON

SIGHTS

FORT JEFFERSON

Fort Jefferson, the well-preserved Civil War fort on Garden Key, is the centerpiece of these remote islands. Nicknamed the "American Gibraltar," the country's largest 19th-century coastal fort was built in 1846 to control navigation in the Gulf of Mexico, though construction was never quite completed. During and after the war, it served as a remote, Union-affiliated military prison for captured deserters. By the 1880s, the U.S. Army had abandoned the facility. It became a wildlife refuge in 1908 and a national monument in 1935.

Within the fortified walls of the historic citadel are the officers' quarters, soldiers' barracks, cistern, magazines, and cannons. From November to May, parts of Fort Jefferson are closed to the public while mason crews work on much-needed preservation projects.

The **Fort Jefferson Harbor Light** was established in 1825 and is still operational today. The lighthouse tower was erected in 1876 and is a favorite among photographers. It is located northeast of the boat dock on Garden Key.

LOGGERHEAD KEY

Accessible only by private boat or charter, **Loggerhead Key** once housed the Carnegie Institute's Laboratory of Marine Ecology. The island features the **Loggerhead Light,** established in 1825, with an existing tower that was erected in 1858. The park is day use only. Public pathways are open to visitors, but all buildings and structures are closed.

MOAT AROUND FORT JEFFERSON

RECREATION

BIRD-WATCHING

Garden Key has excellent bird-watching. More than 200 varieties of birds are spotted annually, especially March-September when nearby **Bush Key** serves as the nesting ground for migratory birds. April-May, more than 85,000 brown noddies and sooty terns nest on Bush Key. In spring, you might spot herons, raptors, and shorebirds; in summer, look for frigatebirds and mourning doves. The fall and winter months bring hawks, merlins, peregrine falcons, gulls, terns, American kestrels, and belted kingfishers. Other possible birds include orioles, warblers, cormorants, masked boobies, black noddies, mangrove cuckoos, and white-crowned pigeons.

Sea-Clusive Charters (1107 Key Plaza, Ste. 315, Key West, 305/744-9928, www.seaclusive.com) features tailored excursions led by professional bird guide Larry Manfredi (www.southfloridabirding.com). While on board, you might also spot sharks, dolphins, and if you're lucky, gigantic sea turtles. The cruises can accommodate 8-11 passengers.

BOATING AND KAYAKING

Kayaking can be a wonderful way to experience the islands; however, the area is only suitable for experienced sea kayakers, as the currents can be very strong. You can bring kayaks aboard the **Yankee Freedom** (800/634-0939, www.drytortugas.com) ferry. Also bring a life vest, an anchor, a bailer, extra paddles, drinking water, waterproof bags for gear, and required safety equipment.

Garden Key and **Loggerhead Key** are both accessible by private vessel, though docking on Garden Key can be problematic. Your best bet is to anchor in the harbor and use a dinghy to reach the island, which has a dinghy beach for that exact purpose. Overnight anchoring is allowed between sunset and sunrise in the designated anchorage area: the sand-and-rubble bottom within one nautical mile of the Fort Jefferson Harbor Light. The dock on Loggerhead Key is only open to government vessels, but visitors are allowed to land south of the boathouse.

FISHING

Anglers can fish from the public dock on Garden Key and the beach west of the dock. (Fishing from a boat is only permitted within a one-mile radius of Garden Key.) Several local fishing charters operate multiday trips to the area; guides are allowed to fish in and around Dry Tortugas.

Andy Griffiths Charters (40 Key Haven Rd., Key West, 305/296-2639, www.fishandy.com) offers three-day, two-night excursions for up to six anglers. **Dream Catcher Charters** (5555 College Rd., Stock Island, 305/292-7702 or 888/362-3474, www.chartersofkeywest.com) offers 10-hour trips for up to six passengers as well as overnight excursions (trip times and rates vary). Another helpful operator is **Lethal Weapon Charters** (245 Front St., Key West, 305/744-8225).

DIVING AND SNORKELING

Snorkelers, scuba divers, and underwater photographers favor this area. On Garden Key, you can snorkel directly off the isolated **Fort Jefferson Beach**, near the moat walls and coaling dock ruins. The warm, shallow waters boast a cornucopia of kaleidoscopic tropical fish, conch shells, lobster, sponges, sea fans, sea anemones, staghorn coral clusters, and the occasional sea turtle. Other spots include patch reefs and the shipwrecks of the 19th-century **Bird Key Wreck** and early 20th-century **Windjammer Wreck**.

CORAL

DIVING CORAL REEFS

For more snorkeling and dive sites, **Sea-Clusive Charters** (1107 Key Plaza, Ste. 315, Key West, 305/744-9928, www.seaclusive.com) offers multiday diving excursions for 6-11 passengers. You can explore the Windjammer Wreck site as well as the overhangs, caves, and swim troughs of coral reefs, which have water depths of 45-80 feet. Look for tropical fish, resident jewfish, black grouper, coral formations, and sponges.

WHERE TO STAY

INSIDE THE PARK

Dry Tortugas National Park has no public lodging. Camping is the only option for overnighting on Garden Key. A short walk from the public dock leads to a primitive 10-site **campground** ($15, first come, first served) with picnic tables and barbecue grills. Each site can accommodate six people and three tents. A group site, which can accommodate 10-40 people, must be reserved in advance.

OUTSIDE THE PARK

Accommodations, restaurants, and services are available in **Key West.**

GETTING THERE AND AROUND

Travelers can reach Key West by flying into the **Key West International Airport (EYW)** (3491 S. Roosevelt Blvd., 305/296-5439, www.keywestinternationalairport.com). Dry Tortugas National Park lies approximately 68 miles west of Key West and is only accessible by ferry or private boat—all of which can be boarded in Key West.

Ferry and seaplanes access Garden Key, but not the other islands (personal boat, kayak, or canoe only). To reach Garden Key by ferry, schedule a day trip on the 100-foot catamaran **Yankee Freedom II** (100 Grinnell St., 800/634-0939, www.drytortugas.com, 8am-5:30pm daily), which docks in the Historic Seaport at Key West Bight. Reservations are recommended. The ferry also offers overnight excursions (reservations required).

If traveling to Garden Key by private vessel (permit required), docking restrictions limit use of the public dock between sunrise and 10am and 3pm and sunset. On Loggerhead Key, you can only land vessels south of the dock and boathouse.

ISLANDS

A handful of national parks lie isolated on remote U.S. islands. The Hawaiian Islands offer the easiest access for visitors. On the Big Island, lava leaps from the Kilauea Crater at Hawai'i Volcanoes National Park. Maui's upcountry is the place to watch the day begin over the 10,023-foot summit of Haleakalā Crater.

East of Puerto Rico, Virgin Islands National Park sits nestled in the Caribbean Sea. More than 60 percent of the island of St. John is national park, with sandy beaches, coral gardens, and peaceful hiking paths.

Hidden deep in the South Pacific, the National Park of American Samoa comprises a handful of tiny islands in the Samoan archipelago. Tenacious visitors can discover its treasures—unique rain forests, coral communities, and a traditional Samoan culture.

◀ LAVA FLOW, HAWAII

ISLANDS

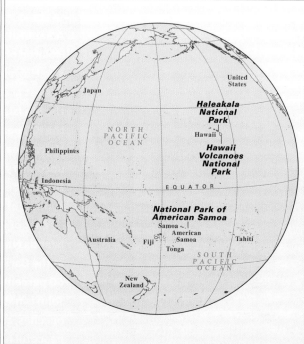

The National Park
ISLANDS

HALEAKALĀ, MAUI

Most visitors go to Haleakalā for sunrise, but there are also trails that tour the colorful crater and a portion of the park that spills to the coast at Kīpahulu (page 661).

HAWAI'I VOLCANOES, HAWAII

The 13,677-foot summit of Mauna Loa looms above the shorter, more easily accessed Kilauea, where you can walk through lava tubes and on trails through lava flows (page 671).

VIRGIN ISLANDS

Surrounded by turquoise water, the island of St. John includes historic plantations, snorkeling beaches, and opportunities for hiking amid tropical forests and boating (page 681).

AMERICAN SAMOA

This tropical paradise has rain forest hiking trails, sandy beaches, coral reefs for snorkeling, and the customs of the 3,000-year-old Samoan culture (page 690).

1: THE SUMMIT AREA, HALEAKALĀ, MAUI
2: HIKING IN HAWAI'I VOLCANOES, HAWAII
3: TRUNK BAY, ST. JOHN ISLAND, VIRGIN ISLANDS

Best OF THE ISLANDS

Sunrise over Haleakalā: Watch the sun rise and then spend the day hiking across the crater floor (page 665).

Crater Rim Drive: See the volcanic forces that created the Hawaiian archipelago (pages 675 and 679).

Trunk Bay: Lounge under coconut palms on this white-sand beach flanking clear, turquoise water for snorkeling (page 685).

National Natural Landmarks: Visit seven of American Samoa's natural landmarks created by volcanoes (page 695).

PLANNING YOUR TRIP

HAWAI'I

Hawai'i Volcanoes is located on the Big Island of Hawai'i, while Haleakalā is located on the island of Maui. Both islands have airports.

The prime tourist season for the Hawaiian Islands starts two weeks before **Christmas** and lasts until **Easter.** It picks up again in early June and ends in late August. Everything is heavily booked, and prices are higher. Hotel, airline, and car reservations are a must. You can generally save money and avoid a lot of hassle if you travel in the off-season (September-early December and late-April-late May).

VIRGIN ISLANDS

There are no airports on St. John. Travelers must fly into St. Thomas Cyril E. King Airport on Charlotte Amalie and then take a car barge or ferry to St. John.

Winter **(December-March)** is high season, which coincides with the dry season in the islands, and the season of the best sailing winds and coolest, most comfortable temperatures. There is no better time to visit than when the weather is clear and sunny, the breezes blow, and there is an array of things to do.

Hurricane season runs June-November with the peak from August to October.

AMERICAN SAMOA

There is one airport on Tutuila Island. All visitors must have a valid passport, a return ticket, and confirmation of funds. A visa may be required. High season is **June-September,** which are the cooler, drier months. October-May is the monsoon season with tropical storms.

▲ TRUNK BAY, VIRGIN ISLANDS

HALEAKALĀ NATIONAL PARK

Hawaii

PASSPORT STAMPS ▼▼▼

WEBSITE:
www.nps.gov/hale

PHONE NUMBER:
808/572-4400

VISITATION RANK:
22

WHY GO:
Watch the sun rise over a volcanic summit.

▲ HALEAKALĀ NATIONAL PARK

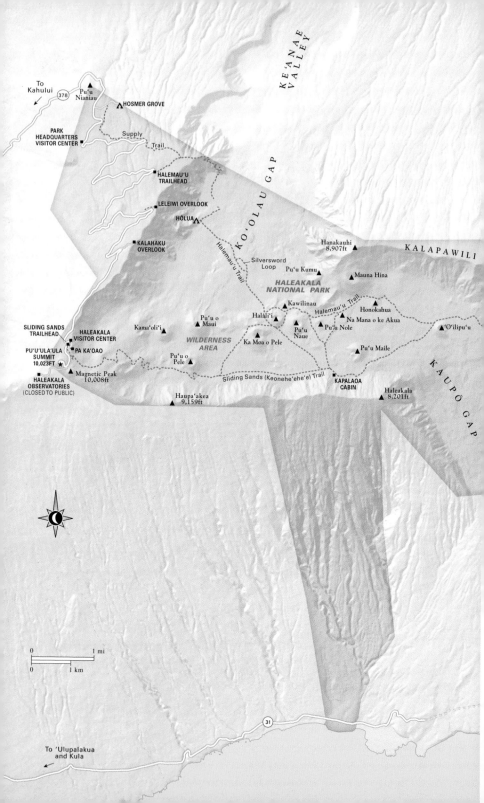

KEʻANAE VALLEY

To Kahului
378
Puʻu Nianiau

▲ HOSMER GROVE

PARK HEADQUARTERS VISITOR CENTER

Supply

Trail

■ HALEMAUʻU TRAILHEAD

KOʻOLAU GAP

■ LELEIWI OVERLOOK

HŌLUA ▲

■ KALAHAKU OVERLOOK

Halemauʻu Trail

Silversword Loop

Hanakauhi 8,907ft ▲

KALAPAWILI

HALEAKALA NATIONAL PARK

Puʻu Kumu

Mauna Hina ▲

Kawilinau ▲

Halali'i ▲

Halemauʻu Trail

Honokahua ▲

SLIDING SANDS TRAILHEAD

HALEAKALA VISITOR CENTER

Kamaʻoliʻi ▲

Puʻu o Maui ▲

WILDERNESS AREA

Ka Moa o Pele ▲

Puʻu Naue ▲

Na Mana o ke Akua ▲

Puʻu Nole ▲

ʻOʻilipuʻu ▲

PUʻUʻULAʻULA SUMMIT 10,023FT ★

PA KAʻOAO

Puʻu o Pele ▲

Puʻu Maile ▲

Magnetic Peak 10,008ft ▲

■ HALEAKALA OBSERVATORIES (CLOSED TO PUBLIC)

Sliding Sands (Keoneheʻeheʻe) Trail

KAPALAOA CABIN

Haleakala 8,201ft ▲

KAUPŌ GAP

Haupaʻakea 9,159ft ▲

0   1 mi
0   1 km

31

To ʻUlupalakua and Kula

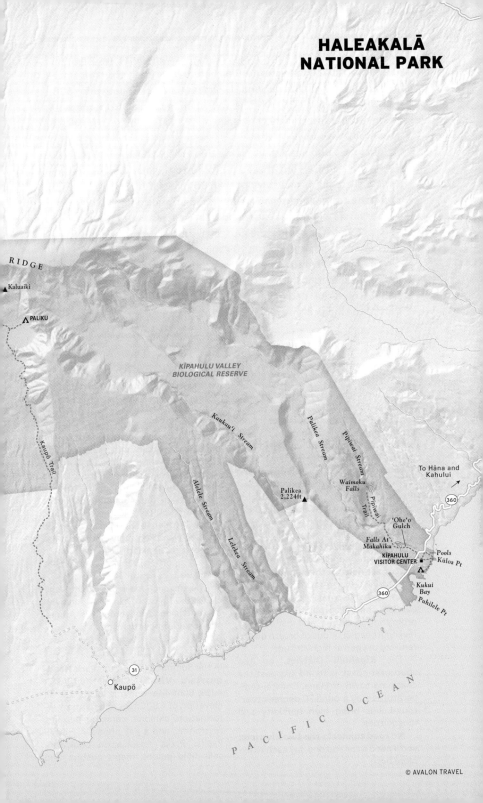

HALEAKALĀ
NATIONAL PARK

RIDGE

▲ Kaluaiki

⌂ PALIKU

KĪPAHULU VALLEY
BIOLOGICAL RESERVE

Kaupo Trail

Kaukau'i Stream

Alelele Stream

Lelekea Stream

Palikea Stream

Pipiwai Stream

Palikea
2,224ft ▲

Waimoku
Falls

Pipiwai
Trail

To Hāna and
Kahului →

360

'Ohe'o
Gulch

Falls At
Makahiku

KĪPAHULU
VISITOR CENTER ⌂

Pools
Kūloa Pt

360

Kukui
Bay

Puhilele Pt

○ Kaupō

31

PACIFIC OCEAN

"Hale-a-ka-la," House of the Sun. Few places are more aptly named than this 10,023-foot volcano. Believed to have been dormant since 1790 (the summit area around the crater has been inactive for 600 years), Haleakalā is 30,000 feet tall when measured from the seafloor—surpassed only by the peaks on the Big Island as the tallest mountains on earth.

The most popular activity is visiting **HALEAKALĀ NATIONAL PARK** for sunrise—but there's far more to this national park than simply the light of dawn. More than 30 miles of hiking trails crisscross the crater, where backcountry cabins and campgrounds provide a classic wilderness experience. The sunsets and stargazing are as spectacular as seeing the crater at sunrise. Views plunge from the crater's seemingly barren volcanic rock down to the rain forest. On the high-elevation pumice slopes, the beautiful yet fragile silversword maintains its foothold. Even the drive leading up to the park—where the road gains 10,000 vertical feet in only 38 miles—is part of the magical, mystical experience of standing atop Haleakalā.

PLANNING YOUR TIME

Haleakalā commandeers the southeast of Maui. The park is divided into two sections. The **Summit District** is deservedly popular: It's the more accessible area, home to the famous Haleakalā crater. The summit of Haleakalā is 20-30 degrees cooler than the warm and tropical coast and the weather is unpredictable. You can leave an 80-degree beach to arrive at the crater in 50-degree weather with wind and rain.

Rain and even snow can fall year-round, but summer (May-Sept.) typically sees better conditions. There are **no visitor services at the summit**—bring food, drinks, warm layers, sunglasses, a hat, and sunscreen. At this high elevation, the solar radiation is strong, prompting sunburns, and visitors may feel lightheaded or out of breath due to reduced oxygen at high altitude.

The **Kīpahulu District,** on the southeast coast, is found just past the charming town of Hana. Coastal temperatures stay around 70 degrees year-round, but bring high humidity and mosquitoes.

No road connects the two districts; you'll need a car and one day each to explore both.

ENTRANCES AND FEES

Access to the **Summit District** is via Route 278 (open year-round), a paved and curvy road; severe weather may temporarily close the road. The entrance station is located prior to the park headquarters and the turnoff to Hosmer Grove Campground. The Park Headquarters Visitor Center is less than one mile farther along the road.

Access to the **Kīpahulu District** is via Route 360 (the Road to Hana) and Route 31 (open year-round). The paved Road to Hana is fraught with potholes and bumps, making it very rough to drive. The official Kīpahulu entrance is at the visitors center.

The entrance fee is $25-30 per vehicle ($20-25 motorcycle, $12-15 individual) and is good for three days. Admission includes both districts.

VISITORS CENTERS

In the Summit District, the **Park Headquarters Visitor Center** (808/572-4459, 8am-4pm daily) is located at an elevation of 6,800 feet and has park information, exhibits, camping permits, restrooms, and a pay phone. A Hawaii Pacific Parks Association bookstore sells field guides, maps, posters, and

Top ❸

1 WATCH SUNRISE FROM HALEAKALĀ CRATER

Everyone should experience a Haleakalā sunrise at least once. But it requires advance planning, **reservations** (877/444-6777, www.recreation.gov, $1.50 per vehicle), and waking up at 3am.

SUNRISE PEEKING UP OVER THE CRATER WALLS OF HALEAKALĀ NATIONAL PARK

The highest observation point for sunrise is **Pu'u 'Ula'ula** (Red Hill), which tops out above 10,000 feet and is the official summit of Haleakalā. It has a glass-sided observation area (open 24 hours daily) and is often the most crowded spot. The **Haleakalā Visitor Center** (9,740 feet) is the second-highest viewing point. Two viewpoints on the road toward the summit—**Leleiwi Overlook** (8,840 feet) and **Kalahaku Overlook** (9,324 feet, only accessible downhill)—offer less-crowded alternatives to the higher-elevation overlooks.

A reservation allows one vehicle access to the Summit District between 3am and 7am. Reservations are not required after 7am. On most mornings, it's clear enough to see the sunrise. For the weather forecast, call the **Hotline for Haleakalā Summit** (808/944-5025, ext. 4). Temperatures are often near or below freezing; bring warm clothes and beach chairs for sitting.

2 BIKE DOWN HALEAKALĀ

Watching the day begin from Haleakalā crater, followed by feeling the crisp air in your face as you weave through cow-speckled pastures via bicycle, is magical. To bike from the summit, you must make **advance reservations** for sunrise access and provide **your own bicycle and transportation.** Some companies do offer bike tours, but these do not leave from the summit.

3 FIND PARADISE AT THE POOLS OF 'OHE'O

The **Pools of 'Ohe'o** (near the Kīpahulu Visitor Center) in 'Ohe'o Gulch are the stuff of a dreamy paradise. Tucked in the rain forest, waterfalls drop into placid pools. Also called the Seven Sacred Pools (there are actually more), they are closed to swimming, but you can still enjoy their serenity.

Access to the pools may close periodically. Stop at the visitor center first for updates.

THE POOLS OF 'OHE'O

THE KIPAHULU COAST

kids games. Stop here to inquire about sunrise-viewing reservations at the summit.

Also in the Summit District, the **Haleakalā Visitor Center** (sunrise-3pm daily) is located at 9,740 feet, 10 miles up the park road from the Park Headquarters Visitor Center. Geology exhibits detail the history of the volcano and maps and field guides are available at the Hawaii Pacific Parks Association bookstore. A ranger-guided walk takes place most days (10am and 11am). From the visitors center parking lot, hike the short **Pa Ka'oao Trail** (0.4 mile) with views toward the crater.

The **Kīpahulu Visitor Center** (808/248-7375, 9am-4:30pm daily) is on the coast in the southeast portion of the park and has exhibits that offer insights into the Hawaiian culture. A Hawaii Pacific Parks Association bookstore is on-site and park naturalists are available to answer questions. Amenities include a pay phone and restrooms.

SCENIC DRIVE

The **Haleakalā Road** (Rte. 378, 10 mi.) from the park entrance to the summit may be short, but it has two overlooks on the ends of switchbacks. Stop at **Leleiwi Overlook** (mile marker 17.5) and walk the 0.5-mile trail to see the massive crater from this 8,840-foot vantage point. Pull off at **Kalahaku Overlook** (mile marker 18.7) to view the crater from the interpretive observation platform at 9,324 feet. The road terminates at the summit and **Haleakalā Visitor Center**.

RECREATION

HIKING

Haleakalā crater is a vast wilderness with 30 miles of trails and Maui's best hiking. Temperatures can range 30-80°F over the course of a single day and the high elevation (7,000-10,000 feet) can tax lungs.

AVOID THE CROWDS

Sunset at Haleakalā is nearly as colorful as sunrise, but without all the crowds: There are often only 20 people instead of 400, and it isn't as cold. The lava rock ridge just in front of the parking area is the best place to watch the sunset. If you can't see the mountain from below, don't bother driving up.

TRAILS CROSS VOLCANIC CINDER VALLEYS.

Hike Maui (808/784-7982, www.hikemaui.com) is the only company that offers commercially guided hiking tours in the park, both at the summit and at Kīpahulu.

Summit District

The **Hosmer Grove Nature Trail** (0.5 mi. rt., 30 min., easy) is at the park's lower boundary just after the park entrance. The short trail loops through a dense grove of sweet-smelling pine and fir. To extend the trip, hike the **Supply Trail** (4.6 mi. rt., 3 hrs., strenuous) to the crater rim. To reach the trailhead, turn left on the road toward the campground.

From its start at 7,990 feet, the first mile of the **Halemau'u Trail** (7.5 mi. rt., 4-5 hrs., strenuous) meanders through scrub brush before reaching the edge of a giant cliff. The view down into the Ko'olau Gap, where the volcano exploded outward, is better than from the summit. Although the 1,000-foot descent on the switchbacked trail is well defined, the drop-offs can be disconcerting. The trail reaches Holua Cabin, where you need a permit to camp overnight.

Near mile marker 17.5 at 8,840 feet, **Leleiwi Overlook** (0.5 mi. rt., 30 min., easy) sees smaller crowds and is usually warmer than the summit. Views look down on the huge floor of the crater and the sheer multihued cliffs.

From the summit visitors center at 9,800 feet, the **Keonehe'ehe'e Trail** (8 mi. rt., 5 hrs., strenuous) descends to the crater floor. This barren and windswept trail is without shade, and with a 2,500-foot elevation loss, but it's a stunning conduit to the cinder cones.

SILVERSWORD

Best Hike

SLIDING SANDS SWITCHBACK LOOP

DISTANCE: 12.2 miles round-trip
DURATION: 7-8 hours
ELEVATION CHANGE: 1,000-2,500 feet
EFFORT: strenuous
TRAILHEAD: Halemau'u

The **Sliding Sands Switchback Loop** is the best day hike in the summit area. Park at the Halemau'u trailhead, then hitch a ride to the top to hike down to the crater floor on the Sliding Sands Trail. Follow the signs toward Holua Cabin and the Halemau'u Trail, where a leg-burning, switchbacking, 1,000-foot climb leads back to the car.

Kīpahulu District

From the Kīpahulu Visitor Center, the **Kuloa Point Trail** (0.5 mi. rt., 30 min., easy) loops past the famed Pools of 'Ohe'o, taking in the ocean views and archeological sites.

The **Pipiwai Trail** (4 mi. rt., 2 hrs., moderate) is a highlight of Kīpahulu. The trail follows boardwalks and footbridges through the rain forest, lending an adventurous feel. The last 0.5 mile winds through bamboo so thick it blocks out the sun. Just when you think it couldn't get any more tropical, the path emerges at the base of 400-foot

WATERFALLS ALONG THE PIPIWAI TRAIL

Waimoku Falls. Plan to camp overnight at the Kīpahulu Campground to hit the trail before the day-trippers arrive. The trailhead is at mile marker 41.7 on the Road to Hana.

BACKPACKING

Backcountry campsites require a permit (free) from the Park Headquarters Visitor Center. The Holua campsite is accessible via a 3.7-mile hike down Halemau'u Trail, while the Paliku campsite requires hiking 9.2 miles from the Sliding Sands Trail at the summit. The Holua campsite is cold and dry; the Paliku campsite is a few degrees warmer and is set in a lush forest.

Three **backcountry cabins** are available at Holua, Kapalaoa, and Paliku and have basic cooking facilities and bunk beds. Reservations (877/444-6777, www.recreation.gov, $75) are required about six months in advance.

BIKING

Bike tours down Haleakalā start at 6,500 feet, outside the national park. If you want to include sunrise at Haleakalā crater, that means waking up early, with pickups at 2am. (After watching the sun rise, it's back in the van for the drive down to the bike start.) Tours without sunrise usually visit the summit at around 10am and then descend to the start of the bike tour.

To rent a bike or book a tour, contact: **Maui Sunriders** (71 Baldwin Ave., Paia, 808/579-8970, www.mauisunriders.com), **Haleakalā Bike Company** (810 Ha'iku Rd., Suite 120, Haiku, 808/575-9575, www.bikemaui.com).

ONE DAY IN HALEAKALĀ

With only one day, aim to drive to the **summit of Haleakalā**. On the road between the Park Headquarters and Haleakalā Summit Visitor Centers, stop to admire the views from roadside overlooks. At the summit, you can stroll to the highest point in the park at 10,023 feet. With advance planning, you can book a reservation to **watch the sunrise** from the summit.

STARGAZING

Haleakalā's elevation and lack of light pollution make the summit a prime location for stargazing. Bring a pair of binoculars or rent them from a local dive shop. Star maps, available at the Haleakalā visitors centers, can help you identify the constellations. Nights can be cold on the summit; bring layers to stay warm.

To observe the night sky through big telescopes with astronomy experts, book a tour with **Maui Stargazing** (808/298-8245, www.mauistargazing.com). The four-hour tour starts at sunset. Their scopes are big enough to see deep-space celestial objects. As a bonus, they bring outerwear and hot chocolate to keep you warm.

BIRD-WATCHING

One of the best bird-watching places is at **Hosmer Grove** on the loop trail. Even if you don't see native honeycreepers (birds whose bills have adapted to extract nectar from native plant species), the treetops chirp with birdsong different from anywhere else on the planet.

Higher up toward the summit, bird-watchers should look for two endangered species: the ʻuʻau (Hawaiian petrel), which burrows in areas near the **summit visitors center**, and the nene (Hawaiian goose), which can be spotted along park roadways and the valley floor. The nene is Hawaii's state bird, and one of the best places to spot it is in the grasslands surrounding **Paliku Cabin**.

VIEW FROM HALEAKALĀ SUMMIT

WHERE TO STAY

INSIDE THE PARK

The park has two first-come, first-served campgrounds. The more accessible is **Hosmer Grove Campground** (drinking water available) at 6,800 feet in the Summit District. Its grassy sites can pack in up to 50 campers. Nights can get close to freezing, but it makes a great staging ground for driving to the summit for sunrise.

Some of Maui's best camping is on the coast at the **Kīpahulu Campground** (drinking water available at the visitors center). The grassy campsites can fit up to 100 people; the best sites are hidden beneath *lauhala* trees on the trail leading toward the pools.

Each has picnic tables, barbecue grills, and pit toilets. Camping fees are included in the park entrance fee.

OUTSIDE THE PARK

Most accommodations in **Makawao, Pa'ia,** and **Kula** are conveniently located within an hour's drive of Haleakalā summit. Near the Kīpahulu coast, the closest services are in **Hana.**

GETTING THERE AND AROUND

AIR

Kahului Airport (OGG, 1 Kahului Airport Rd., 808/872-3830, www.hawaii. gov) has direct flights to a host of mainland cities. Car rentals are at the airport.

CAR

To reach the Summit District from Kahului, take Route 37 to Route 377 where it meets Route 378. The Summit District of Haleakalā National Park is located at the end of Route 378. The curvy drive has multiple switchbacks and will take about 2.5-3 hours to reach the summit. The last gas en route is in Pukalani.

To reach the coastal Kīpahulu District, you'll have to drive the Road to Hana. From Kahului, take Route 36 to Route 360, then to Route 31. Kīpahulu is 12 miles past Hana. The narrow, curvy, and partially unpaved drive will take approximately four hours. Fill up on gas

WILDFLOWERS

before you go; the last gas on the way to Hana is in Paia. Plan to depart Hana early in the day so that you won't be driving the rough road in the dark.

There is no public transit—and no gas stations—within the park.

TOURS

Several tour companies guide trips to Haleakalā summit for sunrise, sunset, or daytime visits, as well as excursions on the Road to Hana and to Kīpahulu. Vehicles range from buses to minivans and all tours include narration. The following guide companies are licensed in the park: **Polynesian Adventures** (888/206-4531, www.polyad.com), **Temptation Tours** (800/817-1234 or 808/877-8888, www.temptationtours. com), **Roberts Hawaii** (808/539-9400, www.robertshawaii.com), and **Maui Tours** (808/871-5224, www.tourmaui. com).

SIGHTS NEARBY

Wai'anapanapa State Park (mile 32, Road to Hana, 808/984-8109, http:// hawaiistateparks.org) has volcanic features from Haleakalā, including a black-sand beach, natural arch, lava tubes, blowholes, and caves.

Polipoli Spring State Recreation Area (Kula, 808/984-8109, http://ha-waiistateparks.org) flanks Haleakalā with a forest preserve, camping, and hiking trails.

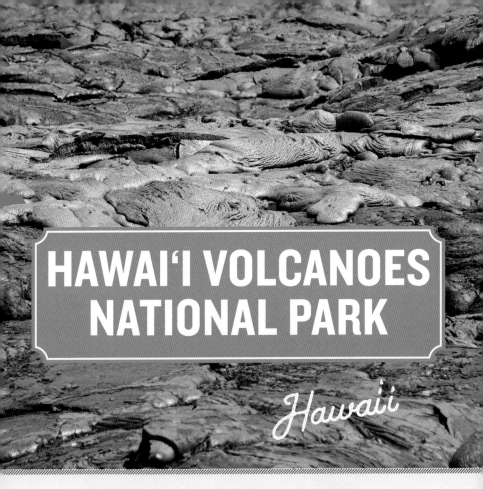

HAWAI'I VOLCANOES NATIONAL PARK

Hawai'i

WEBSITE:
www.nps.gov/havo

PHONE NUMBER:
808/985-6000

VISITATION RANK:
14

WHY GO:
Watch a volcano in action.

▲ LAVA ON THE COASTAL PLAIN

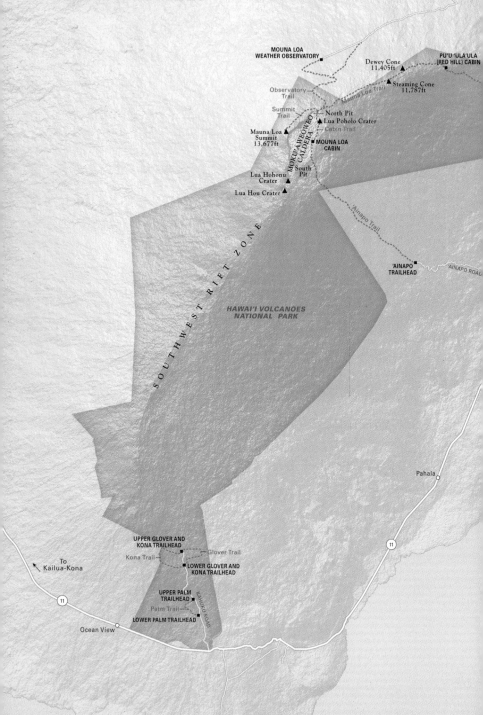

HAWAI'I VOLCANOES
NATIONAL PARK

MOUNA LOA
WEATHER OBSERVATORY

Dewey Cone
11,405ft

PU'U 'ULA'ULA
(RED HILL) CABIN

Observatory
Trail

Steaming Cone
11,787ft

Summit
Trail

North Pit
Lua Poholo Crater

Cabin Trail

Mauna Loa
Summit
13,677ft

MOUNA LOA
CABIN

South
Pit

Lua Hohonu
Crater

Lua Hou Crater

'Ainano Trail

'AINAPO
TRAILHEAD

'AINAPO ROAD

SOUTHWEST RIFT ZONE

HAWAI'I VOLCANOES
NATIONAL PARK

Pahala

UPPER GLOVER AND
KONA TRAILHEAD

Glover Trail

To
Kailua-Kona

Kona Trail

LOWER GLOVER AND
KONA TRAILHEAD

UPPER PALM
TRAILHEAD

Palm Trail

LOWER PALM TRAILHEAD

KAHUKU ROAD

Ocean View

11

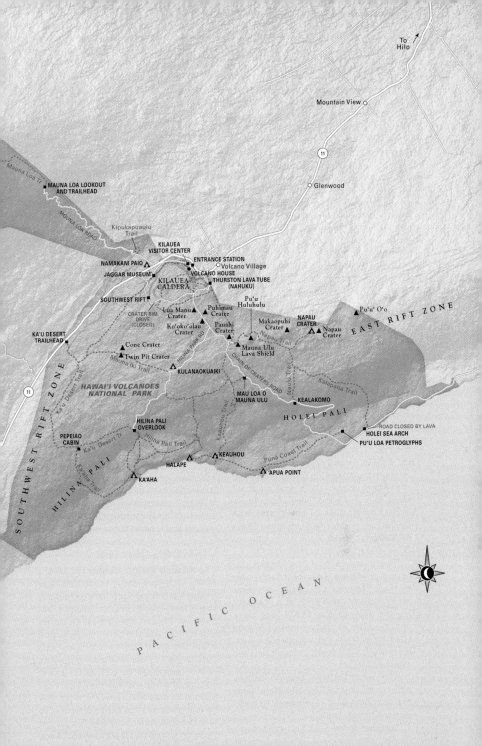

To Hilo

Mountain View

11

Glenwood

Mauna Loa Tr.

MAUNA LOA LOOKOUT
AND TRAILHEAD

MAUNA LOA ROAD

Kipukapuaulu
Trail

KILAUEA
VISITOR CENTER

ENTRANCE STATION

Volcano Village

NAMAKANI PAIO

VOLCANO HOUSE

JAGGAR MUSEUM

THURSTON LAVA TUBE
(NAHUKU)

KILAUEA
CALDERA

Pu'u
Huluhulu

SOUTHWEST RIFT

CRATER RIM
DRIVE
(CLOSED)

Lua Manu
Crater

Puhimau
Crater

Makaopuhi
Crater

NAPAU
CRATER

Pu'u' O'o

KA'U DESERT
TRAILHEAD

Ko'oko'olau
Crater

Pauahi
Crater

Napau
Crater

EAST RIFT ZONE

HILINA PALI ROAD

Cone Crater

Twin Pit Crater

Mauna Iki Trail

Mauna Ulu
Lava Shield

Napau Trail

SOUTHWEST RIFT ZONE

HAWAI'I VOLCANOES
NATIONAL PARK

KULANAOKUAIKI

CHAIN OF CRATERS ROAD

Naulu Trail

Kalapana Trail

Ka'u Desert Trail

MAU LOA O
MAUNA ULU

KEALAKOMO

HOLEI PALI

11

Keauhou Trail

HILINA PALI
OVERLOOK

Hilina Pali Trail

ROAD CLOSED BY LAVA

PEPEIAO
CABIN

HOLEI SEA ARCH

Ka'u Desert Tr.

HILINA PALI

PU'U LOA PETROGLYPHS

KA'AHA

HALAPE

KEAUHOU

Puna Coast Trail

'APUA POINT

PACIFIC OCEAN

0   5 mi

0   5 km

© AVALON TRAVEL

This volcanic landscape fumes steam, pumps sulfur, seethes lava, and lights up a fiery display at night like something out of Dante's Inferno. Viewed from the crater's rim, Kīlauea's volcanic activity highlights the birthing process of the still-growing Hawaiian Islands. **HAWAI'I VOLCANOES NATIONAL PARK** now covers 333,000 acres on the Big Island. Based on its scientific and scenic value, the park was named an International Biosphere Reserve and awarded World Heritage Site status, giving it greater national and international prestige. This is one of the top visitor attractions in the state.

High above Kīlauea, the behemoth Mauna Loa is the largest active volcano on earth. Tiny by comparison, Kīlauea erupts molten lava in the caldera while the ever-changing volcano breaks with fresh cracks spewing lava into the sea. Visitors are impressed by the environmental oddities, such as vastly different landscapes adjacent to each other. Within moments one can pass through a tropical rain forest and into a lunar landscape. Even if this doesn't impress, it will be hard to tear yourself away from the lava flow or glow. It's surreal.

PLANNING YOUR TIME

Located on the Big Island of Hawaii, the park extends north and south off Highway 11. Most visitors head south for the heart of the park: **Kīlauea Caldera.** At 4,000-foot Kīlauea Caldera, expect temperatures 12-15 degrees cooler than the tropical coast, with overcast skies, rain, and wind. The caldera is encircled by 11 miles of the **Crater Rim Drive.** From Crater Rim Drive, the **Chain of Craters Road** leads through lava flows down the *pali* to the coast.

The upper end of the park is the stupendous **Mauna Loa,** reachable only by foot. Mauna Loa Road branches off Highway 11 and ends at a footpath for the trek to the 13,679-foot summit. Weather at the summit of Mauna Loa ranges from freezing to 55°F year-round, with frequent wind, rain, and even blizzards.

The southwestern section of the park is dominated by the **Ka'u Desert**—a desolate, semiarid region crossed by few trails.

Summer (May-Sept.) is high season, though the park appeals year-round. A few tips: Start your visit early. The colors of the park look entirely different in the early morning and it is much quieter before the busloads of tourists arrive. Also, pack a lunch; services within the park are minimal.

ENTRANCE AND FEES

The park entrance is on **Highway 11** (near mile marker 28), west of Volcano Village. The entrance fee is $25-30 per vehicle ($20-25 motorcycle, $12-15 individual) and is good for seven days.

VISITORS CENTER

The **Kīlauea Visitor Center** (808/985-6000, 9am-5pm daily) is located near the park entrance. Stop here to find out the latest conditions on volcanic activity, which can alter access to sights and trails inside the park. Inside, watch a film about the park's geology and volcanism, with tremendous highlights of past eruptions, as well as Hawaiian culture and natural history. The 1959 Kīlauea Iki eruption video (11:30am daily) is a must-see for those planning to hike the trail. Ask about free ranger-led tours and the After Dark in the Park educational interpretive program.

Top ③

1 STAND ON TOP OF KĪLAUEA VOLCANO

Continuously active since 1983, Kīlauea dominates the heart of Hawai'i Volcanoes National Park. Many of the park's sights are along Crater Rim Drive,

KILAUEA CRATER PLUMES

which partly circles the three-mile wide and 400-foot deep **Kīlauea Caldera**. The rumbling volcano steams and spouts lava and is best viewed at night.

2 GAZE OUT FROM MAUNA LOA

At 60 miles long and 30 miles wide, snowcapped Mauna Loa (13,680 feet) occupies the entire southern half of the Big Island. The summit of Mauna Loa contains the giant **Moku'aweoweo Caldera**. Visitors can drive up the 10-mile **Mauna Loa Road** to a lookout at 6,600 feet, but only hikers can reach the summit. This remote mountaintop bastion is the least-visited part of the park but is visible from many locations.

3 TOUR THE CALDERA ALONG CRATER RIM DRIVE

Crater Rim Drive (11 mi., 2-3 hrs.) circles Kīlauea Caldera past steam vents, sulfur springs, and tortured fault lines that always seem on the verge of gaping wide and swallowing the landscape. Along the way, peer into the mouth of Halema'uma'u Crater, home of the fire goddess, Pele.

Start at the **Kīlauea Visitor Center** to get oriented. On the north rim, tour the **Jaggar Museum**, followed by the **Kīlauea Overlook** (marked as a picnic area). Both offer views into the caldera. Afterward, stop at the **steaming vents** pullout, where even the parking lot steams.

To explore the south portion of Crater Rim Dive, return past the visitors center and turn south just before the park entrance. At **Kīlauea Iki Overlook**, the steaming crater floor resembles a desolate desert landscape. Next, stop to walk through the **Nāhuku-Thurston Lava Tube.** Finish at the overlook of the brownish-red cinder cone **Pu'u Pua'i** (Gushing Hill).

KILAUEA IKI VOLCANIC CRATER

ONE DAY IN HAWAI'I VOLCANOES

You can see the park's "greatest hits" in one long day by driving **Crater Rim Road** and **Chain of Craters Road.** Stop at the visitors center and then walk along the **Crater Rim Trail.** Visit the **Thurston Lava Tube** and hike the **Kīlauea Iki Trail.** At night, catch the glow of sunset from the **Jaggar Museum.**

SIGHTS

JAGGAR MUSEUM

Named after the founder of the Hawaiian Volcano Observatory, the **Jaggar Museum** (808/985-6049, 10am-8pm daily, free) has a fantastic multimedia display of the park's geology and volcanology, complete with a miniseries of spectacular photos on movable walls, topographical maps, inspired paintings, and video presentations. Exhibits include an electronic seismograph, lava samples, and volcano monitors. The museum has a bookstore and an interpretive outdoor observation patio for watching Kīlauea eruptions.

VOLCANO ART CENTER GALLERY

Located in the original 1877 Volcano House, the **Volcano Art Center Gallery**

(808/967-8222, http://volcanoartcenter.org, 9am-5pm daily) contains one of the finest art galleries in the state. Featured artists exhibit in a variety of mediums: metal, painting, sculpture, jewelry, photography, and mixed media.

NĀHUKU-THURSTON LAVA TUBE

South of the Kīlauea Iki Overlook is the remarkable **Nāhuku-Thurston Lava Tube.** A paved trail starts as a steep incline that quickly enters a vibrantly green fern forest filled with native birds. The lighted lava tube tunnel takes about 10 minutes to walk through. At the other end, a fantasy world of ferns and moss reappears. From here, the trail leads back to the parking lot.

▼ HAWAI'I VOLCANOES NATIONAL PARK

VIEW FROM CHAIN OF CRATERS ROAD

SCENIC DRIVES
CHAIN OF CRATERS ROAD

At the south end of Crater Rim Drive, the **Chain of Craters Road** (37 mi rt., 1.5 hrs.) drops 3,700 feet in elevation to the coast. En route, the road traverses lava that was laid down about 40 years ago; remnants of the old road can still be seen in spots.

Several craters line the road. **Lua Manu Crater** is a deep depression lined with green vegetation. At **Puhimau Crater,** walk to the viewing stand to peer over the crater's edge. Next, you'll pass **Koʻokoʻolau Crater, Hiʻiaka Crater,** and **Pauahi Crater.** At 9.9 miles is **Kealakomo Lookout,** a picnic area with unobstructed views of the coast. The road then heads over the edge of the *pali* and diagonally down to the flats. The last section of road runs close to the sea, where cliffs rise up from the pounding surf. Near the end of the road is the **Holei Sea Arch,** where wave action has undercut the rock to leave a bridge of stone.

HILINA PALI ROAD

Two miles down Chain of Craters Road, **Hilina Pali Road** (18 mi. rt., 2 hrs.) shoots southwest over a narrow, roughly paved road to Hilina Pali Lookout, on the edge of the rift. Expansive views stretch over the benched coastline. This road is rough, but passable.

MAUNA LOA ROAD

Mauna Loa Road (22 mi. rt., 1.5 hrs.) is a narrow, curvy, and potholed one-lane road that leads to the **Tree Molds** (scattered potholes of entombed tree trunks) and the **Kipuka Puaulu** bird sanctuary, as well as the trailhead for Mauna Loa summit. From its terminus at 6,662 feet, you can overlook Kīlauea below on a clear day. Traveling this road leaves 99 percent of the tourists behind. Find the road 2.5 miles south of the park entrance on Highway 11.

RECREATION
HIKING
Kīlauea Summit

The **Crater Rim Trail** (5 mi. rt., 2.5 hrs., easy) starts at the Jaggar Museum and heads toward the visitors center for unparalleled views of the vast Kīlauea Caldera. Desert-like conditions with sparse vegetation eventually give way to lush native tropical forests. Stops include the **Steam Vents,** where water heated by the volcano rises from cracks in the earth.

Best Hike

KĪLAUEA IKI TRAIL

DISTANCE: 4 miles round-trip
DURATION: 3 hours
ELEVATION CHANGE: 400 feet
EFFORT: moderate
TRAILHEAD: Kīlauea Iki Overlook

In 1959, lava spewed 1,900 feet into the air from a 0.5-mile crack in the Kīlauea crater wall. Within weeks, 17 separate lava flow episodes occurred, creating a lake of lava now known as **Kīlauea Iki** (Little Kīlauea). From the Kīlauea Iki Overlook, the **Kīlauea Iki Trail** (4 mi. rt., 3 hrs., moderate) leads 400 feet from the rim into the crater where lush tropical rain forest fills the volcanic floor.

At the Kīlauea Visitor Center, the paved **Ha'akulamanu Trail** (0.5 mi. rt., 15 min., easy), also called **Sulphur Banks,** explores fumaroles surrounded by red-brown earth covered in yellow-green sulfur.

Behind Volcano House, the paved and wheelchair-accessible **Earthquake Trail** (1 mi rt., 30 min., easy) leads to the **Waldron Ledge** for superb views of Kīlauea Caldera. The trail is so named due to damage this area incurred during a 6.6-magnitude earthquake.

From the Pu'u Pua'I Overlook, the paved **Devastation Trail** (1 mi. rt., 30 min., easy) heads across a field ravaged by the Kīlauea Iki eruption and one of the most photographed areas in the park.

Chain of Craters Road

The **Pu'u Huluhulu Trail** (2.5 mi. rt., 2-3 hrs., moderate) climbs 210 feet to the summit of a steaming volcanic crater with 360-degree panoramic views. Start the hike from the Mauna Ulu Trailhead.

The **Pu'u Loa Petroglyphs** (1.5 mi. rt., 1 hr., easy) trail follows a boardwalk encircling most of the petroglyphs, ensuring protection for the designs. Some rocks are entirely covered with designs, while others have only a symbolic scratch or two.

Guided Hikes

At the visitors center, the ranger-led **Exploring the Summit hike** (45 min., 10:30am and 1:30pm daily) tours the rim and provides information about Hawaiian history and geology.

Friends of Hawaii Volcanoes National Park (808/985-7373, http://fh-vnp.org) tour guides are retired park rangers and wildlife biologists. Tours are on demand and transportation is not provided. Other guided hikes are led by **Native Guide Hawaii** (808/982-7575, www.nativeguidehawaii.com).

BACKPACKING

A permit is required for most trails outside the Crater Rim Drive area and the coastal stretch beyond the end of Chain of Craters Drive. Permits can be obtained in person from the Backcountry Office at the **Visitor Emergency Operations Center** (Crater Rim Dr., daily 8am-4pm) the day prior to your hike. Reservations are not accepted.

Halapē

From the Hilina Pali Overlook on Hilina Pali Road, the **Hilina Pali Trail** (15.4 mi. rt., 2-3 days) descends across hot, dry, rugged terrain. It drops straight down the *pali* (cliff) with multiple switchbacks to a junction, where the hot, steep left fork yo-yos up and down to **Halape**. The reward is a sugary beach and a sheltered lagoon with backcountry campsites and bathroom facilities.

Mauna Loa

An extreme hike, Mauna Loa is a grueling climb to the 13,679-foot summit of the island's largest volcano. There are two trail options.

From the terminus of Mauna Loa Road, the **Mauna Loa Road Trail** (36 mi. rt., 3-4 days) ascends 6,600 feet over 18 miles to the **Pu'u 'Ula'ula cabin**

(Red Hill, 4-6 hrs., 7.5 mi. one-way). The next day, climb 11.5 miles to the **Mauna Loa summit cabin** (8-12 hrs. one-way) on the caldera's rim. Both cabins (permit required, $10) have bunks and pit toilets.

A shorter but still ultra-strenuous trail to the summit goes from Mauna Loa Observatory trailhead outside the park, a two-hour drive via Saddle Road.

The **Mauna Loa Observatory Trail** (7.6 mi. rt., 7-9 hrs.) climbs 1,975 feet over 3.8 miles up the volcano's north slope to the rim of the Moku'aweoweo Caldera (the summit). The Mauna Loa summit cabin is 2.1 miles. The Mauna Loa Observatory trailhead is outside the park, a two-hour drive via Saddle Road.

On either trail, be prepared for altitude sickness, winter conditions, and changes in weather. Staying hydrated is imperative.

BIKING

Bring your bike along to cruise the paved **Crater Rim Drive** (11 mi.), the moderate **Hilina Pali Road** (18 mi. rt.), or the challenging **Mauna Loa Road** (11.5 mi. rt.). The classic challenge follows the **Summit to Sea** (36 mi. rt.)—the path of the Mauna Ulu eruption on the Chain of Craters Road. Biking maps are available from the visitors center.

You can also take a guided bike tour with **Bike Volcano** (808/934-9199, www.bikevolcano.com) or **Nui Pohaku** (808/937-0644, www.nuipohaku.com).

WHERE TO STAY
INSIDE THE PARK

Volcano House (1 Crater Rim Dr., 808/756-9625 or 866/536-7972, www. hawaiivolcanohouse.com, from $250) is the only hotel inside the park. Dating from the 1940s, it has the feel of a country inn, but with updated decor and facilities. From its rim location, you can see the glow of the crater from your window. Inside, **Uncle George's Lounge** (11am-10pm daily) and **The Rim Restaurant** (breakfast 7am-10am, lunch 11am-2pm, dinner 5:30pm-9pm daily) have priceless views of the crater.

North of the caldera at 4,000 feet elevation, **Nāmakanipaio Campground and Cabins** (Hwy. 11, 808/756-9625 or 866/536-7972, www.hawaiivolcanohouse.com, reservations recommended) has Spartan A-frame cabins (from $80) that sleep up to four people with a double bed and two single bunks. Linens, soap, towels, a blanket, and an electric light are provided, but there are no electrical outlets. The campground is a large grassy area surrounded by trees.

THE TRAIL TO THE PU'U LOA PETROGLYPHS

Rent a tent ($55) or bring your own ($15, no hookups). Cabins and campsites have picnic tables, fire pits, and communal restrooms with showers.

South of the caldera off the Chain of Craters Road, **Kulanaokuaiki Campground** (Hilina Pali Rd., $10) has nine first-come, first-served sites at 2,700 feet. Facilities include picnic tables and a vault toilet, but no drinking water.

Kīlauea Military Camp (Hilina Pali Rd., 808/967-8333, http://kilaueamilitarycamp.com) is where military families vacation. Two eateries are open to the public: **Crater Rim Café** (6:30am-1pm Mon.-Fri., 6:30am-11am Sat.-Sun., and 5pm-8pm daily) and **Lava Lounge** (4pm-close Mon.-Sat.).

OUTSIDE THE PARK

Volcano Village has accommodations and restaurants. Most are on Old Volcano Road, the inner road that parallels Highway 11 through town.

GETTING THERE AND AROUND
AIR

Most direct mainland-Big Island flights land at the **Ellison Onizuka Kona International Airport** (KOA, Keahole Airport Rd., 808/329-3423, http://airports.hawaii.gov/koa) on the island's west side. Some planes land on the east side

TREE MOLD

at **Hilo International Airport** (ITO, 808/961-9321, Kekuanaoa St., http://airports.hawaii.gov/ito). Both airports have car rentals.

CAR

From Kailua-Kona, drive southeast on Highway 11 for 96 miles (2.5 hrs.) to the park entrance. From Hilo, take Highway 11 southwest for 30 miles (45 min.).

Hele-On Bus (808/961-8744, www.heleonbus.org) connects Hilo with the Kīlauea Visitor Center and Volcano Village. Once inside the park, there is no public transit.

TOURS
Bus Tours

Bus tours depart from Big Island locations to tour the national park. Hilo-based tours include **Roberts Hawaii** (808/966-5483, www.robertshawaii.com) and **Kapoho Kine Adventures** (25 Waianuenue Ave., Hilo, 808/964-1000, www.kapohokine.com). From the Kona side, **Hawaii Forest and Trails** (808/331-8505, www.hawaii-forest.com) offers a 12-hour round-trip adventure of the main park sights.

Helicopter Tours

A dramatic way to experience the volcano's power is via a helicopter. **Sunshine Helicopters** (808/882-1851 or 866/501-7738, www.sunshinehelicopters.com) fly from the island's north end. **Blue Hawaiian Helicopters** (808/886-1768 in Waikoloa, 800/745-2583, www.bluehawaiian.com) operates tours from the Kona and Hilo sides.

SIGHTS NEARBY

Puʻuhonua O Hōnaunau National Historical Park (Honaunau, Hwy. 160, 808/328-2326, www.nps.gov/puho) preserves the traditional Hawaiian place of refuge for lawbreakers. Sights include a temple, rock walls, and carved wooden statues.

Kaloko-Honokōhau National Historical Park (73-4786 Kanalani St. #14, Kailua-Kona, 808/329-6881, ext. 1329, www.nps.gov/kaho) is the site of a traditional Hawaiian village with petroglyphs, a temple, house sites, and fishponds.

VIRGIN ISLANDS NATIONAL PARK

U.S. Virgin Islands

PASSPORT STAMPS ▼▼▼

WEBSITE:
www.nps.gov/viis

PHONE NUMBER:
340/776-2601

VISITATION RANK:
44

WHY GO:
Snorkel and dive
amid coral reefs.

▲ TRUNK BAY, ST. JOHN ISLAND

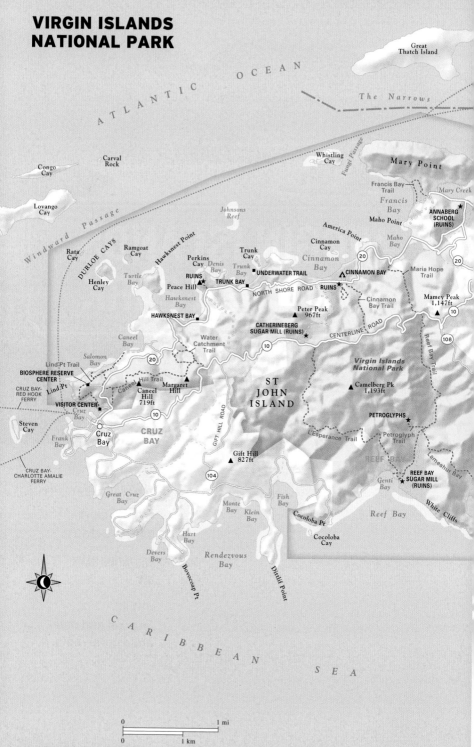

VIRGIN ISLANDS NATIONAL PARK

ATLANTIC OCEAN

Great Thatch Island

The Narrows

Mary Point

Carval Rock

Whistling Cay

Congo Cay

Francis Bay Trail

Mary Creek

Francis Bay

Lovango Cay

ANNABERG SCHOOL (RUINS)

Maho Point

Maho Bay

America Point

Rata Cay

Ramgoat Cay

Hawksnest Point

Cinnamon Cay

Cinnamon Bay

20

Maria Hope Trail

Henley Cay

Turtle Bay

Perkins Cay

Trunk Cay

CINNAMON BAY

Mamey Peak 1,147ft

RUINS

Denis Bay

UNDERWATER TRAIL

Cinnamon Bay Trail

10

Peace Hill

TRUNK BAY

NORTH SHORE ROAD

RUINS

Hawksnest Bay

Trunk Bay

Peter Peak 967ft

Reef Bay Trail

108

HAWKSNEST BAY

CATHERINEBERG SUGAR MILL (RUINS)

CENTERLINE ROAD

Caneel Bay

Water Catchment Trail

Virgin Islands National Park

Salomon Bay

20

10

BIOSPHERE RESERVE CENTER

Lind Pt Trail

Caneel Hill Trail

Margaret Hill

ST JOHN ISLAND

Camelberg Pk 1,193ft

CRUZ BAY–RED HOOK FERRY

Lind Pt

Caneel Hill 719ft

PETROGLYPHS

VISITOR CENTER

10

Petroglyph Trail

Steven Cay

Cruz Bay

CRUZ BAY

L'Esperance Trail

Lameshur Bay

REEF BAY

Frank Bay

GIFT HILL ROAD

104

Gift Hill 827ft

Genti Bay

REEF BAY SUGAR MILL (RUINS)

CRUZ BAY–CHARLOTTE AMALIE FERRY

Great Cruz Bay

Monte Bay

Fish Bay

Cocoloba Pt

Reef Bay

White Cliffs

Klein Bay

Cocoloba Cay

Hart Bay

Devers Bay

Rendezvous Bay

Bovocoup Pt

Ditrlif Point

CARIBBEAN SEA

0   1 mi
0   1 km

© AVALON TRAVEL

Windward Passage

DURLOE CAYS

Johnsons Reef

Fungi Passage

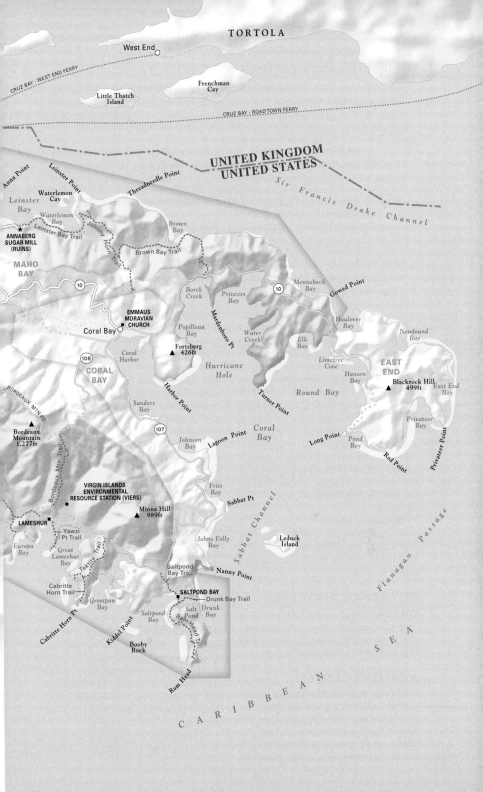

More than 60 percent of the island of St. John is protected within **VIRGIN ISLANDS NATIONAL PARK.** Its 20 square miles are home to beaches, coral reefs, and hiking paths that are peaceful, quiet, and unspoiled. Offshore, the island hosts a tropical marine reserve with 302 species of fish. This unique diversity contributes to the park's utter beauty.

For outdoors enthusiasts, there is no better place to explore a tropical wilderness. St. John may be small, but its bays, hills, and reefs hold a seemingly infinite array of sights, sounds, and abundant, vibrant color. As you peel off the layers, you will be surprised, enchanted, and inspired.

Tucked within St. John's scenic coves, bays, and mountainsides is a remarkable history. In 1733 the island was the site of one of the only successful slave revolts in the Caribbean. Ruins of sugarworks and great houses from the plantation era remain for visitors to explore. But even older than the sugar factories are the Taino petroglyphs, evidence that pre-Columbian people once inhabited the island paradise where turquoise water laps onto white-sand beaches.

PLANNING YOUR TIME

The island of St. John is mountainous, with two laid-back hamlets outside the national park boundary. **Cruz Bay,** on the far western end of the island, is where ferries and boats from neighboring islands arrive. **Coral Bay** is a sprawling settlement along a wide, horseshoe-shaped bay on the far eastern end of the island.

December-March is high season, which coincides with the dry season in the islands and offers the best sailing. August-October is the peak of the hurricane season.

ENTRANCE AND FEES

Cruz Bay serves as the park entrance. There is no entrance fee; however, there are amenity fees for **Trunk Bay** ($5) and for overnight mooring ($26).

VISITORS CENTER

The **Cruz Bay Visitor Center** (8am-4:30pm daily) is a good first stop for visitors to the island. A permanent exhibit describes the human and natural history of St. John, and a three-dimensional map helps you get your bearings.

Park rangers are on duty to answer questions and hand out maps and brochures. Outside, the visitors center has shaded picnic tables and public restrooms.

SIGHTS

HONEYMOON BEACH

Honeymoon Beach is a lovely and secluded beach accessible only by the **Lind Point Trail** (1.1 mi.). Set up on the powdery white sand for pleasant views of Lovango, Mingo, and Henley Cays, or snag one of the half-dozen hammocks spaced around the shady interior of the bay. The trailhead is behind the Cruz Bay Visitor Center.

HAWKSNEST BEACH

Hawksnest Bay is home to glorious **Hawksnest Beach,** a wide, long strip of pale sand fringed by a canopy of mature trees and sandwiched between rock promontories. Hawksnest is the closest beach you can drive to from Cruz Bay.

At the top of the headland between Hawksnest and Trunk Bays is **Peace**

CINNAMON BAY BEACH

Hill, a grassy knoll and windmill ruin with beautiful views.

TRUNK BAY

Trunk Bay (7:30am-4:30pm daily, $4 per person) is St. John's most magnificent beach and its most popular, a vision of fluffy white sand, sea grape trees, and coconut palms. Named for the leatherback turtles that nest here, Trunk Bay is a long beach—even at its most crowded you will find some quiet. Facilities include lifeguards and restrooms. An underwater snorkel trail lies along Trunk Cay, just offshore.

CINNAMON BAY

Cinnamon Bay is home to an excellent beach, extensive ruins, a hiking trail, and some of St. John's best water sports. The long and winding shore gives way to expansive **Cinnamon Beach,** where the fine white sand creates a wide, shallow bank ideal for snorkeling on the reef about 100 yards from shore.

Explore the remains of the bay's 1680 colonial settlement at the **Cinnamon Bay Ruins,** across the street from the beach. A self-guided 0.5-mile walk leads through the ruins of a sugar factory, an estate house, bay rum stills, and a small Danish cemetery.

MAHO BAY BEACH

Maho Bay is a long, narrow beach well protected from surf, which makes it a good destination for stand-up paddleboarding and swimming.

FRANCIS BAY

Francis Bay is a great place for swimming and is home to the best bird-watching on St. John, especially at **Francis Bay Pond.** A small coral reef at the western end of **Francis Bay Beach** is perfect for beginning snorkelers. The **Francis Bay Trail** (0.5 mile) passes through a crumbling great house "ruin" before reaching an overlook with a view of the pond before ending at the beach.

ANNABERG RUINS

In 1844, two government schools were constructed on St. John (then called the Danish West Indies). The **Annaberg School ruins** are a short distance

RUINS OF THE ANNABERG SUGAR MILL

from the road to the Annaberg Plantation. Climb the steps for the best views. A display describes the history of the school.

The ruins of the **Annaberg Sugar Mill** are the best place to learn about the colonial-era life of both planters and slaves on St. John. The site includes the ruins of a windmill, a sugar factory, a mill round, a rum still, and slave quarters. An 0.25-mile paved trail meanders through the grounds past interpretive signs that describe the ruins.

LEINSTER BAY

Calm **Leinster Bay Beach** is covered with packed, coarse yellow sand and fringed by shade trees. It's a decent place to swim and snorkel. From the beach, hike 0.25 mile up the **Johnny Horn Trail** to reach great house ruins once associated with the Annaberg estate.

WATERLEMON CAY

Waterlemon Cay is a tiny offshore islet a 0.2-mile swim (and a 0.8-mile hike) from Leinster Bay Beach—and home to the best snorkeling on St. John. A shallow reef fringes the protected side of the cay, deepening to 20 feet with an intricate diversity of coral life.

HURRICANE HOLE

Hurricane Hole (Borck Creek, Princess Bay, and Water Creek) is a critical mangrove ecosystem best explored by kayak or stand-up paddleboard; it takes about an hour to paddle here from Coral Bay. Bring a snorkel to explore the enchanting world amid the knobbed knees and underwater roots of the mangrove trees.

SALTPOND BAY

Remote and uncrowded, **Saltpond Bay** is located near the end of Route 107. After a 10-minute hike to the beach, you can snorkel the underwater landscape around the jagged rocks in the middle of the bay. The site offers picnic tables and pit toilets and is accessible by public transportation.

The extreme southeastern tip of St. John is a narrow finger of land called **Ram Head,** a dramatic place with views of the Caribbean Sea and the irregular foothills of southern St. John. The only way to get here is a 1.2-mile hike (one-way, difficult) from the Saltpond Bay parking lot.

LAMESHUR BAY

Some of St. John's best snorkeling is found around **Great Lameshur Bay** and **Little Lameshur Bay** along the island's south coast. Great Lameshur is scattered with rock and coral; the best snorkeling is on its east side. Little Lameshur has a sand and rubble beach. There is good snorkeling around the rocks that jut out in the middle of the bay.

REEF BAY

Reef Bay was the site of one of the most productive sugar plantations on St. John. The remains of the **Reef Bay Sugar Mill** consist of a well-preserved mill building, handsome stone smokestack, and cattle round. Large copper pots used in the manufacture of sugar lie on the ground outside of the building. The old sugar factory is also home to bats. The ruins of the **Reef Bay Great House** are a short detour off the Lameshur Bay Trail (0.5 mi.). The old great house was one of the largest on St. John.

SCENIC DRIVE
NORTH SHORE ROAD

If you have time for only one driving tour of St. John, make it **North Shore Road** (Route 20). From Cruz Bay, the road enters Virgin Islands National Park in less than 0.5 mile. This is quintessential St. John: powder-white beaches, pristine coral reefs, hiking trails, and awesome overlooks. You can drive along most of the north shore; the journey takes about 20 minutes one-way.

RECREATION
SNORKELING

Snorkeling is the most popular activity on St. John. On the north shore, the **Trunk Bay Underwater Trail** is a good reef for beginners. The 225-yard underwater snorkel trail lies between a series of buoys off the southwestern tip of Trunk Cay. It's a short swim out to the trail, and the area is normally protected from currents and wind.

Jumbie Beach has a shallow, mazelike reef along the eastern side, where you may see lobsters and nurse sharks. **Waterlemon Cay,** accessible

via Leinster Bay, has excellent coral reef snorkeling but is not for beginners.

On the south shore, **Salt Pond Bay** has good reef snorkeling around the two jagged rocks that break the surface of the bay. At **Great Lameshur Bay,** the snorkeling is best along the eastern shore. **Little Lameshur Bay** has snorkeling for beginners just off the western end of the beach.

Maho Bay has offshore seagrass beds that provide food for green turtles, especially in the early morning and late afternoon. **Leinster Bay,** near Annaberg, has nice seagrass beds where you may see sea stars, conch, and turtles. **Brown Bay,** accessible only on foot, has a seagrass bed just offshore.

Mangroves provide a fascinating glimpse into an important marine habitat. The best place for mangrove snorkeling is **Princess Bay,** along Route 10 (East End Road).

Rent snorkel gear from **Crabby's Watersports** (Cocoloba Shopping Center, Coral Bay, 340/714-2415); **Concordia Eco-Resort** (Concordia, 340/693-5855); **Arawak Expeditions** (Mongoose Junction, 340/693-8312); and **Low Key Watersports** (1 Bay St., Cruz Bay, 340/693-8999, http://divelowkey.com). **Virgin Islands Ecotours** (Honeymoon Beach, 340/779-2155, www.viecotours.com) offers a three-hour hike and snorkel on the grounds of Caneel Bay Resort.

DIVING

St. John has several dive sites, including two sites off Cruz Bay. The *Maj. Gen. Rogers,* a 1940 army freighter, was sunk in 1972 to become an artificial reef. The excellent reefs around **Grass Cay** and **Mingo Cay** are good for beginning divers. There is a dizzying array of sealife at **Witch's Hat** on the southern tip of Steven's Cay, just off Cruz Bay.

South shore dives include **Cocoloba,** an easy, sandy reef dive, and **Maple Leaf,** a large offshore reef east of Reef Bay. The most famous east-end dive site is **Eagle Shoal,** between Ram Head and Leduck Island. Access to Eagle Shoal is limited.

Low Key Watersports (Cruz Bay, 340/693-8999, http://divelowkey.com) offers daily dive trips.

ANCIENT PETROGLYPHS ALONG THE REEF BAY TRAIL

KAYAKING

Kayaking is popular off St. John's north shore, where you can paddle up to beaches or out to offshore islets, like Whistling Cay, Waterlemon Cay, or the Durloe Cays.

On the north shore, rent kayaks at **Virgin Islands Ecotours** (Honeymoon Beach, 340/779-2155, www.viecotours. com). For Coral Bay, **Crabby's Watersports** (Cocoloba Shopping Center, 340/714-2415) rents single and two-seater kayaks.

Outfitters include **Arawak Expeditions** (340/693-8312, www.arawak-exp.com) and **Virgin Islands Ecotours** (Honeymoon Beach, 340/779-2155, www.viecotours.com).

HIKING

The most popular hike on St. John is the 2.6-mile **Reef Bay Trail,** (2.6 mi. rt., 5 hrs.), which descends from Centerline Road to the shore at Reef Bay. The trail passes the remains of four different sugar factories, including the extensive Reef Bay ruins, and visits **petroglyphs** that date to about AD 1300-1450.

The **Cinnamon Bay Trail** (1.1 mi., 1 hr.) is an uphill trek that follows an old Danish road all the way to Centerline Road. The trail passes through land that would have been cultivated with sugarcane during the plantation era, now all secondary forest.

The **Yawzi Point Trail** (0.5 mi., 30 min., easy) follows the headland separating Little Lameshur and Great Lameshur Bays. The trail cuts through a dry forest before reaching the point. People suffering from a tropical skin disease were sent to a quarantine camp here in the 18th and 19th centuries.

THE REFLECTING POOL ON THE REEF BAY TRAIL

NUMEROUS BEACHES OFFER RELAXATION.

WHERE TO STAY

INSIDE THE PARK

Two lodgings on St. John are recovering from the 2017 hurricanes: **Cinnamon Bay Resort** (1 Great Cinnamon Bay, St. John, 669/999-8784, https://cinnamonbayresort.com, from $130) and **Caneel Bay Resort** (Caneel Bay, 340/776-6111, U.S. 212/758-1735, www.caneelbay.com, from $549).

A handful of beaches have outdoor cafes or stands: Honeymoon Beach, Trunk Bay, Cinnamon Bay, and Caneel Bay.

OUTSIDE THE PARK

St. John's hotels and villas are among the priciest in the Virgin Islands. A few moderate hotels in **Cruz Bay** offer affordable options.

GETTING THERE

There is no airport on St. John. The closest airport is on **St. Thomas** (SST, Cyril E. King Airport, Airport Rd., Charlotte Amalie West, 340/774-5100, www.viport.com). **Varlack Ventures** (340/776-6412) operates ferries between St. Thomas and Cruz Bay. Ferries leave Charlotte Amalie daily (10am, 1pm, and 5:30pm, $13 one-way).

GETTING AROUND

TAXIS

Taxis are widely available on St. John, especially in Cruz Bay and at the popular north shore beaches. Try **C&C Taxi Service** (340/693-8164) or **St. John Taxi Services** (340/693-7530).

CAR RENTALS

Rental companies based on St. John only rent 4WD sport-utility vehicles suitable for the island's roads. Numerous rental companies are located in or around Cruz Bay. There are two gas stations on St. John, both on the road between Cruz Bay and the Westin Resort.

BUSES

The air-conditioned **VITRAN buses** (340/774-0165, $1) run hourly from Cruz Bay to Coral Bay and Salt Pond Bay, along Centerline Road.

TOURS

Cruz Bay Watersports (888/492-9923, http://cruisebaywatersports.com) offers catamaran trips for sunsets, snorkeling, and beach visits. A number of day-sail operators offer sailing trips around St. John. Contact the activity desks around St. John for sailing operators, availability, and pricing.

NATIONAL PARK OF AMERICAN SAMOA

American Samoa

American Samoa

WEBSITE:
www.nps.gov/npsa

PHONE NUMBER:
684/633-7082

VISITATION RANK:
51

WHY GO:
Explore a tropical
rain forest and
coral reefs.

▲ POLA ISLAND

Remote and difficult to navigate, the **NATIONAL PARK OF AMERICAN SAMOA** anchors itself in a tiny handful of islands in the Samoan archipelago. Located south of the equator, it claims fame as the southernmost national park in the United States. The islands' natural environment includes lush mountains and tropical beaches that cling to shield volcanoes, and the park preserves unique rain forests and coral reefs. Underwater, a prolific tropical marine ecosystem is the definition of biodiversity: It contains 950 species of fish, 250 species of coral, and one of the planet's largest living coral communities.

The National Park of American Samoa pays tribute to traditional Samoan culture, which has survived for 3,000 years on the islands—long before they became a U.S. territory. American Samoa served as a strategic base for U.S. troops during World Wars I and II, and a few historic military sites remain. This small national park racks up nearly 14,000 visits annually, but only a few from off-island.

PLANNING YOUR TIME

Located in the South Pacific (north of Fiji, Tonga, and Tahiti), American Samoa sits just east of the international date line, far south of the equator. The national park is split across several of the Samoan Islands.

Tutuila Island has the largest tract and is the most visited due to its easier access. Sixty miles east are the tiny Manu'a Islands of **Ta'ū** and **Ofu**, reachable by boat. Bring a sense of adventure and a good dose of self-sufficiency, as there are few services. Most of the island is composed of villages rather than towns, and roads can be rough.

High season is **June-September,** when the months are cooler and dry. October-May is the monsoon season, which sees tropical storms. Temperatures range 75-85°F, but oppressive humidity can make it feel much hotter. Rain is frequent, the mosquitoes are ubiquitous, and acute solar radiation can intensify sunburns.

ENTRANCES AND FEES

Pago Pago on Tutuila serves as the main base for the park; Pago Pago International Airport is at the south end of the island. The villages of Vatia, Fagasa,

and Afono are also close to the park boundaries.

On **Ta'ū Island,** the main access point is the boat harbor at Faleasao and Fiti'uta Airport. The village of **Ofu** is the main access point for Ofu.

For entry into American Samoa, visitors must have a passport, return ticket, and confirmation of funds. Upon arrival, nationals from the UK, Australia, and 14 European Union countries may receive 30-day entry permits. Visas are required for all other international travelers.

There is no entrance fee and no official entrance station.

VISITORS CENTER

The **national park visitors center** (8am-4:30pm Mon.-Fri.) is in Pago Pago across from the Pago Way Service Station. Exhibits explore the island's natural history and Samoan culture and rangers advise for trip planning. Field guides and natural history books are sold in the **Hawaii Pacific Parks Association** (www.hawaiipacificparks. org) bookstore. Kids can pick up Junior Ranger activity books to complete for a certificate and badge.

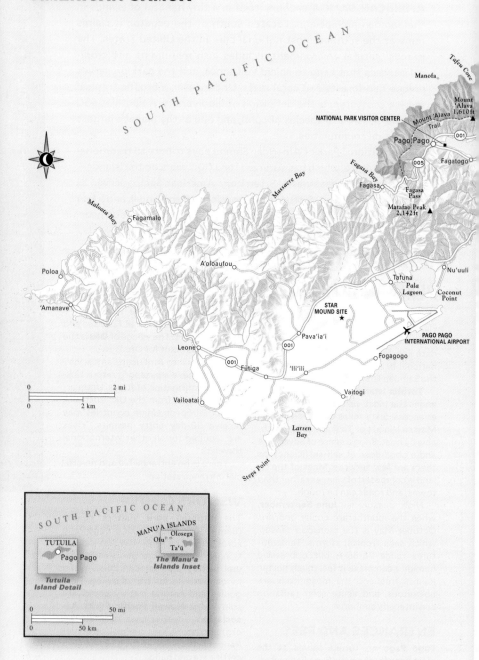

NATIONAL PARK OF AMERICAN SAMOA

SOUTH PACIFIC OCEAN

Manofa

Tafeu Cove

Mount 'Alava 1,610ft

NATIONAL PARK VISITOR CENTER

Mount 'Alava Trail

001

Pago Pago

005

Fagatogo

Fagasa Bay

Fagasa

Fagasa Pass

Matafao Peak 2,142ft

Massacre Bay

Maloata Bay

Fagamalo

A'oloaufou

Nu'uuli

Poloa

Tafuna Pala Lagoon

Coconut Point

'Amanave

STAR MOUND SITE

Pava'ia'i

PAGO PAGO INTERNATIONAL AIRPORT

Leone

001

Fogagogo

Fútiga

'Ili'ili

Vaitogi

Vailoatai

Larsen Bay

| 0 | 2 mi |
| 0 | 2 km |

Steps Point

SOUTH PACIFIC OCEAN

MANU'A ISLANDS

Ofu

Olosega

Ta'ū

The Manu'a Islands Inset

TUTUILA

Pago Pago

Tutuila Island Detail

| 0 | 50 mi |
| 0 | 50 km |

Pola
Island

Vatia Bay
Vatia
Craggy Point
Afono Bay
Amalau
Valley
Ridge
Afono
Maugaloa
Afono Pass
006
Aua
North Pioa
Mountain
1,718ft
Pago Pago
Harbor
Alega
Utulei
001
Faga'alu
001
Fatumafuti
Fatu Rock
Breakers Point

Masefau Bay
Masefau

Masefau Bay

Sa'ilele
'Aoa
Onenoa
Tula
Cape Matatula

Faga'itua

Faga'itua
(bay)

Amouli
Au'asi
001

'Aunu'u
'AUNU'U
ISLAND

Taema Bank

Nafanua Bank

To
Manu'a Islands,
see inset below
→

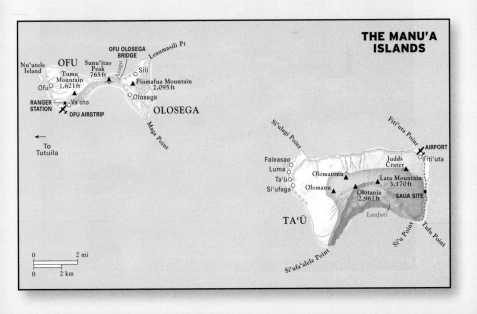

**THE MANU'A
ISLANDS**

Nu'utele
Island
OFU
Sunu'itao
Peak
765ft
OFU OLOSEGA
BRIDGE
Leaumasili Pt
Tumu
Mountain
1,621ft
Ofu
Sili
Piumafua Mountain
2,095ft
RANGER
STATION
Va'oto
Olosega
OFU AIRSTRIP
OLOSEGA

←
To
Tutuila
Maga Point

Si'ulagi Point
Fiti'uta Point
AIRPORT
Faleasao
Fiti'uta
Luma
Ta'ü
Judds
Crater
Si'ufaga
Olomatimu
Olomanu
Lata Mountain
3,170ft
Olotania
2,961ft
SAUA SITE
TA'Ü
Laufuti
Si'u Point
Tufu Point
Si'ufa'alele Point

0   2 mi
0   2 km

TUTUILA ISLAND

VAI'AVA STRAIT

One of the most iconic sights in the national park is **Vai'ava Strait**. Steep, forested, and rocky cliffs plunge into the sea at a gap in between Pola Island and the mainland. Waves cut between the rocks to form the strait while the erosion-resistant volcanic rocks still stand on either side as a geological marvel. The scenic strait is near the village of Vatia on the north coast of the park. For the best views, drive to the pullout 4.1 miles beyond the village of Aüa. You can also see it from the beach at the end of the Lower Sauma Ridge Trail.

MATAFAO PEAK AND RAINMAKER MOUNTAIN

Covered with dense jungle, two landmark mountains stand on either side of Pago Pago Harbor, both created from molten magma. At an elevation of 2,164 feet, **Matafao Peak** is the highest mountain on Tutuila Island. Opposite the harbor sits **Rainmaker Mountain**. To see both, drive Route 001 around the west side of the harbor as it arcs around the base of Matafao. Driving to Äfono Pass from the village of Aüa yields a good view of Rainmaker.

MATAFAO PEAK

BEACHES

Three beaches flank the south and west of Pago Pago International Airport, accessed from Route 001. Take a side trip from Leone Village down Taputima Road to visit **Le'ala Shoreline**, which contains a mix of tropical vegetation, sculpted rocks, and volcanic layers.

NORTH COAST, TUTUILA

POLA ISLAND

West from Leone is the island's westernmost point, **Cape Taputapu**, where waves shaped a conical volcanic rock. To get there, drive west past 'Āmanave Village. When the road veers sharply to the right and uphill, park to the side of the road and walk one mile along the shore to the beach (only accessible at low tide).

Aunu'u Island, located one mile off Tutuila Island, was created from volcanic basalt and tuff. To reach the island, drive to the village of 'Au'asi on the eastern end of Tutuila Island and take the 'Aunu'u Island ferry for the crossing.

HIKING

The **Lower Sauma Ridge Trail** (0.4 mi. rt., moderate) visits archeological sites with interpretive signs en route. The short trail cuts through rain forest until it reaches a beach. At the beach, look across Vatia Bay for views of Vai'ava Strait **National Natural Landmark** and try to spot Pola Island, where seabirds nest.

From the village of Vailoatai, the **Le'ala Shoreline Trail** (3.2 mi. rt., moderate) passes along private land through thick rain forest with broken views of the shore. The steep route weaves through several volcanic craters to finish at the Fagatele Bay Trail. (The trail sits outside the national park, but the shoreline is a National Natural Landmark.)

The **World War II Heritage Trail** (1.7 mi. rt., moderate) passes several World War II historic sites before entering a rain forest loaded with birds. Near the end of the trail, you'll encounter steep steps with rope handrails or ladders and the remains of an old tramway that once carried riders to the top of Mount 'Alava. At 1,610 feet, the summit of the mountain sits on the national park boundary. The trailhead is located between Faga'alu and Utulei on the coast road; a sign next to the IBM Laundromat denotes the path. Park at the nearby public parking lot next to the harbor.

Many trails are primitive or unimproved and cross private land; request permission before hiking.

MANU'A ISLANDS

The remote islands of **Ta'ū** and **Ofu** are located 60 miles east of Tutuila Island. The islands contain half of the National Park of American Samoa, which lines their southern shores. These small, undeveloped islands are home to traditional Samoans who live on farms or in tiny villages. There are no amenities or services. At night, dark skies yield brilliant constellations.

OFU ISLAND

OFU BEACH

HIKING

On Ta'ū, the **Si'u Point Trail** (5.7 mi. rt., moderate) tours a coastal tropical forest on an old dirt roadbed—an extension of the main paved road in Fiti'uta—and passes a cultural history site.

Ofu Island is home to the **Tumu Mountain Trail** (5.5 mi. rt., moderate), which climbs an old road to the top of the highest point on the island at 1,621 feet. From the summit, it follows another trail 0.25 mile to Leolo Ridge where a rocky outcrop overlooks coral lagoons and the three Manu'a Islands. Look for the trailhead near the Ofu Harbor. Though the trail is outside the national park boundary, it yields views inside the national park.

Island trails are rugged, primitive, and undeveloped. Consider hiring a local guide, or check with the park service for options.

SNORKELING

Ofu Beach is one of the best places for snorkeling in American Samoa. Its protected reef lies in easily accessible shallow water, with a diverse range of coral and fish.

WHERE TO STAY

INSIDE THE PARK

The National Park Service runs a **homestay program** for those who want to immerse themselves in Samoan life. Guests live in a Samoan village, learn local customs, and participate in traditional village activities, such as arts and crafts, gardening, collecting fruit, and fishing. Activities vary by location and host family. Each host sets an independent fee for your stay (the transaction is between you and the host, with no park service involvement).

OUTSIDE THE PARK

For lodging outside the park, **Pago Pago** has the most options. Lodging options on the **Manu'a Islands** are extremely limited, but a few are available.

GETTING THERE AND AROUND

The most accessible airport is **Pago Pago International Airport** (PPG, Pago Pago, http://americansamoaport.as.gov) on Tutuila Island. Car rentals are available. From Pago Pago, **Samoa Airways** (684/699-9126 or 684/699-9127, http://samoaairways.com) offers several flights per week to **Fiti'uta Airport** (FAQ), on the island of Ta'ū, or a weekly flight to **Ofu Airport** (Z08) on the island of Ofu.

To get around **Tutuila Island,** take a taxi or the **Agia bus** (Mon.-Sat.), which runs frequently though not on any set schedule. From Fagatogo market, the bus travels to the island's remote corners. Simply flag it down for pickup. The islands of Ta'ū and Ofu have no public transportation or taxis.

SIGHTS NEARBY

National Marine Sanctuary of American Samoa (Pago Pago, 684/633-6500, https://americansamoa.noaa.gov) is the place to go scuba diving in coral reefs with scads of marine life.

ESSENTIALS

THE HISTORY OF THE NATIONAL PARKS

THE FIRST NATIONAL PARK

No country in the world recognized any land as a national park until President Ulysses S. Grant signed a bill in 1872 to create **Yellowstone National Park**. Some countries had nature preserves and lands with national protection, as did the United States, but none set aside national parks for the preservation of unique features and enjoyment by the people.

Yellowstone benefited from champions of preservation such as John Muir and George Bird Grinnell, who laid the groundwork, while artists and photographers documented its features. Expedition leader Ferdinand Hayden in 1871 recommended a national park, an idea suggested to him by Northern Pacific Railway lobbyist A. B. Nettleton, who saw the benefit to train ridership. Hayden's report to Congress included details of Yellowstone's uniqueness, but also pointed out that the land was unsuitable for farming or mining, rendering it useless for development. With Hayden's recommendations also came a warning: to avoid the fate of Niagara Falls, a national treasure surrounded by private development.

In part, the creation of the first national park was a function of bureaucracy. When Yellowstone was created in 1872, the states in which it now resides—Wyoming and Montana—did not yet exist. So, the federal government designated it—a big square on the map with no accommodation for topographical features that would later be included.

But the federal vision fell far short of launching a national park by failing to provide funding or an agency to run Yellowstone. No one really knew what a national park was, except that it was for people to enjoy rather than develop. No legislation protected its natural features and wildlife, and the park's first superintendent—who was unpaid—visited it only twice. Several expeditions surveyed Yellowstone for science, mapping, and exploration, but the park floundered, unfunded and directionless.

Six years after the park's inception, Congress finally appropriated money to "protect, preserve, and improve" Yellowstone. The park's second superintendent, Philetus Norris, built a few primitive roads and constructed a rudimentary station at Mammoth Hot Springs. He hired the park's first gamekeeper to battle poachers. But after Norris, political machinations swapped in a series of useless superintendents, and in its second decade, Yellowstone ran wild. Vandals destroyed natural features, poachers slaughtered wildlife, loggers harvested timber, squatters threw up shelters and camps for tourists, and hot springs facilities were erected as laundries and baths.

The public loved the idea of Yellowstone, but Congress trashed its annual funding in 1886 due to ineffective management. The solution to Yellowstone's lack of oversight turned out to be the **U.S. Army,** already operating out of several forts in the territories of Montana, Idaho, and Wyoming. That year, the army erected Fort Yellowstone in the park to enforce regulations.

Outside the park, bison slaughters fed the booming fur and meat business. The federal government even encouraged them, especially as a means to subdue Native American tribes that relied on bison for food and to force them to move onto reservations. Inside Yellowstone, poachers likewise jeopardized the survival of bison. With eviction from the park as the maximum punishment, the army had no strong clout. After a journalistic outcry at one bison slaughter in Pelican Valley, Congress passed the **National Park Protection Act** in 1894 to protect birds, animals, and natural features in Yellowstone. Guilty violators faced fines and jail.

As the first national park, Yellowstone eventually paved the way for other U.S. national parks. Yosemite and Sequoia National Parks followed in 1890, and Mount Rainier gained parkhood in 1899. With the idea of national parks taking off, the first two decades of the 1900s saw the frenzied addition of 12 more national parks—Crater Lake, Wind Cave, Mesa Verde, Glacier, Rocky Mountain, Lassen Volcanic, Hawai'i Volcanoes, Haleakalā, Denali, Grand Canyon, Zion, and Acadia.

THE NATIONAL PARK SERVICE

Managing the growing number of national parks became problematic. While the U.S. Army units managed Yellowstone and Yosemite, other parks relied on various agencies for oversight. The addition of national monuments, mineral springs, memorials, military parks, and historical sites compounded the problem by taking the total number of federal preservation lands to 35.

By 1910, several national organizations, including the Sierra Club, were lobbying for a new federal agency to take over the national parks and monuments. The U.S. Forest Service opposed the concept, arguing in favor of the timber industry that relied on public lands. Stephen Mather, a conservationist and industrialist, and Horace Albright, a young lawyer, launched a campaign in support of creating the National Park Service, spreading the word via journalist Robert Yard.

Finally, 44 years following the creation of Yellowstone National Park, President Woodrow Wilson put his signature on the 1916 **Organic Act** to establish the **National Park Service**. The act directed the agency to preserve the scenery, natural and historic objects, and wildlife. The act also required the agency provide for the enjoyment of those things in a way that preserved them for future generations.

The new agency was placed under the Department of the Interior, an entirely different branch of the federal government from the Department of Agriculture that oversaw the U.S. Forest Service. To this day, that differentiation in federal management separates the purpose of the national parks and national forests and the way they can be used.

THE PARKS TODAY

National parks were steadily added to the system over the century following the creation of the National Park Service. Today, the NPS oversees 59 national parks and more than 400 public lands. Most recently, since 2000, the Cuyahoga Valley National Recreation Area converted to a national park, as did three national monuments: Congaree, Great Sand Dunes, and Pinnacles.

Many of our parks have gained recognition beyond the country's boundaries. UNESCO (United Nations Educational, Scientific and Cultural Organization) named 15 of the parks as World Heritage Sites and 19 as Biosphere Reserves.

Our national parks protect some of the country's most scenic and unique places. From the first rays of sunlight to hit the country in Acadia to the ice-draped highest peak on the continent in Denali, these national prizes yield visions of raw, uncontrolled beauty. Glacier's ice-scoured mountains, Grand Canyon's deep chasm, and Yosemite's vertical walls remind us of the earth-shaping forces that wrought our landscape. Bison herds wandering in Yellowstone let us connect with our roots, as do the cliff dwellings in Mesa Verde. For those where city lights drown out the stars, the parks are places where the Milky Way still sparkles in the night sky. These parks offer renewal for the human spirit and a regeneration of that deep connection of how we, as humans, fit in the world.

CAR AND RV RENTAL

Most car-rental companies are located in major international airports. To reserve a car in advance, contact **Budget** (U.S. 800/218-7992, outside U.S. 800/472-3325, www.budget.com), **Dollar Rent A Car** (800/800-5252, www.dollar.com), **Enterprise** (855/266-9289, www.enterprise.com), or **Hertz** (U.S. and Canada 800/654-3131, international 800/654-3001, www.hertz.com).

To rent a car, most companies require drivers to be at least 21 years old and have a valid driver's license. Companies may also tack on additional fees for those under age 25. You will also need liability insurance, which you can purchase through the rental company. Private auto insurance also tends to cover rental cars, but check with your insurance company to verify.

The **average cost** of a rental car is $50 per day or $210 per week; however, rates vary greatly based on the time of year and distance traveled. Weekend and summer rentals cost significantly more. Generally, it is more expensive to rent from car rental agencies at an airport. To avoid excessive rates, first plan travel to areas where a car is not required, then rent a car from an agency branch in town to further explore more rural areas. Rental agencies occasionally allow vehicle drop-off at a different location from where it was picked up for an additional fee.

Another option is to rent an **RV.** You won't have to worry about camping or lodging options, and many facilities, particularly farther north, accommodate RVs. However, RVs are difficult to maneuver and park, limiting your access to some trailheads and sights in national parks. Be aware that some national park roads ban RVs or restrict length. They are also expensive, both in terms of gas and the rental rates. Rates during the summer average $1,300 per week and $570 for three days, the standard minimal rental. **Cruise America** (800/671-8042, www.cruiseamerica.com) has branches throughout the United States.

ROAD CONDITIONS

Road closures are not uncommon, especially in winter in mountain parks. Traffic jams, accidents, mudslides, fires, and snow can affect interstates and local highways at any time. Before heading out on your adventure, check road conditions online with the state highway department.

In an emergency, **dial 911** from any phone. The American Automobile Association, better known as **AAA** (800/222-4357, www.aaa.com), offers roadside assistance free to members; others pay a fee.

Be aware of your car's maintenance needs while on the road. The most frequent maintenance needs result from **summer heat.** If the car gets hot or overheats, stop for a while to cool it off. Never open the radiator cap if the engine is steaming. After the engine cools, squeeze the top radiator hose to see if there's any pressure in it; if there isn't, it's safe to open. Never pour water into a hot radiator because it could crack the engine block. If you start to smell rubber, your tires are overheating, and that's a good way to have a blowout. Stop and let them cool off. When descending steep mountain roads, use lower gears for the engine to force a slowdown rather than riding your brakes and wearing them down. During **winter**, a can of silicone lubricant such as WD-40 will unfreeze door locks, dry off humid wiring, and keep your hinges in shape. Mountain parks may require chains or traction devices for winter access.

MAPS AND GPS NAVIGATION

Always travel with a printed map or guide; do *not* rely solely on GPS navigation, which is notoriously unreliable inside the national parks. Some park travelers relying on GPS get led to the wrong location, into dead-ends, or onto closed roads, snowbound passes, or defunct roads. Carry printed, up-to-date road maps and learn how to read them. Check seasonal access and weather conditions for all driving routes prior to travel.

Upon entering any national park and paying the park entrance fee, you'll be offered a free park map. These maps are good for paved road navigation and locating services, but they are not detailed enough for backcountry trails or rough, 4WD roads. For more detailed maps, download maps from **National** Geographic (www.natgeomaps.com) or order them from the **USGS** (http://store.usgs.gov).

INTERNATIONAL DRIVERS LICENSES

If visiting the United States from another country, you need to secure an International Driving Permit from your home country before coming to the United States. (It can't be obtained once you're here.) You must also bring your government-issued driving permit.

Visitors from outside the United States should check the driving rules of the states they will visit at www.usa.gov. Among the most important rules is that traffic runs on the right side of the road in the United States. Note that many states have bans on using handheld cell phones while driving. If caught, expect to pay a hefty fine.

HEALTH AND SAFETY

HOSPITALS AND EMERGENCIES

Most national parks tuck into remote locations, where emergency services take longer to respond. Often, hospitals, emergency rooms, and urgent care facilities are located outside the national parks in nearby towns several hours away. The larger parks with huge visitation numbers may have an urgent care clinic.

If you are injured in a park, **dial 911** (if you have phone service) or the park phone number for emergencies. If phone service is not available, flag down a ranger or passing motorist to get help instead. Due to the remote locations of many national parks, do not rely on having cell phone service to call for help.

WILDERNESS SAFETY

For hikers, backpackers, mountain bikers, climbers, and river travelers, be prepared to handle emergencies on your own. Be competent in administering first aid, self-rescuing, and providing your own evacuation. Rely only on calling for help in life-threatening situations or where severe injuries prevent being able to get out on your own.

HEAT EXHAUSTION AND HEATSTROKE

Being out in the elements can present its own set of challenges. Heat exhaustion and heatstroke can affect anyone during the hot summer months, particularly during a long strenuous hike in the sun. Common symptoms include nausea, lightheadedness, headache, or muscle cramps.

DEHYDRATION

Many first-time hikers to high mountain or arid parks are surprised to find they drink more water than at home. Wind, sun, altitude, and lower humidity can add up to a fast case of dehydration. It manifests first as a headache. While hiking, drink lots of water, even more than you normally would. With children, monitor their fluid intake. For hiking desert parks, plan to carry and drink a gallon of water per person per day. Before launching at a trailhead, consult with rangers about current reliable water sources.

HYPOTHERMIA

Exhausted and physically unprepared hikers are at risk for insidious and subtle hypothermia. The body's inner core loses heat, reducing mental and physical functions. Watch for uncontrolled shivering, incoherence, poor judgment, fumbling, mumbling, and slurred speech. Avoid becoming hypothermic by staying dry. Don rain gear and warm moisture-wicking layers, rather than cottons that won't dry and fail to retain heat. Get hypothermic hikers into dry clothing and shelter. Give warm non-alcoholic and non-caffeinated liquids. If the victim cannot regain body heat, get into a sleeping bag with the victim, both stripped for skin-to-skin contact.

HYPERNATREMIA

Often occurring in hotter, arid parks, hypernatremia is an imbalance of sodium. Taking electrolytes with fluids prevents the onset of nausea, weakness, and loss of appetite that accompanies hypernatremia. More severe symptoms may include confusion and twitching muscles.

POISON OAK, IVY, AND SUMAC

Poison oak, ivy, and sumac are vines or shrubs that inhabit forests. Common in western states, poison oak has three scalloped leaves. Found across the United States except for tropical islands and Alaska, poison ivy has three spoon-shaped leaves and grows along rivers, lakes, and oceans. With 7-13 leaflets, poison sumac grows in wet, swampy zones in the north and Florida. Contact with these plants may cause a rash and itching, which can be transferred to your eyes or face via touch. Your best protection is to wear long sleeves and long pants when hiking, no matter how hot it is. Tecnu can protect your skin from poison oak and ivy. Calamine lotion can help ease the rash and itching.

GIARDIA

Lakes and streams can carry parasites like *Giardia lamblia*. If ingested, it causes cramping, nausea, and severe diarrhea for up to six weeks. Avoid giardia by boiling water (for one minute, plus one minute for each 1,000 feet of elevation above sea level) or using a one-micron filter. Bleach also works (add two drops per quart and wait 30 minutes). Tap water in campgrounds, hotels, and picnic areas has been treated; you'll taste the chlorine.

ALTITUDE

Some visitors from sea-level locales feel the effects of altitude at high elevations in mountain parks of the Rockies and the Sierra. Watch for lightheadedness, headaches, or shortness of breath. To acclimatize, slow down the pace of hiking and drink lots of fluids. If symptoms spike, descend in elevation as soon as possible. Altitude also increases UV radiation exposure: To prevent sunburn, use a strong sunscreen and wear sunglasses and a hat.

WILDLIFE
BEARS

Many of the national parks are home to **black bears** and **grizzly bears.** Food is the biggest bear attractant. Bears are dangerous around food, be it a carcass in the woods, pack on a trail, or cooler in a campsite. Proper use, storage, and handling of food and garbage prevents bears from being conditioned and turning aggressive.

On the trail, pick up any dropped food, including wrappers and crumbs, and pack out all garbage. When camping, use low-odor foods, keep food and cooking gear out of sleeping sites in the backcountry, and store them inside your vehicle in front-country campgrounds.

▶ BLACK BEAR, YELLOWSTONE

WILDLIFE SAFETY TIPS

While you may see bison, elk, moose, deer, pronghorn, wolves, coyote, or bears, remember that wildlife is just that . . . WILD. Though bison, elk, or even bears may appear tame, they are not and gorings are common. Here are a few tips to remain safe.

Do not approach wildlife. Crowding wildlife puts you at risk and endangers the animal, often scaring it off. Seemingly docile bison and elk have suddenly gored people crowding too close. Stay at least **100 yards away** (the length of a football field) from bears and wolves. For all other wildlife, stay at least **25 yards away.**

For spying wildlife up close, use a good pair of **binoculars** or a **spotting scope.** Use telephoto lenses for photography.

Take safe selfies. Bison gorings are more prevalent now, and many are related to taking selfie photos with tablets or cell phones. Avoid getting too close and maintain a distance of 25-100 yards between yourself and all wildlife.

Do not feed any animal. Feeding can amp up their aggression; because human food is not part of their natural diet, they may suffer at foraging on their own.

Follow instructions for food storage. Bears, wolves, and coyote may become more aggressive when acquiring food, and ravens can strew food and garbage, making it more available to other wildlife.

Let the animal's behavior guide your behavior. If the animal appears twitchy, nervous, or points eyes and ears directly at you, back off: You're too close. If you behave like a predator stalking an animal, the creature will assume you are one.

If you see **wildlife along a road,** use pullouts or broad shoulders to drive completely off the road. Use the car as a blind to watch wildlife, and keep pets inside. Watch for cars, as visitors can be injured by inattentive drivers whenever a wildlife jam occurs.

Bear Bells vs. Pepper Spray

On trails in grizzly bear country (Alaska, Washington, Idaho, Montana, and Wyoming), you'll hear jingle bells, sold in gift shops as **bear bells.** While making noise on the trail does prevent surprising a bear, bear bells are not a substitute for human noise on the trail in the form of talking, singing, hooting, and hollering.

Most hikers in grizzly bear country carry an eight-ounce can of **pepper spray,** which deters bear attacks without injuring the bears or humans. Spray it directly into a bear's face, aiming for the eyes and nose. Carry it on the front of your pack where it is easily reached. (If confronted with a bear, you won't have time to dig it out of your pack.)

MOUNTAIN LIONS

Because of their solitary nature, it is unlikely you will see a mountain lion, even on long trips in the backcountry. These large cats rarely prey on humans, but they can, especially small kids. Hike with others, keep kids close, and make noise on the trail. If you do stumble upon a cougar, do not run: Remain calm and gather your group together to appear bigger. Look at the cat with peripheral vision, rather than staring straight on, and back away slowly. If the lion attacks, fight back with rocks, sticks, or by kicking.

HANTAVIRUS

Hantavirus infection is contracted by inhaling dust from deer mice droppings. When camping, store food in rodent-proof containers. If you find rodent dust in your gear, disinfect the gear with water and bleach (1.5 cups bleach to one gallon water). If you contract the virus, which results in flu-like symptoms, seek immediate medical attention.

SPIDERS, MOSQUITOES, AND TICKS

Spiders, mosquitoes, and ticks can carry diseases such as West Nile virus and Rocky Mountain spotted fever. Protect yourself by wearing long sleeves and pants and use insect repellent in spring-summer, when mosquitoes and ticks are common. If you are bitten by a tick, carefully remove it by the head with tweezers, disinfect the bite, and then see a doctor. Some spiders, such as the brown recluse, carry poison in their bites. If symptoms are severe (breathing difficulty, nausea, sweating, and vomiting), seek medical attention immediately.

SNAKES

Rattlesnakes are ubiquitous in prairie and desert parks across the West. When hiking, keep your eyes on the ground and an ear out for the telltale rattle, a warning to keep away. Should you be bitten, seek immediate medical help.

TRAVEL TIPS

ENTERING THE UNITED STATES

PASSPORTS AND VISAS

If you are visiting from another country, you must have a **valid passport** and a **visa** to enter the United States. You may qualify for the **Visa Waiver Program** if you hold a current passport from one of the following countries: Andorra, Australia, Austria, Belgium, Brunei, Chile, Czech Republic, Denmark, Estonia, Finland, France, Germany, Greece, Hungary, Iceland, Ireland, Italy, Japan, Latvia, Liechtenstein, Lithuania, Luxembourg, Malta, Monaco, the Netherlands, New Zealand, Norway, Portugal, San Marino, Singapore, Slovakia, Slovenia, South Korea, Spain, Sweden, Switzerland, Taiwan, and the United Kingdom. To qualify, you must apply online with the Electronic System for Travel Authorization at www.cbp.gov and hold a **return plane or cruise ticket** to your country of origin dated less than **90 days** from your date of entry. Holders of Canadian passports don't need visas or visa waivers.

In most other countries, the local U.S. embassy should be able to provide a **tourist visa.** The application fee for a visa is US$160, plus you'll need to pay an issuance fee. While a visa may be processed in as little as 24 hours on request, plan for at least a couple of weeks, as there can be unexpected delays, particularly during the busy summer season (June-Aug.). For information, visit http://travel.state.gov.

Travelers from Canada and countries in the Western Hemisphere Travel Initiative may use a U.S. passport card, enhanced driver's license, or NEXUS card instead of a passport. Except Canadians, international travelers entering the United States must have a current I-94 form ($6).

MONEY AND CURRENCY EXCHANGE

International travelers should exchange currency at their major port of entry. As you travel, use ATM cards to get more cash. Smaller denominations ($50 and under) work best. Using a credit card while traveling will give you the best exchange rates.

EMBASSIES AND CONSULATES

If you should lose your passport or find yourself in some other trouble while visiting the United States, contact your country's offices for assistance. The website of the **U.S. State Department** (www.state.gov) lists the websites for all foreign embassies and consulates in the United States. Also, a representative can direct you to the nearest embassy or consulate.

CUSTOMS

Before you enter the United States from another country by sea or by air, you'll be required to fill out a customs form. Check with the U.S. embassy in your country or the **Customs and Border Protection** website (www.cbp.gov) for an updated list of items you must declare.

In general, the United States does not allow plants, drugs, firewood, or live bait to cross borders. Some fresh meats, poultry products, fruits, and vegetables are restricted, as are firearms. Pets are permitted to cross the border with a certificate of rabies vaccination dated within 30 days prior to crossing. Bear sprays are not allowed on airplanes in checked or carry-on luggage and are considered firearms in Canada; they must have a U.S. Environmental Protection Agency-approved label to go across the border.

If you require medication administered by injection, you must pack your syringes in a checked bag; syringes are not permitted in carry-ons coming into the United States. Also, pack documentation describing your need for any narcotic medications you've brought with you. Failure to produce documentation for narcotics on request can result in severe penalties in the United States.

PASSES, PERMITS, AND FEES

Many national park passes are available for purchase online at **https://store. usgs.gov/pass.** Entrance fees must be paid in person at the individual park entrances; some unstaffed entrances may be cash-only.

ENTRY FEES

Entrance fees range from free to $30 or more per vehicle; entry fees for motorcycles, bicyclists, and individuals on foot are slightly reduced. Once paid, most entrance fees are good for seven days.

ANNUAL PASSES

The **Annual Pass** ($80) admits entrance to all national parks and federal fee areas for up to one year. Most national parks also offer their own **Annual Pass** ($40-60) granting access to the one park for up to one year. Some neighboring parks such as Yellowstone and Grand Teton offer a **Joint Pass** ($50), which admits entrance for seven days to both.

AMERICA THE BEAUTIFUL SENIOR PASS

U.S. citizens or permanent residents age 62 and older have two pass options: an **Annual Senior Pass** ($20, $10 processing fee), good for one year, or a **Lifetime Senior Pass** ($80, $10 processing fee), which is valid for life. To purchase either pass, apply online (https://your-passnow.com) or bring proof of age (state driver's license, birth certificate, or passport) in person to any national park entrance station (processing fee waived at park entrances). In a private vehicle, the card admits four adults, plus all children under age 16.

The Lifetime Park Pass also grants 50 percent discounts on fees for federally run tours and campgrounds; however, discounts do not apply to park concessionaire services like hotels, boat tours, and bus tours.

ACCESS PASS

Blind or permanently disabled U.S. citizens or permanent residents can request a lifetime **National Parks and Federal Recreational Lands Access Pass** (free, $10 processing fee) for access to all national parks and other federal sites. The pass admits the pass holder plus three other adults in the same vehicle; children under age 16 are free. Pass holders also receive a 50 percent discount on federally run tours and campgrounds. Proof of medical disability or eligibility is required for receiving federal benefits.

MILITARY PASS

U.S. military personnel can get a lifetime **National Parks and Federal Recreational Lands Access Pass** (free) for access to all national parks and other federal sites. The pass admits the pass holder plus three other adults in the same vehicle; children under age 16 are free. Pass holders also get 50 percent discounts on federally run tours and campgrounds. Passes must be acquired in person at entrance stations; proof of service is required.

FEE-FREE DAYS

Admission is free on Fee-Free Days: Martin Luther King Day (Jan.), the first day of National Park Week (Apr.), National Public Lands Day (Sept.), and Veterans Day (Nov. 11).

VOLUNTEER PASS

Those volunteering in national parks or other federal lands can get an annual pass to all national parks by reaching 250 service hours. Service hours maybe be accrued in one year or across several years.

WILDERNESS PERMITS

If you're planning a backcountry expedition, follow all rules and guidelines for obtaining **wilderness permits** for specific parks (www.nps.gov). Rules vary between parks, especially regarding fees, reservations, and procedures for picking up permits. Park-specific backcountry offices will have information on any health, trail, bear, or other alerts in the area. For your safety, let someone outside your party know your route and expected date of return.

TRAVELING WITHOUT RESERVATIONS

During the busy summer months, accommodations can be hard to come by. It's not unusual for national park lodgings and campgrounds to be full days, weeks, and even months in advance. While it may be possible to find a last-minute campsite at one of the nearby national forests, savvy travelers book lodging, campsites, and wilderness permits **up to 13 months in advance.**

Don't have reservations for camping? Here are a few tips to snagging a campsite in summer.

Make a base camp and stay put rather than shuffling campgrounds every day or so. You'll spend a little more time driving to some destinations, but you'll experience the park more with the time you save from searching campground after campground only to be confronted with Full signs.

On any day you plan to move camp, change locations in early morning to get a campsite before campgrounds fill up. Make getting your next campsite the first priority rather than sightseeing.

At campgrounds that allow self-selection of campsites, plan to begin prowling to nab a site when someone departs an hour or more before the fill times mentioned on the park's website.

TRAVELING WITH CHILDREN

The National Park Service has designed ways to pique the interest of kids through educational activities online (www.nps.gov, under "Learn About the Park"), in-park activities, and visitors center hands-on exhibits.

Hiking with kids can either be a nightmare or a hoot. To make it more fun, take water and snacks along to prevent hunger and thirst from zapping their energy. Take extra layers to keep kids warm if the weather turns. Help them connect with the environment while hiking by asking them about what they see and why things are the way they are. If you make hiking a fun experience for them, they'll want to do it again.

JUNIOR RANGER PROGRAMS

Junior Ranger Programs (www.nps. gov/kids/jrRangers.cfm) mix educational activities with experiences for families to do in the park. Most activities target ages 6-12. Pick up Junior Ranger activity guides ($3) at any visitors center. Kids complete the self-guided activities and receive a Junior Ranger badge after stopping at a visitors center to get sworn in.

TRAVELING WITH PETS

Pets are allowed inside national parks, but only in limited areas: campgrounds, parking lots, and roadsides. They are not allowed on most trails and beaches, off-trail in the backcountry, or at most park lodges or motor inns. When outside a vehicle or in a campground, pets must be on a leash or caged. Be kind enough to avoid leaving them unattended in a car anywhere. Be considerate of wildlife and other visitors by keeping your pet under control and disposing of waste in garbage cans. Some national parks (such as Grand Canyon) provide kennel services for a fee.

ACCESSIBILITY

While some national park structures have been refitted with ramps and wider doors, many historic or remote structures remain inaccessible. Many hiking trails are accessible to wheelchairs and most campgrounds designate specific campsites that meet the Americans with Disabilities Act standards.

If you are traveling with a disability, there are many resources to help you plan your trip. Check on the specific park's website (www.nps.gov) for services pertinent to that park. Many parks have facilities, programs, and trails designed for those with physical or mobility challenges. Most park brochures are also available in large print or braille. With enough notice, some parks can provide services for those with hearing impairments, and park videos often have captioned versions. Trained service dogs are permitted in many parks, but check on requirements; some parks with prevalent grizzly bear populations discourage them in the backcountry.

FIREARMS

Federal law allows people that can legally carry firearms under federal, state, and local laws to bring their guns into the national parks. However, federal law prohibits firearms in government offices, visitors centers, ranger stations, fee-collection buildings, and maintenance facilities. Those places are marked with signs at all public entrances. Discharging firearms in the park is illegal except when presented with "imminent danger."

WI-FI AND CELL SERVICE

Cell-phone service and Internet connectivity within the national parks tends to be limited. In general, plan to be out of reach while you travel in the parks, where service is unavailable on many roads, trails, campgrounds, picnic areas, and lodges. Internet is equally limited. National park visitors centers, ranger stations, and campgrounds rarely have Wi-Fi. Some park lodges may offer limited Wi-Fi (fee) for overnight guests, but connectivity will often be very slow.

MOBILE APPS

The National Park Service has **mobile phone apps** for individual parks that contain information on visitors centers, hikes, geyser predictions, road construction, ranger programs, and interactive park maps. **Download the apps before** you begin your trip because Internet is limited inside the parks.

Be aware that you will have dead zones for phones and that mobile phone apps don't account for seasonal road or trail closures. Your first stop for accurate, up-to-date information should always be a national park visitors center and the national park website.

LEAVE NO TRACE

To keep the national parks pristine, visitors to these parks need to take an active role in maintaining them.

Plan ahead and prepare. Hiking in the backcountry is inherently risky. Three miles hiking at the high elevations in Wyoming may be much harder than three miles through your neighborhood park back home. Choose appropriate routes for mileage and elevation gain with this in mind, and carry hiking essentials.

Travel and camp on durable surfaces. In front-country and backcountry campgrounds, camp in designated sites. Protect fragile plants by staying on trails even in mud, refusing to cut switchbacks, and walking single file. If you must walk off the trail, step on rocks, snow, or dry grasses rather than wet soil and delicate plants.

Leave what you find. Flowers, rocks, and fur tufts on shrubs are protected park resources, as are historical and cultural items. For lunch stops and camping, sit on rocks or logs where you find them rather than moving them to accommodate comfort.

Properly dispose of waste. Pack out whatever you bring, including all garbage. If toilets are not available, pack out toilet paper. Urinate on rocks, logs, gravel, or snow to protect soils and plants from salt-starved wildlife, and bury feces 6-8 inches deep at least 200 feet from water.

RESPECT WILDLIFE.

Minimize campfire impacts. Make fires in designated fire pits only, not on beaches. Use small wrist-size dead and downed wood, not live branches. Be aware: Fires and collecting firewood are not permitted in some places in the parks.

Respect wildlife. Bring along binoculars, spotting scopes, and telephoto lenses to aid in watching wildlife. Keep your distance. Do not feed any wildlife, even ground squirrels. Once fed, they become more aggressive.

Be considerate of other visitors. Particularly be aware of cell phones and how their use or noise cuts into the natural soundscapes of the parks.

For more Leave No Trace information, visit www.LNT.org.

INDEX

LIST OF MAPS

PHOTO CREDITS

TEXT CREDITS

Alaska

Text for the Alaska national parks adapted from *Moon Alaska,* first edition, by Lisa Maloney.

California

Text for Death Valley National Park adapted from *Moon Death Valley National Park,* first edition, by Jenna Bough

Text for Joshua Tree National Park adapted from *Moon Palm Springs & Joshua Tree,* first edition, by Jenna Bough

Text for Redwoods National and State Parks and for Channel Island National Park adapted from *Moon Coastal California,* fifth edition, by Stuart Thornton

Text for Pinnacles National Park adapted from *Moon Northern California,* seventh edition, by Elizabeth Linhart Veneman & Christopher Arns, and from *Moon Monterey & Carmel,* fifth edition, by Stuart Thornton

Pacific Northwest

Text for Crater Lake National Park adapted from *Moon Oregon,* 11th edition, by Judy Jewell & W. C. McRae

Text for the Washington national parks adapted from *Moon Washington,* 10th edition, by Matthew Lombardi

Southwest

Text for the Arizona national parks adapted from *Moon Arizona & the Grand Canyon,* 13th edition, by Tim Hull

Text for the Colorado national parks adapted from *Moon Colorado,* ninth edition, by Terri Cook

Text for Great Basin National Park adapted from *Moon Nevada,* eighth edition, by Scott Smith

Text for the Texas national parks adapted from *Moon Texas,* ninth edition, by Andy Rhodes

Text for the Utah national parks adapted from *Moon Utah,* 12th edition, by W. C. McRae & Judy Jewell

Rocky Mountains

Text for the Colorado national parks adapted from *Moon Colorado,* ninth edition, by Terri Cook

Text for the South Dakota national parks adapted from *Moon Mount Rushmore & the Black Hills,* third edition, by Laural A. Bidwell

Great Lakes and Northeast

Text for Acadia National Park adapted from *Moon Maine,* seventh edition, by Hilary Nangle

Text for Cuyahoga Valley National Park adapted from *Moon Cleveland,* second edition, by Douglas Trattner

Text for Isle Royale National Park adapted from *Moon Michigan,* sixth edition, by Paul Vachon

Text for Voyageurs National Park adapted from *Moon Minnesota,* fourth edition, by Tricia Cornell

South

Text for Great Smoky Mountains National Park adapted from *Moon Great Smoky Mountains National Park,* first edition, by Jason Frye

Text for Shenandoah National Park adapted from *Moon Blue Ridge Parkway Road Trip,* first edition, by Jason Frye

Text for Mammoth Cave National Park adapted from *Moon Kentucky,* second edition, by Theresa Dowell Blackinton

Text for Congaree National Park adapted from *Moon South Carolina,* sixth edition, by Jim Morekis

Text for Everglades National Park adapted from *Moon Sarasota & Naples,* second edition, by Jason Ferguson

Text for Biscayne National Park and Dry Tortugas National Park adapted from *Moon Florida Keys,* third edition, by Joshua Lawrence Kinser

Islands

Text for Hawai'i Volcanoes National Park adapted from *Moon Big Island of Hawai'i,* eighth edition, by Bree Kessler

Text for Virgin Islands National Park adapted from *Moon U.S. & British Virgin Islands,* sixth edition, by Susanna Henighan Potter

ACKNOWLEDGMENTS

A huge thank-you goes out to all past and present members of the National Park Service. It's through their labors that we have access to such treasures. For many in the park service, their work is a devotion to the park they love.

I thank my parents for introducing me to the national parks. Before I was born, my father served as a ranger at Mount Rainier National Park. On one of my parents' first dates, he took my mom bushwhacking to see a secret cluster of ancient trees. After they were married, my parents led us kids to the giant trees, which later became known as Grove of the Patriarchs (after the trail and bridge were installed). As grandparents, my folks took their small grandchildren to hug the no-longer-secret trees trees. After my father passed away, my mother, along with all of the kids and grandkids, returned to our grove to honor his memory amid those sacred trees. Experiencing the national parks is one of the greatest gifts parents can give their children.

I thank the regional writers who contributed mounds of their expertise. Their valuable insight into their "home" parks provided the backbone of this project; without it, this book could not be. Cheers also go to my editor, Sabrina Young, for her tireless curating of national park details. She provided the building blocks for me to develop this guidebook for you.

MORE NATIONAL PARKS GUIDES FROM MOON

Craft a personalized journey through the top National Parks in the U.S. and Canada with Moon Travel Guides.

In these books:
- Full coverage of gateway cities and towns
- Itineraries from one day to multiple weeks
- Advice on where to stay (or camp) in and around the parks

MOON.COM
@MOONGUIDES

MOON USA NATIONAL PARKS

Avalon Travel
Hachette Book Group
1700 Fourth Street
Berkeley, CA 94710, USA
www.moon.com

Editor: Sabrina Young
Copy Editor: Brett Keener
Graphics Coordinators: Kathryn Osgood, Darren Alessi
Avalon Production: Darren Alessi, Jane Musser
Cover Design: Kimberly Glyder Design
Interior Design and Production: Megan Jones Design
Moon Logo: Tim McGrath
Map Editor: Mike Morgenfeld
Cartographers: Moon Street Cartography, Durango, CO., Brian Shotwell, Mike Morgenfeld
Proofreader: Caroline Trefler
Indexer: Greg Jewett

ISBN-13: 978-1-64049-279-0

Printing History
1st Edition — October 2018
5 4 3 2

Special thanks to Tom Patterson of the National Park Service.

Front cover photo: String Lake in Grand Teton National Park, Wyoming © Robert Garrigus / Alamy Stock Photo
Back cover photos (top to bottom): Arches National Park, Utah © Larry Geddis / Alamy Stock Photo; Mormon Row, Grand Teton National Park, Wyoming © Niebrugge Images / Alamy Stock Photo; Glacier National Park, Montana © YinYang /Getty Images.

Printed in China by R. R. Donnelley

MAP SYMBOLS

▦ Expressway	○ City/Town	✈ Airport	♪ Golf Course
▦ Primary Road	◉ State Capital	✗ Airfield	🅿 Parking Area
▦ Secondary Road	⊛ National Capital	▲ Mountain	⬭ Archaeological Site
▦ Unpaved Road	★ Point of Interest	✦ Unique Natural Feature	♟ Church
▬ Feature Trail	• Accommodation		⌷ Gas Station
▬ Other Trail	▼ Restaurant/Bar	⬎ Waterfall	
▬ Ferry	■ Other Location	▲ Park	⬭ Glacier
▦ Pedestrian Walkway	Λ Campground	☗ Trailhead	⬭ Mangrove
▦ Stairs		⛷ Skiing Area	⬭ Reef
			⬭ Swamp

CONVERSION TABLES

°C = (°F - 32) / 1.8
°F = (°C x 1.8) + 32
1 inch = 2.54 centimeters (cm)
1 foot = 0.304 meters (m)
1 yard = 0.914 meters
1 mile = 1.6093 kilometers (km)
1 km = 0.6214 miles
1 fathom = 1.8288 m
1 chain = 20.1168 m
1 furlong = 201.168 m
1 acre = 0.4047 hectares
1 sq km = 100 hectares
1 sq mile = 2.59 square km
1 ounce = 28.35 grams
1 pound = 0.4536 kilograms
1 short ton = 0.90718 metric ton
1 short ton = 2,000 pounds
1 long ton = 1.016 metric tons
1 long ton = 2,240 pounds
1 metric ton = 1,000 kilograms
1 quart = 0.94635 liters
1 US gallon = 3.7854 liters
1 Imperial gallon = 4.5459 liters
1 nautical mile = 1.852 km

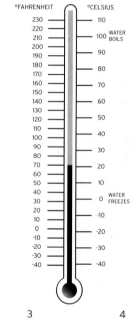

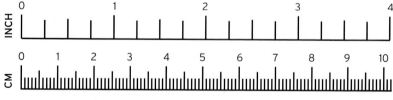